All inquiries be addressed to:
Barron's Educational Series, Inc.
113 Crossways Park Drive
Woodbury, New York 11797

Library of Congress Catalog Card No. 84-12446

International Standard Book No. 0-8120-5611-6

Library of Congress Cataloging in Publication Data

Harris, Jack C.
    Barron's real estate handbook.

1. Real estate business—Handbooks, manuals, etc.
2. Real estate business—Dictionaries. 3. Business
mathematics—Real estate business—Tables. I. Friedman,
Jack P. II. Title. III. Title: Real estate handbook.
HD1375.F77 1984   333.33   84-12446
ISBN 0-8120-5611-6

PRINTED IN THE UNITED STATES OF AMERICA
    5 6 7   880   9 8 7 6 5 4 3 2

BARRON'S
REAL ESTATE
HANDBOOK

Jack C. Harris, Ph.D.
Assistant Research Economist, Texas Real Estate Research Center
and Member of the Graduate Faculty
Texas A&M University

and

Jack P. Friedman, Ph.D, C.P.A., S.R.P.A.
Senior Research Economist, Texas Real Estate Research Center
and Member of the Graduate Faculty
Texas A&M University

BARRON'S

Woodbury, New York • London • Sydney • Toronto

CONTENTS

PREFACE

Real estate, like most business fields, has its own unique jargon. You must speak the language in order to understand and be understood. Real estate is also a field of numbers and formulas. Closing a simple transaction may involve calculating future mortgage payments and depreciation allowances or prorating closing costs. Furthermore, new terminology, types of mortgage loans and depreciation methods emerge constantly, taxing the ability of the professional to keep up.

Whether you are a real estate professional or someone who occasionally gets involved, the *Real Estate Handbook* will be indispensible. Reading through the glossary with its numerous examples will provide a course in the essentials of real estate. As a reference, this handbook will serve you in numerous situations where you encounter a term or problem for which you need an explanation or where you need the answer to a financial question. In addition to the illustrated real estate glossary, this handbook contains a series of helpful tables that allow you to handle most real estate finance and investment problems.

The glossary contains more than 1300 terms with concise, up to date definitions. All these terms have examples which show how they are used and many include illustrations to make them easy to understand. You will find legal terms to help take the mystery out of contract documents, financial terms to aid in structuring deals, architectural terms for traditional and contemporary buildings, and other helpful real estate words.

The tables will allow you to solve real estate problems using only simple mathematics. Monthly mortgage payment and amortization schedules can be constructed for mortgage loans with a variety of interest rates and terms. The critical early years of a graduated payment mortgage can be analyzed. Depreciation schedules can be computed whether the old or new rules apply. The effects of discount points can be determined. Property sellers who provide financing will find special tables for estimating the premium they should receive for the financing and be able to estimate how much their loan is worth in the secondary market. Each table has been specially prepared to make its use as simple as possible. Instructions precede each table stating the information needed to use the table and including example solutions to common real estate problems.

We hope that you, the reader, have an enjoyable experience whether you use this handbook as a reference guide or as a way to learn about real estate and its business environment.

Jack C. Harris
Jack P. Friedman

GLOSSARY

HOW TO USE THIS GLOSSARY EFFECTIVELY

Alphabetization: All words are alphabetized by letter rather than by word. Thus, for the purpose of arrangement, all multiple word terms are treated as if they were one word. For example, the word "ad valorem" follows "adult," rather than preceding as would be the case if "ad" were treated as a separate word. Abbreviations, in the rare instance that they appear as entries, are treated as if they were a word. The term "MAI," which stands for "Member, Appraisal Institute," appears before "maintenance fee." A separate list of abbreviations is included, so as a general rule, abbreviations and acronyms do not appear as entries. In the case of "MAI," the initials are understood by many who are not familiar with the formal name. Thus, MAI becomes the entry.

Parentheses: Parentheses are used in two instances. The first application is to indicate an abbreviation commonly applied to the term. For example, "ADJUSTABLE RATE MORTGAGE (ARM)" indicates that the abbreviation "ARM" commonly refers to adjustable rate mortgages. The second application is to indicate the context of the term as defined. For example, "TO RETIRE (A DEBT)" indicates the context under which the word "retire" is defined is when it is applied to retiring a debt. The definition is not appropriate to other legitimate uses of the word retire, such as in the expression "retirement benefits."

Cross References: When an entry is used in the definition or example for another entry, the term is printed in **boldface type.** This provides a cross reference in case the term is used in the definition is unclear to the reader. In general, the term is printed in boldface only the first time it appears in the definition. Occasionally, when a term is a closely related concept or provides contrast, it is cross-referenced, even though not used in the definition. In the former case, the term is referenced as follows: "See **cash flow.**" In the latter case, the reference appears as: "Contrast with **net lease.**" When an entry is merely another expression for a term defined elsewhere in the book, a reference rather than a definition is provided; for example, "NOMINAL RATE same as **face rate.**"

Examples and Addresses: At least one example is given for each definition in the book. In the case of organizations listed as entries, a current address is supplied in lieu of an example. The examples are intended to illustrate how the term is used in a sentence or to provide a sample of specific things which fall under the purview of the term. For example, under the entry for "closing costs" a list of specific closing cost items is provided. When an entry has more than one definition, an example is provided for each definition. Where applicable, an illustration is provided as an example. e.g., under "cluster housing," an illustration of a sample cluster housing plan is included.

A

ABANDONMENT the voluntary surrender of property, owned or leased, without naming a successor as owner or tenant. The property will generally revert to one holding a prior interest or, in cases where no owner is apparent, to the state. Abandonment does not relieve obligations associated with lease or ownership unless the abandonment is accepted by the entity to which the obligation is owed.
Example: Abel owns a dilapidated apartment house with 2 years delinquent property taxes. Rather than pay the back taxes, Abel *abandons* the building by disclaiming ownership.

ABATEMENT a reduction in amount or intensity.
Example: A manufacturing plant may install equipment for pollution *abatement*.
Example: Tenants may ask for an *abatement* in rent over a period when their use of the property has been interrupted or inhibited by actions of the landlord, such as renovation of the structure.

ABSENTEE OWNER an owner who does not personally manage or reside at property owned.
Example: Abel, living in New York, purchases an apartment building in Houston. Abel is an *absentee owner*.

ABSORPTION RATE an estimate of the expected annual sales or new occupancy of a particular type of land use.
Example: The demand for new homes in a market area is estimated to be 500 per year. Developer Abel's new subdivision, when completed, is expected to capture 10% of the market. Therefore Abel's subdivision has an expected *absorption rate* of 50 homes per year (10% of 500 = 50).

ABSTRACT OF TITLE a historical summary of all of the recorded instruments and proceedings that affect the title to property.
Example: A title insurance company will have an attorney prepare an *abstract of title* prior to granting a title insurance policy.
Example: An abstract company will compile an *abstract of title* with copies of all recorded instruments affecting title to a specific tract.

ABUT adjoining or meeting. See also **adjacent.**
Example: The 2 properties shown in Figure 1 *abut* one another. The property on the right also *abuts* the road.

1

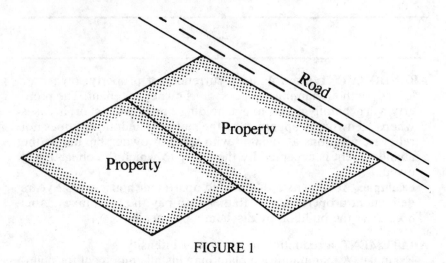

FIGURE 1

ACCELERATED COST RECOVERY SYSTEM (ACRS) a method of **depreciation** introduced by the Economic Recovery Tax Act of 1981 and modified by the Tax Reform Act of 1984. Under it, most buildings acquired in 1984 and thereafter may be depreciated using an 18-year life. See Table 1 for depreciable lives and methods. If the **straight-line** method is chosen, there will be no **depreciation recapture** upon resale. Owners may also select 35- and 45-year lives. **Accelerated depreciation** approximating 175% **declining balance** may be used; however, that will result in depreciation recapture.

Example: Under the *accelerated cost recovery system,* buildings can be depreciated over 18 years without regard to their **economic life.** Thus, the concept of depreciation is changed from an allowance for loss in value to become a cost recovery method.

ACCELERATED DEPRECIATION depreciation methods, chosen for income tax or accounting purposes, that offer greater deductions in early years. See **accelerated cost recovery system, double declining balance, sum-of-years-digits depreciation.**

Example: One method of *accelerated depreciation* is the double declining balance method (DDB). If straight-line deductions equal 5% of depreciable basis, DDB allows a deduction of 10% (200% of 5%), but applied to the undepreciated basis. Thus the deductions decline each year (Figure 2).

ACCELERATION CLAUSE a loan provision giving the lender the right to declare the entire amount immediately due and payable upon the violation of a specific loan provision, such as failure to make payments on time.

Example: Collins sells her house to Baker, who assumes the existing 8% interest rate mortgage. They do not notify the lender of the sale. Clause 17 in the mortgage states that the full principal *accel-*

TABLE 1

RECOVERY CLASS AND ALLOWABLE DEPRECIATION METHODS FOR BUILDINGS ACQUIRED AFTER MARCH 15, 1984

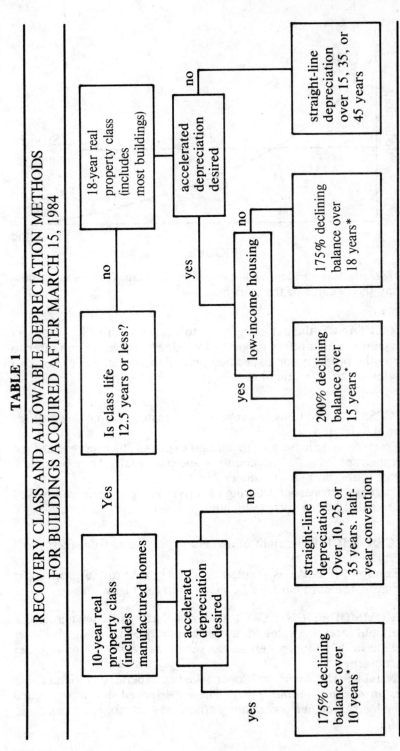

*The accelerated rate changes to the straight-line method at the optimal time to maximize recovery deductions.

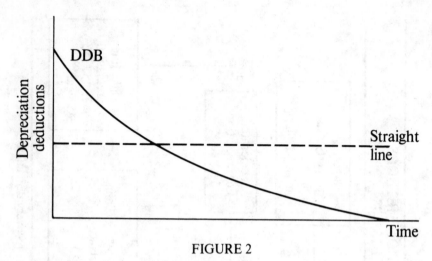

FIGURE 2

erates unless the lender approves of the sale. Collins must now pay the balance of the principal.

ACCEPTANCE the act of agreeing to accept an offer.
Example: Abel offers property for sale, Baker makes an offer to buy the property for a specified price. Upon Abel's *acceptance* a sales contract is complete.

ACCESSION additions to property as a result of annexing fixtures or alluvial deposits.
Example: The lease on a restaurant expires. The proprietor of the restaurant leaves some counters and bar stools. They become a part of the property by *accession*.
Example: Property bordering on a river is legally enlarged by soil deposited by the river **(alluvium).**

ACCESS RIGHT the right of owners to get to and from their property.
Example: If Baker is granted an *access right* to the property in Figure 3, a curb cut may be made onto the highway.

ACCOMMODATION PARTY one who has signed an agreement without receiving value for it, for the purpose of lending his or her name so that another person can secure a necessary loan or other arrangement.
Example: The young developer asked an experienced friend to act as an *accommodation party*. The experienced developer signed the loan agreement even though there was no monetary benefit to him.

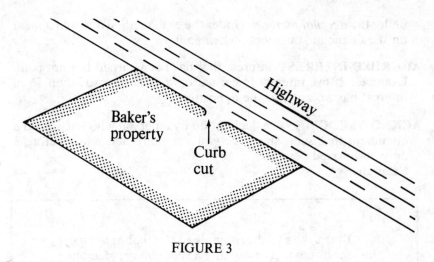

FIGURE 3

ACCRETION the addition to land through processes of nature, such as deposits of soil carried by streams. See **alluvium**.
Example: Figure 4.

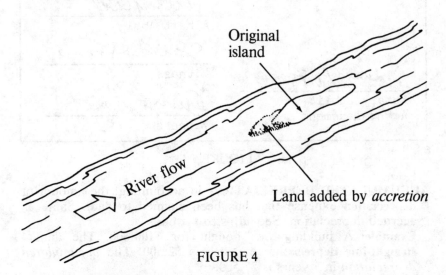

FIGURE 4

ACCRUAL METHOD a method of accounting that requires income or expense to be entered when the amount is earned or the obligation is payable. Distinguished from **cash method** in which amounts are posted when paid or received.
Example: The home buyer bought and paid for a 3-year hazard insurance policy at closing. On the *accrual method*, only the current year's expense is indicated.
Example: Interest on a loan is 3 months delinquent. The expense, though unpaid, appears in the current year's financial statement

under the *accrual method*. Under the cash method it would appear on the financial statements when paid.

ACCRUED INTEREST interest that has been earned but not paid. **Example:** If 6% interest is earned on a $100 deposit, then $6 of interest has *accrued* to the depositer.

ACKNOWLEDGMENT a declaration by a person who has signed a document that such signature is a voluntary act, made before a duly authorized person.
Example:

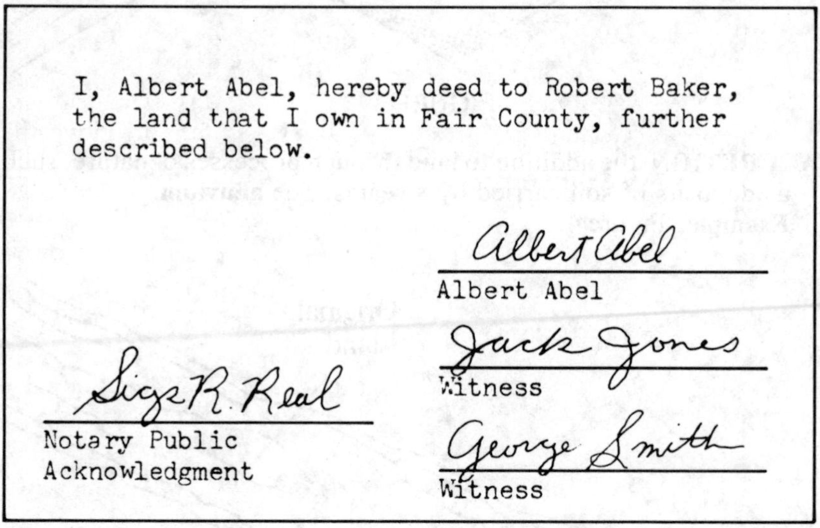

```
   I, Albert Abel, hereby deed to Robert Baker,
   the land that I own in Fair County, further
   described below.
```

Albert Abel
Albert Abel

Jack Jones
Witness

Sigz R. Real
Notary Public
Acknowledgment

George Smith
Witness

FIGURE 5

ACCUMULATED DEPRECIATION in accounting, the amount of **depreciation** expense that has been claimed to date. Same as accrued depreciation. See **adjusted tax basis.**
Example: A building was bought for $100,000. The annual **straight-line depreciation** expense is $2,500. The *accumulated depreciation* in 3 years is $7,500.

ACQUISITION COST the price and all fees required to obtain a property.
Example: Abel purchases a property for $90,000 plus $5,000 in **closing costs** (attorney's fees, loan fees, **appraisal** costs, **title insurance**, and loan **discount points**). Abel's *acquisition cost* is $95,000.

ACRE a 2-dimensional measure of land equaling 160 square rods, 10 square chains, 4,840 square yards, or 43,560 square feet.

Example: A land survey shows that Abel owns 1.3774 *acres* of land (Figure 6).

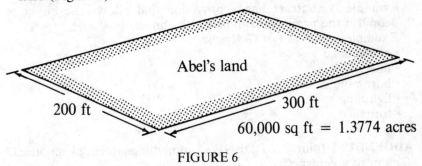

FIGURE 6

ACTIVE SOLAR HEATING a system that uses energy from sunlight to heat a structure and/or provide hot water. Contrasted with **passive solar heating** by the use of pumps or fans to move the energy-transporting medium through the system. Installation of active solar heating equipment is eligible for certain income tax credits.

Example: A schematic of a typical *active solar heating* system is shown in Figure 7.

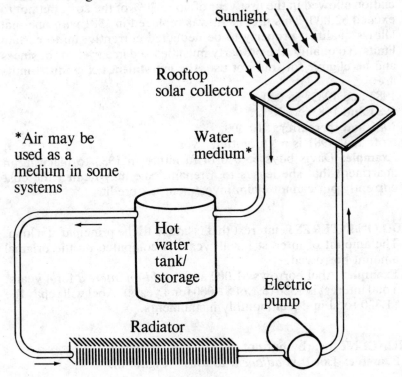

FIGURE 7

ACT OF GOD an unpreventable destructive occurrence of the natural world.

Example A **contract** has a provision that allows the buyer to **default** if the property is damaged by an *act of God*.

Examples of an *act of God* are:
• earthquake
• flood
• hurricane
• lightning
• tornado

ADDENDUM (plural: ADDENDA) something added, as an attachment to a **contract**.

Example: An *addendum* to the **contract of sale** described the type of **financing** that the buyer must secure to be required to purchase the property.

Commonly added *addenda* in real estate purchase agreements are for financing terms and property **inspection** requirements.

ADDITIONAL FIRST-YEAR DEPRECIATION (TAX) for depreciable personal property placed in service before 1981, extra depreciation allowed in the first year of up to 20% of the cost, but not to exceed $2,000. This provision was replaced in 1981 with one that allows qualified property to be deducted currently, up to certain limits. To qualify, the property must be used in a trade or business and be eligible for, but not use, the **investment tax credit**. Limits are:

1982 and 1983: $5,000
1984 and 1985: $7,500
1986 and thereafter: $10,000
Note that 1981 is a "forgotten" year.

Example: Davis buys $5,000 of furniture in 1983 to place in an apartment that she leases to a tenant. She may deduct the cost currently but cannot claim investment tax credit.

ADD-ON INTEREST interest that is added to the principal of a loan. The amount of interest for all years is computed on the original amount borrowed.

Example: Abel borrows $1,000 at 8% *add-on interest* for 4 years. Total interest is $320 (8% of $1,000 for 4 years). Abel will repay the $1,320 total in equal monthly installments.

ADJACENT nearby but not necessarily **adjoining**.

Example: Lot B is *adjacent* to lot A (Figure 8).

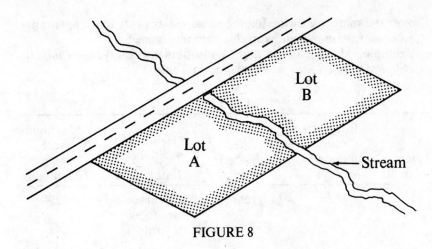

FIGURE 8

ADJOINING contiguous; attaching; sharing a common border.
   Example: A warehouse with *adjoining* office space (Figure 9).

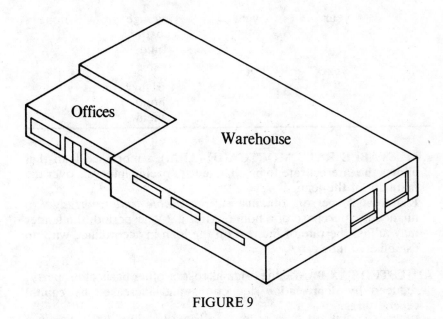

FIGURE 9

ADJUSTABLE MORTGAGE LOAN (AML) a mortgage instrument
authorized by the Federal Home Loan Bank Board in 1981 for use
by all federally chartered savings and loan associations. The *AML*
provides to local associations maximum flexibility in selecting the
terms under which interest rates and payments may be adjusted

over the maturity of the loan. See **adjustable rate mortgage, renegotiated rate mortgage, variable rate mortgage.**

Example: Major Savings and Loan offers several types of *adjustable mortgage loans* as described in Table 2.

TABLE 2

Loan plan	Interest rate adjusted every:	Payments adjusted every:	Index used	Maximum rate change each year
1	year	year	average mortgage rate	2%
2	6 months	3 years	6-month treasury bill rate	none
3	year	year	average cost of funds	none
4	3 years	3 years	3-year treasury bond yield	1%

ADJUSTABLE RATE MORTGAGE (ARM) a mortgage loan that allows the interest rate to be changed at specific intervals over the maturity of the loan.

Example: A person obtains an *adjustable rate mortgage* to finance the purchase of a home. After a 2-year period, the lender may adjust the rate of interest on the loan in accordance with an established index.

ADJUSTED TAX BASIS the original cost or other basis of property, reduced by **depreciation** deductions and increased by **capital expenditures.**

Example: Collins buys a lot for $10,000. She erects a retail facility for $60,000, then depreciates the improvements for tax purposes at the rate of $4,000 per year. After 3 years her *adjusted tax basis* is $58,000. ($10,000 + $60,000 − 3 × $4,000)

ADJUSTMENTS (IN APPRAISAL) dollar value or percentage amounts that, when added to or subtracted from the sales price of

a **comparable,** provide an indication of the value of a subject property. *Adjustments* are necessary to compensate for variation in the features of the comparable relative to the subject.
Example: An appraisal is to be made of a three-bedroom house. One **comparable** is a similar house with two bedrooms which sold for $50,000. The appraiser makes an adjustment of $1,000 to the comparable to account for the difference of bedrooms. The adjusted sales price of the **comparable** is $51,000.

ADMINISTRATOR a person appointed by a court to administer the estate of a deceased person who left no will.
Example: The *administrator* of the estate called a meeting of the deceased's relatives for the purpose of dividing the property.

ADMINISTRATOR'S DEED a **deed** conveying the property of one who died without a will **(intestate).**
Example: At the hearing called by the administrator, the heir received an *administrator's deed* to her father's home.

ADULT one who has attained the age of **majority.**
Example: Abel enters into a contract to purchase land. Because he is 17 years of age he is a **minor** (not an *adult*) and may **void** the contract.

AD VALOREM according to value. See **ad valorem tax.**

AD VALOREM TAX a tax based on the value of the thing being taxed.
Example: If the *ad valorem tax* rate is 1%, the tax would be $1 per $100 of assessed value.

ADVERSE POSSESSION a means of acquiring title to real estate where an occupant has been in actual, open, **notorious,** exclusive, and continuous occupancy of property for the period required by state law.
Example: Although the elderly Ms. Davis held no official **deed** to the land, she was awarded title by *adverse possession,* since she had lived on the property all her life and the legal owner was unknown.

AFFIDAVIT a written statement, sworn to or **affirmed** before an officer who is authorized to administer an oath or affirmation.
Example: The *affidavit* affirmed that the landlord was solely entitled to lease out the property.

AFFIRM to confirm; to ratify; to verify.
Example: At a meeting between the buyer, seller, and broker, the voidable sales contract was *affirmed* by the party who could have

voided it. All parties are now bound by the stipulations of the contract.

"A" FRAME a post World War II style house with a frame in the shape of one or more "A's."
Example: Figure 10.

"A" shape frame

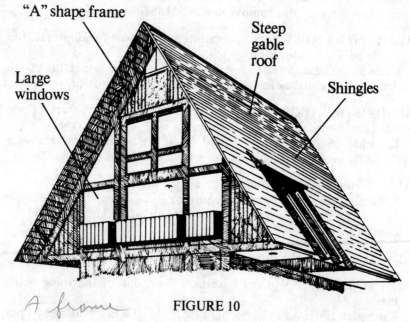

Steep gable roof

Large windows

Shingles

A frame   FIGURE 10

AFTER-TAX CASH FLOW **cash flow** from income-producing property, less income taxes if any attributable to the property's income. The tax saving from the shelter of income earned outside the property is added to the **cash flow** that is earned by the property.
Example: A property generates $1,000 per year of cash flow. In the first year of ownership, depreciation and interest deductions provide a tax loss of $3,000. The loss saves $900 of income taxes that the investor would otherwise pay on salary earned as a teacher. The *after-tax cash flow* is $1,900.

AGENCY the legal relationship between a principal and his **agent** arising from a contract in which the principal engages the agent to perform certain acts on the principal's behalf.
Example: Under the law of *agency,* agents must be loyal to their employers. Therefore broker Roberts submits to employer Davis all offers on property.

AGENT one who undertakes to transact some business or to manage some affair for another, with the authority of the latter.

Example: An owner engages a **broker** to act as *agent* in selling real property; the broker in turn engages salespersons to act as *agents* to sell the same property.

AGREEMENT OF SALE a written agreement between seller and purchaser in which the purchaser agrees to buy certain real estate and the seller agrees to sell upon terms of the agreement. Also called **offer and acceptance, contract of sale, earnest money** contract.

Example: Abel's **broker** prepared an *agreement of sale* to sell a home to Baker. Both principals signed it. It states that the price of $50,000 is to be paid in cash at closing, subject to Baker's ability to arrange a $40,000 loan at a 12% interest rate.

AIR RIGHTS the right to use, control, or occupy the space above a designated property. Air rights can be leased, sold, or donated to another party.

Example: The Pan Am building in New York City is situated in the *air rights* of Grand Central Station (Figure 11).

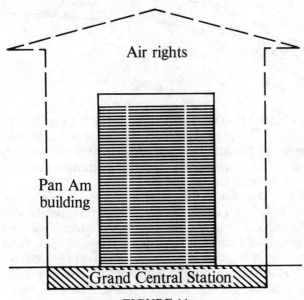

FIGURE 11

ALIENATION to convey or transfer **title** and **possession** of property. May be voluntary (by the owner) or involuntary (without the owner's consent) such as in **condemnation**.

Example: By signing a **deed,** there is an *alienation* of property.

alienation clause (due on sale) allows balance

ALLODIAL SYSTEM a legal system that allocates full property ownership rights to individuals. The allodial system is the basis for

of loan to be paid in full if collateral is sold. (mortgage man at closing)

property rights in the United States.

Example: Under the *allodial system,* an individual may obtain **fee simple** ownership of a parcel of real estate. This allows the individual to enjoy the full set of rights entailed in property ownership, subject to restriction only by governmental powers of taxation, **police power,** and **eminent domain.**

ALLUVIUM (or ALLUVION) soil deposited by **accretion.** Usually considered to belong to the owner of the land to which it is added.

Example: Figure 12.

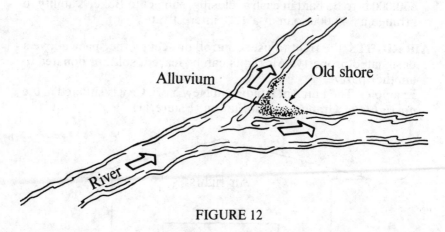

FIGURE 12

ALTERNATIVE MINIMUM TAX a type of flat-rate tax that applies to individual taxpayers who have certain types of income. A 20% rate applies to broadly based income. If this tax exceeds the regular income tax, then this (alternative minimum tax) is to be paid instead of the regular income tax.

To derive the alternative minimum tax, certain items must be added to adjusted gross income. These include the 60% capital gains deduction, the excess of accelerated over straight-line depreciation, and certain other deductions. A specific exemption is subtracted from that total. The exemption is $40,000 for married taxpayers filing a joint return, $20,000 for married taxpayers filing separate returns, and $30,000 for others. A 20% tax rate is applied to the balance. If this results in a greater tax than the regular tax, this is paid.

Example: Collins is a single taxpayer. Her adjusted gross income for 1984 is $60,000. Her personal exemptions and deductions result in a regular taxable income of $55,300, requiring a regular tax of $16,115 in 1984.

She claimed excess accelerated depreciation of $15,000, and had a net capital gains deduction of $40,000. These two items are added to her $60,000 adjusted gross income. The result is $115,000. Subtracting a $30,000 exemption leaves $85,000 to be taxed at 20%. The result is $17,000 in tax. This will be paid since it exceeds the $16,115 regular tax.

ALTERNATIVE MORTGAGE INSTRUMENT (AMI) any mortgage other than a fixed interest rate, level payment **amortizing** loan.
Examples:
Various types of *AMI's:*
• **variable rate mortgages**
• **rollover loans**
• **graduated payment mortgages**
• **shared appreciation mortgages**
• **adjustable rate mortgages**
• **growing equity mortgages**

AMENITIES in **appraisal,** the nonmonetary benefits derived from property ownership, such as pride of home ownership.
Example: Graham bought a **condominium** overlooking Lake Michigan with a prestige address, thus enhancing the *amenities* of ownership.

AMERICAN INSTITUTE OF REAL ESTATE APPRAISERS (AIREA) a professional organization of real estate appraisers affiliated with the **National Association of Realtors®**. AIREA publishes the *Appraisal Journal* and several reference works on appraisal, provides educational services, and confers the professional designations of **MAI** (Member, Appraisal Institute) and RM **(Residential Member).**
Address:
American Institute of Real Estate Appraisers
430 North Michigan Avenue
Chicago, Illinois 60611

AMERICAN LAND TITLE ASSOCIATION (ALTA) a national association of title companies, abstractors, and attorneys established to promote uniformity and quality in **title abstract** and insurance policies.
Example: The title company employed in the purchase of the property is a member of the *American Land Title Association* and, therefore, used standard ALTA forms when underwriting the title policy.

AMERICAN MANSARD OR SECOND EMPIRE STYLE a nineteenth century style house whose main and distinguishing characteristic is the roof design. The mansard roof slopes gently back from the wall line and then is topped with an invisible (from the street) section resembling a conventional hip roof. Multiple dor-

mers protrude through the roof.
Example: Figure 13.

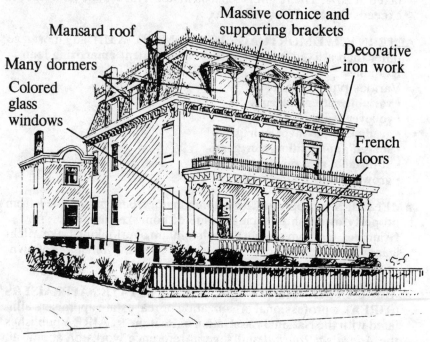

Mansard roof

Massive cornice and
supporting brackets

Decorative
iron work

Many dormers

Colored
glass
windows

French
doors

FIGURE 13

AMERICAN PLANNING ASSOCIATION (APA) a professional
organization of regional and urban planners for the purpose of
promoting professional standards, research, and education. APA
was formed by the merger of the American Institute of Planners
(AIP) and the American Society of Planning Officials (ASPO).
APA publishes a monthly magazine, *Planning,* and a quarterly
journal, *Journal of the APA.*
Address:
American Planning Association
1313 East 60th Street
Chicago, Illinois 60637

**AMERICAN REAL ESTATE AND URBAN ECONOMICS ASSOCI-
ATION (AREUEA)** an organization of scholars, researchers, and
practitioners concerned with economic analysis of real estate
related problems. Publishes the *AREUEA Journal* quarterly.
Address:
Jeffrey Fisher
Secretary-Treasurer
College of Business Administration

Indiana University
Bloomington, Indiana 47401

AMERICAN SOCIETY OF APPRAISERS (ASA) a professional organization of appraisers (not restricted to real estate). ASA publishes the biannual journal, *Valuation*.
Address:
American Society of Appraisers
International Headquarters
Dulles International Airport
P.O. Box 17265
Washington, D.C. 20041

AMERICAN SOCIETY OF REAL ESTATE COUNSELORS (ASREC) a professional organization of real estate investment counselors and consultants. Affiliated with the **National Association of Realtors®**. Awards the designation of Counselor of Real Estate (CRE). Publishes the biannual journal, *Real Estate Issues*.
Address:
American Society of Real Estate Counselors
430 North Michigan Avenue
Chicago, Illinois 60611

AMORTIZATION a gradual paying off of a debt by periodic installments.
Example: A $100,000 loan is arranged at a 12% interest rate. The borrower pays $13,500 in the first year. Of the payment, $12,000 is for interest, $1,500 for *amortization*. After the payment, the loan balance is amortized to $98,500.

AMORTIZATION SCHEDULE a table that shows the periodic payment, interest and principal requirements, and unpaid loan balance for each period of the life of a loan.
Example: An *amortization schedule* for a $1,000 principal, 5-year self-amortizing loan at 10% interest with annual payments is shown in Table 3.

TABLE 3

End of year	Payment required	Interest at 10% of unpaid balance	Principal retirement	Unpaid balance at end of year
1	$263.80	$100.00	$163.80	$836.20
2	263.80	83.62	180.18	656.02
3	263.80	65.60	198.20	457.82
4	263.80	45.78	218.02	239.80
5	263.78	23.98	239.80	0
Total retired			$1000.00	

ANCHOR TENANT the main tenant in a shopping center.
　Example: Big Buy Foods is the *anchor tenant* in Figure 14. (Note: Large scale centers may have more than one anchor tenant).

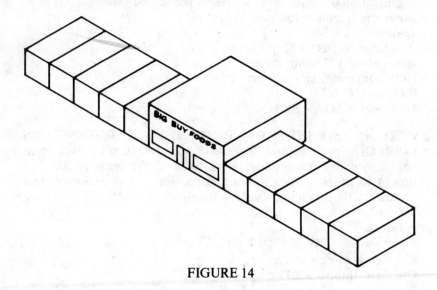

FIGURE 14

ANNEXATION the process by which an incorporated city expands its boundaries to include a specified area. The rules of annexation are established by state law and generally require a public ballot within the city and the area to be annexed. Other incorporated areas are generally protected from annexation by an adjacent city.
　Example: *Annexation* is generally sought by a city to expand its boundaries by taking in an area to which it may already be providing services. Many unincorporated suburban areas, however, resist efforts to annex them into the city because of possibly higher tax rates and loss of local control over schools and other services.

ANNUAL DEBT SERVICE required annual principal and interest payments for a loan.
　Example: A loan of $100,000 calls for 300 equal monthly payments to fully **amortize** the principal. Interest is 15% annually. Monthly payments are $1280.83. *Annual debt service* is the sum of 12 monthly payments, or $15,369.96.

ANNUAL MORTGAGE CONSTANT the amount of **annual debt service** compared to the principal; also expressed as a dollar amount. The formula is:

$$\text{Annual mortgage constant} = \frac{\text{annual debt service}}{\text{mortgage principal}}$$

Example: A loan, at a 15% interest rate, is amortizing over 30 years with monthly payments. The *annual mortgage constant* is 15.1733%. Total principal and interest payments in a year are 15.18 per $100 borrowed. Note: the annual mortgage constant must exceed the interest rate for **amortization** to occur.

ANNUAL PERCENTAGE RATE the effective rate of interest for a loan per year, disclosure of which is required by the **Truth-In-Lending** Law. See **yield to maturity.**
Example: Abel gets a loan for $50,000 at 10% interest plus 2 **discount points,** payable over 30 years. Because of the discount points $49,000 has been effectively borrowed but $50,000 must be repaid with 10% interest on $50,000. Considering the effective amount borrowed, the *annual percentage rate* is 10.25%.

ANNUITY a series of equal or nearly equal periodic payments or receipts.
Example: The receipt of $100 per year for the next 5 years constitutes a $100 five-year *annuity.*

ANNUITY DUE same as **ordinary annuity.**

ANNUITY IN ADVANCE a series of equal or nearly equal payments, each payable at the beginning of the period.
Example: A landlord leases property for 5 years. The rent, payable at the beginning of each period, constitutes an *annuity in advance* (Figure 15).

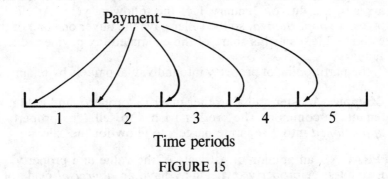

Time periods

FIGURE 15

ANNUITY IN ARREARS same as **ordinary annuity.**

ANNUITY FACTOR a mathematical figure that shows the present value of an income stream that generates one dollar of income each period for a specified number of periods.

Example: Collins is to receive $1,000 each year for 10 years for rental of her land. To value this income, she used an *annuity factor* at a 10% rate that is 6.144. The estimated rent has a present value of $6,144 (6.144 × $1,000).

$$\text{Annuity factor} = \frac{(1 + i)^n - 1}{i}$$

where *i* is the periodic interest rate in decimal form and *n* is the number of periods that the income stream will last.

ANTITRUST LAWS federal and state acts to protect trade and commerce from monopolies and restrictions.
Example: In the early 1960's several real estate boards required all members to charge the same rate of commission. Some boards were found to be in violation of *antitrust laws*. Now there are no boards that require specific commission rates.

APARTMENT (BUILDING) a dwelling unit within a multifamily structure, generally provided as rental housing. An apartment building is a structure with individual apartment units but a common entrance and hallway. See **multifamily housing.**
Example: *Apartments* may vary in size from small, 1-room efficiencies to large, multibedroom units. *Apartment buildings* may be as small as a 1-story, 4-unit building to a high-rise building with hundreds of units and retail and office space included.

APPORTIONMENT 1. the **prorating** of property expenses, such as taxes and insurance, between buyer and seller.
Example: A house is sold on July 1. Property taxes, paid in **arrears,** are due on January 1 of the following year. At closing taxes are *apportioned,* so the seller pays the buyer one half of the estimated taxes as his share of the estimated tax payment due in January.
2. the partitioning of property into individual parcels by tenants in common.
Example: A sister and a brother inherit a property and hold it as tenants in common. The brother wishes to sell. The property is *apportioned* into 2 separate parcels to allow for the sale.

APPRAISAL an opinion or estimate of the value of a property.
Examples: A property owner may have an *appraisal* made of a specific property to:

• determine a reasonable offering price in a sale
• determine the value at death for estate tax purposes
• allocate the purchase price to the land and improvements
• determine the amount of **hazard insurance** to carry

APPRAISAL APPROACH one of 3 methods to estimate the value of property: **cost approach, income approach,** and **market comparison approach.**
Example: An independent fee appraiser generally uses each of the 3 *appraisal approaches* when preparing an appraisal report.

APPRAISAL BY SUMMATION same as **cost approach.**

APPRAISER one qualified to estimate the value of real property.
Example: One may hire an *appraiser* to render an opinion of a property's market value. In a court of law, an *appraiser* may be called upon for expert testimony.

APPRECIATION an increase in the value of property.
Example: Abel sold for $100,000 land that he purchased 10 years ago for $60,000. During that time the amount of *appreciation* was $40,000.
Appreciation gains from investment property are generally subject to favorable **capital gains** tax rates.

APPROPRIATION setting aside land for a public use.
Example: Abel plans to develop a subdivision in Pleasantville. In order to obtain permission from the city council, Abel is required to *appropriate* 2 acres to the city for construction of an elementary school.

APPURTENANCE something that is outside the property itself but is considered a part of the property and adds to its greater enjoyment, such as the right to cross another's land (i.e., **easement** or **right-of-way**).
Example: *Appurtenances* (Figure 16).

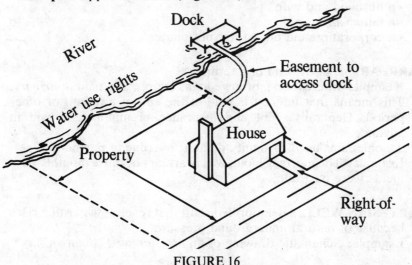

FIGURE 16

ARBITRAGE 1. buying in one market, selling simultaneously in another to make a profit.
Example: Graham bought gold in London for $500 per ounce; simultaneously she sold it in New York for $502. The *arbitrage* allowed $2 profit per ounce, less transaction costs.
2. buying one type of security and selling an equivalent to make a profit.
Example: Baker bought bonds for $5000 that could be converted into 500 shares of stock. Simultaneously, he sold 500 shares of stock at $11 per share. He earned $500 for this *arbitrage,* minus transaction costs.

arbitration clause — 3rd person to referee

ARCHITECTURE the manner in which a building is constructed, including the layout, **floor plan,** style and appearance, materials used, and the building technology used.
Example: The *architecture* of the houses in the neighborhood is characteristic of the design common to the 1930's: small rooms, much attention to detail, an elaborate **facade,** high ceilings, and thick walls.

AREA a 2-dimensional space defined by boundaries; such as floor area, area of a lot, and market area.
Example: A rectangular lot is 50 × 100 feet in dimension. Its *area* is 5,000 square feet or 0.11 acre.

ARM'S LENGTH TRANSACTION a transaction among parties, each of whom acts in his or her own best interest.
Examples: Transactions between the following parties would, in most cases, *not* be considered arm's length:
• a husband and wife
• a father and son
• a corporation and one of its subsidiaries

ARREARS 1. at the end of a term.
Example: Interest on mortgage loans is normally paid in *arrears*. This means that interest is paid at the end of a month or other period. Generally, rent and insurance premiums are paid in advance.
2. sometimes used to signify default; overdue in payment.
Example: The mortgage loan was in arrears because monthly payments were past due.

ARTESIAN WELL a deep-drilled shaft that reaches water that rises because of natural underground pressure.
Example: Schematic drawing of an *artesian well* (Figure 17).

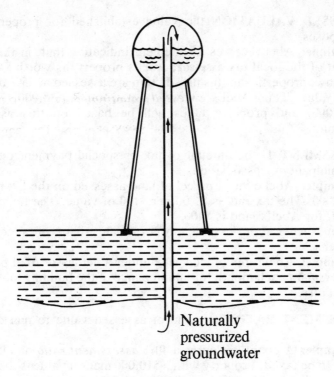

Naturally
pressurized
groundwater

FIGURE 17

AS IS without guarantees as to condition, as in a sale.
  Example: Baker purchases a building from Abel with the under-
  standing that the building is to be conveyed *as is*. When Baker
  discovers that the roof leaks, Abel is not legally responsible for
  repairs.

ASKED the amount a property owner sets as a selling price for his
  property.
  Example: Abel has *asked* $75,000 for 20 acres of land, even
  though its **appraised** value is only $60,000.

ASKING PRICE the list price that an owner would like to
  receive.
  Example: Abel advertises a property for sale at a price of
  $100,000. The advertised price is Abel's *asking price*.

ASSEMBLAGE combining of 2 or more parcels of land. See **plottage
  value.**
  Example: Abel buys 2 **adjoining** properties of land for $10,000
  each. The large unified tract is worth $25,000. The process is
  assemblage.

ASSESSED VALUATION the value established for property tax purposes.

Example: Abel receives a statement indicating that, in the judgment of the local tax **assessor,** Abel's property is worth $40,000. By law, properties in this jurisdiction are assessed at 75% of **market value.** Thus Abel's *assessed valuation* is $30,000 (75% of $40,000) and property taxes will be based on this assessed amount.

ASSESSMENT 1. the amount of tax or special payment due to a municipality or association. *to cover portionate cost for improvement*

Example: Abel owns a parcel of land assessed on the tax roll for $40,000. The tax rate is $1.00 per $100 of value. The tax *assessment* for Abel's land is $400.

2. an owner's or lessee's proportionate share of a common expense.

Example: Abel rents office space under a **net lease.** Abel pays an *assessment* each month for maintenance of the building lobby and elevators.

ASSESSMENT RATIO the ratio of assessed value to **market value.**

Example: A county requires a 40% *assessment ratio* on all property to be taxed. Property with a $10,000 market value is therefore assessed at $4000 (40% of $10,000), and the **tax rate** is applied to $4000.

ASSESSMENT ROLL a public record of the assessed value of property in a taxing jurisdiction.

Example: The *assessment roll* of Anytown, USA lists each individual tract of land within its taxing jurisdiction and shows the assessed value of each. The total assessed value of property is $10 million.

ASSESSOR an official who determines property tax assessments.

Example: Jones inspects Abel's property and estimates its value at $50,000 for property tax purposes. Jones is an *assessor.*

ASSET something of value.

Example: Land, houses, cars, furniture, cash, bank deposits, and securities owned are *assets.*

ASSET DEPRECIATION RANGE generally applies to property purchased before 1981. Limitations on the period over which assets may be depreciated. Generally allows depreciable lives 20% longer or shorter than the guidelines provided by the Internal Revenue Service. Also provides maximum amounts that can be spent annually on assets and still be a deductible repair.

Example: Farm buildings purchased before 1981 may be depreciated over 25 years or within a range of 20 to 30 years, according to the *asset depreciation range*. Up to 5% of the cost can be spent annually and be treated as repair, not as a capital improvement.

ASSIGNEE the person to whom an agreement or contract is sold or transferred.
Example: See **assignor**.

ASSIGNMENT the method by which a right or contract is transferred from one person to another.
Example: A tenant signs an *assignment* giving another the rights to use the leased space.

ASSIGNMENT OF LEASE the transfer of rights to use leased property. The **assignee** acquires the same rights and privileges as the **assignor.** The assignor remains liable unless released by the landlord.
Example: Abel signs a 20-year lease for a warehouse. After 5 years, Abel no longer needs the warehouse and *assigns the lease* to Baker.

ASSIGNOR a party who assigns or transfers an agreement or contract to another.
Example: Davis has an option to buy certain land. She assigns her rights to Baker, so that Baker now has the same rights. Davis is the *assignor*. Baker is the **assignee.**

ASSUMPTION OF MORTGAGE the purchase of mortgaged property whereby the buyer accepts liability for the debt that continues to exist. The seller remains liable to the lender unless the lender agrees to release him.
Example: Abel owes a 30-year mortgage loan of $50,000 against his house. Baker wants to buy the house and keep the same mortgage. Baker pays $20,000 cash for the **equity** and *assumes* the mortgage. Baker becomes liable for the debt, but Abel remains liable also.

AT-RISK RULES tax laws that limit tax losses to the amount that an investor (particularly a **limited partner**) can lose. Generally does not apply to real estate owners or partnerships whose principal asset is real estate.
Example: Partners contribute $10,000 and borrow another $15,000 on a **nonrecourse** basis. Because of *at-risk rules* they cannot deduct tax losses above $10,000 in:

• equipment leasing
• farming
• movie production
• oil and gas exploration

ATTACHMENT legal seizure of property to force payment of a debt.
Example: The landlord obtained an *attachment* that created a **lien** on the tenant's property to enforce payment of back rent.

ATTEST to witness by observation and signature.
Example: Many contracts require a third party to *attest* to the signing by the principals.

ATTORNEY-IN-FACT one who is authorized to act for another under a **power of attorney,** which may be general or limited in scope.
Example: Collins wishes to sell her home but is planning a 6-month vacation in the Middle East. She gives authorization to her friend Baker to sign the **deed** over to a buyer. Baker becomes her *attorney-in-fact* for this situation.

ATTORNMENT a tenant's formal agreement to be a tenant of a new landlord.
Example: Abel defaulted on the mortgage against his shopping center, so the Happy Life Insurance Company **foreclosed** and became the landlord. Happy Life asked all tenants to sign an *attornment* recognizing the new landlord.

AUCTION a way of marketing property to the highest bidder. **Bids** are taken verbally or simultaneously through mail or telegrams, and the property is sold to the highest bidder. Auctioning real estate may require both an auctioneer's license and a real estate license.
Example: Land in Iowa, since it is relatively homogeneous, lends itself to *auction* sales where it is sold to the highest verbal bidder.
Example: Fannie Mae agrees to buy mortgages once a week via an *auction*. Mortgage sellers state the price or yield they want, and Fannie Mae accepts the highest yields offered.

AVULSION the sudden removal of land from one parcel to another, when a body of water, such as a river, abruptly changes its channel. Contrast to **accretion.**
Example: Because of the change in the river's channel, in Figure 18 parcel A gains use of a portion of the land in the original river bed through *avulsion*. Similarly, parcel B loses land which is now covered by the river.

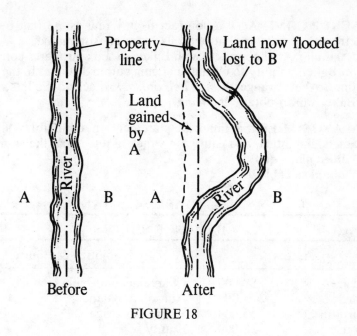

FIGURE 18

B

BACKFILL the replacement of excavated earth into a hole or against a structure.
Example: Figure 19.

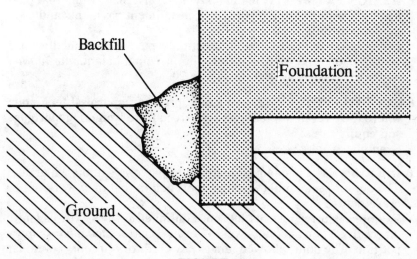

FIGURE 19

BACKUP CONTRACT a contract to buy real estate that becomes effective if a prior contract fails to be consummated.
Example: Abel contracts with Baker to sell a property contingent on Baker's ability to obtain financing within 30 days. In the meantime, Abel arranges a *backup contract* to sell to Collins, should Baker fail to obtain financing.

BALANCE SHEET a financial statement in table form showing **assets**, liabilities, and **equity**, in which assets equal the sum of **liabilities** plus **equity**.
Example: Table 4:

TABLE 4

BALANCE SHEET

Assets		Liabilities & Equity	
Cash	$1,000	Charge account debts	$500
Cars	5,000	Auto loan balance	2,000
Furniture	5,000	Home mortgage	28,500
House	50,000	Equity	40,000
Stocks	10,000		
Total assets	$71,000	Total liabilities & equity	$71,000

BALLOON MORTGAGE a mortgage with a **balloon payment**.
Example: The *balloon mortgage* called for payments of $500 per month for 5 years, followed by a **balloon payment** of $50,000.

BALLOON PAYMENT the final payment on a loan, when that payment is greater than the preceding installment payments and pays the loan in full.
Example: A debt requires interest-only payments annually for 5 years, at the end of which time the principal balance (a *balloon payment*) is due, as seen in Figure 20.

BAND OF INVESTMENT an income property **appraisal** technique where the overall interest rate is derived from weighting **mortgage** and **equity** rates.
Example: Table 5.

BANKRUPTCY the financial inability to pay one's debts when due. The debtor seeks relief through court action that may work out or erase debts.
Example: Carter lost his job but continued to live extravagantly on **credit**. When accounts were overdue, Carter filed a *bankruptcy* petition. The court allowed him to pay creditors 10 cents per dollar of debt, payable over 3 years.

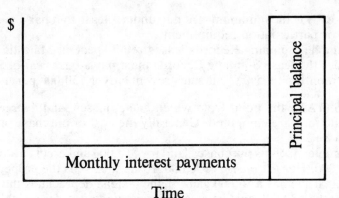

FIGURE 20

TABLE 5

Source of purchase capital	Percentage contributed	×	Rate of interest	=	Weighted rate
Mortgage	60%		15%		9%
Equity	40%		20%		8%
Band of investment rate					17%

BASE AND MERIDIAN imaginary lines used by **surveyors** to find and describe the location of land. The base line is east-west; the meridian line is north-south.
Example: Principal *base and meridian* lines for Oklahoma (Figure 21).

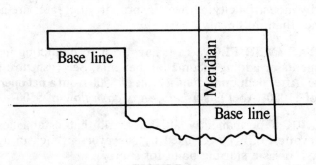

FIGURE 21

BASE LINE part of the **Rectangular Survey** or **Government Rectangular Survey** method of land description. The *base line* is the major east-west line to which all north-south measurements refer.
Example: See **base and meridian.**

BASE RENT the minimum rent due under a lease that has a percentage or participation requirement.
Example: Spinning Records leases retail space in Majestic Mall. Under the lease Spinning Records must pay a *base rent* of $2,000 per month plus 5% of all sales revenue over $50,000 per month.

BASIS (TAX) the point from which gains, losses, and **depreciation** deductions are computed. Generally the cost or purchase price of an asset.
Example: Collins purchases land for $10,000 and erects a store for $80,000. Her *tax basis* is $90,000. If she then sells the property for $95,000 she has a $5,000 gain. If she instead depreciates the property, the $80,000 cost basis of improvements are depreciable; the $10,000 *basis* of the land remains because land is not depreciable.

BASIS POINT one 100th of 1%.
Example: Mortgage loan interest rates are 12.75% this week. They were 12.25% last week. The increase was 50 *basis points* (1275 minus 1225 equals 50).

BEARER INSTRUMENT a **security** that does not indicate the owner; payable to whoever presents it.
Example: A *bearer instrument* is open to theft because it can be redeemed without proof of legitimate ownership.

BEDROOM COMMUNITY a residential community in the **suburbs,** often near an employment center, but itself providing few employment opportunities.
Example: *Bedroom communities* frequently offer uncrowded schools, uncongested streets, and less noise and air pollution than the nearby industrial city. However, property tax rates are generally higher than in the city.

BEFORE-TAX CASH FLOW **cash flow** prior to deducting income tax payments or adding income tax benefits. See **cash throw-off.**
Example: After deducting **debt service** of $500 from a **net operating income** of $1000, Abel has a *before-tax cash flow* of $500.

BENCHMARK a permanently affixed mark that establishes the exact elevation of a place; used by **surveyors** in measuring site elevations, or as a starting point for **surveys.**
Example: The U.S. Coast and Geodetic Survey implants brass markers in the sidewalks of downtown areas to serve as *benchmarks.* The benchmark indicates the official elevation above sea level for the spot at which the marker is placed.

BENEFICIARY the person who receives or is to receive the benefits resulting from certain acts.

Example: Whitman takes out a $10,000 life insurance policy with her husband as the *beneficiary*. Should Whitman die, her husband will receive the benefits from the policy.

BEQUEATH to specify by **will** the recipient of personal property. Compare **devise**.
Example: In Abel's will he *bequeaths* his automobile and wrist watch to his son.

BEQUEST that personal property given by the terms of a **will**.
Example: Collins received a set of sterling silverware as a *bequest* from her deceased aunt.

BETTERMENT an improvement to real estate.
Example: Abel purchases a **site** and constructs a building. The building is considered a *betterment* to the site.

BIANNUAL occurring twice a year. Same as **semiannual**. Contrast **biennial**.
Example: Under a lease, Abel is required to make *biannual* rent payments, one in January and one in July (Figure 22).

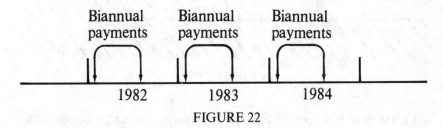

FIGURE 22

BID the amount someone offers to pay.
Example: Abel places a property for sale at an **asking price** of $90,000. Baker makes a *bid* of $65,000 for the property, indicating he is willing to pay that amount for the property.

BIENNIAL occurring every 2 years.
Example: Abel arranges to pay premiums on a property insurance policy on a *biennial* basis. If the current premium is paid in 1984, the next premium is due in 1986 (Figure 23).

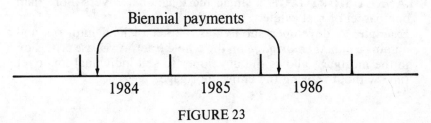

FIGURE 23

BILATERAL CONTRACT a contract under which each party promises performance. See **unilateral contract.**
Example: A sales contract is a *bilateral contract,* since the seller promises to **convey** a property and the buyer agrees to pay a specified sum, given certain conditions.

BI-LEVEL a house built on 2 levels in which the main entrance is situated above the lower level but below the upper level.
Example: Drawing of a *bi-level* house (Figure 24):

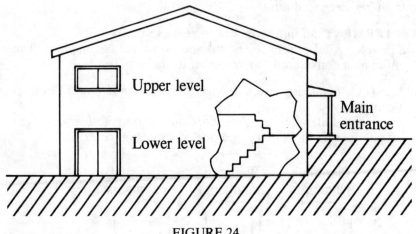

FIGURE 24

BILL OF SALE a written **instrument** given to pass **title** of personal property from a seller to a buyer. Used when furniture and portable appliances are sold.
Example: Figure 25.

BINDER an agreement, accompanied by a **deposit,** for the purchase of real estate, to evidence **good faith** on the part of the purchaser.
Example: Abel gave Baker a *binder* on the house; Abel then contacted his attorney to prepare the papers for a contract.

BLANKET MORTGAGE a single **mortgage** that covers more than one parcel of real estate.
Example: A developer subdivides a tract of land into lots and obtains a *blanket mortgage* on the whole tract. A **release** provision in the mortgage allows the developer to sell individual lots over time without **retiring** the entire mortgage.

```
                        Bill of Sale

        I, Ernest Abel, do hereby sell my dining
        room suite, which I represent to be free
        and clear, to Bill Baker.

                        Signed,

                        Ernest Abel
```

FIGURE 25

BLENDED RATE an **interest rate,** applied to a **refinanced** loan, that is higher than the rate on the old loan but lower than the rate offered on new loans. Generally offered by the lender to induce home buyers to refinance existing, low-interest rate loans as an alternative to assuming the existing loan. Compare **assumption of mortgage.**
Example: Jones wishes to sell a home to Brown. Brown can assume the existing loan of $20,000 at an interest rate of 8%. Jones' lender offers the alternative of refinancing the loan for $40,000 at a *blended rate* of 10%. Brown could get a new loan at a rate of 12%.

BLIGHTED AREA a section of a city in which a majority of the structures are dilapidated.
Example: Urban renewal is planned for several *blighted areas* of the city. Within these areas, houses that do not meet **housing codes** are to be rehabilitated or demolished and new buildings constructed.

BLIND POOL an investment program in which monies are invested into an association without investors knowing which properties will be purchased.
Example: Each of 100 investors contributes $5,000 into a joint venture. The **syndicator** has not located the property to be purchased, so the investment money is said to be a *blind pool*.

BLOCKBUSTING a racially discriminatory and illegal practice of coercing a party to sell a home to someone of a minority race or ethnic background, then using scare tactics to cause others in the neighborhood to sell at depressed prices.

Examples: A sales agent arranges a sale in which a minority family enters a previously all-white neighborhood. The agent then engages in *blockbusting* by contacting other owners in the neighborhood and informing them that their property's value will fall if they don't sell right away at a depressed offered price.

BLUE-SKY LAWS state laws requiring the offeror of securities to give full disclosure, and register the offering as required by federal and state law.
Example: A **syndicator** wishes to sell 10,000 units of a partnership to investors throughout the U.S. He registers the offering with the **Securities and Exchange Commission** and complies with *blue-sky laws* in 50 states. The term comes from fraudulent practices of exaggerated offerings to investors, including part of the blue sky.

BOARD OF EQUALIZATION a government entity whose purpose is to assure uniform property tax assessments.
Example: A *board of equalization* at the local level may review **assessments** to be certain that the assessment for each parcel is fair; at the state level, the board will assure that each county is assessing property at the mandated proportion of market value.

BOARD OF REALTORS® a local group of real estate licensees who are members of the State and **National Association of Realtors®**.
Example: The Springfield *Board of Realtors®* has 200 members. They meet monthly to discuss business matters, and form the **multiple listing** service in Springfield.

BOILER PLATE standard language found in contracts. Preprinted material.
Example: Collins decided to lease her property. At a stationery store she finds a preprinted *boiler plate* form. She fills in rental rates and dates in the blank places, than asks her tenant, Baker, to sign the lease.

BONA FIDE in **good faith,** without fraud.
Example: To be certain that the signatures to the deed were *bona fide,* the county clerk insisted they be **notarized.**

BOND a certificate that serves as evidence of a debt and of the terms under which it is undertaken. See **promissory note.**
Example: Abel loans $10,000 to Baker, who gives a **note** or *bond* to evidence the debt (Figure 26).

BOOK VALUE the carrying amount of an **asset,** as shown on the books of a company. Generally the amount paid for an asset, less depreciation.

Example: X Corporation purchases a building for $100,000, then **depreciates** it by $10,000 on its financial statements. The *book value* was $100,000 and is now $90,000.

Bill Baker owes Ernest Abel $10,000, payable
at maturity in 10 years with interest payable
semiannually at 10%.

Signed

Bill Baker

Bill Baker
August 15, 1983

FIGURE 26

BOOT unlike property included to balance the value of like properties exchanged.
Example: In an exchange of property under **Section 1031** of the **Internal Revenue Code,** Collins exchanges her warehouse worth $100,000 and receives Baker's land worth $125,000. Collins pays $15,000 cash and a car worth $10,000 to *boot* in order to equalize the values of properties exchanged. The car and cash are *boot* (Figure 27).

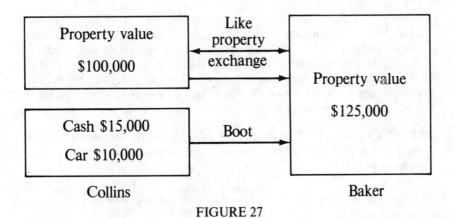

FIGURE 27

BOTTOMLAND 1. low land near a river, lake, stream, which is often flooded, see **flood plain.**
Example: Figure 28.

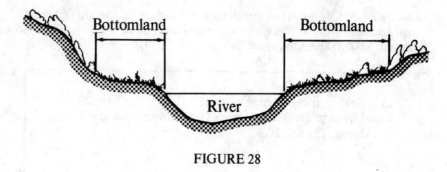

FIGURE 28

2. land in a valley or dale.
Example: Figure 29.

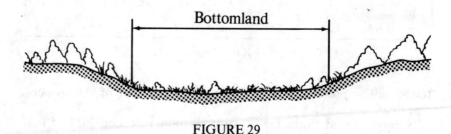

FIGURE 29

BOUNDARY same as **property line.**

BREACH OF CONTRACT a violation of the terms of a legal agreement; **default.** Breach of contract allows the nonbreaching party to rescind the contract, sue for damages, or sue for performance of the contract.
Example: Baker contracts with owner Brown to purchase a property. When the closing date arrives, Brown refuses to **convey** title to the property. Brown's action is not supported by any special conditions in the sales contract and therefore constitutes a *breach of contract*. Baker may rescind the contract and recover his **deposit,** may sue Brown for any expenses and damages incurred, or may sue to force Brown to sell.

BREAK-EVEN POINT the amount of **rent** or the **occupancy level** needed to pay **operating expenses** and **debt service.** Also called **default** point.

$$\text{Break-even point} = \frac{\text{operating expenses and debt service}}{\text{potential gross income}}$$

Example: Annual operating expenses for a 100-unit apartment complex are estimated at $200,000 per year. Debt service requirements are $250,000 per year. Therefore, total cash requirements are $450,000. If all apartments are rented all year, the **gross income** would be $600,000. The *break-even point* is at 75% occupancy. At that level, gross income would exactly equal cash requirements.

BRIDGE LOAN mortgage financing between the termination of one loan and the beginning of another loan.
Example: Collins, who is a developer, has a construction loan outstanding. She is in the process of negotiating better terms for permanent financing than the commitment previously arranged. She has arranged a *bridge loan* to pay off the construction loan when it is due. When new permanent financing is arranged, that loan will pay off the bridge loan.

BROKER a state-licensed **agent** who, for a fee, acts for property owners in real estate transactions, within the scope of state law.
Example: A person wishing to sell or lease property often engages a *broker* to arrange the sale or locate tenants. A broker may also be engaged by a prospective buyer or tenant to locate acceptable property.

BROKERAGE 1. the business of being a **broker.**
Example: One may open a *brokerage* office, upon receiving a broker's license, for the purpose of engaging in brokerage.
2. the **commission** received by a broker for his services.
Example: The *brokerage* was $6,000 on the sale of a $100,000 house.

BROWNSTONE, BRICK ROW HOUSE, OR EASTERN TOWNHOUSE a nineteenth century style house, usually having 4 or 5 stories with a stoop leading up to the first floor. They have common side walls with the house on either side.
Example: Figure 30.

BUDGET MORTGAGE a **mortgage** that requires monthly payments for taxes and insurance in addition to interest and principal.
Example: Abel borrows $50,000 on a *budget mortgage* at 12% interest. His monthly mortgage payment is $700, which consists of $514 principal and interest, $150 taxes, and $36 insurance.

BUFFER ZONE a transitional area between 2 areas of different predominant land uses.
Example: In Figure 31 a *buffer zone* of **apartments** separates an area of **single-family** houses from a **commercial property** area:

BUILDING AND LOAN ASSOCIATIONS see **savings and loan associations.**

BUILDING CODES regulations established by local governments describing the minimum structural requirements for buildings;

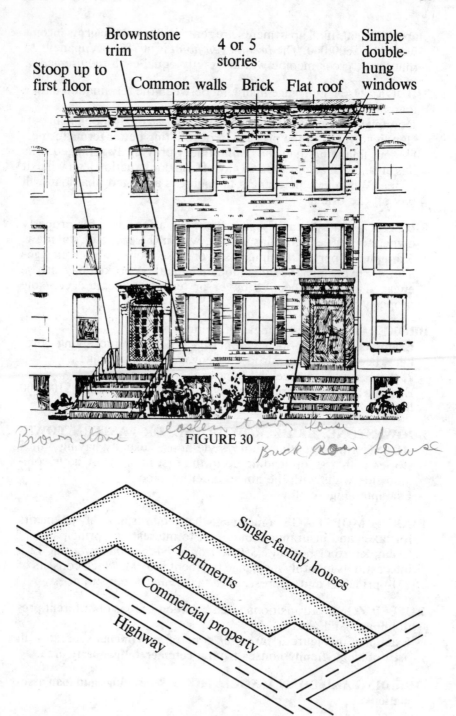

Brownstone trim

4 or 5 stories

Simple double-hung windows

Stoop up to first floor

Common walls

Brick

Flat roof

FIGURE 30

Brownstone   eastern town house

Brick Row house

Single-family houses

Apartments

Commercial property

Highway

FIGURE 31

includes foundation, roofing, plumbing, electrical, and other specifications for safety and sanitation.

Example: Abel is developer who wishes to construct houses. He must comply with the standards of the local *building codes* and submit to inspections by a building inspector.

BUILDING LINE a line fixed at a certain distance from the front and/or sides of a lot, beyond which the building may not project.

Example: Figure 32.

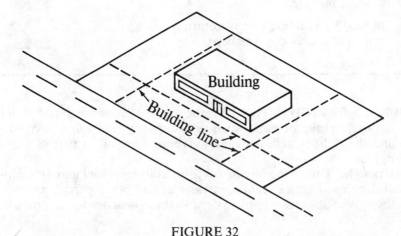

FIGURE 32

BUILDING LOAN AGREEMENT an agreement whereby the lender advances money to an owner at specified stages of construction, i.e., upon completion of the foundation, framing, etc. Same as **construction loan** agreement.

BUILDING OWNERS AND MANAGERS ASSOCIATION (BOMA) an organization of practitioners who own and manage buildings, notably office space.

Address:
1221 Massachusetts Ave., N.W.
Washington, D.C. 20005

BUILDING PERMIT permission granted by a local government to build a specific structure at a particular site.

Example: Abel desires to construct a small office building at the corner of First and Main. A *building permit* must be obtained from the city to allow the construction to proceed legally.

BUILDING RESIDUAL TECHNIQUE an **appraisal** technique whereby income to land is subtracted from **net operating income** to

result in the building income. Building income is capitalized into building value.
Example: Table 6:

TABLE 6

Net operating income	$13,000
Less: Land income (Land value $50,000×10% rate of return)	− 5,000
Building income	$8,000
Divided by building rate of return (10%+2% **depreciation**)	÷ .12
Building value	$66,666

BUNDLE OF RIGHTS THEORY the theory that ownership of realty implies a group of rights such as occupancy, use and enjoyment, and the right to sell, **bequeath**, give, or **lease** all or part of these rights.
Example: Under the *bundle of rights* concept, Abel may sell mineral rights, hunting rights, **easements**, and other partial interest, then give a **life estate** to his wife with the **remainder** to their daughter.

BUNGALOW a small, early twentieth century style, 1-story house that usually has an open or enclosed front porch.
Example: Figure 33.

BUSINESS DAY a standard day for conducting business. Excludes weekends and holidays.
Example: On Monday, July 1, Abel agrees to buy real estate. Closing will be 5 *business days* later, which is July 9 (Table 7):

TABLE 7

		Business days
Tuesday	July 2	1
Wednesday	July 3	2
Thursday	July 4	holiday
Friday	July 5	3
Saturday	July 6	weekend
Sunday	July 7	weekend
Monday	July 8	4
Tuesday	July 9	5

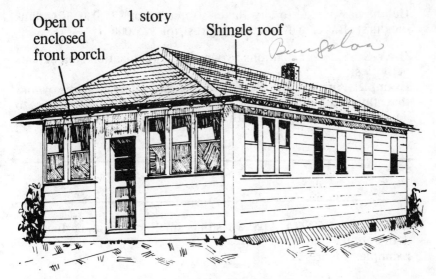

Open or enclosed front porch

1 story

Shingle roof

Bungalow

FIGURE 33

BUY-BACK AGREEMENT a provision in a contract under which the seller agrees to repurchase the property at a stated price upon the occurrence of a specified event within a certain period of time.
Example: The *buy-back agreement* in the sales contract requires the builder-seller to buy the property back if Collins, the buyer-occupant, is transferred by her company within 6 months.

BUY DOWN 1. the action to pay additional **discount points** to a lender in exchange for a reduced rate of interest on a loan. The reduced rate may apply for all or a portion of the loan term. 2. a loan that has been bought down by the seller of the property for the benefit of the buyer.
Example: In order to achieve a sale of a property, Jones arranged for a *buy down* loan. If a seller agreed to Jones' price, Jones would *buy down* the interest rate for the first 3 years by paying the lender 5% of the loan amount at closing.

BUYER'S MARKET a situation where buyers have a wide choice of properties and may negotiate lower prices. Often caused by over-building, local population decreases, or economic slump.
Example: Abel can purchase properties below their appraised values because of the existence of a *buyer's market*.

BUY-SELL AGREEMENT a pact among partners or stockholders under which some agree to buy the interests of others upon some event.
Example: Collins and Baker are partners. In the event Baker dies,

Collins has agreed to buy Baker's interest for $25,000. If Collins dies first, Baker will buy her interest for $25,000.

BYLAWS a set of regulations by which an organization conducts its activities.
Example: An association of **condominium** owners prepares *bylaws* that state the minimum number of owners to conduct a meeting, to decide on policies, to elect officers, and other matters.

C

CALIFORNIA BUNGALOW a 1-story, small, compact, early twentieth century house.
Example: Figure 34

Small, compact shape   1 story

FIGURE 34

CALIFORNIA RANCH a post-World War II style, 1-story, ground-hugging house with a low, pitched roof.
Example: Figure 35.

CALL PROVISIONS clauses in a loan that give the lender the right to accelerate the debt upon the occurrence of a specific event or date. See **acceleration clause.**
Example: Abel, the **mortgage** lender, notices that Baker, the homeowner, has begun to demolish the property. *Call provisions* in the loan allow Abel to claim that the full debt is now due.

CANCELLATION CLAUSE a contract provision that gives the right to terminate obligations upon the occurrence of specified conditions or events.
Example: a *cancellation clause* in a **lease** may allow the landlord to break the lease upon the sale of the building.

1 story   Low-pitched roof   Picture windows   Ground-hugging   Sliding windows

FIGURE 35

CAPE COD COLONIAL an early American style 1½ story compact house that is small and symmetrical with a central entrance. The roof is the steep gable type covered with shingles. The authentic types have low central chimneys, but end chimneys are very common in the new versions. Bedrooms are on the first floor. The attic may be finished into additional bedrooms and a bath. A vine covered picket fence is traditional.
Example: Figure 36.

Gable roof   1½ stories

Shingles

Central entrance

FIGURE 36

Capital appreciation

CAPITAL ASSET an asset defined in **Section 1221** of the **Internal Revenue Code** that can receive favorable tax treatment upon sale. Excludes **inventory,** property held for resale, property used in a trade or business, copyrights in certain instances, and certain U.S. government obligations.
Example: The dwelling that one owns and lives in, investment land, a limited partnership interest, or securities held for investment are *capital assets.*

CAPITAL EXPENDITURE an improvement (as distinguished from a **repair**) that will have a life of more than one year.
Example: Collins adds a new 25-room wing to her motel, at a cost of $250,000. The new wing is a *capital expenditure.*
Example: Baker, a rancher, has a fence that is in such poor condition it cannot be repaired. He makes a $50,000 *capital expenditure* to replace the fence.

CAPITAL GAIN gain on the sale of a **capital asset.** If long-term (generally over one year), capital gains are favorably taxed. Contrast with **ordinary income.**

Example: Collins purchases land, for investment purposes, for $10,000. Thirteen months later she sells it for $14,000. She reports the $4,000 profit as a long-term *capital gain* on her income tax return.

CAPITAL IMPROVEMENT same as **capital expenditure.**

CAPITAL RECOVERY see **recapture rate.**

CAPITALIZATION 1. in finance, a process whereby anticipated future income is converted to one lump sum capital value. A **capitalization rate** is divided into the expected periodic income to derive a capital value for the expected income. Sum of **interest rate** and **recapture rate.** See **capitalization rate.**
Example: A property is expected to produce an annual income of $10,000. It is judged to have a value of $80,000, which represents *capitalization* of the $10,000 per year income stream. Also, when taxes on the property increased by $500 per year, the property's value was reduced by $6,000 due to the *capitalization* process.
2. in accounting, setting up an **asset** on the financial records, rather than deducting it currently.
Example: *Capitalization* is required for an asset that has a 15-year **depreciable life;** the cost will be deducted over that time period, not deducted currently.

CAPITALIZATION RATE a rate of return used to derive the capital value of an **income stream.** The formula is

$$\text{Value} = \frac{\text{annual income}}{\text{capitalization rate}}$$

Example: The estimated net operating income of an office building is $12,000 per year. An appraiser decides the appropriate *capitalization rate* is 12%, comprised of a 10% return on investment and 2% for **depreciation.** The estimated value of the building is $100,000.

CAPITALIZE 1. to estimate the present lump sum value of an **income stream..** See **capitalization rate.**
Example: An **income stream** of $1,000 per year expected for 20 years is *capitalized to result in a value of $8,513, based on a 10% interest rate.*
2. *to set up the cost of an* **asset** *on financial records.*
Example: *Abel acquires a building at a cost of $100,000. Since the cost cannot be deducted in the year paid, the $100,000 is capitalized as an asset and* **depreciates** *over its estimated useful life.*

CAPITAL LOSS loss from the sale of a **capital asset.**
Example: Collins, an investor, purchases land for $10,000. Two years later she sells it for $8,000. The $2,000 difference is a *capital loss,* since the land is a capital asset. Note: There are limitations on the amount of loss that can be used to offset **ordinary income.**

capital recapture

CAP RATE same as **capitalization rate.**

CARRYING CHARGES expenses necessary for holding property, such as taxes and interest on idle property or property under construction.
Example: The annual *carrying charges* on a $100,000 tract of land are: $2,000 for taxes and $12,000 for interest.

CARRYOVER BASIS in a tax-deferred exchange, the **adjusted tax basis** of the property surrendered that is used to determine the tax basis of the property acquired. See **basis (tax)..**
Example: Abel exchanges land with Baker in a tax-deferred exchange. Abel's **adjusted tax basis** in the **land** given up was $10,000. The *carryover basis* will therefore be $10,000 and (in the absence of **boot**) that will be Abel's tax basis in the land acquired from Baker.

CASH BASIS a method of accounting based on cash receipts and disbursements.
Example: Abel, a *cash method* taxpayer, has the carpets in his

office building shampooed on December 20 and immediately gets a bill for the service. He pays the bill on January 1 so the tax deduction is taken in the next year.

CASH FLOW periodic amounts available to an **equity** investor after deducting all periodic cash payments from rental income. See **before-tax cash flow, cash throw-off, after-tax cash flow.**
Example: Table 8.

TABLE 8

potential gross income	$10,000
less: vacancy and collection allowance	− 1,000
add: miscellaneous income	+ 500
effective gross income	9,500
less: operating expenses	− 3,000
less: replacement reserve	− 500
net operating income	6,000
less: interest	− 4,000
less: principal payment	− 500
cash flow	$1,500

CASH THROW-OFF same as **cash flow.**

CAVEAT EMPTOR "let the buyer beware." The buyer must examine the goods or property and buy at his own risk, except for **latent defects.**
Example: Often a property is offered "as is," with no expressed or implied guarantee of quality or condition. When entering such transactions, *caveat emptor* is a worthy admonishment.

CENTRAL BUSINESS DISTRICT (CBD) the downtown section of a city, generally consisting of retail, office, hotel, entertainment, and governmental land uses with some high **density** housing.
Example: Elaine chose to live in the suburb of Great Neck because it is only 30 minutes from the Manhattan CBD.

CERTIFICATE OF DEPOSIT (CD) a type of savings account that carries a specified minimum deposit and **term** and generally provides a higher **yield** than passbook-type savings accounts.
Example: Carny purchases a 3-year *certificate of deposit* from Local Savings and Loan. Carny must deposit at least $1000 and may not withdraw the money for 3 years without forfeiting a portion of the interest earned. Carny receives a yield of 8% annually.

Cease & Desist Order
Cease & Desist Petition

CERTIFICATE OF ELIGIBILITY issued by the Veterans Administration to those who qualify for a **VA loan.**
Example: A person honorably discharged after serving a certain
number of days on active duty in the armed forces is entitled to a
certificate of eligibility. It indicates eligibility for a VA mortgage
loan.

CERTIFICATE OF INSURANCE a document issued by an insurance company to verify the coverage.
Example: Under the **net lease,** the tenant had to keep adequate
insurance and provide the landlord with a *certificate of insurance*
as evidence.

CERTIFICATE OF NO DEFENSE same as **estoppel certificate.**

CERTIFICATE OF OCCUPANCY a document issued by a local
government to a **developer** permitting the structure to be occupied
by members of the public. Issuance of the certificate generally
indicates that the building is in compliance with public health and
building codes.
Example: Upon obtaining **zoning** and **subdivision** approvals and
passing inspection by code enforcement officials, the developer is
issued a *certificate of occupancy.*

CERTIFICATE OF REASONABLE VALUE a document issued by
the Veteran's Administration, based on an approved **appraisal.**
Establishes a ceiling on the maximum **VA mortgage loan** principal.
Example: A *certificate of reasonable value* (CRV) was received
for a home that was under a **contract of sale.** Since the CRV was
$1,000 more than the contracted price, the VA lent the full pur-
chase price.

CERTIFICATE OF TITLE an opinion rendered by an attorney as to
the status of **title** to a property, according to the public records.
See **title search.**
Example: Abel's attorney issues a *certificate of title* that indicates
no public record of claims against Abel's ownership of the property.

CERTIFIED COMMERCIAL INVESTMENT MEMBER (CCIM) a
designation awarded by the **Realtors National Marketing Institute,**
which is affiliated with the **National Association of Realtors®.**
Address:
Realtors National Marketing Institute
430 N. Michigan Ave.
Chicago, Illinois 60611

CERTIFIED HISTORIC STRUCTURE see **historic structure.**

CERTIFIED PROPERTY MANAGER (CPM) a professional designation awarded to real estate managers by the **Institute of Real Estate Management,** an affiliate of the **National Association of Realtors®.**
Address:
Institute of Real Estate Management
430 N. Michigan Ave.
Chicago, Illinois 60611.

CERTIFIED RESIDENTIAL BROKER (CRB) a designation awarded by the **Realtors National Marketing Institute,** which is affiliated with the **National Association of Realtors®.**
Example: Upon completing the necessary requirements, Abel was awarded the title of *Certified Residential Broker.*

CERTIFIED RESIDENTIAL SPECIALIST (CRS) a professional designation awarded by the **Realtors National Marketing Institute,** based on education and experience in residential sales. Candidates must hold the **GRI** designation.

CHAIN a linear unit of land measurement used in surveying: 66 feet in length. Each chain consists of 100 links.
Example: A plot 66 ft square measures 1 chain by 1 chain.

CHAIN OF TITLE a history of **conveyances** and **encumbrances** affecting a **title** from the time that the original **patent** was granted, or as far back as records are available. See **abstract of title, certificate of title.**
Example: An abstractor can research title to property going back to the date that the property was granted to the United States. This *chain of title* is helpful in preparing an attorney's **opinion of title,** as to whether the owner has a marketable or **insurable interest.** See **marketable title.**

CHATTEL personal property. Anything owned and tangible, other than real estate. See **personalty.**
Example: Furniture, automobiles, and jewelry are all *chattels.*

CHATTEL MORTGAGE a pledge of personal property as **security** for a **debt.**
Example: Abel borrows money against his automobile; the lender grants a *chattel mortgage.*

CLEAR TITLE a **marketable title;** one free of **clouds** and disputed interests.
Example: It is necessary to obtain *clear title* in order to convey a general **warranty deed** in a transaction.

CLIENT the one who engages a **broker,** lawyer, accountant, **appraiser,** etc.

Example: Unless otherwise specified in the sales contract, the *client* of the broker, most often the seller, pays the **brokerage** commission.

CLOSING 1. the act of transferring ownership of a property from seller to buyer in accordance with a sales contract. 2. the time when a closing takes place.
Example: Abel agrees to purchase a property from Baker. A *closing* is set up for June 15, at which time Abel and Baker will sign all documents and pay all expenses necessary to transfer ownership and secure financing.

CLOSING COSTS various fees and expenses payable by the seller and buyer at the time of a real estate **closing** (also termed transaction costs).
Examples: The following are some *closing costs:*
• **brokerage** commissions
• lender **discount points**/other fees
• **title insurance** premium
• deed **recording** fees
• loan **prepayment penalty**
• **inspection** and **appraisal** fees
• attorney's fees

CLOSING DATE the date on which the seller delivers the **deed** and the buyer pays for the property.
Example: The sales contract generally establishes a *closing date*, at which time the parties will meet and settle all accounts necessary to transfer **title** to the property.

CLOSING STATEMENT an accounting of funds from a real estate sale, made to both the seller and the buyer separately. Most states require the **broker** to furnish accurate closing statements to all parties to the transaction.
Example: Table 9

TABLE 9

	Seller		Buyer	
	Debit	Credit	Debit	Credit
Real property		$40,000	$40,000	
Prepaid taxes		670	670	
Sales commission	$ 2,400			
Survey fee			75	
Cash paid by buyer to close				$40,745
Cash received by seller	38,270			
Totals	$40,670	$40,670	$40,745	$40,745

CLOUD ON THE TITLE an outstanding claim or **encumbrance** that, if valid, would affect or impair the owner's **title.** Compare **clear title.**
Example: Abel dies and in his will leaves land to Baker. Abel's widow is contesting the validity of Abel's will. During this period there is a *cloud on* Baker's *title* to the land.

CLUSTER HOUSING a **subdivision** technique in which detached dwelling units are grouped relatively close together, leaving open spaces as **common areas..**
Example: A *cluster housing* development (Figure 37).

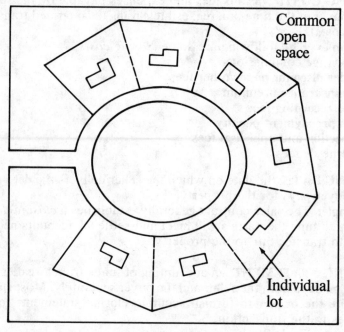

FIGURE 37

CODE see **building code, code of ethics, housing code.**

CODE OF ETHICS a statement of principles concerning the behavior of those who subscribe to the code.
Example: All Realtors® are required to subscribe to a *code of ethics* that defines proper professional behavior and practices that are considered unbecoming a professional real estate **agent.**

COINSURANCE a clause in an insurance policy stating the minimum percentage of value to be insured in order to collect the full amount of loss.

Example: Abel has a building worth $100,000. He figures that the maximum loss in the event of a disastrous fire will be $60,000, and insures it to $60,000. The policy has an 80% *coinsurance* clause. Since he did not insure it to 80% of its value, he will not receive the full amount of loss. The ratio he will receive is:

$$\frac{\text{Amount carried}}{\substack{\text{Amount should carry} \\ (\text{property value} \times \text{coinsurance rate})}} = \frac{\$60,000}{\$80,000} \times \text{loss}$$

$$= \text{maximum recovery, subject to maximum carried}$$

codicil

COLD CANVASS the process of contacting homeowners in an area in order to solicit **listings.**
Example: Abel discovers a growing demand for older homes that are close to the central business district. To increase the number of listings of such homes, Abel *cold canvasses* several older neighborhoods to determine owners' interest in selling.

COLLAPSIBLE CORPORATION a term that applies to some corporations that are dissolved within 3 years. The IRS treats gain on the sale or **liquidation** of the corporation as **ordinary income** to the stockholder.
Example: Abel forms a corporation and is the sole stockholder. The corporation builds 50 houses and estimates that each is worth $10,000 more than it costs. Abel liquidates the corporation and claims a $500,000 **capital gain** on the corporate stock. The **Internal Revenue Service** claims the gain is ordinary income because of the existence of a *collapsible corporation*.

COLLATERAL property pledged as **security** for a **debt.**
Example: A borrower who arranges a **mortgage** loan pledges the property as *collateral*.

COLOR OF TITLE that which appears to be good title but is not.
Example: Abel gives Baker a **deed** to land that he has never actually owned; Baker farms the land under a *color of title*.

COMMERCIAL BANK a financial institution authorized to provide a variety of financial services, including consumer and business loans (generally short-term), checking services, credit cards and savings accounts. Certain deposits at most commercial banks are insured by the **Federal Deposit Insurance Corporation.** Commercial banks may be members of the **Federal Reserve System.**

Example: Although *commercial banks* do make long-term mortgage loans, they have traditionally concentrated on short-term loans and are good sources for home-improvement loans and second loans secured by home equity.

COMMERCIAL BROKER one who **lists** and sells **commercial property,** which may include shopping, office, industrial and apartment projects. Contrast **residential broker.**
Example: Collins sells apartment complexes to earn a brokerage fee. She is considered a *commercial broker* despite the fact that apartments are residences.

COMMERCIAL PROPERTY property designed for use by retail, wholesale, office, hotel, or service users.
Example: An investor is interested in purchasing *commercial property* for investment. A **broker** might show the investor shopping centers, office buildings, hotels and motels, resorts or restaurants.

COMMINGLE to mingle or mix, such as the deposit of another's money in a broker's personal account.
Example: State law prohibits the *commingling* of **earnest money** deposits with a broker's own money. Most states require a separate account for earnest money held by a **broker.**

COMMISSION 1. an amount earned by a real estate broker for his services.
Example: Broker Roberts sells a $50,000 home for a client. At a 6% commission rate the client owes the broker a $3,000 *commission.*
2. the official body that enforces real estate license laws. See Figure 38.
Example: The State Real Estate *Commission* administers the real estate licensing examination, collects license fees, hears testimony from those who claim misconduct on the part of a licensee, and may punish offenders.

COMMISSIONER the head administrator of the State **Real Estate Commission.**
Example: As *commissioner,* Jones is responsible for maintaining records of licensees and administering examinations (Figure 38).

COMMITMENT a pledge or promise; a firm agreement.
Example: Collins obtains a *commitment* from a **savings and loan association** for a $50,000 loan on a house she wants to buy. She is then assured of the loan so business will proceed to **closing.**

COMMON AREAS areas of a property that are used by all owners or tenants.

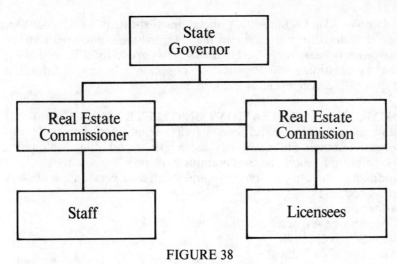

FIGURE 38

Example: The following are examples of *common areas.*
• the clubhouse and pool of a condominium development
• the hallways and stairs of an apartment building
• the elevators in an office building
• the mall area of a shopping center

COMMON ELEMENTS in a **condominium,** those portions of the property not owned individually by unit owners but in which an indivisible interest is held by all unit owners. Generally includes the grounds, parking areas, recreational facilities, and external structure of the building. See **community association.**
Example: In a condominium building, each resident unit owner owns the interior space within that unit. The remainder of the building and **site** are *common elements* enjoyed by each resident according to the condominium bylaws. The common elements are maintained by the owners' association, to which each owner pays a fee.

COMMON LAW the body of law that has grown out of legal customs and practices that developed in England. Common law prevails unless superseded by other law.
Example: In many disputes between neighboring landowners over damages from the activities of one or the other, the courts apply *common law* to reach a settlement.

COMMUNITY ASSOCIATION general name for any organization of property owners to oversee some common interest. In a **condominium** or planned unit development, the association has the responsibility of managing the **common elements** in the project. A **homeowners' association** may be established in a **subdivision** to enforce deed **covenants.**

Example: The **Community Associations Institute (CAI)** is a not-for-profit organization to assist in the establishment and operation of *community associations*. Their materials are helpful in setting up the association, maintenance of common elements, enforcing bylaws, and collecting monthly fees.

COMMUNITY ASSOCIATIONS INSTITUTE (CAI) a nonprofit educational and research organization concerned with the problems of managing homeowners' associations and other community associations (such as **condominium** owners associations). CAI sponsors educational seminars and publishes various handbooks and brochures.
Address:
Community Associations Institute
3000 South Eads St.
Arlington, Va. 22202

COMMUNITY PROPERTY property accumulated through joint efforts of husband and wife and owned by them in equal shares. This doctrine of ownership now exists in Arizona, California, Idaho, Louisiana, Nevada, New Mexico, Texas, and Washington State.
Example: Mary and Jim are getting divorced. During their marriage she inherited $100,000, which is kept in a separate bank account. All other property was acquired during their marriage. Although she never worked outside the home, half of all property acquired by joint effort during the marriage is hers under the *community property* laws of the state. Her $100,000 is entirely her separate property.

CO-MORTGAGOR one who signs a **mortgage** contract with another party or parties and is thereby jointly obligated to repay the loan. Generally a co-mortgagor provides some assistance in meeting the requirements of the loan and receives a share of ownership in the encumbered property.
Example: Brown and Jones agree to purchase and share residence in a home. They jointly apply for and receive a mortgage loan to make the purchase and, thereby, become *co-mortgagors*.
Example: Sims wishes to assist her son to purchase a home. Sims provides a portion of the **down payment** money and signs the loan contract as a *co-mortgagor*.

COMPARABLES properties that are similar to the one being sold or appraised. See **market approach.**
Example: A subject property is a detached, 3-bedroom house that is 30 years old and will be bought with an **FHA loan.** *Comparables* would be recently sold houses with similar styling, age, location,

and financing. Slight variations in characteristics may be taken into account when making the analysis.

COMPETENT PARTIES persons legally capable of entering a **contract.** Must be of legal age, not be insane or a drunkard.
Example: If Abel is a **minor** he may generally **void** contracts he entered to buy or sell real estate because the law does not consider him to be a *competent party.*

COMPLETION BOND a legal instrument used to guarantee the completion of a development according to specifications. More encompassing than a **performance bond,** which assures that one party will perform under a contract on condition that the other party performs. The completion bond assures production of the development without reference to any contract and without the requirement of payment to the **contractor.**
Example: A developer proposes to build a **subdivision** that necessitates a rezoning. The **zoning** commission requires the developer to post a *completion bond* prior to granting a permit for the development.

COMPONENT DEPRECIATION dividing real estate improvements into various parts such as the roof, plumbing, electrical system, and shell, then depreciating each component separately for tax purposes. Eliminated by the 1981 Tax Act, for acquisitions after 1980.
Example: Abel builds a shopping center. The $1 million total cost was spent on the components with useful lives indicated in Table 10. Abel claims *component depreciation* on each part based on its estimated useful life.

TABLE 10

roof	$100,000	15-year life
plumbing	$100,000	20-year life
electrical	$100,000	15-year life
heating & A/C	$100,000	10-year life
paving	$100,000	15-year life
building foundation and structure	$500,000	50-year life

COMPOUND INTEREST interest paid on the original principal and also on the unpaid interest that has accumulated. Contrast with **simple interest.**
Example: $100 deposited in a 5% savings account earns $5 interest the first year. Its second-year earnings are 5% of $105, or $5.25. Each year, interest is received on previously earned but undistributed interest, so interest compounds.

CONCESSIONS benefits granted by a seller/**lessor** to induce a sale/ **lease.**
Example: Abel is leasing out space in an office building. In order to get the Granite Insurance Co. to sign a lease, Abel offers a *concession* in the form of a $2000 remodeling allowance.
Example: Baker is converting apartments to **condominium** units. In order to induce tenants to purchase their units, Baker offers a *concession* of a 20% discount on the sales price, available only to tenants.

CONDEMNATION 1. taking private property for public use with compensation to the owner under **eminent domain.** Used by governments to acquire land for streets, parks, schools, etc., and by utilities to acquire necessary property. Compare **appropriation.**
Example: Abel's home is in the **right-of-way** of the new highway. When Abel refused to sell, the highway department acquired the property through *condemnation,* paying Abel an amount based on a **fair market value** appraisal.
2. declaring a structure unfit for use.
Example: The state health department, acting through its *condemnation* powers, prevented use of an old, dilapidated shack because of violations of the **housing code.**

CONDITION(S) provision(s) in a contract that some or all terms of the contract will be altered or cease to exist upon a certain event. See **cancellation clause.**
Example: If a house is destroyed by fire before closing, the buyer is not obligated to complete the purchase.
Example: If a loan that is described as a *condition* cannot be arranged, the buyer is not required to complete the transaction and may receive a refund of any **earnest money.**

CONDITIONAL SALES CONTRACT a contract for the sale of property stating that the seller retains **title** until the conditions of the contract have been fulfilled.
Example: A **contract for deed** or a **land contract** is a *conditional sales contract.* Until the buyer makes full payment, the seller retains title to the property.

CONDOMINIUM a system of ownership of individual units in a multiunit structure, combined with joint ownership of commonly used property (sidewalks, hallways, stairs, etc.). See **common elements.**
Example: A midrise *condominium* (Figure 39).

CONDOMINIUM OWNERS ASSOCIATION an organization of all unit owners in a **condominium** to oversee the **common elements** and enforce the bylaws. See **community association.**

Example: When Vivian and Paul Carter purchase a unit in the condominium, they are automatically members of the *owners association*. As such, they are entitled to vote on decisions before the association regarding changes in bylaws, development and repair of common elements, and other matters. They are also required to pay a monthly fee to cover expenses of the association.

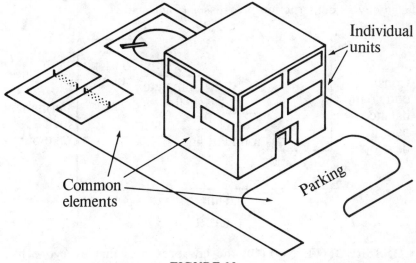

Individual units

Common elements

Parking

FIGURE 39

CONFORMITY PRINCIPLE an **appraisal** principle that holds that property tends to reach maximum value when the neighborhood is reasonably homogeneous in social and economic activity.
Example: Under the *conformity principle,* a house that cost $300,000 in a neighborhood of $50,000 homes is not worth as much as if it were in a neighborhood of $300,000 homes.

CONSIDERATION anything of value given to induce entering into a **contract;** it may be money, personal services, love and affection, etc.
Example: Abel ran out of gasoline while driving down the highway. Baker, a passing motorist, gave him a ride to the nearest filling station. Abel promised Baker a $50,000 tract of land for his help, but Baker cannot enforce the promise because of the absence of *consideration*.

CONSTANT PAYMENT LOAN a loan on which equal payments are made periodically so as to pay off the debt when the last payment is made. See **level payment mortgage, variable payment plan.**
Example: Baker obtains a *constant payment loan* to purchase a home. The loan requires a payment of $450.00 per month (princi-

pal and interest) for 30 years. At the end of 30 years, the principal balance will be zero.

CONSTRUCTION LOAN one that finances **subdivision** costs and/or improvements to real estate. See **building loan agreements.**
Example: Collins plans to develop an office building. She receives a **commitment** for permanent financing and approaches a **commercial bank** for a *construction loan*. The bank agrees to advance money as construction progresses (Figure 40).

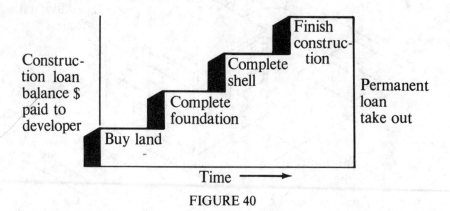

FIGURE 40

CONSTRUCTIVE NOTICE the law presumes that everyone has knowledge of a fact when the fact is a matter of public record.
Example: Abel buys land from Baker, believing that Baker is the owner. Since Carter's **deed** had been properly recorded, Abel had *constructive notice* of Carter's ownership and cannot claim ownership against Carter.

CONTIGUOUS actually touching; contiguous properties have a common boundary.
Example: Lots A and B in Figure 41 are *contiguous*. Lot C is **adjacent** to A and B but not *contiguous*.

CONTINGENCY CLAUSE see **condition.**

CONTOUR MAP a map that displays the **topography** of the **site.** A map with contour lines that indicate various elevations of the land.
Example: A *contour map* of a building **site** (Figure 42).

CONTRACT an agreement between competent parties to do or not to do certain things for a **consideration.**
Example: To have a valid *contract* for the sale of real estate there must be:

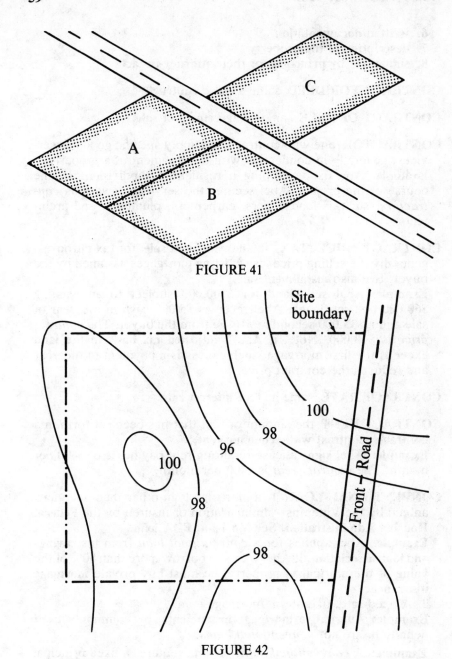

FIGURE 41

FIGURE 42

1. an **offer**
2. an **acceptance**
3. **competent parties**
4. **consideration**
5. **legal purpose**

6. **written documentation**
7. **description of the property**
8. **signatures by principals** or their **attorney-in-fact**

CONTRACT FOR DEED same as **land contract.**

CONTRACT OF SALE same as **agreement of sale.**

CONTRACTOR one who contracts to supply specific goods or services, generally in connection with development of a property.
Example: Abel is developing a residential **subdivision.** In the course of the project, Abel secures the services of various *contractors,* such as landscapers, carpenters, plumbers, and architects.

CONTRACT PRICE (TAX) in an **installment sale,** for tax purposes, generally the selling price less existing mortgages assumed by the buyer. See also **installment sale.**
Example: Abel sells land for $100,000 subject to an existing $60,000 first mortgage. Abel receives $5,000 cash in the year of sale and a $35,000 second mortgage from the buyer. The *contract price* is $40,000. Note, if Abel's **adjusted tax basis** in the land exceeds the first mortgage, such excess is a payment in the year and reduces the contract price.

CONTRACT RATE same as **face interest rate.**

CONTRACT RENT the amount of rent that has been set forth in a contract. Contrast with **economic rent.**
Example: Abel signs a lease requiring rent payments of $400 per month. The *contract rent* is $400 per month.

CONVENTIONAL LOAN 1. a mortgage loan other than one guaranteed by the Veterans Administration or insured by the **Federal Housing Administration.** See **VA loan, FHA loan.**
Example: Abel applies for a *conventional loan* from his **savings and loan association.** If Abel wants to borrow more than 80% of the value of the mortgaged property, he must buy private **mortgage insurance.**
2. A fixed-rate, fixed-term mortgage loan.
Example: Alternative mortgage instruments, by commonly used definition, are not *conventional loans.*

Example: A *conventional mortage loan* requires a fixed principal and interest payment over its term.

CONVERSION 1. changing property to a different use or form of ownership, such as when **apartments** are transformed to **condominiums.**

Example: A **condominium** *conversion* allows existing tenants to remain until the expiration of their **lease** and often allows them to purchase the unit at terms more favorable than those offered to general public.
2. the taking away of property that belongs to another person. See also **involuntary conversion.**
Example: An illegal *conversion* of the landlord's property occurred when the tenant removed the landlord's light fixture from the apartment.
3. a change in the ownership form of a **savings and loan association.**
Example: Friendly Savings applies to the **Federal Home Loan Bank** Board for *conversion* from a **mutual savings bank** to a stockholder-owned company.

CONVEY to **deed** or transfer **title** to another.
Example: At the **closing,** Abel will *convey* the property to Baker.

CONVEYANCE the transfer of the **title** of real estate from one to another; the means or medium by which title of real estate is transferred.
Example: A **warranty deed** is most often used as a *conveyance* at the **closing.**

CO-OP 1. an arrangement between 2 real estate **agents** that generally results in splitting the **commission** between them.
Example: Abel obtains a **listing** contract on a piece of property. Baker agrees to find a buyer in exchange for a portion of the commission. Abel and Baker have arranged a *co-op* agreement.
2. a type of housing in which each tenant is a shareholder in a **corporation** that owns the building. Also termed **cooperative.**
Example: Upon moving to New York, Abel obtains an apartment in a *co-op*. This requires purchase of shares in the apartment corporation.

COOPERATIVE a type of corporate ownership of real property whereby stockholders of the corporation are entitled to use a certain dwelling unit or other units of space. Special income tax laws allow the tenant stockholders to deduct interest and property taxes paid by the corporation. See **co-op.**
Example: Apartment buildings in New York City are occasionally converted to *cooperatives*. In simple terms, this requires forming a **corporation** to own the building and selling shares to those who wish to live in the building.

Co

CORPORATION a legal entity properly registered with the secretary of state. Can have **limited liability,** perpetual life, freely transferable shares, and centralized management.
Example: Abel wants to start a real estate **brokerage** business with $10,000 of his own money. He asks his attorney to form a *corporation* with Abel as the sole stockholder. The corporation may **bankrupt** but Abel's other assets are not affected.

CORPOREAL visible or tangible real or personal property.
Example: Buildings, pavement, fences, and the like are *corporeal*. **Easements** are incorporeal.

Correlation

COSIGNER same as **accommodation party.**

COST APPROACH a method of **appraising** property based on the **depreciated** reproduction or replacement cost (new) of improvements, plus the market value of the **site.**
Example: Table 11:

TABLE 11

Reproduction cost (new)		$100,000
Minus: Physical deterioration	$25,000	
Functional obsolescence	$10,000	
Economic obsolescence	$5,000	
Total accrued depreciation	$40,000	−$40,000
Depreciated value of improvements		$60,000
Add: Site value		$20,000
Value indicated by *cost approach*		$80,000

COST OF LIVING INDEX an indicator of the current price level for goods and services related to some base year.
Example: The Consumer Price Index (CPI), published by the Bureau of Labor Statistics, indicates that the price level for goods and services in 1982 was 289.1 This means that, on average, prices were 189% higher in 1982 than in 1967 (when the CPI was 100). A **lease** made in 1967 with initial annual payments of $1000 and indexed to the CPI, would call for payments of $2891 in 1982. See **index lease.**

COTENANCY any of a number of forms of multiple ownership such as **tenancy in common** and **joint tenancy.**

Example: Abel and Baker decide to invest in a parcel of land. Both names are to be on the **deed.** Abel and Baker join together as *cotenants;* each owns one half of the property.

COUNSELING the act of advising clients on a variety of real estate investment or development matters.
Example: Abel wishes to invest in an office building. Baker offers *counseling* by advising Abel on how to select a property, how to legally structure the investment and how to maximize after-tax returns from the investment.

COUNSELOR OF REAL ESTATE (CRE) a member of the **American Society of Real Estate Counselors (ASREC).** Membership is based on experience and professional conduct as a real estate counselor.

COUNTEROFFER rejection of an **offer** to buy or sell, with a simultaneous substitute offer.
Example: A property is put on the market. An investor offers $75,000 in cash. The owner rejects the offer but submits a *counteroffer* to sell for $80,000. Offers and counteroffers may be negotiated on factors other than price, e.g., **financing** arrangements, **apportionment** of **closing costs,** inclusion of personal property.

COVENANT NOT TO COMPETE a clause in an agreement where one party promises not to offer to sell or produce the same goods and services in proximity to the other party.
Example: Abel sells his realty firm to Baker. In the sales contract, Abel gives Baker a *covenant not to compete*. This bars Abel from opening a competing realty firm in the same immediate area as Baker.

COVENANTS promises written into **deeds** and other instruments agreeing to performance or nonperformance of certain acts, or requiring or preventing certain uses of the property.
Examples: Deed *covenants* are often used to:
• maintain a land parcel in a specified use, such as residential
• enforce architectural and design standards
• control the **density** of future development
• prohibit certain practices, such as the sale of liquor

CREATIVE FINANCING any **financing** arrangement other than a traditional **mortgage** from a third-party lending institution.
Example: *Creative financing* devices include:
• loans from the seller
• **balloon payment** loans
• **wraparound mortgages**
• **assumption of mortgage**

- **sale-leasebacks**
- **land contracts**
- alternative mortgage instruments

CREDIT 1. in finance, the availability of money.
Example: When money and *credit* are readily available, it is easier to buy real estate. Credit policy is determined to a large extent by the **Federal Reserve System.**
2. in accounting, a **liability** or **equity** entered on the right side of the ledger.
Example: In **closing statements,** the *credit* column shows what is due and payable. The buyer is *credited* with amounts paid, the seller is *credited* with the price of the real property and prepaid items.

CREDITOR one who is owed money.
Examples: *Creditors* include:
- bond holders
- loan companies
- mortgage lenders

CREDIT RATING (REPORT) an evaluation of a person's capacity (or history) of debt repayment. Generally available for individuals from a local retail credit association; for businesses by companies such as Dunn & Bradstreet; and for publicly held bonds by Moody's, Standard & Poors, and Fitch's. Individuals have access to their own files.
Example: Goodmoney Savings Association received and studied the *credit report* on Collins before they issued her a mortgage loan. The report stated credit limits at various stores, current balances, and repayment terms in days. It would have noted **defaults** and slow repayments.

CUL-DE-SAC a street with an intersection on one end and a closed turning area on the other. Often valued in the design of residential **subdivisions** for the privacy provided to homes on the street.
Example: A **subdivision** plan showing a *cul-de-sac* (Figure 43).

CURABLE DEPRECIATION depreciation or deterioration that can be corrected at a cost less than the value that will be added.
Example: An apartment owner estimates that remodeling the dwelling units would allow an increase in rent of $20 per month. The cost of remodeling is $1,500 per unit. The prevailing **gross rent multiplier** in the neighborhood is 100. Thus the value added by remodeling is $100 \times \$20 = \$2,000$ per unit. Thus, the outmoded appearance of the units is a form of *curable depreciation*.

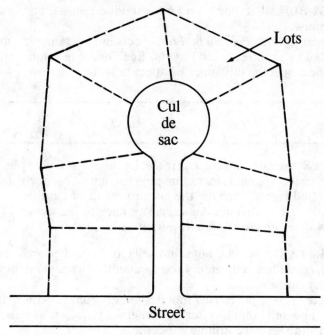

Lots

Cul
de
sac

Street

FIGURE 43

CURRENT YIELD a measurement of investment returns based on
the percentage relationship of annual cash income to the investment cost. The formula is

$$\text{Current yield} = \frac{\text{current income}}{\text{investment cost}}$$

Example: Abel purchases a parking lot for $10,000. It provides
$5,000 of parking revenues each year. Property taxes and insur-
ance total $3,500, leaving $1,500 of annual before-income-tax **cash
flow.** The *current yield* is 15%:

$$\frac{\$1,500}{\$10,000} = 15\%$$

CURTESY the right of a husband to all or part of his deceased wife's
realty regardless of the provisions of her will. Exists in only a few
states.
Example: Under the *curtesy* law of some states, a widower may
claim a **life estate** to part of the property left by his deceased wife,
provided they had a child in their marriage.

CUSTOM BUILDER one who builds unique houses; contrast with
tract house.
Example: Abel, a *custom builder,* erects unique homes from plans
provided by architects and buyers. Each home is unique, whether
built for a specific customer or speculatively.

D

DAMAGES the amount recoverable by a person who has been
injured in any manner, including physical harm, property damage,
or violated rights, through the act or default of another.
Example: Abel forfeited his **earnest money** to the owner of property as *damages* for failing to purchase as agreed.

DEALER (TAX) one who buys and sells for his or her own account.
The merchandise is **inventory,** consequently any gain on the sale is
ordinary income.
Example: Davis purchases mobile homes from several manufac-
turers, and sells them to her customers. Davis is a *dealer* and all
gains from sales are ordinary income.

DEBENTURE an unsecured **note** or **bond.**
Example: Abel invests in *debentures* of the XYZ Corporation;
Baker invests in a **first mortgage** on a building owned by XYZ
Corporation. The XYZ Corporation **bankrupts.** Ultimately Baker
receives full payment for the mortgage upon the **foreclosure sale.**
Abel is a general creditor and receives only 18 cents per dollar
owed to him.

DEBIT 1. in a **closing statement** (settlement), an item that is charged
to a party. Contrast with **credit.**
Examples: The buyer is charged with these typical *debits:*
• purchase price
• taxes prepaid by seller
• deed recording fees
The seller is charged with these typical *debits:*
• cost to **retire** existing mortgage principal.
• **accrued interest** on mortgage being relieved
• **termite inspection** fee
2. in accounting, entries on the left side of the general ledger.
Contrast with **credit.**
Examples: Debits include:
• acquisition cost of **assets**
• amounts of deductible expenses

DEBT an obligation to pay.
Example: Abel borrows $1,000 from Baker and thereby incurs a *debt*.

DEBT COVERAGE RATIO the relationship between **net operating income** (NOI) and **annual debt service** (ADS). Often used as an **underwriting** criterion for **income property** mortgage loans.
Example: Annual debt service for a mortgage loan on a certain office building is $10,000. The property generates $25,000 in annual gross rent, and requires $7,000 for expenses of operation, leaving $18,000 net operating income. The *debt coverage ratio* is 1.80, calculated by the following formula:

$$\frac{\text{NOI}}{\text{ADS}} = \frac{\$18,000}{\$10,000} = 1.8$$

DEBT SERVICE see **annual debt service.**
Decedent - one who is dead
DECLARATION 1. formal pleadings by a plaintiff as to the facts and circumstances that gave rise to his cause of action. Also, a statement made out of court.
Example: The unhappy land buyer offered a *declaration* explaining the claim that the property was misrepresented.
2. a legal document used to create a **condominium.** Includes a description of the property and the uses to which it is restricted, a description of individual ownership units, **common elements,** and procedures for amending the declaration.
Example: A developer constructs apartments and wishes to market them as a condominium. He prepares and records a *declaration,* which describes the division of individual and common ownership, a set of bylaws and a master **deed** for the project.

DECLARATION OF TRUST a written statement by a **trustee** to acknowledge that the property is held for the benefit of another.
Example: A *declaration of trust* was signed by a **trustee** to state that certain valuable land was being held in **trust** for certain orphaned children.

DECLINING BALANCE DEPRECIATION a method of **depreciation,** often used for income tax purposes, whereby a rate is applied to the remaining balance to derive the depreciation deduction. Compare **accelerated depreciation.**
Example: Table 12 shows the depreciation schedule for a property with a **tax basis** of $10,000 and **depreciable** life of 5 years, using the 125% *declining balance* method:

TABLE 12

Year	Remaining balance	Rate*	Annual deduction
1	$10,000	0.25	$2,500
2	7,500	0.25	1,875
3	5,625	0.25	1,406
4	4,219	0.25	1,055
5	3,164	0.25	791

*A 5-year life results in 20% per year depreciation using the straight-line method. The 125% declining balance method results in an annual percentage of 25 for an asset with this life (125% of 20% = 25%).

DECREE an order issued by one in authority; a court order or decision.
Example: The court issued a *decree* stating that Abel owed $10,000 to Baker for failing to perform under a **contract.**

DEDICATION the gift of land by its owner for a public use and the acceptance of it by a unit of government. See also **appropriation.**
Example: A **developer** of a large **subdivision** makes to the local government a *dedication* of the streets, the flood-prone areas and one **acre** of land for a public school. This obligates the government to **maintenance** of these areas and relieves the developer of a property tax liability on the dedicated lands.

DEED a written document, properly signed and delivered, that conveys **title** to real property. See **general warranty deed, quitclaim deed, special warranty deed.**
Example: In exchange for the agreed upon terms of a **contract,** including the purchase price, at **closing** the seller delivers a *deed* to the buyer.

DEED IN LIEU OF FORECLOSURE the act of giving property back to a lender without **foreclosure.**
Example: Abel, a builder, has a **construction loan** with a $100,000 balance against the house he is building. He offers the house for sale at $100,000 but no one buys it. He does not have the cash to continue to pay interest on the construction loan, and is in **default.** The lender asks for a *deed in lieu of foreclosure.*

DEED OF TRUST an instrument used in many states in lieu of a **mortgage.** Legal title to the property is **vested** in one or more **trustees** to secure the repayment of the loan.
Example: Abel borrows $50,000 on his property in Texas from the

Good Money Savings Association. He gives a *deed of trust* that is held in the name of I.M. Honest, a trustee. If Abel **defaults** it will not be difficult for Good Money to gain possession.

DEED RESTRICTION a clause in a deed that limits the use of land. See **covenants.**
Example: A deed might stipulate that alcoholic beverages are not to be sold on the land for 20 years. This is a *deed restriction.*

DEFAULT failure to fulfill an obligation or promise, or to perform specified acts.
Example: The **contract** required the buyer to close within 3 business days. His failure to appear at **closing** constituted a *default* under the contract.

DEFEASANCE a clause in a **mortgage** that gives the borrower the right to redeem the property after **default,** usually by paying the full indebtedness and fees incurred.
Example: Graham defaults on the **balloon payment** of the mortgage. Three days later she pays the balance in cash. The *defeasance* clause allows her to redeem the property. It overrides the provision that grants the property to the lender upon default.

DEFECT IN TITLE any recorded **instrument** that would prevent a **grantor** from giving a **clear title.**
Example: A **mechanic's lien** that was recorded against the property when it was remodeled was a *defect in title.* The grantor had to clear the **lien** by paying the amount due the electrician who filed the lien.

DEFENDANT the party sued in an action at law.
Example: Abel brings suit against a former landlord, Baker, for refusing to return a **security deposit.** In the suit, Baker is the *defendant.*

DEFERRED MAINTENANCE in appraisal, a type of physical **depreciation** owing to lack of normal upkeep.
Example: The appraiser found the following examples of *deferred maintenance* on the subject property:
• broken window glass
• missing roof shingles
• peeling paint
• broken guttering

DEFERRED PAYMENT METHOD, OTHER (TAX) a method to report the gain on a sale when **promissory notes** taken by the seller are worth less than their face value.
Example: Abel sells land for $40,000 cash plus a promissory note for $60,000 at 9% interest. Using the *deferred payment method,*

Abel reports on his tax return that the note has a **market value** that is $15,000 less than its $60,000 **face value,** and therefore the selling price of the property was $85,000 ($40,000 cash plus a note worth $45,000). As Abel collects the **principal** of the note, the part of the collections that represent the **discount** of the note is **ordinary income.**

DEFERRED PAYMENTS payments to be made at some future date.
Example: On a **graduated payment mortgage** the **principal** payments and some interest payments are *deferred* for the first 3 to 5 years.

DEFICIENCY JUDGMENT a court order stating that the borrower stills owes money when the **security** for a loan does not entirely satisfy a defaulted debt.
Example: Upon **default** by the **mortgagor,** a lender **forecloses** on the mortgage. The unpaid balance of the loan is $60,000. The property is sold at public **auction** and brings $50,000. The lender then seeks a *deficiency judgment* against the mortgagor to recover the $10,000 shortage.

DELIVERY transfer of the **possession** of a thing from one person to another.
Example: A man dies leaving no will. A search of his possessions uncovers a **deed** giving valuable land to his nephew. Since the deed has not been *delivered,* the court ruled that the land does not belong to the nephew.

DEMOGRAPHIC pertaining to characteristics of the population, such as race, sex, age, household size, and to population growth and **density.**
Example: As a first step in estimating the demand for new housing units, a **developer** commissions a *demographic* study. The study describes the current population density and rate of growth, the age distribution of the population, and average size of households in the local **market area.**

DEMOLITION destruction and removal of an existing structure from a **site;** necessary to prepare a site for new construction.
Example: A block of old houses in the city is to be converted into a new shopping mall. This conversion will require *demolition* of the houses, site preparation and construction of the mall.

DENSITY the intensity of a land use. See also **land use intensity.**
Example: A 10-acre **subdivision** contains 30 single-family houses. The *density* is 3 dwelling units per **acre.**

Demising Clause - landlord leases tenant takes property

DENSITY ZONING laws that restrict **land use intensity.**
   Example: A **zoning ordinance** states that all zones designated "R-2" may contain no more than 4 **detached housing** units per **acre.** This is an example of *density zoning*.

DEPLETION a **tax deduction** to account for reduced **land** value due to removing minerals.
   Example: The $10,000 tax deduction for *depletion* was allowed because coal was being removed and the land would become virtually worthless when all of the coal was gone.

DEPOSIT money paid in **good faith** to assure performance of a contract. Deposits are commonly used with **sales contracts** and **leases.** If the person who put up the deposit fails to perform, the deposit is forfeited, unless conditions in the contract allow a refund. **Brokers** are to put deposits in a separate checking account pending completion of the contract. See **earnest money.**
   Example: Whitman presented a $1,000 check as an earnest money *deposit* on a home she would buy provided she could get a 10% rate, 30-year loan for 80% of the price. The broker deposited the check in an **escrow account,** and refunded it when Whitman could not arrange said loan.

DEPOSITORY INSTITUTIONS DEREGULATION AND MONETARY CONTROL ACT federal law that represents significant decontrol of federally regulated banks and savings institutions, including gradual phase out of limits on interest rates paid on passbook accounts. **(Regulation Q).**
   Example: The *Depository Institutions Deregulation and Monetary Control Act* is a major effort to reform the nation's banking regulations. Among its effects are:
   • standardized reserve requirements for banks and **savings and loan associations**
   • phase out of deposit interest rate limitations
   • authorization for interest-bearing checking accounts
   • increased ability for savings and loan associations to make consumer loans
   • reduced applicability of state **usury** laws

DEPRECIABLE BASIS see **basis (tax)**; see **adjusted tax basis.**

DEPRECIABLE LIFE 1. for tax purposes, the number of years over which the cost of an **asset** may be spread. See **accelerated cost recovery system.**
   Example: Abel buys an apartment complex. For tax purposes the carpets have a 3-year *depreciable life* and the building shell has a 15-year *depreciable life*.
   2. for **appraisal** purposes, the estimated useful life of an asset.

Example: Baker buys an apartment complex. An appraiser estimates that the roof will last for 15 years, so it has a 15-year *depreciable life*.

DEPRECIABLE REAL ESTATE (TAX) realty that is subject to deductions for **depreciation.** Generally includes property used in a trade or business, or an investment, subject to an allowance for depreciation under **Section 167** of the **Internal Revenue Code.**
Example: Abel buys an apartment complex for $1 million. Of the purchase price, $100,000 is the value of the land, the remaining $900,000 is the value of *depreciable real estate.* Abel uses the **straight-line** method and a 35-year remaining depreciable life.

DEPRECIATION (ACCOUNTING) allocating the cost of an **asset** over its estimated **useful life.**
Example: Collins buys a warehouse for $550,000. Of the price, $50,000 is for land, which is not subject to depreciation. Of the remaining $500,000, she claims accounting *depreciation* of $10,000 per year over a 50-year **depreciable life,** despite the fact that the property is expected to increase in value because of the location of the land.

DEPRECIATION (APPRAISAL) a charge against the **reproduction cost** (new) of an **asset** for the estimated wear and **obsolescence.** Depreciation may be physical, functional, or economic.
Example: The estimated reproduction cost (new) of a theater being appraised is $500,000. **Wear and tear** sustained during its life is estimated at $100,000. Functional obsolescence caused by lack of air-conditioning and high ceilings causes an estimated loss of $100,000. It is in a decaying area of the city estimated at causing $100,000 of economic obsolescence. Total *depreciation* is estimated at $300,000.

DEPRECIATION RECAPTURE when real property is sold at a gain and **accelerated depreciation** had been claimed, the owner may be required to pay a tax at ordinary rates to the extent of the excess accelerated depreciation. Excess depreciation on residential real estate after 1980 is recaptured; all depreciation on commercial property after 1980 is recaptured when an accelerated method had been used, under **Section 1250** of the **Internal Revenue Code.** See Table 13. Also for personal property under **Section 1245.**
Example: Collins buys an apartment building for $1 million and depreciates it to a $600,000 **adjusted tax basis** using accelerated depreciation. Had she used **straight-line depreciation,** the adjusted tax basis would have been $700,000. She sells the property for $1,050,000. Of the $450,000 gain, $100,000 is *recaptured* as **ordinary income** (Figure 44).

TABLE 13

DEPRECIATION RECAPTURE ON BUILDINGS UNDER ACRS
(DISPOSITIONS AFTER DECEMBER 31, 1980)

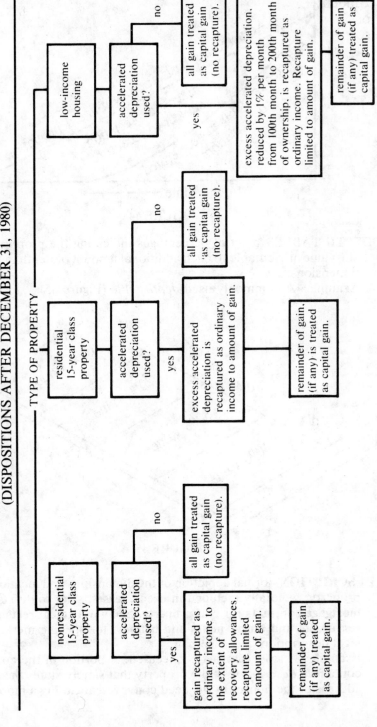

TYPE OF PROPERTY

low-income housing

accelerated depreciation used?

- no → all gain treated as capital gain (no recapture).
- yes → excess accelerated depreciation, reduced by 1% per month from 100th month to 200th month of ownership, is recaptured as ordinary income. Recapture limited to amount of gain. → remainder of gain (if any) treated as capital gain.

residential 15-year class property

accelerated depreciation used?

- no → all gain treated as capital gain (no recapture).
- yes → excess accelerated depreciation is recaptured as ordinary income to amount of gain. → remainder of gain (if any) is treated as capital gain.

nonresidential 15-year class property

accelerated depreciation used?

- no → all gain treated as capital gain (no recapture).
- yes → gain recaptured as ordinary income to the extent of recovery allowances. recapture limited to amount of gain. → remainder of gain (if any) treated as capital gain.

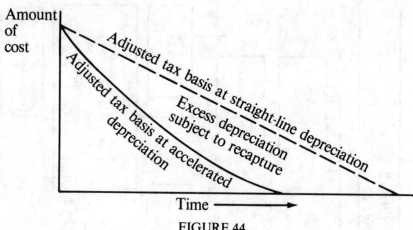

FIGURE 44

DEPTH TABLES a set of percentages indicating the proportion of **site** value attributable to each additional amount of depth in the lot dimensions.

Example: A commonly used *depth table* (Figure 45).

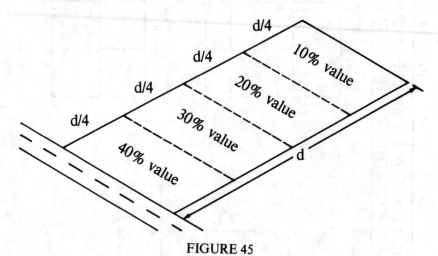

FIGURE 45

DESCRIPTION formal depiction of the dimensions and location of a property; generally included in **deeds, leases, sales contracts,** and **mortgage** contracts for **real property.** See **government rectangular survey, lot and block, metes and bounds,** for specific methods of legal description. See also **plat.**

Example: A **sales contract** is executed. A portion of the contract contains a *description* of the property that simply states the street address of the house. In the deed conveyed at **closing** a more precise metes and bounds *description* is included based upon a **survey** of the property.

DESCRIPTIVE MEMORANDUM a term used to describe an offering circular of property or securities when a **prospectus** is not required.
Example: A **syndicator** prepared a *descriptive memorandum* about the property after receiving an exemption from registering the offering by the **Securities and Exchange Commission (SEC).**

DESCENT the acquisition of property by an heir when the deceased leaves no will.
Example: Abel dies without having prepared a will. His wife and son are awarded **title** to Abel's estate by the courts. They are said to acquire title by *descent*.

Desist + Refrain order

DETACHED HOUSING **residential** buildings in which each **dwelling** unit is surrounded by freestanding walls and is generally sited on a separate lot. Contrast with **duplex, row house, town house.**
Example: Figure 46.

Detached housing   Townhouses

FIGURE 46

DEVELOPER one who transforms **raw land** to **improved** property by use of labor, capital, and **entrepreneur** efforts.
Example: Abel buys 25 acres of land for $10,000 per **acre.** After putting in streets and utilities, dividing it into 100 lots, and building homes on each lot, Abel sells the homes. Abel is a *developer*.

DEVELOPMENT LOAN same as **construction loan.**

DEVISE a gift of real estate by **will** or last testament. Compare **bequeath.**
Example: In his will, Abel *devises* his home to his daughter. He **bequeaths** his automobile to his son.

DEVISEE one who inherits real estate through a will.
Example: Abel dies. The *devisee* in his will receives his land.

Divisor

DIRECTIONAL GROWTH the location or direction toward which a city is growing.

Example: the *directional growth* of Boom Town is toward the northeast (Figure 47).

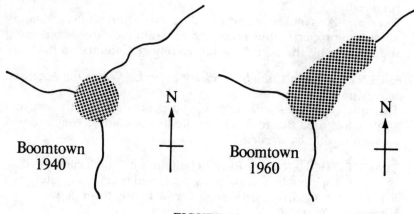

FIGURE 47

DIRECT REDUCTION MORTGAGE a loan that requires both **interest** and **principal** with each payment such that the level payment will be adequate for **amortization** over the loan's term. See **level payment mortgage.**

Example: Collins borrows $50,000 at 10% interest over a 30-year term, using a *direct reduction mortgage*. Her monthly principal and interest payment of $438.79 will fully amortize (pay off) the loan over 30 years.

DISCHARGE IN BANKRUPTCY the release of a bankrupt party from the obligation to repay **debts** that were, or might have been, proved in a **bankruptcy** proceeding.

Example: A real estate resort **developer** filed for bankruptcy. He owned 2,000 unsold vacation lots, and owed $2 million on land acquisition loans. The court granted a *discharge in bankruptcy* for these loans and allowed the creditor to dispose of the lots.

DISCLAIMER 1. a statement whereby responsibility is rejected.

Example: Abel, a certified public accountant, is asked to write up the **financial statements** of Baker without testing (auditing) the validity of the statements. Abel's report provides a *disclaimer* in which he states that he did not examine the financial statements and does not accept responsibility for their accuracy.

2. Renunciation of ownership of **property.**

Example: Because it was no longer profitable, Baker *disclaimed* apartments that had become dilapidated.

DISCOUNT the difference between the **face amount** of an obligation and the amount advanced or received.
Example: Abel sells land for $100,000 and receives a $60,000 mortgage at 7% interest as part of the payment. Abel then sells the mortgage (the right to collect payments on the mortgage) at a $15,000 *discount,* thereby receiving $45,000.

DISCOUNT POINTS amounts paid to the lender (usually by the seller) at the time of origination of a loan, to account for the difference between the market interest rate and the lower face rate of the note (often required when **VA loans** are used).
Example: At the time of loan application, conventional mortgages are being made at 15%. The maximum rate on an FHA loan is 14½% with 4 *discount points* added to compensate for the lower face rate of interest. If the loan is for $50,000, the points will require an additional payment of $2,000 at closing. (The 4 points equals 4% of $50,000, which is $2,000.)

DISCOUNT RATE 1. a **compound interest** rate used to convert expected future income into a present value. See **capitalization rate, present value of annuity, present value of one.**
Example: A *discount rate* of 10% applied to a $100 sum expected to be received in one year results in a present value of $90.90. (The **present value of one** for one year is 0.909.)
2. the rate charged member banks who borrow from the **Federal Reserve System.** Same as **rediscount rate.**
Example: See **rediscount rate.**

DISCRIMINATION applying special treatment (generally unfavorable) to an individual solely on the basis of the person's race, religion, or sex.
Example: Abel is accused of *discrimination* under the Fair Housing Laws because he refused to rent apartments to nonwhite families.

DISINTERMEDIATION situation when deposits are removed from a financial intermediary, such as a **savings and loan association,** and invested in other **assets,** generally for the purpose of obtaining higher yields.
Example: Figure 48.

DISPOSSESS PROCEEDINGS the legal process by a **landlord** to remove a **tenant** and regain possession of property. See **eviction.**
Example: After not having received rent for 3 months, the landlord began *dispossess proceedings* to eject the tenant.

DISTRAINT the legal right of a **landlord** to seize a tenant's personal property to satisfy payment of back rent.

distributee

Example: Abel is 6 months in **arrears** on rent. Landlord Baker obtains a court order to seize Abel's furniture to satisfy the rent due. Baker is exercising his right of *distraint*.

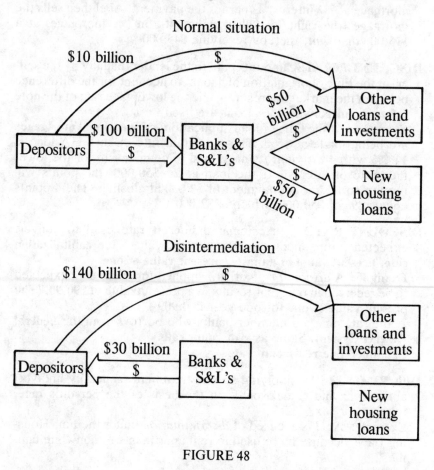

FIGURE 48

DISTRESSED PROPERTY real estate that is under **foreclosure** or impending foreclosure because of insufficient income production. See **workout**.

Example: An **apartment building** is financed with **mortgages** that require $25,000 in **annual debt service**. Because of high vacancies and rising expenses, **net operating income** drops to $20,000. The owners have ceased making loan payments because their resources are insufficient to pay the **negative cash flow**. The property is considered *distressed property*.

DOCUMENTARY EVIDENCE evidence in the form of written or printed papers.

Example: During court proceedings, a **sales contract** was entered in the record as *documentary evidence* of the agreement made between the **plaintiff** and the **defendant.**

DOMICILE the state in which one makes his or her principal residence.
Example: Mason's job requires her to travel throughout the United States. Although she owns property in several states, Mason's *domicile* is New York, where she has her principal residence. Mason is subject to the laws of New York concerning automobile registration, voting rights, payment of taxes, and other matters.

DOMINANT TENEMENT land that benefits from an **easement** on another property. The other property, which usually is **adjacent,** is the **servient tenant.**
Example: In Figure 49 the owner of Parcel A has a right-of-way easement to the road by going across Parcel B.

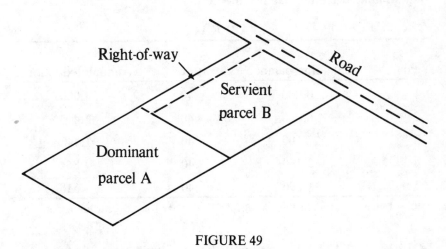

FIGURE 49

DONEE a recipient; as of a gift.
Example: Collins was the *donee* of an **estate;** she takes the **property** as a gift.

DONOR one who gives.
Example: Whitman was the *donor* of land that she gave to charity; she had owned the land in **fee simple.**

DORMER 1. a window projecting through a sloping roof (single dormer); 2. the roofed structure containing such a window (shed dormer).
Example: Figure 50.

DOUBLE DECLINING BALANCE a method of **depreciation** for tax purposes whereby twice the **straight-line** rate is applied to the

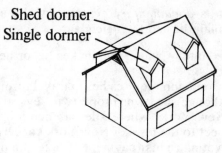

Shed dormer
Single dormer

FIGURE 50

remaining depreciable balance of an asset. See **declining balance depreciation.**

Example: Table 14 is a depreciation schedule for a property with depreciable basis of $10,000 and **depreciable life** of 5 years, using the **double declining balance** method.

TABLE 14

Year	Remaining balance	Rate*	Annual deduction
1	$10,000	.40	$4,000
2	6,000	.40	2,400
3	3,600	.40	1,440
4	2,160	.40	864
5	1,296	.40	518

*.40 = twice the straight-line rate of 20% per year for a 5-year life asset.

DOUBLE TAXATION taxation of the same income at 2 levels.
  Example: A corporation earns $25,000 of **net income.** The corporation pays a $5,000 corporate income tax, then distributes $20,000 in dividends to its shareholders, who pay an $8,000 tax on this dividend income. The corporation's earnings are subject to *double taxation.*

DOWER under **common law,** the legal right of a wife or child to part of a deceased husband's or father's property. See **curtesy.**
  Example: In some states a widow can enforce *dower* rights to claim part of her deceased husband's **estate,** regardless of provisions in his will.

DOWN PAYMENT the amount one pays for property in addition to the **debt** incurred.
  Example: Abel buys a house for $50,000. He arranges a $30,000

first mortgage and a $5,000 **second mortgage.** The *down payment* he needs is $15,000, which he pays in cash at **closing.**

DOWNZONING the act of **rezoning** a tract of land for a less inten- sive use than the existing use or permitted use.
Example: Arlington had a booming single-family residential mar- ket, but was not attracting industry. The owner of a large tract of land zoned for industrial use asked for a *downzoning* to **single- family housing** use to develop the land immediately.

DRAGNET CLAUSE a provision in a **mortgage** that pledges several properties as **collateral.** A **default** on one mortgage constitutes a default on the one with the *dragnet.*
Example: A real estate investor was in financial straits. She failed to pay a certain **mortgage.** The holder of the mortgage on a differ- ent property, which was not in **default,** enforced the *dragnet* clause in its mortgage by **foreclosing.**

DRAW a periodic advance of funds from a construction lender to a **developer. Construction loans** generally provide for a schedule of draws, either at regular intervals during construction or pending construction of specific segments of the structures.
Example: A developer arranges a construction loan of $500,000. The funds are to be advanced in a series of *draws* as follows:
• $50,000 upon completion of final plans and **specifications**
• $200,000 upon completion of the foundation
• $150,000 upon completion of the frame, external surfaces, and roof
• $100,000 upon internal finishing

DRY MORTGAGE same as **nonrecourse** mortgage.

DUE-ON-SALE CLAUSE a provision in a **mortgage** that states the loan is due upon the sale of the property.
Example: Collins owes on a $30,000 mortgage loan against her house at an 8% interest rate. She wants to sell the house to a buyer who will assume the mortgage. The lender says that the $30,000 loan is *due upon the sale* of the house so it cannot be assumed by the buyer. The lender adds that he will **waive** the due-on-sale pro- vision if the interest rate is escalated to 16%.

DUAL CONTRACT the illegal or unethical practice of providing 2 different **contracts** for the same transaction.
Example: Abel wants to purchase a home from a builder for $50,000 but has no cash for the **down payment.** The builder sug- gests that they prepare a fictitious contract for $60,000 and try to borrow 90% of $60,000. The bank's attorney discusses the *dual contract* and explains that they could be guilty of attempted **fraud.**

DUMMY an individual or **entity** that stands in the place of the **principal** to a transaction.
Example: Abel wants to borrow from a bank $100,000 to build houses to sell. Abel requests his attorney to establish a *dummy* **corporation** with $500 of **equity.** The dummy borrows the $100,000 from the bank and, in turn, lends it to Abel as a **nonrecourse** loan.

DUPLEX 1. two dwelling units under one roof.
Example: General floor plan for a *duplex* (Figure 51).
2. an apartment having rooms on two floors.
Example: An artist in a Manhattan *duplex* apartment enjoyed the sunlight that came in from the upper floor to his studio below.

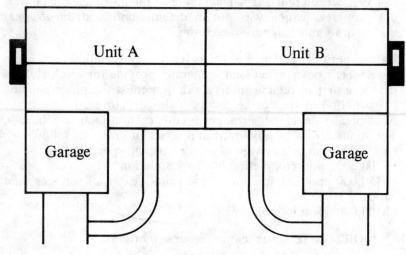

FIGURE 51

DURESS compulsion to do something because of a threat.
Example: Abel tells Baker that unless Baker will sell his property to Abel for $1,000, Abel will physically harm Baker. Baker signs the **contract** under *duress,* but can later **void** it by showing he acted under duress.

DUTCH COLONIAL an early American style, moderate sized, 2 to 2½ story house with a gambrel roof and eaves that flare outward.
Example: Figure 52.

DWELLING a place of residence.
Examples: The following are *dwellings:*
• apartment
• hotel

- mobile home
- nursing home
- single-family house

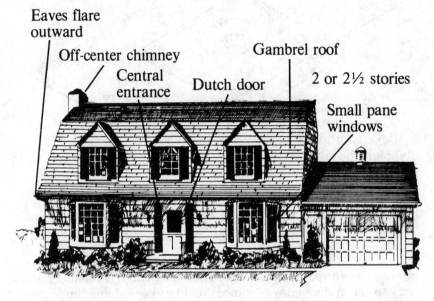

Eaves flare outward

Off-center chimney

Central entrance

Dutch door

Gambrel roof

2 or 2½ stories

Small pane windows

FIGURE 52

E

EARNEST MONEY a **deposit** made by a purchaser of real estate to evidence **good faith.**
Example: It is customary for the buyer to give the seller *earnest money* at the time a **sales contract** is signed. The earnest money generally is credited to the **down payment** at **closing.** Until closing a **broker** must hold earnest money in a separate account. See also **commingle.**

EASEMENT the right, privilege, or interest that one party has in the land of another.
Example: The right of public utility companies to lay their lines across others' property is a utility *easement.*

EASEMENT BY NECESSITY the right of an owner to cross over another's property for a special necessary purpose.
Example: Figure 53.

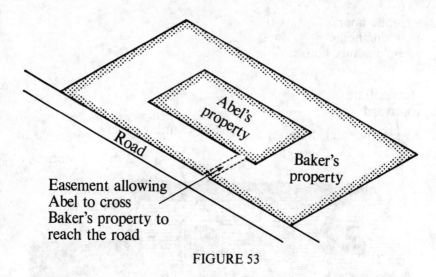

FIGURE 53

EASEMENT BY PRESCRIPTION continued use of another's property for a special purpose can ripen into a permanent use if conditions are met.

Example: Although Abel can reach the highway by another path, for the last 10 years, Abel has been traveling across Baker's property to reach the highway. Since Abel has been doing this for the length of time required by state law, Abel can continue to do so despite Baker's protests, because Abel has achieved an *easement by prescription* (Figure 54).

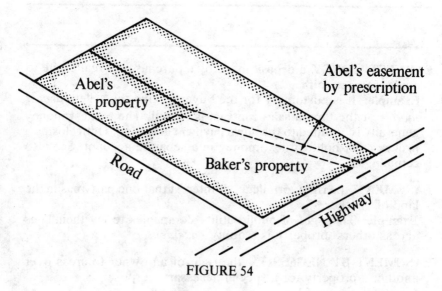

FIGURE 54

EASTLAKE HOUSE a nineteenth century style house with three-dimensional ornamentation made with a chisel, gouge, and lathe rather than the scroll saw. Many of the parts of the ornamentation resemble furniture legs and knobs. This distinctive type of orna-mentation is the major characteristic of this style and separates the Eastlake style house from the Queen Anne or Carpenter Gothic style.
Example: Figure 55.

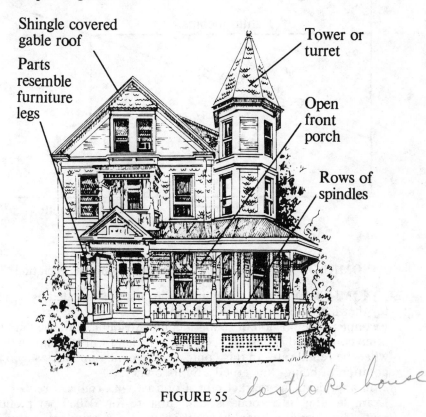

Shingle covered gable roof

Parts resemble furniture legs

Tower or turret

Open front porch

Rows of spindles

FIGURE 55 *Eastlake house*

ECONOMIC BASE industry within a geographic **market area** that provides employment opportunities that are essential to support the community.
Example: Steel is the *economic base* for Pittsburgh. For each steelworker added to the economic base there is another job added in service employment (physician, lawyer, switchboard operator, barber). Each new job brings 2 people to the community (spouse, children, nonworking parents, etc.).

ECONOMIC DEPRECIATION loss of value from all causes outside the property itself. See **depreciation (appraisal).**
Example: An expensive private home may drop in value when an

industrial plant is built nearby. This is a form of *economic depreciation* that must be considered in the appraisal of the property.

ECONOMIC LIFE that remaining period for which real estate **improvements** are expected to generate more income than **operating expenses** cost. See **useful life.**
Example: Figure 56. *yield investor return on the investment.*

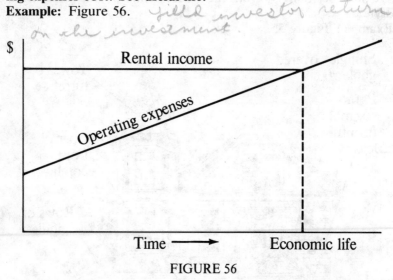

FIGURE 56

ECONOMIC OBSOLESCENCE Same as **economic depreciation.**
loss of value due to outside changes

ECONOMIC RENT 1. in economics, the cost commanded by a factor that is unique or inelastic in supply.
Example: The portion of rental income attributable to the land is often considered *economic rent,* since the land will exist no matter what the rental rate. In this context, *economic rent* carries a connotation of being "unearned" by its owner.
2. in appraisal, the **market rent.** Contrast with **contract rent.**
Example: Big Buy Foods is using a store for $1,000 per month rent. If the landlord could rent the store on a new **lease** now, it would command $4,000 per month. The $1,000 is the **contract rent** and the $4,000 is the *economic rent.*

EFFECTIVE AGE the age of a property based on the amount of **wear and tear** it has sustained.
Example: Collins' house was built twelve years ago. Because she keeps it in excellent condition it shows only as much wear as a typical 5-year-old house. Collins' house therefore has an *effective age* of 5 years.

EFFECTIVE RATE the true rate of return considering all relevant **financing** expenses. See **annual percentage rate.**

Example: Abel borrows $10,000 on a one-year bank loan. He pays 2 **discount points** and a 10% **face interest rate.** He repays the loan at the end of the year, with interest. Since he really received only $9,800 at the start of the loan and repaid $11,000, the *effective rate* was greater than 10%. It was approximately 12.25%.

EGRESS access from a land parcel to a public road or other means of exit.
Example: Figure 57.

A lot with *egress*   A lot without *egress*

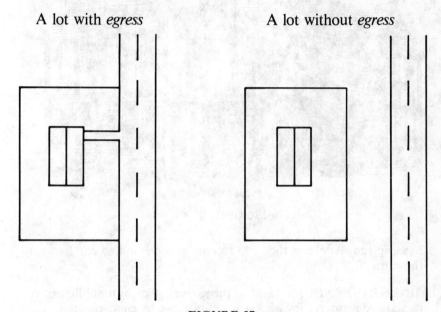

FIGURE 57

EJECTMENT action to regain possession of **real property,** when there is no **lease.**
Example: The holder of a **conditional sales contract,** through an action in *ejectment,* regains possession when the buyer **defaults.**

ELIZABETHAN OR HALF TIMBER STYLE an English style, 2- or 2½-story house, often with part of the second story overhanging the first. It has less stone work and is less fortlike than the Tudor. Stone and stucco walls with half timbers are most common.
Example: Figure 58.

EMBLEMENT a growing crop. Annual crops are generally considered **personal property.**
Example: Abel, a **tenant,** planted corn on Baker's, land. Three days prior to harvesting, Baker informs Abel that the **land lease**

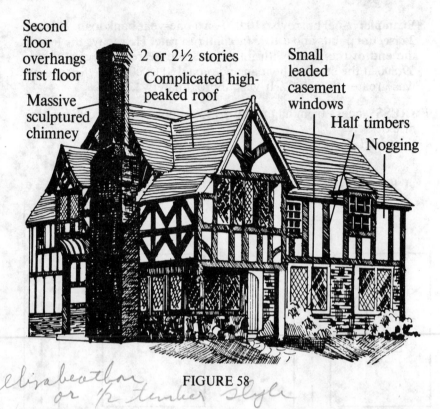

Second floor overhangs first floor

Massive sculptured chimney

2 or 2½ stories

Complicated high-peaked roof

Small leaded casement windows

Half timbers

Nogging

FIGURE 58

Elizabethan or ½ timber style

has expired. Abel has the right to *emblements* and so can harvest the corn.

EMINENT DOMAIN the right of the government or a public utility to acquire property for necessary public use by **condemnation**; the owner must be fairly compensated.
Example: Ready Watts Electric Company is granted the power of *eminent domain* by the state government. This allows the company to acquire private property for specified purposes through the process of condemnation.

EMPTY NESTERS a couple whose children have established separate households; important segment of the housing market, since empty nesters often seek to reduce the amount of housing space they occupy. Thus empty nesters are one source of demand for smaller housing units.
Example: The Etons have raised 2 children who are now grown and have families of their own. As *empty nesters*, the Etons no longer have need for the big 4-bedroom home they occupy. They purchase a 2-bedroom **town house,** which provides all the space they require.

ENCROACHMENT a building, a part of a building, or an obstruction that physically intrudes upon, overlaps, or **trespasses** upon the property of another.
Example: A part of the building on lot A is an *encroachment* on lot B. This situation probably occurred because of a faulty **survey** of lot A (Figure 59).

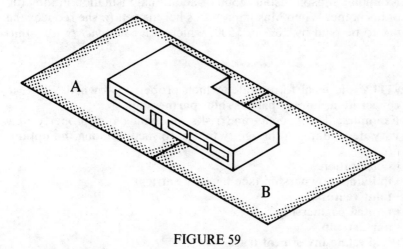

FIGURE 59

ENCUMBRANCE any right to or interest in land that affects its value. Includes outstanding **mortgage** loans, unpaid taxes, **easements, deed restrictions.**
Example: *Encumbrances* on Blackacres include 3 mortgages, 4 **leases, a mechanic's lien,** and a deed restriction preventing the sale of alcoholic beverages on the land.

END LOAN same as **permanent mortgage.**

ENDORSEMENT 1. the act of signing one's name, as the payee, on the back of a check or **note,** with or without further qualification; the signature itself.
Example: Figure 60.
2. offering support or credibility to a statement.

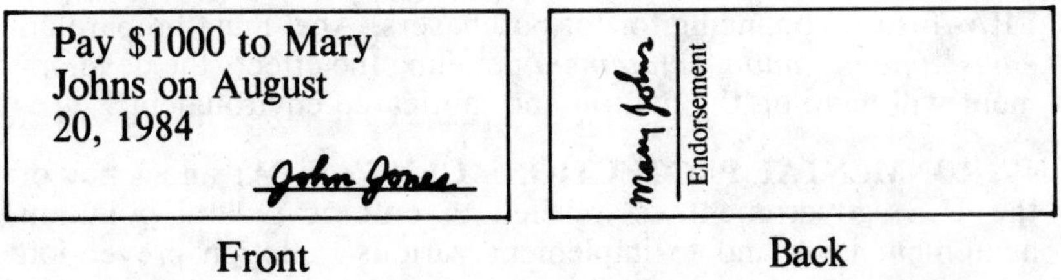

Pay $1000 to Mary
Johns on August
20, 1984
                    John Jones

Mary Johns   Endorsement

Front   Back

FIGURE 60

Example: The American Association of Homebuilders *endorses* the use of brick as a construction material.

ENERGY TAX CREDITS a reduction in income tax, generally based on the cost of installing insulation and other energy-saving devices.
Example: Mason installs $500 of additional insulation in the attic of his home. When Mason prepares her tax return she reduces the tax to be paid by 20% of $500, which is a $100 *energy tax credit*.

ENTITY the legal form under which property is owned. See also **corporation, limited partnership, partnership.**
Examples: The benefits and risks of owning real property may vary depending on the *entity* that is formed. Among the options are:
• corporation
• individual ownership (see **tenancy** entries)
• **joint venture**
• **limited partnership**
• **partnership**
• **real estate investment trust**

ENTREPRENEUR an individual who generates business activity. A businessman or businesswoman. Often associated with one who takes business risks.
Example: Business owned by *entrepreneurs* include:
• auto dealerships
• restaurants
• retail stores
• wholesale distributing companies

ENVIRONMENTAL IMPACT STATEMENT (EIS) an analysis of the expected effects of a development or action on the surrounding natural and fabricated environment. Such statements are required for many federally supported developments under the National Environmental Policy Act of 1969.
Example: Abel seeks to develop a large **subdivision** and obtain **FHA-** insured financing for lot purchasers. Abel must prepare an *environmental impact statement* detailing the effects the development will have on the natural and fabricated environment.

ENVIRONMENTAL PROTECTION AGENCY (EPA) an agency of the U.S. government established to enforce federal pollution abatement laws and to implement various pollution prevention programs.
Example: The *Environmental Protection Agency* requires **permits**

for the siting of manufacturing facilities that may introduce pollution into the air or public waters. The *EPA* also provides grants to local governments to assist in construction of sewage treatment plants.

EQUAL CREDIT OPPORTUNITY ACT a federal law, enacted in 1974, to discourage discrimination by lenders on the basis of sex or marital status. Amended in 1976 to prohibit discrimination on the basis of age, race, color, religion, national origin, or receipt of public assistance.
Example: Collins, a divorced woman, is denied a **mortgage** loan by a local **savings and loan association.** She feels she would have obtained the loan if she were a man. She sues the savings and loan under the *Equal Credit Opportunity Act*. Her steady, permanent part-time earnings are to be considered in granting the loan.

EQUALIZATION BOARD a government agency that determines the fairness of taxes levied against properties.
Example: Abel feels the **market value** estimate of his property made by the tax **assessor** is too high. Appeals to the assessor do not result in satisfying Abel's complaint. Abel may take his case to the *Equalization Board* in the hope of reducing the amount of his **assessment.**

EQUITABLE CONVERSION a legal doctrine in some states in which, under a **contract of sale,** buyers and sellers are treated as though the **closing** had taken place in that the seller in possession has an obligation to take care of the property. See **equitable title.** Note: A contract of sale may specify which party incurs risk of loss until closing.
Example: Though the legal **title** has not passed, the law holds that there has been an *equitable conversion* that effectively **vests** the property in the buyer.

EQUITABLE TITLE the interest held by one who has agreed to purchase but has not yet closed the transaction.
Example: Collins has agreed in writing to buy Baker's house, with **closing** to be arranged in 2 weeks. In the interim valuable minerals are found on the property. Since Collins has *equitable title,* the minerals belong to her. Similarly, if the property were **condemned** for public use, the value gain or loss would be hers.

EQUITY the interest or value that the owner has in real estate over and above the **liens** against it.
Example: A property has a **market value** of $100,000. The owner currently owes $60,000 in **mortgage** loans that are against the property. The owner's *equity* is $40,000. See Table 15

EQUITY OF REDEMPTION the right of an owner to recover property that has been **foreclosed.**
Example: Abel's property has been foreclosed because he has not met his **mortgage** obligation. If he raises enough money within the period of time set by state laws, he may reclaim the property by paying the **principal, interest,** and legal expenses, under *equity of redemption* laws.

TABLE 15

Market value	$100,000
Liens	−60,000
Equity	$ 40,000

EROSION the gradual wearing away of land through processes of nature, as by streams and winds.
Examples:
• Deep gullies cut into unvegetated earth, caused by rainwater *erosion*
• The Grand Canyon formed by *erosion* from the Colorado River
• The Sphinx in Egypt, disfigured by wind *erosion*

ESCALATOR CLAUSE a provision in a **lease** that requires the **tenant** to pay more rent based on an increase in costs. Same as stop **clause.**
Example: A lease requires the tenant to pay increases in real estate taxes over the amount in the base year. Taxes were $1000 for the base year; and were $1,250 the following year. The tenant's rent is *escalated* by $250.

ESCHEAT the **reversion** of property to the state in the event that the owner dies without leaving a will and has no legal heirs.
Example: Abel dies without a will. No heirs are found. His property *escheats* to the state.

ESCROW an agreement between 2 or more parties providing that certain instruments or property be placed with a third party for safekeeping, pending the fulfillment or performance of a specified act or condition.
Example: The **deed** to the property and the **earnest money** were both placed in *escrow* pending fulfillment of other conditions to the **contract.**

ESCROW ACCOUNT same as **trust account.**

ESCROW AGENT any person engaged in the business of receiving **escrows** for deposit or delivery.
Example: The **title** company is serving as the *escrow agent*. It holds the **earnest money** and **deed,** pending fulfillment of other conditions to the **contract** (Figure 61).

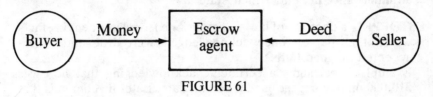

FIGURE 61

ESTATE the degree, nature, and extent of interest that a person has in **real property.**
Example: The highest form of an *estate* is **fee simple,** under which the owner can use the property at will and dispose of it without restriction.

ESTATE AT SUFFERANCE the wrongful occupancy of property by a tenant after the **lease** has expired. See **dispossess proceedings.**
Example: Abel's lease expired and he remained on the property. He has an *estate at sufferance* and may be ejected at the landlord's whim.

ESTATE AT WILL the occupation of real estate by a tenant for an indefinite period, terminable by one or both parties at will.
Example: Under an *estate at will,* the landlord may evict the tenant at any time, and the tenant may vacate at any time. The tenant may have certain rights, however, such as ownership of **emblements** (crops as a result of annual cultivation).

ESTATE FOR LIFE an interest in property that terminates upon the death of a specified person. See **life estate.**
Example: Abel deeded his wife an *estate for her life*. When she dies the property will go to Abel's son. She may use the property and may not commit **waste,** but normal **wear and tear** is acceptable.

ESTATE FOR YEARS an interest in land allowing possession for a specified and limited time.
Example: The **tenant** under a 5-year **lease** holds an *estate for years*.

ESTATE IN REVERSION an **estate** left by the **grantor** for himself or herself, to begin after the termination of some particular estate granted by him or her.
Example: All landlords have an *estate in reversion* which becomes theirs to possess when the **lease** expires.

ESTATE TAX a tax based on the value of property left by the deceased. By 1987, the estate and gift tax laws will exempt up to $600,000 of property.
Example: Abel dies, leaving $800,000 worth of **assets.** The estate of Abel will pay an *estate tax.* Abel's heirs may also be liable for an **inheritance tax** under their state law.

ESTOPPEL a doctrine of law that stops one from later denying facts which that person once acknowledged were true and others accepted on **good faith.**
Example: Abel signs a certificate acknowledging that he owes $10,000 on a **mortgage** as of a certain date. Later he contends that he owed only $5,000. Abel is prevented from asserting this new contention under *estoppel.*

ESTOPPEL CERTIFICATE a document by which the **mortgagor** (borrower) certifies that the mortgage debt is a **lien** for the amount stated. The debtor is thereafter prevented from claiming that the balance due differs from the amount stated.
Example: The Good Money Savings Association asks Abel to sign an *estoppel certificate,* which he does. Good Money Savings then sells the mortgage to Baker, who buys with confidence. Abel is later estopped (prevented) from denying that he owed the money.

ESTOVERS the legally supported right to take necessities from property. Contrast with **waste.**
Example: Mason has a **life estate** on property. She needs to cut timber for firewood to heat the residence. The **remainderman,** Baker, complains that Mason is damaging the property. The law supports Mason's use of the *estovers* as she has been doing.

ET AL. abbreviation of the Latin *et alii,* "and others."
Example: Property owned by John Jones and several others may be referenced as "John Jones, *et al.*"

ET CON legal term signifying "and husband." See **et ux.**
Example: Hereby signed and delivered by Ellen Smith *et con.*

ET UX abbreviation of the Latin *et uxor,* which means "and wife."
Example: A house is sold by Bill Baker *et ux.* Baker and his wife both must sign the **deed.**

EVICTION a legal proceeding by a **lessor** (landlord) to recover possession of property.
Example: When the **tenant** fails to comply with the **lease** agreement (skipping rent payments, unauthorized use of the property, etc.), the landlord may seek *eviction* of the tenant. If successful,

this action will terminate the rights of the tenant to use the property.

EVICTION, ACTUAL exists where one is removed from the property, either by force or by process of law.
Example: An apartment tenant may be subject to *actual eviction,* in which case, a notice will be served requiring the tenant to vacate the apartment within a specified time interval.

EVICTION, CONSTRUCTIVE exists when, through the fault of the landlord, physical conditions of the property render it unfit for the purpose for which it was leased.
Example: A landlord may allow the physical condition of an apartment building to deteriorate to the point that the premises are no longer safe for occupancy. A tenant may be able to terminate the **lease,** order *constructive eviction,* and end **liability** for future rent payments.

EVICTION, PARTIAL exists where the possessor of the property, such as a tenant, is deprived of a portion thereof.
Example: A law firm leases a floor of an office building. The **landlord** wishes to make substantial modifications to one side of the building. Because of the disruption caused by the work, the tenant and landlord agree to a *partial eviction* from the property affected by construction. The tenant's rent is reduced accordingly.

EVIDENCE OF TITLE documents, such as **deeds,** that demonstrate ownership.
Example: The property owner kept the **deed** in a bank vault because it is important *evidence of title*.

EXCHANGE under **Section 1031** of the **Internal Revenue Code, like-kind property** used in a trade or business can be exchanged tax-free. See also **boot, realized gain, recognized gain.**
Example: Collins *exchanges* her farm worth $100,000, but subject to a $20,000 **mortgage,** for Baker's apartments worth $80,000.

EXCLUSIVE AGENCY LISTING employment **contract** giving only one **broker,** for a specified time, the right to sell the property and also allowing the owner alone to sell the property without paying a **commission.**
Example: Graham gives Quick Sale Realty an *exclusive agency listing* on her house. If an agent of Quick Sale or any other **brokerage** firm sells the house during the time of the listing, Quick Sale is entitled to a commission. If Graham sells the house herself, no commission is earned.

EXCLUSIVE RIGHT TO SELL LISTING employment **contract** giving the **broker** the right to collect **commission** if the property is sold

by anyone, including the owner, during the term of the agreement. See also **multiple listing service.**
Example: Abel give Quick Sale Realty an *exclusive right to sell listing* on his house. If the house is sold during the time of the listing, Quick Sale is entitled to a commission.

EXCULPATORY CLAUSE a provision in a **mortgage** allowing the borrower to surrender the property to the lender without personal **liability** for the loan.
Example: Abel buys land for $100,000, paying $40,000 cash and gives a $60,000 mortgage to the seller with an *exculpatory clause.* The **market value** of the land drops suddenly to $55,000. Abel abandons the mortgaged property, losing the $40,000 investment but keeping everything else he owns.

EXECUTE to sign a **contract;** sometimes, to perform a contract fully.
Example: Generally when a buyer and seller sign a **sales contract,** they *execute* the contract.

EXECUTED CONTRACT a **contract** whose terms have been completely fulfilled.
Example: At the **closing,** all parties signed the contract, which made it an *executed contract.*

EXECUTOR a person named in a **will** to carry out its provisions for the disposition of the estate.
Example: Abel specifies in his will that his attorney shall serve as its *executor.* The attorney, at the appropriate time, assures that Abel's property is distributed according to the will.

EXECUTORY CONTRACT a **contract** under which one or more parties has not yet performed.
Example: Abel orally has agreed to buy Baker's land, and Baker's attorney has drafted a contract. At this stage it is *executory* because neither Abel nor Baker has signed it.

EXECUTRIX a woman who performs the duties of an **executor.**
Example: Abel appoints his wife as *executrix* for his estate. She will not need a real estate **license** to sell the property he leaves.

EXEMPTION an amount provided by law that reduces taxable income or taxable value.
Example: Personal exemptions, generally based on the number of people in a household, reduce taxable income.
Example: Homestead exemptions, offered in many jurisdictions, reduce the value of real estate that would otherwise be subject to **ad valorem tax.**

EXPOSURE (MARKET) the advertising, whether free or paid, of property that is for sale.
Example: Real estate agents provide market *exposure* through such devices as:
• classified ads in local papers
• for sale signs on the premises
• inclusion in **multiple listing service**
• displays in their office

EXTENDED COVERAGE insurance that covers specific incidences normally excluded from standard insurance policies.
Example: A homeowner who lives **adjacent** to a golf course discovers that the standard homeowners' insurance policy does not cover damage due to errant golf balls. An *extended coverage* policy may be obtained, however, to cover such damage.

EXTENSION an agreement between 2 parties to extend the time period specified in a **contract.**
Example: When a tenant is unable to **vacate** the property at the termination of the **lease,** an *extension* may be granted by the **landlord.**
Example: When a seller fails to clear the **title** in time for a **closing,** an *extension* of the closing date may be granted.

F

FACADE the outside front wall of a building.
Example: *Facade* materials for a building include:
• aluminum
• brick
• glass
• masonry
• wood

FACE AMOUNT same as **face value.**

FACE INTEREST RATE the percentage interest that is shown on the loan document. Compare with **annual percentage rate, effective rate.**
Example: A mortgage has an 8% *face interest rate,* $10,000 **face value,** and 30-year **amortization** term. If market interest rates are 12%, the **market value** of the loan is $7,200.

FACE VALUE the dollar amount, shown by words and/or numbers, on a document. Compare with **market value;** see **amortization.**

Example: A **mortgage** has a *face value* of $10,000, **amortization** term of 30 years, and 8% **face interest rate.** It will be amortized in 13 years to $8,000 by annual payments.

FAIR CREDIT REPORTING ACT a federal law that allows individuals to examine and correct information used by **credit** reporting services.
Example: Abel wishes to purchase property from Baker under an **installment land contract.** Baker refuses to make the contract because of Abel's poor **credit rating.** Under the *Fair Credit Reporting Act,* Abel may demand disclosure of Baker's source of information and then take steps to correct any misinformation in the report.

FAIR MARKET RENT the amount that a property would command if it were now available for **lease.** Contrast with **contract rent.** See **economic rent, rent control, Section 8 housing.**
Example: The *fair market rent* for an apartment is estimated at $400 per month. Under **Section 8,** the **tenant** is required to pay 20% of income toward rent; the **landlord** would receive a payment from the government to make up the difference.

FAIR MARKET VALUE a term, generally used in **property tax** and **condemnation** legislation, meaning the **market value** of a property.
Example: Property taxes generally are assessed at some ratio of *fair market value.*
Example: When property is condemned for public use, the owner is entitled to be compensated at *fair market value.*

FALSE ADVERTISING describing property in a misleading fashion.
Example: Examples of false advertising might include:
• representing a property as not being in a **floodplain** when, in fact, it is
• stating, without **caveat,** that a property will appreciate in value
• denying structural flaws that are known to exist

FANNIE MAE nickname for **Federal National Mortgage Association.**

FARMER'S HOME ADMINISTRATION (FmHA) an agency, within the U.S. Department of Agriculture, that administers assistance programs for purchasers of homes and farms in small towns and rural areas.
Example: Abel wishes to develop housing for the elderly in a rural area. He may apply to the *Farmer's Home Administration* for a special 40-year **mortgage** loan.

FEASIBILITY STUDY a determination of the likelihood that a proposed development will fulfill the objectives of a particular investor.
Example: A *feasibility study* of a proposed **subdivision** should:
• estimate the demand for housing units in the area
• estimate the **absorption rate** for the project
• discuss legal and other considerations
• forecast **cash flows**
• approximate investment returns likely to be produced

FEDERAL an early American style of house that is box-shaped and has a flat roof.
Example: Figure 62.

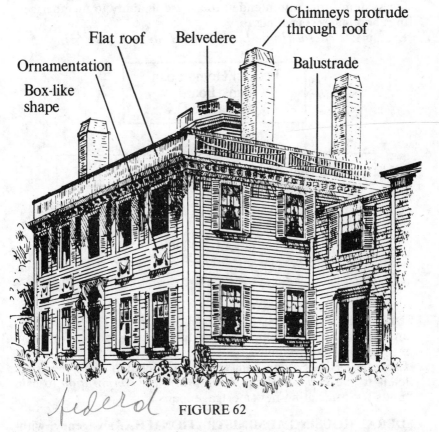

Chimneys protrude
through roof

Flat roof   Belvedere

Ornamentation   Balustrade

Box-like
shape

federal   FIGURE 62

FEDERAL DEPOSIT INSURANCE CORPORATION (FDIC) a public corporation, established in 1933; insures up to $100,000 for each depositor in most **commercial banks.** Has own reserves and can borrow from the U.S. Treasury.
Example: The First National Bank has a **liquidity** difficulty and

cannot pay depositors who want to withdraw their money. The *FDIC* pays each depositor the full **prinicpal** amount, up to $100,000.

FEDERAL FAIR HOUSING LAW a federal law that forbids **discrimination** on the basis of race, color, sex, religion, or national origin in the selling or renting of homes and apartments. See **steering.**
Example: Broker Abel is contacted by a black couple wishing to purchase a home. Although homes are currently for sale in several all-white neighborhoods, Abel maintains there are no houses available in these areas. Abel may be prosecuted under the *Federal Fair Housing Law*.

FEDERAL HOME LOAN BANK SYSTEM a federally created banking system primarily intended to assure **liquidity** to member **savings and loan associations.**
Example: *Federal Home Loan Bank System* (Figure 63).

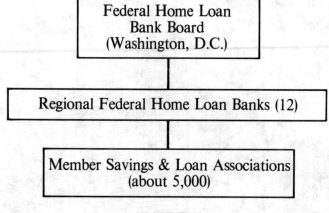

Federal Home Loan
Bank Board
(Washington, D.C.)

Regional Federal Home Loan Banks (12)

Member Savings & Loan Associations
(about 5,000)

FIGURE 63

FEDERAL HOME LOAN MORTGAGE CORPORATION (FHLMC) an organization that purchases **mortgage** loans, mostly from **savings and loan associations.**
Example: ABC Savings and Loan Association sells mortgage loans to the *Federal Home Loan Mortgage Corporation* to gain funds for originating new mortgage loans.

FEDERAL HOUSING ADMINISTRATION (FHA) an agency, within the U.S. Department of Housing and Urban Development, that administers many loan programs, loan **guarantee** programs, and **loan insurance** programs designed to make more housing available.
Example: Abel wishes to purchase a home but lacks funds for a

large **down payment.** Through a program provided by the *Federal Housing Administration,* Abel may obtain a loan for up to 97% of the purchase price.

FEDERAL NATIONAL MORTGAGE ASSOCIATION (FNMA) a corporation that specializes in buying mortgage loans, mostly from **mortgage bankers.** It adds **liquidity** to the mortgage market. Nicknamed **Fannie Mae,** FNMA is owned by its stockholders, who elect 10 to its Board of Directors. The U.S. president appoints the other 5 directors.
Example: A mortgage banker originates conventional and **FHA loans** and periodically sells them to the *Federal National Mortgage Association.*

FEDERAL RESERVE SYSTEM the central federal banking system that regulates and provides services to member **commercial banks.** Also has the responsibility for conducting federal monetary policy.
Example: The system consists of the Federal Reserve Board and a series of regional Federal Reserve Banks.

FEDERAL SAVINGS & LOAN ASSOCIATION a member of the **Federal Home Loan Bank System** and the **Federal Savings and Loan Insurance Corporation.**
Example: City Federal Savings and Loan is a *federal savings and loan association.* Its activities are regulated by the Federal Home Loan Bank Board. Home Savings is a state chartered savings and loan association regulated by state government.

FEDERAL SAVINGS AND LOAN INSURANCE CORPORATION (FSLIC) an agency of the federal government that insures depositors in **savings and loan associations** against loss of **principal.** Most deposits, including passbooks and saving certificates, are insured up to a maximum amount per account.
Address: Federal Savings and Loan Insurance Corporation
1700 G Street, N.W.
Washington, D.C. 20552
Example: Graham may deposit savings in a **savings and loan association** without fear of losing her money, since her deposit, up to $100,000, is insured by the *Federal Savings and Loan Insurance Corporation.*

FEDERAL TRADE COMMISSION (FTC) a federal agency, headquarters in Washington, D.C., that regulates advertising and other promotion and sales practices of firms engaged in interstate commerce. The FTC does *not* regulate interstate land sales (HUD), anticompetitive activities (JUSTICE), or sale of securities (SEC).

Example: Abel, a builder, was found guilty of false television advertising by the *FTC*.

FEE SIMPLE or FEE ABSOLUTE or FEE SIMPLE ABSOLUTE absolute ownership of **real property;** owner is entitled to the entire property with unconditional power of disposition during the owner's life, and upon his death the property descends to the owner's designated heirs.

Example: The only power that can require Abel to sell his land is **eminent domain;** he owns the property in *fee simple*, so there is no other interest.

FEE SIMPLE DEFEASIBLE a type of property ownership in which the grant of **title** or duration of ownership is dependent on a specified condition.

Example: A *fee simple defeasible* may be granted on the condition that the property be used for an orphanage home (termed "fee simple subject to a condition subsequent").

Example: A *fee simple defeasible* may be granted as long as the property is held as a wildlife refuge (termed "fee simple determinable").

FHA MORTGAGE LOAN a **mortgage** loan insured by the FHA. The FHA charges ½% of the balance each year as an insurance fee. See **Federal Housing Administration.**

Example: Abel wishes to purchase a home but has insufficient cash to make a large down payment. By obtaining an *FHA loan*, Abel may borrow more than the customary 80% of value, with the FHA insuring the loan amount.

FHLB Federal Home Loan Bank; a federally chartered bank that supplies **credit** to member banks. See **Federal Home Loan Bank System.**

FIDELITY BOND an assurance, generally purchased by an employer, to cover employees who are entrusted with valuable property or funds.

Example: A landlord employs a resident manager who, among other duties, collects the **rent.** To safeguard these funds during the collection process, the landlord purchases a *fidelity bond* on the resident manager.

FIDUCIARY one who acts, in a financial role, in the best interests of others.

Example:
• a **broker** is a *fiduciary* for the seller
• a banker is a *fiduciary* for the bank's depositors
• an attorney may be a *fiduciary* for the client
• a **trustee** is a *fiduciary* for the **beneficiaries**

FILTERING DOWN the process whereby, over time, a housing unit or neighborhood is occupied by progressively lower-income residents.

Example: Many older residences near the downtown of big cities were once occupied by the upper classes, but have *filtered down* to the relatively poor. At some point in the filtering process, many large houses may be converted into rented **multifamily housing.**

FINANCE CHARGE interest or certain other fees charged to a **credit** customer.

Example: A customer makes purchases of $400 on credit. Payment is made one month later. Based on an annual percentage rate of interest of 18%, a *finance charge* of $6.00 ($.\frac{18}{12} \times \$400$) is added to the bill.

FINANCIAL LEVERAGE the use of borrowed money to complete an investment purchase.

Example: The effects of *financial leverage* on return on **equity** are shown in Table 16.

(Note: If **debt service** required is high compared to income, effect of leverage may be to *reduce* return to equity.)

TABLE 16

No Leverage		Leverage with 50% Debt	
Cost	$100,000	Cost	$100,000
Debt	0	Debt	$50,000
Equity	$100,000	Equity	$50,000
Income	$20,000	Income	$20,000
Debt service	0	Debt service	−7,500
Cash to equity	$20,000	Cash to equity	$12,500
Return on equity	$\frac{20,000}{100,000} = 0.20$	Return on equity	$\frac{12,500}{50,000} = 0.25$

FINANCIAL MANAGEMENT RATE OF RETURN (FMRR) a method of measuring investment performance that is a variation on the **internal rate of return** method. The user specifies 2 after-tax reinvestment rates:

i_L: a safe, liquid rate, obtainable for liquid deposits.

i_R: a run-of-the-mill rate, which can be earned from typical investments over a long term.

Negative cash flows are generally **discounted** to a present value at the i_L rate, inflows are compounded to the investment resale date at i_R. The FMRR is the rate that equates the present value of negative cash flows to the future value of inflows.

Example: An investment requires a $10,000 negative cash flow for the first 3 years, then offers $8,500 of cash inflows for years 4-10. If i_L is 5%, the negative cash flows have a present value of $27,232. If i_R is 10%, the cash inflows will become $80,641. The *FMRR* is 11.47% because that is the rate at which $27,232 would grow to $80,641 in 10 years with **compound interest.**

FINANCIAL STATEMENT one that shows income and expense for an accounting period, or **assets, liabilities** and **equity** as of a point in time.

Example: Table 17.

Table 17

Income statement		Balance sheet		
Rental income	$5,000	Assets		Liabilities & equity
Interest expense	−2,000			
Depreciation	−1,000	Buildings $40,000	Mortgage $30,000	
Real estate taxes	− 500	Land 10,000	Equity 20,000	
Net income	$1,500	Total $50,000	Total $50,000	

FINANCING borrowing money to buy property. See **creative financing.**

Example: The following are examples of *financing:*
• obtaining a **mortgage** loan on a purchase
• **assumptions of a mortgage** from a seller
• arranging for the seller to take a loan as part of the purchase price
• arranging an **installment sale**

FINDER'S FEE money paid to someone other than a **broker** who locates suitable property or a purchaser. Prohibited or limited in most states.

Example: Broker Abel has a **listing** on a particular property. Baker knows several people interested in such property. Abel arranges with Baker to provide a *finder's fee* should one of the **prospects** identified by Baker purchase the property.

FIREPROOF having all exposed surfaces constructed of noncombustible materials or protected by such materials.

Example: The exterior surface of the building was composed of brick, aluminum siding, and asbestos shingles, thereby making the exterior *fireproof.*

FIRE-RESISTIVE able to withstand exposure to flame of a specified intensity or for a specified time. Compare **fireproof.**

Example: The interior walls in the house were made of *fire-resistive* material. The walls were designed to resist igniting at temperatures below 1,000 degrees if not exposed for more than one hour.

FIRST MORTGAGE a **mortgage** that has priority as a **lien** over all other mortgages. In cases of **foreclosure** the first mortgage will be satisfied before other mortgages. See **junior mortgage, second mortgage.**
Example: A property costing $100,000 is financed with a *first mortgage* of $75,000, a second mortgage of $15,000, and $10,000 in cash. If the borrower **defaults** and the property is sold upon foreclosure for $80,000, the holder of the *first mortgage* will receive the full amount of the unpaid **principal** plus legal expenses. The second mortgage holder will receive any excess after the first mortgage has been satisfied.

FIRST REFUSAL RIGHT same as **right of first refusal.**

FIRST-YEAR DEPRECIATION same as **additional first-year depreciation.**

FISCAL YEAR a 12-month time interval used for financial reporting; the period starts on any date after January 1 and ends one year later.
Example: For agencies of the federal government, *fiscal year* 1981 refers to the time between October 1, 1980 to September 31, 1981.

FIXING-UP EXPENSES (TAX) expenses incurred for the purpose of physically preparing a personal residence for sale. Qualified fixing-up expenses may be deducted from the sales price to determine the price that must be spent in the purchase of another residence to defer **capital gains** taxes on the sale of the old one.
Example: Abel spends $500 for painting and repairs on a home prior to sale. The house sells for $75,500 and costs $7,000 in transaction costs. The adjusted sales price is calculated in Table 18.

TABLE 18

Sale price	$75,500
Fixing-up expenses	− 500
Selling expenses	− 7,000
Adjusted sales price	$68,000

Abel must spend at least $68,000 on a new residence to avoid **capital gains** on the sale.

FIXTURES improvements or **personal property** attached to the land so as to become part of the real estate. Tests to determine whether an item is a fixture include:
- intent of the parties (was it intended to remain?)
- method of annexation (how is it affixed?)
- relation of the parties (was it expected to be part of a tenant's business?)
- adaptation of the article (is it essential to the building?)

Example: Abel sells his house. The contract of sale includes all of the real estate. Baker, the buyer, believes that the ceiling fan in the dining room is a *fixture*, but Abel claims it as **personal property.**

FLAT 1. an apartment, generally on one level.
Example: A 2-room *flat* is an apartment having 2 rooms.
2. a **level payment mortgage** or **lease** requirement.
Example: A **flat lease** is one that requires level payments each month or other specified period.

FLAT LEASE a rental agreement that requires periodic level rent payments.
Example: Pattern of payments for a one-year *flat lease* with monthly payments (Figure 64).

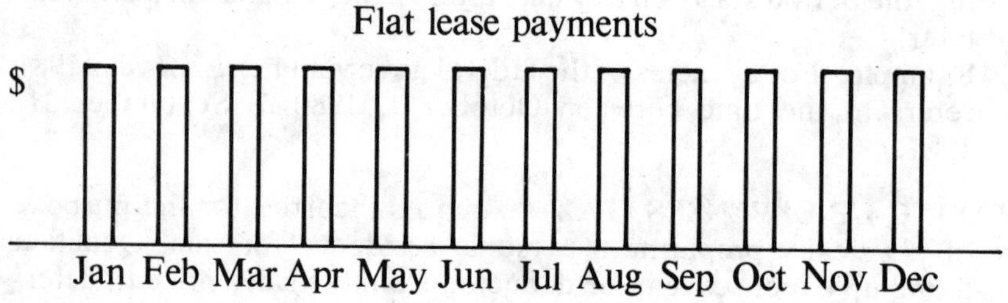

Flat lease payments

FIGURE 64

FLEXIBLE PAYMENT MORTGAGE (FPM) a home-purchase loan plan that allows the borrower to pay interest-only for the first several years of the term. FPM's were authorized by the **Federal Home Loan Bank** Board in 1974 with 2 restrictions:
1. monthly payments must be sufficient to cover **interest** on the **principal**
2. after 5 years, payments must be sufficient to amortize the principal over the remaining term

Example: A young couple purchases a home with a *flexible payment mortgage*. The principal is $50,000, interest rate at 14%, and term of 30 years. For the first 5 years, the monthly payments are $583.33. For years 6 through 30, payments will be $601.88. If they had obtained a **level payment mortgage,** monthly payments would have been $592.44 over the entire loan. See the mortgage tables in the Appendix.

FLOAT 1. the interval of time after a deposit or withdrawal is made and before the transaction is credited or deducted.
Example: Abel writes a check to pay a **debt** to Baker. Baker deposits the check in a bank other than the one used by Abel. Abel's bank may have a *float* of 2 or 3 days before Baker's bank collects the money.
2. the difference between a **variable interest rate** and the **index** to which it is pegged.
Example: A bank makes construction loans at 3% over the **prime rate.** The 3% is the *float*.
3. to incur a debt.
Example: To fund a project, Atlas Company may *float* a loan or *float* a **bond** issue.

FLOOD INSURANCE an insurance policy that covers property damage due to natural flooding. Flood insurance is offered by private insurers but is subsidized by the federal government.
Example: Abel owns a home within an area defined as a 100-year **floodplain.** If the local community is participating in a special federal program, Abel may purchase *flood insurance* to cover damage from periodic flooding.

FLOODPLAIN a level land area subject to periodic flooding from a **contiguous** body of water. Floodplains are delineated by the expected frequency of flooding. For example, an annual floodplain is expected to flood once each year.
Example: Figure 65.

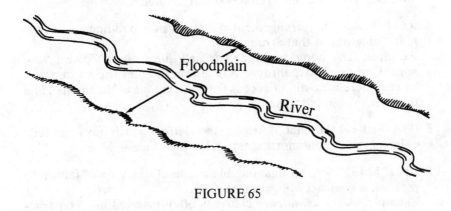

FIGURE 65

FLOOR-AREA RATIO the arithmetic relationship of the total square feet of a building to the square footage of the land area.

Formula: floor-area ratio $= \dfrac{\text{building area}}{\text{land area}}$

The floor-area ratio is $0.25 \left(\dfrac{50' \times 50'}{100' \times 100'} \right)$

Example: Figure 66.

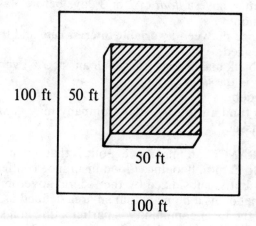

100 ft | 50 ft

50 ft

100 ft

FIGURE 66

FLOOR LOAN the minimum that a lender is willing to advance. See also **gap loan.**
Example: Abel, a lender, agrees to a $700,000 floor on a $1,000,000 permanent loan. When construction is complete, the borrower will receive a $700,000 *floor loan;* when the property is 80% occupied the full $1,000,000 will be loaned.

FLOOR PLAN the arrangement of rooms in a building, or a one-plane diagram of that arrangement.
Example: The home is difficult to sell due to its awkward *floor plan*. One must pass through a bedroom to enter the master bedroom. There is no direct access from the garage to the kitchen and the living room is too small.

FNMA Federal National Mortgage Association, which buys and sells existing residential mortgages; nicknamed **Fannie Mae.**

FORCE MAJEURE an unavoidable cause of delay or of failure to perform a **contract** obligation in time.
Example: A *force majeure* clause is often inserted in a construction contract to protect the **contractor** from delays due to weather, labor disputes, and other unavoidable incidents.

FORECLOSURE a termination of all rights of a **mortgagor** or the **grantee** in the property covered by the **mortgage**. Statutory foreclosure is effected without recourse to courts, but must conform to laws (statutes). Strict foreclosure forever bars **equity of redemption**. See **default**.

Example: The lender *forecloses* to gain possession of mortgaged land after the borrower missed 3 payments.

FORFEITURE loss of money or anything else of value because of failure to perform under **contract**.

Example: Because Baker, the prospective purchaser, failed to keep up payments under the **land contract**, he *forfeited* all his rights to the property.

FRAME HOUSE a house constructed with a wooden frame over which is placed some form of siding or **veneer**.

Example: A *frame house* (Figure 67).

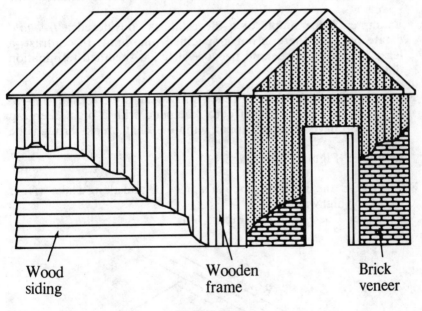

Wood
siding

Wooden
frame

Brick
veneer

FIGURE 67

FRANCHISE a **license** for a person or group to operate a business under someone else's company name.

Example: **Broker** Abel obtains a *franchise* from Century 21. This allows the broker to use the name and logo of the company and participate in all training and assistance programs offered by the company.

FRAUD the intentional use of deception to cause another person to suffer loss.
Example: Abel purchases property from Baker. Abel later discovers that Baker did not hold **title** to the property and had no right to sell. Baker was guilty of *fraud* and is liable for damages suffered by Abel in the purchase of the property.

FREDDIE MAC nickname for **Federal Home Loan Mortgage Corporation.**

FREE AND CLEAR TITLE title to a property without **encumbrances.** Generally used to refer to a property free of **mortgage** debt. See **clear title, marketable title.**
Example: *Free and clear title* is generally desired by the purchaser of a property. This requires clearing any **clouds on the title** and satisfying any **liens** that may exist.

FREEHOLD an interest in **real estate** without a predetermined time span.
Example: A **fee simple** or a **life estate** is considered a *freehold* estate because there is not a specified time limit. In contrast, a **lease** is less than freehold because it has a specified termination date.

FRENCH PROVINCIAL a French Provincial style formal, 1½- to 2½-story house that is perfectly balanced with a high steep hip roof and curved-headed upper windows that break through the cornice.
Example: Figure 68 on page 111.

FRONTAGE the linear distance of a piece of land along a lake, river, street, or highway.
Example: Road *frontage* (Figure 69).

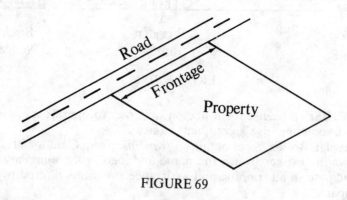

FIGURE 69

Example: Lake *frontage* (Figure 70).

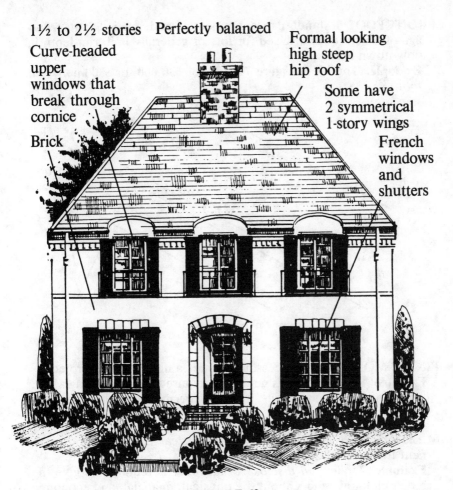

1½ to 2½ stories   Perfectly balanced

Curve-headed
upper
windows that
break through
cornice

Brick

Formal looking
high steep
hip roof

Some have
2 symmetrical
1-story wings

French
windows
and
shutters

FIGURE 68

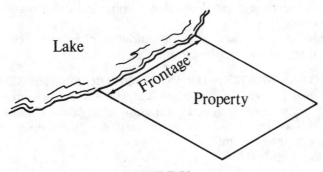

Lake

Frontage

Property

FIGURE 70

FRONT FOOT a standard measurement of land, applied at the **front-age** of its street line. Used for lots of generally uniform depth in downtown arces.
Example: The lot in Figure 71 sold for $30,000, or $300 per *front foot*.

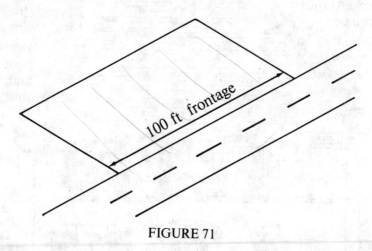

FIGURE 71

FRONT MONEY cash necessary to start a development project.
Example: *Front money* is generally required for purchasing a **site**, preparing plans and studies, obtaining **permits**, and obtaining loan **commitments.**

FULL DISCLOSURE a requirement to reveal all information pertinent to a transaction.
Example: Under *full disclosure,* a **broker** is required to give the buyer all known facts about the physical, financial, and economic condition of the subject property.

FUNCTIONAL DEPRECIATION loss of value from all causes within the property, except those due to physical deterioration. See **obsolescence.**
Example: A poor **floor plan** or outdated plumbing fixtures are types of *functional depreciation*.

FUNCTIONAL MODERN OR CONTEMPORARY HOUSE a post World War II style house with an exterior style that is an integral part of the overall design. Its function is to enclose some living areas with modern materials while integrating the indoor and outdoor space into one unit.
Example: Figure 72.

FUNCTIONAL OBSOLESCENCE same as **functional depreciation.**

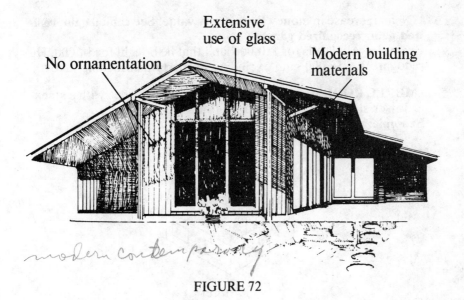

No ornamentation

Extensive
use of glass

Modern building
materials

modern contemporary

FIGURE 72

FUTURE INTEREST a property right or estate that may not be
enjoyed until some time in the future.
Example: When a **life estate** is created, the **remainder** is a *future
interest*.
Example: The lender's right to a portion of net **appreciation,** under
a **shared appreciation mortgage**, is a *future interest*.

G

GABLE ROOF one with a triangle, with the ridge forming an angle
at the top and each eave forming an angle at the bottom.
Example: Figure 73.

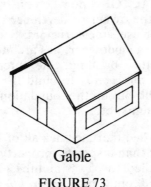

Gable

FIGURE 73

GAIN an increase in money or **property** value. See **capital gain, realized gain, recognized gain.**
Example: Abel sells for $10,000 land that he bought for $4,000. He recognizes a $6,000 gain excluding property and income taxes.

GAMBREL ROOF one having two slopes on two sides with a steeper lower slope than the upper, flatter sections.
Example: Figure 74.

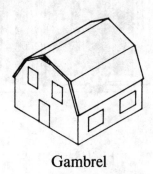

Gambrel

FIGURE 74

GAP LOAN one that fills the difference between the **floor loan** and the full amount of the **permanent loan.**
Example: A **developer** arranges a permanent **mortgage** that will fund $1,000,000 when the apartments she is building are 80% occupied. From completion of construction until 80% occupancy is reached, the mortgage is only $700,000. The developer arranges a *gap loan* of $300,000 for the **rent-up period.**

GARDEN APARTMENTS a housing complex whereby some or all **tenants** have access to a lawn area.
Example: Abel is now enjoying a steak that he grilled outside his *garden apartment* (Figure 75).

GENERAL CONTRACTOR one who constructs a building or other **improvement** for the owner or **developer.** May retain a construction labor force or use **subcontractors.** See **contractor.**
Example: Collins, a landowner, has architectural plans and **specifications** for an office building. She enters into a **contract** with Baker, a *general contractor,* to build the structure. Baker hires subcontractors who put up the foundation, walls, roof, electrical and plumbing systems, etc.

GENERAL LIEN a **lien** that includes all of the property owned by the debtor, rather than a specific property.
Example: Abel failed to pay 3 months of rent and moved out. Baker, the **landlord,** obtained a *general lien* against Abel by going

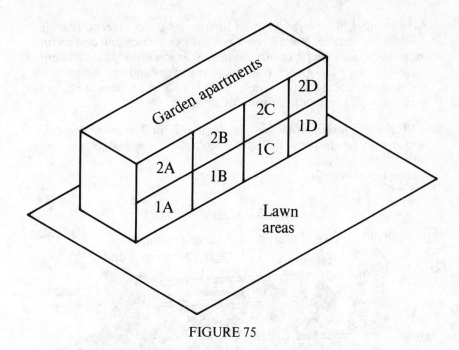

FIGURE 75

to secure a **judgment** against Abel. If Abel doesn't pay the back rent, Baker will apply for a specific lien against Abel's furniture and then have it sold.

GENERAL PARTNER in a **partnership**, a partner whose **liability** is not limited. All partners in an ordinary partnership are general partners. A **limited partnership** must have at least one general partner.
Example: The *general partner* in a limited partnership is the **syndicator** who arranges the purchase, seeks investors, and assumes all liabilities of the partnership.

GENERAL WARRANTY DEED a **deed** in which the **grantor** agrees to protect the **grantee** against any other claim to **title** of the property and provides other promises. See **warranty deed**.
Example: Abel received a *general warranty deed* for land he bought from Baker. Five years later a defect is found. Mrs. Cabel, whose deceased husband sold the land to Baker, actually owns one half of the property. Abel can claim restitution from Baker for the half because the deed warranties against all defects.

GENTRIFICATION the displacement of lower-income residents by higher-income residents in a neighborhood. Generally occurs when an older neighborhood is rehabilitated or revitalized.
Example: In the past, many large older homes in Inman Park,

Atlanta, had been converted to boarding houses. Recently, middle-income families have been buying these houses and converting them back into **single-family homes.** The lower-income residents are often forced to move to surrounding areas and are replaced by the middle-income renovators. As this process is repeated, *gentrification* of the neighborhood occurs.

GEORGIAN a large, English style, formal 2- or 3-story rectangular house that is characterized by its classic lines and ornamentation.
Example: Figure 76.

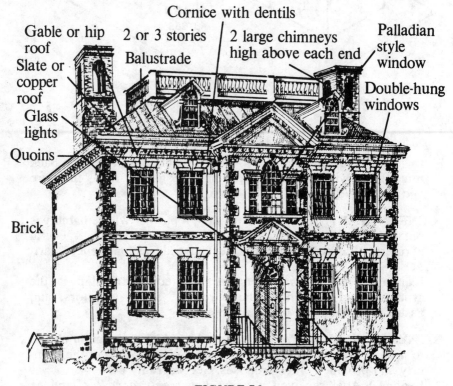

Cornice with dentils

Gable or hip roof
2 or 3 stories
2 large chimneys high above each end
Palladian style window

Slate or copper roof
Balustrade
Double-hung windows

Glass lights

Quoins

Brick

FIGURE 76

GIFT DEED a **deed** for which **consideration** is love and affection, and no material consideration is involved.
Example: Abel, who is on the brink of **bankruptcy, executes** a *gift deed* to his wife. Since there is no consideration and the apparent reason for the transfer was to remove the property from the reach of Abel's creditors, the deed might not be valid. In other situations the gift deed would be upheld.

GIFT TAX federal tax upon a monetary gift to a relative or friend. Generally, each person may give up to $10,000 per year to each **donee** without imposition of a federal gift tax. On higher gifts, there may be a gift tax, or the gift may affect the **donor's estate tax.**
Example: Mr. and Mrs. Abel together give $20,000 this year to each of 3 sons ($60,000 total). There will be no *gift tax* imposed.

GI LOAN same as **VA loan.**

GINNIE MAE nickname for **Government National Mortgage Association.**

GOOD FAITH an act done honestly.
Example: Abel pays $1,000 to Baker as a *good faith* **deposit** on land Baker offers for sale. Baker doesn't own the land and doesn't plan to buy it, so his acceptance of the deposit was not in *good faith.*

GOODWILL a business **asset** of **intangible value** created by customer and supplier relations.
Example: Diversified Enterprises, Inc. bought Acme Hardware Co. They paid a total of $200,000, which included $100,000 for the **property**, $50,000 for **inventory**, and $50,000 for *goodwill.*

GOVERNMENT NATIONAL MORTGAGE ASSOCIATION (GNMA) market. a government organization to assist in housing finance. There are 2 main programs:
1. to **guarantee** payments to investors in mortgage-backed securities
2. to absorb the **write-down** of low-interest rate loans that are used to finance **low-income housing**
   See **secondary mortgage morlat.**
Example: Good Money Mortgage Bankers, who have originated $3,000,000 of **FHA** and **VA mortgages**, have issued **participation mortgage** certificates, backed by the mortgages, to investors. *GNMA* guarantees the participation certificates (Figure 77).

GOVERNMENT RECTANGULAR SURVEY a rectangular system of land **survey** that divides a district into 24-square mile **quadrangles** from the **meridian** (north-south line) and the **base line** (east-west line); the tracts are divided into 6-mile-square parts called *townships,* which are in turn divided into 36 tracts, each 1 mile square, called **sections.**
Example: *Government Rectangular Survey* System (Figure 78).

GRACE PERIOD the period during which one party may fail to perform without being considered in **default.**

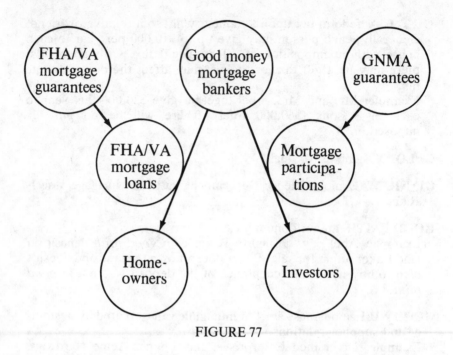

FIGURE 77

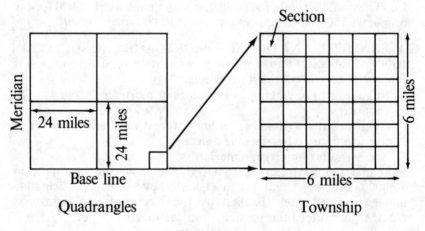

FIGURE 78

Example: Rent is due on the first of each month, but the tenant requested and received a 10-day *grace period* from the landlord. If rent is paid on or before the 10th, the tenant is not in default.

GRADE 1. ground level at the foundation.
Example: Part A of the building in Figure 79 is above *grade;* Part B is below *grade*.

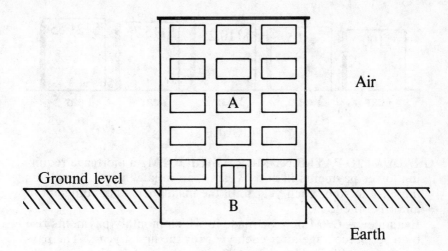

FIGURE 79

2. to prepare a smooth surface on a site.

Example: Machinery was brought to the **site** to *grade* the **land** in preparation for the foundation.

GRADED LEASE same as **graduated lease.**

GRADIENT the slope, or rate of increase or decrease in the elevation of a surface; usually expressed as a percentage:

$$\text{Gradient} = \frac{\text{vertical rise or fall}}{\text{horizontal distance}}$$

Example: The lot in Figure 80 has a 10% *gradient:*

$$\frac{10'}{100'} = 0.10$$

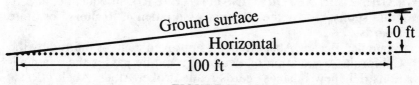

FIGURE 80

GRADUATED LEASE a lease that provides for graduated changes, at stated intervals, in the amount of rent.
Example: A 5-year *graduated lease* calls for annual rent increases of 5%. The yearly payments are shown in Figure 81.

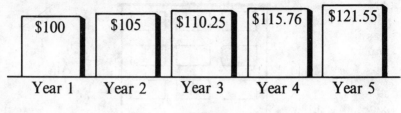

FIGURE 81

GRADUATED PAYMENT MORTGAGE (GPM) a mortgage requiring lower payments in early years than in later years. Payments increase in steps each year until the installments are sufficient to amortize the loan.

Example: A *GPM* may be made in which monthly payments rise by a set percentage after each year for the first 4 years. The payments would look like Figure 82.

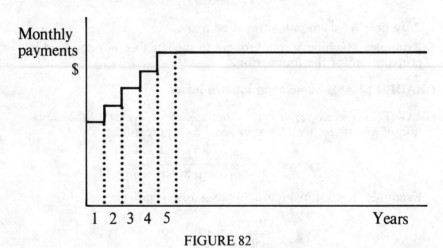

FIGURE 82

GRADUATE REALTORS® INSTITUTE (GRI) an educational program sponsored by the **National Association of Realtors®** or State Boards.

Example: Broker Abel attends 3 approved courses offered by the California Association of Realtors®, and he passes the examinations. His new business cards read: Broker Albert Abel, *GRI*.

GRANDFATHER CLAUSE when a law is changed or a new law is passed, those whose specific activity was legal under the previous law are often allowed to continue, by virtue of this provision.

Example: All real estate **brokers** are allowed to continue to practice as brokers after licensure requirements increase. The new law affects only new **licensees**; old licensees are *grandfathered*.

GRANT a technical term used in deeds of **conveyance** of property to indicate a transfer.
Example: In a **deed**, Abel *grants* his land to his daughter in **fee simple**.

GRANTEE the party to whom the **title** to **real property** is conveyed; the buyer.
Example: Edith Andrew Abel is the *grantee* under a **deed** from her father, Albert Abel.

GRANTOR anyone who gives a **deed**.
Examples: *Grantors* include:
• an individual (former) owner
• a bankruptcy **trustee**
• a **guardian** for an **incompetent**

G.R.I. graduate of the Realtors® Institute, which is affiliated with the **National Association of Realtors®. See Graduate Realtors Institute**.

GROSS AREA the total floor area of a building, usually measured from its outside walls.
Example: The *gross area* of a 2-story office building (Figure 83) that completely covers a 100′ X 100′ tract of land is 20,000 square feet (10,000 square feet for each story). Exterior walls, interior hallways, stairwells, and utility rooms absorb 4,000 square feet, so the **net leasable area** is 16,000 square feet.

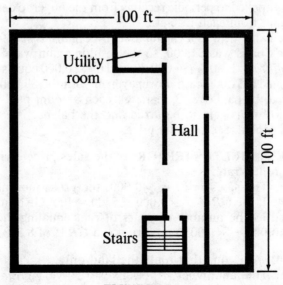

FIGURE 83

GROSS INCOME total income from property before any expenses are deducted.

Example: A building with 10,000 net rentable square feet of floor space rents for an average of $10 per square foot. **Concessions** in the lobby produce an additional $20,000 in annual income. An average 5% **vacancy rate** is maintained. Two measures of *gross income* are shown in Table 19.

Table 19

Total **rent** income	$100,000	(10,000 × $10)
Concession income	20,000	
Potential gross income	$120,000	
Vacancy loss	− 5,000	(.05 × $100,000)
Effective gross income	$115,000	

GROSS INCOME MULTIPLIER (GIM) same as **gross rent multiplier.**

GROSS LEASE a lease of property whereby the landlord **(lessor)** is responsible for paying all property expenses, such as taxes, insurance, utilities, and repairs.

Example: In a certain apartment complex the **landlord** pays for all utilities and taxes. The lease is a *gross lease*, since the landlord receives rent as a gross figure and must pay **operating expenses.**

GROSS PROFIT RATIO in an **installment sale,** the relationship between the gross profit (gain) and the **contract price.** The resulting fraction is applied to periodic receipts from the buyer to determine the taxable gain from each receipt.

Example: Land, held as a **capital asset** by Collins, is sold for $10,000. Collins tax basis was $4,000, so the resulting gain was $6,000. The *gross profit ratio* is 60% ($6,000 divided by $10,000 equals 60%). Collins accepted a $1,000 cash **downpayment** with the $9,000 balance of the price to be paid over 3 years. Of each amount paid toward the principal, 60% is gain to be taxed and the balance is a nontaxable return of capital. See **contract price.**

GROSS RENT MULTIPLIER (GRM) the sales price divided by the **contract** rental rate.

Example: The sales price is $40,000; the gross monthly **contract rent** is $400; the *GRM* = $40,000 ÷ $400 = 100. GRM may also be expressed as the number of years of rent equaling the purchase price ($40,000 ÷ $4,800 annual rent = a *GRM* of 8.333).

GROUND LEASE one that rents the land only.

Example: The landowner, Abel, gives a 50-year *ground lease* to Baker. Baker must pay $5,000 per year rent. At the end of the

50-year period, Abel owns the land **free and clear** and whatever **improvements** that Baker left on the property.

GROUND RENT the rent earned by leased land.
Example: The Good Title Company owns an office building situated on a **site** owned by the Widget Makers Retirement Fund. The site is leased to Good Title on a long-term basis and requires the payment of *ground rent* to the Widget Makers Retirement Fund on a semiannual basis.

GROWING EQUITY MORTGAGE (GEM) a **mortgage** loan in which the payment is increased by a specific amount each year, with the additional payment amount applied to **principal** retirement. As a result of the added principal retirement, the **maturity** of the loan is significantly shorter than a comparable **level payment mortgage.**
Example: Long purchased her home with a *growing equity mortgage.* Long's monthly payments will increase by 5% each year, with the increased amount applied to principal. Long will **retire** the loan in about half the time required to retire a comparable loan with fixed payments.

(TO) GUARANTEE (A LOAN) to agree to **indemnify** the holder of a loan all or a portion of the unpaid **principal** balance in case of **default** by the borrower. See also **VA mortgage loan.**
Example: Abel takes out a **VA mortgage loan** to purchase a home. The Veterans Administration *guarantees* the loan. In case foreclosure is threatened because Abel fails to make the payments, the VA will reimburse the lender for losses up to the amount guaranteed.

GUARANTY an assurance provided by one party that another party will perform under a contract.
Example: Fred Garrison is an experienced developer. His daughter, Ruth, decides to branch out and start her own company. The construction lender requires a *guaranty* from Fred Garrison before granting Ruth Garrison a loan for her first project.

GUARDIAN one appointed by a court to administer the personal affairs or property of an individual who is not capable of such duties.
Example: The *guardian* of an orphan **minor** signs a **deed** to sell property inherited by the minor, to pay the minor's educational expenses.

GUIDELINE LIVES **depreciable lives**, for buildings and equipment, that are used in trade or business. Generally applied to **assets** bought before 1981; the **accelerated cost recovery system** applies to

depreciable assets bought since then.
Example: *Guideline lives* for certain assets:
• apartments—40 years
• dwellings—45 years
• hotels—40 years
• warehouses—60 years

H

HABENDUM CLAUSE the "to have and to hold" clause that
defines or limits the quantity of the **estate** granted in the **deed**.
Example: The *habendum clause* "to have and to hold for one's
lifetime" creates a **life estate**.

HANGOUT the remaining balance of a loan when the **term** of the
loan is beyond the term of a **lease**.
Example: A lender offers a 30-year loan on property that is leased
to Big Buy Foods for the next 25 years. In 25 years the loan balance will be $100,000, which is the *hangout*. The lender estimates
that the land value in 25 years will greatly exceed $100,000, so
concern for the hangout is minimized.

HAZARD INSURANCE a form of insurance that protects against
certain risks, such as from fires or storms.
Example: **Mortgage** lenders frequently require that owners maintain *hazard insurance*, at least to the extent of the mortgage
debt.

HEARING a formal procedure, with issues of fact or law to be tried,
in which parties have a right to be heard. Similar to a trial and may
result in a final order.
Example: State **real estate commissions** hold *hearings* to investi-
gate complaints filed against licensed salespersons.

HECTARE a metric land measurement equal to about 2.471 **acres** or
about 107,637 square feet.
Example: Abel sold 6 *hectares* of land in Puerto Rico for
$20,000.

HEIR one who inherits **property**.
Example: A person can decide on *heirs* by leaving a **valid** will. If
one dies **intestate**, state laws determine who the heirs are.

HEIRS AND ASSIGNS a term often found in **deeds** and **wills** to grant
a **fee simple** estate.
Example: Abel wills property to "Baker, *heirs and assigns*."

Upon inheriting the property, Baker can sell it or will it to **heirs**.

HEREDITAMENTS any property, whether real or personal, tangible or intangible, that may be inherited.
Example: Buildings, lands, and **leaseholds** are examples of *hereditaments*.

HIGHEST AND BEST USE an **appraisal** term meaning the legally and physically possible use that, at the time of appraisal, is most likely to produce the greatest net return to the land and/or buildings over a given period.
Example: A vacant lot in the city is valued at $10,000 if developed for a **single-family house**, $20,000 as an **apartment building**, $25,000 as a retail store, and $30,000 as a small chemical processing plant. Because of **restrictions** on water supply and disposal, the chemical plant is not physically or legally possible. **Zoning** laws prohibit commercial development. Therefore, the *highest and best use* of the lot is for an apartment building.

HIGH RISE generally a building that exceeds 6 stories in height and is equipped with elevators.
Example: A *high-rise* building is constructed to include retail space on the first floor, 8 floors of office space, 10 floors of **condominium** units, and a club/restaurant on the 20th floor.

HIGH VICTORIAN ITALIANATE a nineteenth century style house with three different kinds of window arches, the primary distinguishing characteristic of this style. The arches are straight-sided, flat-topped and rectangular.
Example: Figure 84.

HIP ROOF one formed by four walls sloped in different directions with the two longer sides forming a ridge at the top.
Example: Figure 85.

HISTORIC STRUCTURE a building that is officially recognized for its historic significance has special status under the 1976 Tax Reform Act, which encourages **rehabilitation** and discourages **demolition** or substantial alteration of the structure. In 1981 a special tax law allowed a 25% **tax credit** for rehabilitation of **certified historic structures**.
Example: Because the old office building was designated a certified *historic structure*, its owner decided to restore the building to take advantage of allowable tax deductions.

HOLDBACK money not paid until certain events have occurred, such as a **floor loan** of a **loan commitment** or **retainage** on a construction contract.

Rectangular
arch

Straight-
sided arch

Flat-topped arch

Entrance way with
columns supporting
entablature

Large brackets

Hip roof

Three
different
types
of arches

Symmetrical
bays

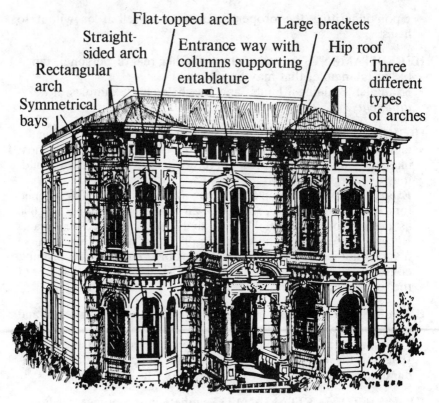

FIGURE 84

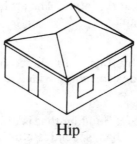

Hip

FIGURE 85

Example: On a $1,000,000 loan the lender has a $300,000 *holdback* until the property is 80% rented.

Example: The developer has a 10% *holdback* from subcontractors until the building **inspection** is complete.

HOLDER IN DUE COURSE one who acquires a **bearer instrument** in **good faith** and is eligible to keep it even though it may have been stolen.

EXAMPLE: Abel receives from Baker a $100 bill in payment of rent on his apartment. Police inform Abel that the bill was stolen by Baker from Cobb. Since the bill is bearer paper and Abel accepted it without knowing about the theft, he became a *holder in due course* and is allowed to keep it.

HOLD HARMLESS CLAUSE in a **contract**, a clause whereby one party agrees to protect another party from claims.
Example: Big Buy Foods is leasing property from its landlord, Lucky Lessors. A customer is injured by a falling light fixture, and she sues both Big Buy Foods and Lucky Lessors. In the **lease**, Big Buy Foods agreed to a *hold harmless clause* whereby they **indemnified** Lucky Lessors against such events.

HOLDING COMPANY one that owns or controls another company(ies).
Example: Banks and public utilities are often owned or controlled by a *holding company*. Sometimes this arrangement allows more latitude for business practices than the operating company can achieve alone.

HOLDING COSTS same as **carrying costs**.

HOLDING PERIOD the time span of ownership, often for investment real estate.
Example: Some investors prefer short *holding periods* (under 5 years) in an attempt to retain high levels of financial **leverage**. Others hold property longer to reduce frequent **transaction costs** and avoid **depreciation recapture**.

HOLDOVER TENANT a **tenant** who remains in possession of leased property after the expiration of the lease **term**. See **tenancy at sufferance**.
Example: Abel leases an apartment for one year. At the end of the year, Abel is still in the process of finding a new home. As a *holdover tenant*, Abel may be evicted or allowed to remain on a month-to-month basis by continuing to pay rent, at the landlord's discretion.

HOME LOAN see **mortgage**.

HOMEOWNER'S ASSOCIATION an organization of the homeowners in a particular **subdivision**, planned unit development, or **condominium**; generally for the purpose of enforcing **deed** restrictions or managing the **common elements** of the development. See **community association**.
Example: All unit owners of the Lakefront Condominiums are members of the Lakefront *Homeowners' Association*. The Asso-

ciation maintains the pool, grounds, and building structure, and regulates use of common elements. They assess each owner a $75 monthly fee.

HOMEOWNERSHIP the state of living in a structure that one owns. Contrasted with being a renter or **tenant** in one's home.
Example: *Homeownership* is a goal of many families. It provides security from the decisions of landlords, pride of ownership, and investment advantages in exchange for undertaking the responsibilities of a property owner.

HOMEOWNER'S POLICY an insurance policy designed especially for homeowners. Usually protects the owner from losses caused by most common disasters, theft, and **liability**. Coverage and costs vary widely.
Example: Whitman acquired a *homeowner's policy* for an annual premium of $500. It insures her home from fire losses (up to $100,000), theft (of household goods, excluding jewelry, paintings, stamp collections, silverware), and gives up to $300,000 of **liability** protection.

HOMEOWNERS' WARRANTY PROGRAM (HOW) a private insurance program that protects purchasers of newly constructed homes, when the builder participates in the program, against structural and mechanical faults.
Example: Abel purchases a new home. The builder participates in the HOW program and provides Abel with a *homeowner's warranty* to cover any faults or oversights in the construction.

HOMEOWNER WARRANTY INSURANCE same as **homeowner warranty program.**

HOMESTEAD status provided to a homeowner's principal residence by some state statutes; protects home against **judgments** up to specified amounts.
Example: *Homestead* laws in Texas prevent a lender, other than the **mortgage** lender, from forcing the sale of one's principal residence to satisfy a **debt**.

HOMESTEAD EXEMPTION in some jurisdictions, a reduction in the **assessed value** allowed for one's principal residence.
Example: The *homestead exemption* in Georgia enables a homeowner, upon application, to get $5,000 subtracted from the assesor's **appraisal** of the home. This reduces the property tax burden.

HORIZONTAL PROPERTY LAWS state statutes that enable **condominium** ownership of property. Whereas property laws generally recognize **ownership rights** to all space from the center of the earth to some distance in the air, condominium laws allow individual ownership to be split on a horizontal plane that generally limits the unit owner's interest to the inside dimensions of the unit. See **common elements**.

Example: Before passage of *horizontal property laws*, all owners in a condominium were obligated under each individual mortgage loan in the complex. If one owner **defaulted**, the lender could **foreclose** on the entire condominium. Now, to secure a loan, each owner pledges only his or her limited interest in the condominium.

HOUSING AND URBAN DEVELOPMENT (HUD) DEPARTMENT
a U.S. government agency established to implement certain federal housing and community development programs.

Example: Mason desires to develop a housing project for low-income families. She applies to the *Department of Housing and Urban Development* for a special low-interest loan for the development.

HOUSING CODE a local government **ordinance** that sets minimum standards of safety and sanitation for existing residential buildings. Contrast to **building codes**, which pertain to new construction.

Example: Because of violations of the *housing code*, including a badly leaking roof and rat infestation, the old apartment building was condemned.

HOUSING STARTS an estimate of the number of dwelling units on which construction has begun during a stated period.

Example: During the last month, *housing starts* were 20% lower than the same month a year ago, reflecting a lower demand for new houses caused by high **mortgage** rates.

HYPOTHECATE to pledge a thing as **security** without having to give up possession of it.

Example: Through use of a **mortgage** or **deed of trust**, the buyer *hypothecates* a newly acquired home to the lender or **trustee**. The buyer uses and controls the property.

I

IMPLIED CONTRACT created by actions but not necessarily written or spoken. See also **Statute of frauds**.

Example: Abel posts a for-sale sign on his property that says, "See Your Broker." Davis submits an offer through her **broker** and buys the property. Abel refuses to pay the broker, who then goes to court contending that the sign created an *implied contract*.

IMPLIED WARRANTY one that is not written but exists under the law. Contrasted with "expressed."
Example: Under the law in several states there is an *implied warranty* **of habitability** for apartments leased to tenants. This means that the tenant has the right to a dwelling that is fit for living, i.e., there are no **building code** violations.

IMPOUND ACCOUNT same as **escrow account.**

IMPROVED LAND land that has some improvements. Land that has been partially or fully developed for use.
Examples: Any of the following activities on a piece of **raw land** will result in *improved land*:
• landscaping and grading
• installation of utilities
• construction of roads, curbs, and/or gutters
• contruction of buildings

IMPROVEMENTS those additions to **raw land**, such as buildings, streets, sewers, etc., tending to increase value.
Example: A hypothetical example of how *improvement* costs may affect property and land values is shown in Table 20.

TABLE 20

Improvement	Cost of improvement	Total property value	Value of land
None	$ 0	$ 500	$ 500
Curbs, drainage, & utilities	3,000	5,000	2,000
House	70,000	85,000	15,000
Apartment building	250,000	290,000	40,000

IMPOUND ACCOUNT a fund set aside for future needs. See **reserve fund.**
Example: Each month a homeowner deposits $1/12$ of the estimated annual **property tax** and insurance premium requirements into an *impound account*, so that the balance will be sufficient to pay amounts when they come due.

IMPUTED INTEREST implied interest. In a **mortgage** that states an insufficient interest rate, the law will impute that the rate is higher, and the **principal** is less.
Example: Abel sells property to Baker. Baker gives Abel a portion of the price in cash and Abel takes a **note** for the remainder. Since the gain on the sale is taxable at **capital gains** rates and the interest paid on the note is taxed as **ordinary income**, it is in Abel's favor to set a higher price in exchange for charging a low rate of interest on the note. If this is done, the **Internal Revenue Service** will consider a portion of the principal paid on the note as *imputed interest* and tax that portion as ordinary income.

INCHOATE unfinished, begun but not completed. In real estate, this can apply to **dower** or **curtesy** rights prior to the death of a spouse.
Example: Collins dies, leaving dower rights *inchoate*. Her children by a former marriage sue her widower to recover her share of property he sold.

INCOME the money or other benefit coming from the use of property, skill, or business.
Examples: In real estate, *income* may be produced by:
• rents
• fees
• royalties
• sales of crops, timber, or livestock
• revenues derived from business activities on the property

INCOME APPROACH a method appraising real estate based on the property's anticipated future income. The formula for appraisal by the income approach is

$$\frac{\text{Expected annual income}}{\text{Capitalization rate}} = \text{Market value}$$

See **capitalization** and **gross rent multiplier**.
Example: A property is expected to produce a **net operating income** of $100,000 yearly. Recent sales data indicate that the **capitalization rate** for **comparable** properties is 10%. By the *income approach,* the property has a market value of

$$\frac{\$100,000}{.10} = \$1,000,000$$

INCOME PROPERTY real estate that generates rental income.
Examples: The following are types of *income property:*
• apartment buildings
• shopping centers
• office buildings
• industrial properties and warehouses

- resort and recreational properties
- hotels, motels, and restaurants

The following are generally not considered *income property:*

- personal residences
- undeveloped land (rental income is minimal)
- schools, churches, parks

INCOME STREAM a regular flow of money generated by a business or investment.
Example: A **net lease** that pays $1,000 per month **rent** for 10 years provides an *income stream.*

INCOMPETENT one not legally capable of completing a **contract**. Includes the mentally ill, **minors**, and others considered incapable.
Example: Abel, a moron, inherited $100,000, and wants to buy a tract of land. He enters into a contract, but his legal guardian **voids** it because the land is worth under $5,000. It is voidable because Abel is *incompetent.*

INCORPORATE 1. to form a **corporation** under regulations provided by the Secretary of State.
Example: Abel intends to enter the real estate **brokerage** business and wishes to protect his personal **assets**. He retains a lawyer whom he pays a $1,000 fee to *incorporate* the business. Abel is the sole stockholder and chairman of the board of directors. Abel's personal assets are protected because **liability** is limited to the assets owned by the corporation.
2. to provide a geographic area the legal status of a political subdivision of the state.
Example: A large **subdivision** outside a large city petitions the state legislature to *incorporate* as an independent city. The residents of the incorporated area may elect representatives and tax themselves to provide services.

INCURABLE DEPRECIATION a defect that cannot be cured or that is not financially practical to cure; a defect in the "bone structure" of a building. Compare **curable depreciation**.
Example: It is estimated that if a specific house had a more convenient **floor plan**, it would sell for an additional $5,000. The cost of rearranging the partitions to improve the plan is $10,000. The poor floor plan is *incurable depreciation.*

INDEMNIFY 1. to protect another person against loss or damage.
Example: **FHA mortgage loans** *indemnify* the lender against the risk of a buyer's **default**.
2. to compensate a party for loss or damage.
Example: Upon **foreclosure**, the FHA *indemnified* the lender for losses on the defaulted loan.

INDENTURE a written agreement made between 2 or more persons having different interests.
Example: The *indenture* **trustee** enforces the agreement made between the **bond** issuer (borrower) and the lender.

INDEPENDENT CONTRACTOR a **contractor** who is self-employed.
Example: Collins, a real estate salesperson, is an *independent contractor* engaged by **broker** Baker. She has not received any income in the last 3 months but is unable to collect unemployment insurance because she is an *independent contractor*. Last year she paid a self-employment tax instead of social security.

INDEX 1. a statistic that indicates some current economic or financial condition. Indexes are often used to make adjustments in wage rates, rental rates, loan interest rates, and pension benefits set by long-term contracts.
Example: Office building rental rates are sometimes adjusted in relation to the consumer price *index*.
2. to adjust contract terms according to an index. See **indexed loan**.
Example: Mortgage interest rates on **adjustable rate mortgages** are often *indexed* to the average mortgage rate for all lenders or the average cost of funds for all lenders.

INDEXED LOAN a long-term loan in which the **term**, payment, **interest rate**, or **principal** amount may be adjusted periodically according to a specific **index**. The index and the manner of adjustment are generally stated in the loan contract.
Example: An **adjustable rate mortgage** is an *indexed loan*. At specific intervals the **face interest rate** on the loan may be changed according to variations in the specified **index**.

INDEX LEASE a rental agreement that requires changes in rent based on a published record of cost changes. See **cost of living index**.
Example: A landlord makes an *index lease* with initial rent at $10,000 per year, adjusted annually by the Consumer Price Index (CPI). If the CPI is 100 at the time of the lease and increases to 110 in the second year, the rent for the second year will be 10,000 × 1.10 = $11,000.

INDIVIDUAL RETIREMENT ACCOUNT (IRA) a special account available to all employees through private financial organizations (banks, **savings and loans**, credit unions, insurance companies, and securities firms) for the purpose of retirement savings. Deposits to an IRA, up to a maximum annual amount, are exempt from income taxation in the year of deposit. Funds may not be withdrawn without penalty until the depositor reaches the age of 59½.

Example: Rollins, a 40-year-old schoolteacher, opens an *Individual Retirement Account* with Local Savings and Loan. Each year she deposits into the account $2,000, which is deducted from her taxable income. The account earns 10% interest each year. She is in a 20% tax bracket. At age 60 her IRA balance is $114,550. If she didn't use an IRA, she would have paid taxes on the $2,000 each year and on any taxable interest earned.

INDUSTRIAL PARK an area designed and **zoned** for manufacturing and associated activities.
Example: Figure 86.

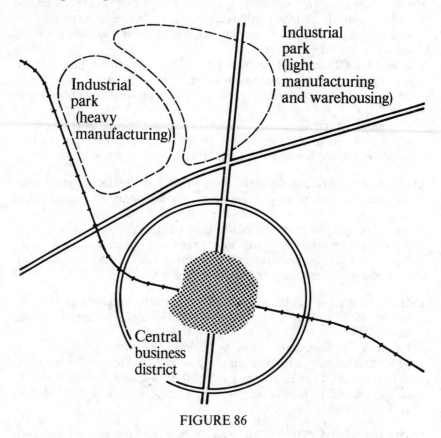

FIGURE 86

INDUSTRIAL PROPERTY property used for industrial purposes, such as factories.
Examples: Types of *industrial property:*
• factory-office multiuse property
• factory-warehouse multiuse property

- heavy manufacturing buildings
- industrial parks
- light manufacturing buildings
- research and development parks

INHERITANCE TAX a tax, based on property **value**, imposed in some states on those who acquire property from a decedent. Compare **estate tax**.
Example: An estate tax is based on the value of all property left by the decedent, whereas an *inheritance tax* is based on the amount that an **heir** receives.

INJUNCTION an order issued under the seal of a court to restrain one or more parties to a legal proceeding, from performing an act deemed inequitable to another party or parties in the proceeding.
Example: Abel begins serving alcoholic drinks on property he bought from Baker. Baker claims that a **deed restriction** prevents consumption of such beverages on the property, and sues Abel. Since the trial is set several months ahead, Baker requests an *injunction* to prevent the sale of drinks until the trial.

INNER CITY generally the older and more urbanized area of a large city surrounding the **central business district.** The term often refers to densely populated blighted **areas** characterized by low-income residents and a high proportion of minority racial and ethnic groups.
Examples:
- Many *inner city* neighborhoods have been **rehabilitated** by **urban renewal** projects.
- Violence is a problem in some *inner city* schools.
- The mayor promises a construction program to rehabilitate the *inner city.*

IN REM Latin: "against the thing." A proceeding against the property directly, as distinguished from a proceeding against a person (used in taking land for nonpayment of taxes, etc.)
Example: Baker cannot collect on his past due loan from Abel. Baker, through court action, secures a **judgment** *in rem* against a building lot owned by Abel, which causes a lien against the lot.

INSIDE LOT in a **subdivision,** a lot surrounded on each side by other lots, as opposed to a corner lot, which has road **frontage** on at least 2 sides.
Example: An *inside lot* **adjoining** a corner lot (Figure 87).

INSPECTION a physical scrutinizing review of property or of documents.

Example: *Inspections* may be required for the following purposes:
- compliance with **building codes**
- sale requirements as to property conditions, such as wood-destroying insects or structural soundness
- legal review of documents such as **leases** and **mortgages** to determine whether they are as purported

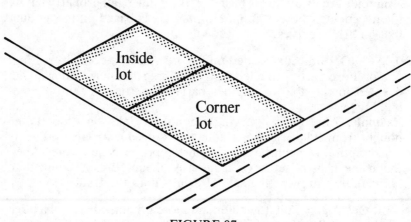

FIGURE 87

INSTALLMENTS parts of the same **debt**, payable at successive periods as agreed; payments made to reduce a **mortgage**.
Example: Abel purchases a property with a **land contract**. The contract calls for a payment of $30,000 at **closing**, with 10 annual *installments* of $15,000 each.

INSTALLMENT CONTRACT same as **land contract**.

INSTALLMENT SALE when a seller accepts a **mortgage** for part of the sale, the tax on the gain is paid as the mortgage **principal** is collected. See also **contract price, gross profit ratio, imputed interest.**
Example: Collins sells for $10,000 her land that she bought 3 years ago for $4,000. Her gain is $6,000. She received 10% ($1,000) as a cash **down payment** and a 90% ($9,000) **purchase money mortgage**. She will report 10% of the gain in the year of sale and the balance as she collects the principal of the purchase money mortgage. To do so, on her tax return she reports the sale as an installment sale. See Table 21.

INSTITUTE OF REAL ESTATE MANAGEMENT (IREM) a professional organization of property managers. Affiliated with the **National Association of Realtors®**. Publishes the *Journal of Property Management*.

Address:
Institute of Real Estate Management
430 North Michigan Avenue
Chicago, Illinois 60611

TABLE 21

	Year of sale	Year 1	Year 2	Year 3
Principal paid	$1000	$3000	$3000	$3000
Taxable gain	600	1800	1800	1800
Interest income	0	900	600	300

INSTITUTIONAL LENDER financial intermediaries who invest in loans and other securities on behalf of their depositors or customers; lending and investment activities are regulated by laws to limit risk.
Example: *Institutional lenders* are a prime source of real estate loans. Many organizations, such as **savings and loan associations** and **commerical banks**, originate loans directly; others, such as insurance companies, lend through **mortgage brokers**.

INSTRUMENT a written legal document, created to establish the rights and liabilities of the parties to it.
Examples: The following are examples of instruments:
• **deed**
• mortgage
• land contract
• lease
• assignment

INSURABLE INTEREST an **interest** in a person or property that would cause one a loss if that person or property were injured. Must be present to collect from an insurance policy.
Example: The Good Money Savings Association lent $50,000 on Abel's house. Yesterday it was destroyed by fire. Good Money can collect on its insurance policy, because they were insured and had an *insurable interest*. Five Star Savings also had an insurance policy on the home but had no **lien**, so they couldn't collect.

INSURABLE TITLE a **title** that can be insured by a **title insurance** company.
Example: In some **contracts** for the sale of **real estate** the buyer must receive *insurable title* or he is not obligated to purchase the property.

INSURANCE COVERAGE total amount and type of insurance carried.

Example: The owner maintained $100,000 of hazard *insurance coverage* on the property, and $300,000 of **liability** *insurance coverage*. The **hazard insurance** coverage was adequate to meet the 80% **coinsurance** requirement in the policy.

INSURANCE (MORTGAGE) a service, generally purchased by a borrower, that will **indemnify** the lender in case of **foreclosure** of the loan. Indemnification is generally limited to losses suffered by the lender in the foreclosure process. See **FHA mortgage loan**, **private mortgage insurance**.
Example: Abel took out a **home loan** covered by *mortgage insurance*. After one year, Abel **defaulted** on the loan and the lender foreclosed. Abel owed $50,000, but the foreclosure sale produced only $40,000 in proceeds. The insurance company paid the lender the difference of $10,000.

INTANGIBLE VALUE value that cannot be seen or touched.
Example: The **goodwill** of an established business is an *intangible value*.

INTEREST 1. cost of the use of money.
Example: Lenders require payment of *interest* at a specified rate, to compensate for risk, deferment of benefits, inflation, and administrative burdens.
2. the type and extent of ownership.
Example: One may hold either a partial or **fee simple** *interest* in a property. That *interest* entitles one to specific ownership rights.

INTEREST-ONLY LOAN a loan in which interest is payable at regular intervals until loan **maturity**, when the full loan balance is due. Does not require **amortization**. Contrast **self-amortizing mortgage**.
Example: Land was bought with a 5-year *interest-only loan* of $100,000 at 12%. The **interest** of $1,200 was paid annually for 4 years. The $100,000 **principal**, together with the last $1,200 interest payment, was due at the end of the fifth year.

INTEREST RATE 1. the percentage of a sum of money charged for its use.
2. the **rate of return** on an investment.
Example: A $50,000 mortgage loan is made at 12% interest and 4 **discount points**. The contract *interest rate* is 12% and determines the monthly payment amount. The **effective rate** of interest, which incorporates the effects of the discount points, is 12.55% and is the rate of return to the lender if the loan runs to maturity.

INTERIM FINANCING a loan, including a **construction loan**, used when the property owner is unable or unwilling to arrange perma-

nent financing. Generally arranged for less than 3 years, used to gain time for financial or market conditions to improve.
Example: Monroe developed an office building but, in the expectation of falling **interest rates**, does not wish to use permanent financing at this time. He arranges a 2-year *interim* loan, during which time he seeks favorable permanent financing.

INTERNAL RATE OF RETURN (IRR) the true annual rate of earnings on an investment. Equates the value of cash returns with cash invested. Considers the application of **compound interest** factors. Requires a trial-and-error method for solution. The formula is

$$\sum_{t=1}^{n} \frac{\text{periodic } cash\ flow}{(1+i)^t} = \text{investment amount}$$

where i = internal rate of return
$\quad t$ = each time interval
$\quad n$ = total time intervals
$\quad \Sigma$ = summation

Example: Abel sells for $20,000 land that he bought 4 years earlier for $10,000. There were no **carrying charges** or **transaction costs**. The *internal rate of return* was about 19%. That is the annual rate at which compound interest must be paid for $10,000 to become $20,000 in 4 years.
Example: Baker received $3,000 per year for 5 years on a $10,000 investment. The *internal rate of return* was about 15%.

INTERNAL REVENUE CODE the law, passed by Congress, that specifies how and what income is to be taxed, and what may be deducted from taxable income.
Example: Court cases, regulations, revenue rules, and revenue procedures attempt to properly interpret the *Internal Revenue Code*.

INTERNAL REVENUE SERVICE (IRS) an agency of the federal government that is responsible for the administration and collection of federal income taxes. The IRS prints and distributes tax forms and audits tax returns.
Addresses:
   Regional Offices

- Andover, MA 05501
- Atlanta, GA 31101
- Austin, TX 73301
- Cincinnati, OH 45999
- Fresno, CA 93888
- Holtsville, NY 00501

- Kansas City, MO 64999
- Memphis, TN 37501
- Ogden, UT 84201
- Philadelphia, PA 19255

INTERNATIONAL ARCHITECTURE an early twentieth century style house whose design is very simple with no ornamentation. The windows appear to be continuous rather than appearing to be holes in the walls.
Example: Figure 88.

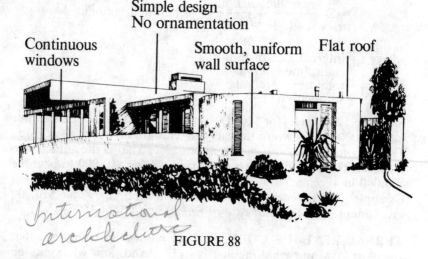

Simple design
No ornamentation

Continuous windows

Smooth, uniform wall surface

Flat roof

FIGURE 88

INTERNATIONAL ASSOCIATION OF ASSESSING OFFICERS (IAAO) a professional organization of property tax **assessors**. Awards the designation of Certified Assessment Evaluator (CAE). Publishes the quarterly *Assessors Journal*.
Address:
International Association of Assessing Officers
1313 East 60th Street
Chicago, Illinois 60637

INTERNATIONAL RIGHT OF WAY ASSOCIATION (IR/WA) an individual membership association (no corporate membership) that offers courses covering various phases of **right-of-way** work. Educational curriculum includes law, engineering, **appraisal**. Offers a designation, SR/WA, and a bimonthly magazine.
Address:
International Right of Way Association
6133 Bristol Parkway, Suite 270
Culver City, California 90230

INTERSTATE LAND SALES ACT a federal law, administered by the Department of **Housing and Urban Development** (HUD), which requires certain disclosures and advertising procedures when selling land to purchasers in other states.
Example: Rollins, a developer, has a 200-acre **subdivision** in Florida and wishes to market lots nationally. Under the *Interstate Land Sales Act,* she must register with the Office of Interstate Land Sales Registration (OILSR, a division of HUD), and make certain disclosures in the **prospectus** sent to prospective purchasers.

INTER VIVOS during one's life.
Example: Abel makes an *inter vivos* gift of $10,000 to each of 3 children. The children spend the $10,000 and may inherit more money if Abel names them in the **will** he is preparing.

INTESTATE 1. (adj.) having made no valid will 2. (noun) a person who dies leaving no will or leaving one that is defective. Property goes to the legal **heirs** of the intestate.
Example: If Doris dies *intestate,* her heirs under state law will inherit her property. If she leaves no heirs her property will **escheat**.

INVENTORY property held for sale or to be used in the manufacture of goods held for sale. Does not qualify for **capital gains** tax treatment.
Examples: Examples of *inventory* are:
• raw materials
• work-in-progress
• finished goods
To a builder, property under construction and property completed are *inventory.* To a **subdivider**, vacant lots are *inventory.*

INVERSE CONDEMNATION a legal procedure to obtain compensation when a property **interest** has been taken or diminished in value by a government activity.
Example: Abel owns a home near a public airport. The city constructs a new runway that sends air traffic directly over Abel's house, seriously diminishing Abel's enjoyment of his property. Abel may sue for *inverse condemnation* and, if successful, may force the airport authority to take Abel's house in exchange for just compensation.

INVESTMENT INTEREST EXPENSE interest paid to carry passive investments such as undeveloped land and net-leased rental property. Tax deductions for interest are limited.
Example: Abel buys undeveloped land. He pays with a $200,000 **purchase money mortgage** at 10% interest. The resulting $20,000

investment interest expense is not fully deductible this year; only $10,000 plus net investment income is. The undeducted portion carries forward.

INVESTMENT LIFE CYCLE the time span from acquisition of an investment to final disposition.
Example: The best way to measure the **rate of return** from an *investment* is over its *life cycle*. All relevant investment contributions, **cash flows**, and resale proceeds are known (Figure 89).

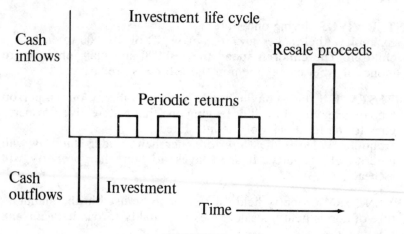

FIGURE 89

INVESTMENT TAX CREDIT a reduction in income tax generally based on the cost and life of certain assets purchased.
Example: Fun Living Furnished Apartments acquires, for $10,000, furniture for a new apartment complex. The furniture has a life of over 7 years, which allows them to claim a 10% *investment tax credit*. Federal income taxes paid are reduced by $1,000. (10% of $10,000 cost = $1,000 credit).

INVOLUNTARY CONVERSION condemnation or sudden destruction by nature.
Example: A property is taken by **eminent domain** for the purpose of constructing a public highway. This *involuntary conversion* of the property is contrasted with a sale that the owner enters into voluntarily.

INVOLUNTARY LIEN a **lien** imposed against property without consent of the owner (unpaid taxes, special assessments, etc.). Compare **mortgage lien**.
Example: The **absentee** land **owner** was not notified of the past-due tax bill. The tax **assessor** placed a lien on the property that was an

involuntary lien, since the owner did not take action to cause the lien.

INWOOD ANNUITY FACTOR a number that, when multiplied by the periodic payment from a **level payment income stream**, indicates the present value of the income stream, based on a specific interest rate. Same formula as that for **annuity factor**.
Example: An investment is expected to provide income of $100 per month for 10 years. At the end of 10 years the investment has no value. At an interest rate of 10%, the present value (PV) of the investment is

$$PV = \$100 \times 75.67 = \$7,567$$

where 75.67 is the *Inwood annuity factor.*

INWOOD TABLES a set of **annuity factors** for various **interest rates** and **maturities**. See **Inwood annuity factor**.
Example: The *Inwood tables* show that the right to receive $1.00 at the end of each year for 10 years at 15% interest is worth $5.02 as of the beginning of the first year.

IRREVOCABLE incapable of being recalled or revoked; unchangeable.
Example: The bank issued an *irrevocable* **letter of credit** stating that if the terms of the **contract** were met the bank would lend the money requested.

ITALIAN VILLA a Latin style, massive 2- or 3-story house of masonry with large overhanging eaves.
Example: Figure 90.

J

JEOPARDY danger, **risk**.
Example: Property pledged as **security** for a delinquent loan is in *jeopardy* of **foreclosure**.

JOINT AND SEVERAL LIABILITY a **creditor** can demand full repayment from any and all of those who have borrowed. Each borrower is **liable** for the full debt, not just the **prorated** share.
Example: Abel and Baker are **general partners**. Together they borrow (or the **partnership** borrows) $10,000 from a bank, agreeing to *joint and several liability*. Upon **default**, the bank can collect the remaining balance of the $10,000 from either party.

JOINT TENANCY ownership of **realty** by 2 or more persons, each of whom has an **undivided interest** with the **right of survivorship**.

Typically used by related persons.
Example: Abel and Baker own land in *joint tenancy*. Each owns
half of the entire (undivided) property. Upon Abel's death, Baker
will own the entire property, and vice versa.

Some have
quoins

Massive

Decorative
iron work

2 or 3 story

Large
overhanging
eaves

Heavy
cornice
line

Brackets

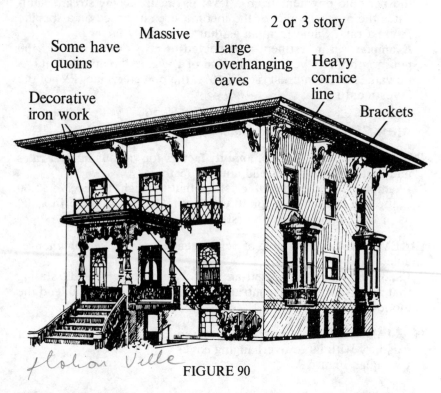

florian Ville

FIGURE 90

JOINT VENTURE an agreement between 2 or more parties who
invest in a single business or property. See also **limited partnership**, **tenancy in common**.
Example: Abel and Baker form a *joint venture* to explore for minerals on Cobb's land. Abel and Baker use a **tenancy in common**
arrangement for ownership of the mineral rights.

JUDGMENT a decree of a court stating that one individual is indebt-
ed to another and fixing the amount of the indebtedness.
Example: As a result of Abel's failure to pay disputed rent, the
landlord obtained a court decision, or *judgment,* against Abel.

JUDGMENT CREDITOR one who has received a court decree or
judgment for money due from the **judgment debtor**.
Example: To enforce the judgment awarded by court, the *judgment creditor* filed a **lien** against the **judgment debtor** Abel.

JUDGMENT DEBTOR one against whom a **judgment** has been issued by a court for money owed, and that remains unsatisfied.
Example: A judgment was entered into against Abel for nonpayment of rent. Abel is the *judgment debtor*.

JUDGMENT LIEN the claim upon the property of a debtor resulting from a **judgment**.
Example: Abel won't pay his debt to Baker. After establishing the debt in court, Baker may be allowed by the court to put a *judgment lien* on Abel's **real estate**.

JUDICIAL FORECLOSURE having a defaulted debtor's property sold where the court ratifies the price paid.
Example: Happy Mortgage Company is owed $50,000 on a first mortgage by Mr. Baker. At *judicial foreclosure,* Happy Mortgage Company **bids** $30,000 for the property, which is more than anyone else bids. They then claim the property and are awarded a $20,000 **deficiency judgment** against Mr. Baker.

JUNIOR MORTGAGE a **mortgage** whose claim against the property will be satisfied only after prior mortgages have been repaid. See **first mortgage, second mortgage**.
Example: Property is purchased for $100,000. A first mortgage is obtained covering $75,000 of the price. To reduce the cash requirements, a *junior mortgage* is arranged to cover $15,000 of the price. The remaining $10,000 is cash **equity**.

JUST COMPENSATION the amount paid to the owner of a property when it is acquired under **eminent domain**. See **condemnation**.
Example: Property is condemned to construct a sewage treatment plant. The owner is entitled to *just compensation* equal to the **fair market value** of the property taken.

K

KICKER a payment required by a **mortgage** in addition to normal **principal** and **interest**. See **participation loan**.
Example: Abel obtains a loan to purchase a retail store building. The lender requires a *kicker* equal to 10% of gross sales in excess of $100,000 per month, in addition to principal and interest.

L

LACHES undue delay or negligence in asserting one's legal rights, possibly leading to **estoppel** of the negligent party's suit.
Example: Abel was estopped by *laches* after he knowingly delayed telling an **adjacent** property owner of an **encroachment**.

LAND the surface of the earth; any part of the surface of the earth. (Note: Legal definitions often distinguish land from water.)
Example: Extent of *land* as **real property** (Figure 91). **Air rights** may be limited to some defined altitude. Added **improvements** are distinguished from *land*.

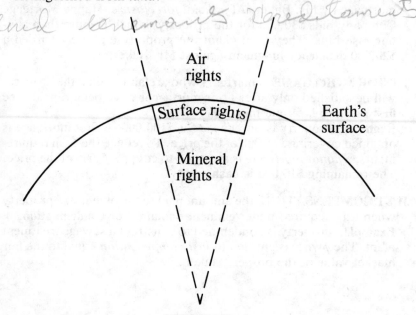

FIGURE 91

LAND BANKING the activity of purchasing land that is not presently needed for use.
Example: The Burger Company buys 8 **sites** that they plan to use 10 years from now. Wendy Ronald is in charge of *land banking* for The Burger Company.

LAND CONTRACT a real estate **installment** selling arrangement whereby the buyer may use, occupy, and enjoy land, but no **deed** is given by the seller (so no **title** passes) until all or a specified part of the sale price has been paid. Same as **contract for deed** and **installment land contract**.
Example: Collins buys a recreational lot. Under the *land contract*

she signed, she must pay $500 down and $100 per month for 7 years; then she is to receive a **general warranty deed**.

LAND LEASE only the ground is covered by the lease. See **ground lease**.
Example: Abel arranges a *land lease* from Baker for 50 years at a net annual rent of $5,000. Abel builds a shopping center on the land. At the end of 50 years the entire property will revert to Baker (Figure 92).

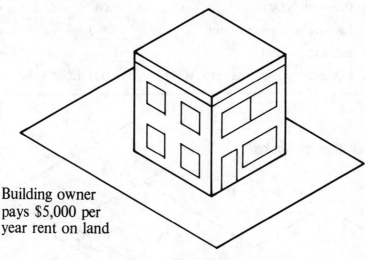

Building owner pays $5,000 per year rent on land

FIGURE 92

LANDLOCKED the condition of a lot that has no access to a public thoroughfare except through an **adjacent** lot. See **egress**. Compare **easement, right-of-way**.
Example: Figure 93.

LANDLORD one who rents property to another; a **lessor**. A property owner who surrenders the right to use property for a specific time in exchange for the receipt of rent.
Example: *Landlord*-tenant relationship (Figure 94).

LANDMARK a fixed object serving as a **boundary** mark for a tract of land. Same as **monument**.
Example: The tree and rail line may serve as *landmarks* in a land **description** (Figure 95).

LAND RESIDUAL TECHNIQUE in **appraisal**, a method of estimating the value of land when given **the net operating income (NOI)** and value of **improvements**. Used for **feasibility** analysis and **highest and best use**. See **income approach**.

Example: A property generates $10,000 net operating income ($15,000 rent less $5,000 operating expenses). The improvements cost $70,000 to construct and claim a 12% rate of return (10% interest plus 2% depreciation), which is $8,400. The remaining $1,600 income is capitalized at a 10% rate (divided by .10) to result in a $16,000 land value, using the *land residual technique*. See Table 22.

Table 22

Property NOI	$10,000
Income to improvement	− $8,400
Income to land	$1,600
Divided by required rate (10%)	$16,000 Land value

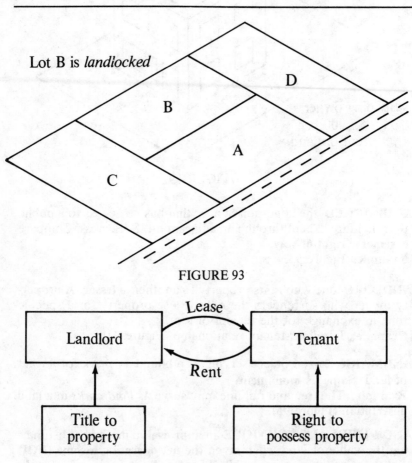

Lot B is *landlocked*

FIGURE 93

FIGURE 94

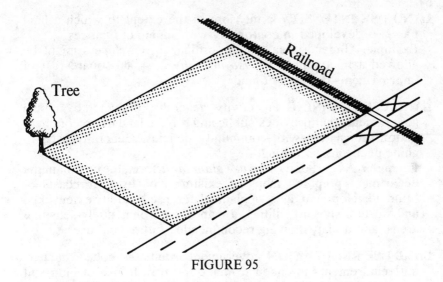

FIGURE 95

LAND SALE-LEASEBACK the sale of land and simultaneous leasing of it by the seller, who becomes the **tenant**.

Example: Collins owns land and wants to raise cash to build a shopping center on it. She sells the land for $100,000 to Baker and leases it back for 50 years at a $5,000 annual rent. Collins can use the land for the lease **term** provided she pays the annual rent, so she builds the shopping center after the *land sale-leaseback* (Figure 96).

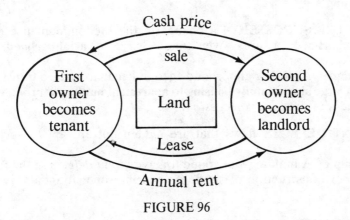

FIGURE 96

LAND, TENEMENTS, AND HEREDITAMENTS a phrase used in early English law to express all sorts of **real estate**.

Example: The **bundle of rights** in real estate is expressed by the phrase *land, tenements and hereditaments*. It includes all **interests** in real estate.

LAND USE INTENSITY a measure of the extent to which a land parcel is developed in conformity with **zoning** ordinances.
Example: Under a local zoning ordinance, **developers** might be allowed a maximum *land use intensity* of 4,000 square feet of **improvements** per **acre** of land.

LAND USE PLANNING an activity, generally conducted by a local government, that provides public and private land use recommendations consistent with community policies. Generally used to guide decisions on **zoning**.
Example: As part of its *land use planning* efforts, the city planning department prepared maps of existing land uses, forecasts of future development, a list of planned new roads, **utility** extensions, and waste disposal facilities, a map of environmentally sensitive areas, and a map showing recommended future land uses.

LAND USE REGULATION government **ordinances**, codes, and permit requirements intended to make the private use of land and natural resources conform to policy standards. See also **zoning**.
Example: Local governments have several types of *land use regulation*. Commonly used types are:
• building codes
• curb-cut permit systems
• historic preservation laws
• housing codes
• subdivision regulations
• tree-cutting laws
• zoning

LAND USE SUCCESSION a change in the predominant use of a **neighborhood** or area over time. See also **neighborhood life cycle**.
Example: As the neighborhood aged, it began to make a transition from large **single-family housing** to **apartment buildings** through the process of *land use succession*.

LATENT DEFECTS flaws that are hidden but are apt to surface later.
Example: A building was found to have *latent defects* in the form of poor construction of subfloors and improper foundation support.

LEASE a **contract** in which, for a payment called **rent,** the one entitled to the **possession** of real property (**lessor**) transfers those rights to another (**lessee**) for a specified period of time.
Example: Abel leases office space from Baker. Under the *lease* signed by the parties, Abel is allowed to conduct business activities within the office space, subject to specified **restrictions**, for a

specified period of time. Baker is entitled to receive a specified amount of rent payments according to a specified schedule of payments.

LEASEHOLD the **interest** or **estate** on which a **lessee (tenant)** of **real estate** has a **lease**.
Example: Mason possesses a long-term lease on a property. She may obtain a loan with the *leasehold* pledged as **collateral**. If the **contract rent** required by the lease is lower than **market rents**, Mason's *leasehold* will have a positive value.

LEASEHOLD MORTGAGE a **lien** on the tenant's **interest** in **real estate**.
Example: Abel is leasing land from Baker under a 50-year lease. Abel builds a shopping center and borrows money from the Big Money Assurance Company to do so. Big Money Assurance Company secures the loan with a leasehold mortgage. The mortgage will be lower in priority (subordinate) to land lease because the lease was contracted first. Had the mortgage been arranged before the lease, the mortgage would have priority. The holder of a prior **lien** has first claim to the income and assets if in default.

LEASE WITH OPTION TO PURCHASE a lease that gives the **lessee (tenant)** the right to purchase the property at an agreed-upon price under certain conditions.
Example: Abel *leases* property with an *option to purchase*. He must pay $500 per month rent for 5 years; after that he may buy the property (but is not forced to buy) for $100,000.

LEGAL DESCRIPTION legally acceptable identification of **real estate** by one of the following:
• the **government rectangular survey**
• metes and bounds
• recorded **plat (lot and block** number)
Example: The seller was required to include a *legal description* in the **deed**.

LEGAL NAME the name one has for official purposes.
Example: Though friends call him Fast Buck Jones, his *legal name* is Ferdinand Buchanan Jones. He may sign **contracts** with the name Ferdinand B. Jones.
Example: The *legal name* of GM is General Motors, Incorporated.

LEGAL NOTICE notification of others using the method required by law. See **constructive notice, notice**.
Example: Abel wishes to **rescind** an **offer** to buy real estate that has not been accepted by Baker. Abel sends a telegram and reg-

istered letter to Baker as *legal notice*.

Example: Collins bought land. She recorded the **deed** in the county courthouse as *legal notice* of ownership.

LEGATEE one who receives property by **will**. See **devisee**.

Example: Garrison wills all her property to Baker. Upon Garrison's death, Baker is the *legatee*.

LESSEE a person to whom property is rented under a **lease**. A **tenant**. Compare **lessor**.

Example: In the arrangement shown in Figure 97, Baker is the *lessee*.

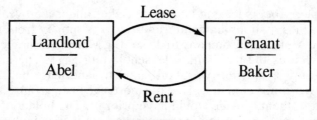

FIGURE 97

LESSOR one who rents property to another under a **lease**. A **landlord**. Compare **lessee**.

Example: In the arrangement shown in Figure 98, Abel is the *lessor*.

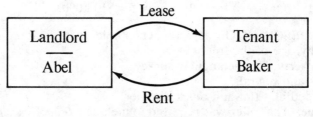

FIGURE 98

LETTER OF CREDIT an arrangement, with specified conditions, whereby a bank agrees to substitute its credit for a customer's.

Example: Abel, from Atlanta, wishes to buy property from Baker, in Boston. Abel arranges a *letter of credit* with the Atlanta Trust Company Bank to pay Baker upon **closing** in Boston.

LETTER OF INTENT the expression of a desire to enter into a **contract** without actually doing so.

Example: After a preliminary meeting, the Five Stars Development Company writes to a landowner, "We wish to enter into a contract to buy your land and will further pursue this matter in coming days. This *letter of intent* does not commit either party to purchase, sell, or lease.''

LEVEL PAYMENT INCOME STREAM see **annuity**.

LEVEL PAYMENT MORTGAGE requires the same payment each month (or other period) for full **amortization**. See **mortgage constant, flat**.
Example: Abel borrows $50,000 to buy a house. The *level payment mortgage* at 15% interest, payable over 30 years, requires a $632.50 monthly payment for **principal** and **interest**. That payment will be constant over the life of the loan.

LEVERAGE use of borrowed funds to increase purchasing power and, ideally, to increase the profitability of an investment. See **positive leverage, reverse leverage**.
Example: Collins wishes to invest in real estate. The property costs $100,000 and produces **net operating income** of $10,000 per year. If purchased with all cash, Collin's annual **rate of return** is 10% ($10,000÷$100,000). If she *leverages* the investment by borrowing $75,000, her return may be higher. If the debt cost is 8% ($6,000) annually, the *leverage* results in a return of 16% ($4,000÷$25,000). However, if the debt cost is 12% ($9,000), the *leverage* produces a return of 4% ($1,000÷$25,000).

LEVY to legally impose or collect that which is due.
Example: A tax assessor *levies* a tax.
Example: A judge *levies* a fine.

LIABILITY 1. a **debt** or financial obligation. Contrast with **asset**.
Example: One who borrows $75,000 for a **mortgage** loan incurs a *liability* to repay that loan.
Example: A **general partner** in a **partnership** has a personal *liability* for debts of the partnership in the event the partnership cannot repay its debt.
2. a potential loss.
Example: One should purchase sufficient *liability* insurance to protect against possible legal claims of someone who gets injured on one's property.

LIABILITY INSURANCE protection for a property owner from claims arising from injuries or damage to other people or property.
Example: Abel slipped on a broken step on the walkway in an apartment complex owned by Baker. Baker's *liability insurance* pays Abel for the doctor and hospital fees.

LIABLE responsible or obligated. Contrast with **exculpatory clause** and **nonrecourse**.
Example: One who borrows a **mortgage** loan generally becomes personally *liable* for its repayment. The lender can look to the **property** or the borrower personally for repayment.

LICENSE 1. permission
Example: If Abel did not secure *license* to cross Baker's property, it would be a **trespass**.
2. a right granted by a state to an individual to operate as a real estate **broker** or salesperson.
Example: The **real estate commission** issued a salesperson *license* to Rollins (Figure 99). Working under the supervision of her broker, Rollins can sell and lease real estate owned by others.

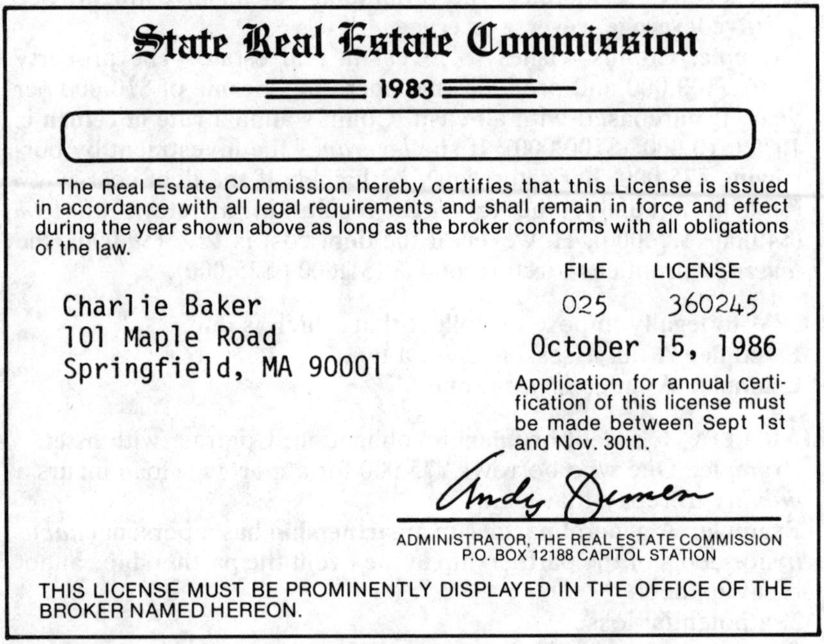

𝕾𝖙𝖆𝖙𝖊 𝕽𝖊𝖆𝖑 𝕰𝖘𝖙𝖆𝖙𝖊 𝕮𝖔𝖒𝖒𝖎𝖘𝖘𝖎𝖔𝖓
══ 1983 ══

The Real Estate Commission hereby certifies that this License is issued in accordance with all legal requirements and shall remain in force and effect during the year shown above as long as the broker conforms with all obligations of the law.

	FILE	LICENSE
Charlie Baker	025	360245
101 Maple Road		
Springfield, MA 90001	October 15, 1986	

Application for annual certification of this license must be made between Sept 1st and Nov. 30th.

Andy Demen

ADMINISTRATOR, THE REAL ESTATE COMMISSION
P.O. BOX 12188 CAPITOL STATION

THIS LICENSE MUST BE PROMINENTLY DISPLAYED IN THE OFFICE OF THE BROKER NAMED HEREON.

FIGURE 99

LICENSEE one who holds a real estate **license**; a licensed salesperson or **broker**. See **licensing examination**.
Example: A pocket card is held by *licensees*. The employing broker displays licenses in the office.

LICENSE LAWS laws that govern the activities of real estate salespersons.
Example: Abel, an unlicensed individual, sold a farm for Baker

and a house owned by Collins. Under state *license laws* each violation subjects Abel to a $10,000 fine and a year imprisonment, or both.

LICENSING EXAMINATION a written test given to a prospective real estate **broker** or salesperson to determine ability to represent the public in a real estate transaction. Most states offer examinations on at least 5 dates each year.
Example: Educational Testing Services (ETS) in Princeton, New Jersey, and American College Testing (ACT) in Iowa City, Iowa, prepare *licensing examinations* for most states. Some states prepare their own *licensing examination*.

LIEN a charge against property making it **security** for the payment of a **debt, judgment, mortgage**, or taxes; it is a type of **encumbrance**. A specific lien is against certain property only. A **general lien** is against all of the property owned by the debtor.
Example: Abel failed to pay the **contractor** for work performed on his home. The contractor files a **mechanic's lien** against the property for the amount due.

LIEN, JUNIOR a **lien** that will be paid after earlier liens have been paid. See **junior mortgage, subordination**.
Example: Abel obtains a **mortgage** loan from Solid Savings to finance the acquisition of a property. To reduce the **down payment,** he takes out a **second mortgage** with Baker, an investor. Solid Savings has a first lien and has first **priority** to **foreclosure** sale proceeeds in case of a **default**. Baker has a *junior lien* and is entitled to whatever remains, up to the debt and costs, after Solid Savings is **indemnified**.

LIEN-THEORY STATES states whose laws give a **lien** on property to secure debt. Contrasted with **title theory states** in which the lender becomes the **title** owner. In either case the borrower has the right to use and enjoy the property in the absence of **default**; in the event of default, lenders may **foreclose**.
Example: After **closing** the sale of a home in a *lien-theory state,* the lender acquires a **first mortgage** and may foreclose upon certain default.

LIFE ESTATE a **freehold** interest (in **real property**) that expires upon the death of the owner or some other specified person (**pur autre vie**).
Example: A retired couple purchase a *life estate* in a retirement village apartment unit. Upon death of both husband and wife, ownership of the unit will revert to the owner's association, who may then resell to another couple.

LIFE TENANT one who is allowed to use property for life or the lifetime of another designated person. See **life estate**.
Example: Graham owns a life estate in a home. As a *life tenant*, Graham may enjoy full ownership rights to the home during her lifetime.

LIKE-KIND PROPERTY property having the same nature. See also **Section 1031** and **tax-free exchange**.
Example: Under the **Internal Revenue Code**, apartments and land are considered *like-kind property*, but animals of different sexes are not.

LIMITED LIABILITY the restriction of one's potential losses to the amount invested. The absence of personal liability. See **at-risk rules**.
Example: *Limited liability* is provided to stockholders in a **corporation** and limited partners of a **limited partnership**. Those parties cannot lose more than they contribute to the corporation, unless they agree to become personally liable. For example, if Collins buys stock in a corporation for $1,000, she cannot lose more than that amount. However, many lenders require personal guarantees of major stockholders before lending to corporations.

LIMITED PARTNERSHIP one in which there is at least one partner who is passive and limits **liability** to the amount invested, and at least one partner whose liability extends beyond monetary investment. See **general partner**, **partnership**.
Example: Abel, a **syndicator**, forms a *limited partnership* with Price, Stone, and Wise. Abel invests his time and talent, is the general partner, and owns 10% of the partnership. Price, Stone, and Wise each invested $30,000 cash and were limited partners. They buy property with a $90,000 **down payment** and a $500,000 mortgage. The property drops in value by $250,000. Price, Stone, and Wise lose their **equity**, and Abel, the general partner, is responsible for additional losses (Figure 100).

Limited partnership

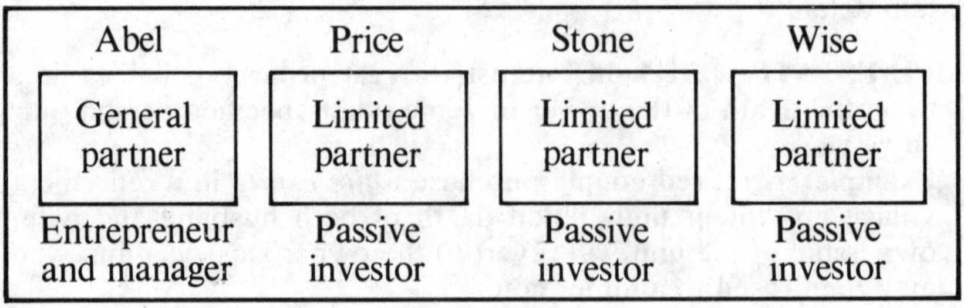

Abel	Price	Stone	Wise
General partner	Limited partner	Limited partner	Limited partner
Entrepreneur and manager	Passive investor	Passive investor	Passive investor

FIGURE 100

LINE OF CREDIT an agreement whereby a financial institution promises to lend up to a certain amount without the need to file another application.
Example: Happy Homes Brokers, Inc., has a *line of credit* under which they can borrow up to $50,000 at 3% above the **prime rate** through The Goodmoney National Bank.

LIQUIDATE 1. to dissolve a business.
Example: A **corporation's** only asset is **real estate** which is encumbered by a **mortgage**. The stockholders decide to *liquidate* the corporation. They may have the corporation sell the real estate, **retire** the mortgage, and distribute the **resale proceeds** to stockholders. The corporation is said to be *liquidated*.
2. to **retire debts**.
Example: Abel *liquidates* a $1,000 **debt** by paying it off in full with cash.

LIQUIDATED DAMAGES an amount agreed upon in a contract that one party will pay the other in the event of a **breach of the contract**.
Example: Abel engages a builder to erect a house. The **contract** says that if the builder fails to complete it by March 1, 1985, the builder will pay $50 per day thereafter until completion, as *liquidated damages*.

LIQUIDITY ease of converting **assets** to cash.
Example: Common stocks and U.S. savings bonds have good *liquidity*. **Real estate** and many types of collectibles generally have poor *liquidity*.

LIS PENDENS Latin: "suit pending." Recorded **notice** of the filing of a suit, the outcome of which may affect **title** to a certain land.
Example: The unpaid **mortgage** holder filed a **foreclosure** suit. She gave notice of *lis pendens* to make others aware of the suit pending.

LIST to obtain a **listing**.
Example: Baker wanted to *list* as many properties as possible under an **exclusive right to sell** so he would earn a commission no matter who sold the property.

LISTING 1. a written engagement **contract** between a principal and an **agent**, authorizing the agent to perform services for the principal involving the latter's property. 2. a record of property for sale by a **broker** who has been authorized by the owner to sell. 3. the property so listed.
Example: Abel employs Baker to find a buyer for his home by

giving Baker a *listing* contract. When prospective buyers visit
Baker, they will examine the *listings* in Baker's office. If interested, a prospective buyer may wish to visit the *listing*.

LISTING BROKER (AGENT) the licensed real estate **broker** (agent)
who secures a **listing** of the property. Contrast with **selling broker
(agent)**.
Example: For most sales, the *listing broker* and the **selling broker**
share **commissions** equally. In some locales, notably for new
homes, the *listing broker* earns only 1%, whereas the **selling broker** earns 3% of the selling price.

LITIGATION the act of carrying on a lawsuit.
Example: *Litigation* is a contest in court to enforce a right.

LITTORAL part of the shore zone of a large body of water. Compare **riparian rights**.
Example: Lot A has *littoral* land. Lot B has **riparian** land (Figure
101).

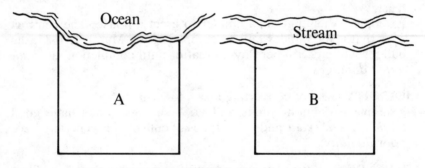

FIGURE 101

LOAN APPLICATION document required by a lender prior to issuing a **loan commitment**. The application generally includes the following information:
1. name of the borrower
2. amount and terms of the loan
3. description of the subject property to be mortgaged
4. borrower's financial and employment data
Example: Lowry wishes to borrow money to purchase a home. At
Friendly Savings, she completes a *loan application* and pays an
application fee. Friendly Savings will **appraise** the house, examine
Lowry's **credit rating**, and verify certain information on the application prior to approving or disapproving the application.

LOAN COMMITMENT an agreement to lend money, generally of a
specified amount, at specified terms at some time in the future.
Example: Before commencing development, Abel obtained a *loan*

commitment from the local **savings and loan association** for permanent financing.

LOAN-TO-VALUE RATIO (LTV) the portion of the amount borrowed compared to the cost or value of the property purchased. **Example:** Abel bought a $100,000 house and arranged a $90,000 **mortgage** loan, resulting in a 90% *loan-to-value ratio*. Home mortgages at more than an 80% *LTV* ratio generally require **mortgage insurance**.

LOG CABIN an early American style house built of unfinished logs.
Example: Figure 102.

Chimneys
at ends   Shingle covered gable roof

                                                    Unfinished logs

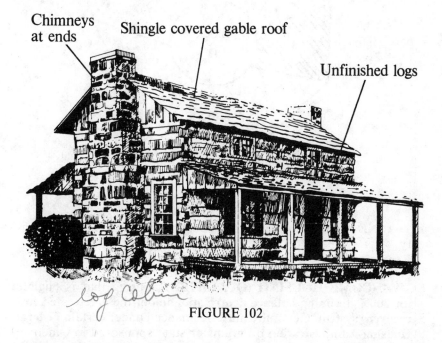

FIGURE 102

LONG-TERM CAPITAL GAIN for income tax purposes, the gain on a **capital asset** held long enough to qualify for special tax considerations. Over one year is enough for most capital assets. See **capital gain**.
Example: Abel sells land for $15,000, purchased 367 days ago for $4,000. The $11,000 profit is a *long-term capital gain*, and only 40% of the gain is taxed at ordinary rates.

LOT AND BLOCK a method of locating a parcel of land. See **legal description**.
Example: The shaded property in Figure 103 is lot 4, block B of Rolling Acres **subdivision**, in Lincoln County, New Mexico.

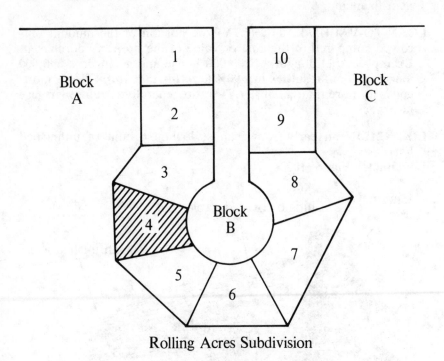

Rolling Acres Subdivision

FIGURE 103

LOT LINE a line bounding a lot as described in a **survey** of property.
Example: Figure 104

LOW-INCOME HOUSING (QUALIFIED) housing that is eligible
for 200% **declining balance depreciation** under the **accelerated cost
recovery system.** Generally must be financed under certain **Federal
Housing Administration** programs or state sponsored low-income
housing programs.
Example: Tax incentives are offered to owners of qualified *low-
income housing.* They can claim fast depreciation of their property, and **depreciation recapture** rules are more liberal.

M

MAI (Member, Appraisal Institute) a member of the **American Institute of Real Estate Appraisers,** which is affiliated with the **National
Association of Realtors**®.

Example: To acquire the designation *MAI,* an **appraiser** must pass several written proficiency examinations, perform acceptable appraisal work for a specific period of time, and prepare a demonstration narrative appraisal report. The *MAI* signifies the appraiser is qualified to appraise a broad range of **real estate** types.
Address:
American Institute of Real Estate Appraisers
430 North Michigan Avenue
Chicago, Illinois 60611

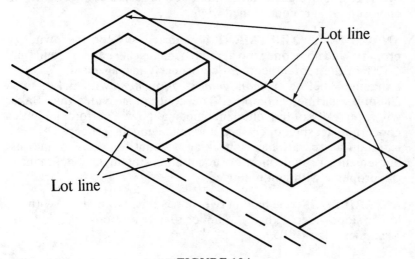

FIGURE 104

MAINTENANCE activities required to compensate for **wear and tear** on a property. See **deferred maintenance.**
Example: Among the duties of **property management** is *maintenance* of the property. This includes routine upkeep of the building, repair and periodic painting as needed, keeping all mechanical parts in working order, and lawn maintenance.

MAINTENANCE FEE an assessment by a **homeowners' association** or a **condominium owners' association,** to pay costs of operating the **common elements.**
Example: A condominium association assesses each owner a *maintenance fee* of $100 per month for lawn maintenance and insurance costs.

MAJORITY 1. the age at which one is no longer a **minor** and is fully able to conduct one's own affairs; majority (full legal age) is 18 to 21 years, depending on the state.
Example: Abel, under 18 years of age, enters into a **contract** to buy land. Because he has not attained *majority,* he may **void** the

contract if he chooses. Baker, the seller, is bound to the contract unless Abel voids it.

2. more than half.

Example: The bylaws of the **condominium owners' association** require a *majority* of the owners who vote to change to another management firm.

MALL a public area connecting individual stores in a **shopping center;** generally enclosed. Also, an enclosed shopping center.

Example: A large shopping *mall* was being developed south of town. It was designed to include over 40 stores connected by an enclosed and air-conditioned *mall*.

MANAGEMENT AGREEMENT a **contract** between the owner of property and someone who agrees to manage it. Fees are generally 4-10% of the rental income. See **property management.**

Example: Abel has a *management agreement* with Baker for a 200-unit apartment complex. The contract provides that Baker will receive 5% of the rental income, and he will perform all duties concerning leasing, operating, and managing the property. He will maintain a separate bank checking account for receipts and disbursements, provide monthly accounting statements, and manage the property with competence.

MANSARD ROOF one having two slopes on all four sides, with the lower slope steeper than the upper, flatter sections.

Example: Figure 105

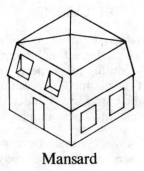

Mansard

FIGURE 105

MARGINAL PROPERTY property that is barely profitable to use.

Example: The sale of cotton that has been efficiently raised **yields** $100; yet the cotton cost $99.99 to raise. The land on which the cotton was raised is therefore considered *marginal property*.

Example: A tract of undeveloped land is deemed *marginal property* because of lack of access to a roadway.

MARITAL DEDUCTION the tax-free amount one transfers by **will** to one's spouse. The 1981 Tax Act allows an unlimited amount to be transferred without tax.
Example: The concept of a *marital deduction* is to treat husband and wife as one economic unit. Since 1981, a federal **estate tax** will be due only on taxable property that passes to another generation.

MARKETABLE TITLE a **title** so free from defect that a court will enforce the title's acceptance by a purchaser. Compare **cloud on the title.**
Example: Through a divorce settlement, Collins obtained certain ownership rights to a property. She now wished to sell the property. To obtain a *marketable title,* she must obtain a **quitclaim deed** from her former husband, thereby curing a defect in her title.

MARKET APPROACH same as **market comparison approach.**

MARKET AREA a geographic region from which one can expect the primary demand for a specific product or service provided at a fixed location.
Example: A regional shopping center has a larger *market area* than a neighborhood shopping center.
Example: A developer estimates that the *market area* for a **subdivision** covers the northeast section of the metropolitan area.

MARKET COMPARISON APPROACH one of 3 **appraisal approaches.** Value is estimated by analyzing sales prices of similar properties (**comparables**) recently sold.
Example: The subject property is a 3-bedroom, 2-bath house. Two recently sold comparables are found. The appraiser, using the *market comparison approach,* sets up Table 23.

TABLE 23

Subject	Comparable #1	Comparable #2
Sale price	$70,500	$69,000
Date of sale	last week	3 months ago (+$1000)
3 bedrooms	3 bedrooms	3 bedrooms
2 baths	2½ baths (−$500)	2 baths
Adjusted price	$70,000	$70,000

The subject property is appraised for $70,000.

MARKET DATA APPROACH same as **market comparison approach.**

MARKET PRICE the actual price paid in a market transaction. Contrast with **market value.**
Example: A home was offered for sale at $100,000. It was appraised for $93,000, and actually sold for $95,000 in an **arm's length transaction.** The *market price* is $95,000.

MARKET RENT the **rent** that a comparable unit would command if offered in the competitive market. Contrast with **contract rent.**
Example: Long rents an apartment to Towns for $400 per month. Similar units are renting for $450 per month. The apartment's *market rent* is $450 per month.

MARKET VALUE the theoretical highest price a buyer, willing but not compelled to buy, would pay, and the lowest price a seller, willing but not compelled to sell, would accept.
Example: An **appraisal** of a home indicates its *market value* is $75,000. In a normally active market, the home should sell for this amount if allowed to stay on the market for a reasonable time. The owner may, however, **deed** the home to a relative for $250. The owner may also grow impatient and sell for $70,000. Conversely, an anxious buyer may be found who pays $80,000. Finally, the owner may provide favorable financing and sell for $85,000.

MASONRY construction made from brick, cement block, or stone.
Example: The ground floor of the house shown in Figure 106 is made of *masonry*. The upper floor is wooden frame with wooden siding.

MASTER LEASE a controlling **lease.** Contrast with **sublease.** Note that one cannot grant a greater interest in real estate than one has; so if a *master lease* is for a 5-year term, a sublease cannot legally exceed 5 years.
Example: Abel leases 10,000 square feet of retail space to Baker. Baker then subleases the space to 5 different **tenants.** The lease between Abel and Baker is the *master lease*.

MASTER PLAN a document that describes, in narrative and with maps, an overall development concept. The master plan is used to coordinate the preparation of more detailed plans or may be a collection of detailed plans. The plan may be prepared by a local government to guide private and public development or by a **developer** on a specific project.
Example: The city planners checked to see if the **zoning** request complied with the city's *master plan*.
Example: The *master plan* for further development of the resort **condominium** is displayed in the sales office.

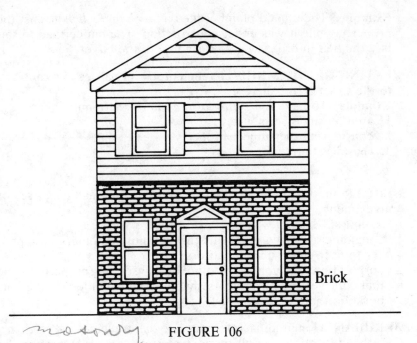

masonry   FIGURE 106

MATERIAL FACT a fact that is germane to a particular situation; one that participants in the situation such as a trial, may reasonably be expected to consider.
Example: If *material facts* about the investment property lying in a **floodplain** had been communicated to the buyer, he would not have bought. He is now charging **misrepresentation** against the seller and the **broker.**

MATERIALMAN a person who supplies materials used in the construction or repair of a building or other property.
Example: Since the *materialman* was not paid for lumber, he filed a **mechanic's lien** against the property.

MATURITY the due date of a loan.
Example: A **mortgage** loan may have a *maturity* of 30 years. Periodic payments are established so that the loan **principal** will **amortize** by the *maturity* date.
Example: A bond may have a *maturity* of 20 years. Generally, **interest** only will be paid, with the full principal repaid at *maturity*.

MECHANIC'S LIEN a **lien** given by law upon a building or other **improvement** upon land, and upon the land itself, as **security** for the payment for labor done and materials furnished for improvement.

Example: The unpaid plumber filed a *mechanic's lien* against the property while it was under construction. The builder had to satisfy the lien in order to give **clear title** to the buyer.

MEETING OF THE MINDS agreement, by all parties to a **contract,** to the exact terms thereof.
Example: To have a *meeting of the minds* there must be:
1. an **offer** and **acceptance**
2. considering the subject property
3. **consideration**
4. **terms**

MERGER the fusion of 2 or more interests, such as businesses or investments.
Examples: Examples of *mergers* are:
• conglomerates—corporations that are not customers or suppliers to each other or competitors
• corporations—union of 2 or more by transferring property to one that survives, and issuing its shares to stockholders of the corporation that ceases to exist

MERIDIAN a longitudinal reference line that traverses the earth in a north-south direction; all meridians circle the earth through the equator and converge at the north and south poles; used by **surveyors** in describing property under the **government rectangular survey method.**
Example: Figure 107

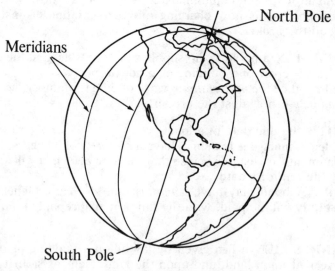

FIGURE 107

METES AND BOUNDS a land **description** method that details all the **boundary** lines of land, together with their terminal points and angles.

Example: *Metes and bounds* description: Beginning at a point on the northeasterly corner of the intersection of South St. and West Rd.; running thence northerly along West Rd. 200 feet; thence easterly parallel to South St. 150 feet; thence southerly parallel to West Rd. 200 feet; thence westerly along South St. 150 feet to the point of beginning (Figure 108).

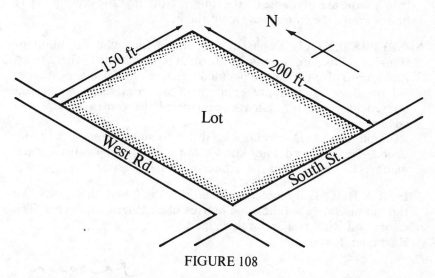

FIGURE 108

METROPOLITAN AREA generally the developed region economically attached to a large central city; same as **standard metropolitan statistical area.**

Example: The *metropolitan area* of Atlanta, Georgia covers 15 counties and contains over 2 million people.

MILL one tenth of a cent. Used in expressing tax rates on a per-dollar basis.

Example: A tax rate of 60 *mills* means that taxes are 6 cents per dollar of **assessed valuation.**

MINERAL RIGHTS the privilege of gaining **income** from the sale of oil, gas, and other valuable resources found on land.

Example: Abel purchases a property that contains underground oil deposits. Abel may:
• develop these *mineral rights* by drilling a well
• sell the rights for a price to an oil company
• **lease** the rights to an oil company in exchange for a **royalty**

MINIMUM LOT AREA the smallest building lot area allowed in a **subdivision,** generally specified by a **zoning ordinance.**
Example: Baker owns land that is zoned "R-4." If Baker develops the land, it must be used for residential purposes and lots must have a *minimum lot area* of ¼ acre.

MINOR a person under the age of **majority** specified by law (18 to 21 years, depending on the state).
Example: Contracts for the sale or use of real estate, entered into by a *minor,* are voidable by the minor. Note that the other party is bound; only the minor may void them.

MISREPRESENTATION an untrue statement, whether unintentional or deliberate. It may be a form of nondisclosure where there is a duty to disclose or the planned creation of a false appearance. Where there is misrepresentation of **material fact,** the person injured may sue for **damages** or **rescind** the **contract.** See **false advertising.**
Example: The **broker** represented the home as being structurally sound. The broker did not know that **termites** were destroying the wood. The buyer sued the broker for *misrepresentation.*

MISSION HOUSE a nineteenth century style house that looks like the old mission churches and houses of Southern California. The doors and windows are arch-shaped.
Example: Figure 109

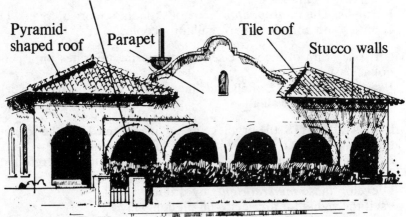

FIGURE 109

MISTAKE an unintentional error made in preparing a **contract;** may be corrected by mutual consent of all parties without voiding contract.
Example: Abel and Baker agree to a sales contract for a property located at 100 Main Street. In preparing the contract the address is listed as 100 Main Blvd. The *mistake* is discovered at the **closing,** and correction is made with the consent of both parties.

MOBILE HOME a dwelling unit (Figure 110) manufactured in a factory and designed to be transported to a **site** and semipermanently attached.

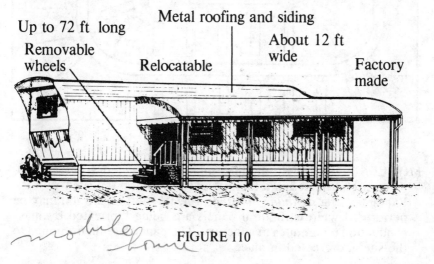

Up to 72 ft long

Metal roofing and siding

About 12 ft wide

Removable wheels

Relocatable

Factory made

FIGURE 110

Example: One option for low-cost housing is purchase of a *mobile home,* which generally costs much less than site-built housing. *Mobile homes* may be placed on the purchaser's lot or in a **mobile home park** for a monthly rental.

MOBILE HOME PARK a **subdivision** of plots designed for siting of mobile homes. Plots are generally leased to mobile home owners and include **utilities,** parking space, and access to utility roads. Many parks also include such **amenities** as swimming pools and clubhouses.
Example: A typical *mobile home park* design (Figure 111).

MODEL UNIT a representative home, apartment, or office space used as part of a sales campaign to demonstrate the design, structure, and appearance of units in a development.
Example: A **developer** constructs a *model unit* in an effort to **prelease** units in a development. Prospective tenants are invited to tour the *model unit* to gain an appreciation for the design and appearance of the development.

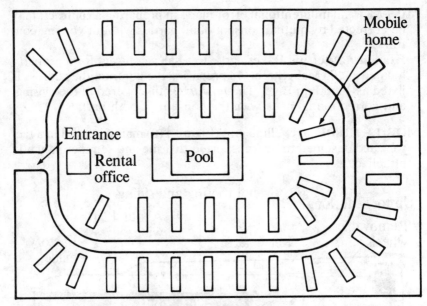

FIGURE 111

MODULAR HOUSING dwelling units constructed from components **prefabricated** in a factory and erected on the **site.**
Example: In a *modular housing* project, site preparation may be
performed while structural panels are being fabricated by mass
production techniques in a factory. The panels are then shipped to
the site and erected in place.

MOISTURE BARRIER a layer of foil, plastic, or paper used in the
construction of exterior walls, ceilings, and foundations to prevent
moisture penetration into wooden members or insulation.
Example: The *moisture barrier* in an exterior wall (Figure 112).

MONETARY INSTITUTION DEREGULATION ACT same as **Depository Institutions Deregulation and Monetary Control Act.**

MONEY MARKET CERTIFICATE (MMC) a type of **certificate of
deposit** offered by banks and **savings and loan associations.** A fixed
interest rate is determined, for certificates issued that week, by
rates offered by U.S. treasury bills. Carries a 6-month term,
requires a $10,000 deposit.
Example: Mercer purchases a *money market certificate* with
$10,000. It carries a 10% interest rate, and matures in 6 months.

MONTEREY ARCHITECTURE a nineteenth century style, 2-story
house with a balcony across the front at the second floor level.
Example: Figure 113

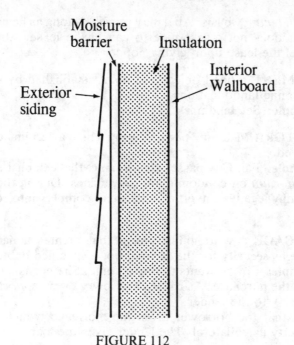

Moisture barrier

Insulation

Exterior siding

Interior Wallboard

FIGURE 112

monterey architecture

Balcony across front at second floor

Shingle roof

2 stories

Rail simple iron or wood

FIGURE 113

MONTH-TO-MONTH TENANCY lease agreement extendable or cancelable each month.

Example: Abel rents an apartment from Baker on a *month-to-*

month tenancy basis. Abel may remain as long as he pays rent and Baker does not give notice to cancel the lease. Abel may also cancel the lease upon giving notice.

MONUMENT a fixed object and point established by **surveyors** to determine land locations.
Example: See **landmark.**

MORATORIUM a time period during which a certain activity is not allowed.
Example: Fair City passes an **ordinance** that establishes a 6-month *moratorium* on condominium **conversions.** During the period, no one may legally convert an apartment complex into **condominium** units.

MORTGAGE a written **instrument** that creates a **lien** upon **real estate** as **security** for the payment of a specified debt.
Example: Lowry wants to buy a home. She needs a loan to complete the purchase. As **collateral,** Lowry offers a *mortgage* on the property to the lender.
Note that the borrower gives the mortgage, which pledges the property as collateral. The lender gives the loan.

MORTGAGE ASSUMPTION same as **assumption of mortgage.**

MORTGAGE BANKER one who originates, sells, and services **mortgage** loans. Most loans are insured or guaranteed by a government agency or private mortgage insurer. See **mortgage insurance.**
Example: The Mortgage Store, a *mortgage banker,* originates 100 loans totaling $5,000,000. They sell this package of loans to an out-of-state investor for $5,010,000. They continue to collect monthly payments from homeowners and assure that property taxes are paid and insurance is maintained. They charge the investor an annual fee of ⅜ of 1% of the loan **principal,** each month remitting to the investor the rest of the monthly payments from homeowners.

MORTGAGE BANKERS ASSOCIATION (MBA) an organization that provides educational programs and other services for **mortgage bankers.** Offers the Certified Mortgage Banker (CMB) designation. Publishes *Mortgage Banker* magazine.
Address: Mortgage Bankers Association of America
1125 Fifteenth Street, N.W.
Washington, D.C. 20005

MORTGAGE BONDS tax-exempt securities sold by municipal and state authorities for the purpose of providing low-interest rate **mortgage** loans to qualified individuals. For most programs, mortgage borrowers must be first-time home buyers with moderate income.

Example: In 1981, the city of Houston sold $100 million of *mortgage bonds*. The proceeds from the sale were used to originate loans through local mortgage lenders for first-time home buyers within the city. Interest on the bonds was tax-exempt to the bondholders, thereby allowing the city to borrow money at an **interest rate** below 10%. The mortgage loans could be originated at rates below 12% at a time when **conventional mortgage loans** carried a much higher rate.

MORTGAGE BROKER one who, for a fee, places loans with investors, but does not service such loans.

Example: The Ace Development Company wants to build a shopping center. A *mortgage broker* charges a 1% fee for each construction loan (placed with a commercial bank) and the permanent loan (placed with an insurance company).

MORTGAGE COMMITMENT an agreement between a lender and a borrower to lend money at a future date, subject to the conditions described in the agreement.

Example: Baker wishes to build a home. Construction will require 6 months. Baker obtains a *mortgage commitment* from Home Town Savings and Loan for permanent financing of the home at the time of its completion.

MORTGAGE CONSTANT the percentage ratio between the annual **debt service** and the loan **principal.** The formula is

$$\frac{\text{Ann. debt serv.}}{\text{Loan prin.}} = \text{mort. const.}$$

where

$$\text{Mort. const.} = \frac{\text{int. rate}}{(1 + \text{int. rate})^{\text{loan term}} - 1}$$

Example: A loan of $10,000 at 12% interest for 5 years has a *mortgage constant* of

$$\frac{0.12}{(1.12)^5 - 1} = 0.1574$$

Annual debt service for the loan is

$$0.1574 \times \$10,000 = \$1,574$$

MORTGAGE CORRESPONDENT one who services loans for a fee. Compare **mortgage broker.**

Example: The Good Money Savings Association bought a package of 1,000 loans in another state. They arrange with a *mortgage* *correspondent* to collect monthly payments, pay real estate taxes, and assure that the property is insured. The *mortgage correspondent* keeps as a fee ⅜ of 1% of the mortgage balance each year.

MORTGAGE DISCOUNT amount of **principal** that lenders deduct at the beginning of the loan. See **discount points.**
Example: Abel obtains a mortgage loan in the amount of $50,000. The loan is discounted by 2 **points,** each point equaling 1% of the **principal.** At **closing** Abel will receive $49,000, yet will owe $50,000. The $1,000 difference is the *mortgage discount.*

MORTGAGEE one who holds a **lien** on property or **title** to property, as **security** for a debt.
Example: Abel obtains a **mortgage** loan from Homebuyers Savings. Homebuyers Savings serves as the *mortgagee.*

MORTGAGE GUARANTEE INSURANCE CO. (MGIC) a private company that insures, to lenders, loan repayment in the event of **default** and/or **foreclosure.** See **mortgage insurance.**
Example: Collins wants to arrange a loan for 90% of the cost of the home she is buying. The lender applies to *MGIC* for **private mortgage insurance.** MGIC accepts and, for a **premium,** stands willing to accept any losses on the mortgages up to 25% of the **principal.**

MORTGAGE INSURANCE 1. a policy that guarantees repayment of a mortgage loan in the event of death or, possibly, disability of the **mortgagor.** 2. protection for the lender in the event of **default,** usually covering the top 25% of the amount borrowed. See **private mortgage insurance.**
Example: Manning obtains a mortgage loan and, for an additional monthly **premium,** purchases *mortgage insurance.* Should Manning die before loan **maturity,** the policy will pay the remaining balance of the loan. This protects Manning's survivors from losing the property because of inability to continue the loan payments, and also protects the **mortgagee.**

MORTGAGE LIEN an **encumbrance** on property used to secure a loan. The holder of the **lien** has a claim to the property in case of loan **default.** The **priority** of the claim depends on the order of **recording** and any **subordination** agreements. Thus a **first mortgage** generally has prior claim to all other mortgage lien holders. See also **second mortgage.**
Example: Minton obtains a mortgage loan to purchase a house. Minton signs a **note** and mortgage contract. The lender obtains a *mortgage lien* on the house. Should Minton default on the loan, the lender may **foreclose** and exercise the lien to force a sale, the proceeds of which are used to satisfy Minton's debt.

MORTGAGE OUT to obtain financing in excess of the cost to construct a project. In the early 1970's **developers** could mortgage out by obtaining a permanent **loan commitment** based on a high percentage of the completed project's value. This enabled the developer to borrow more than the cost of developing the project. Since then opportunities to mortgage out have been virtually eliminated by lower **loan-to-value ratios,** higher **capitalization rates** and higher construction costs.
Example: A proposed office building is projected to produce annual **net operating income** of $100,000. At a capitalization rate of 10%, the building is worth $1,000,000. A **takeout** loan commitment is obtained for 80% of value, or $800,000. The developer requires only $750,000 to purchase the land and construct the building. The $50,000 excess represents the results of the developer *mortgaging out*.

MORTGAGE RELIEF acquired freedom from mortgage debt, generally through **assumption of mortgage** by another party or **debt** retirement. In a tax-free exchange, mortgage relief is considered **boot** received.
Example: Collins exchanged her mortgaged office building, receiving land worth $25,000 and *mortgage relief* of $75,000. The total value received was $100,000.

MORTGAGOR one who pledges property as **security** for a loan.
Example: Abel obtains a mortgage loan from Homebuyers Savings. Abel serves as a *mortgagor*.

MULTIFAMILY HOUSING a type of residential structure with more than one **dwelling** unit in the same building.
Example: *Multifamily housing* is divided into 2 categories:
2-4 dwelling units: **duplexes,** triplexes, and quadraplexes
5 or more units: apartment buildings
Multifamily housing may be tenant-occupied, owner-occupied (as in a **condominium** or cooperative project), or mixed (as many duplexes with the owner occupying one side).

MULTIPLE LISTING an arrangement among a group of real estate brokers; they agree in advance to provide information about some or all of their **listings** to the others and also agree that **commissions** on sales of such listings will be split between listing and selling brokers.
Example: A broker lists a home under an **exclusive right to sell.** The broker belongs to a *multiple listing* association. After 5 days the broker turns in a description of the home to the association. Any cooperating broker can sell the home and will receive half of the commission. The broker who obtained the **exclusive right to sell** is assured of earning half the commission upon the sale.

MULTIPLE LISTING SERVICE (MLS) an association of real estate **brokers** that agrees to share **listings** with one another. The listing broker and the selling broker share the **commission.** The MLS usually distributes a book with all listings to its members, updating the book frequently. Prospective buyers benefit from the ability to select from among many homes from any member broker.
Example: Abel and Baker, both brokers, are members of the *multiple listing service.* A home that was listed by Abel under an **exclusive right to sell** is sold by Baker. The two brokers share the commission.

MUNIMENTS OF TITLE documents, such as **deeds** or **contracts,** one uses to indicate ownership.
Example: In order to register **title** under the **Torrens system,** the owner offered *muniments of title.*

MUTUAL SAVINGS BANKS mostly in the northeastern U.S., these state-chartered banks are owned by the depositors and operated for their benefit. Most of these banks hold a large portion of their **assets** in home mortgage loans.
Example: Abel deposits his savings in a *mutual savings bank* in New York. As a depositor-shareholder, Abel receives a proportionate distribution of the bank's earnings.

N

NATIONAL APARTMENT ASSOCIATION (NAA) an organization of apartment owners, with local chapters in metropolitan areas, that provides information and services for members concerning apartment rentals, **lease** forms, occupancy rates, and other matters.
Address:
National Apartment Association
1825 K Street, N.W.
Washington, D.C. 20006

NATIONAL ASSOCIATION OF CORPORATE REAL ESTATE EXECUTIVES (NACORE) membership includes those active with purchasing, selling, and managing **real estate** held by **corporations.**
Address:
National Association of Corporate Real Estate Executives
7799 Southwest 62nd Avenue
South Miami, Florida 33143, N.W.

NATIONAL ASSOCIATION OF HOME BUILDERS (NAHB) an organization of home builders, providing educational, political information and research services. Publishes a monthly magazine, *Builder*.
Address:
National Association of Home Builders
15th and M Street, N.W.
Washington, D.C. 20005

NATIONAL ASSOCIATION OF REAL ESTATE BROKERS (NAR-EB) an organization of minority real estate salespersons and **brokers** who are called **realtists**.
Address:
National Association of Real Estate Brokers
9th floor, Suite 900
1101 14th Street, N.W.
Washington, D.C. 20005

NATIONAL ASSOCIATION OF REAL ESTATE LICENSE LAW OFFICIALS (NARELLO) membership is composed of commissioners from state real estate licensing agencies.
Address:
National Association of Real Estate License Law Officials
2580 South 90th Street
Omaha, Nebraska 68124

NATIONAL ASSOCIATION OF REALTORS® (NAR) an organization of **Realtors®,** devoted to encouraging professionalism in **real estate** activities. There are over 600,000 members of NAR, 50 state associations, and several affiliates. Members are required to abide by the **Code of Ethics** of the NAR.
Address:
National Association of Realtors®
430 N. Michigan Avenue
Chicago, Illinois 60611

NEGATIVE AMORTIZATION an increase in the **outstanding balance** of a loan resulting from the failure of periodic **debt service** payments to cover required interest charged on the loan. Generally occurs under **indexed loans** for which the applicable **interest rate** may be changed without affecting the monthly payments. *Negative amortization* will occur if the indexed interest rate is increased.
Example: A loan is originated at 15% interest with a **maturity** of 30 years. The interest rate may be adjusted each 6 months, but monthly payments remain a constant $632. After 6 months, the interest rate is raised to 16.5%, which would require a monthly payment of $692 to fully amortize the loan. At the new interest

rate, $687 is required to pay interest. The $55 difference between the payment and interest due is added to the principal in month 7 as *negative amortization* (Figure 114).

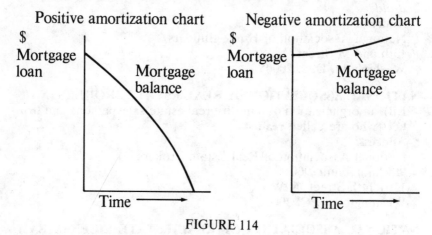

FIGURE 114

NEGATIVE CASH FLOW situation in which a property owner must make an outlay of funds to operate a property.
Example: Baker acquires an apartment building with the first year income statement shown in Table 24.

TABLE 24

Potential **gross income:**	$50,000
Vacancy loss	– 5,000
Effective gross income	45,000
Operating expenses	–30,000
Net operating income	15,000
Debt service	–20,000
Negative cash flow before tax	$5,000

Baker must spend $5,000 to operate the building for the first year, because of a *negative cash flow*.

NEGATIVE LEVERAGE same as **reverse leverage.**

NEGOTIABLE INSTRUMENT a promise to pay money, transferable from one person to another.
Example: Abel gave Baker a *negotiable instrument* that contained a promise to pay $1000 on July 22 of this year. Baker sold the note for $900 cash to Collins by endorsing and delivering it. Collins became a **holder in due course.**

NEGOTIABLE ORDER OF WITHDRAWAL (NOW) an **instrument,** offered by financial institutions, that is printed to appear as a check but generally represents a withdrawal from a savings account.

Example: The ABC financial institution pays 5% interest on deposits. Depositors are supplied with *negotiable orders of withdrawal,* which are accepted in most instances in the same manner as a check. Sums represented by *NOWs* earn interest until the NOWs clear.

NEGOTIATION the process of bargaining that precedes an agreement. Successful negotiation generally results in a **contract** between the parties.

Example: Nelson wishes to purchase a property from Newman. Nelson is willing to pay up to a certain price and desires certain **conditions** placed on the sale. Newman will accept anything over a certain price and may be willing to help finance the purchase for a higher price. In *negotiation* Nelson and Newman attempt to come to an agreement over the price and conditions. When they agree, a sales contract is **executed.**

NEIGHBORHOOD a district or locality characterized by similar or compatible land uses. Neighborhoods are often identified by a place name and have boundaries composed of major streets, barriers, or abrupt changes in land use.

Example: Residential *neighborhoods* are often identified with a **subdivision,** an elementary school attendance zone, a major public facility, such as a college, or a small town within a larger urban area. Homes in the neighborhood are of similar style, age, and value.

Example: Commercial *neighborhoods* are generally associated with a major road, shopping center, or **central business district.**

Example: Industrial *neighborhoods* are generally identified by common use of a transportation linkage.

NEIGHBORHOOD LIFE CYCLE a generalized pattern that describes the physical and social changes that residential areas experience over time. See also **abandonment, filtering down, urban renewal, land use succession.**

Example: Richard Andrews' *neighborhood life cycle* (Figure 115).

NET INCOME 1. in accounting, the amount remaining after all expenses have been met.

Example: Table 25

2. in **appraisal,** same as **net operating income.**

NET LEASABLE AREA in a building or project, floor space that may be rented to tenants. The area upon which rental payments are based. Generally excludes common areas and space devoted

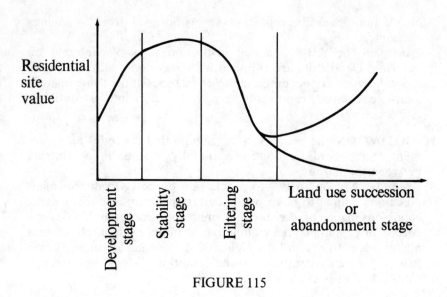

FIGURE 115

TABLE 25

Rental income		$10,000
Less:		
Utilities	$1,500	
Property taxes	1,000	
Management fee	500	
Maintenance expenses	2,000	
Interest	2,000	
Depreciation	1,000	
Income taxes	1,000	
Subtotal		− 9,000
Net income		$1,000

to the heating, cooling, and other equipment of a building.
Example: A building with 10 floors, each containing 3,000 square feet of space, may have a *net leasable area* of 25,000 square feet. Elevators, hallways, and utility spaces absorb the remaining 5,000 square feet. If the average rental is $10 per net leasable square foot, the building has a potential **gross income** of $250,000 per year.

NET LEASE a **lease** whereby, in addition to the rent stipulated, the **lessee** (tenant) pays such expenses as taxes, insurance, and **maintenance.** The landlord's rent receipt is thereby "net" of those expenses.
Example: Baker leases retail space from Abel on a *net lease*. Abel

can expect to receive the full rent without deducting for **operating expenses,** which are paid by Baker. In practice, various levels of net leases are often used to designate arrangements where the tenant pays only some types of expenses and the landlord pays other types.

NET LISTING a listing in which the brokers's **commission** is the excess of the sale price over an agreed-upon (net) price to the seller; illegal in some states.
Example: Abel agrees to sell Baker's house on a *net listing*. They set the net price at $70,000. Abel finds a buyer willing to pay $75,000. Abel's commission is $5,000. Note that should Abel find a buyer offering $70,000, Abel would earn no commission.

NET OPERATING INCOME (NOI) income from property or business after **operating expenses** have been deducted, but before deducting income taxes and financing expenses (**interest** and **principal** payments). The formula is:
$$NOI = \text{gross income} - \text{operating expenses}$$
Example: A property produces rental income of $100,000 during the year. The expenses incurred are shown in Table 26.

TABLE 26

Operating expenses:	
Maintenance	$20,000
Insurance	5,000
Property taxes	10,000
Management	10,000
Utilities	15,000
	$60,000

Debt service:*	
Interest	$18,000
Principal	2,000
	$20,000
Income taxes*	($5,000)

*Excluded from the computation.

NOI = $100,000 − $60,000 = $40,000 (*net operating income*)

NET PRESENT VALUE a method of determining whether expected performance of a proposed investment promises to be adequate. See also **internal rate of return, present value of one.**
Example: A proposed land investment requires $10,000 of cash now, and is expected to be resold for $25,000 in 4 years. For the **risks** involved, the investor seeks a 20% **discount rate** (same as

compounded rate of return). The $25,000 amount to be received in 4 years, when discounted by 20% annually, is worth $12,056 now. Since the investment costs $10,000, the *net present value* is $2,056.

$$\frac{\$25,000}{(1 + 0.24)^4} - \$10,000 = \$2,056$$

NET WORTH the excess of **assets** over **liabilities.** The amount of **equity.**
Example: Table 27:

TABLE 27

Balance Sheet

Assets		Liabilities	
Land	$10,000	Mortgage	$75,000
Buildings	90,000	Net worth	25,000
Total	$100,000	Total	$100,000

NET YIELD the return on an investment after subtracting all expenses. See also **current yield, yield to maturity.**
Example: Equity paid for an investment is $10,000. **Net income** is $1,000. Therefore, the investment generates a $1,000 *net yield*.

NEW ENGLAND COLONIAL an early American style, 2½ story boxlike house that is generally symmetrical, square, or rectangular with side or rear wings. The traditional material is narrow clapboard siding. The roof is usually the gable type covered with shingles.
Example: Figure 116.

NEW ENGLAND FARM HOUSE an early American style of house that is simple and box-shaped. The traditional material for the exterior siding is white clapboard. A steep pitched roof is used to shed heavy snow.
Example: Figure 117.

NEW TOWN a large mixed-use development designed to provide residences, general shopping, services, and employment. The basic concept of a new town is to construct a community in a previously undeveloped area under a central plan, to avoid unplanned development. Some European and South American countries use new towns to attract population into less developed regions.
Example: The popularity of *new towns* reached a peak in the early 1970's under financial assistance from the federal government.

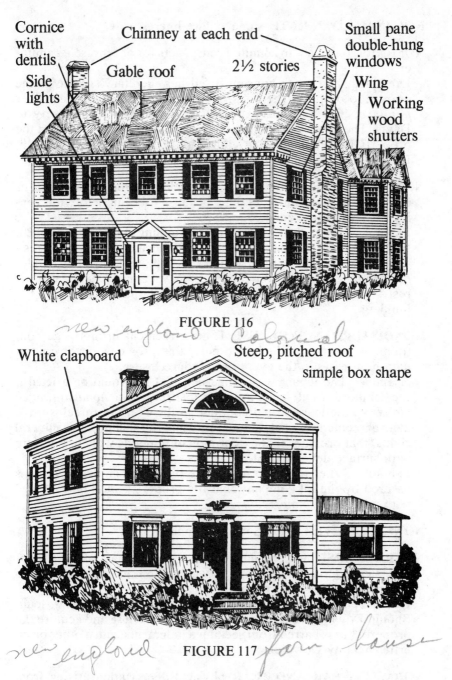

Cornice with dentils
Side lights
Chimney at each end
Gable roof
2½ stories
Small pane double-hung windows
Wing
Working wood shutters

FIGURE 116

new england Colonial

White clapboard
Steep, pitched roof
simple box shape

new england FIGURE 117 *farm house*

Possibly the most famous modern *new towns* in the U.S. are Columbia, Maryland and Reston, Virginia. *New towns* have been developed to serve as national capitals, such as Washington, D.C., Brasilia, Brazil, and Canberra, Australia.

NOMINAL LOAN RATE same as **face interest rate.**

NOMINEE one who, in a limited sense, acts for or represents another.
Example: Davis with consent, used her secretary's name as the **grantee** to property she buys. Her secretary was considered her *nominee.* Simultaneously, her secretary **deeded** the property to Davis. There was a **mortgage** on the property. Davis acquired the property from the *nominee* **subject to** the mortgage. By doing so, Davis is not personally liable for the mortgage loan.

NONCONFORMING USE a use that violates **zoning** regulations or codes but is allowed to continue because it began before the zoning **restriction** was enacted.
Example: Carter owns a commercial building constructed in 1920. In 1935, the city enacted a **zoning ordinance** that prescribes residential use for the area in which the building is located. Under *noncomforming use,* the building may remain, but Carter is restricted in the extent to which he may improve or restore the building.

NONDISTURBANCE CLAUSE 1. an agreement in mortgage contracts on income-producing property that provides for the continuation of **leases** in the event of loan **foreclosure.**
Example: The tenant was concerned that he would be **evicted** if the landlord went **bankrupt.** He insisted on a *nondisturbance clause* so the lease would continue in the event of foreclosure.
2. an agreement in a sales contract, when the seller retains **mineral rights,** that provides that exploration of minerals will not interfere with surface development.
Example: When the seller negotiated the **oil and gas lease,** she was assured by the oil company that the property could be **conveyed** with a *nondisturbance clause.*

NONEXCLUSIVE LISTING same as **open listing.**

NONRECOURSE no personal **liability.** Lenders may take the property pledged as **collateral** to satisfy a **debt,** but have no **recourse** to other **assets** of the borrower.
Example: Downing purchases a property with a *nonrecourse* loan. Should Downing **default,** the lender may **foreclose** and acquire the property but is barred from seeking a **judgment** against other properties held by Downing.

NORMAL WEAR AND TEAR physical **depreciation** arising from age and ordinary use of the property.
Example: An **appraiser** estimates that a certain type of carpeting, subject to *normal wear and tear,* should have a physical life of 5 years.

NOTARIZE to attest, in one's capacity as a **notary public,** to the genuineness of a signature.
Example: Before a county clerk will record certain types of documents, they must be *notarized* to assure the signature is not forged.

NOTARY PUBLIC an officer who is authorized to take **acknowledgments** to certain types of documents, such as **deeds, contracts,** and **mortgages,** and before whom **affidavits** may be sworn.
Example: Eakins and Finwick agree to transfer a piece of property. At the **closing,** a *notary public* serves to witness the signing of all documents.

NOTE a written **instrument** that acknowledges a **debt** and promises to pay.
Example: Greer borrows money from Thrifty Savings to purchase a home. Greer signs a *note* to acknowledge the debt, to promise to pay under specified terms, and to prescribe a procedure for curing **default.** A **mortgage** will also be signed that pledges the home to the lender as **security** for the note.

NOTICE official communication of a legal action or one's intent to take an action. See also **public offering, public sale.**
Example: A landlord may be required to give a tenant 30 days *notice* before terminating the **lease.**
Example: A lender may be required to give a debtor *notice* that a **default** has occurred before initiating **foreclosure** proceedings. See **notice of default.**
Example: Recording a deed serves to give **constructive notice** to the public of one's ownership of a property.

NOTICE OF DEFAULT a letter sent to a defaulting party as a reminder of the **default.** May state a **grace period** and the **penalties** for failing to cure the default.
Example: Vacation Lot Sales Corp. sent a *notice of default* to Abel. It offered a 7-day grace period, after which they would consider his **interest** as forfeited unless he paid the delinquent **installment.**

NOTICE TO QUIT 1. a notice to a tenant to **vacate** rented property.
Example: After the lease expired the tenant remained in **possession.** The landlord sent a *notice to quit* by January 31.
2. sometimes used by a tenant who intends to vacate on a certain date.

NOTORIOUS POSSESSION generally acknowledged **possession** of **real estate.** One of the requirements to gain ownership of real estate through **adverse possession.**

Example: A squatter, who was in *notorious possession* of land, was thought by neighbors to be the owner of record.

NOVATION a 3-party agreement whereby one party is released from a **contract** and another party is substituted.
Example: Baker wants to buy Abel's home and assume the mortgage. Abel wants to be released from all mortgage **liability.** Good Money Savings Association cooperates. The 3 sign a *novation* whereby Baker is substituted for Abel on the mortgage.

NUISANCE a land use whose associated activities are incompatible with surrounding land uses.
Example: Zoning laws and private **deed restrictions** are used to prevent the development of *nuisances,* such as:
• activities that produce noxious fumes or air pollution in residential areas
• commercial uses that generate large volumes of automobile traffic in residential areas
• junkyards in highly visible areas
• activities considered socially offensive, such as sale of pornographic materials, in residential areas

NULL AND VOID that which cannot be legally enforced, as with a **contract** provision that is not in conformance with the law.
Example: Ivenson sells a property and places in the **deed** a **covenant** that the property may never be sold to someone of a minority race. Since this provision is in defiance of the U.S. Constitution, it could never be enforced and is thereby *null and void.*

O

OBLIGEE the person in whose favor an obligation is entered into.
Example: Jackson promises to manage the property of Kindall, an out-of-town investor. In this arrangement, Kindall is the *obligee;* Jackson is the **obligor.**

OBLIGOR the person who binds himself or herself to another; one who has engaged to perform some obligation; one who makes a **bond.**
Example: See **obligee.**

OBSOLESCENCE a loss in value due to reduced desirability and usefulness of a structure because its design and construction has become obsolete; loss due to a structure's becoming old-fash-

ioned, not in keeping with modern needs, with consequent loss of income. See **economic depreciation, functional depreciation, functional obsolescence.**
Example: An old house may suffer from the following examples of *obsolescence:*
• rooms of improper size
• features no longer useful, such as a coal chute with a gas-fired furnace
• out-of-date plumbing, heating, and electrical fixtures and systems
• inadequate insulation
• unsuitable architectural style
• construction materials that require excessive **maintenance**
• undesirable location

OCCUPANCY AGREEMENT, LIMITED one that allows a prospective buyer to obtain **possession** under a temporary arrangement, usually prior to **closing.**
Example: Abel, the seller, signs a *limited occupancy agreement* with Baker that allows Baker possession of the property at rent of $25 per day for up to 30 days or the day of closing, whichever occurs first.

OCCUPANCY LEVEL percentage of currently rented units in a building, city, neighborhood, or complex. Contrast with **vacancy rate.**
Example: Today the Holiday Hotel has 90 of its 100 rooms booked and filled. Its *occupancy level* is 90%. Conversely, its vacancy rate is 10%.

OFFER an expression of willingness to purchase a property at a specified price.
Example: Lincoln places a property on the market. Murray makes an *offer* to buy the property for $150,000. Lincoln may accept the offer, reject the offer, or propose a **counteroffer.**

OFFER AND ACCEPTANCE see **agreement of sale.**

OFFICE OF INTERSTATE LAND SALES REGISTRATION (OILSR) a division of the U.S. Department of **Housing and Urban Development** that regulates offerings of land for sale across state lines. See **Interstate Land Sales Act.**
Example: Norwood **subdivides** a large land parcel in Arizona and wishes to market the lots to investors across the nation. Norwood is required to register the offering with *OILSR* and follow certain procedures intended to inform buyers of the characteristics of their investment.

OFF-SITE COSTS expenditures related to construction that are spent away from the place of construction.
Example: Owens is developing a **subdivision.** Certain *offsite costs* are incurred, such as the costs of extending roads, sewers, and water lines to the **site.** Site costs include landscaping and other site **improvements.**

OFF-SITE IMPROVEMENTS the portions of a **subdivision** or development that are not directly on the lots to be sold.
Example: Access streets, curbs, sewers, and utility connections are common examples of *off-site improvements.*

OIL AND GAS LEASE an agreement that gives the right to explore for oil, gas, and sometimes other minerals and to extract them from the ground. Provisions include the granting of subsurface and surface rights, **lease** duration, **extension** terms, **royalties,** surface damages, **assignments,** and **warranties.** See **mineral rights.**
Example: In an *oil and gas lease,* the owner is to receive $100 per acre as a bonus payment, and one eighth of the value of minerals found on the property.

ONE-HUNDRED-PERCENT LOCATION a point in space where a retail establishment would achieve maximum sales volume compared to other locations in the local market area.
Example: The corner of First and Main is the busiest intersection downtown. It represents the *hundred-percent location* for a department store.

OPEN-END MORTGAGE a **mortgage** under which the **mortgagor** (borrower) may secure additional funds from the **mortgagee** (lender), usually stipulating a ceiling amount that can be borrowed.
Example: Poole obtains an *open-end mortgage* to purchase a home. Under the mortgage agreement, Poole may borrow additional funds over the **maturity** of the loan as long as the unpaid **principal** does not exceed 80% of the home's **appraised** value.

OPEN HOUSE a method of showing a home for sale whereby the home is left open for inspection by interested parties.
Example: A **broker** advertises an *open house* to promote the sale of a **listing.** On the specified date, prospective buyers may inspect the house during the hours of the *open house.*

OPEN HOUSING a condition under which housing units may be purchased or **leased** without regard for racial, ethnic, color, or religious characteristics of the buyers or tenants.
Example: The intent of government antidiscrimination laws applied to housing is to provide *open housing* under which anyone with sufficient funds may purchase or rent available housing units.

OPEN LISTING a **listing** given to any number of **brokers** without **liability** to compensate any except the one who first secures a buyer who is ready, willing, and able to meet the terms of the listing or secures the seller's **acceptance** of another **offer.** The sale of the property automatically terminates all open listings.
Example: Quarry offers an *open listing* to 2 brokers, Ridley and Sims. Ridley presents a buyer who eventually purchases the property. Ridley is entitled to a **commission;** Sims is not.

OPEN MORTGAGE a **mortgage** that has **matured** or is overdue and is therefore open to **foreclosure** at any time.
Example: Towns sells a property to Udall. Towns provides financing for the sale in the form of a 5-year, **interest-only** loan. At the end of 5 years, Udall does not pay the **principal** and Towns allows the loan to become an *open mortgage*. This arrangement allows Udall to pay off the loan at any time or Towns to call the loan at any time.

OPEN SPACE land, within a developed area, that is left undeveloped and serves as an **amenity** to surrounding occupants.
Example: A 20-acre **planned unit development** contains 12 acres that are covered by structures and pavement. The remaining 8 acres are left in *open space*.

OPERATING EXPENSES amounts paid to maintain property, such as **property taxes, utilities, hazard insurance.** Excludes **financing** expenses and **depreciation.**
Example: The following are expenses incurred in operating a property:
Operating expenses
  • maintenance
  • management
  • real estate taxes
  • hazard and liability insurance
  • utilities
  • supplies
The following are not categorized as operating expenses:
debt service
  • principal payments
  • interest
  • loan fees
  • participation payments
depreciation
income taxes

OPERATING LEASE a **lease** between the **lessee** and the sublessee who actually occupies and uses the property. See **sublease.**
Example: Figure 118.

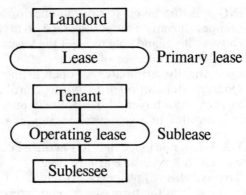

FIGURE 118

OPINION OF TITLE a certificate, generally from an attorney, as to the validity of **title** to property being sold. See **title abstract.**
Example: Based upon the attorney's *opinion of title,* the **title insurance** company insured title to the property.

OPTION the right to purchase or **lease** a property upon specified terms within a specified period.
Example: Moore purchases an *option* on a piece of land. The option runs 90 days and costs $500 per acre. If Moore wishes to purchase the land, she has 90 days to exercise her right and may buy the land for $5,000 per acre. If she decides not to purchase, she **forfeits** the $500 per acre.

ORAL CONTRACT a verbal agreement. With few exceptions, verbal agreements for the sale or use of **real estate** are unenforceable. In most states, contracts for the sale or rental of real estate are, unless they are in writing, unenforceable under the **Statute of Frauds.** Verbal leases for a year or less are often acceptable.
Example: Abel agrees to sell property to Baker. Their contract is oral. Abel changes his mind. He faces no **penalty** because *oral contracts* for the sale of real estate are unenforceable.

ORDINANCES municipal rules governing the use of land.
Examples: Local governments may pass *ordinances* to:
• specify certain land uses in certain areas
• regulate **nuisances**
• specify the manner in which structures are constructed or maintained
• specify the manner in which **subdivisions** are designed
• regulate rental practices
• regulate condominium **conversion** practices

ORDINARY AND NECESSARY BUSINESS EXPENSES a tax term that allows a current deduction for business expenses. Contrasted

with **capital expenditures** and unreasonable expenses.
Example: Each day the apartment manager enjoyed a 3-martini lunch with his friend. He claimed a tax deduction for the lunch expense. The **Internal Revenue Service** contests the deductions because they were not *ordinary and necessary business expenses.*

ORDINARY ANNUITY a series of equal payments, each payment occurring at the end of each equally spaced period.
Example: For a lender the **income stream** from a standard, fixed rate mortgage loan provides an *ordinary annuity* (Figure 119).

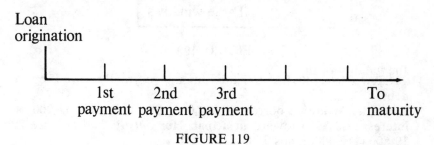

FIGURE 119

ORDINARY INCOME defined by the **Internal Revenue Code** to include salaries, fees, **commissions,** interests, dividends, and many other items. Taxed at regular tax rates. Contrasted with long-term **capital gains,** which receive more favorable tax treatment.
Example: Abel would prefer to convert *ordinary income* into long-term capital gains. He wants to change the nature of property he has from **inventory** to investment.

ORDINARY LOSS for income tax purposes a loss that is deductible against **ordinary income.** Usually more beneficial to a taxpayer than a **capital loss,** which has limitations on deductibility.
Example: The sale of **inventory** at a loss results in an *ordinary loss,* whereas the sale of an investment at a loss results in a capital loss.

ORIENTATION the position of a structure on a **site** relative to sunlight angles and prevailing winds.
Example: A house in Figure 120 has a north-south *orientation* designed to maximize the natural heating effect of the sun in the winter:

ORIGINATION FEES charges to a borrower to cover the costs of issuing the loan, such as **credit** checks, **appraisal,** and **title** expenses.
Example: The lender issued a $50,000 **mortgage** loan and charged a 1% *origination fee* ($500).

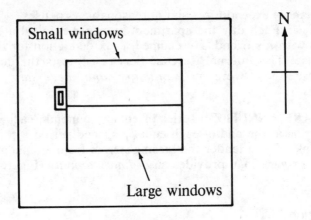

FIGURE 120

OUTSTANDING BALANCE the amount currently owed on a
debt.
Example: Whitman borrowed $10,000. She then paid $1,200 of
interest and $500 toward **principal.** Her *outstanding balance* is
$9,500 ($10,000 minus $500).

OVERAGE in leases for retail stores, amounts to be paid, based on
gross sales, over the **base rent.** See **percentage lease.**
Example: Winfield leases retail space in a shopping center. The
lease calls for a base rent of $2,500 per month plus 5% of gross
sales over $10,000. The first month, Winfield has sales of $20,000.
In addition to the $2,500 base rent, Winfield pays an *overage* of
$500 [.05 × ($20,000 − $10,000)].

OVER AGE 55 HOME SALE EXEMPTION in taxation, an individual over age 55 can sell principal residence at a gain and exclude up
to $125,000 of the gain from taxation. Allowed regardless of the
purchase of another home. Must have used the property as a **principal residence** for 3 of the last 5 years.
Example: Abel, *over age 55*, sells his principal residence, which
he has lived in for the last 3 years, at a $150,000 gain. He may
exclude $125,000 of the gain from taxation. The rest of the gain is
taxable as a **capital gain.**

OVERALL RATE OF RETURN (OAR) the percentage relationship
of **net operating income** divided by the purchase price of property.
See **capitalization rate.**
Example: Property that sells for $1,000,000 is anticipated to
produce a net operating income of $100,000 per year. The indi-

cated *overall rate of return* is 0.10 or 10% $\left(\dfrac{\$100,000}{\$1,000,000}\right)$.

OVERIMPROVEMENT a land use considered too intense for the land.
Example: A proposed house costs $100,000 to construct on a **site** valued at $20,000. It is estimated that the completed house would have a market value of only $110,000. The proposed house is an *overimprovement* of the site.

OVERRIDE 1. a fee paid to someone higher in the organization, or above a certain amount.
Example: In the agreement the salesman was required to pay an *override* of 10% of his gross **commissions** to the managing **broker.**
2. an **estate** carved out of a working interest in an **oil or gas lease.**
Example: The *overriding* **royalty** required 2% of the production of the well be paid to the attorney who negotiated the oil lease.

OWNERSHIP FORM methods of owning **real estate,** which affect **income** tax, **estate tax,** continuity, **liability, survivorship,** transferability, disposition at death and at **bankruptcy.**
Example: *Ownership* forms include:
• **corporation**
• joint tenancy
• **limited partnership**
• **partnership**
• **Subchapter S corporation**
• **tenancy by the entireties**
• **tenancy in common**
• **tenancy in severalty**

OWNERSHIP RIGHTS TO REALTY possession, enjoyment, control, and disposition. See also **fee tail, interest, tenancy.**
Example: By virtue of **title** to the property, Overton enjoys full *ownership rights to realty.* This enables Overton to use the property, **lease** out the property, pledge it as **security** on loans, and sell the property within the restrictions of the law.

P

PACKAGE MORTGAGE a **mortgage** arrangement whereby the **principal** amount loaned is increased because **personalty** (e.g., appliances), as well as **realty** serve as **collateral.**
Example: Simmons applied for a *package mortgage* in order to spread the cost of appliances over 25 years and to pay for them with her home mortgage payment.

PAPER credit given, evidenced by a written obligation that is backed by **property.**
Example: Dunn sells his property for $100,000. He receives $20,000 cash and $80,000 of *paper* that is payable over 20 years at 10% interest.

PARCEL a piece of property under one ownership; a lot in a **subdivision.**
Example: In order to construct the highway, the state must acquire parts of *parcels* A and C in Figure 121. *Parcels* B and D are unaffected.

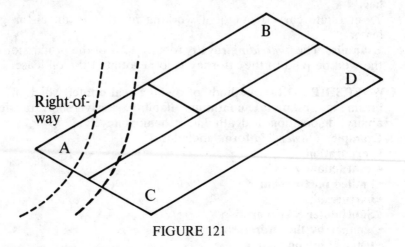

FIGURE 121

PAROL EVIDENCE oral evidence, rather than that contained in documents. The parol evidence rule states that when parties put their agreement in writing, all previous oral agreements merge into the written agreement. The written agreement cannot be contradicted by oral testimony, unless there was a **mistake** or **fraud.**
Example: Carter agrees to buy a house from Dooley, and both sign a written agreement. Carter later argues that Dooley said he'd pay all the loan **discount points.** Under the *parol evidence* rule, courts will interpret the **contract** as it is written.

PARTIAL RELEASE a provision in a **mortgage** that allows some of the property pledged to be freed from serving as **collateral.**
Example: Baker sold 3 acres of land (Figure 122), and accepted a $30,000 purchase money mortgage. *Partial releases* in the mortgage require that, upon each $10,000 **principal** payment, one acre be freed from serving as collateral. The sequence of release was **platted,** and described in the mortgage.

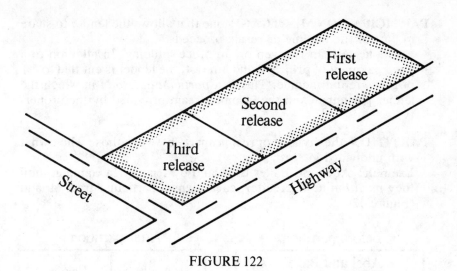

FIGURE 122

PARTIAL TAKING acquisition by **condemnation** of only part of the property or some property rights.
   Examples: Situations calling for *partial takings* (Figure 123).

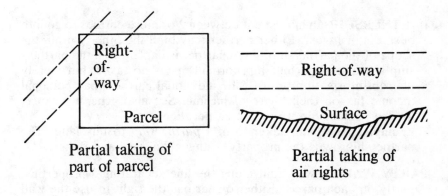

FIGURE 123

PARTICIPATION MORTGAGE one that allows the lender to share in part of the income or resale proceeds.
Example: A loan is given on an office building. In addition to a fixed payment of **principal** and **interest,** the lender is entitled to 2% of gross rental income. This is a *participation loan* in which the lender participates in the **income stream** provided by the property.

PARTITION the division of **real property** between those who own it with **undivided interest.**
Example: Abel and Baker own land by **tenancy in common** until they *partition* it. Thereafter, each owns a particular tract of land (Figure 124).

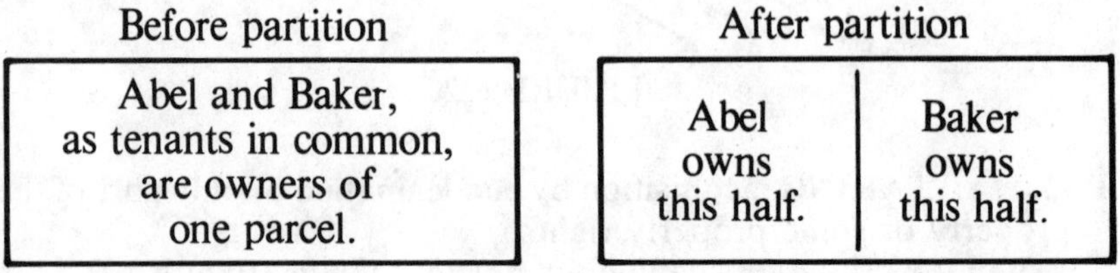

Before partition	After partition	
Abel and Baker, as tenants in common, are owners of one parcel.	Abel owns this half.	Baker owns this half.

FIGURE 124

PARTNERSHIP an agreement between 2 or more entities to go into business or invest. Either partner may bind the other, within the scope of the partnership. Each partner is liable for all the partnership's debts. A partnership normally pays no taxes, but merely files an information return. The individual partners pay personal income tax on their share of **income.** See also **general partner, limited partnership.** Compare **corporation.**
Example: Abel and Baker form a *partnership* to buy land. The partnership owns the property, rather than Abel and Baker.

PARTY WALL a wall built along the line separating 2 properties, partly on each **parcel.** Either owner has the right to use the wall and has an **easement** over that part of the **adjoining** owner's land covered by the wall.
Example: The structures built on lots A and B in Figure 125 are separated by a *party wall*.

PASSIVE INCOME generally, income from **rents, royalties,** dividends, interest, and gains from the sale of securities. **Subchapter S corporations** may not receive more than 20% of their income from passive sources. Regular closely held corporations that receive most of their income from passive sources and have few stockholders may be personal **holding companies.**
Example: *Passive income* includes:

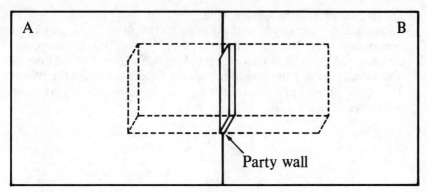

FIGURE 125

- dividends from stocks
- interest from bonds and bank accounts
- **lease** rentals (except for an actively managed rental business, such as for tool rentals)
- **royalties** from book sales
  Active income includes:
- **commissions**
- fees
- **inventory** sales
- salaries
- wages

PASSIVE INVESTOR one who invests money but does not manage the business or property.
Example: Dooley has neither time nor skills to manage the property that he wants to invest in. He forms a **partnership** with a real estate **syndicator** who will devote time and expertise to manage the property for profit. Dooley contributes money but not effort, so he is a *passive investor.*

PASSIVE SOLAR HEATING a system of features incorporated into a building's design to use and maximize the effects of the sun's natural heating capability. See **active solar heating.**
Example: *Passive solar heating* systems use some type of collection and storage element, such as a water-filled partition, which is exposed to the sun during the day and radiates heat to the structure at night. Other features, such as south-facing windows, site **orientation,** roof overhangs, are included to enhance the effects of the sun's heat.

PASS-THROUGH CERTIFICATES interests in a pool of mortgages sold by **mortgage bankers** to investors. Money collected as monthly mortgage payments is distributed to those who own certificates.

Often **guaranteed** by **Ginnie Mae.**
Example: A mortgage banker sells $5,000,000 of *pass-through certificates* in $10,000 denominations, supported by an equal amount of **VA** and **FHA mortgages.** Monthly collections of **interest** and **principal** are remitted to certificate holders, except for ⁴⁴/₁₀₀ of 1% of the annual principal, kept by the mortgage banker as a **servicing** fee (Figure 126).

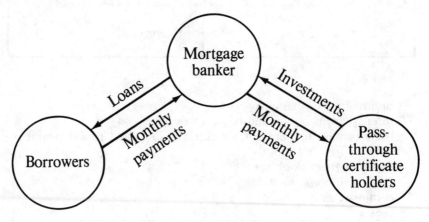

FIGURE 126

PATENT conveyance of **title** to government land.
　Example: The federal government grants a *patent* on land they sell to a mining company.

PENALTY money one will pay for breaking a law or violating part or all of the **terms** of a **contract.**
　Example: *Penalties* are often imposed for:
　• prepaying a loan
　• failing to complete a contract of sale
　• breaking a lease

PENTHOUSE a luxury housing unit located on the top floor of a high-rise building.
　Example: A *penthouse* (Figure 127).

PERCENTAGE LEASE a **lease** of property in which the rental is based on a percentage of the volume of sales made upon the leased premises. It usually stipulates a minimum rental and is regularly used for retailers who are **tenants.** See **overage.**
　Example: The *percentage lease* required the jewelry store to pay as additional rent 6% of annual sales in excess of $100,000. The **base rent** is $6,000 per year.

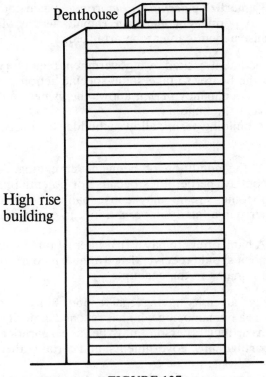

Penthouse

High rise
building

FIGURE 127

PERCOLATION TEST a procedure to measure the drainage characteristics of the soil on a lot. Required in the proper design of
septic tank drainfields.
Example: Carter is developing a **subdivision** in the county. As part
of site preparation, Carter runs *percolation tests* on the soil. From
this information, the engineer can determine the proper size of the
lots and placement of septic tanks.

PERFORMANCE BOND issued by an insurance company; posted
by a party who is to perform certain work. If the work is not
performed, the insurer promises to complete the work or pay damages up to the amount of the bond. Contrast with **completion
bond.**
Example: The contract requires the **contractor** to put up a $10,000
performance bond. If the contractor fails to do the job, the property owner has assurances of compensatory payment from the
insurance company.

PERMANENT MORTGAGE a mortgage for a long period of time
(over 10 years).
Example: The **savings and loan association** promises to originate a

25-year **self-amortizing** *permanent mortgage* when construction is completed. A permanent **mortgage commitment** is often needed before a **construction** loan can be arranged.

PERMIT a document, issued by a government regulatory authority, that allows the bearer to take some specific action.
Example: An occupancy *permit* allows the owner of a building to occupy or rent the building.
Example: A building *permit* allows a builder to construct or modify a structure.

PERPETUITY the condition of being never ending. Most states attempt to outlaw perpetuities because of potential problems. A perpetual income stream may cause bankruptcy. A **deed** that keeps property in a family in *perpetuity* can cause financial hardship.
Example: A bank offers to pay a 10% interest rate in *perpetuity*. A $10,000 deposit should receive $1,000 annual income for as long as the deposit remains in the account.

PERSON in law, an **entity** having legal responsibility. Legally, a natural person is a human being who has reached **majority.** (Compare **minor.**) An artificial person may be a **corporation;** in some instances **partnerships,** governments, and certain other bodies are considered persons.
Example: When negotiating a contract it is important to deal with a **person;** otherwise the contract may be unenforceable.

PERSONAL HOLDING COMPANY in taxation, a term that applies to certain **corporations.** A personal holding company is required to either pay a high tax in addition to the corporate income, or pay out most of the corporate earnings to shareholders each year. Personal holding companies are those that 1) derive most of their earnings from passive sources such as **interest,** dividends, rents, and **royalties,** and 2) have the 5 (or fewer) largest stockholders together own more than 50% of the corporation. See **passive income.**
Example: Abel and Baker are the sole stockholders of the Laid Back Corporation. The corporation's income derives entirely from dividends, interest, and royalties. The corporation is a *personal holding company.* To avoid the personal holding company tax, it pays its earnings to Abel and Baker as a dividend.

PERSONAL PROPERTY same as **personalty.**

PERSONALTY personal property, i.e., all **property** that is not **realty.** Property that is movable, not fixed to land. See **chattel**
Example: The following are *personalty:*

201 PLANNED UNIT DEVELOPMENT

- appliances not permanently attached to **real property**
- cash and securities
- furniture and household items
- **mobile homes** not permanently affixed to a **site**
- vehicles

PER STIRPES a legal method of distributing an **estate** to include the descendants of a deceased legatee, whose share is apportioned among linear descendants.
Example: A person dies intestate. State law requires a *per stirpes* distribution of assets. The decedent had 4 children. Three are surviving; the fourth child died as an adult and left 5 children. The estate is divided into 4 equal parts. Each surviving child of the decedent gets one fourth, and the 5 orphaned grandchildren, as a group, share one fourth.

PHYSICAL DEPRECIATION OR DETERIORATION the loss of value from all causes of age and action of the elements.
Example: Sources of *physical depreciation:*
- breakage
- deferred maintenance
- effects of age on construction material
- normal wear and tear

PIGGYBACK LOAN 1. a combination of the **construction loan** with the permanent **loan commitment.**
Example: The permanent lender would issue a commitment at a 15% rate, effective upon completion of construction. As assurance that the loan will be borrowed even if rates are lower later, the commitment is *piggybacked* to the construction loan, and must be drawn down upon **retiring** the construction loan.
2. one mortgage held by more than one lender, with one lender holding the rights of the others in **subordination.**
Example: A loan is made for 90% of the home price; 80% of the price is supplied by a **savings and loan association,** 10% by an individual, who then has a *piggyback loan.* The piggyback agreement allows the S&L to have priority in **foreclosure.**

PLAINTIFF the person who brings a lawsuit. Contrast with **defendant.**
Example: A *plaintiff* sued for **specific performance** to force the owner of land to sell at the agreed upon terms.

PLANNED UNIT DEVELOPMENT (PUD) a **zoning** classification that allows flexibility in the design of a **subdivision.** Planned Unit Development zones generally set an overall **density** limit for the entire subdivision, allowing the dwelling units to be clustered to provide for common open space. See also **cluster housing, common**

areas.
Example: A typical *planned unit development* (Figure 128).

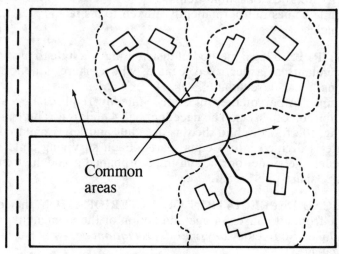

Common
areas

FIGURE 128

PLANNING COMMISSION a group of citizens appointed by local government officials to conduct hearings and recommend amendments to the **zoning ordinance.** The planning commission generally oversees the work of a professional planning department, which prepares a comprehensive plan. May also be called a planning board, zoning commission, or zoning board, depending on locality.
Example: Moore wishes to have her land **rezoned** from low **density** to high density **residential.** She submits her request to the *planning commission.* The commission holds a public hearing and asks the planning department to evaluate the change. Following the review, the commission makes a recommendation to the city council on whether or not to grant the request.

PLAT a plan or map of a specific land area. See also **description, government rectangular survey.**
Example: *Plat* of a **subdivision** (Figure 129).

PLAT BOOK a public record containing maps of land, showing the division of the land into streets, blocks, and lots and indicating the measurements of the individual **parcels.**
Example: Sample entry in a *plat book* for property number 001 in district 07-510-AZ (Figure 130).

PLEDGED ACCOUNT MORTGAGE (PAM) a type of home purchase loan under which a sum of cash contributed by the owner is

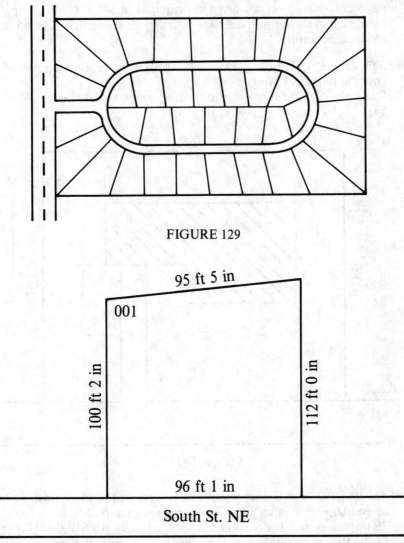

FIGURE 129

FIGURE 130

set aside in an account pledged to the lender. The account is drawn down during the initial years of the loan to supplement periodic mortgage payments. The effect is to reduce the payment amounts in early years. See **graduated payment mortgage.** Compare **collateral.**

Example: Abel obtains a *pledged account mortgage.* The loan **principal** is $40,000 and Abel makes a down payment of $10,000. $5,000 of this amount is put in a pledged account. Abel makes payments based on a mortgage principal of $45,000 but the payments are reduced in the first 3 years by drawing upon the $5,000 pledged account.

PLOT PLAN a diagram showing the proposed or existing use of a specific **parcel** of land.
Example: A *plot plan* submitted to a **zoning** review board (Figure 131).

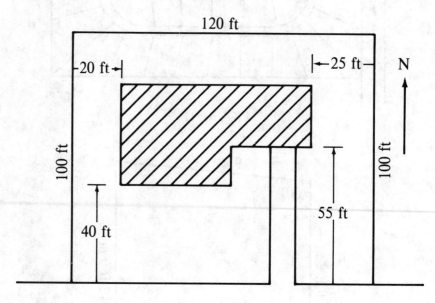

FIGURE 131

PLOTTAGE VALUE increment in the value of land comprised by **assemblage** of smaller plots into one ownership.
Example: A and B are **adjacent** lots, each worth $10,000 (Figure 132). By combining them under one owner the entire **tract** becomes large enough for use as a restaurant **site,** worth $50,000. The *plottage value* is $30,000.

POCKET CARD required for salespersons and **brokers** in most states. Issued by the state licensing agency, it identifies its holder as a **licensee** and must be carried at all times.
Example: Figure 133

POINTS fees paid to induce lenders to make a **mortgage** loan. Each point equals 1% of the loan **principal.** Points have the effect of reducing the amount of money advanced by the lender. Same as *discount points*.

Example: Mortgage lenders commonly charge one *point* as a loan **origination fee.** Additional points may be charged to raise the loan **yield** to current **market interest rates.** If only one point is required,

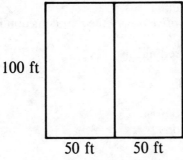

100 ft

50 ft   50 ft

Two lots valued at $10,000 each

100 ft

100 ft

Lots combined with value of $50,000

FIGURE 132

Real Estate Broker Identification Card

Expires 3-1-33

Charlie Baker
101 Maple Road
Springfield, MA 90001

FILE   025   LICENSE   360245

(NOT A LICENSE — FOR IDENTIFICATION ONLY)

FIGURE 133

a borrower requesting a loan of $50,000 would actually receive only $49,500. The $500 cost of the point is a **closing** cost.

POLICE POWER the right of any governmental body to enact and enforce regulations for the order, safety, health, morals, and general welfare of the public.
Example: Types of *police power* mechanisms applied to **real property:**
• **condemnation** proceedings
• **housing codes**
• public **nuisance** ordinances
• **rent controls**
• special operating **licenses**
• **subdivision** regulations
• **zoning**

POSITIVE LEVERAGE the use of borrowed funds that increases the return on an investment.
Example: See **leverage.**

POSSESSION the holding, control, or custody of property for one's use, either as owner or person with another right. See also **ownership rights to realty, title.**
Example: Actual *possession:* within immediate occupancy
Adverse *possession:* see definition
Constructive *possession:* as stated in the public record

POWER OF ATTORNEY an **instrument** authorizing a person to act as the **agent** of the person granting it. See **attorney-in-fact.**
Example: Abel is going on a 6-month vacation to China. He wants to sell his house in Colorado for $75,000 but will not be present to sign the **deed.** He gives his trusted friend Baker the *power of attorney* so Baker may deed the property to a **grantee** while Abel is in China.

POWER OF SALE a clause sometimes inserted in **mortgages** or **deeds of trust;** grants the lender (or **trustee**) the right to sell the property upon certain **default.** The property is to be sold at **auction** but court authority is unnecessary.
Example: The **savings and loan association** exercises the *power of sale* clause in the mortgage by selling the defaulted property at public auction for $100,000. Since the debt was $60,000 and expenses of sale $5,000, the $35,000 surplus belongs to the borrower.

PRAIRIE HOUSE an early twentieth century style house with a long, low roof line, continuous row of windows and an unornamented exterior. Designed to satisfy the physical and psychologi-

cal needs of the inhabitants, it is unlike the traditional concept of a house that is a box subdivided into smaller boxes (rooms), each with some doors and windows.
Example: Figure 134.

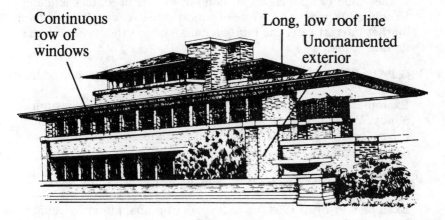

Continuous row of windows

Long, low roof line
Unornamented exterior

FIGURE 134

PRECLOSING a rehearsal of the **closing** whereby **instruments** are prepared and signed by some or all parties to the **contract.** Used when closings are expected to be complicated.
Example: *Preclosings* are used when there are many parties to an agreement. This sometimes occurs when there are multiple loans to be arranged and/or multiple buyers or sellers, as when **syndicating** property or converting an apartment complex to a **condominium.**

PREFABRICATED 1. constructed, as building components, in a factory prior to being erected or installed on the construction site. 2. constructed, as a house, of prefabricated components. See **modular housing.**
Example: The **subdivision** is developed with *prefabricated* housing. The roof, exterior walls, and interior partitions are *prefabricated* in a factory in Dallas.

PRELEASE to obtain **lease** commitments in a building or complex prior to its being available for occupancy.
Example: As a requirement for obtaining a **permanent mortgage,** a developer must *prelease* 50% of the space in the office building.

PREMISES land and **tenements;** an **estate;** the subject matter of a **conveyance.**
Example: In selling the property, Carter **deeds** the *premises* to Dawson. Dawson later **leases** the *premises* to Enwright.

PREMIUM 1. the cost of an insurance policy.
Example: Annual or monthly *premiums* are generally required for **hazard insurance, liability insurance,** and life insurance. **Title insurance** *premiums* are paid only once.
2. the value of a **mortgage** or **bond** in excess of its **face amount.**
Example: When the face rate of a mortgage exceeds the prevailing **market interest rate,** the mortgage may be worth a *premium* over its **face value.**

PREPAID EXPENSES amounts that are paid prior to the period they cover.
Example: Simmons pays the full **premium** on a 3-year insurance policy. When her accountant prepares Abel's financial statement, the proportionate value of the unused premium is presented as a *prepaid expense.*

PREPAID INTEREST interest paid in advance of the time it is earned.
Example: Prior to 1968, up to 5 years of prepaid interest could be deducted from taxable income; until 1976 up to one year could be deducted. Since then *prepaid interest* has not been deductible. An exception is for **points** paid on one's residence, provided that the practice and amount is customary in the local area.

PREPAYMENT CLAUSE a clause in a **mortgage** that gives a **mortgagor** (borrower) the privilege of paying the mortgage indebtedness before it becomes due. Sometimes there is a **penalty** for prepayment, with **waiver** of the interest that is not yet due.
Example: The *prepayment clause* in the mortgage allows the unpaid **principal** to be **retired** by the owner with a 1% penalty.

PREPAYMENT PENALTY fees paid by borrowers for the privilege of **retiring** a loan early.
Example: Abel borrowed $50,000 last year at 15% interest on a 30-year mortgage. If he pays the remaining **principal** now, in one lump sum, there will be a 5% *prepayment penalty* that amounts to $2,500.

PREPAYMENT PRIVILEGE the right of a borrower to **retire** a loan before **maturity.**
Example: A loan on **commercial property** is closed (no *prepayment privilege*) for the first 5 years. Afterwards it can be prepaid without **penalty.**

PRESALE sale of proposed properties, such as **condominiums,** before construction begins.
Example: The developer *presold* 40% of the condominium units at a $5,000 **discount** for each unit before construction began. Based

on the *presales,* the developer was able to get a favorable **construction loan.**

PRESCRIPTION acquiring rights through **adverse possession.**
Example: For years, Fulson, owner of a **landlocked** parcel, has continually and openly crossed the property of Grissom to reach the highway. Fulson eventually acquires an **easement** by *prescription* to the access route, thus preventing Grissom from blocking his way.

PRESENT VALUE OF ANNUITY the value now of a level stream of income to be received each period for a finite number of periods. See **ordinary annuity.**

$$\text{Present value of annuity} = \frac{1 - \dfrac{1}{(1 + i)^n}}{i}$$

where i = interest rate
n = number of periods
Example: The *present value of an annuity* of \$1.00 per year for 10 years, discounted at 12%, is \$5.65. Selected present values of annuity factors for annual income of 1 are shown in Table 28.

Table 28

Life of the Annuity (years)	Discount Rates			
	5%	10%	15%	20%
1	.952	.909	.870	.833
2	1.859	1.736	1.626	1.528
3	2.723	2.487	2.283	2.016
4	3.546	3.170	2.855	2.589
5	4.329	3.791	3.352	2.991
10	7.722	6.144	5.019	4.192
15	10.380	7.606	5.847	4.675
20	12.462	8.514	6.259	4.870
25	14.094	9.077	6.464	4.948
30	15.372	9.427	6.566	4.979

PRESENT VALUE OF ONE the value today of an amount to be received in the future, based on a **compound interest** rate.
Example: At a 12% interest rate, the receipt of one dollar one year from now has a *present value* of \$.89286 (slightly more than 89 cents). One dollar to be received in 2 years has a *present value* of \$.79719 (under 80 cents). Factors are based on the following formula:

$$\text{Present worth (1 factor)} = \frac{1}{(1 + i)^n}$$

where i = interest rate

n = number of periods

See Table 29.

TABLE 29

Number of Years until $1 Is Received

	Rates			
	5%	10%	15%	20%
1	.952381	.909091	.869565	.833333
2	.907029	.826446	.756144	.694444
3	.863838	.751315	.657516	.578704
4	.822702	.683014	.571753	.482253
5	.783526	.620921	.497177	.401878
10	.613913	.385543	.247185	.161506
15	.481017	.239392	.122894	.0649055
20	.376889	.148644	.0611003	.0260841
25	.295302	.092296	.0303776	.0104826
30	.231377	.057308	.015103	.004212

PRIMARY LEASE a **lease** between the owner and a tenant whose **interest,** all or in part, has been sublet.
Example: Figure 135.

PRIME RATE the lowest commercial **interest rate** charged by banks on short-term loans to their most credit-worthy customers. The prime rate is not the same as the long-term mortgage rate, though it may influence long-term rates. Also, it is not the same as the consumer loan rate that is charged on personal property loans and credit cards. Mortgage rates and consumer loan rates are generally higher than the prime rate, but exceptions occur at times.
Example: The Chemical Bank and the Chase Manhattan Bank offer a *prime rate* of 12%. Gulf Oil is a prime customer and at that rate may borrow loans up to 270 days. Chemical Bank offers construction loans at 4 **points** over the *prime rate.*

PRIME TENANT in a shopping center or office building, the tenant who occupies the most space. Prime tenants are considered credit worthy and attract customers or traffic to the center. See also **anchor tenant.**
Example: Huntley is developing an office building with 40,000 square feet of leasable space. Of this, 20,000 square feet are **prel-**

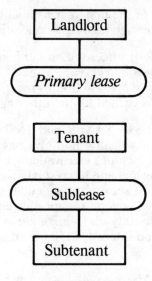

FIGURE 135

eased to a *prime tenant,* Diesoil. The **credit rating** and prestige of the prime tenant allow Huntley to obtain **financing** and prelease the remaining space to other tenants.

PRINCIPAL 1. the one who owns or will use property.
Example: The *principals* to the **lease** are the **landlord** and **tenant;** *principals* to a sale are the buyer and seller.
2. One who contracts for the services of an **agent** or **broker,** the broker's or agent's **client.**
Example: Grey wishes to purchase a shopping center. Grey engages Jamison, a mortgage broker, to arrange **financing.** Jamison arranges a loan in the name of the *principal,* Grey. The loan is payable as **interest** only for 5 years, with the *principal* payable as a **balloon payment** at the end of year 5.
3. the amount of money raised by a mortgage or other loan, as distinct from the **interest** paid on it.
Example: Abel arranged a loan with $100,000 principal on his home. The first monthly payment is $1,200 including $1,000 interest and $200 that **amortized** the *principal.*

PRINCIPAL AND INTEREST PAYMENT (P&I) a periodic payment, usually paid monthly, that includes the **interest** charges for the period plus an amount applied to **amortization** of the **principal** balance. Commonly used with amortizing loans. See **mortgage constant, amortization.**
Example: A $1,200 annual *principal and interest payment* is required by a $10,000 **face value** amortizing mortgage at a 10%

interest rate. $1,000 of the first year payment is required for interest; $200 reduces the outstanding balance to $9,800.

PRINCIPAL BROKER the licensed broker responsible for the operations conducted by the **brokerage** firm.
Example: As *principal broker,* Collins receives a 10% **override** on all sales **commissions** earned by the other **agents.**

PRINCIPAL, INTEREST, TAXES and INSURANCE PAYMENT (PITI) the periodic (typically monthly) payment required by an amortizing loan that includes **escrow** deposits. Each periodic payment includes a **principal and interest payment** plus a contribution to the escrow account set up by the lender to pay insurance premiums and property taxes on the mortgaged property.
Example: Abel's monthly *PITI payment* is $950. This includes $750 for **principal and interest,** $150 for **ad valorem taxes** and $50 for insurance.

PRINCIPAL MERIDIAN one of the prime **meridians** used in the **government rectangular survey** method of land **description** to locate **range lines.**
Example: *Principal meridians* within the state of California are shown in Figure 136.

PRINCIPAL RESIDENCE the place one lives in most of the time. May be a single-family house, **condominium,** trailer, or houseboat. To defer **capital gain** taxes on the profit from a home, the home must be used as the taxpayer's *principal residence.*
Example: Collins spends 10 months each year living in a rented apartment in downtown Seattle. She spends 2 months in a home she owns in San Diego. The rented apartment is her *principal residence.*

PRIORITY legal precedence; having preferred status. Generally, upon **foreclosure,** lenders are repaid according to priority.
Example: Abel's home was foreclosed and sold for $25,000. Unpaid taxes and attorney's fees were accorded *priority,* and paid in full. The rest of the sales proceeds was applied against the **first mortgage.** There was nothing for the **second mortgage,** because it was lower in *priority.*

PRIVATE MORTGAGE INSURANCE **default** insurance on conventional loans, provided by private insurance companies. See **mortgage insurance.**
Example: Lawton wishes to obtain a home purchase loan covering 90% of value. The lender requires Lawton to acquire *private mortgage insurance* as a condition for granting any loan for more than 80% of value.

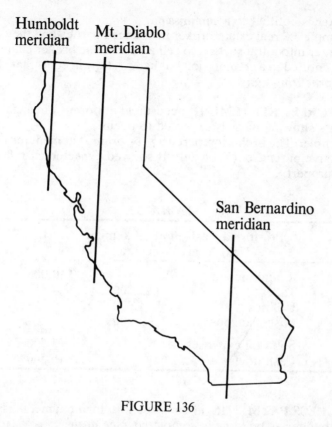

Humboldt
meridian

Mt. Diablo
meridian

San Bernardino
meridian

FIGURE 136

PRIVATE OFFERING an investment or business offered for sale to
a small group of investors, generally under exemptions to registration allowed by the **Securities and Exchange Commission** and state
securities registration laws.
Example: The **syndicator** prepared a *private offering* of the **equity**
in the apartments. Up to 35 persons are allowed to participate in
the purchase. If more persons are allowed, the **syndicator** must
register a **public offering** with the state securities commissioner or
the U.S. Securities and Exchange Commission (SEC).

PROBATE OR PROVE to establish the validity of the **will** of a
deceased person.
Example: Hughes died. The **executor** appealed to the *probate*
court that a certain document was the **valid** will that Hughes
left.

PROCEEDS FROM RESALE same as **resale proceeds.**

PROCURING CAUSE a legal term that means the cause resulting in
accomplishing a goal. Used in **real estate** to determine whether a

broker is entitled to a **commission.**
Example: A real estate broker introduced parties and they agreed to enter into a transaction to sell a home. The broker claimed she was entitled to a commission but had to show in court that she was the *procuring cause.*

PRO-FORMA STATEMENT according to form. Financial statements showing what is expected to occur.
Example: The **broker** prepared a *pro-forma* statement for the prospective purchaser (Table 30). It showed expected cash flows for the property:

TABLE 30

Pro-forma Cash Flow Statement
Next Year, Projected

Rental income		$10,000
Taxes	−$2,000	
Utilities	−1,000	
Miscellaneous	− 500	
Subtotal expenses		−3,500
Cash flow		$6,500

PROGRESS PAYMENTS in construction, loan payments issued to the builder as building is completed. See **draw.**
Example: For the $100,000 **construction loan,** the *progress payments* were $20,000 upon buying the lot and a like amount upon pouring the foundation, roofing, wiring, and completion of all work.

PROMISSORY NOTE a promise to pay a specified sum to a specified **person** under specified **terms.** See also **note.**
Example: Figure 137.

PROPERTY 1. the rights that one individual has in lands or goods to the exclusion of all others; rights gained from the ownership of wealth. See **real property, personalty; possession, title.**
Example: An individual may own *property* with the associated rights to enjoyment, control over others' use of the property, and disposition, subject to government-imposed **restrictions.** Groups of individuals may own *property,* with ownership rights shared collectively. Governments may also own *property,* held for public use.
2. real estate

Example: The appraiser needed to inspect the *property* prior to establishing its value.

```
              Promissory Note

    I, June Monroe, do promise to pay City
Finance Co. the sum of $50,000.  Repayment is
to be made in the form of 300 equal payments
at 12% interest, or $526.61 payable on the
1st of each month, beginning 8/1/84 until the
total debt is satisfied.
                       Signed,

                       June Monroe
                          7/15/84
```

FIGURE 137

PROPERTY LINE the recorded **boundary** of a plot of land.
  Example: Figure 138.

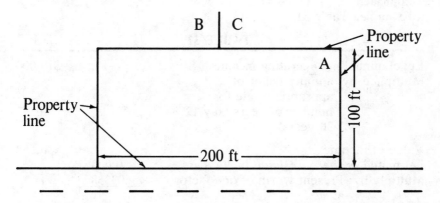

FIGURE 138

PROPERTY MANAGEMENT the operation of property as a business, including rental, rent collection, **maintenance,** etc.
  Example: The following tasks are often required in the ownership of property:
Property management
• accounting and reporting
• leasing
• maintenance and repair

- paying taxes
- provision of utilities and insurance
- remodeling
- rent rate setting and collection
Investment management
- acquisition and disposition
- development and rehabilitation feasibility
- financing
- income tax accounting

PROPERTY REPORT required by the **Interstate Land Sale Act** for the sale of **subdivisions** of 50 lots or more, if the subdivisions are not otherwise exempt. Filed with HUD's **Office of Interstate Land Sales Registration (OILSR).**
Example: A **subdivider** wishes to sell lots in a 55-lot development, through an interstate commerce promotional plan. She is required to file a *property report* with OILSR.

PROPERTY RESIDUAL TECHNIQUE in **appraisal,** a method for estimating the value of property based on estimated future income and the **reversionary value** of the building and land. See **income approach**.
Example: Table 31.

TABLE 31

Level annual **net operating income**		$10,000
Multiplied by: **annuity factor** of appropriate rate for number of years (say 12%, 30 years)		× 8.0552
Value of income		$80,552
Estimated *property residual* in 30 years	$50,000	
Multiply by: Present worth of one factor at 12%	× .03338	
Present worth of reversion		$1,669
Estimated property value		$82,221

PROPERTY TAX a government **levy** based on the **market value** of privately owned property. Sometimes referred to as **ad valorem tax** or real estate tax.
Example: Homeville assesses a *property tax* at the rate of $.50 per $100 of market value. Kilmer pays a tax of $500 on a property valued at $100,000.

Proration - allocating of closing costs + credits to buyers + sellers

PRORATE to allocate between seller and buyer their proportionate share of an obligation paid or due; for example, to prorate real

dividing monies:

? same as opportionment

property taxes or insurance.

Example: Property taxes were $730, assessed for the calendar year and paid by the seller on April 30. The property was sold on September 15 (Figure 139). It is necessary to *prorate* property taxes so that the buyer and seller each pay a proportionate share for his or her ownership period. There are 107 days from September 15 to December 31. Therefore the buyer must pay $214 at **closing,** based on a daily rate of $2.00.

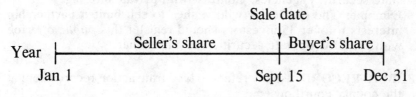

FIGURE 139

PROSPECT a **person** considered likely to buy. A prospective purchaser.

Example: All of the persons who request further information about the advertised property are considered *prospects*.

PROSPECTUS a printed descriptive statement about a business or investment that is for sale, to invite the interest of prospective investors.

Example: A **syndicator** prepared a *prospectus* that disclosed all **material facts** about the property being offered. Before it is approved by the SEC or state securities commissioner, it is called a **red herring.** If it need not be approved, it is called a **descriptive memorandum.**

PROXY a person who represents another, particularly in some meeting. Also, the document giving to another the authority to represent.

Example: Abel could not be at the **cooperative** apartment association's annual meeting, so he cast his vote by *proxy*.

PUBLIC HOUSING government-owned housing units made available to low-income individuals and families at no cost or for nominal rental rates. Contrast to **low-income housing.**

Example: The Metropolitan Housing Authority operates several *public housing* projects for those who cannot afford decent housing on the rental market.

PUBLIC LANDS acreage held by the government for conservation purposes. Public lands are generally undeveloped, with limited activities such as grazing, wildlife management, recreation, timbering, mineral development, water development, and hunting.

Example: Many western states, such as Alaska and Nevada, have large amounts of *public lands*. A part of this area is held by the federal government and is dedicated to national parks, wilderness, and wildlife refuges. Some oil and mineral exploration is allowed under **lease** to private firms.

PUBLIC OFFERING soliciting the general public for the sale of investment units. Generally requires approval by the SEC and/or state securities agencies. Contrast with **private offering.**
Example: The **syndicator** who wishes to sell **limited partnership** interests to over 35 investors should register this *public offering* with the SEC or state securities commissioner.

PUBLIC RECORD usually refers to land transaction records kept at the county courthouse.
Example: Documents that are evidence of real estate transactions should be taken to the county courthouse to be officially entered in the *public record*. Recording gives **constructive notice** of a document's existence.

PUBLIC SALE an **auction** sale of property with **notice** to the general public.
Example: After **foreclosure**, a *public sale* was effected. It was advertised in the local newspaper in advance. The property was auctioned off on the courthouse steps to the highest bidder.

PUEBLO OR ADOBE an early twentieth century house that is made of adobe brick or some other material made to look like adobe brick. The characteristic projecting roof beams are called viga.
Example: Figure 140.

PUFFING overstating the qualities of a property.
Example: ''This house has the most efficient floor plan of any home in the world'' is an example of a salesperson's *puffing*.

PUNCH LIST an enumeration of items that need to be corrected prior to a sale.
Example: The buyer refuses to close the purchase until the builder fixes the leaky roof and replaces the defective carpeting—the 2 items on the buyer's *punch list*.

PUR AUTRE VIE for the life of another. An **estate** one person grants to another, only for the duration of the life of a third person.
Example: Abel grants a **life estate** to Baker to use Abel's ranch until Baker's wife dies. Baker has a life estate *pur autre vie*.

PURCHASE AGREEMENT same as **contract of sale.**

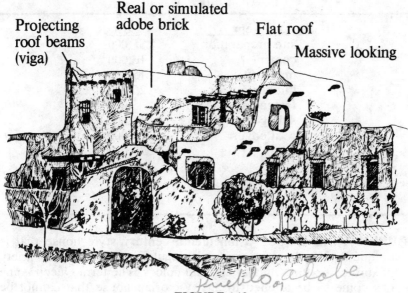

Projecting roof beams (viga)

Real or simulated adobe brick

Flat roof

Massive looking

FIGURE 140

PURCHASE MONEY MORTGAGE a **mortgage** given by a **grantee** (buyer) to a **grantor** (seller) in part payment of the purchase price of **real estate**.
Example: Lamar wishes to purchase a house from Murphy. The sale price is $75,000. Lamar will assume Murphy's existing mortgage in the amount of $50,000. In addition, Lamar gives Murphy a *purchase money mortgage* of $15,000, plus $10,000 in cash to close the sale.
(note: a purchase money mortgage can be a **first mortgage** or junior **lien,** depending on its **priority**).

Q

QUADRANGLE a square-shaped land area, 24 miles on each side, used in the **government rectangular survey** method of land **description**. Each quadrangle contains 16 **townships**.
Example: See example for **government rectangular survey**.

QUANTITY SURVEY a method used by **appraisers** to estimate **reproduction cost** (new) of an **improvement;** detailed cost estimate of all materials, labor, and overhead required to reproduce a structure. See **cost approach**.
Example: A simplified *quantity survey* estimate of reproduction cost (new) is shown in Table 32.

TABLE 32

Item	Cost
site preparation	$5,000
cement	10,000
masonry	15,000
lumber	25,000
fasteners	5,000
siding	15,000
roof cover	10,000
labor	30,000
fees	5,000
financing	10,000
Total cost	$130,000

QUEEN ANNE HOUSE a nineteenth century style house that is unique-looking, multi-story, and irregular in shape with a variety of surface textures, materials, and colors. The term Queen Anne has come to be applied to any Victorian house that cannot be otherwise classified.
Example: Figure 141.

QUIET ENJOYMENT the right of an owner or any other **person** legally entitled to **possession** to the use of property without interference.
Example: The landlord, unhappy with a low rental rate, continually blocks the driveway of the tenant. The tenant sues for *quiet enjoyment.*

QUIET TITLE (ACTION) court action to settle a title dispute.
Example: People may use quiet **title** action to:
• substantiate the **title** of a squatter
• extinguish **easements**
• release a **dower** interest
• remove any **cloud on title**

QUIET TITLE SUIT (OR ACTION) a suit in court to remove a defect, **cloud on the title,** or suspicion regarding legal rights of an owner to a certain **parcel** of **real property.**
Example: In an *action to quiet title,* the landowner of record brought the **adverse possessor** to court that required him to establish his claim or be forever barred from claiming the property.

QUITCLAIM DEED a **deed** that conveys only the **grantor's** rights or interest in real estate, without stating the nature of the rights and with no **warranties** of ownership. Often used to remove a possible **cloud on the title.** Contrast with **general warranty deed.**

Projecting
upper stories

Unique looking

Multi-story

Turrets

Bay windows

Big chimneys

Variety of
surface textures

Various forms
of windows

Many
small
details

Queen Ann House

FIGURE 141

Example: It is discovered during a **title** search that a certain property was at one time held by a **partnership** that later **abandoned** the property. To obtain a **marketable title,** the current owner obtains *quitclaim deeds* from all partners in the old partnership.

R

Racial Steering ~ influencing a persons choice based on race

RANGE LINES lines parallel to a **principal meridian,** marking off the land into 6-mile strips known as ranges; they are numbered east or west of a principal meridian in the **Government Rectangular Survey.** See **base line.**
Example: Figure 142.

RATE OF RETURN the percentage relationship between the earnings and the cost of an investment. See **internal rate of return, overall rate of return.**
Example: Nickson deposits $100 in a savings account. At the end

of the year Nickson receives a payment of $10. Nickson's *rate of return* is 10%.

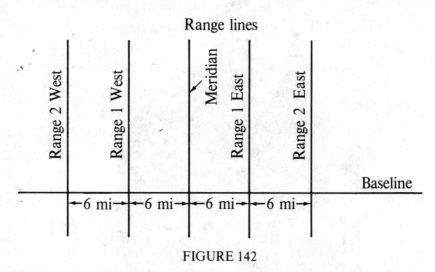

FIGURE 142

RATE OF RETURN OF INVESTMENT same as **recapture rate.**

RAW LAND acreage with no added **improvements,** such as landscaping, drainage, streets, **utilities,** and structures.
Example: The developer bought 50 acres of *raw land* upon which to develop a **subdivision.**

READY, WILLING, AND ABLE capable of an action and disposed to act.
Example: A home is listed with a **broker** who finds a *ready, willing and able* person who agrees to buy under the terms of the **listing.** The seller refuses to sell. The broker has earned a **commission** because she fulfilled the requirements of the listing.

REAL ESTATE 1. in law, land and everything more or less attached to it. Ownership below to the center of the earth and above to the heavens. Distinguished from **personal property.** Same as **realty.**
Example: Figure 143.

2. in business, the activities concerned with ownership and use transfers of the physical property.
Example: The following are engaged in *real estate* business activities:
- **accountants**
- **appraisers**
- attorneys
- **brokers**
- counselors

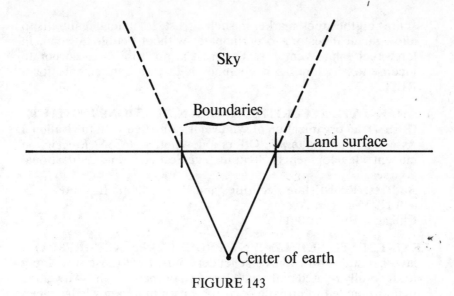

FIGURE 143

- government regulators
- **mortgage brokers**
- mortgage lenders
- salespersons
- **surveyors**
- **title** companies

REAL ESTATE COMMISSION state agency that enforces real estate **license** laws.

Example: The *Real Estate Commission* is usually comprised of between 5 and 15 members who are appointed for a term (2 to 6 years) by the governor, generally confirmed by the state senate. They enforce the real estate laws and regulations, subject to judicial authority. The real estate **commissioner,** a full time employee of the Real Estate Commission, conducts the routine activities of licensing, collecting fees, and other matters.

REAL ESTATE INVESTMENT TRUST (REIT) a real estate mutual fund, allowed by income tax laws to avoid the corporate income tax. It sells shares of ownership and must invest in real estate or **mortgages.** It must meet certain other requirements, including minimum number of shareholders, widely dispersed ownership, **asset** and income tests. If it distributes 90% of its income to shareholders, it is not taxed on that income, but shareholders must include the income in their personal tax returns.

Example: During the early 1970's, many *real estate investment trusts* were created. They raised money from investors for investment in mortgages and real estate **equities.** An individual could buy shares on the stock market in such a **trust.** Its unique feature is to allow small investors to participate, without **double taxation,** in large real estate ventures. The trust is not subject to corporate income tax as long as it complies with the requirements for a REIT.

REAL ESTATE SECURITIES AND SYNDICATIONS INSTITUTE (RESSI) an organization of **syndicators** affiliated with the **National Association of Realtors®.** Offers a newsletter, *RESSI Review,* on current developments affecting **syndications,** and educational courses.
Address: Real Estate Securities and Syndications Institute
430 N. Michigan Avenue
Chicago, Illinois 60611

? Real estate Syndicate - partnership for real estate venture

REAL ESTATE SETTLEMENT PROCEDURES ACT (RESPA) a law that states how **mortgage** lenders must treat those who apply for federally related real estate loans on property with 1-4 dwelling units. Intended to provide borrowers with more knowledge when they comparison shop for mortgage money.
Example: Within 3 days after Abel applies for a loan on a house he wants to buy, the lender is to provide a **good faith** estimate of settlement **(closing)** costs, and a booklet about *RESPA.* In addition, one day before closing, the borrower is entitled to review the closing papers, including all amounts that are known at that time.

also

REALIZED GAIN in a tax-free exchange, a gain that has occurred financially, but is not necessarily taxed. See **boot, recognized gain, Section 1031.**
Example: Abel's land has a tax **basis** of $10,000. Its **market value** is $75,000. He exchanges the land, tax-free under Section 1031, for Baker's warehouse, which was appraised at $75,000. Abel's *realized gain* is $65,000. None of Abel's *realized gain* is recognized, because he did not receive boot.

REAL PROPERTY the rights to use real estate.   Sometimes also defined as **real estate.** *land & what is erected on it*
Example: *Real property* includes, but is not limited to:
• personal residence owned in **fee simple**
• a **life estate** to a farm
• rights to use land under a **lease**
• **easements** and other partial interests

REALTIST a member of the **National Association of Real Estate Brokers,** a group comprised of mainly minority brokers.
Example: Abel, a black real estate broker, paid dues to the

National Association of Real Estate Brokers and subscribed to its code of ethics. Abel is a *Realtist*.

REALTOR® a professional in real estate who subscribes to a strict **Code of Ethics** as a member of the local and state boards and of the **National Association of Realtors®.**
Example: Much of the general public are surprised to discover that only about 40% of licensed real estate **brokers** are eligible to use the designation *Realtor®*.

REALTOR®-ASSOCIATE a licensed salesperson (not **broker**) who is a member of the **National Association of Realtors®.**
Example: Downing passed the salesman's **licensing exam** and is sponsored by a **Realtor®**-broker. Upon being sworn in to the national and state association, Downing is appropriately described as a *Realtor®-Associate*.

REALTORS® NATIONAL MARKETING INSTITUTE (RMNI) an affiliate of the **National Association of Realtors®;** mainly concerned with educational programs and literature for members. Publishes *Real Estate Today* (monthly) and *Real Estate Perspectives* (bimonthly).
Address:
Realtors® National Marketing Institute
430 N. Michigan Avenue
Chicago, Illinois 60611

REALTY same as **real estate.**

REAPPRAISAL LEASE a **lease** where the rental level is periodically reviewed by independent **appraisers.** Often, the **lessor** and **lessee** will each select an appraiser; if they do not agree on a value, they will choose a third appraiser.
Example: In the 20-year *reappraisal lease,* Big Buy Foods agrees to pay the landlord an annual rent of 12% of the property value. Every 5 years the property will be reappraised to determine the rent.

REASSESSMENT the process of revising or updating the value estimate of property for **ad valorem tax** purposes.
Example: Local **property tax** assessors are required to periodically conduct a *reassessment* of all property. Value estimates are revised based on recent sales and other data, and tax **assessments** are based on the new estimates.

REBATE 1. a refund resulting from a purchase or tax.
Example: To encourage sales of the **condominium** project, the developer offered a $2,500 *rebate* to each purchaser.

2. a kickback of a charge, often illegal if done without knowledge of all parties.
Example: the broker accepted a $50 *rebate* from the insurer each time he sold a home carrying a homeowner's **warranty.**

RECAPTURE CLAUSE in a contract, a clause permitting the party who grants an **interest** or right to take it back under certain conditions.
Example: Carter grants a **lease** to Frank's Furniture, with rent set at 6% of retail sales. The lease contains a *recapture clause* whereby Carter can regain the property unless sales are over $1 million per year.

RECAPTURE OF DEPRECIATION same as **depreciation recapture.**

RECAPTURE RATE in **appraisal,** a term used to describe the rate of recovery of an investment in a **wasting asset.** This rate is added to the **discount rate** to derive a **capitalization rate** in appraisal terminology. May be based on the straight line, **sinking fund,** or annuity method.
Example: A building with a 50-year estimated **useful life** has a 2% straight-line *recapture rate*. At a discount rate of 10%, the capitalization rate is 12%.

RECASTING the process of adjusting a loan arrangement, especially under the threat of **default.** See **workout.**
Example: Pope owns an apartment building with a **mortgage** loan requiring **debt service** of $25,000 per year. Because of a period of high vacancies, Pope's **net operating income** falls to $20,000 per year. To eliminate the **negative cash flow,** Pope appeals to the lender to *recast* the loan by extending the **maturity** and reducing the **interest rate** for the next 2 years.

RECIPROCITY mutual agreement to accept, such as a state's **acceptance,** as **valid** the real estate **license** one has earned in another state.
Example: In the absence of *reciprocity,* Moore must take a new examination to obtain a real estate license in the state which she moves. With *reciprocity* she needs only to present her previously earned license.

RECOGNIZED GAIN in a **tax-free exchange,** the portion of gain that is taxable. A **realized gain** will generally be recognized to the extent of **boot** received. See **Section 1031.**
Example: Abel's land has a tax **basis** of $10,000. It is worth $75,000. He exchanges the land under Section 1031 for Baker's warehouse worth $70,000 and $5,000 of cash. Of Abel's $65,000 realized gain, $5,000 will be *recognized.*

RECONCILIATION in **appraisal,** the process of adjusting **comparables** to estimate the value of the subject being appraised.
Example: An **appraiser** arrives at the market value estimates shown in Table 33 following application of the 3 traditional approaches.

TABLE 33

market comparison:	$85,000
cost approach:	$89,000
income approach:	$84,000

In *reconciliation,* the appraiser considers the appropriateness of each approach to the subject, the quality of available data, and the amount of judgmental **adjustment** required to reach each estimate. Following this review, the appraiser settles on an estimate of $85,000 as her opinion of **market value.**

RECONVEYANCE occurs when a **mortgage** debt is **retired.** The lender **conveys** the property back to the **equity** owner, free of the debt.
Example: The *reconveyance* took place after Abel paid off the loan; Abel promptly **recorded** the *reconveyance* **instrument.**

RECORDING the act of entering in a book of public records **instruments** affecting the **title** to **real property.** Recording in this manner gives **notice** to the world of facts recorded. See **constructive notice, ownership rights to realty.**
Example: By *recording* the **deed** from a sale of property, the purchaser assumes that all subsequent interested parties are given notice of the purchaser's ownership **interests** in the property. **Leases** and **liens** may also be recorded.

RECOURSE the ability of a lender to claim money from a borrower in **default,** in addition to the property pledged as **collateral.**
Example: Ross obtains a **mortgage** loan from Local Savings. Should Ross default on the loan, Local Savings may **foreclose** and force the sale of the mortgaged property. Should the sale fail to satisfy the unpaid loan **principal,** Local Savings has *recourse* to other assets of Ross.

RECOVERY FUND generally administered by the **Real Estate Commission.** Requires **licensees** to contribute, then reimburses aggrieved persons who are unable to collect from **brokers** for wrongdoings.
Example: A typical state's *recovery fund* law requires all new licensees to contribute $10 to the fund. Anytime the fund account balance drops below $500,000, all licensees will be assessed. Payments from the fund to an aggrieved person may not exceed

$10,000; total payments on behalf of any licensee may not exceed $25,000. The recovery fund pays only when the broker does not.

RECTANGULAR SURVEY same as **government rectangular survey method.**

REDEMPTION, EQUITY OF same as **equity of redemption.**

REDEMPTION PERIOD the period during which a former owner can reclaim **foreclosed** property. See **equity of redemption.**
Example: Collins' property was foreclosed. If she acts within her state's *redemption period,* she can reclaim her property by paying the **debt** and legal fees.

RED HERRING a proposed **prospectus** that has not been approved by the **Securities and Exchange Commission** (SEC) or state securities commission. See **public offering.**
Example: A *red herring* is shown in Table 34.

TABLE 34

Proposed Prospectus

A registration statement has been filed with the Securities and Exchange Commission but is subject to change. The securities described herein may not be sold until approval becomes effective.

REDISCOUNT RATE the rate of interest charged to member banks when they borrow from the **Federal Reserve System.** Also called **discount rate.**
Example: The First and Citizens Banks borrows funds from the Federal Reserve for one day and is charged interest at the *rediscount rate.*

REDLINING the illegal practice of refusing to originate **mortgage** loans in certain **neighborhoods** on the basis of race or ethnic composition.
Example: A **savings and loan association** may be accused of practicing *redlining* if it is found that no loans have been originated in predominantly nonwhite neighborhoods. The term derives from the alleged practice of drawing a red line on a map around certain neighborhoods to designate them as off limits for loan approvals.

REDUCTION CERTIFICATE a document in which the **mortgagee** (lender) acknowledges the sum due on the **mortgage** loan. Used when mortgaged property is sold and the buyer assumes the debt.
Example: Abel buys Baker's home and agrees to assume the existing mortgage. They obtain a *reduction certificate* from the mortgage lender stating that the remaining balance is $34,567.89.

REFERRAL the act of suggesting the use of a certain **broker.**
Example: Smith receives several **listings** based on *referrals* from former customers.
Example: A broker agrees to pay a 1% *referral* fee to out-of-state brokers who suggest families that are moving into the area.

REFINANCE the substitution of an old loan(s) with a new loan(s).
Example: Garner has a $30,000 loan against her house. She desires cash to pay for a college education. By *refinancing* the home with a new $40,000 loan, she will realize $9,000 in cash after paying $1,000 in **transaction costs.** See Table 35.

TABLE 35

New loan	$40,000
Old debt	−30,000
Cost of loan	− 1,000
Refinancing: cash proceeds	$9,000

REGENCY an English style 2- or 3-story, symmetrical house with a hip roof. A small octagonal window over the front door is traditional.
Example: Figure 144

REGISTRAR the person who is to maintain accurate official records, such as for **deeds, mortgages,** and other recorded **documents.**
Example: After **closing,** the buyer brought the deed to the *registrar* of deeds for **recording** in the county records.

REGULATION D a regulation of the **Securities and Exchange Commission** that sets forth conditions necessary for a **private offering** exemption.
Example: **Syndicator** Stuart wants to sell 35 **limited partnership** interests in an office building. He applies for an exemption under *Rule 146* to avoid the need of registering a **public offering;** he thereby saves over $100,000 and avoids a 4-month delay.

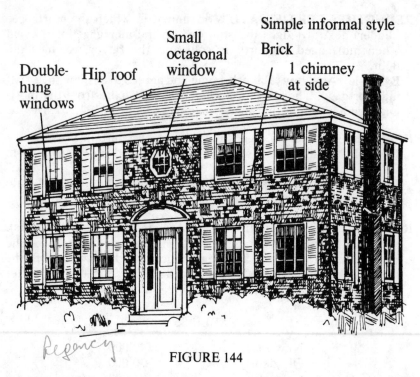

Double-hung windows — Hip roof — Small octagonal window — Simple informal style — Brick — 1 chimney at side

Regency

FIGURE 144

REGULATION Q a federal law that specifies the maximum interest rates that banks and **savings and loan associations** can pay on various types of deposits. Being phased out in the 1980's.
Example: Under *Regulation Q*, a savings and loan association can pay a ¼% higher interest rate than a **commercial bank** for passbook accounts and certain other deposits.

REGULATION Z a federal regulation requiring **creditors** to provide full disclosure of the terms of a loan. Compliance is compulsory for anyone who arranges **credit** for more than 5 sales of **residential** real estate in a year. **Terms** of the loan must be disclosed. The **interest rate** must be stated as an **annual percentage rate** (APR). See also **rescind, rescission.**
Example: Figure 145.

REHABILITATE to restore a structure to a condition of good repair.
Example: An old building has deteriorated to the point of prohibiting profitable operation. The owner faces the choice of **demolition** of the structure and rebuilding or *rehabilitation* to restore the building to a competitive position.

RELEASE to free real estate from a **mortgage**. See **partial release.**
Example: Reynolds owns 100 **acres** of land that is mortgaged for

Convenient Savings and Loan   Account number: 4862-88

Michael Jones
500 Walnut Court, Little Creek, U.S.A.

Annual Percentage Rate The cost of your credit as a yearly rate	Finance Charge The dollar amount the credit will cost you	Amount Financed The amount of credit provided to you or on your behalf	Total of Payments The amount you will have paid after you have made all payments as scheduled
15.37%	$177,970.44	$43,777	$221,548.44

Your payment schedule will be:

Number of Payments	Amount of Payments	When Payments Are Due	
12	$446.62	Monthly beginning	6/1/81
12	$479.67	" "	6/1/82
12	$515.11	" "	6/1/83
12	$553.13	" "	6/1/84
12	$593.91	" "	6/1/85
300 }	Varying from $637.68 to $627.37	" "	6/1/86

Security: You are giving a security interest in the property being purchased.

Late Charge: If a payment is late, you will be charged 5% of the payment.

Prepayment: If you pay off early, you
☒ may   ☐ will not   ☐ have to pay a penalty.
☒ may   ☐ will not   ☐ be entitled to a refund of part of the finance charge.

Assumption: Someone buying your home cannot assume the remainder of the mortgage on the original terms.

See your contract documents for any additional information about nonpayment, default, any required repayment in full before the scheduled date, and prepayment refunds and panalties.

---
e means an estimate

FIGURE 145

$10,000. If she pays the $10,000, the land will be *released* from the lender's **lien** on the property.

RELEASE CLAUSE in a **mortgage,** a clause that gives the owner of the property the privilege of paying off a portion of the mortgage indebtedness, thus freeing a portion of the property from the mortgage. See **partial release.**
Example: Smith, a **developer,** is **subdividing** land that is **financed** under a mortgage. A *release clause* in the mortgage allows Smith

to sell individual lots from the **tract** by retiring portions of the loan. Without the clause, Smith would have to **retire** the entire loan before selling any lots.

RELICTION gradual subsidence of waters, leaving dry land.
Example: As the Great Salt Lake in Utah becomes smaller by evaporation, *reliction* occurs. Generally the new land belongs to the party who owned the rights to the water area (Figure 146).

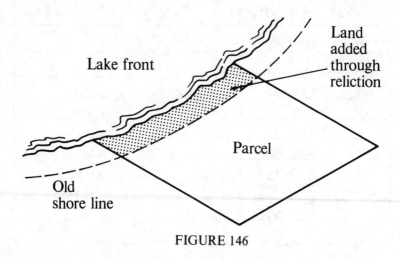

FIGURE 146

RELOCATION CLAUSE a **lease** stipulation that allows the landlord to move the tenant within the building.
Example: The landlord of an office building requires *relocation clauses* in all leases for space that does not include an entire floor. When a new client wishes to lease an entire floor, the landlord may relocate tenants in such a way as to provide the desired space.

REMAINDER an **estate** that takes effect after the termination of a prior estate, such as a **life estate**.
Example: At the death of her husband, Polly Rowen inherits a **life estate** in their home. The *remainder* is **devised** to their son, Paul Rowen. When Polly dies, Paul will gain **title** to the house. Paul is the **remainderman**.

REMAINDERMAN the person who is to receive **possession** of the property after the death of a **life tenant**.
Example: See example under **remainder**.

RENEGOTIATE to legally revise the **terms** of a **contract**.
Example: Abel owes $10,000 to Baker at 7% interest. Abel and Baker *renegotiate* so that Baker agrees to lend $15,000 at 13% interest instead of the original loan.

RENEGOTIATED RATE MORTGAGE (RRM) a long-term **home loan** in which the **interest rate** may be adjusted over the **term.** Adjustments are made at intervals of 3, 4, or 5 years, as specified in the loan agreement. The interest rate may not be adjusted more than ½ **point** per year or 5 points over the loan term. See **rollover loan.**
Example: Abel obtains a *renegotiated rate mortgage* from a federal **savings and loan association.** The adjustment interval is set for 3 years on the 30-year loan term. The interest rate, and thus the monthly payment amount, may be adjusted after year 3, 6, 9, and so on until **maturity.**

RENEWAL OPTION the right, but not the obligation, of a **tenant** to continue a **lease** at specified **term** and **rent.**
Example: Abel leases property from Baker for 20 years at $500 monthly rent. A *renewal option* in the lease gives Abel the right to continue leasing for 5 years beyond the original term (Figure 147).

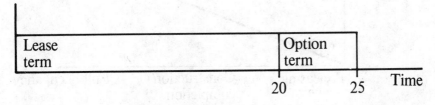

FIGURE 147

RENT a charge for the use of space. See **contract rent, economic rent.**
Example: Abel allows Baker to use property, provided that Baker pays $500 per month (Figure 148). The charge is *rent.*

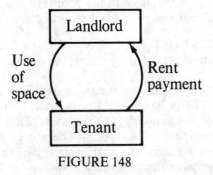

FIGURE 148

RENTABLE AREA same as **net leasable area.**

RENT CONTROL laws that govern the rate that may be charged for
space.
Example: Since the 1940's, apartment owners in New York City
have been restricted by law in the rent that they may charge.
Rent control laws have been adopted by Boston, Washington,
D.C., Los Angeles, and many cities in New Jersey, among others.

RENT-UP PERIOD the time it takes for newly constructed properties to be fully occupied.
Example: Figure 149

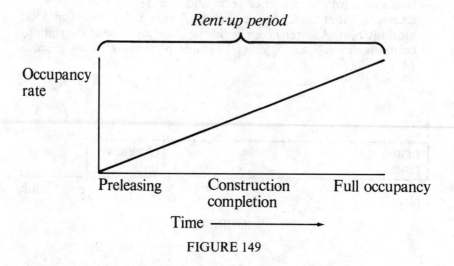

FIGURE 149

REPAIRS work performed to return property to a former condition
without extending its **useful life,** as distinguished from **capital
improvements.** In **income property,** repairs are an **operating
expense** for accounting and tax purposes.
Examples: Patching a hole in the roof (but not replacing the roof)
and mending (but not rebuilding) a fence are *repairs.*

REPLACEMENT COST the cost of erecting a building to replace or
serve the functions of a previous structure. See **reproduction
cost.**
Example: Abel wishes to insure a building against accidental
destruction. The policy should be written so that in the event of
destruction of the building, Abel may replace it with a structure
that serves an identical function. Therefore, Abel should insure
the building in an amount equal to its *replacement cost,* which is
likely to be greater than its **market value.**

REPLACEMENT RESERVE an amount set aside from **net operating income** to pay for the eventual wearing out of short-lived **assets**. See **reserve fund**.
Example: Singer buys new apartments, each containing $1,000 worth of carpeting and appliances that have a 10-year **useful life**. Each year she deposits $100 in a *replacement reserve* account to pay for recarpeting in 10 years.

REPRODUCTION COST the cost of exact duplication of a property as of a certain date. Reproduction differs from replacement in that replacement requires the same functional utility for a property, whereas reproduction is an exact duplication. See **replacement cost**.
Example: In the **cost approach** to property valuation, the **appraiser** estimates the *reproduction cost* of the subject structure. Various deductions are then made to account for **depreciation** in value from the time the building was constructed. These deductions reflect the fact that the building is not new, may not be of modern design, and may have suffered adverse effects due to its location.

RESALE PROCEEDS the amount a former owner receives upon a sale after paying **transaction costs,** remaining debt, and, sometimes, income taxes. Same as **proceeds from resale**.
Example: Table 36.

TABLE 36

Selling price		$100,000
Less: Commissions	$5,000	
Closing costs	1,000	
Unpaid mortgage	60,000	
Capital gains tax	$14,000	− $80,000
Resale proceeds		$20,000

RESCIND to withdraw an **offer** or contract. **Regulation Z** allows a 3-day period in which to *rescind* certain credit transactions.
Example: Abel offers to buy a certain house from Baker. Before Baker accepts, Abel *rescinds* the offer and, therefore, is not obligated to follow through on the purchase.

RESCISSION the act of cancelling or terminating a **contract**. Rescission is allowed when the contract was induced by **fraud, duress, misrepresentation,** or **mistake. Regulation Z** allows one to **rescind** certain credit transactions within 3 business days (not applicable to **first mortgages** on a home); purchasers of certain land that must be registered by **Department of Housing and Urban Development (HUD)** may rescind within 3 business days. See **rescind**.

Example: *Rescission* was allowed by the court for a contract that Abel was induced to enter on the threat of death.

RESERVE FUND an account maintained to provide funds for anticipated expenditures required to maintain a building. A reserve may be required by a lender in the form of an **escrow** to pay upcoming taxes and insurance costs. A **replacement reserve** may be maintained to provide for **replacement cost** of short-lived components, such as carpets, heating equipment, or roofing. Deposit of money into such a fund does not achieve a tax deduction.
Example: A **property management** firm anticipates that property taxes will be due in 6 months, insurance must be renewed in 2½ years, and carpeting must be replaced in 6 years. Accordingly, she establishes a *reserve fund* by depositing a portion of monthly revenues in an account. Monies from the fund will be used at the appropriate time to meet the future expenditures.

RESIDENCE the place where one lives, particularly the **dwelling** in which one lives. See **domicile.**
Example: Baker owns several houses, one of which is Baker's *residence,* another is a vacation home, and the others are **income properties** rented to tenants.

RESIDENTIAL pertaining to housing. See **residential property.**

RESIDENTIAL BROKER one who **lists** and sells houses or **condominiums.** Contrast **commercial broker.**
Example: Baker earned a livelihood as a *residential broker* selling **single-family housing.**

RESIDENTIAL MEMBER (RM) a professional designation offered by the **American Institute of Real Estate Appraisers.**
Example: Collins passed several examinations, prepared demonstration **appraisal** reports, and acquired several years of experience in the appraisal of **residential property.** She has been awarded the *RM* designation, which acknowledges her skills as a residential appraiser.

RESIDENTIAL PROPERTY 1. in real estate **brokerage** terminology, owner-occupied housing.
Example: Rollins is in *residential* real estate. She secures **listings** for **single-family housing** and sells homes.
2. in income taxation terminology, rental units used for **dwelling** purposes, not of a transient (hotel, motel) nature. To qualify as residential, at least 80% of a building's income should be derived from dwelling units.
Example: *Residential* rental *property* owners may be subject to different methods of **depreciation (accelerated cost recovery)** and/or **depreciation recapture** than **commercial property** owners.

RESIDENTIAL SERVICE CONTRACT an insurance **contract** or home **warranty,** generally for one year, covering the plumbing, mechanical, and electrical systems of a home. It is available in most areas upon the purchase of an existing home. Either the buyer or seller can pay for the contract.
Example: Ricky and Rebecca Miller purchase a home. The sellers paid $300 for a *residential service contract*. Three months later, the air-conditioner compressor breaks and costs $800 to repair. The Millers must pay the $100 deductible, and the contract covers the balance of the cost of repair.

RESIDENT MANAGER one who supervises the care of an apartment complex while living in one of the units in the complex.
Example: Carter employs Downs as a *resident manager*. Downs' duties include showing vacant units to prospective tenants, making sure the building is kept clean, and providing entry to repair persons. In return, Downs receives an apartment rent-free.

RESIDUAL value or income remaining after deducting an amount necessary to meet fixed obligations.
Example: After deducting **operating expenses, debt service,** and income taxes from **gross income,** the **equity** investor is entitled to the *residual*. Note, there is no assurance that a residual will exist.
In **appraisal,** a portion of stabilized **net operating income** is deducted to support the value of the **improvements.** The *residual* net operating income is then left to support the value of the **site.**

RESPONDEAT SUPERIOR in **agency** law, the doctrine that a **principal** is liable for the acts of an **agent.**
Example: A real estate **agent** misrepresented the facts about property that was offered for sale. The injured party sued the **agent** and the **broker.** The **broker** was held liable under the doctrine of *respondeat superior*.

RESTRAINT ON ALIENATION a limiting condition on the right to transfer property. If the condition is against public policy or is unreasonable, courts will **void** the condition.
Example: The **deed** that Lowell received when she bought property specifies that she may not resell the property to certain ethnic minorities. Since the clause is illegal, she went to court to remove this *restraint on alienation*.

RESTRICTION a limitation placed upon the use of property, contained in the **deed** or other written **instrument** in the **chain of title** or in local **ordinances** pertaining to land use. See **encumbrance.**
Example: The ownership of property is subject to several *restrictions*. A deed **covenant** may restrict development alternatives, as

may a local **zoning ordinance. Easements** may restrict use of parts of the property. **Liens** may restrict sales. **Building** codes may restrict construction practices.

RESTRICTIVE COVENANT see **restriction.**

RETAINAGE in a construction **contract,** money earned by a **contractor** but not paid to the contractor until the completion of construction or some other agreed-upon date.
Example: The **general contractor** earns $5,000 upon pouring the foundation, plus $15,000 upon completion of the frame, plus $10,000 upon completion of the roof. Of each payment, 10% is held back as *retainage*. It is paid after a **certificate of occupancy** is issued.

RETALIATORY EVICTION the requirement that a tenant vacate a unit in response to a complaint from the tenant concerning the condition of the building. Landlord-tenant laws in many states forbid such **evictions** if proper channels are taken to lodge the complaint.
Example: Six months after Romney moved into an apartment, the heating system stopped operating. The landlord failed to repair the system, and Romney filed a formal complaint with the city **housing code** enforcement office. When the landlord received notice from the city to repair the system, he evicted Romney in a *retaliatory eviction*. The eviction was stopped in court.

RETIRE (A DEBT) to pay off the **principal** on a loan, thereby fulfilling the obligation under the loan contract. See also **amortization.**
Example: When Smith made the last monthly payment on his mortgage loan, he *retired* the debt.
Example: Jones arranged to *retire* her home improvement loan by paying an amount equal to the remaining principal balance.

REVALUATION CLAUSE see **reappraisal lease.**

REVERSE ANNUITY MORTGAGE a type of **mortgage,** designed for elderly homeowners with substantial **equity,** by which a lender periodically (monthly, for example) pays an amount to the borrower. The loan balance increases with interest and periodic payments, causing **negative amortization.**
Example: Roper, age 70, who retired from his job, owns his home **free and clear** of any **liens.** His pension is inadequate to pay expenses. He seeks a *reverse annuity mortgage* that will pay him $200 per month. At a 15% interest rate, he will owe $55,043 in 10 years.

REVERSE LEVERAGE a situation in which financial benefits from ownership accrue at a lower rate than the mortgage interest rate. See **leverage**.

Example: Net-leased property is purchased for $100,000 with a $75,000 mortgage at 12% interest and $25,000 of **equity**. The net rent is $10,000 per year; interest expense is $9,000 per year. The $1,000 difference **(cash flow)** provides a 4% return to the equity owner. In the absence of debt, the owner would receive a 10% return. *Reverse leverage* works against the property owner.

REVERSION the right of a **lessor** to **possess** leased property upon the termination of a **lease**.

Example: Evans purchases the home of Felker, a senior citizen, and leases the home back to Felker for life. Evans has the right to receive rental payments from Felker plus a *reversion* in the property at Felker's death.

REVERSIONARY FACTOR the mathematical factor that indicates the present worth of one dollar to be received in the future. Same as **present value of one**. The formula is

$$\text{Reversionary factor} = \frac{1}{(1 + i)^n}$$

where i = interest rate
  n = number of years (or periods)

Example: The *reversionary factor* for 30 years at 12% is .03338. The present value of the receipt of land that will be worth $50,000 in 30 years is $1,690 (.03338 x $50,000).

REVERSIONARY VALUE the value of property at the expiration of a certain time period.

Example: A **lease** will expire in 30 years. The landlord estimates that the *reversionary value* of the property will be $50,000; that is, the property can be sold in 30 years for $50,000.

REVERSIONARY INTEREST the **interest** a person has in property upon the termination of the preceding **estate**.

Example: Abel is the **remainderman** in property that was granted to Baker for life. Abel has a *reversionary interest* in the property.

REVOCATION an act of recalling a power of authority conferred, as a revocation of a **power of attorney**, a **license**, an **agency**, etc.

Example: The *revocation* of Abel's broker's license, caused by his fraudulent acts, prevented him from earning a living in **real estate**.

REZONING an action to change the designation of a subject **parcel** or group of parcels on the **zoning** map. The effect of a rezoning is to change the permitted uses for the affected parcels. See **down-zoning**.
Example: Brown, whose property was zoned for low-**density** residential, petitioned the city for a *rezoning* to allow construction of an **apartment building**.

RIDER an amendment or **attachment** to a **contract**.
Example: A *rider* to Owen's **homeowner's policy** insured the valuable paintings against fire and theft losses.

RIGHT OF FIRST REFUSAL the opportunity of a party to match the **terms** of a proposed contract before the contract is **executed**.
Example: In some states, tenants whose apartments are converted to **condominium** are given a *right of first refusal* for the unit when it is sold. This means the tenant may purchase the unit at the same price and terms of any outside purchaser.

RIGHT OF SURVIVORSHIP the right of a surviving joint tenant to acquire the **interest** of a deceased joint owner; the distinguishing feature of both **joint tenancy** and **tenancy by the entirety**.
Example: Frank Adams and Anna Adams own property as joint tenants with the *right of survivorship*. When either dies, the entire property will pass to the other without **probate**.

RIGHT-OF-WAY 1. the right to use a particular path for **access** or passage; a type of **easement**.
Example: Lot A has acquired a *right-of-way* across lot B (Figure 150).

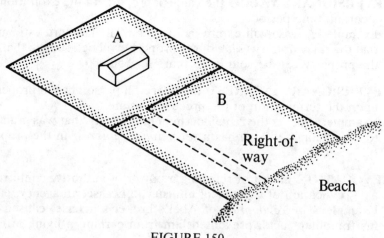

FIGURE 150

2. the areas of subdivisions **dedicated** to government for use for streets, roads, and other public access to lots.

Example: A section of a subdivision with a *right-of-way* for a public road (Figure 151).

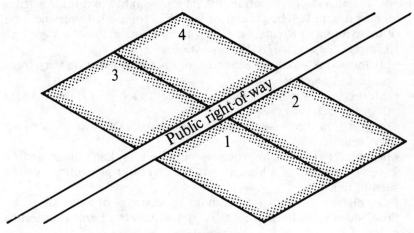

FIGURE 151

Riparian grant

RIPARIAN OWNER one who owns land bounding upon a lake, river, or other body of water. See also **littoral.**

Example: The owner of lot A in Figure 152 is a *riparian owner,* whose ownership rights include access to the river and use of its waters, or **riparian rights.** The owner of lot B has no riparian rights.

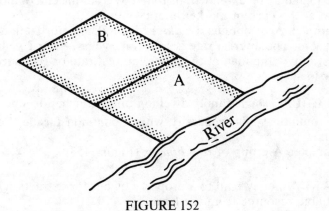

FIGURE 152

RIPARIAN RIGHTS rights pertaining to the use of water on, under, or **adjacent** to one's land. May be qualified to avoid **nuisance** and

pollution. Riparian rights are recognized in most eastern states but rarely in western states, where they recognize **usufructory rights.**
Example: See **riparian owner.**

RISK 1. uncertainty or variability. The possibility that returns from an investment will be greater or less than forecast. Diversification of investments provides some protection against risk.
Example: Types of *risk* in real estate:
• business risk—rents, vacancies, or **operating expenses** vary from projected amounts
• interest risk—property may be subject to a higher rate **mortgage** than the **market rate**
• market rental rate—a long-term lease may lock the owner into low rents
• principal risk—resale proceeds may be less than anticipated
2. the possibility of a loss. Insurance can offer protection against certain risks.
Example: Owners insure buildings against *risk* of loss caused by fires, storms, and other hazards by taking out a **hazard insurance** policy.

ROD a linear unit of measurement equal to 16½ feet.
Example: A certain lot has 165 feet, or 10 *rods,* of road **frontage.**

ROLLOVER LOAN a type of **mortgage** loan, commonly used in Canada, in which the **amortization** of **principal** is based on a long **term** but the **interest rate** is established for a much shorter term. The loan may be extended, or rolled over, at the end of the shorter term at the current market interest rate.
Example: Abel obtains a *rollover loan.* The amortization term is 30 years. The interest rate is 14% for 2 years. After 2 years, Abel must renew the loan at the going interest rate or **refinance** with a new loan.

ROW HOUSE single-family dwelling units attached to one another by common walls, generally with a common **facade.** See **townhouse.**
Example: A group of *row houses* (Figure 153).

ROYALTY money paid to a property owner for extraction of some valuable resource from the land.
Example: Richman owns a 500-**acre** ranch in west Texas. An oil company negotiates a **lease** with Richman to explore for oil on the ranch. Under the agreement, Richman will receive a *royalty* in proportion to the number of barrels of oil pumped from the ranch.

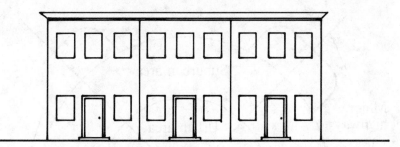

A group of *row houses*

FIGURE 153

RULE OF 72's an approximation of the time it takes for money to double when earning **compound interest.** Divide the percentage rate into 72 to derive the number of years to double the **principal.**
Example: A $1,000 **certificate of deposit** pays a 9% interest rate with annual compounding. In about 8 years the balance will be $2,000. (72 ÷ 9% = 8 years)

RULE OF 78's a method for computing unearned interest used on installment loans with **add-on interest.** The number 78 is based on the sum of the digits from 1 to 12.
Example: A 12-month loan is made for $1,000 with 8% add-on interest. The loan payments are based on a total of $1,080, payable at the rate of $90 per month for 12 months. If the borrower prepays the loan at the end of 1 month, $\frac{12}{78}$ of the $80 interest is charged; the balance of interest is refunded. If the borrower prepays at the end of the second month, $\frac{12+11}{78} = \frac{23}{78}$ is charged. Prepayment at the end of the eleventh month results in a $\frac{1}{78}$ refund.

RUN WITH THE LAND an expression indicating a right or **restriction** that affects all current and future owners of a property. Contrasted to an agreement, between a current owner and other parties, that is not passed on to future owners in a **deed.**
Example: A **covenant,** written into the **deed,** prohibits the property from being used as a liquor store. The restriction *runs with the land,* and all future owners are restrained from violating the covenant.

RURBAN areas, on the fringe of urban development, that are in the process of being developed for urban uses.
Example: Figure 154.

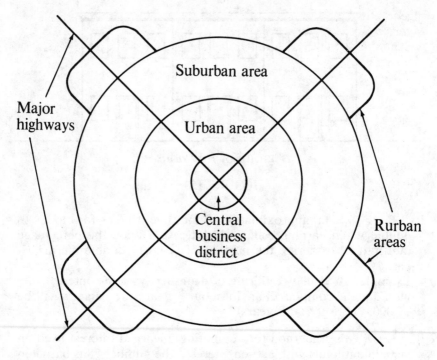

FIGURE 154

RURAL pertaining to the area outside the larger and moderate-sized
cities and surrounding population concentrations. Generally characterized by farms, ranches, small towns and unpopulated
regions. Compare **suburb.**
Example: Garrison grew up on a farm in a *rural* area of Indiana.
She later moved to Chicago and lived in a suburban town nearby.
Garrison invested in *rural* land, hoping to be able to return at
retirement.

S

SALES CONTRACT a **contract** by which the buyer and seller agree
to the **terms** of sale. Same as **agreement of sale, earnest money**
contract.
Example: Carter and Dooley sign a *sales contract,* which specifies
the property to be sold, type of **deed, closing date,** price, **financing**
conditions, and other details.

SALE-LEASEBACK the simultaneous purchase of property and
lease back to the seller. The lease portion of the transaction is

generally long-term. The seller-lessee in the transaction is converted from an owner to a tenant.

Example: ABC Corporation owns an office building. It arranges a *sale-leaseback* for the building **site** with the Carpenters Pension Fund. ABC receives cash and a 25-year lease to the site. In addition, ABC might **depreciate** the value of the building for income taxes. The Fund receives an **income stream** for 25 years and a **reversion** to the property at the end of the lease.

SALESPERSON one who is licensed to deal in real estate or perform any other act enumerated by state real estate **license** laws, while under the supervision of a **broker** licensed by the state.

Example: A *salesperson* arranges a 90-day **listing** on a house, which is accepted by the broker. Another *salesperson* shows the home to a prospective buyer. The sale is closed, and **commissions** are collected by the broker and shared with the *salespersons*.

SALT BOX COLONIAL OR CATSLIDE (IN SOUTH) an early American style, 2 or 2½-story house that is square or rectangular with a steep gable roof that extends down to the first floor in the rear.

Example: Figure 155:

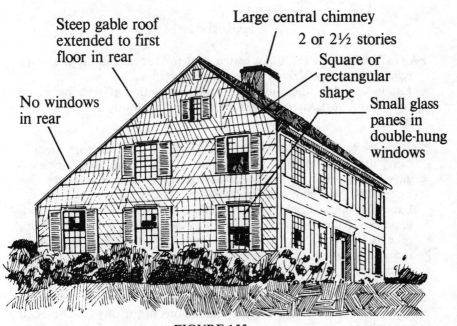

Steep gable roof
extended to first
floor in rear

Large central chimney

2 or 2½ stories

Square or
rectangular
shape

No windows
in rear

Small glass
panes in
double-hung
windows

FIGURE 155

SALVAGE VALUE the estimated **value** that an **asset** will have at the end of its **useful life.**

Example: An appraiser estimates the useful life of a building at 40 years; she also estimates that the building's *salvage value* would be $10,000 in 40 years. Consequently, all but $10,000 of the building cost is to be **depreciated** over 40 years.

SANDWICH LEASE lease held by a **lessee** who becomes a **lessor** by subletting. Typically, the sandwich leaseholder is neither the owner nor the user of the property. See **sublease.**
Example: Figure 156

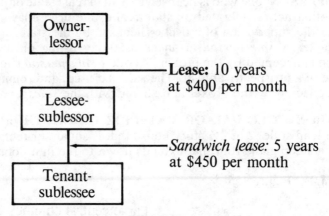

Lease: 10 years at $400 per month

Sandwich lease: 5 years at $450 per month

FIGURE 156

SATISFACTION PIECE an **instrument** for recording and acknowledging final payment of a **mortgage** loan.
Example: After the mortgage loan was paid off, the borrower received a *satisfaction piece,* which she promptly **recorded,** officially.

SAVINGS & LOAN ASSOCIATIONS (S&Ls) depository institutions that specialize in originating, servicing, and holding **mortgage** loans, primarily on owner-occupied, **residential property.** See **Federal Savings and Loan Association.**
Example: Most home buyers finance the purchase with a mortgage loan from a *savings and loan association.* Such associations receive most of their investment funds from the deposits of small individual savers. All savings and loan associations are subject to regulation from federal or state government.

SCALE the proportional relationship between the dimensions of a drawing, plan, or model to the dimensions of the physical object it represents.
Example: A **subdivision** plan is prepared at a *scale* in which one inch equals 1,000 feet. A distance of one inch on the drawing is intended to signify 1,000 feet on the **site.**

Example: A *scale* model of a building has a *scale* of one to 25. Each inch on the model represents 25 inches on the actual building.

SCENIC EASEMENT an **encumbrance** on the **title** to a property to preserve it in a more-or-less natural or undeveloped state. See **easement.**

Example: Smith owns a house with a view of the ocean (Figure 157). Snyder owns the property between the Smith house and the beach. To preserve the view of the ocean, Smith purchases a *scenic easement* to Snyder's property. Snyder is then prevented from developing the property in such a manner as to obstruct Smith's view.

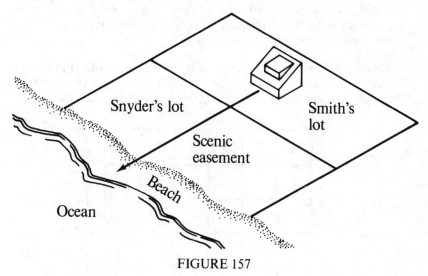

FIGURE 157

SEASONED LOAN a loan on which several payments have been collected.

Example: The seller accepts a **second mortgage** on the property sold. After he collects 12 months of payments, the loan is considered *seasoned* and can more easily be sold to a second mortgage investor.

SECONDARY FINANCING see **junior mortgage, second mortgage.**

SECONDARY MORTGAGE MARKET the mechanisms available to buy and sell mortgages, mainly residential **first mortgages.** There is no set meeting place for the secondary mortgage market. **FNMA** and **Freddie Mac** hold **auctions** weekly to buy those mortgages offered at the highest **effective rate. Bids** are collected from all over the country.

Example: The Good Money Mortgage Bankers originated 100 residential first mortgages with a total **face value** of $5 million. They sell the mortgages in the *secondary mortgage market* for a $1,000 profit on each.

SECOND MORTGAGE a **subordinated lien,** created by a mortgage loan, over the amount of a **first mortgage.** Second mortgages are used at purchase to reduce the amount of a cash **down payment** or in **refinancing** to raise cash for any purpose. See **subordination.**
Example: A house costs $100,000. Available **financing** is a mortgage loan covering 80% of value, or $80,000. The required cash **down payment** is $20,000. A *second mortgage* is available for an additional $10,000 of value, reducing the down payment to $10,000. The *second mortgage* will generally carry a higher **interest rate** than the first mortgage to reflect the inferior position and greater **risk** of the second mortgage.

SECTION (OF LAND) one square mile in the **government rectangular survey.** There are 36 sections in a 6-mile square **township.**
Example: A township, containing 36 *sections* (Figure 158).

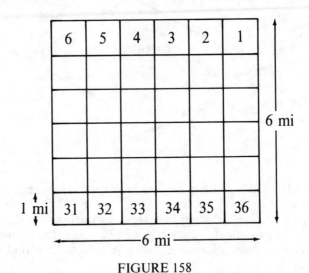

FIGURE 158

SECTION 8 HOUSING privately owned rental **dwelling** units participating in the low-income rental assistance program created by 1974 amendments to Section 8 of the 1937 Housing Act. Under the program, landlords receive rent subsidies on behalf of qualified low-income tenants, allowing the tenants to pay a limited proportion of their incomes toward the rent.
Example: A **landlord** elects to participate in the *Section 8 housing* program. A prospective tenant's income is $800 per month—low

enough to qualify for the program. A **fair market rent** for the unit is established by the **Department of Housing and Urban Development** as $200 per month. The tenant pays 20% of income, or $160 per month, and HUD supplements $40 per month to the landlord.

SECTION 167 the part of the **Internal Revenue Code** that deals with **depreciation.**
Example: Improvements to **real estate** are depreciable in accordance with *Section 167* of the Internal Revenue Code.

SECTION 1031 the section of the **Internal Revenue Code** that deals with tax-free exchanges of certain property. General rules for a tax-free exchange of real estate are:
The properties must be:
1. exchanged
2. **like-kind property** (real estate for real estate)
3. held for use in a trade or business or held as an investment
See also **tax-free exchange, boot.**
Example: Under *Section 1031,* Lowell trades her **appreciated** land for Baker's shopping center. **Equities** are the same. Lowell's **adjusted tax basis** in the land becomes her **adjusted tax basis** in the shopping center.

SECTION 1034 the section of the **Internal Revenue Code** dealing with sales of personal residences. Generally, there is no **recognized gain** or loss on the sale of a personal residence, provided another one is purchased within 2 years of the sale date of the old one. The new one must cost at least as much as the adjusted sales price of the old one (sales price, less expenses of sale, less fixing-up expenses).
Example: Under *Section 1034,* Abel can defer tax on the $10,000 gain on the home he sold for $65,000 by buying a new one that costs more.

SECTION 1221 the part of the **Internal Revenue Code** that defines a **capital asset.** It actually states what is not a capital asset.
Examples: Under *Section 1221* the following are not **capital assets:**
• inventory (such as lots of a subdivider)
• receivables collected in the course of business (such as **notes** received from the sale of lots by a **subdivider**)
• copyrights and the like held by the creator or certain other parties
• certain U.S. securities
The following are capital assets:
• the personal **residence** that one owns
• **raw land** held as an investment
• **mortgages** held as investments

SECTION 1231 the section of the **Internal Revenue Code** that deals with **assets** used in a trade or business. Generally, gains on Section 1231 assets are taxed at **capital gains** rates (except for **depreciation recapture)** and losses are **tax deductible** as **ordinary income.** See also **Section 1245, Section 1250.**
Example: *Section 1231* assets include:
• vehicles used in business
• machinery used in business
• hotels, office buildings, warehouses, apartments

SECTION 1245 the section of the **Internal Revenue Code** dealing with **gains** from **personal property** on which **depreciation** had been claimed. Generally, gains are taxed at **capital gains** rate except to the extent of depreciation claimed.
Example: The furniture of a hotel was purchased for $50,000. Depreciation of $20,000 was claimed in 2 years, causing an **adjusted tax basis** of $30,000. The furniture is sold for $55,000. There is a $25,000 gain of which $20,000 represents *Section 1245* **depreciation recapture,** and $5,000 is taxed at capital gains rates.

SECTION 1250 the section of the **Internal Revenue Code** dealing with **gains** from **real estate** on which **accelerated depreciation** had been claimed. Generally, gains on **residential property** are treated as **capital gains** except to the extent of accelerated depreciation claimed (Figure 159 and Table 37). Gains on nonresidential property on which accelerated depreciation was claimed are all **recaptured** to the extent of gain or depreciation, whichever is less.
Example: An apartment building is purchased for $500,000, then depreciated by $200,000 to a $300,000 **basis.** Of the depreciation, $150,000 is the **straight-line** amount, $50,000 the excess accelerated depreciation. The building is sold for $555,000 after 2 years. Of the $255,000 taxable gain, $50,000 is taxed as **ordinary income** under *section 1250,* and $205,000 is taxed at capital gains rates.

TABLE 37

TREATMENT OF GAIN
AFTER USE OF DEPRECIATION METHOD

1. Accelerated Method

	Nonresidential	Residential
Capital gain	A − B	A − C
Ordinary income	B − D	C − D

2. Straight-line

	Nonresidential	Residential
Capital gain	A − C	A − C
Ordinary income	none	none

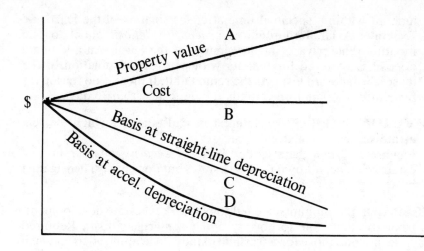

FIGURE 159

SECURITIES AND EXCHANGE COMMISSION (SEC) the federal
agency created in 1934 to carry out the provisions of the Securities
Exchange Act. Generally, the agency seeks to protect the invest-
ing public by preventing **misrepresentation, fraud,** manipulation,
and other abuses in the securities markets.
Example: The **Securities and Exchange Commission** requires their
review of proposed **public offerings** of securities, registration of
listed securities, and other matters. They do not, however, guarantee the investor against loss.

SECURITY 1. property that serves as **collateral** for a **debt.**
Example: Real estate serves as *security* for a **mortgage** loan. In the
event of **default** on the loan, the lender may sell the property to
satisfy the debt.
2. a document that serves as evidence of ownership.
Examples: The following are securities:
• common and preferred stocks
• **bonds**
• **mortgages**
   The **Securities and Exchange Commission** defines **limited partnership** interests and **condominiums** and **cooperatives** in certain situations as *securities*.

SECURITY DEPOSIT a cash payment required by a landlord, to be
held during the **term** of a **lease** to offset damages incurred due to
actions of the tenant. Such damages may include physical damage
to the property, theft of property, failure to pay back rent and
breaking the lease. **Forfeiture** of the deposit does not absolve the
tenant of further financial **liability.** Laws in most states require
landlords to hold the deposit in a separate account and refund the

amount within a specified time after termination of the lease.

Example: A landlord requires a *security deposit* equal to one month's rent, payable at the signing of the lease. An additional deposit is required for tenants with pets. At termination of the lease, the landlord inspects the rented unit. If there is no reason for forfeiture, the landlord refunds the deposit within 30 days.

SECURITY INTEREST an interest in **real estate** in which the real estate serves as **collateral.**

Example: A **mortgage** lender holds a *security interest* in real estate. He doesn't own the real estate, but does have a **lien** against it.

SEED MONEY amounts needed to begin a real estate development, prior to being able to borrow under a **mortgage** loan. Required costs include those for a **feasibility study, loan application** and **loan commitment** fees, attorney and accountant fees, land **option** costs, and others. See **front money.**

Example: To begin a $2,000,000 **condominium** development, about 2% of the total cost is needed as *seed money.*

SEISIN the **possession** of **realty** by one who claims to own a **fee simple** estate or a **life estate** or other salable **interest.** See also **ownership rights to realty, title.**

Example: *Seisin* is used to describe the **possession** of real estate by one who claims a **freehold** interest.

SELF-AMORTIZING MORTGAGE one that will **retire** itself through regular **principal and interest payments.** Contrast with **balloon mortgage, interest-only loan.**

Example: Collins borrowed $100,000 with a *self-amortizing mortgage* at 12% **interest** with a 30-year **term. Principal and interest payments** are $1,029 each month for the 30 years, at the end of which her loan will be amortized fully.

SELF-HELP the efforts of a landlord to cure a **default** on the **lease** without aid of legal proceedings. In most states, self-help remedies are not considered a legitimate substitute for a legal **eviction.**

Example: When Simmons' tenant fell 3 months behind in rent, Simmons changed the locks on the apartment and cut off the heat. The tenant took Simmons to court and forced him to follow eviction procedures in lieu of these *self-help* activities.

SELLER'S MARKET economic conditions that favor sellers, reflecting rising prices and market activity. Contrast with **buyer's market.**

Example: *Seller's markets* in real estate are often caused by:
• population influx

- lower interest rates
- lack of building activity

SELLING BROKER (AGENT) the licensed real estate **broker (agent)** that brings forth the buyer. Contrast with **listing broker (agent).**
Example: Abel was the *selling broker* under a **multiple listing** agreement. He showed the property to Collins, the buyer. Abel will share the **commission** with the listing broker.

SEMIANNUAL twice a year; same as **biannual.**

SEPARATE PROPERTY property acquired by either spouse prior to marriage or by gift or **devise** after marriage, as distinct from **community property.**
Example: At a divorce trial, each party tries to show that property owned prior to marriage or acquired in his or her own right is *separate property.*

SERVICING the act of billing, collecting payment, and filing reports for a **mortgage** loan; may also include loan analysis, **default** follow-up, and management of tax and insurance **escrow** accounts. Often performed for a fee by **mortgage bankers** after loans are sold to investors.
Example: Gray, a mortgage banker, originates loans and markets them in groups to large investors. On each loan originated, Gray receives a monthly fee for *servicing,* thereby freeing the investors of loan management burdens. The fee is ⅜ of 1% of the loan balance.

SERVIENT TENANT contrast with **dominant tenant.**

SETBACK the distance from the curb or other established line within which no buildings may be erected. See also **building line.**
Example: A 50-ft setback is shown in Figure 160.

SETTLEMENT same as **closing.**

SETTLEMENT STATEMENT same as **closing statement.**

SEVERALTY the ownership of **real property** by an individual as an individual. See **tenancy in severalty.**
Example: The owner in *severalty* enjoys working the land without partners in its ownership.

SEVERANCE DAMAGES an element of **value** arising out of a **condemnation** to which a **tract** was a part.
Example: The state highway department needed a strip of land 100 feet wide from the middle of Dooley's farm. They awarded $1,000

per **acre** for the land taken, plus $15,000 *severance damages* for Dooley's inconvenience in getting from one side of the highway to the other.

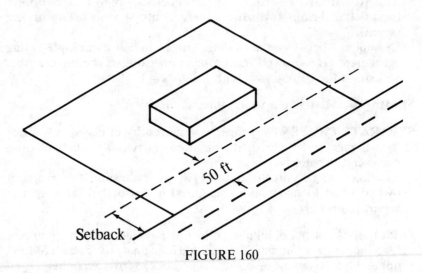

Setback

FIGURE 160

SEWER a system of pipes, containments, and treatment facilities for the disposal of plumbing wastes.
Example: A sanitary *sewer* collects waste water from individual buildings and homes, for treatment and disposal at a public facility.
Example: To prevent flooding, a storm *sewer* collects water drainage from streets and other surfaces.

SHARED APPRECIATION MORTGAGE a residential loan with a fixed **interest rate** set below **market rates,** with the lender entitled to a specified share of **appreciation** in property **value** over a specified time interval. Loan payments are set to **amortize** the loan over a long-term **maturity,** but repayment is generally required after a much shorter term. The amount of appreciation is established by sale of the home or by **appraisal** if no sale is made.
Example: Hogan obtains a *shared appreciation mortgage.* The interest rate on the loan is 10%, with the lender receiving ⅓ of any appreciation after 10 years. At the end of 10 years, Hogan does not wish to sell the home. An appraisal is made to establish the appreciation amount. Hogan must **retire** the loan by **refinancing** with a new loan the amount of the unpaid balance plus the appreciation share.

SHARED EQUITY MORTGAGE a home **loan** in which the lender is granted a share of the **equity,** thereby allowing the lender to participate in the proceeds from resale. After satisfying the unpaid balance of the loan, the borrower splits the residue of the proceeds with the lender. Shared equity plans often require the lender to buy a portion of the equity by providing a portion of the **down payment.**

Example: Ingram obtains a *shared equity mortgage* from a **mortgage banker.** The lender provides one half of the necessary down payment. Ingram makes loan payments on a fixed-rate, level payment basis. At resale, Ingram and the lender split the proceeds after repayment of the balance of the loan.

SHED ROOF one having a single, sloped side.
Example: Figure 161.

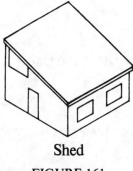

Shed

FIGURE 161

SHOPPING CENTER a collection of retail stores with a common parking area and generally one or more large department, discount, or food stores; sometimes including an enclosed **mall** or walkway. See also **anchor tenant.**
Example: *Shopping centers* developed after World War II as population shifted to the suburbs. Providing a variety of stores with easy access and ample parking, the centers became a strong alternative to downtown retail centers. Types of shopping centers are shown in Table 38.

SHORT-FORM an **instrument,** seldom more than 2 pages, that refers to another document. The short form is often recorded in lieu of a cumbersome longer document.
Example: The Giant Development Company leased part of a shopping center to Malee's Department Store. The **lease** required 150 printed pages. A *short-form* lease was recorded.

SHORT-TERM CAPITAL GAIN gain on the sale of a **capital asset** that was held, generally, for less than one year. A taxpayer's short-term **capital gains** and losses are merged, the net is then merged with net long-term capital gains. If the result is a net short-

term capital gain, it is taxed as **ordinary income.**
Example: An investor sold land at a $10,000 profit. She owned it
for 10 months. The sale was the only capital transaction for her
that year, so the $10,000 *short-term capital gain* is added to ordi-
nary income.

TABLE 38

	Building area, sq ft	Anchor tenant
Neighborhood	30,000–100,000	supermarket or drugstore
Community	100,000–500,000	junior department store and supermarket
Regional	500,000–1,000,000	at least one major department store
Superregional	over 1,000,000	several major department stores

SIMPLE INTEREST a method of calculating the future value of a
sum assuming that interest paid is not compounded, i.e., that
interest is paid only on the **principal.** See also **compound interest.**
Example: An account is established paying *simple interest* of 10%
on a principal of $1,000. Table 39 shows the current value of the
account for the next 5 years.

TABLE 39

Year	Value
1	$1100
2	1200
3	1300
4	1400
5	1500

SINGLE-FAMILY HOUSING a type of residential structure
designed to include one **dwelling.** Adjacent units may share walls
and other structural components but generally have separate

access to the outside and do not share plumbing and heating equipment.
Example: *Single-family housing* includes:
• **detached housing** units
• **town houses**
• **zero lot line** homes

SINKING FUND an account that, when compounded, will equal a specified sum after a specified time period. See **compound interest.**
Example: The Johnsons wish to buy a home 3 years from now. They estimate the **down payment** will equal $5,000. To accumulate the necessary money, they set up a *sinking fund* at the local bank. At 5% interest, the fund requires monthly deposits of $129. After 36 payments, the account will contain $5,000.

SITE a plot of land prepared for or underlying a structure or development. The location of a property.
Example: The Smith Building is located on a half-**acre** *site* in downtown Smithville. Several new buildings are being constructed on *sites* nearby.

SMALL BUSINESS ADMINISTRATION (SBA) a federal government agency in Washington, D.C. that encourages small business.
Example: The *SBA* offers low-interest rate loans to qualified businessmen and businesswomen.
Address:
Small Business Administration
1441 L Street, N.W.
Washington, D.C. 20416

SOCIETY OF INDUSTRIAL REALTORS® (SIR) an organization, affiliated with the **National Association of Realtors®,** whose members are mainly concerned with the sale of warehouses, factories, and other **industrial property.** Confers SIR designation. Publishes *SIR Market Letter* (bimonthly) and *SIR Newsletter* (monthly).
Address:
Society of Industrial Realtors®
925 Fifteenth Street, N.W.
Washington, D.C. 20005

SOCIETY OF REAL ESTATE APPRAISERS (SREA) an organization in Chicago, Illinois dedicated to professionalism in real estate **appraisal.** They award designations, **SRA, SRPA, SREA.**
Address:
Society of Real Estate Appraisers
645 N. Michigan Avenue
Chicago, Illinois 60611

SOFT MONEY 1. in a development or an investment, money contributed that is **tax-deductible.**
Example: Equity required for a development is $100,000, of which 50% is promised to be tax-deductible and therefore is *soft money*.
2. sometimes used to describe costs that do not physically go into construction, such as interest during construction, architect's fees, legal fees, etc.

SOIL BANK land held out of agricultural production in an effort to stabilize commodity prices and promote soil conservation. Subsidies to farmers participating in the soil bank program are provided by the U.S. Department of Agriculture.
Example: A farmer normally plants her land in corn. To avoid a surplus of corn production, the federal government pays the farmer to hold the land out of production for a year. The farmer is participating in the *soil bank* program.

SOLAR HEATING, HOT WATER see **active solar heating, passive solar heating.**

SOUTHERN COLONIAL a large, early American style, 2 or 3-story frame house with a characteristic colonnade extending across the front. The roof extends over the colonnade.
Example: Figure 162.

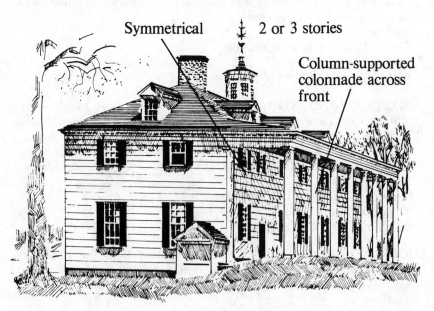

Symmetrical   2 or 3 stories

Column-supported colonnade across front

FIGURE 162

SPANISH VILLA a Latin style, asymmetrical, 1- to 3-story house with painted stucco exterior walls and red tile roof.
Example: Figure 163.

Painted stucco exterior walls

1 to 3 stories

Red tile roof

Oval-top doors

FIGURE 163

SPEC HOUSE a **single-family** dwelling constructed in anticipation of finding a buyer.
Example: Keene, a **developer,** is convinced there is local demand for 3-bedroom houses priced in the $80,000 range. Keene therefore constructs a number of *spec houses* and mounts a marketing campaign.

SPECIAL AGENT one who is engaged to act for another, with limited authority.
Example: A real estate **broker,** engaged by an owner to find a buyer, is considered a *special agent* of the owner.

SPECIAL ASSESSMENT an **assessment** made against a property to pay for a public **improvement** by which the assessed property is supposed to be especially benefited.
Example: The Lawsons own a house in a developing section of the city. When the city constructs curbs and gutters along their street, the Lawsons are levied a *special assessment,* in the form of a one-time tax, to pay for the construction.

SPECIALIST IN REAL ESTATE SECURITIES (SRS) a professional designation awarded by the **Real Estate Securities and Syndication Institute (RESSI).** Qualification is based on experience, education, examination, and demonstration of expertise in preparing a **syndication** report.

SPECIAL USE PERMIT a right granted by a local **zoning** authority to conduct certain activities within a zoning district. Such activities are considered conditional uses, which are permitted within the zone only upon special approval of the zoning authority. Also termed a "conditional use permit."

Example: A local government allows, as a conditional use, the operation of parking lots within its high-**density** residential zoning districts. A landowner wishing to operate a parking lot must obtain a *special use permit* following review of the plans of the development.

SPECIAL WARRANTY DEED a **deed** in which the **grantor** limits the title **warranty** given to the **grantee** to anyone claiming by, from, through, or under him, the grantor. The grantor does not warrant against **title** defects arising from conditions that existed before he owned the property. See **warranty deed.**

Example: Because of **bankruptcy** of its owner, a property goes under trusteeship. When the property is sold to satisfy creditor claims, the **trustee** conveys a *special warranty deed* to the buyer. This provides the buyer with warranty against claims incurred only during the time the property was held by the trustee.

SPECIFICATIONS detailed instructions provided in conjunction with plans and blueprints for construction. Specifications may stipulate the type of materials to be used, special construction techniques, dimensions, and colors.

Example: The building *specifications* state that:
• number 3 lumber shall be used for all framing
• studs are to be on 16-inch centers
• all exterior surfaces shall be painted white

SPECIFIC PERFORMANCE a legal action in which the court requires a party to a **contract** to perform the **terms** of the contract when he has refused to fulfill his obligations. Used in real estate, since each **parcel** of land is unique.

Example: Baker agrees in writing to sell his house to Abel. Baker changes his mind when his adult daughter decides to buy the house. Baker offers to refund Abel's **earnest money** and pay living expenses for one month, but Abel insists on buying the house as agreed and sues for *specific performance.*

SPECULATOR one who invests with the anticipation that an event or series of events wil occur to increase the value of the investment.

Example: The value of **single-family houses** has been appreciating rapidly for several months. Munson, a *speculator,* purchases several houses in anticipation that this rapid rate of **appreciation** will continue.

SPENDABLE INCOME same as **after-tax cash flow.**

SPOT ZONING the act of rezoning a **parcel** of land where all surrounding parcels are zoned for a different use, in particular where the rezoning creates a use which is incompatible with surrounding land uses. Spot **zoning** is generally disallowed in the courts.
Example: Figure 164 may be construed as *spot zoning*.

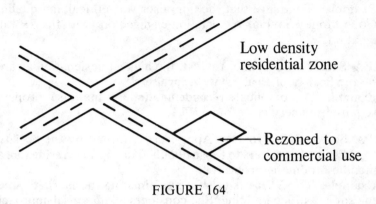

Low density
residential zone

Rezoned to
commercial use

FIGURE 164

SPREAD 1. the difference between the **bid** price and **asking price.**
Example: The buyer offers to pay $1,000 per **acre,** but the seller asks $1,300. The *spread* is $300.
2. the difference between the cost of money and the earnings rate.
Example: Good Money Savings and Loan pays an average interest rate of 10% to its depositors. It earns an average of 12% on its investments. The 2 point *spread* is adequate to pay **operating expenses** and leave some profit.

SPREADING AGREEMENT an agreement that extends the **collateral** of a loan to include several properties.
Example: Abel owns 7 shopping centers; all have **first mortgages.** He wants to borrow $5 million from a lender. The lender insists he sign a *spreading agreement* that gives a second **lien** on all 7 shopping centers.

SQUARE FOOTAGE the area, measured in square feet, of a piece of **real estate.** Generally measured from outside the exterior walls in the case of structures.
Example: The outside dimension of a rectangular home is 40 × 50 feet. Its *square footage* is 2,000.

SQUATTER'S RIGHTS the legal allowance to use the property of another in absence of an attempt by the owner to force **eviction;** this right may eventually be converted to **title** to the property over time by **adverse possession,** if recognized by state law.

Example: Various poor families take up residence in a vacant building, acquiring *squatter's rights.* Since ownership of the property is uncertain, no one attempts to evict the families.

SRA a person who is a Senior Residential Appraiser, a designation awarded by the **Society of Real Estate Appraisers** for residential **appraisers.**
Example: To assure that the appraiser was ethical and qualified, Good Money Savings Association engaged one with the *SRA* designation.

SREA Senior Real Estate Analyst, the highest designation awarded by the **Society of Real Estate Appraisers.**
Example: A complicated **condemnation** of multiuse properties required the services of an *SREA.*

SRPA Senior Real Property Appraiser. Awarded by the **Society of Real Estate Appraisers** to those qualified to appraise **residential** and income-producing **property.**
Example: The *SRPA* is careful in estimating the **market value** of the subject office building. She considers all **appraisal** approaches before arriving at a value estimate.

STANDARD METROPOLITAN STATISTICAL AREA (SMSA) a designation of the U.S. Census Bureau for **metropolitan areas** with a central city having a specified minimum population (50,000 in the 1970 census) and including all counties that are economically linked to the central city. Statistics compiled for the SMSA are considered more descriptive of the importance of a city than those for the political jurisdiction of the city only.
Example: In 1980, the city of Houston had a population of 1.5 million. The Houston *standard metropolitan statistical area,* which included 6 counties, had a population of almost 3 million.

STANDBY FEE the sum required by a lender to provide a standby **commitment.** See **standby loan.** The fee is **forfeited** should the loan not be closed within a specified time.
Example: A **developer** obtains a **standby loan** on a project to be developed. The developer hopes **interest rates** will decline during the construction period so that permanent **financing** may be arranged with **terms** better than those on the standby loan. However, a permanent loan commitment is required to obtain a **construction loan.** The developer pays a *standby fee* to compensate the lender for making the standby loan commitment. At the completion of construction, the developer has the **option** of exercising the standby commitment or forfeiting the fee.

STANDBY LOAN a **commitment** by a lender to make available a sum of money at specified terms for a specified period. A **standby**

fee is charged for this commitment. The borrower retains the **option** of closing the loan or allowing the commitment to lapse.
Example: See **standby fee.**

STATUTE a law established by an act of legislature.
Example: When a bill is passed by the legislature and signed by the governor, it becomes a state *statute*. Similarly, when a bill is passed by Congress and signed by the President, it becomes a federal *statute*.

STATUTE OF FRAUDS a state law that provides that certain **contracts** must be in writing in order to be enforceable. Applied to **deeds, mortgages,** and other **real estate** contracts, with the exception of **leases** for periods shorter than one year.
Example: An oral contract for the sale of land is considered unenforceable under the *statute of frauds*.

STATUTE OF LIMITATIONS a specified statutory period after which a claimant is barred from enforcing his claim by suit.
Example: Abel bought a **limited partnership** interest in a real estate transaction. The **syndicator** failed to mention in the **prospectus** that the land is in a flood-prone area. Abel discovers the fact and sues 4 years later but is barred from collecting under the *statute of limitations*.

STEERING an illegal practice of limiting the housing shown to a certain ethnic group.
Example: Though the minority couple wanted to be shown all available rental housing that they could afford, the unlicensed person *steered* them from certain neighborhoods.

STEPPED-UP BASIS an income tax term used to describe a change in the **adjusted tax basis** of property, allowed for certain transactions. The old basis is increased to **market value** upon inheritance, as opposed to a **carry-over basis** in the event of a **tax-free exchange.**
Example: Dooley dies, leaving land worth $100,000. The land was purchased for $20,000, but the heirs receive a *stepped-up basis* to the **fair market value** at death. The $80,000 **unrealized gain** to Dooley escapes **capital gains** tax.

STEP-UP LEASE see **graduated lease.**

STICK STYLE OR CARPENTER GOTHIC a nineteenth century style house with exposed framing members, high steep roofs, complex silhouettes, diagonal braces, and a large amount of gingerbread trim.
Example: Figure 165.

Exposed framing members

High steep roof

Lots of "Gingerbread"

Ornate windows and doors

Complex silhouette

slick style of carpenter gothic

FIGURE 165

STIPULATIONS the **terms** within a written **contract.**
   Example: A sales contract contains *stipulations* concerning the type of **financing** the buyer must be able to obtain, the price, proration of **closing** cost between buyer and seller, and the date and location of the closing.

STOP CLAUSE in a **lease,** stipulates an amount of **operating expense** above which the tenant must bear. Often the base amount is the amount of expense for the first full year of operation under the lease.
   Example: The *stop clause* requires the tenant to pay all **utilities** in excess of $2,500 per year. If utilities are less than that amount, the landlord pays them.

STRAIGHT-LINE DEPRECIATION equal annual reductions in the **book value** of property. Used in accounting for replacement and tax purposes. See **depreciation (accounting).**
   Example: A property has a **depreciable basis** of $150,000. For tax

purposes, a **useful life** of 15 years is used with no **salvage value.** Using *straight-line depreciation,* the book value of the property is decreased by \$10,000 $\left(\dfrac{150,000}{15}\right)$ per year. The tax deduction for depreciation is \$10,000 per year.

STRAIGHT-LINE RECAPTURE RATE the part of a **capitalization rate** that accounts for the annual erosion of a **wasting asset** by assuming an equal amount of loss in value each year of the **useful life** of the asset.
Example: A retail building's **useful life** is estimated at 50 years. The *straight-line recapture rate* is 2% per year, which will recover the asset cost over its estimated useful life. The 2% should be added to the **discount rate** to derive the **capitalization rate.**

STRAW MAN one who purchases property that is, in turn, **conveyed** to another for the purpose of concealing the identity of the eventual purchaser.
Example: A **developer** is assembling land, for a **subdivision,** from a large number of individually owned plots. To avoid the possibility that a few landowners will hold out for high prices, the developer uses *straw men* to purchase the **parcels. Agents** of the developer purchase plots in their own names and later convey the land to the developer.

STRIP DEVELOPMENT a form of commercial land use in which each establishment is afforded direct access to a major thoroughfare; generally associated with intensive use of signs to attract passersby.
Example: Map of *strip development* (Figure 166).

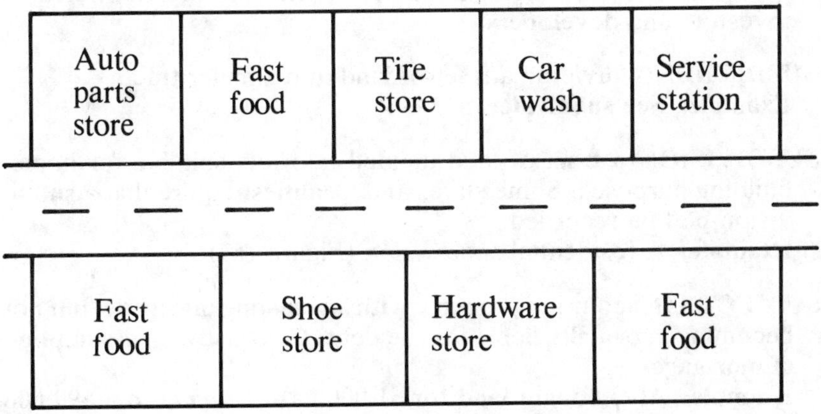

Auto parts store	Fast food	Tire store	Car wash	Service station

Fast food	Shoe store	Hardware store	Fast food

FIGURE 166

STRUCTURE any constructed improvement to a **site**.
Examples: *Structures* include:
- buildings
- fencing and enclosures
- garages
- gazebos, greenhouses, and kiosks
- sheds and utility buildings

SUBCHAPTER S CORPORATION a **corporation** with a limited number of stockholders (35 or fewer) that elects not to be taxed as a regular corporation, and meets certain other requirements. Shareholders include, in their personal tax return, their pro-rata share of **capital gains, ordinary income, tax preference** items, and so on. See **passive income.**
Example: To avoid **double taxation,** the ABC Real Estate Corporation elects *Subchapter S* status. Its shareholders will include corporate income in their own tax return, whether or not they receive a dividend. The corporation itself will not pay an income tax, but will file a tax return.

SUBCONTRACTOR one who performs services under **contract** to a **general contractor.**
Example: A general contractor agrees to construct a building for a **developer.** The contractor arranges with individual *subcontractors* who are specifically responsible to the contractor for performance of carpentry, plumbing, electrical, and masonry work.

SUBDIVIDER one who partitions a **tract** of land for the purpose of selling the individual plots. If the land is improved in any way, the subdivider becomes a **developer.**
Example: Olsen, a *subdivider,* purchases a 100-acre tract of land. The tract is subdivided into 5-acre plots that are marketed to investors and developers.

SUBDIVIDING dividing a **tract** of land into smaller tracts.
Example: See **subdivider.**

SUBDIVISION a **tract** of land divided into lots suitable for home-building purposes. Some states and localities require that a subdivision **plat** be recorded.
Example: A residential *subdivision* (Figure 167).

SUBJECT TO acquiring property with an existing mortgage, but not becoming **personally liable** for the debt. Contrast with **assumption of mortgage.**
Example: Abel bought **land** for $1,000 cash, *subject to* a $99,000 mortgage. If Abel defaults on the **mortgage** he will lose the cash **down payment** but is not responsible for the $99,000 **debt.**

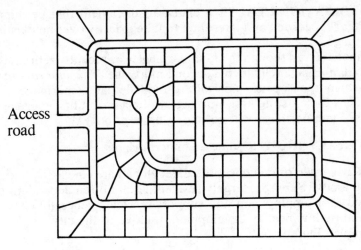

Access
road

FIGURE 167

SUBJECT TO MORTGAGE circumstance in which a buyer takes
title to mortgaged **real property** but is not personally liable for the
payment of the amount due. The buyer must make payments in
order to keep the property; however, with default, only the buyer's **equity** in that property is lost. Contrast **assumption of mortgage.**
Example: Queen purchases a house from Parsons *subject to* the
existing *mortgage.* Parson's mortgage has an outstanding balance
of $40,000 and the sales price is $60,000. Queen pays Parsons
$20,000 in cash and takes over the payments on the mortgage.
Should Queen **default,** Parsons is liable under the **promissory note**
given to the lender.

SUBLEASE a **lease** from a **lessee** to another lessee. The new lessee is
a sublessee or subtenant. See **sandwich lease.**
Example: Acme, Inc., leases office space under a 10-year lease.
Acme wishes to relocate but cannot break the lease. With the landlord's permission, Acme finds a subtenant, Medcorp, to sign a
sublease for the space. Medcorp pays rent to Acme, which, in
turn, continues to pay rent to the landlord.

SUBLET see **sublease.**

SUBORDINATION moving to a lower **priority,** as a **lien** would if it
changes from a **first mortgage** to a **second mortgage.**
Example: The land seller who held a first mortgage allowed *subordination* so the **development loan** could be arranged. In return,
the seller is promised mortgage **retirement** in 2 years.

SUBORDINATION CLAUSE a clause or document that permits a **mortgage** recorded at a later date to take **priority** over an existing mortgage.

Example: Even though the **first mortgage** was recently **retired,** the **second mortgage** remained a second mortgage. The *subordination clause* in the second mortgage provided that a mortgage that replaces the existing first mortgage will become a first mortgage; the second mortgage will not move up in priority.

SUBSURFACE RIGHTS same as **mineral rights.**

SUBURB a town or unincorporated developed area in close proximity to a city. Suburbs, largely residential, are often dependent on the city for employment and support services; generally characterized by low-**density** development relative to the city.
Example: Figure 168.

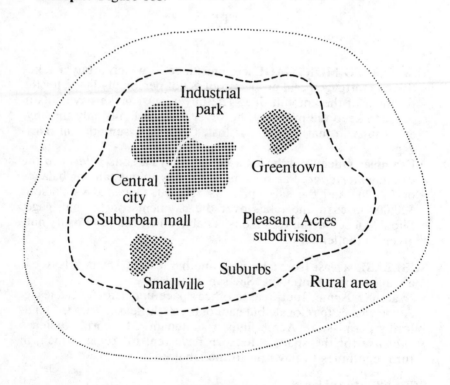

FIGURE 168

SUMMARY POSSESSION same as **eviction, actual.**

SUM-OF-YEARS-DIGITS DEPRECIATION in tax and accounting, a method of allocating the cost of an **asset** over its **useful life.** It requires a fraction to be computed each year, which is applied against the depreciable amount. The numerator is the number of years left to be depreciated. The denominator is the sum of the years digits of the depreciable life. The formula for the denominator is:

$$\frac{N(N + 1)}{2}$$

where N = the depreciable life. See **accelerated depreciation.**
Example: An automobile used in business cost $10,000 and has a 4-year depreciable life. *Sum-of-the-years-digits depreciation* results in the deductions shown in Table 40.

TABLE 40

Year	Fraction	Asset	Depreciation deduction
1	4/10	$10,000	$4,000
2	3/10	10,000	3,000
3	2/10	10,000	2,000
4	1/10	10,000	1,000

SUMP as part of a drainage system, a pit in the basement to collect excess moisture and liquids. To avoid flooding, a *sump* pump may be installed to remove accumulated water in the sump pit.
Example: Figure 169

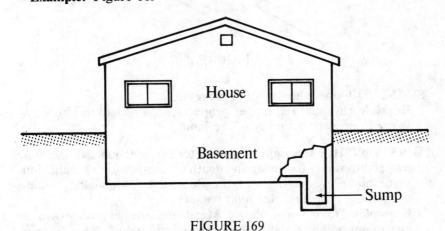

FIGURE 169

SURETY one who guarantees the performance of another.
Example: Ridley employs a **contractor** to construct a house. Under the **contract,** the contractor is required to obtain a **perfor-**

mance bond against failure to perform the work. Ace Bonding Co. provides the bond, thereby acting as a *surety*. Should the contractor fail to perform, Ace compensates Ridley for damages.

SURRENDER the cancellation of a **lease** by mutual consent of the **lessor** and the **lessee.**
Example: Simmons rents a house under a 2-year lease. Simmons is forced to move due to a job transfer. The landlord agrees to allow Simmons to *surrender* the **premises** if Simmons finds an acceptable new tenant.

surrogate Court (Probate Court)

SURVEY 1. the process by which a **parcel** of land is measured and its area ascertained. 2. the plan showing the measurements, boundaries, area, and contours.
Example: A simplified *survey* (Figure 170).

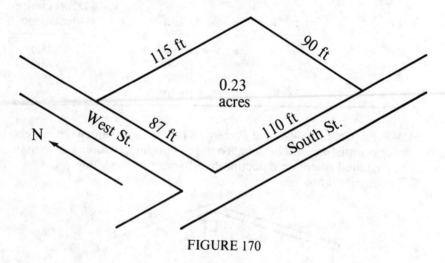

FIGURE 170

SURVEYOR one who prepares **surveys.**
Example: Prior to selling her property, Collins had to hire a *surveyor* to prepare a survey of the land.

SURVIVORSHIP the right of a joint tenant or tenants to maintain ownership rights following the death of another joint tenant. Survivorship prevents heirs of the deceased from making claims against the property. See **joint tenancy.**
Example: Travers and Vance Mead are brothers who own an apartment building, with the right of survivorship. When Travers Mead dies, Vance Mead, through *survivorship,* becomes sole owner of the building.

SWEAT EQUITY value added to a property due to **improvements** as a result of work performed personally by the owner.

Example: The Watsons purchase an old house for $20,000. Working in their spare time, the Watsons repair and repaint the structure to the point that the property is valued at $30,000. The $10,000 increment is *sweat equity*.

SWISS CHALET a Swiss style 1½- to 2½-story, gable roof house with extensive natural decorative woodwork on the exterior.
Example: Figure 171.

1½ to 2½ stories

Large glass windows

Gable roof

Decorative wood work

Natural wood look

Open porches

Curved cornice

FIGURE 171

SYNDICATION a method of selling property whereby a sponsor (or **syndicator**) sells interests to investors. May take the form of a **partnership, limited partnership, tenancy in common, corporation,** or **subchapter S Corporation.**
Example: A *syndication* was formed whereby limited partnership interests were sold to investors. The partnership bought land with the **equity** raised.

SYNDICATOR a person in business who sells an investment in shares or units.
Example: Collins, licensed as both a real estate **broker** and a **securities** salesperson, is a *syndicator*. She contracts with investors to buy shopping centers, then sells **partnership** interests conveying ownership in the centers to 30 different investors.

T

TACKING adding on to a time period.
Example: A squatter was on property for 10 years, moved away for one year, then returned for 10 years. If he were allowed to *tack* both 10-year periods, his claim to **squatter's rights** to the land would be a strong one.

TAKEOUT FINANCING a **commitment** to provide permanent **financing** following construction of a planned project. The takeout commitment is generally predicated upon specific conditions, such as a certain percentage of unit sales or leases, for the permanent loan to "takeout" the **construction loan.** Most construction lenders require takeout financing.
Example: Young, a developer, applied for a construction loan on a small office building. The construction lender requires Young to obtain *takeout financing* in the form of a commitment from a permanent lender. The takeout loan will be granted following construction and leasing of at least 65% of **net rentable area** to creditworthy tenants.

TAKING 1. acquisition of a **parcel** of land through **condemnation.**
Example: The Highway Department acquires much of its **right-of-way** for new roads through *takings*. These are usually parcels whose owners are unwilling to settle on a price through negotiation.
2. in land use law, application of **police power** restrictions to a parcel of land that are so restrictive as to preclude any reasonable use.
Example: A local community zones a parcel of land for agricultural use. The owner argues the land is unsuitable for growing crops but could be used for building homes. The owner's argument is the **zoning** is a *taking* of the property without just compensation, which is contrary to the Fourteenth Amendment to the U.S. Constitution.

TANDEM PLAN a program of the **Government National Mortgage Association (GNMA)** working together with the **Federal National Mortgage Association (FNMA)** to provide low interest rate home loans.
Example: Under the *tandem* plan, FNMA purchases qualified low-interest rate mortgages at a discount from GNMA. GNMA absorbs the loss as a subsidy to the qualified low-income home buyer.

TAX a charge levied upon persons or things by a government.
  Example:
  • ad valorem *tax*
  • county *tax*
  • excise *tax*
  • income *tax*
  • property *tax*
  • sales *tax*
  • school *tax*
  • use *tax*

TAX BASIS same as **basis (tax)**; see **adjusted tax basis.**

TAX BRACKET marginal rate for income taxes; the percentage of
  each additional dollar in income required to be paid as income
  taxes.
  Example: Abel is considering an investment that will produce
  $1,000 in taxable income for the next year. Abel's taxable income
  is currently $20,000, which places Abel in the 28% *tax bracket.*
  Thus, should Abel make the investment, $280 of the $1,000 will
  be paid in taxes.

TAX CREDIT a reduction against income tax payments that would
  otherwise be due. Contrasted with tax deductions that reduce taxable income.
  Example: *Tax credits* that are available to **real estate** owners
  include:
  • energy conservation tax credits
  • investment tax credit
  • rehabilitation tax credits for older properties and **historic struc-
    tures**

TAX DEDUCTIBLE a type of expense that can be used to reduce
  taxable income. See **tax deduction.**
  Example: Interest and **ad valorem** taxes are generally *tax deductible* for all types of property. **Depreciation,** repairs, **maintenance,
  utilities,** and other ordinary and necessary expenses are *tax
  deductible* for **income property.**

TAX DEDUCTION one that can be used to reduce taxable income.
  See **tax deductible.** Contrast with **tax credit.**
  Example: Abel has a $75,000 annual salary and $25,000 worth of
  tax deductions. Taxes for the year are figured on taxable income
  of $50,000.

TAX DEED the type of instrument given to a **grantee** by a government that had claimed the **property** for unpaid taxes.
  Example: The city acquired a **parcel** of land because the former

owner failed to pay **ad valorem** taxes. The city then auctioned it. Baker, the highest bidder, received a *tax deed* as evidence of ownership.

TAX-EXEMPT PROPERTY real property that is not subject, in whole or in part, to **ad valorem** property taxes.
Examples: In many local communities, the following types of property are *tax-exempt property:*
• churches
• government land and buildings
• **homesteads** (in part)
• solar-powered heating systems

TAX-FREE EXCHANGE same as tax-deferred exchange.

TAX LIEN a **debt** attached against **property** for failing to pay taxes.
Example: A *tax lien* may be imposed for failing to pay the following taxes:
• city
• county
• estate
• income
• payroll
• sales
• school

TAX MAP a document showing the location, dimensions, and other information pertaining to a **parcel** of land subject to **property taxes.** Maps are generally bound into books and kept as public records at the local tax office.
Example: A *tax map* showing parcel 65 in district A5-300 (Figure 172).

TAX PREFERENCE ITEMS certain types of **income** or deductions that are added to adjusted **gross income** to calculate the **alternative minimum tax.**
Examples: Tax preference items in 1984 include:
• certain dividends and **interest** income
• **accelerated depreciation** on **real estate** to the extent it exceeds **straight-line depreciation**
• **accelerated depreciation** on leased **personal property** to the extent it exceeds **straight-line depreciation**
• **amortization** of certified pollution control facilities in excess of normal depreciation
• the 60% **capital gains** deduction
• bargain element of an incentive stock option
• percentage **depletion** in excess of adjusted basis
• certain rapid write-offs.

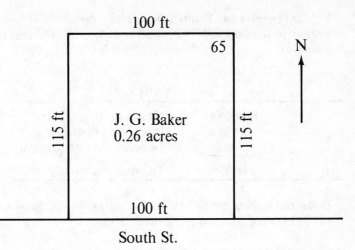

A5-300-65

FIGURE 172

TAX RATE the ratio of a tax **assessment** to the amount being taxed.
Example: In a certain community, the *tax rate* for **property taxes** is $0.35 per $100 of **assessed value**. A home is valued at $20,000. A **homestead exemption** of $2,000 is allowed for this type of property. The tax collected is

$$\$0.35 \times \frac{(\$20,000 - \$2,000)}{\$100} = \$63.00$$

TAX SALE the sale of property after a period of nonpayment of taxes. The **grantee** receives a **tax deed.** In most states the **defaulting** party has a **redemption period** during which he may pay the unpaid taxes, interest, court costs, and the purchase price to redeem the property.
Example: The failure to pay property **ad valorem** taxes resulted in a *tax sale* of Abel's land. Since the property was worth more than the back taxes, Abel erred by failing to pay.

TAX SHELTER an investment that produces after-tax income that is greater than before-tax income. The investment may produce **before-tax cash flow** while generating losses to shield, from taxation, income from sources outside the investment.
Example: Dunn purchases an income-producing property which provides *tax shelter*. In the first year, the property produces a **net operating income** of $100,000. **Debt service** is $80,000, of which

$75,000 is **interest**. Dunn's before-tax **cash flow** is $20,000. First-year **depreciation** is $50,000, so that taxable income is shown in Table 41.

TABLE 41

$100,000	Net operating income
75,000	Interest deduction
50,000	Depreciation deduction
(25,000)	Taxable income

Dunn not only pays no tax on the $20,000 cash flow but may shelter $25,000 of income from other sources.

TAX STOP a clause in a **lease** that stops a **lessor** from paying **property taxes** above a certain amount. See **escalator clause, stop clause**.
Example: The *tax stop* in the lease required the tenant to pay all property taxes in excess of $1,200.

TENANCY AT SUFFERANCE tenancy established when a person who had been a lawful tenant wrongfully remains in **possession** of property after expiration of a **lease**.
Example: A *tenant at sufferance* may be ejected from the property anytime the landlord decides to do so.

TENANCY AT WILL a **license** to use or occupy lands and buildings at the will of the owner. The tenant may decide to leave the property at any time or must leave at the landlord's will. Agreement may be oral or written. See also **emblements**.
Example: Under an oral agreement, Abel is using Baker's property. Baker may ask Abel to leave at any time; Abel may leave at any time.

TENANCY BY THE ENTIRETY an **estate** that exists only between husband and wife with equal right of **possession** and enjoyment during their joint lives and with the **right of survivorship,** i.e., when one dies, the property goes to the surviving tenant. Recognized in some states.
Example: A married couple owns property as *tenants by the entirety*. Neither can convey his or her part of the property during their lives unless the other consents. Divorced spouses become tenants in common. See **tenancy in common**.

TENANCY FOR YEARS created by a **lease** for a fixed term, such as 2 months, 3 years, 10 years, and so on.
Example: Big Buy Groceries leased a building for 10 years, beginning April 1, 1984 and ending March 31, 1994, 10 years later. The company has a *tenancy for years*.

TENANCY IN COMMON an ownership of **realty** by 2 or more persons, each of whom has an **undivided interest,** without the right of survivorship. Upon the death of one of the owners, the ownership share of the decedent is inherited by the party or parties designated in the decedent's **will.** Compare **partition.** See **syndication.**
Example: A syndicate is formed using a *tenancy in common.* Under this arrangement all of the investors have to sign the **deed** for the entire property to be conveyed. Each tenant may convey his or her share independently.

TENANCY IN SEVERALTY ownership of property by one person or one legal entity (corporate ownership).
Example: Abel owns land as a *tenant in severalty.* He enjoys the absence of partners or cotenants.

TENANT one who is given **possession** of real estate for a fixed period or at will. See **lessee, tenancy at will.**
Example: Enwright signs a **lease** to rent office space. Enwright is a *tenant* of the office building.

TENDER 1. an **offer** to perform an obligation, together with actual performance or evidence of present ability to perform. 2. to perform under a contract 3. to pay or deliver.
Example: Abel thought Baker would **default** under the **sales contract** but did not know for certain until Baker *tendered* the **deed.**

TENEMENTS 1. possessions that are permanent and fixed; structures attached to land.
Example: Real property consists of *tenements* and hereditaments: tenements are the physical and legal property that may be enjoyed by the owner; hereditaments are property one can pass on to one's heirs.
2. older apartment units.
Example: In the inner city, many people live in *tenements*.

TENURE the nature of an occupant's ownership rights; an indication of whether one is an owner or a tenant.
Example: For economic analysis, one may differentiate the occu-

pied housing stock by *tenure:* one portion may be owner-occupied; the other portion may be renter-occupied.

TENURE IN LAND the mode in which a person holds an **estate** in lands.
Example: If one purchases all rights to real estate, *tenure in land* is **fee simple** ownership. A tenant's *tenure in land* is a **leasehold.**

TERM the period of time during which something is in effect.
Example: Fowler leases an apartment for a *term* of one year. At the end of the year, Fowler moves from the apartment and buys a house. To finance the purchase, Fowler gets a mortgage loan with a *term* of 30 years. At the end of 30 years, the loan will be paid off.

TERM, AMORTIZATION for a loan, the period of time during which **principal and interest** payments must be made; generally the time needed to amortize the loan fully.
Example: *Amortization terms* of 25 and 30 years are commonly used on real estate mortgage loans. Monthly principal and interest payments are set to fully liquidate loans over the **term.**

TERMITE INSPECTION an examination of a structure by qualified personnel to determine the existence of infestation by **termites.** Often required by the **terms** of a **sales contract.** See **wood-destroying insect.**
Example: Gross sells a house to Handy. As protection for Handy, the sales contract stipulates that a *termite inspection* will be performed at Gross' expense and the sale is contingent on a finding of no termite infestation.

TERMITES insects that bore into wood and destroy it.
Example: *Termites* are a threat to any wooden structure or members of a structure. *Termites* generally act to weaken support members in proximity to the ground or in contact with it. *Termites* are often confused with winged adult ants. The differences are shown in Figure 173.

TERMS conditions and arrangements specified in a **contract.**
Example: A **sales contract** will generally include *terms* relating to the price, **financing** available to the buyer, contingencies based on the condition of the property, **how to prorate closing costs,** and items of personal property included in the sale. See also **as is, cancellation clause, contingency clause.**

TESTAMENT a **will.** Generally to dispose of **personal property.**

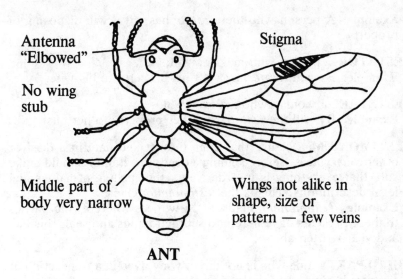

Antenna "Elbowed"

No wing stub

Middle part of body very narrow

Stigma

Wings not alike in shape, size or pattern — few veins

ANT

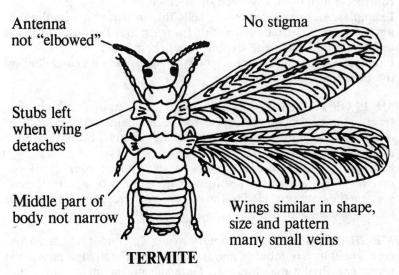

Antenna not "elbowed"

Stubs left when wing detaches

Middle part of body not narrow

No stigma

Wings similar in shape, size and pattern many small veins

TERMITE

FIGURE 173

Common usage employs the words **will,** *testament,* and *last will and testament* as synonyms.
Example: Ewen wrote her *testament* that directed the disposition of her property upon her death.

TESTATE having made a valid **will.** Contrast **intestate.**

Example: A person who dies *testate* has left a will disposing of property.

TESTATOR a person who makes a **will.**
Example: By will the *testator* left his property to his wife.

TESTATRIX a woman who makes a **will.**
Example: By will the *testatrix* left her property to her husband.

TESTIMONIUM a clause that cites the act and date in a **deed** or other **conveyance.** Before signing a deed, the grantor should make sure that everything is in order, e.g., the spelling of names and legal descriptions. This is the *testimonium* clause.
Example: *Testimonium* clause: "In witness whereof, the parties to these presents have hereunto set their hands and seals this day and year written above."

THIRD PARTY one who is not directly involved in a transaction or **contract** but may be involved or affected by it.
Example: An apartment owner sells the property to a **condominium** converter. The **tenants,** as *third parties,* may be forced to move or buy their units at the expiration of their **lease.**
Example: A trusted *third party* was designated as **escrow** agent by the **principals.**

TIME IS OF THE ESSENCE a phrase that, when inserted in a **contract,** requires that all references to specific dates and times of day noted in the contract be interpreted exactly. In its absence extreme delays might be acceptable.
Example: A **sales contract** contains the clause: *time is of the essence.* This statement reinforces the content of other clauses, such as the time provided to the buyer to arrange **financing** and the date of **closing.**

TIME-SHARING a form of property ownership under which a **property** is held by a number of people, each with the right of **possession** for a specified time interval. Time-sharing is most commonly applied to resort and vacation properties.
Example: Ingram is an owner in a *time-sharing* arrangement for a lakefront cottage. Ingram is entitled to use the cottage each year from July 1 to July 15. Use of the property during the remainder of the year is divided among other owners. All property expenses are paid by an owner's association to which Ingram pays an annual fee.

TITLE evidence that the owner of land is in lawful **possession** thereof; evidence of ownership. See also **adverse possession, certificate of title, clear title, color of title, cloud on the title, marketable title.**

Example: *Title* to land does not merely imply that a person has the right of **possession,** because one may have the right to possession and have no title. Title does ordinarily signify rights to possession in addition to evidence of ownership.

Example: Abel sold land to Baker. *Title* to the **property** was transferred at closing by the deed Baker received.

TITLE ABSTRACT see **abstract of title.**

TITLE COMPANY one in the business of examining **title** to real estate and/or issuing **title insurance.**

Example: The Chicago Lawyer Title Company searched courthouse records to be sure that Whitman would get **marketable title** on a house she planned to buy. They charged a $500 one-time **premium.** The bank wouldn't issue a loan without the policy.

TITLE INSURANCE an insurance policy that protects the holder from loss sustained by **defects in the title.**

Example: When property is purchased, most **mortgage** lenders require the buyer to obtain *title insurance.* After a satisfactory **title search** and in exchange for a one-time **premium,** the title company insures the buyer against most claims to the title of the property.

TITLE REPORT a document indicating the current state of the **title,** such as **easements, covenants, liens** and any **defects.** The title report does not describe the **chain of title.** See **abstract of title.**

Example: A buyer wishes to assure receipt of **clear title** to a property. The buyer authorizes a *title search* by an experienced attorney. The attorney examines the public records for all recorded encumbrances and past claims. The attorney renders to the buyer an **abstract of the title.**

TITLE SEARCH an examination of the public records to determine the ownership and **encumbrances** affecting **real property.**

Example: A buyer wishes to assure receiving **clear title** to a property. The buyer authorizes a *title search* by an experienced attorney. The attorney examines the public records for all recorded encumbrances and past claims. The attorney renders to the buyer an **abstract of the title.**

TITLE THEORY STATES states in which the law splits the **title** of mortgaged property into legal title, held by the lender, and **equitable title,** held by the borrower. The borrower gains full title to the property upon **retiring** the mortgage debt. The lender is granted more immediate cure to a **default** than in **lien theory states.** Contrast **lien theory states.**

Example: In *title theory states,* mortgage lenders may possess the property upon default of the borrower. **In lien theory states,** lenders must go through the process of **foreclosure.**

TOPOGRAPHY the state of the surface of the land; may be rolling, rough, flat, etc.
Example: The *topography* in Oklahoma is mostly flat; in West Virginia, mountainous; in Ohio, rolling.

TORRENS SYSTEM a **title** registration system used in some states; the condition of the **title** can easily be discovered without resorting to a **title search.**
Example: A property owner in Chicago wishes to register the property under the *Torrens System.* An application is made with the appropriate court. Following a title examination and **notice** to all who wish to make a claim, the court issues a **certificate of title** setting forth the nature of the applicant's title. When the owner sells the property, a new certificate is issued to the buyer. Anyone establishing a claim to the property following registration is compensated from a special fund for any losses suffered.

TORT a wrongful act that is neither a crime nor a **breach of contract,** but that renders the perpetrator **liable** to the victim for damages.
Examples:
• **nuisance**
• **trespass**
• negligence
An example of negligence is a landlord's failure to fix reported defective wiring. The law provides remedy for damages from resulting fire.

TOWN HOUSE a **dwelling** unit, generally having 2 or more floors and attached to other similar units via **party walls.** Town houses are often used in **planned unit developments** and **condominium** developments, which provide for clustered or attached housing and common open space. See **cluster housing, row house, brownstone.**
Example: Figure 174.

TOWNSHIP a 6-mile square **tract** delineated by **government rectangular survey.**
Example: 16 *townships* (Figure 175).

TRACT a **parcel** of land, generally held for **subdividing;** a **subdivision.**
Example: Reynolds, a **subdivider** purchases a *tract* of land. For marketing purposes, she subdivides the *tract* into lots (Figure 176).

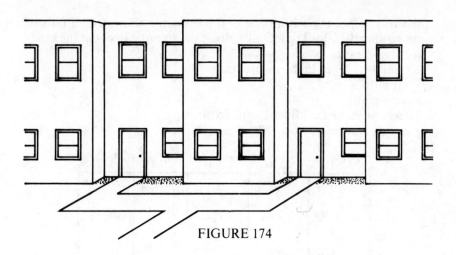

FIGURE 174

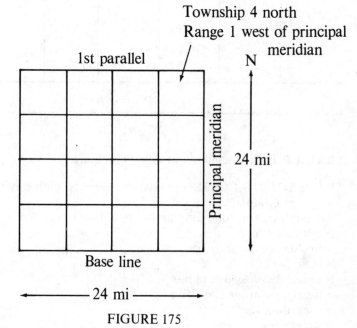

FIGURE 175

TRACT HOUSE a dwelling that has a similar style and **floor plan** to those of all other houses in a development. Contrast **custom builder.**
Example: Pleasant Acres is a **subdivision** of *tract houses*. Each home is a 3-bedroom ranch style house with the same basic floor plan.

TRADE FIXTURE articles placed in rented buildings by the tenant to help carry out trade or business. The tenant can remove the

fixtures before the expiration of the **lease,** but if the tenant fails to do so shortly after the lease expires, the fixtures become the landlord's property.

Examples: *Trade fixtures* include:
• bar stools
• neon signs
• decorative or functional light fixtures
• stoves and refrigerators

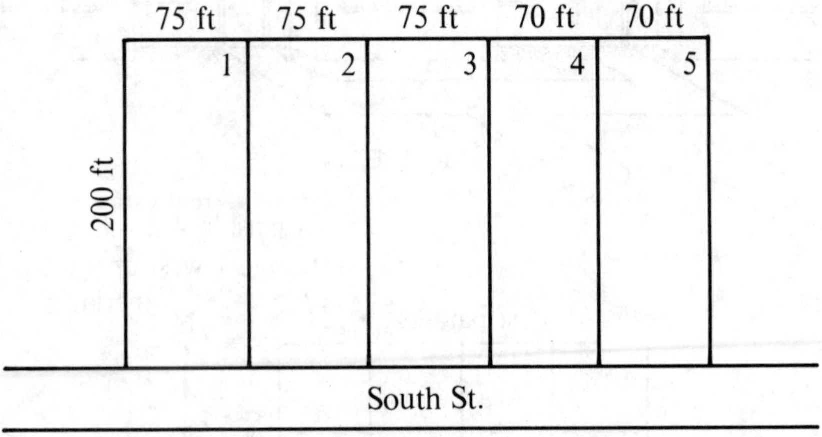

FIGURE 176

TRAILER PARK same as **mobile home park.**

TRANSACTION COSTS the costs associated with buying and selling **real estate.**
   Examples: The following are *transaction costs:*
   • **appraisal** fees
   • **brokerage** commission
   • legal fees
   • mortgage **discount points**
   • mortgage **origination fees**
   • **recording** fees
   • **survey** fees
   • **title search**

TRANSFER DEVELOPMENT RIGHTS a type of **zoning ordinance** that allows owners of property zoned for low-density development or conservation use to sell development rights to other property owners. The development rights purchased permit the landowners to develop their **parcels** at higher **densities** than otherwise. The system is designed to provide for low-density uses, such as historic preservation, without unduly penalizing some landowners.
   Example: Under a *transfer development rights* system, a land-

owner whose property is restricted to open space is assigned development rights in proportion to some overall desirable density for the jurisdiction. The landowner cannot utilize the rights but may sell them on the open market to landowners in other locations who are allowed to develop their properties. The rights may be used to develop additional structures on the unrestricted properties. In this way, restricted areas may be maintained as open space without completely destroying the development value of the properties.

TRANSFER TAX one paid upon the passing of **title** to property or to a valuable **interest.**
Example: In a state that imposes a high *transfer tax* on the sale of **real estate,** the seller formed a **corporation** as the owner of a valuable building and sold stock that was subject to a lower transfer tax. The state is claiming that it was a sale of real estate.

TRESPASS unlawful entry or **possession** of property.
Example: Thompson rents an apartment from Turner. When Thompson is away, Turner enters with a passkey and checks on the apartment's condition. Even though Turner owns the property, he is guilty of *trespass,* since the right to possession has been granted to Thompson exclusively. It is possible for Turner to reserve the right to enter the property periodically.
Example: Smith fenced in his farm and posted signs to prevent *trespass* by hunters.

TRIPLE-NET LEASE one in which the tenant is to pay all **operating expenses** of the property; the landlord receives a net rent.
Example: Big Buy Supermarkets enters into a *triple-net lease.* They are to pay for all the taxes, **utilities,** insurance, repairs, janitorial services, and license fees; any **debt service** and the landlord's income taxes are the responsibility of the landlord.

TRUST an arrangement whereby property is transferred to a trusted **third party** (trustee) by a **grantor** (trustor). The **trustee** holds the property for the benefit of another **(beneficiary).**
Example: An **inter vivos** *trust* was established by a living person who gave her warehouse to a trustee for the benefit of her children.
Example: A testamentary *trust* was established upon the death of a trustor, according to his **will.**

TRUST ACCOUNT a separate bank account segregated from a broker's own funds, in which the **broker** is required by state law to deposit all monies collected for clients. In some states called an **escrow** account.
Example: A broker who fails to deposit **earnest money** into a sep-

arate *trust account* may be held **liable** for penalties under the state's real estate **license** laws.

TRUST DEED a **conveyance** of real estate to a **third party** to be held for the benefit of another. Commonly used in some states in place of **mortgages** that conditionally convey **title** to the lender.
Example: Same as **deed of trust.**

TRUSTEE one who holds property in **trust** for another to secure performance of an obligation; the neutral party in a **trust deed** transaction.
Example: Johnson purchases property and finances it with a **deed of trust** from a lender. The **title company** is the *trustee,* holding legal title to the property pending Johnson's satisfaction of the debt. Should Johnson **default** on the loan, the trustee may sell the property to satisfy the debt.

TRUTH IN LENDING see **Regulation Z.**

TUDOR an English style imposing looking house with fortress-lines. Siding is chiefly stone and brick with some stucco and half timbers. Windows and doors have moulded cement or stone trim around them.
Example: Figure 177.

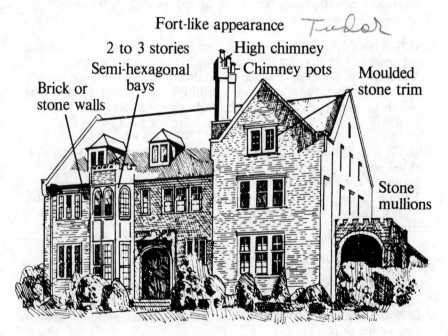

Fort-like appearance   Tudor
2 to 3 stories   High chimney
Semi-hexagonal   Chimney pots
Brick or   bays   Moulded
stone walls   stone trim
Stone
mullions

FIGURE 177

TURNKEY PROJECT a development in which a **developer** completes the entire project on behalf of a buyer; the developer turns over the keys to the buyer at completion.
Example: Many government-owned public housing projects are *turnkey projects*. A private developer undertakes all activities necessary to producing the project, including land purchases, **permits,** plans, and construction, and sells the project to the housing authority.

U

UNDERIMPROVEMENT a structure or development of lower cost than the **highest and best use** of the site. Compare **overimprovement.**
Example: Construction of a $40,000 bungalow on a vacant lot in a **neighborhood** of $100,000 homes would represent an *underimprovement* of the **site.**

UNDERWRITER one who insures another or takes certain **risks.** In **mortgage** lending, the one who approves or denies a loan based on the property and the applicant. In securities, it is the **broker** that sells the issue and, unless sold on a "best efforts" basis, agrees to purchase the shares not bought by the public.
Example: The *underwriter* analyzed the loan submission package carefully, because she didn't want her firm to accept excessive risk.

UNDIVIDED INTEREST an ownership right to use and possession of a property that is shared among co-owners, with no one co-owner having exclusive rights to any portion of the property. Compare **partition.**
Example: Ten investors form a **tenancy in common** and purchase a 100-**acre** tract of land. Each cotenant obtains an *undivided interest* in the property. All decisions as to the use and disposition of the land are made collectively by all cotenants. No one cotenant may unilaterally mortgage, develop, or sell a portion of the **tract.**

UNEARNED INCREMENT an increase in the **value** of real estate unrelated to effort on the part of the owner; often due to an increase in population.
Example: Murphy buys a **tract** of land in the county for $2,000 per **acre.** As the city grows, the surrounding county begins to develop, with paved highways eventually extended to Murphy's land. Murphy sells the land for $5,000 per acre, realizing an *unearned increment* in value of $3,000 per acre.

UNENCUMBERED PROPERTY real estate with **free and clear title.**
Example: Nash owns an *unencumbered property*. Nash's **interest** is **fee simple,** there are no **mortgage, vendor, mechanic's** or **tax liens** on the property, no **restrictive covenants** exist, and no **easements** have been granted.

UNIFORM COMMERCIAL CODE (UCC) a group of laws to standardize the state laws that are applicable to commercial transactions. Few of the laws have relevance to **real estate.**
Example: The *Uniform Commercial Code* applies to **chattel mortgages, promises, commercial paper, securities, etc.**

UNILATERAL CONTRACT an obligation given by one party contingent on the performance of another party, but without obligating the second party to perform. Compare **bilateral contract.**
Example: A **broker** makes a *unilateral contract* with her associates. She offers a trip to Hawaii to any salesman who sells one million dollars of property during the month. None of the salesmen is obligated to meet the goal, but the broker is obligated to provide the trip should any salesman perform the feat.

UNIMPROVED PROPERTY land that has received no development, construction, or **site** preparation. See **raw land.**
Example: O'Brien is **subdividing** a **tract** of land and selling lots to investors. In all marketing materials, O'Brien must disclose the fact that the land is *unimproved property* that must receive extensive development before being suitable for urban uses.

UNINCORPORATED ASSOCIATION an organization formed by a group of people. If the organization has too many characteristics of a **corporation** it may be treated like one for income tax purposes.
Example: Many **condominium** associations, **limited partnerships,** and real estate investment **trusts** are examples of *unincorporated associations.*

UNIT-IN-PLACE METHOD a technique used by **appraisers** to estimate the **reproduction cost** (new) of a structure. The method involves estimating the cost of producing and installing individual components, such as the foundation, exterior walls, and plumbing. Similar methods include the trade-breakdown method and segregated-costs method. See **cost approach.**
Example: A simplified cost estimate using the *unit-in-place method* is shown in Table 42.

UNREALIZED GAIN the excess of current **market value** over cost for an asset that is unsold.

Example: Collins bought land for $10,000; she had an offer to sell it for $15,000, but decided to keep the land. Her *unrealized gain* is $5,000.

TABLE 42

Item	Cost per unit ($/ft^2)	Cost
Foundation 1500 ft^2	2	$3,000
Walls 1600 ft^2	4	6,400
Roof 1500 ft^2	3	4,500
Flooring 1500 ft^2	2	3,000
Plumbing		2,500
Heating		1,500
Electrical		2,000
Total		$22,900
Fees, interest and overhead (10%)		2,290
Reproduction cost (new)		$25,190

UNRECORDED DEED an **instrument** that transfers **title** from one party **(grantor)** to another party **(grantee)** without providing public **notice** of change in ownership. **Recording** is essential to protect one's **interest** in **real estate.**
Example: Uncas purchases a lakefront lot from Upson. At **closing,** Uncas receives a **deed** but fails to record it at the county courthouse. In the meantime, Upson fradulently sells the lot to Ustinov. Ustinov's attorney does a **title search** but, because of the *unrecorded deed,* does not turn up the sale to Uncas. When Uncas discovers what has occurred, he is forced to pursue legal proceedings against Upson for recovery. Ustinov, who purchased in **good faith,** owns the land.

UPSET PRICE the minimum acceptable price for property being auctioned. See also **asking price, bid.**
Example: If the bidding at **auction** fails to reach the *upset price,* the property will not be sold.

URBAN LAND INSTITUTE (ULI) a nonprofit organization providing research and information on land use and development. Among the many publications of the ULI are the periodicals, *Urban Land* and *Environmental Comment,* and several development guides for specific types of land use.
Address:
Urban Land Institute
1200 18th St. N.W.
Washington, D.C. 20036

URBAN PROPERTY real estate located in an urban area, generally characterized by relatively high-**density** development and extensive availability of city water and sewer services.
Example: Typical development of 3 types of property is shown in Table 43.

TABLE 43

Urban	Suburban	Rural
High-rise office	Office parks	Farms
High-rise apartment	Industrial parks	Low-density housing
Department stores	Shopping centers	Recreational lands
Public buildings	Garden apartments	Summer camps
Moderate density single-family housing	Low-density housing	

URBAN RENEWAL the process of redeveloping deteriorated sections of the city, often through **demolition** and new construction. Although urban renewal may be privately funded, it is most often associated with government renewal programs.
Example: Most large cities have experienced some *urban renewal* in the last 20 years. The typical program attempts to demolish concentrations of dilapidated housing and attract **developers** of middle-income or mixed housing. Often, however, urban renewal areas become **sites** for new public buildings, such as civic auditoriums, sports arenas, and universities.

USEFUL LIFE the period of time over which a building is expected to provide a competitive return. Useful life provides the basis for allowable **depreciation** deductions on properties acquired prior to 1981. See **accelerated cost recovery system.**
Example: A property acquired in 1980 has a **depreciable basis** of $100,000 and a *useful life* of 25 years. Using **straight-line depreciation,** the owner may deduct $4,000 per year for tax reporting.

USUFRUCTORY RIGHTS interests that provide for the use of property that belongs to another. Compare **emblement.**
Example: The owner of land that bounds or contains a natural water channel has a *usufructory right* to use of the water. The water itself is considered to be held by the public with all **adjacent** property owners holding rights to its use. **Restrictions** on that use vary under state law.

USURY charging a rate of interest greater than that permitted by state law. In most states, usury limits vary according to the type of lender and type of loan. Federal laws have passed to preempt certain usury limits under certain conditions.
Example: The **interest rate** that must comply with *usury* limitation is defined differently in the various states. The stated maximum rate may apply to the **face interest rate, effective rate** to the borrower, or the actual **yield** to the lender. If a loan is found to be usurious, severe penalties may be imposed, including loss of the **principal,** interest, a multiple of the interest, and/or damages.

UTILITIES 1. services, such as water, sewer, gas, electricity, and telephones, that are generally required to operate a building.
2. the periodic charges for such services.
Example: The building will be ready for occupancy as soon as the *utilities* are connected. When available, the *utility* bill is expected to average $100 per month. All *utilities* are paid for by the **landlord.**

UTILITY EASEMENT use of another's property for the purpose of laying gas, electric, water, and sewer lines.
Example: A property owner grants a *utility easement* to the electric power company to extend power lines to the owner's home.

V

VACANCY RATE the percentage of all units or space that is unoccupied or not rented. On a **pro-forma** income **statement** a projected vacancy rate is used to estimate the vacancy allowance, which is deducted from potential **gross income** to derive effective gross income.
Example: The *vacancy rate* for apartment units in Boom City is currently 4.5%. For the Hightower Building, the *vacancy rate* is 9.5% (of 100,000 square feet of **net leasable area,** 9,500 square feet are not rented). If this 9.5% *vacancy rate* is expected to be the average through next year, a vacancy allowance of $95,000 (at $10 per square foot) should be deducted from potential rent when projecting income.

VACANT LAND land not currently being used. May have **utilities** and **off-site improvements.** Contrast with **raw land.**
Example: *Vacant land* was cleared and graded for future use as a **shopping center.**

VACATE to move out.
Example: A tenant *vacates* an apartment by terminating occupan-

cy and removing all possessions. The tenant is responsible for **rent** to the end of the **lease** term.

VALID having legally binding force; legally sufficient and authorized by law.
Examples: A *valid* **deed, will, lease, mortgage,** or other **contract.**

VA LOAN home loan **guaranteed** by the U.S. **Veterans Administration (VA)** under the Servicemen's Readjustment Act of 1944 and later. The VA **guarantees** restitution to the lender in the event of **default.** The **guaranty** is 60% of the loan, but not more than $27,500. Home must be a principal residence.
Example: Abel, a veteran of the U.S. Army, wishes to purchase a home. Abel may apply for a *VA loan* with the Veterans Administration and, if qualified, may obtain a **mortgage** loan from a lending institution with no **down payment.**

VALUABLE CONSIDERATION a type of promised payment upon which a promisee can enforce a claim against an unwilling promisor. Includes money, extension of time, and other equivalents for the grant. Distinguished from good **consideration,** which may be love and affection toward a relative, generosity, and the like.
Example: A man promised to give certain land to a suitor of his daughter, provided they marry. This was not considered *valuable consideration,* so the suitor could not enforce it and he did not marry the daughter.

VALUATION 1. estimated worth or price.
Example: The *valuation* of the land is $100,000.
2. the act of estimating the worth of a thing. See **appraisal.**
Example: The *valuation* was prepared in accordance with instructions provided by the tax **assessor.**

VALUE the worth of all the rights arising from ownership; the quantity of one thing that will be given in exchange for another.
Example: A property may have a certain *value* to its owner (value in use) equal to the amount of other property (typically cash) that the owner would be willing to accept in exchange for the property without loss in wealth or well-being. The same property may have a different **market value** (value in exchange) equal to the amount of other property exchanged for the property when many typically motivated buyers and sellers are allowed to interact.

VARIABLE INTEREST RATE an amount of compensation to a lender that is allowed to vary over the **maturity** of a loan. The amount of variation is generally governed by an appropriate index. See **variable rate mortgage, renegotiated rate mortgage.**
Example: A 20-year loan is made with a *variable interest rate.* The

initial rate is 14% but may be changed each year in relation to changes in a published index of average loan rates. If, at the end of the first year, the index has risen one percentage **point,** the rate on the loan may be raised to 15%. Similarly, a fall in the index at one point would allow a decrease in the loan rate to 13%.

VARIABLE MATURITY MORTGAGE a long-term **mortgage** loan, under which the **interest rate** may be adjusted periodically. Payment levels remain the same but the loan **maturity** is lengthened or shortened to achieve the adjustment.
Example: Abel obtains a *variable maturity mortgage* originated at 12% with a **term** of 25 years. At the end of one year, the interest rate is increased to 12¼%. Abel's monthly payment of $527 remains the same after the adjustment; however, the remaining term is no longer 24 years, but is increased to 27 years.

VARIABLE PAYMENT PLAN any **mortgage** repayment schedule that provides for periodic change in the amount of monthly payments. Changes may occur as a result of: the expiration of an interest-only period **(flexible payment mortgage),** a planned step-up in payments **(graduated payment mortgage),** or a change in the **interest rate** due to fluctuation in an index **(variable rate mortgage).**
Example: A loan is made with a *variable payment plan.* The interest rate on the loan may be adjusted once a year according to a published index. As the interest rate is changed, the monthly payment is adjusted to provide for full **amortization** of the outstanding **principal** over the remaining life of the loan.

VARIABLE RATE MORTGAGE (VRM) a long-term **mortgage** loan applied to residences, under which the **interest rate** may be adjusted on a 6-month basis over the **term** of the loan. Rate increases are restricted to no more than ½ **point** per year and 2½ points over the term.
Example: Abel obtains a *variable rate mortgage* originated at a 12% interest rate. In 6 months, the index upon which the rate is based increases by one percentage point. Abel's rate is adjusted to 12½% and cannot be further increased during the year because of the ½% annual cap.

VARIANCE permission granted by a **zoning** authority to a property owner to allow for a specified violation of the zoning requirements. Variances are generally granted when compliance is impossible without rendering the property virtually unusable.
Example: Sherman owns a lot that is zoned for low-**density** housing. Because of the peculiar shape and **topography** of the lot, Sherman cannot build a home with the required minimum floor area without violating the **setback** requirements for the area. Sherman

may be granted a *variance* to either construct a smaller dwelling or encroach on the setback line.

VENDEE a buyer. Generally used for **real estate;** one who purchases **personal property** is usually called the buyer.
Example: The *vendee* is the party that pays for the real estate bought.

VENDEE'S LIEN a **lien** against property under a **contract of sale,** to secure the **deposit** paid by a purchaser.
Example: Moore, the vendee (buyer), gave a substantial deposit. Since Moore did not trust the seller, she secured a *vendee's lien* against the property. The lien provides the vendee with a claim against the property should the seller attempt to sell to another party prior to closing.

VENDOR a seller, usually of **real estate.** The term *seller* is commonly used for **personal property.**
Example: The *vendor* receives cash, **notes,** and **mortgage relief** from the **vendor.**

VENEER wood or brick exterior that covers a less attractive and less expensive surface.
Example: Beneath the sturdy-looking oak *veneer* was low-grade hollow board (Figure 178).

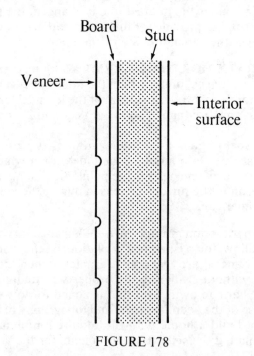

FIGURE 178

VENTURE CAPITAL money raised for high-risk investments.
Example: Money raised for oil exploration, theatrical productions, and the like is considered *venture capital*.

VERIFICATION sworn statements before a duly qualified officer that the contents of an **instrument** are correct.
Example: A tenant takes a landlord to court to recover a **security** deposit. The tenant files a claim describing the **conditions** under which the **deposit** is to be refunded and the manner in which the tenant complied with the conditions. The tenant then supplies *verification* of this description by a sworn statement.

VEST to create an entitlement to a privilege or right.
Example: By crossing Baker's property regularly for 20 years, Abel's right to an easement became *vested*. Baker can no longer prevent Abel from crossing.
Example: If she stays employed by the same **brokerage** firm for 10 years, Collins' right to a pension will *vest*.

VETERANS ADMINISTRATION (VA) an agency of the federal government that provides services for eligible veterans. Generally, a veteran who has served (beyond basic training) more than 120 days active duty in the armed forces is eligible for a **home loan** with no **down payment.**
Address:
Veterans Administration
810 Vermont Avenue
Washington, D.C. 20420

VIOLATION an act or a condition contrary to law or to permissible use of **real property.**
Example: According to most **zoning ordinances,** operating a business from one's home is a *violation* of the restriction for a residential zone. In many cities, owning an occupied **apartment building** with nonfunctioning plumbing is a *violation* of the **housing code.**

VOID having no legal force or effect; unenforceable. See **null and void.**
Example: In a **listing** contract with a **broker,** Smith stipulates that the property be sold only to a person of a certain race. Since the stipulation is contrary to antidiscrimination laws, it is *void* and thereby unenforceable.

VOIDABLE capable of being voided, but not **void** unless action is taken to void it. A **contract** to **real estate** entered into by a **minor** is voidable only by the minor.
Example: A **landlord** leases an apartment to a minor. The minor

may honor the **lease** and rent the apartment. However, should the minor decide not to rent the apartment, he may void the lease without **liability** for performance. The lease is a *voidable* contract.

VOLUNTARY LIEN a **debt** that the property owner agrees to have recorded. Typically a **mortgage.** Contrast **involuntary lien.**
Example: The **mortgage** was a *voluntary lien,* since the real estate owner agreed to pledge the property as **security.**

W

WAIVER the voluntary renunciation, **abandonment,** or surrender of some claim, right, or privilege.
Example: A **violation** of a contract causes the need for a *waiver* from the other party who does not feel injured.

WAREHOUSING (LOAN) the packaging of a number of **mortgage** loans for sale in the **secondary mortgage market** by a financial institution or **mortgage banker** who has originated the loans.
Example: Willard, a mortgage banker, is regularly engaged in loan *warehousing.* He would originate a number of FHA-insured mortgages and sell the package to **FNMA** at **auction.** After origination but before the sale to FNMA, the loans are considered to be in Willard's *warehouse.*

WARRANTY a promise contained in a **contract.**
Example: The **vendee** received a one-year *warranty* from the builder as to the structural soundness of the property.

WARRANTY DEED one that contains a **covenant** that the **grantor** will protect the **grantee** against any and all claims. Usually contains covenants assuring good **title,** freedom from **encumbrances,** and **quiet enjoyment.** See also **general warranty deed** and **special warranty deed.**
Example: The grantor was willing to give a *warranty deed* because she was confident that she had good title to the property and would defend the grantee against future claims.

WARRANTY OF HABITABILITY an implied assurance given by a **landlord** that an apartment offered for rent is free from safety and health hazards.
Example: Todd signed a one-year **lease** to rent an apartment from Landon. Todd later discovered that the apartment's heating system was not functioning. Todd sought to break the lease, claiming

the apartment was deficient under Landon's implied *warranty of habitability.*

WASTE unauthorized use or neglect of property by a party with the right to **possession** when another party owns an **interest** in the property. The party may be a **tenant, a mortgagor,** or a **life tenant.**
Example: A tenant neglecting to heat an apartment in the winter with the result of damage to the plumbing.
Example: A mortgagor failing to pay property taxes, thereby risking a tax **foreclosure.**
Example: A life tenant converting a residential property into a production center for some specialized product.

WASTING ASSET something of value that deteriorates over time.
Example: Improvements to land will not last forever, so they are *wasting assets;* in contrast **land** is not wasting because it will last forever.

WATER RIGHTS see **riparian rights, usufructory** rights.

WATER TABLE the upper level at which underground water is normally encountered in a particular area.
Example: Cross section showing the *water table* (Figure 179).

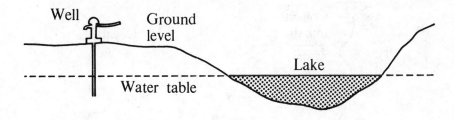

FIGURE 179

WEAR AND TEAR physical deterioration of property as the result of use, weathering, and age.
Example: A carpet is expected to last only 8 years because of *wear and tear,* or deterioration resulting from foot traffic and cleaning.

WESTERN ROW HOUSE OR WESTERN TOWNHOUSE a nineteenth century style house usually built to cover an entire street or block. It has common side walls with the house on either side.
Example: Figure 180

WETLANDS land, such as a marsh or swamp, normally saturated with water.
Example: A typical coastal *wetlands* (Figure 181):

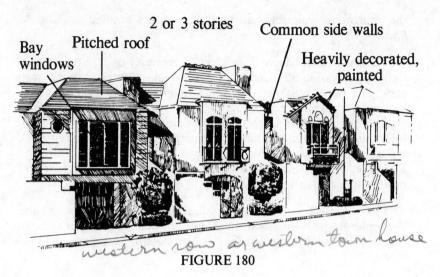

Bay windows

Pitched roof

2 or 3 stories

Common side walls

Heavily decorated, painted

western row or western town house

FIGURE 180

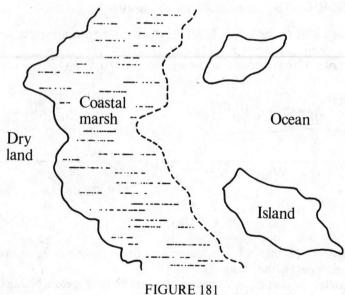

Coastal marsh

Dry land

Ocean

Island

FIGURE 181

WILL the disposition of one's property, to take effect after one's death. Same as **testament.**
Example: If one does not prepare a *will*, state law will govern the disposition of one's property after death.

WILLIAMSBURG GEORGIAN OR EARLY GEORGIAN an English style house built in Williamsburg and representative of the early Georgian houses built in America throughout the early 1700s. They had simple exterior lines and generally fewer of the

decorative devices characteristic of the later Georgian houses. Most were 2- or 3-story rectangular houses with two large chimneys rising high above the roof at each end.
Example: Figure 182.

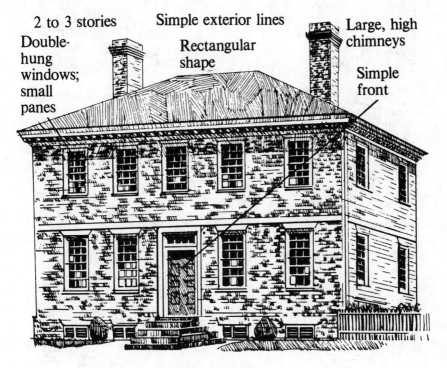

2 to 3 stories
Double-hung windows; small panes
Simple exterior lines
Rectangular shape
Large, high chimneys
Simple front

FIGURE 182

WINDOW an opening in the wall of a building to let in light and air. Most are made of transparent material and have the ability to be opened and closed.
Example: Figure 183.

WITHOUT RECOURSE words used in endorsing a **note** or bill to denote that the holder is not to look to the debtor personally in the event of nonpayment: the creditor has **recourse** only to the property. A form of exculpation. Same as **nonrecourse**. See **endorsement, exculpatory clause.**
Example: Abel insisted that the **mortgage** to the seller be *without recourse.* In the event that the value of the property declines, Abel may lose the property but he loses nothing else.

WOMEN'S COUNCIL OF REALTORS® (WCR) an organization, affiliated with the **National Association of Realtors®,** devoted to preparing women in **real estate** for their emerging roles in society,

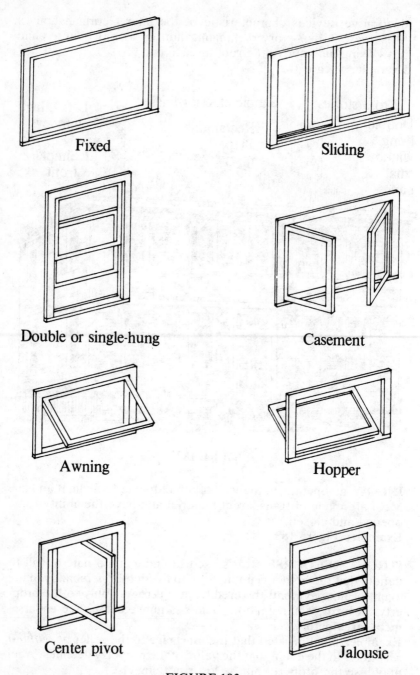

Fixed

Sliding

Double or single-hung

Casement

Awning

Hopper

Center pivot

Jalousie

FIGURE 183

to encouraging members to a productive career in real estate, and
to developing leadership potential. Publishes *The Real Estate*

Scene (monthly) and the *WCR Communiqué* (quarterly).
Address:
Women's Council of Realtors®
430 N. Michigan Avenue
Chicago, Illinois 60611

WOOD-DESTROYING INSECT a term used in certain home **inspection** forms; as a condition for purchase, the property must be free of these insects.
Examples:
• subterranean termites
• dry wood termites
• powder post beetles

WORKING CAPITAL the difference between current **assets** and current **liabilities.**
Example: The *working capital* is $2,500 ($4,000 minus $1,500) according to the balance sheet in Table 44.

TABLE 44

Assets		Liabilities & equity	
Current		Current	
cash	$1,000		
acc'ts receivable	1,000	accounts payable	$ 500
inventory	2,000	3-month note	1,000
Current assets	$4,000	Current liabilities	$1,500
Fixed		Long-term	
Land	6,000	Mortgage	$10,000
Buildings	10,000	Equity	8,500
Total assets	$20,000	Total liabilities and equity	$20,000

WORKOUT a mutual effort by a property owner and lender to avoid **foreclosure** or **bankruptcy** following a **default;** generally involves substantial reduction in the **debt service** burden during an economic depression. See **distressed property.**
Example: Because of an economic slowdown, the hotel suffered high **vacancy rates** and failed to generate enough income to meet **mortgage** payments. The owner approached the lender about a *workout.* It was agreed to reduce the outstanding loan **principal** and extend the **maturity** date to reduce the debt service. In turn the lender would participate in the income when the economy recovered and hotel income exceeded a specified amount. See **participation mortgage.**

WRITE-DOWN to diminish in amount on the records, generally to reflect a **market value** loss.

Example: Bank auditors, upon discovering that a certain **mortgage** was worthless, insisted on a *write-down*. The bank recorded the value decline as a bad debt expense.

WRAPAROUND MORTGAGE a loan arrangement in which an existing loan is retained and an additional loan, larger than the existing loan, is made. The new lender accepts the obligation to make payments on the old loan. The existing loan generally carries an **interest rate** below the rate available on new loans. Consequently, the **yield** to the wraparound lender is higher than the rate charged on the new loan. Sellers are the most common wraparound lenders.

Example: Figure 184 and Table 45.

TABLE 45

Wraparound mortgage

Seller gets $10,000 from buyer
    and $20,000 from wraparound
    lender.
Wraparound lender makes
    payments on existing
    mortgage.
Buyer makes payments on
    wraparound mortgage.
Lender gets payment of
    $632
    -336
    _____
    $296 per month on $20,000
    outlay for a yield over 25
    years of 17.5%.

WRIT OF EJECTMENT see **ejectment.**

wraparound loan

Y

YIELD 1. a measurement of the rate of earnings from an investment. See **current yield, yield to maturity.**

Example: A loan is arranged to *yield* 15% a year to the lender.

2. the productivity of agricultural land.

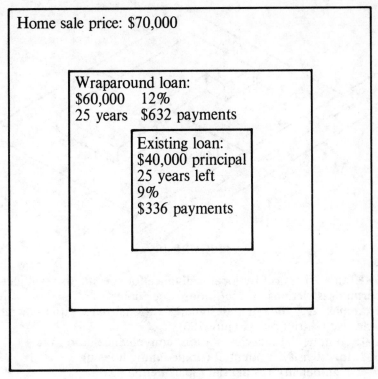

Home sale price: $70,000

Wraparound loan:
$60,000   12%
25 years $632 payments

Existing loan:
$40,000 principal
25 years left
9%
$336 payments

FIGURE 184

Example: A farm produces a *yield* of 5,000 bushels of corn per acre.

YIELD TO MATURITY the **internal rate of return** on an investment. Considers all inflows and outflows of investment returns and their timing.
Example: An income-producing property requires a $10,000 investment. It promises a $1,000 annual return for 5 years, then resale proceeds of $15,000. The *yield to maturity* is 17.1%. See **internal rate of return** for formulas.

Z

ZERO LOT LINE a form of **cluster housing** development in which individual dwelling units are placed on separately platted lots but are attached to one another. See **planned unit development, plat, row house, town-house.**
Example: A representative *zero lot line* development (Figure 185).

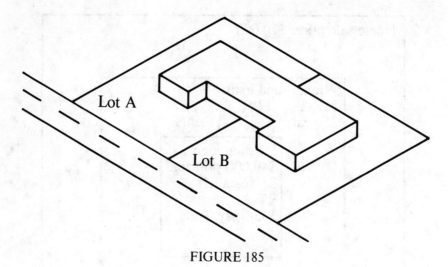

FIGURE 185

ZONE an area set off by local **ordinance** for specific use, subject to certain **restrictions** or conditions. See **zoning.**
Example: A zoning map designates various *zones* with associated land use restrictions (Figure 186).
C-1: commercial (service station, convenience store, etc.)
R-2: low-**density** residential **(single-family** housing)
R-4: high-density residential (apartments)

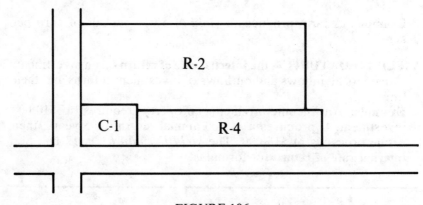

FIGURE 186

ZONING a legal mechanism for local governments to regulate the use of privately owned **real property** by specific application of **police power** to prevent conflicting land uses and promote orderly development. All privately owned land within the jurisdiction is placed within designated zones that limit the type and intensity of development permitted. See **zone.**

Example: Before a **tract** of land may be developed, the intended use must be permitted under the existing *zoning* classification. If the proposed use is not permitted, the developer must apply for an amendment to the **zoning ordinance,** or for rezoning. Such amendments are granted by the local governing body, generally following a public hearing and recommendation from the **planning commission.**

ZONING MAP a map of the local jurisdiction that indicates current **zoning** designations.

Example: A typical *zoning* map (Figure 187).

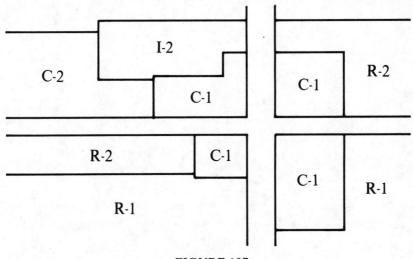

FIGURE 187

ZONING ORDINANCE act of city or county or other authorities specifying the type of use to which property may be put in specific areas. See **zone, zoning.**

Example: A typical *zoning ordinance* defines:
• the purpose for which the ordinance is adopted
• the various zoning classifications and permitted uses within each
• **restrictions,** such as height limitations
• the procedure for handling nonconforming uses
• the procedure for granting amendments, **variances,** and hearing appeals
• penalties for **violation** of the ordinance

TABLES

MONTHLY MORTGAGE PAYMENTS

The monthly payments table allows you to find out how much you would pay in interest and principal per month on an amortizing mortgage loan. To use the table you must know the following:

1. *The loan interest rate.* Each page is for a different interest rate as shown in the table's heading. Rates range from 7% to 21.75% by .25% intervals.

2. *The amount borrowed.* Amounts are shown in the column on the far left side of each table. To find the payment for an amount in between those shown, add up the payments as shown in the example below.

3. *The maturity or term of the loan.* This is the length of time over which the payments are set to run. Maturities of 15, 20, 25, and 30 years are shown in the top row of each table.

The body of the table shows the monthly payment amount in dollars. This payment does not include escrow payments which may be required by the lender for insurance and property taxes. Such payments would be in addition to the amount shown in the table.

Example: Suppose you wish to borrow $47,850 to buy a home. The maturity of the loan is 25 years and the annual interest rate is 7%. To find the monthly payment, look at the first table where the annual interest rate is 7%. First look at where the row for "40,000" intersects the column for "25" years. The amount is 282.72. Next locate the row for "7,000" and column for "25" and see the amount of 49.48 at their intersection. Likewise, find the "800" row and "25" column (amount is 5.66) and the "50" row and "25" column (amount is .36). The total payment is the sum of these amounts:

40,000	282.72
7,000	49.48
800	5.66
50	.36
47,850	338.22

The total loan amount is $47,850 and the total monthly payment is $338.22.

Example: Suppose your monthly income is $2,000 and you can afford to pay up to 25% of that amount ($500) on mortgage payments. How big a loan can you get?

Assume the loan interest rate is 7% and 30 year loans are available. Look once again at the first table. Find the amount in the table under the "30" column which is closest but lower than 500. You should see the amount of 465.72 in the "70,000" row. The difference between 500 and 465.72 is 34.28. Find the closest lower amount in the "30" column. The answer is 33. 27 in the "5,000" row. You still have 34.28 minus 33.27, or 1.01 to

spend. In the "100" row you will find an amount of .67. You still have
1.01 −.67, or .34 to spend. In the "50" row you will find an amount of .34.
Now add up all the amounts:

465.72	70,000
33.27	5,000
.67	100
.34	50
500.00	75,150

The highest payment you could afford is $500.00 which, at 7% over 30
years, will provide for a loan of $75,150.

MONTHLY PAYMENTS
ANNUAL INTEREST RATE: 7 %

LOAN AMOUNT	LOAN MATURITY (YEARS)			
	15	20	25	30
50	0.45	0.39	0.36	0.34
100	0.90	0.78	0.71	0.67
200	1.80	1.56	1.42	1.34
300	2.70	2.33	2.13	2.00
400	3.60	3.11	2.83	2.67
500	4.50	3.88	3.54	3.33
600	5.40	4.66	4.25	4.00
700	6.30	5.43	4.95	4.66
800	7.20	6.21	5.66	5.33
900	8.09	6.98	6.37	5.99
1,000	8.99	7.76	7.07	6.66
2,000	17.98	15.51	14.14	13.31
3,000	26.97	23.26	21.21	19.96
4,000	35.96	31.02	28.28	26.62
5,000	44.95	38.77	35.34	33.27
6,000	53.93	46.52	42.41	39.92
7,000	62.92	54.28	49.48	46.58
8,000	71.91	62.03	56.55	53.23
9,000	80.90	69.78	63.62	59.88
10,000	89.89	77.53	70.68	66.54
20,000	179.77	155.06	141.36	133.07
30,000	269.65	232.59	212.04	199.60
40,000	359.54	310.12	282.72	266.13
50,000	449.42	387.65	353.39	332.66
60,000	539.30	465.18	424.07	399.19
70,000	629.18	542.71	494.75	465.72
80,000	719.07	620.24	565.43	532.25
90,000	808.95	697.77	636.11	598.78
100,000	898.83	775.30	706.78	665.31
150,000	1348.25	1162.95	1060.17	997.96

MONTHLY PAYMENTS
ANNUAL INTEREST RATE: 7.25 %

LOAN AMOUNT	LOAN MATURITY (YEARS)			
	15	20	25	30
50	0.46	0.40	0.37	0.35
100	0.92	0.80	0.73	0.69
200	1.83	1.59	1.45	1.37
300	2.74	2.38	2.17	2.05
400	3.66	3.17	2.90	2.73
500	4.57	3.96	3.62	3.42
600	5.48	4.75	4.34	4.10
700	6.40	5.54	5.06	4.78
800	7.31	6.33	5.79	5.46
900	8.22	7.12	6.51	6.14
1,000	9.13	7.91	7.23	6.83
2,000	18.26	15.81	14.46	13.65
3,000	27.39	23.72	21.69	20.47
4,000	36.52	31.62	28.92	27.29
5,000	45.65	39.52	36.15	34.11
6,000	54.78	47.43	43.37	40.94
7,000	63.91	55.33	50.60	47.76
8,000	73.03	63.24	57.83	54.58
9,000	82.16	71.14	65.06	61.40
10,000	91.29	79.04	72.29	68.22
20,000	182.58	158.08	144.57	136.44
30,000	273.86	237.12	216.85	204.66
40,000	365.15	316.16	289.13	272.88
50,000	456.44	395.19	361.41	341.09
60,000	547.72	474.23	433.69	409.31
70,000	639.01	553.27	505.97	477.53
80,000	730.30	632.31	578.25	545.75
90,000	821.58	711.35	650.53	613.96
100,000	912.87	790.38	722.81	682.18
150,000	1369.30	1185.57	1084.22	1023.27

MONTHLY PAYMENTS
ANNUAL INTEREST RATE: 7.5 %

LOAN AMOUNT	LOAN MATURITY (YEARS)			
	15	20	25	30
50	0.47	0.41	0.37	0.35
100	0.93	0.81	0.74	0.70
200	1.86	1.62	1.48	1.40
300	2.79	2.42	2.22	2.10
400	3.71	3.23	2.96	2.80
500	4.64	4.03	3.70	3.50
600	5.57	4.84	4.44	4.20
700	6.49	5.64	5.18	4.90
800	7.42	6.45	5.92	5.60
900	8.35	7.26	6.66	6.30
1,000	9.28	8.06	7.39	7.00
2,000	18.55	16.12	14.78	13.99
3,000	27.82	24.17	22.17	20.98
4,000	37.09	32.23	29.56	27.97
5,000	46.36	40.28	36.95	34.97
6,000	55.63	48.34	44.34	41.96
7,000	64.90	56.40	51.73	48.95
8,000	74.17	64.45	59.12	55.94
9,000	83.44	72.51	66.51	62.93
10,000	92.71	80.56	73.90	69.93
20,000	185.41	161.12	147.80	139.85
30,000	278.11	241.68	221.70	209.77
40,000	370.81	322.24	295.60	279.69
50,000	463.51	402.80	369.50	349.61
60,000	556.21	483.36	443.40	419.53
70,000	648.91	563.92	517.30	489.45
80,000	741.61	644.48	591.20	559.38
90,000	834.31	725.04	665.10	629.30
100,000	927.01	805.60	738.99	699.22
150,000	1390.52	1208.39	1108.49	1048.83

MONTHLY PAYMENTS
ANNUAL INTEREST RATE: 7.75 %

LOAN AMOUNT	LOAN MATURITY (YEARS)			
	15	20	25	30
50	0.48	0.42	0.38	0.36
100	0.95	0.83	0.76	0.72
200	1.89	1.65	1.52	1.44
300	2.83	2.47	2.27	2.15
400	3.77	3.29	3.03	2.87
500	4.71	4.11	3.78	3.59
600	5.65	4.93	4.54	4.30
700	6.59	5.75	5.29	5.02
800	7.54	6.57	6.05	5.74
900	8.48	7.39	6.80	6.45
1,000	9.42	8.21	7.56	7.17
2,000	18.83	16.42	15.11	14.33
3,000	28.24	24.63	22.66	21.50
4,000	37.66	32.84	30.22	28.66
5,000	47.07	41.05	37.77	35.83
6,000	56.48	49.26	45.32	42.99
7,000	65.89	57.47	52.88	50.15
8,000	75.31	65.68	60.43	57.32
9,000	84.72	73.89	67.98	64.48
10,000	94.13	82.10	75.54	71.65
20,000	188.26	164.20	151.07	143.29
30,000	282.39	246.29	226.60	214.93
40,000	376.52	328.39	302.14	286.57
50,000	470.64	410.48	377.67	358.21
60,000	564.77	492.58	453.20	429.85
70,000	658.90	574.67	528.74	501.49
80,000	753.03	656.77	604.27	573.14
90,000	847.16	738.86	679.80	644.78
100,000	941.28	820.96	755.34	716.42
150,000	1411.92	1231.43	1133.00	1074.63

MONTHLY PAYMENTS
ANNUAL INTEREST RATE: 8 %

LOAN AMOUNT	LOAN MATURITY (YEARS)			
	15	20	25	30
50	0.48	0.42	0.39	0.37
100	0.96	0.84	0.78	0.74
200	1.92	1.68	1.55	1.47
300	2.87	2.51	2.32	2.21
400	3.83	3.35	3.09	2.94
500	4.78	4.19	3.86	3.67
600	5.74	5.02	4.64	4.41
700	6.69	5.86	5.41	5.14
800	7.65	6.70	6.18	5.88
900	8.61	7.53	6.95	6.61
1,000	9.56	8.37	7.72	7.34
2,000	19.12	16.73	15.44	14.68
3,000	28.67	25.10	23.16	22.02
4,000	38.23	33.46	30.88	29.36
5,000	47.79	41.83	38.60	36.69
6,000	57.34	50.19	46.31	44.03
7,000	66.90	58.56	54.03	51.37
8,000	76.46	66.92	61.75	58.71
9,000	86.01	75.28	69.47	66.04
10,000	95.57	83.65	77.19	73.38
20,000	191.14	167.29	154.37	146.76
30,000	286.70	250.94	231.55	220.13
40,000	382.27	334.58	308.73	293.51
50,000	477.83	418.22	385.91	366.89
60,000	573.40	501.87	463.09	440.26
70,000	668.96	585.51	540.28	513.64
80,000	764.53	669.16	617.46	587.02
90,000	860.09	752.80	694.64	660.39
100,000	955.66	836.44	771.82	733.77
150,000	1433.48	1254.66	1157.73	1100.65

315

MONTHLY PAYMENTS
ANNUAL INTEREST RATE: 8.25 %

LOAN AMOUNT	LOAN MATURITY (YEARS)			
	15	20	25	30
50	0.49	0.43	0.40	0.38
100	0.98	0.86	0.79	0.76
200	1.95	1.71	1.58	1.51
300	2.92	2.56	2.37	2.26
400	3.89	3.41	3.16	3.01
500	4.86	4.27	3.95	3.76
600	5.83	5.12	4.74	4.51
700	6.80	5.97	5.52	5.26
800	7.77	6.82	6.31	6.02
900	8.74	7.67	7.10	6.77
1,000	9.71	8.53	7.89	7.52
2,000	19.41	17.05	15.77	15.03
3,000	29.11	25.57	23.66	22.54
4,000	38.81	34.09	31.54	30.06
5,000	48.51	42.61	39.43	37.57
6,000	58.21	51.13	47.31	45.08
7,000	67.91	59.65	55.20	52.59
8,000	77.62	68.17	63.08	60.11
9,000	87.32	76.69	70.97	67.62
10,000	97.02	85.21	78.85	75.13
20,000	194.03	170.42	157.69	150.26
30,000	291.05	255.62	236.54	225.38
40,000	388.06	340.83	315.38	300.51
50,000	485.07	426.04	394.23	375.64
60,000	582.09	511.24	473.07	450.76
70,000	679.10	596.45	551.92	525.89
80,000	776.12	681.66	630.76	601.02
90,000	873.13	766.86	709.61	676.14
100,000	970.14	852.07	788.45	751.27
150,000	1455.21	1278.10	1182.68	1126.90

MONTHLY PAYMENTS
ANNUAL INTEREST RATE: 8.5 %

LOAN AMOUNT	LOAN MATURITY (YEARS)			
	15	20	25	30
50	0.50	0.44	0.41	0.39
100	0.99	0.87	0.81	0.77
200	1.97	1.74	1.62	1.54
300	2.96	2.61	2.42	2.31
400	3.94	3.48	3.23	3.08
500	4.93	4.34	4.03	3.85
600	5.91	5.21	4.84	4.62
700	6.90	6.08	5.64	5.39
800	7.88	6.95	6.45	6.16
900	8.87	7.82	7.25	6.93
1,000	9.85	8.68	8.06	7.69
2,000	19.70	17.36	16.11	15.38
3,000	29.55	26.04	24.16	23.07
4,000	39.39	34.72	32.21	30.76
5,000	49.24	43.40	40.27	38.45
6,000	59.09	52.07	48.32	46.14
7,000	68.94	60.75	56.37	53.83
8,000	78.78	69.43	64.42	61.52
9,000	88.63	78.11	72.48	69.21
10,000	98.48	86.79	80.53	76.90
20,000	196.95	173.57	161.05	153.79
30,000	295.43	260.35	241.57	230.68
40,000	393.90	347.14	322.10	307.57
50,000	492.38	433.92	402.62	384.46
60,000	590.85	520.70	483.14	461.35
70,000	689.32	607.48	563.66	538.25
80,000	787.80	694.27	644.19	615.14
90,000	886.27	781.05	724.71	692.03
100,000	984.75	867.83	805.23	768.92
150,000	1477.12	1301.74	1207.85	1153.38

MONTHLY PAYMENTS
ANNUAL INTEREST RATE: 8.75 %

LOAN AMOUNT	LOAN MATURITY (YEARS)			
	15	20	25	30
50	0.50	0.45	0.42	0.40
100	1.00	0.89	0.83	0.79
200	2.00	1.77	1.65	1.58
300	3.00	2.66	2.47	2.37
400	4.00	3.54	3.29	3.15
500	5.00	4.42	4.12	3.94
600	6.00	5.31	4.94	4.73
700	7.00	6.19	5.76	5.51
800	8.00	7.07	6.58	6.30
900	9.00	7.96	7.40	7.09
1,000	10.00	8.84	8.23	7.87
2,000	19.99	17.68	16.45	15.74
3,000	29.99	26.52	24.67	23.61
4,000	39.98	35.35	32.89	31.47
5,000	49.98	44.19	41.11	39.34
6,000	59.97	53.03	49.33	47.21
7,000	69.97	61.86	57.56	55.07
8,000	79.96	70.70	65.78	62.94
9,000	89.96	79.54	74.00	70.81
10,000	99.95	88.38	82.22	78.68
20,000	199.89	176.75	164.43	157.35
30,000	299.84	265.12	246.65	236.02
40,000	399.78	353.49	328.86	314.69
50,000	499.73	441.86	411.08	393.36
60,000	599.67	530.23	493.29	472.03
70,000	699.62	618.60	575.51	550.70
80,000	799.56	706.97	657.72	629.37
90,000	899.51	795.34	739.93	708.04
100,000	999.45	883.72	822.15	786.71
150,000	1499.18	1325.57	1233.22	1180.06

MONTHLY PAYMENTS
ANNUAL INTEREST RATE: 9 %

LOAN AMOUNT	LOAN MATURITY (YEARS)			
	15	20	25	30
50	0.51	0.45	0.42	0.41
100	1.02	0.90	0.84	0.81
200	2.03	1.80	1.68	1.61
300	3.05	2.70	2.52	2.42
400	4.06	3.60	3.36	3.22
500	5.08	4.50	4.20	4.03
600	6.09	5.40	5.04	4.83
700	7.10	6.30	5.88	5.64
800	8.12	7.20	6.72	6.44
900	9.13	8.10	7.56	7.25
1,000	10.15	9.00	8.40	8.05
2,000	20.29	18.00	16.79	16.10
3,000	30.43	27.00	25.18	24.14
4,000	40.58	35.99	33.57	32.19
5,000	50.72	44.99	41.96	40.24
6,000	60.86	53.99	50.36	48.28
7,000	71.00	62.99	58.75	56.33
8,000	81.15	71.98	67.14	64.37
9,000	91.29	80.98	75.53	72.42
10,000	101.43	89.98	83.92	80.47
20,000	202.86	179.95	167.84	160.93
30,000	304.28	269.92	251.76	241.39
40,000	405.71	359.89	335.68	321.85
50,000	507.14	449.87	419.60	402.32
60,000	608.56	539.84	503.52	482.78
70,000	709.99	629.81	587.44	563.24
80,000	811.41	719.78	671.36	643.70
90,000	912.84	809.76	755.28	724.16
100,000	1014.27	899.73	839.20	804.63
150,000	1521.40	1349.59	1258.80	1206.94

MONTHLY PAYMENTS
ANNUAL INTEREST RATE: 9.25 %

LOAN AMOUNT	LOAN MATURITY (YEARS)			
	15	20	25	30
50	0.52	0.46	0.43	0.42
100	1.03	0.92	0.86	0.83
200	2.06	1.84	1.72	1.65
300	3.09	2.75	2.57	2.47
400	4.12	3.67	3.43	3.30
500	5.15	4.58	4.29	4.12
600	6.18	5.50	5.14	4.94
700	7.21	6.42	6.00	5.76
800	8.24	7.33	6.86	6.59
900	9.27	8.25	7.71	7.41
1,000	10.30	9.16	8.57	8.23
2,000	20.59	18.32	17.13	16.46
3,000	30.88	27.48	25.70	24.69
4,000	41.17	36.64	34.26	32.91
5,000	51.46	45.80	42.82	41.14
6,000	61.76	54.96	51.39	49.37
7,000	72.05	64.12	59.95	57.59
8,000	82.34	73.27	68.52	65.82
9,000	92.63	82.43	77.08	74.05
10,000	102.92	91.59	85.64	82.27
20,000	205.84	183.18	171.28	164.54
30,000	308.76	274.77	256.92	246.81
40,000	411.68	366.35	342.56	329.08
50,000	514.60	457.94	428.20	411.34
60,000	617.52	549.53	513.84	493.61
70,000	720.44	641.11	599.47	575.88
80,000	823.36	732.70	685.11	658.15
90,000	926.28	824.29	770.75	740.41
100,000	1029.20	915.87	856.39	822.68
150,000	1543.80	1373.81	1284.58	1234.02

MONTHLY PAYMENTS
ANNUAL INTEREST RATE: 9.5 %

LOAN AMOUNT	LOAN MATURITY (YEARS)			
	15	20	25	30
50	0.53	0.47	0.44	0.43
100	1.05	0.94	0.88	0.85
200	2.09	1.87	1.75	1.69
300	3.14	2.80	2.63	2.53
400	4.18	3.73	3.50	3.37
500	5.23	4.67	4.37	4.21
600	6.27	5.60	5.25	5.05
700	7.31	6.53	6.12	5.89
800	8.36	7.46	6.99	6.73
900	9.40	8.39	7.87	7.57
1,000	10.45	9.33	8.74	8.41
2,000	20.89	18.65	17.48	16.82
3,000	31.33	27.97	26.22	25.23
4,000	41.77	37.29	34.95	33.64
5,000	52.22	46.61	43.69	42.05
6,000	62.66	55.93	52.43	50.46
7,000	73.10	65.25	61.16	58.86
8,000	83.54	74.58	69.90	67.27
9,000	93.98	83.90	78.64	75.68
10,000	104.43	93.22	87.37	84.09
20,000	208.85	186.43	174.74	168.18
30,000	313.27	279.64	262.11	252.26
40,000	417.69	372.86	349.48	336.35
50,000	522.12	466.07	436.85	420.43
60,000	626.54	559.28	524.22	504.52
70,000	730.96	652.50	611.59	588.60
80,000	835.38	745.71	698.96	672.69
90,000	939.80	838.92	786.33	756.77
100,000	1044.23	932.13	873.70	840.86
150,000	1566.34	1398.20	1310.55	1261.29

MONTHLY PAYMENTS
ANNUAL INTEREST RATE: 9.75 %

LOAN AMOUNT	LOAN MATURITY (YEARS)			
	15	20	25	30
50	0.53	0.48	0.45	0.43
100	1.06	0.95	0.90	0.86
200	2.12	1.90	1.79	1.72
300	3.18	2.85	2.68	2.58
400	4.24	3.80	3.57	3.44
500	5.30	4.75	4.46	4.30
600	6.36	5.70	5.35	5.16
700	7.42	6.64	6.24	6.02
800	8.48	7.59	7.13	6.88
900	9.54	8.54	8.03	7.74
1,000	10.60	9.49	8.92	8.60
2,000	21.19	18.98	17.83	17.19
3,000	31.79	28.46	26.74	25.78
4,000	42.38	37.95	35.65	34.37
5,000	52.97	47.43	44.56	42.96
6,000	63.57	56.92	53.47	51.55
7,000	74.16	66.40	62.38	60.15
8,000	84.75	75.89	71.30	68.74
9,000	95.35	85.37	80.21	77.33
10,000	105.94	94.86	89.12	85.92
20,000	211.88	189.71	178.23	171.84
30,000	317.81	284.56	267.35	257.75
40,000	423.75	379.41	356.46	343.67
50,000	529.69	474.26	445.57	429.58
60,000	635.62	569.12	534.69	515.50
70,000	741.56	663.97	623.80	601.41
80,000	847.50	758.82	712.92	687.33
90,000	953.43	853.67	802.03	773.24
100,000	1059.37	948.52	891.14	859.16
150,000	1589.05	1422.78	1336.71	1288.74

MONTHLY PAYMENTS
ANNUAL INTEREST RATE: 10 %

LOAN AMOUNT	LOAN MATURITY (YEARS)			
	15	20	25	30
50	0.54	0.49	0.46	0.44
100	1.08	0.97	0.91	0.88
200	2.15	1.94	1.82	1.76
300	3.23	2.90	2.73	2.64
400	4.30	3.87	3.64	3.52
500	5.38	4.83	4.55	4.39
600	6.45	5.80	5.46	5.27
700	7.53	6.76	6.37	6.15
800	8.60	7.73	7.27	7.03
900	9.68	8.69	8.18	7.90
1,000	10.75	9.66	9.09	8.78
2,000	21.50	19.31	18.18	17.56
3,000	32.24	28.96	27.27	26.33
4,000	42.99	38.61	36.35	35.11
5,000	53.74	48.26	45.44	43.88
6,000	64.48	57.91	54.53	52.66
7,000	75.23	67.56	63.61	61.44
8,000	85.97	77.21	72.70	70.21
9,000	96.72	86.86	81.79	78.99
10,000	107.47	96.51	90.88	87.76
20,000	214.93	193.01	181.75	175.52
30,000	322.39	289.51	272.62	263.28
40,000	429.85	386.01	363.49	351.03
50,000	537.31	482.52	454.36	438.79
60,000	644.77	579.02	545.23	526.55
70,000	752.23	675.52	636.10	614.31
80,000	859.69	772.02	726.97	702.06
90,000	967.15	868.53	817.84	789.82
100,000	1074.61	965.03	908.71	877.58
150,000	1611.92	1447.54	1363.06	1316.36

MONTHLY PAYMENTS
ANNUAL INTEREST RATE: 10.25 %

LOAN AMOUNT	LOAN MATURITY (YEARS)			
	15	20	25	30
50	0.55	0.50	0.47	0.45
100	1.09	0.99	0.93	0.90
200	2.18	1.97	1.86	1.80
300	3.27	2.95	2.78	2.69
400	4.36	3.93	3.71	3.59
500	5.45	4.91	4.64	4.49
600	6.54	5.89	5.56	5.38
700	7.63	6.88	6.49	6.28
800	8.72	7.86	7.42	7.17
900	9.81	8.84	8.34	8.07
1,000	10.90	9.82	9.27	8.97
2,000	21.80	19.64	18.53	17.93
3,000	32.70	29.45	27.80	26.89
4,000	43.60	39.27	37.06	35.85
5,000	54.50	49.09	46.32	44.81
6,000	65.40	58.90	55.59	53.77
7,000	76.30	68.72	64.85	62.73
8,000	87.20	78.54	74.12	71.69
9,000	98.10	88.35	83.38	80.65
10,000	109.00	98.17	92.64	89.62
20,000	217.99	196.33	185.28	179.23
30,000	326.99	294.50	277.92	268.84
40,000	435.98	392.66	370.56	358.45
50,000	544.98	490.83	463.20	448.06
60,000	653.97	588.99	555.83	537.67
70,000	762.97	687.15	648.47	627.28
80,000	871.96	785.32	741.11	716.89
90,000	980.96	883.48	833.75	806.50
100,000	1089.95	981.65	926.39	896.11
150,000	1634.93	1472.47	1389.58	1344.16

MONTHLY PAYMENTS
ANNUAL INTEREST RATE: 10.5 %

LOAN AMOUNT	LOAN MATURITY (YEARS)			
	15	20	25	30
50	0.56	0.50	0.48	0.46
100	1.11	1.00	0.95	0.92
200	2.22	2.00	1.89	1.83
300	3.32	3.00	2.84	2.75
400	4.43	4.00	3.78	3.66
500	5.53	5.00	4.73	4.58
600	6.64	6.00	5.67	5.49
700	7.74	6.99	6.61	6.41
800	8.85	7.99	7.56	7.32
900	9.95	8.99	8.50	8.24
1,000	11.06	9.99	9.45	9.15
2,000	22.11	19.97	18.89	18.30
3,000	33.17	29.96	28.33	27.45
4,000	44.22	39.94	37.77	36.59
5,000	55.28	49.92	47.21	45.74
6,000	66.33	59.91	56.66	54.89
7,000	77.38	69.89	66.10	64.04
8,000	88.44	79.88	75.54	73.18
9,000	99.49	89.86	84.98	82.33
10,000	110.55	99.84	94.42	91.48
20,000	221.09	199.68	188.84	182.95
30,000	331.63	299.52	283.26	274.43
40,000	442.17	399.36	377.68	365.90
50,000	552.71	499.20	472.10	457.37
60,000	663.25	599.03	566.51	548.85
70,000	773.79	698.87	660.93	640.32
80,000	884.33	798.71	755.35	731.80
90,000	994.87	898.55	849.77	823.27
100,000	1105.41	998.39	944.19	914.74
150,000	1658.11	1497.58	1416.28	1372.11

MONTHLY PAYMENTS
ANNUAL INTEREST RATE: 10.75 %

LOAN AMOUNT	LOAN MATURITY (YEARS)			
	15	20	25	30
50	0.57	0.51	0.49	0.47
100	1.13	1.02	0.97	0.94
200	2.25	2.04	1.93	1.87
300	3.37	3.05	2.89	2.81
400	4.49	4.07	3.85	3.74
500	5.61	5.08	4.82	4.67
600	6.73	6.10	5.78	5.61
700	7.85	7.11	6.74	6.54
800	8.97	8.13	7.70	7.47
900	10.09	9.14	8.66	8.41
1,000	11.21	10.16	9.63	9.34
2,000	22.42	20.31	19.25	18.67
3,000	33.63	30.46	28.87	28.01
4,000	44.84	40.61	38.49	37.34
5,000	56.05	50.77	48.11	46.68
6,000	67.26	60.92	57.73	56.01
7,000	78.47	71.07	67.35	65.35
8,000	89.68	81.22	76.97	74.68
9,000	100.89	91.38	86.59	84.02
10,000	112.10	101.53	96.21	93.35
20,000	224.19	203.05	192.42	186.70
30,000	336.29	304.57	288.63	280.05
40,000	448.38	406.10	384.84	373.40
50,000	560.48	507.62	481.05	466.75
60,000	672.57	609.14	577.26	560.09
70,000	784.67	710.67	673.47	653.44
80,000	896.76	812.19	769.68	746.79
90,000	1008.86	913.71	865.89	840.14
100,000	1120.95	1015.23	962.10	933.49
150,000	1681.43	1522.85	1443.14	1400.23

MONTHLY PAYMENTS
ANNUAL INTEREST RATE: 11 %

| LOAN AMOUNT | LOAN MATURITY (YEARS) | | | |
	15	20	25	30
50	0.57	0.52	0.50	0.48
100	1.14	1.04	0.99	0.96
200	2.28	2.07	1.97	1.91
300	3.41	3.10	2.95	2.86
400	4.55	4.13	3.93	3.81
500	5.69	5.17	4.91	4.77
600	6.82	6.20	5.89	5.72
700	7.96	7.23	6.87	6.67
800	9.10	8.26	7.85	7.62
900	10.23	9.29	8.83	8.58
1,000	11.37	10.33	9.81	9.53
2,000	22.74	20.65	19.61	19.05
3,000	34.10	30.97	29.41	28.57
4,000	45.47	41.29	39.21	38.10
5,000	56.83	51.61	49.01	47.62
6,000	68.20	61.94	58.81	57.14
7,000	79.57	72.26	68.61	66.67
8,000	90.93	82.58	78.41	76.19
9,000	102.30	92.90	88.22	85.71
10,000	113.66	103.22	98.02	95.24
20,000	227.32	206.44	196.03	190.47
30,000	340.98	309.66	294.04	285.70
40,000	454.64	412.88	392.05	380.93
50,000	568.30	516.10	490.06	476.17
60,000	681.96	619.32	588.07	571.40
70,000	795.62	722.54	686.08	666.63
80,000	909.28	825.75	784.09	761.86
90,000	1022.94	928.97	882.11	857.10
100,000	1136.60	1032.19	980.12	952.33
150,000	1704.90	1548.29	1470.17	1428.49

MONTHLY PAYMENTS
ANNUAL INTEREST RATE: 11.25 %

LOAN AMOUNT	LOAN MATURITY (YEARS)			
	15	20	25	30
50	0.58	0.53	0.50	0.49
100	1.16	1.05	1.00	0.98
200	2.31	2.10	2.00	1.95
300	3.46	3.15	3.00	2.92
400	4.61	4.20	4.00	3.89
500	5.77	5.25	5.00	4.86
600	6.92	6.30	5.99	5.83
700	8.07	7.35	6.99	6.80
800	9.22	8.40	7.99	7.78
900	10.38	9.45	8.99	8.75
1,000	11.53	10.50	9.99	9.72
2,000	23.05	20.99	19.97	19.43
3,000	34.58	31.48	29.95	29.14
4,000	46.10	41.98	39.93	38.86
5,000	57.62	52.47	49.92	48.57
6,000	69.15	62.96	59.90	58.28
7,000	80.67	73.45	69.88	67.99
8,000	92.19	83.95	79.86	77.71
9,000	103.72	94.44	89.85	87.42
10,000	115.24	104.93	99.83	97.13
20,000	230.47	209.86	199.65	194.26
30,000	345.71	314.78	299.48	291.38
40,000	460.94	419.71	399.30	388.51
50,000	576.18	524.63	499.13	485.64
60,000	691.41	629.56	598.95	582.76
70,000	806.65	734.49	698.77	679.89
80,000	921.88	839.41	798.60	777.01
90,000	1037.12	944.34	898.42	874.14
100,000	1152.35	1049.26	998.25	971.27
150,000	1728.52	1573.89	1497.37	1456.90

MONTHLY PAYMENTS
ANNUAL INTEREST RATE: 11.5 %

LOAN AMOUNT	LOAN MATURITY (YEARS)			
	15	20	25	30
50	0.59	0.54	0.51	0.50
100	1.17	1.07	1.02	1.00
200	2.34	2.14	2.04	1.99
300	3.51	3.20	3.05	2.98
400	4.68	4.27	4.07	3.97
500	5.85	5.34	5.09	4.96
600	7.01	6.40	6.10	5.95
700	8.18	7.47	7.12	6.94
800	9.35	8.54	8.14	7.93
900	10.52	9.60	9.15	8.92
1,000	11.69	10.67	10.17	9.91
2,000	23.37	21.33	20.33	19.81
3,000	35.05	32.00	30.50	29.71
4,000	46.73	42.66	40.66	39.62
5,000	58.41	53.33	50.83	49.52
6,000	70.10	63.99	60.99	59.42
7,000	81.78	74.66	71.16	69.33
8,000	93.46	85.32	81.32	79.23
9,000	105.14	95.98	91.49	89.13
10,000	116.82	106.65	101.65	99.03
20,000	233.64	213.29	203.30	198.06
30,000	350.46	319.93	304.95	297.09
40,000	467.28	426.58	406.59	396.12
50,000	584.10	533.22	508.24	495.15
60,000	700.92	639.86	609.89	594.18
70,000	817.74	746.51	711.53	693.21
80,000	934.56	853.15	813.18	792.24
90,000	1051.38	959.79	914.83	891.27
100,000	1168.20	1066.43	1016.47	990.30
150,000	1752.29	1599.65	1524.71	1485.44

MONTHLY PAYMENTS
ANNUAL INTEREST RATE: 11.75 %

LOAN AMOUNT	LOAN MATURITY (YEARS)			
	15	20	25	30
50	0.60	0.55	0.52	0.51
100	1.19	1.09	1.04	1.01
200	2.37	2.17	2.07	2.02
300	3.56	3.26	3.11	3.03
400	4.74	4.34	4.14	4.04
500	5.93	5.42	5.18	5.05
600	7.11	6.51	6.21	6.06
700	8.29	7.59	7.25	7.07
800	9.48	8.67	8.28	8.08
900	10.66	9.76	9.32	9.09
1,000	11.85	10.84	10.35	10.10
2,000	23.69	21.68	20.70	20.19
3,000	35.53	32.52	31.05	30.29
4,000	47.37	43.35	41.40	40.38
5,000	59.21	54.19	51.74	50.48
6,000	71.05	65.03	62.09	60.57
7,000	82.89	75.86	72.44	70.66
8,000	94.74	86.70	82.79	80.76
9,000	106.58	97.54	93.14	90.85
10,000	118.42	108.38	103.48	100.95
20,000	236.83	216.75	206.96	201.89
30,000	355.25	325.12	310.44	302.83
40,000	473.66	433.49	413.92	403.77
50,000	592.07	541.86	517.40	504.71
60,000	710.49	650.23	620.88	605.65
70,000	828.90	758.60	724.36	706.59
80,000	947.31	866.97	827.84	807.53
90,000	1065.73	975.34	931.32	908.47
100,000	1184.14	1083.71	1034.80	1009.42
150,000	1776.21	1625.57	1552.20	1514.12

MONTHLY PAYMENTS
ANNUAL INTEREST RATE: 12 %

LOAN AMOUNT	LOAN MATURITY (YEARS)			
	15	20	25	30
50	0.61	0.56	0.53	0.52
100	1.21	1.11	1.06	1.03
200	2.41	2.21	2.11	2.06
300	3.61	3.31	3.16	3.09
400	4.81	4.41	4.22	4.12
500	6.01	5.51	5.27	5.15
600	7.21	6.61	6.32	6.18
700	8.41	7.71	7.38	7.21
800	9.61	8.81	8.43	8.23
900	10.81	9.91	9.48	9.26
1,000	12.01	11.02	10.54	10.29
2,000	24.01	22.03	21.07	20.58
3,000	36.01	33.04	31.60	30.86
4,000	48.01	44.05	42.13	41.15
5,000	60.01	55.06	52.67	51.44
6,000	72.02	66.07	63.20	61.72
7,000	84.02	77.08	73.73	72.01
8,000	96.02	88.09	84.26	82.29
9,000	108.02	99.10	94.80	92.58
10,000	120.02	110.11	105.33	102.87
20,000	240.04	220.22	210.65	205.73
30,000	360.06	330.33	315.97	308.59
40,000	480.07	440.44	421.29	411.45
50,000	600.09	550.55	526.62	514.31
60,000	720.11	660.66	631.94	617.17
70,000	840.12	770.77	737.26	720.03
80,000	960.14	880.87	842.58	822.90
90,000	1080.16	990.98	947.91	925.76
100,000	1200.17	1101.09	1053.23	1028.62
150,000	1800.26	1651.63	1579.84	1542.92

MONTHLY PAYMENTS
ANNUAL INTEREST RATE: 12.25 %

LOAN AMOUNT	LOAN MATURITY (YEARS)			
	15	20	25	30
50	0.61	0.56	0.54	0.53
100	1.22	1.12	1.08	1.05
200	2.44	2.24	2.15	2.10
300	3.65	3.36	3.22	3.15
400	4.87	4.48	4.29	4.20
500	6.09	5.60	5.36	5.24
600	7.30	6.72	6.44	6.29
700	8.52	7.83	7.51	7.34
800	9.74	8.95	8.58	8.39
900	10.95	10.07	9.65	9.44
1,000	12.17	11.19	10.72	10.48
2,000	24.33	22.38	21.44	20.96
3,000	36.49	33.56	32.16	31.44
4,000	48.66	44.75	42.87	41.92
5,000	60.82	55.93	53.59	52.40
6,000	72.98	67.12	64.31	62.88
7,000	85.15	78.30	75.03	73.36
8,000	97.31	89.49	85.74	83.84
9,000	109.47	100.68	96.46	94.32
10,000	121.63	111.86	107.18	104.79
20,000	243.26	223.72	214.35	209.58
30,000	364.89	335.57	321.53	314.37
40,000	486.52	447.43	428.70	419.16
50,000	608.15	559.29	535.88	523.95
60,000	729.78	671.14	643.05	628.74
70,000	851.41	783.00	750.23	733.53
80,000	973.04	894.86	857.40	838.32
90,000	1094.67	1006.71	964.57	943.11
100,000	1216.30	1118.57	1071.75	1047.90
150,000	1824.45	1677.85	1607.62	1571.85

MONTHLY PAYMENTS
ANNUAL INTEREST RATE: 12.5 %

LOAN AMOUNT	LOAN MATURITY (YEARS)			
	15	20	25	30
50	0.62	0.57	0.55	0.54
100	1.24	1.14	1.10	1.07
200	2.47	2.28	2.19	2.14
300	3.70	3.41	3.28	3.21
400	4.94	4.55	4.37	4.27
500	6.17	5.69	5.46	5.34
600	7.40	6.82	6.55	6.41
700	8.63	7.96	7.64	7.48
800	9.87	9.09	8.73	8.54
900	11.10	10.23	9.82	9.61
1,000	12.33	11.37	10.91	10.68
2,000	24.66	22.73	21.81	21.35
3,000	36.98	34.09	32.72	32.02
4,000	49.31	45.45	43.62	42.70
5,000	61.63	56.81	54.52	53.37
6,000	73.96	68.17	65.43	64.04
7,000	86.28	79.53	76.33	74.71
8,000	98.61	90.90	87.23	85.39
9,000	110.93	102.26	98.14	96.06
10,000	123.26	113.62	109.04	106.73
20,000	246.51	227.23	218.08	213.46
30,000	369.76	340.85	327.11	320.18
40,000	493.01	454.46	436.15	426.91
50,000	616.27	568.08	545.18	533.63
60,000	739.52	681.69	654.22	640.36
70,000	862.77	795.30	763.25	747.09
80,000	986.02	908.92	872.29	853.81
90,000	1109.28	1022.53	981.32	960.54
100,000	1232.53	1136.15	1090.36	1067.26
150,000	1848.79	1704.22	1635.54	1600.89

MONTHLY PAYMENTS
ANNUAL INTEREST RATE: 12.75 %

LOAN AMOUNT	LOAN MATURITY (YEARS)			
	15	20	25	30
50	0.63	0.58	0.56	0.55
100	1.25	1.16	1.11	1.09
200	2.50	2.31	2.22	2.18
300	3.75	3.47	3.33	3.27
400	5.00	4.62	4.44	4.35
500	6.25	5.77	5.55	5.44
600	7.50	6.93	6.66	6.53
700	8.75	8.08	7.77	7.61
800	10.00	9.24	8.88	8.70
900	11.24	10.39	9.99	9.79
1,000	12.49	11.54	11.10	10.87
2,000	24.98	23.08	22.19	21.74
3,000	37.47	34.62	33.28	32.61
4,000	49.96	46.16	44.37	43.47
5,000	62.45	57.70	55.46	54.34
6,000	74.94	69.23	66.55	65.21
7,000	87.42	80.77	77.64	76.07
8,000	99.91	92.31	88.73	86.94
9,000	112.40	103.85	99.82	97.81
10,000	124.89	115.39	110.91	108.67
20,000	249.77	230.77	221.82	217.34
30,000	374.66	346.15	332.72	326.01
40,000	499.54	461.53	443.63	434.68
50,000	624.42	576.91	554.53	543.35
60,000	749.31	692.29	665.44	652.02
70,000	874.19	807.67	776.34	760.69
80,000	999.07	923.05	887.25	869.36
90,000	1123.96	1038.44	998.15	978.03
100,000	1248.84	1153.82	1109.06	1086.70
150,000	1873.26	1730.72	1663.58	1630.04

MONTHLY PAYMENTS
ANNUAL INTEREST RATE: 13 %

LOAN AMOUNT	LOAN MATURITY (YEARS)			
	15	20	25	30
50	0.64	0.59	0.57	0.56
100	1.27	1.18	1.13	1.11
200	2.54	2.35	2.26	2.22
300	3.80	3.52	3.39	3.32
400	5.07	4.69	4.52	4.43
500	6.33	5.86	5.64	5.54
600	7.60	7.03	6.77	6.64
700	8.86	8.21	7.90	7.75
800	10.13	9.38	9.03	8.85
900	11.39	10.55	10.16	9.96
1,000	12.66	11.72	11.28	11.07
2,000	25.31	23.44	22.56	22.13
3,000	37.96	35.15	33.84	33.19
4,000	50.61	46.87	45.12	44.25
5,000	63.27	58.58	56.40	55.31
6,000	75.92	70.30	67.68	66.38
7,000	88.57	82.02	78.95	77.44
8,000	101.22	93.73	90.23	88.50
9,000	113.88	105.45	101.51	99.56
10,000	126.53	117.16	112.79	110.62
20,000	253.05	234.32	225.57	221.24
30,000	379.58	351.48	338.36	331.86
40,000	506.10	468.64	451.14	442.48
50,000	632.63	585.79	563.92	553.10
60,000	759.15	702.95	676.71	663.72
70,000	885.67	820.11	789.49	774.34
80,000	1012.20	937.27	902.27	884.96
90,000	1138.72	1054.42	1015.06	995.58
100,000	1265.25	1171.58	1127.84	1106.20
150,000	1897.87	1757.37	1691.76	1659.30

MONTHLY PAYMENTS
ANNUAL INTEREST RATE: 13.25 %

LOAN AMOUNT	LOAN MATURITY (YEARS)			
	15	20	25	30
50	0.65	0.60	0.58	0.57
100	1.29	1.19	1.15	1.13
200	2.57	2.38	2.30	2.26
300	3.85	3.57	3.45	3.38
400	5.13	4.76	4.59	4.51
500	6.41	5.95	5.74	5.63
600	7.70	7.14	6.89	6.76
700	8.98	8.33	8.03	7.89
800	10.26	9.52	9.18	9.01
900	11.54	10.71	10.33	10.14
1,000	12.82	11.90	11.47	11.26
2,000	25.64	23.79	22.94	22.52
3,000	38.46	35.69	34.41	33.78
4,000	51.27	47.58	45.87	45.04
5,000	64.09	59.48	57.34	56.29
6,000	76.91	71.37	68.81	67.55
7,000	89.73	83.27	80.27	78.81
8,000	102.54	95.16	91.74	90.07
9,000	115.36	107.05	103.21	101.32
10,000	128.18	118.95	114.68	112.58
20,000	256.35	237.89	229.35	225.16
30,000	384.53	356.83	344.02	337.74
40,000	512.70	475.78	458.69	450.31
50,000	640.87	594.72	573.36	562.89
60,000	769.05	713.66	688.03	675.47
70,000	897.22	832.61	802.70	788.05
80,000	1025.39	951.55	917.37	900.62
90,000	1153.57	1070.49	1032.04	1013.20
100,000	1281.74	1189.44	1146.71	1125.78
150,000	1922.61	1784.15	1720.06	1688.67

MONTHLY PAYMENTS
ANNUAL INTEREST RATE: 13.5 %

LOAN AMOUNT	LOAN MATURITY (YEARS)			
	15	20	25	30
50	0.65	0.61	0.59	0.58
100	1.30	1.21	1.17	1.15
200	2.60	2.42	2.34	2.30
300	3.90	3.63	3.50	3.44
400	5.20	4.83	4.67	4.59
500	6.50	6.04	5.83	5.73
600	7.79	7.25	7.00	6.88
700	9.09	8.46	8.16	8.02
800	10.39	9.66	9.33	9.17
900	11.69	10.87	10.50	10.31
1,000	12.99	12.08	11.66	11.46
2,000	25.97	24.15	23.32	22.91
3,000	38.95	36.23	34.97	34.37
4,000	51.94	48.30	46.63	45.82
5,000	64.92	60.37	58.29	57.28
6,000	77.90	72.45	69.94	68.73
7,000	90.89	84.52	81.60	80.18
8,000	103.87	96.59	93.26	91.64
9,000	116.85	108.67	104.91	103.09
10,000	129.84	120.74	116.57	114.55
20,000	259.67	241.48	233.13	229.09
30,000	389.50	362.22	349.70	343.63
40,000	519.33	482.95	466.26	458.17
50,000	649.16	603.69	582.83	572.71
60,000	778.99	724.43	699.39	687.25
70,000	908.83	845.17	815.96	801.79
80,000	1038.66	965.90	932.52	916.33
90,000	1168.49	1086.64	1049.08	1030.88
100,000	1298.32	1207.38	1165.65	1145.42
150,000	1947.48	1811.07	1748.47	1718.12

MONTHLY PAYMENTS
ANNUAL INTEREST RATE: 13.75 %

LOAN AMOUNT	LOAN MATURITY (YEARS)			
	15	20	25	30
50	0.66	0.62	0.60	0.59
100	1.32	1.23	1.19	1.17
200	2.63	2.46	2.37	2.34
300	3.95	3.68	3.56	3.50
400	5.26	4.91	4.74	4.67
500	6.58	6.13	5.93	5.83
600	7.89	7.36	7.11	7.00
700	9.21	8.58	8.30	8.16
800	10.52	9.81	9.48	9.33
900	11.84	11.03	10.67	10.49
1,000	13.15	12.26	11.85	11.66
2,000	26.30	24.51	23.70	23.31
3,000	39.45	36.77	35.55	34.96
4,000	52.60	49.02	47.39	46.61
5,000	65.75	61.28	59.24	58.26
6,000	78.90	73.53	71.09	69.91
7,000	92.05	85.78	82.93	81.56
8,000	105.20	98.04	94.78	93.21
9,000	118.35	110.29	106.63	104.87
10,000	131.50	122.55	118.47	116.52
20,000	263.00	245.09	236.94	233.03
30,000	394.50	367.63	355.41	349.54
40,000	526.00	490.17	473.87	466.05
50,000	657.50	612.71	592.34	582.56
60,000	789.00	735.25	710.81	699.07
70,000	920.50	857.79	829.27	815.58
80,000	1052.00	980.33	947.74	932.10
90,000	1183.50	1102.87	1066.21	1048.61
100,000	1315.00	1225.41	1184.67	1165.12
150,000	1972.49	1838.12	1777.01	1747.67

MONTHLY PAYMENTS
ANNUAL INTEREST RATE: 14 %

LOAN AMOUNT	LOAN MATURITY (YEARS)			
	15	20	25	30
50	0.67	0.63	0.61	0.60
100	1.34	1.25	1.21	1.19
200	2.67	2.49	2.41	2.37
300	4.00	3.74	3.62	3.56
400	5.33	4.98	4.82	4.74
500	6.66	6.22	6.02	5.93
600	8.00	7.47	7.23	7.11
700	9.33	8.71	8.43	8.30
800	10.66	9.95	9.64	9.48
900	11.99	11.20	10.84	10.67
1,000	13.32	12.44	12.04	11.85
2,000	26.64	24.88	24.08	23.70
3,000	39.96	37.31	36.12	35.55
4,000	53.27	49.75	48.16	47.40
5,000	66.59	62.18	60.19	59.25
6,000	79.91	74.62	72.23	71.10
7,000	93.23	87.05	84.27	82.95
8,000	106.54	99.49	96.31	94.79
9,000	119.86	111.92	108.34	106.64
10,000	133.18	124.36	120.38	118.49
20,000	266.35	248.71	240.76	236.98
30,000	399.53	373.06	361.13	355.47
40,000	532.70	497.41	481.51	473.95
50,000	665.88	621.77	601.89	592.44
60,000	799.05	746.12	722.26	710.93
70,000	932.22	870.47	842.64	829.42
80,000	1065.40	994.82	963.01	947.90
90,000	1198.57	1119.17	1083.39	1066.39
100,000	1331.75	1243.53	1203.77	1184.88
150,000	1997.62	1865.29	1805.65	1777.31

MONTHLY PAYMENTS
ANNUAL INTEREST RATE: 14.25 %

LOAN AMOUNT	LOAN MATURITY (YEARS)			
	15	20	25	30
50	0.68	0.64	0.62	0.61
100	1.35	1.27	1.23	1.21
200	2.70	2.53	2.45	2.41
300	4.05	3.79	3.67	3.62
400	5.40	5.05	4.90	4.82
500	6.75	6.31	6.12	6.03
600	8.10	7.58	7.34	7.23
700	9.45	8.84	8.57	8.44
800	10.79	10.10	9.79	9.64
900	12.14	11.36	11.01	10.85
1,000	13.49	12.62	12.23	12.05
2,000	26.98	25.24	24.46	24.10
3,000	40.46	37.86	36.69	36.15
4,000	53.95	50.47	48.92	48.19
5,000	67.43	63.09	61.15	60.24
6,000	80.92	75.71	73.38	72.29
7,000	94.41	88.33	85.61	84.33
8,000	107.89	100.94	97.84	96.38
9,000	121.38	113.56	110.07	108.43
10,000	134.86	126.18	122.30	120.47
20,000	269.72	252.35	244.59	240.94
30,000	404.58	378.52	366.88	361.41
40,000	539.44	504.69	489.18	481.88
50,000	674.29	630.86	611.47	602.35
60,000	809.15	757.04	733.76	722.82
70,000	944.01	883.21	856.05	843.29
80,000	1078.87	1009.38	978.35	963.75
90,000	1213.73	1135.55	1100.64	1084.22
100,000	1348.58	1261.72	1222.93	1204.69
150,000	2022.87	1892.58	1834.40	1807.04

MONTHLY PAYMENTS
ANNUAL INTEREST RATE: 14.5 %

LOAN AMOUNT	LOAN MATURITY (YEARS)			
	15	20	25	30
50	0.69	0.64	0.63	0.62
100	1.37	1.28	1.25	1.23
200	2.74	2.56	2.49	2.45
300	4.10	3.84	3.73	3.68
400	5.47	5.12	4.97	4.90
500	6.83	6.40	6.22	6.13
600	8.20	7.68	7.46	7.35
700	9.56	8.96	8.70	8.58
800	10.93	10.24	9.94	9.80
900	12.29	11.52	11.18	11.03
1,000	13.66	12.80	12.43	12.25
2,000	27.32	25.60	24.85	24.50
3,000	40.97	38.40	37.27	36.74
4,000	54.63	51.20	49.69	48.99
5,000	68.28	64.00	62.11	61.23
6,000	81.94	76.80	74.53	73.48
7,000	95.59	89.60	86.96	85.72
8,000	109.25	102.40	99.38	97.97
9,000	122.90	115.20	111.80	110.22
10,000	136.56	128.00	124.22	122.46
20,000	273.11	256.00	248.44	244.92
30,000	409.66	384.00	372.65	367.37
40,000	546.21	512.00	496.87	489.83
50,000	682.76	640.00	621.09	612.28
60,000	819.31	768.00	745.30	734.74
70,000	955.86	896.00	869.52	857.19
80,000	1092.41	1024.00	993.74	979.65
90,000	1228.96	1152.00	1117.95	1102.11
100,000	1365.51	1280.00	1242.17	1224.56
150,000	2048.26	1920.00	1863.25	1836.84

MONTHLY PAYMENTS
ANNUAL INTEREST RATE: 14.75 %

LOAN AMOUNT	LOAN MATURITY (YEARS)			
	15	20	25	30
50	0.70	0.65	0.64	0.63
100	1.39	1.30	1.27	1.25
200	2.77	2.60	2.53	2.49
300	4.15	3.90	3.79	3.74
400	5.54	5.20	5.05	4.98
500	6.92	6.50	6.31	6.23
600	8.30	7.80	7.57	7.47
700	9.68	9.09	8.84	8.72
800	11.07	10.39	10.10	9.96
900	12.45	11.69	11.36	11.21
1,000	13.83	12.99	12.62	12.45
2,000	27.66	25.97	25.23	24.89
3,000	41.48	38.96	37.85	37.34
4,000	55.31	51.94	50.46	49.78
5,000	69.13	64.92	63.08	62.23
6,000	82.96	77.91	75.69	74.67
7,000	96.78	90.89	88.31	87.12
8,000	110.61	103.87	100.92	99.56
9,000	124.43	116.86	113.54	112.01
10,000	138.26	129.84	126.15	124.45
20,000	276.51	259.68	252.30	248.90
30,000	414.76	389.51	378.44	373.35
40,000	553.01	519.35	504.59	497.80
50,000	691.26	649.18	630.74	622.24
60,000	829.51	779.02	756.88	746.69
70,000	967.76	908.85	883.03	871.14
80,000	1106.01	1038.69	1009.18	995.59
90,000	1244.26	1168.53	1135.32	1120.03
100,000	1382.51	1298.36	1261.47	1244.48
150,000	2073.76	1947.54	1892.20	1866.72

MONTHLY PAYMENTS
ANNUAL INTEREST RATE: 15 %

LOAN AMOUNT	LOAN MATURITY (YEARS)			
	15	20	25	30
50	0.70	0.66	0.65	0.64
100	1.40	1.32	1.29	1.27
200	2.80	2.64	2.57	2.53
300	4.20	3.96	3.85	3.80
400	5.60	5.27	5.13	5.06
500	7.00	6.59	6.41	6.33
600	8.40	7.91	7.69	7.59
700	9.80	9.22	8.97	8.86
800	11.20	10.54	10.25	10.12
900	12.60	11.86	11.53	11.38
1,000	14.00	13.17	12.81	12.65
2,000	28.00	26.34	25.62	25.29
3,000	41.99	39.51	38.43	37.94
4,000	55.99	52.68	51.24	50.58
5,000	69.98	65.84	64.05	63.23
6,000	83.98	79.01	76.85	75.87
7,000	97.98	92.18	89.66	88.52
8,000	111.97	105.35	102.47	101.16
9,000	125.97	118.52	115.28	113.80
10,000	139.96	131.68	128.09	126.45
20,000	279.92	263.36	256.17	252.89
30,000	419.88	395.04	384.25	379.34
40,000	559.84	526.72	512.34	505.78
50,000	699.80	658.40	640.42	632.23
60,000	839.76	790.08	768.50	758.67
70,000	979.71	921.76	896.59	885.12
80,000	1119.67	1053.44	1024.67	1011.56
90,000	1259.63	1185.11	1152.75	1138.00
100,000	1399.59	1316.79	1280.84	1264.45
150,000	2099.38	1975.19	1921.25	1896.67

MONTHLY PAYMENTS
ANNUAL INTEREST RATE: 15.25 %

LOAN AMOUNT	LOAN MATURITY (YEARS)			
	15	20	25	30
50	0.71	0.67	0.66	0.65
100	1.42	1.34	1.31	1.29
200	2.84	2.68	2.61	2.57
300	4.26	4.01	3.91	3.86
400	5.67	5.35	5.21	5.14
500	7.09	6.68	6.51	6.43
600	8.51	8.02	7.81	7.71
700	9.92	9.35	9.11	9.00
800	11.34	10.69	10.41	10.28
900	12.76	12.02	11.71	11.57
1,000	14.17	13.36	13.01	12.85
2,000	28.34	26.71	26.01	25.69
3,000	42.51	40.06	39.01	38.54
4,000	56.68	53.42	52.02	51.38
5,000	70.84	66.77	65.02	64.23
6,000	85.01	80.12	78.02	77.07
7,000	99.18	93.48	91.02	89.92
8,000	113.35	106.83	104.03	102.76
9,000	127.51	120.18	117.03	115.61
10,000	141.68	133.53	130.03	128.45
20,000	283.36	267.06	260.06	256.90
30,000	425.03	400.59	390.08	385.34
40,000	566.71	534.12	520.11	513.79
50,000	708.38	667.65	650.13	642.23
60,000	850.06	801.18	780.16	770.68
70,000	991.73	934.71	910.19	899.13
80,000	1133.41	1068.24	1040.21	1027.57
90,000	1275.08	1201.77	1170.24	1156.02
100,000	1416.76	1335.30	1300.26	1284.46
150,000	2125.13	2002.95	1950.39	1926.69

MONTHLY PAYMENTS
ANNUAL INTEREST RATE: 15.5 %

LOAN AMOUNT	LOAN MATURITY (YEARS)			
	15	20	25	30
50	0.72	0.68	0.66	0.66
100	1.44	1.36	1.32	1.31
200	2.87	2.71	2.64	2.61
300	4.31	4.07	3.96	3.92
400	5.74	5.42	5.28	5.22
500	7.17	6.77	6.60	6.53
600	8.61	8.13	7.92	7.83
700	10.04	9.48	9.24	9.14
800	11.48	10.84	10.56	10.44
900	12.91	12.19	11.88	11.75
1,000	14.34	13.54	13.20	13.05
2,000	28.68	27.08	26.40	26.10
3,000	43.02	40.62	39.60	39.14
4,000	57.36	54.16	52.79	52.19
5,000	71.70	67.70	65.99	65.23
6,000	86.04	81.24	79.19	78.28
7,000	100.38	94.78	92.39	91.32
8,000	114.72	108.32	105.58	104.37
9,000	129.06	121.85	118.78	117.41
10,000	143.40	135.39	131.98	130.46
20,000	286.80	270.78	263.95	260.91
30,000	430.20	406.17	395.93	391.36
40,000	573.60	541.56	527.90	521.81
50,000	717.00	676.94	659.88	652.26
60,000	860.40	812.33	791.85	782.72
70,000	1003.80	947.72	923.83	913.17
80,000	1147.20	1083.11	1055.80	1043.62
90,000	1290.60	1218.50	1187.78	1174.07
100,000	1433.99	1353.88	1319.75	1304.52
150,000	2150.99	2030.82	1979.62	1956.78

MONTHLY PAYMENTS
ANNUAL INTEREST RATE: 15.75 %

LOAN AMOUNT	LOAN MATURITY (YEARS)			
	15	20	25	30
50	0.73	0.69	0.67	0.67
100	1.46	1.38	1.34	1.33
200	2.91	2.75	2.68	2.65
300	4.36	4.12	4.02	3.98
400	5.81	5.50	5.36	5.30
500	7.26	6.87	6.70	6.63
600	8.71	8.24	8.04	7.95
700	10.16	9.61	9.38	9.28
800	11.62	10.99	10.72	10.60
900	13.07	12.36	12.06	11.93
1,000	14.52	13.73	13.40	13.25
2,000	29.03	27.46	26.79	26.50
3,000	43.54	41.18	40.18	39.74
4,000	58.06	54.91	53.58	52.99
5,000	72.57	68.63	66.97	66.24
6,000	87.08	82.36	80.36	79.48
7,000	101.60	96.08	93.76	92.73
8,000	116.11	109.81	107.15	105.97
9,000	130.62	123.53	120.54	119.22
10,000	145.14	137.26	133.93	132.47
20,000	290.27	274.51	267.86	264.93
30,000	435.40	411.77	401.79	397.39
40,000	580.53	549.02	535.72	529.85
50,000	725.66	686.27	669.65	662.31
60,000	870.79	823.53	803.58	794.78
70,000	1015.92	960.78	937.51	927.24
80,000	1161.05	1098.03	1071.44	1059.70
90,000	1306.18	1235.29	1205.37	1192.16
100,000	1451.31	1372.54	1339.30	1324.62
150,000	2176.97	2058.81	2008.94	1986.93

MONTHLY PAYMENTS
ANNUAL INTEREST RATE: 16 %

LOAN AMOUNT	LOAN MATURITY (YEARS)			
	15	20	25	30
50	0.74	0.70	0.68	0.68
100	1.47	1.40	1.36	1.35
200	2.94	2.79	2.72	2.69
300	4.41	4.18	4.08	4.04
400	5.88	5.57	5.44	5.38
500	7.35	6.96	6.80	6.73
600	8.82	8.35	8.16	8.07
700	10.29	9.74	9.52	9.42
800	11.75	11.14	10.88	10.76
900	13.22	12.53	12.24	12.11
1,000	14.69	13.92	13.59	13.45
2,000	29.38	27.83	27.18	26.90
3,000	44.07	41.74	40.77	40.35
4,000	58.75	55.66	54.36	53.80
5,000	73.44	69.57	67.95	67.24
6,000	88.13	83.48	81.54	80.69
7,000	102.81	97.39	95.13	94.14
8,000	117.50	111.31	108.72	107.59
9,000	132.19	125.22	122.31	121.03
10,000	146.88	139.13	135.89	134.48
20,000	293.75	278.26	271.78	268.96
30,000	440.62	417.38	407.67	403.43
40,000	587.49	556.51	543.56	537.91
50,000	734.36	695.63	679.45	672.38
60,000	881.23	834.76	815.34	806.86
70,000	1028.10	973.88	951.23	941.34
80,000	1174.97	1113.01	1087.12	1075.81
90,000	1321.84	1252.14	1223.01	1210.29
100,000	1468.71	1391.26	1358.89	1344.76
150,000	2203.06	2086.89	2038.34	2017.14

MONTHLY PAYMENTS
ANNUAL INTEREST RATE: 16.25 %

LOAN AMOUNT	LOAN MATURITY (YEARS)			
	15	20	25	30
50	0.75	0.71	0.69	0.69
100	1.49	1.42	1.38	1.37
200	2.98	2.83	2.76	2.73
300	4.46	4.24	4.14	4.10
400	5.95	5.65	5.52	5.46
500	7.44	7.06	6.90	6.83
600	8.92	8.47	8.28	8.19
700	10.41	9.88	9.65	9.56
800	11.89	11.29	11.03	10.92
900	13.38	12.70	12.41	12.29
1,000	14.87	14.11	13.79	13.65
2,000	29.73	28.21	27.58	27.30
3,000	44.59	42.31	41.36	40.95
4,000	59.45	56.41	55.15	54.60
5,000	74.31	70.51	68.93	68.25
6,000	89.18	84.61	82.72	81.90
7,000	104.04	98.71	96.50	95.55
8,000	118.90	112.81	110.29	109.20
9,000	133.76	126.91	124.07	122.85
10,000	148.62	141.01	137.86	136.50
20,000	297.24	282.01	275.71	272.99
30,000	445.86	423.02	413.57	409.49
40,000	594.47	564.02	551.42	545.98
50,000	743.09	705.03	689.28	682.47
60,000	891.71	846.03	827.13	818.97
70,000	1040.32	987.04	964.98	955.46
80,000	1188.94	1128.04	1102.84	1091.95
90,000	1337.56	1269.05	1240.69	1228.45
100,000	1486.17	1410.05	1378.55	1364.94
150,000	2229.26	2115.07	2067.82	2047.41

MONTHLY PAYMENTS
ANNUAL INTEREST RATE: 16.5 %

| LOAN AMOUNT | LOAN MATURITY (YEARS) | | | |
	15	20	25	30
50	0.76	0.72	0.70	0.70
100	1.51	1.43	1.40	1.39
200	3.01	2.86	2.80	2.78
300	4.52	4.29	4.20	4.16
400	6.02	5.72	5.60	5.55
500	7.52	7.15	7.00	6.93
600	9.03	8.58	8.39	8.32
700	10.53	10.01	9.79	9.70
800	12.03	11.44	11.19	11.09
900	13.54	12.87	12.59	12.47
1,000	15.04	14.29	13.99	13.86
2,000	30.08	28.58	27.97	27.71
3,000	45.12	42.87	41.95	41.56
4,000	60.15	57.16	55.93	55.41
5,000	75.19	71.45	69.92	69.26
6,000	90.23	85.74	83.90	83.11
7,000	105.26	100.03	97.88	96.97
8,000	120.30	114.32	111.86	110.82
9,000	135.34	128.61	125.85	124.67
10,000	150.38	142.90	139.83	138.52
20,000	300.75	285.79	279.65	277.03
30,000	451.12	428.68	419.48	415.55
40,000	601.49	571.57	559.30	554.06
50,000	751.86	714.46	699.13	692.58
60,000	902.23	857.35	838.95	831.09
70,000	1052.60	1000.24	978.78	969.61
80,000	1202.97	1143.13	1118.60	1108.12
90,000	1353.34	1286.02	1258.43	1246.64
100,000	1503.71	1428.91	1398.25	1385.15
150,000	2255.57	2143.36	2097.37	2077.73

MONTHLY PAYMENTS
ANNUAL INTEREST RATE: 16.75 %

LOAN AMOUNT	LOAN MATURITY (YEARS)			
	15	20	25	30
50	0.77	0.73	0.71	0.71
100	1.53	1.45	1.42	1.41
200	3.05	2.90	2.84	2.82
300	4.57	4.35	4.26	4.22
400	6.09	5.80	5.68	5.63
500	7.61	7.24	7.09	7.03
600	9.13	8.69	8.51	8.44
700	10.65	10.14	9.93	9.84
800	12.18	11.59	11.35	11.25
900	13.70	13.04	12.77	12.65
1,000	15.22	14.48	14.18	14.06
2,000	30.43	28.96	28.36	28.11
3,000	45.64	43.44	42.54	42.17
4,000	60.86	57.92	56.72	56.22
5,000	76.07	72.40	70.90	70.27
6,000	91.28	86.87	85.08	84.33
7,000	106.50	101.35	99.26	98.38
8,000	121.71	115.83	113.44	112.44
9,000	136.92	130.31	127.62	126.49
10,000	152.14	144.79	141.80	140.54
20,000	304.27	289.57	283.60	281.08
30,000	456.40	434.35	425.40	421.62
40,000	608.53	579.13	567.20	562.16
50,000	760.67	723.91	709.00	702.70
60,000	912.80	868.70	850.80	843.24
70,000	1064.93	1013.48	992.60	983.78
80,000	1217.06	1158.26	1134.40	1124.32
90,000	1369.19	1303.04	1276.20	1264.86
100,000	1521.33	1447.82	1418.00	1405.40
150,000	2281.99	2171.73	2127.00	2108.10

MONTHLY PAYMENTS
ANNUAL INTEREST RATE: 17 %

LOAN AMOUNT	LOAN MATURITY (YEARS)			
	15	20	25	30
50	0.77	0.74	0.72	0.72
100	1.54	1.47	1.44	1.43
200	3.08	2.94	2.88	2.86
300	4.62	4.41	4.32	4.28
400	6.16	5.87	5.76	5.71
500	7.70	7.34	7.19	7.13
600	9.24	8.81	8.63	8.56
700	10.78	10.27	10.07	9.98
800	12.32	11.74	11.51	11.41
900	13.86	13.21	12.95	12.84
1,000	15.40	14.67	14.38	14.26
2,000	30.79	29.34	28.76	28.52
3,000	46.18	44.01	43.14	42.78
4,000	61.57	58.68	57.52	57.03
5,000	76.96	73.34	71.89	71.29
6,000	92.35	88.01	86.27	85.55
7,000	107.74	102.68	100.65	99.80
8,000	123.13	117.35	115.03	114.06
9,000	138.52	132.02	129.41	128.32
10,000	153.91	146.68	143.78	142.57
20,000	307.81	293.36	287.56	285.14
30,000	461.71	440.04	431.34	427.71
40,000	615.61	586.72	575.12	570.28
50,000	769.51	733.40	718.90	712.84
60,000	923.41	880.08	862.68	855.41
70,000	1077.31	1026.76	1006.46	997.98
80,000	1231.21	1173.44	1150.24	1140.55
90,000	1385.11	1320.12	1294.02	1283.11
100,000	1539.01	1466.80	1437.80	1425.68
150,000	2308.51	2200.20	2156.70	2138.52

MONTHLY PAYMENTS
ANNUAL INTEREST RATE: 17.25 %

LOAN	LOAN MATURITY (YEARS)			
AMOUNT	15	20	25	30
50	0.78	0.75	0.73	0.73
100	1.56	1.49	1.46	1.45
200	3.12	2.98	2.92	2.90
300	4.68	4.46	4.38	4.34
400	6.23	5.95	5.84	5.79
500	7.79	7.43	7.29	7.23
600	9.35	8.92	8.75	8.68
700	10.90	10.41	10.21	10.13
800	12.46	11.89	11.67	11.57
900	14.02	13.38	13.12	13.02
1,000	15.57	14.86	14.58	14.46
2,000	31.14	29.72	29.16	28.92
3,000	46.71	44.58	43.73	43.38
4,000	62.28	59.44	58.31	57.84
5,000	77.84	74.30	72.89	72.30
6,000	93.41	89.16	87.46	86.76
7,000	108.98	104.01	102.04	101.22
8,000	124.55	118.87	116.62	115.68
9,000	140.11	133.73	131.19	130.14
10,000	155.68	148.59	145.77	144.60
20,000	311.36	297.17	291.53	289.20
30,000	467.03	445.76	437.30	433.80
40,000	622.71	594.34	583.06	578.40
50,000	778.38	742.93	728.83	723.00
60,000	934.06	891.51	874.59	867.60
70,000	1089.74	1040.09	1020.35	1012.20
80,000	1245.41	1188.68	1166.12	1156.79
90,000	1401.09	1337.26	1311.88	1301.39
100,000	1556.76	1485.85	1457.65	1445.99
150,000	2335.14	2228.77	2186.47	2168.98

MONTHLY PAYMENTS
ANNUAL INTEREST RATE: 17.5 %

LOAN AMOUNT	LOAN MATURITY (YEARS)			
	15	20	25	30
50	0.79	0.76	0.74	0.74
100	1.58	1.51	1.48	1.47
200	3.15	3.01	2.96	2.94
300	4.73	4.52	4.44	4.40
400	6.30	6.02	5.92	5.87
500	7.88	7.53	7.39	7.34
600	9.45	9.03	8.87	8.80
700	11.03	10.54	10.35	10.27
800	12.60	12.04	11.83	11.74
900	14.18	13.55	13.30	13.20
1,000	15.75	15.05	14.78	14.67
2,000	31.50	30.10	29.56	29.33
3,000	47.24	45.15	44.33	43.99
4,000	62.99	60.20	59.11	58.66
5,000	78.73	75.25	73.88	73.32
6,000	94.48	90.30	88.66	87.98
7,000	110.23	105.35	103.43	102.65
8,000	125.97	120.40	118.21	117.31
9,000	141.72	135.45	132.98	131.97
10,000	157.46	150.50	147.76	146.64
20,000	314.92	300.99	295.51	293.27
30,000	472.38	451.49	443.26	439.90
40,000	629.84	601.98	591.02	586.54
50,000	787.29	752.48	738.77	733.17
60,000	944.75	902.97	886.52	879.80
70,000	1102.21	1053.46	1034.28	1026.43
80,000	1259.67	1203.96	1182.03	1173.07
90,000	1417.13	1354.45	1329.78	1319.70
100,000	1574.58	1504.95	1477.53	1466.33
150,000	2361.87	2257.42	2216.30	2199.49

MONTHLY PAYMENTS
ANNUAL INTEREST RATE: 17.75 %

LOAN AMOUNT	LOAN MATURITY (YEARS)			
	15	20	25	30
50	0.80	0.77	0.75	0.75
100	1.60	1.53	1.50	1.49
200	3.19	3.05	3.00	2.98
300	4.78	4.58	4.50	4.47
400	6.37	6.10	5.99	5.95
500	7.97	7.63	7.49	7.44
600	9.56	9.15	8.99	8.93
700	11.15	10.67	10.49	10.41
800	12.74	12.20	11.98	11.90
900	14.34	13.72	13.48	13.39
1,000	15.93	15.25	14.98	14.87
2,000	31.85	30.49	29.95	29.74
3,000	47.78	45.73	44.93	44.61
4,000	63.70	60.97	59.90	59.47
5,000	79.63	76.21	74.88	74.34
6,000	95.55	91.45	89.85	89.21
7,000	111.48	106.69	104.83	104.07
8,000	127.40	121.93	119.80	118.94
9,000	143.33	137.17	134.78	133.81
10,000	159.25	152.41	149.75	148.67
20,000	318.50	304.82	299.50	297.34
30,000	477.75	457.24	449.24	446.01
40,000	636.99	609.64	598.99	594.68
50,000	796.24	762.06	748.74	743.35
60,000	955.49	914.47	898.48	892.02
70,000	1114.73	1066.88	1048.23	1040.69
80,000	1273.98	1219.28	1197.97	1189.36
90,000	1433.23	1371.70	1347.72	1338.03
100,000	1592.47	1524.11	1497.47	1486.70
150,000	2388.71	2286.15	2246.20	2230.04

MONTHLY PAYMENTS
ANNUAL INTEREST RATE: 18 %

LOAN AMOUNT	LOAN MATURITY (YEARS)			
	15	20	25	30
50	0.81	0.78	0.76	0.76
100	1.62	1.55	1.52	1.51
200	3.23	3.09	3.04	3.02
300	4.84	4.63	4.56	4.53
400	6.45	6.18	6.07	6.03
500	8.06	7.72	7.59	7.54
600	9.67	9.26	9.11	9.05
700	11.28	10.81	10.63	10.55
800	12.89	12.35	12.14	12.06
900	14.50	13.89	13.66	13.57
1,000	16.11	15.44	15.18	15.08
2,000	32.21	30.87	30.35	30.15
3,000	48.32	46.30	45.53	45.22
4,000	64.42	61.74	60.70	60.29
5,000	80.53	77.17	75.88	75.36
6,000	96.63	92.60	91.05	90.43
7,000	112.73	108.04	106.23	105.50
8,000	128.84	123.47	121.40	120.57
9,000	144.94	138.90	136.57	135.64
10,000	161.05	154.34	151.75	150.71
20,000	322.09	308.67	303.49	301.42
30,000	483.13	463.00	455.23	452.13
40,000	644.17	617.33	606.98	602.84
50,000	805.22	771.66	758.72	753.55
60,000	966.26	925.99	910.46	904.26
70,000	1127.30	1080.32	1062.21	1054.96
80,000	1288.34	1234.65	1213.95	1205.67
90,000	1449.38	1388.99	1365.69	1356.38
100,000	1610.43	1543.32	1517.44	1507.09
150,000	2415.64	2314.97	2276.15	2260.63

MONTHLY PAYMENTS
ANNUAL INTEREST RATE: 18.25 %

LOAN AMOUNT	LOAN MATURITY (YEARS)			
	15	20	25	30
50	0.82	0.79	0.77	0.77
100	1.63	1.57	1.54	1.53
200	3.26	3.13	3.08	3.06
300	4.89	4.69	4.62	4.59
400	6.52	6.26	6.15	6.12
500	8.15	7.82	7.69	7.64
600	9.78	9.38	9.23	9.17
700	11.40	10.94	10.77	10.70
800	13.03	12.51	12.30	12.23
900	14.66	14.07	13.84	13.75
1,000	16.29	15.63	15.38	15.28
2,000	32.57	31.26	30.75	30.56
3,000	48.86	46.88	46.13	45.83
4,000	65.14	62.51	61.50	61.11
5,000	81.43	78.13	76.88	76.38
6,000	97.71	93.76	92.25	91.66
7,000	114.00	109.39	107.63	106.93
8,000	130.28	125.01	123.00	122.21
9,000	146.56	140.64	138.37	137.48
10,000	162.85	156.26	153.75	152.76
20,000	325.69	312.52	307.49	305.51
30,000	488.54	468.78	461.24	458.26
40,000	651.38	625.04	614.98	611.01
50,000	814.23	781.29	768.72	763.76
60,000	977.07	937.55	922.47	916.51
70,000	1139.91	1093.81	1076.21	1069.26
80,000	1302.76	1250.07	1229.96	1222.01
90,000	1465.60	1406.33	1383.70	1374.76
100,000	1628.45	1562.58	1537.44	1527.51
150,000	2442.67	2343.87	2306.16	2291.26

MONTHLY PAYMENTS
ANNUAL INTEREST RATE: 18.5 %

LOAN AMOUNT	LOAN MATURITY (YEARS)			
	15	20	25	30
50	0.83	0.80	0.78	0.78
100	1.65	1.59	1.56	1.55
200	3.30	3.17	3.12	3.10
300	4.94	4.75	4.68	4.65
400	6.59	6.33	6.23	6.20
500	8.24	7.91	7.79	7.74
600	9.88	9.50	9.35	9.29
700	11.53	11.08	10.91	10.84
800	13.18	12.66	12.46	12.39
900	14.82	14.24	14.02	13.94
1,000	16.47	15.82	15.58	15.48
2,000	32.94	31.64	31.15	30.96
3,000	49.40	47.46	46.73	46.44
4,000	65.87	63.28	62.30	61.92
5,000	82.33	79.10	77.88	77.40
6,000	98.80	94.92	93.45	92.88
7,000	115.26	110.74	109.03	108.36
8,000	131.73	126.56	124.60	123.84
9,000	148.19	142.38	140.18	139.32
10,000	164.66	158.19	155.75	154.80
20,000	329.31	316.38	311.50	309.59
30,000	493.96	474.57	467.25	464.39
40,000	658.61	632.76	623.00	619.18
50,000	823.27	790.95	778.75	773.98
60,000	987.92	949.14	934.50	928.77
70,000	1152.57	1107.33	1090.24	1083.57
80,000	1317.22	1265.52	1245.99	1238.36
90,000	1481.88	1423.71	1401.74	1393.16
100,000	1646.53	1581.90	1557.49	1547.95
150,000	2469.79	2372.85	2336.23	2321.92

MONTHLY PAYMENTS
ANNUAL INTEREST RATE: 18.75 %

LOAN AMOUNT	LOAN MATURITY (YEARS) 15	20	25	30
50	0.84	0.81	0.79	0.79
100	1.67	1.61	1.58	1.57
200	3.33	3.21	3.16	3.14
300	5.00	4.81	4.74	4.71
400	6.66	6.41	6.32	6.28
500	8.33	8.01	7.89	7.85
600	9.99	9.61	9.47	9.42
700	11.66	11.21	11.05	10.98
800	13.32	12.82	12.63	12.55
900	14.99	14.42	14.20	14.12
1,000	16.65	16.02	15.78	15.69
2,000	33.30	32.03	31.56	31.37
3,000	49.95	48.04	47.33	47.06
4,000	66.59	64.06	63.11	62.74
5,000	83.24	80.07	78.88	78.43
6,000	99.89	96.08	94.66	94.11
7,000	116.53	112.09	110.43	109.79
8,000	133.18	128.11	126.21	125.48
9,000	149.83	144.12	141.99	141.16
10,000	166.47	160.13	157.76	156.85
20,000	332.94	320.26	315.52	313.69
30,000	499.41	480.38	473.27	470.53
40,000	665.87	640.51	631.03	627.37
50,000	832.34	800.64	788.79	784.21
60,000	998.81	960.76	946.54	941.05
70,000	1165.27	1120.89	1104.30	1097.89
80,000	1331.74	1281.02	1262.06	1254.73
90,000	1498.21	1441.14	1419.81	1411.57
100,000	1664.67	1601.27	1577.57	1568.41
150,000	2497.01	2401.90	2366.35	2352.62

MONTHLY PAYMENTS
ANNUAL INTEREST RATE: 19 %

LOAN AMOUNT	LOAN MATURITY (YEARS)			
	15	20	25	30
50	0.85	0.82	0.80	0.80
100	1.69	1.63	1.60	1.59
200	3.37	3.25	3.20	3.18
300	5.05	4.87	4.80	4.77
400	6.74	6.49	6.40	6.36
500	8.42	8.11	7.99	7.95
600	10.10	9.73	9.59	9.54
700	11.79	11.35	11.19	11.13
800	13.47	12.97	12.79	12.72
900	15.15	14.59	14.38	14.31
1,000	16.83	16.21	15.98	15.89
2,000	33.66	32.42	31.96	31.78
3,000	50.49	48.63	47.94	47.67
4,000	67.32	64.83	63.91	63.56
5,000	84.15	81.04	79.89	79.45
6,000	100.98	97.25	95.87	95.34
7,000	117.81	113.45	111.84	111.23
8,000	134.64	129.66	127.82	127.12
9,000	151.46	145.87	143.80	143.01
10,000	168.29	162.07	159.77	158.89
20,000	336.58	324.14	319.54	317.78
30,000	504.87	486.21	479.31	476.67
40,000	673.16	648.28	639.08	635.56
50,000	841.44	810.35	798.84	794.45
60,000	1009.73	972.42	958.61	953.34
70,000	1178.02	1134.48	1118.38	1112.23
80,000	1346.31	1296.55	1278.15	1271.12
90,000	1514.59	1458.62	1437.92	1430.01
100,000	1682.88	1620.69	1597.68	1588.90
150,000	2524.32	2431.03	2396.52	2383.34

MONTHLY PAYMENTS
ANNUAL INTEREST RATE: 19.25 %

LOAN AMOUNT	LOAN MATURITY (YEARS)			
	15	20	25	30
50	0.86	0.83	0.81	0.81
100	1.71	1.65	1.62	1.61
200	3.41	3.29	3.24	3.22
300	5.11	4.93	4.86	4.83
400	6.81	6.57	6.48	6.44
500	8.51	8.21	8.09	8.05
600	10.21	9.85	9.71	9.66
700	11.91	11.49	11.33	11.27
800	13.61	13.13	12.95	12.88
900	15.32	14.77	14.57	14.49
1,000	17.02	16.41	16.18	16.10
2,000	34.03	32.81	32.36	32.19
3,000	51.04	49.21	48.54	48.29
4,000	68.05	65.61	64.72	64.38
5,000	85.06	82.01	80.90	80.47
6,000	102.07	98.41	97.07	96.57
7,000	119.09	114.82	113.25	112.66
8,000	136.10	131.22	129.43	128.76
9,000	153.11	147.62	145.61	144.85
10,000	170.12	164.02	161.79	160.94
20,000	340.23	328.04	323.57	321.88
30,000	510.35	492.05	485.35	482.82
40,000	680.46	656.07	647.14	643.76
50,000	850.58	820.08	808.92	804.70
60,000	1020.69	984.10	970.70	965.64
70,000	1190.81	1148.11	1132.48	1126.58
80,000	1360.92	1312.13	1294.27	1287.52
90,000	1531.03	1476.14	1456.05	1448.46
100,000	1701.15	1640.16	1617.83	1609.40
150,000	2551.72	2460.23	2426.75	2414.10

MONTHLY PAYMENTS
ANNUAL INTEREST RATE: 19.5 %

LOAN AMOUNT	LOAN MATURITY (YEARS)			
	15	20	25	30
50	0.86	0.83	0.82	0.82
100	1.72	1.66	1.64	1.63
200	3.44	3.32	3.28	3.26
300	5.16	4.98	4.92	4.89
400	6.88	6.64	6.56	6.52
500	8.60	8.30	8.20	8.15
600	10.32	9.96	9.83	9.78
700	12.04	11.62	11.47	11.41
800	13.76	13.28	13.11	13.04
900	15.48	14.94	14.75	14.67
1,000	17.20	16.60	16.39	16.30
2,000	34.39	33.20	32.77	32.60
3,000	51.59	49.79	49.15	48.90
4,000	68.78	66.39	65.53	65.20
5,000	85.98	82.99	81.91	81.50
6,000	103.17	99.58	98.29	97.80
7,000	120.37	116.18	114.67	114.10
8,000	137.56	132.78	131.05	130.40
9,000	154.76	149.37	147.43	146.70
10,000	171.95	165.97	163.81	163.00
20,000	343.90	331.94	327.61	325.99
30,000	515.85	497.90	491.41	488.98
40,000	687.79	663.87	655.21	651.97
50,000	859.74	829.84	819.01	814.97
60,000	1031.69	995.80	982.81	977.96
70,000	1203.63	1161.77	1146.61	1140.95
80,000	1375.58	1327.74	1310.41	1303.94
90,000	1547.53	1493.70	1474.21	1466.93
100,000	1719.47	1659.67	1638.01	1629.93
150,000	2579.21	2489.50	2457.01	2444.89

MONTHLY PAYMENTS
ANNUAL INTEREST RATE: 19.75 %

LOAN AMOUNT	LOAN MATURITY (YEARS)			
	15	20	25	30
50	0.87	0.84	0.83	0.83
100	1.74	1.68	1.66	1.66
200	3.48	3.36	3.32	3.31
300	5.22	5.04	4.98	4.96
400	6.96	6.72	6.64	6.61
500	8.69	8.40	8.30	8.26
600	10.43	10.08	9.95	9.91
700	12.17	11.76	11.61	11.56
800	13.91	13.44	13.27	13.21
900	15.65	15.12	14.93	14.86
1,000	17.38	16.80	16.59	16.51
2,000	34.76	33.59	33.17	33.01
3,000	52.14	50.38	49.75	49.52
4,000	69.52	67.17	66.33	66.02
5,000	86.90	83.97	82.92	82.53
6,000	104.28	100.76	99.50	99.03
7,000	121.65	117.55	116.08	115.54
8,000	139.03	134.34	132.66	132.04
9,000	156.41	151.14	149.24	148.55
10,000	173.79	167.93	165.83	165.05
20,000	347.58	335.85	331.65	330.10
30,000	521.36	503.77	497.47	495.14
40,000	695.15	671.69	663.29	660.19
50,000	868.93	839.62	829.11	825.24
60,000	1042.72	1007.54	994.93	990.28
70,000	1216.50	1175.46	1160.76	1155.33
80,000	1390.29	1343.38	1326.58	1320.37
90,000	1564.08	1511.31	1492.40	1485.42
100,000	1737.86	1679.23	1658.22	1650.47
150,000	2606.79	2518.84	2487.33	2475.70

MONTHLY PAYMENTS
ANNUAL INTEREST RATE: 20 %

LOAN AMOUNT	LOAN MATURITY (YEARS)			
	15	20	25	30
50	0.88	0.85	0.84	0.84
100	1.76	1.70	1.68	1.68
200	3.52	3.40	3.36	3.35
300	5.27	5.10	5.04	5.02
400	7.03	6.80	6.72	6.69
500	8.79	8.50	8.40	8.36
600	10.54	10.20	10.08	10.03
700	12.30	11.90	11.75	11.70
800	14.06	13.60	13.43	13.37
900	15.81	15.29	15.11	15.04
1,000	17.57	16.99	16.79	16.72
2,000	35.13	33.98	33.57	33.43
3,000	52.69	50.97	50.36	50.14
4,000	70.26	67.96	67.14	66.85
5,000	87.82	84.95	83.93	83.56
6,000	105.38	101.93	100.71	100.27
7,000	122.95	118.92	117.50	116.98
8,000	140.51	135.91	134.28	133.69
9,000	158.07	152.90	151.07	150.40
10,000	175.63	169.89	167.85	167.11
20,000	351.26	339.77	335.70	334.21
30,000	526.89	509.65	503.54	501.31
40,000	702.52	679.53	671.39	668.41
50,000	878.15	849.42	839.23	835.51
60,000	1053.78	1019.30	1007.08	1002.62
70,000	1229.41	1189.18	1174.92	1169.72
80,000	1405.04	1359.06	1342.77	1336.82
90,000	1580.67	1528.95	1510.61	1503.92
100,000	1756.30	1698.83	1678.46	1671.02
150,000	2634.45	2548.24	2517.68	2506.53

MONTHLY PAYMENTS
ANNUAL INTEREST RATE: 20.25 %

LOAN AMOUNT	LOAN MATURITY (YEARS)			
	15	20	25	30
50	0.89	0.86	0.85	0.85
100	1.78	1.72	1.70	1.70
200	3.55	3.44	3.40	3.39
300	5.33	5.16	5.10	5.08
400	7.10	6.88	6.80	6.77
500	8.88	8.60	8.50	8.46
600	10.65	10.32	10.20	10.15
700	12.43	12.03	11.90	11.85
800	14.20	13.75	13.59	13.54
900	15.98	15.47	15.29	15.23
1,000	17.75	17.19	16.99	16.92
2,000	35.50	34.37	33.98	33.84
3,000	53.25	51.56	50.97	50.75
4,000	71.00	68.74	67.95	67.67
5,000	88.74	85.93	84.94	84.58
6,000	106.49	103.11	101.93	101.50
7,000	124.24	120.30	118.92	118.42
8,000	141.99	137.48	135.90	135.33
9,000	159.74	154.67	152.89	152.25
10,000	177.48	171.85	169.88	169.16
20,000	354.96	343.70	339.75	338.32
30,000	532.44	515.55	509.62	507.48
40,000	709.92	687.39	679.49	676.64
50,000	887.40	859.24	849.36	845.80
60,000	1064.88	1031.09	1019.23	1014.96
70,000	1242.36	1202.93	1189.11	1184.12
80,000	1419.84	1374.78	1358.98	1353.28
90,000	1597.32	1546.63	1528.85	1522.44
100,000	1774.80	1718.47	1698.72	1691.60
150,000	2662.20	2577.71	2548.08	2537.39

MONTHLY PAYMENTS
ANNUAL INTEREST RATE: 20.5 %

LOAN AMOUNT	LOAN MATURITY (YEARS)			
	15	20	25	30
50	0.90	0.87	0.86	0.86
100	1.80	1.74	1.72	1.72
200	3.59	3.48	3.44	3.43
300	5.39	5.22	5.16	5.14
400	7.18	6.96	6.88	6.85
500	8.97	8.70	8.60	8.57
600	10.77	10.43	10.32	10.28
700	12.56	12.17	12.04	11.99
800	14.35	13.91	13.76	13.70
900	16.15	15.65	15.48	15.41
1,000	17.94	17.39	17.20	17.13
2,000	35.87	34.77	34.39	34.25
3,000	53.81	52.15	51.58	51.37
4,000	71.74	69.53	68.77	68.49
5,000	89.67	86.91	85.96	85.61
6,000	107.61	104.29	103.15	102.74
7,000	125.54	121.68	120.34	119.86
8,000	143.47	139.06	137.53	136.98
9,000	161.41	156.44	154.72	154.10
10,000	179.34	173.82	171.91	171.22
20,000	358.67	347.64	343.81	342.44
30,000	538.01	521.45	515.71	513.66
40,000	717.34	695.27	687.61	684.88
50,000	896.68	869.08	859.51	856.10
60,000	1076.01	1042.90	1031.41	1027.31
70,000	1255.35	1216.71	1203.31	1198.53
80,000	1434.68	1390.53	1375.21	1369.75
90,000	1614.02	1564.34	1547.11	1540.97
100,000	1793.35	1738.16	1719.01	1712.19
150,000	2690.03	2607.24	2578.52	2568.28

MONTHLY PAYMENTS
ANNUAL INTEREST RATE: 20.75 %

LOAN AMOUNT	LOAN MATURITY (YEARS) 15	20	25	30
50	0.91	0.88	0.87	0.87
100	1.82	1.76	1.74	1.74
200	3.63	3.52	3.48	3.47
300	5.44	5.28	5.22	5.20
400	7.25	7.04	6.96	6.94
500	9.06	8.79	8.70	8.67
600	10.88	10.55	10.44	10.40
700	12.69	12.31	12.18	12.13
800	14.50	14.07	13.92	13.87
900	16.31	15.83	15.66	15.60
1,000	18.12	17.58	17.40	17.33
2,000	36.24	35.16	34.79	34.66
3,000	54.36	52.74	52.18	51.99
4,000	72.48	70.32	69.58	69.32
5,000	90.60	87.90	86.97	86.64
6,000	108.72	105.48	104.36	103.97
7,000	126.84	123.06	121.76	121.30
8,000	144.96	140.64	139.15	138.63
9,000	163.08	158.21	156.54	155.96
10,000	181.20	175.79	173.94	173.28
20,000	362.40	351.58	347.87	346.56
30,000	543.59	527.37	521.80	519.84
40,000	724.79	703.16	695.73	693.12
50,000	905.98	878.94	869.67	866.40
60,000	1087.18	1054.73	1043.60	1039.68
70,000	1268.37	1230.52	1217.53	1212.95
80,000	1449.57	1406.31	1391.46	1386.23
90,000	1630.76	1582.10	1565.40	1559.51
100,000	1811.96	1757.88	1739.33	1732.79
150,000	2717.93	2636.82	2608.99	2599.18

MONTHLY PAYMENTS
ANNUAL INTEREST RATE: 21 %

LOAN AMOUNT	LOAN MATURITY (YEARS)			
	15	20	25	30
50	0.92	0.89	0.88	0.88
100	1.84	1.78	1.76	1.76
200	3.67	3.56	3.52	3.51
300	5.50	5.34	5.28	5.27
400	7.33	7.12	7.04	7.02
500	9.16	8.89	8.80	8.77
600	10.99	10.67	10.56	10.53
700	12.82	12.45	12.32	12.28
800	14.65	14.23	14.08	14.03
900	16.48	16.00	15.84	15.79
1,000	18.31	17.78	17.60	17.54
2,000	36.62	35.56	35.20	35.07
3,000	54.92	53.33	52.79	52.61
4,000	73.23	71.11	70.39	70.14
5,000	91.54	88.89	87.99	87.68
6,000	109.84	106.66	105.58	105.21
7,000	128.15	124.44	123.18	122.74
8,000	146.45	142.22	140.78	140.28
9,000	164.76	159.99	158.37	157.81
10,000	183.07	177.77	175.97	175.35
20,000	366.13	355.53	351.94	350.69
30,000	549.19	533.30	527.90	526.03
40,000	732.25	711.06	703.87	701.37
50,000	915.31	888.83	879.84	876.71
60,000	1098.37	1066.59	1055.80	1052.05
70,000	1281.43	1244.35	1231.77	1227.39
80,000	1464.49	1422.12	1407.74	1402.73
90,000	1647.56	1599.88	1583.70	1578.07
100,000	1830.62	1777.65	1759.67	1753.41
150,000	2745.92	2666.47	2639.50	2630.11

MONTHLY PAYMENTS
ANNUAL INTEREST RATE: 21.25 %

LOAN AMOUNT	LOAN MATURITY (YEARS)			
	15	20	25	30
50	0.93	0.90	0.90	0.89
100	1.85	1.80	1.79	1.78
200	3.70	3.60	3.57	3.55
300	5.55	5.40	5.35	5.33
400	7.40	7.19	7.13	7.10
500	9.25	8.99	8.91	8.88
600	11.10	10.79	10.69	10.65
700	12.95	12.59	12.47	12.42
800	14.80	14.38	14.25	14.20
900	16.65	16.18	16.03	15.97
1,000	18.50	17.98	17.81	17.75
2,000	36.99	35.95	35.61	35.49
3,000	55.48	53.93	53.41	53.23
4,000	73.98	71.90	71.21	70.97
5,000	92.47	89.88	89.01	88.71
6,000	110.96	107.85	106.81	106.45
7,000	129.46	125.83	124.61	124.19
8,000	147.95	143.80	142.41	141.93
9,000	166.44	161.78	160.21	159.67
10,000	184.94	179.75	178.01	177.41
20,000	369.87	359.49	356.01	354.81
30,000	554.80	539.24	534.01	532.21
40,000	739.73	718.98	712.02	709.62
50,000	924.67	898.73	890.02	887.02
60,000	1109.60	1078.47	1068.02	1064.42
70,000	1294.53	1258.22	1246.02	1241.83
80,000	1479.46	1437.96	1424.03	1419.23
90,000	1664.40	1617.71	1602.03	1596.63
100,000	1849.33	1797.45	1780.03	1774.03
150,000	2773.99	2696.17	2670.04	2661.05

MONTHLY PAYMENTS
ANNUAL INTEREST RATE: 21.5 %

LOAN AMOUNT	LOAN MATURITY (YEARS)			
	15	20	25	30
50	0.94	0.91	0.91	0.90
100	1.87	1.82	1.81	1.80
200	3.74	3.64	3.61	3.59
300	5.61	5.46	5.41	5.39
400	7.48	7.27	7.21	7.18
500	9.35	9.09	9.01	8.98
600	11.21	10.91	10.81	10.77
700	13.08	12.73	12.61	12.57
800	14.95	14.54	14.41	14.36
900	16.82	16.36	16.21	16.16
1,000	18.69	18.18	18.01	17.95
2,000	37.37	36.35	36.01	35.90
3,000	56.05	54.52	54.02	53.85
4,000	74.73	72.70	72.02	71.79
5,000	93.41	90.87	90.03	89.74
6,000	112.09	109.04	108.03	107.69
7,000	130.77	127.21	126.03	125.63
8,000	149.45	145.39	144.04	143.58
9,000	168.13	163.56	162.04	161.53
10,000	186.81	181.73	180.05	179.47
20,000	373.62	363.46	360.09	358.94
30,000	560.43	545.19	540.13	538.41
40,000	747.24	726.92	720.17	717.87
50,000	934.05	908.65	900.21	897.34
60,000	1120.86	1090.37	1080.25	1076.81
70,000	1307.66	1272.10	1260.29	1256.27
80,000	1494.47	1453.83	1440.33	1435.74
90,000	1681.28	1635.56	1620.37	1615.21
100,000	1868.09	1817.29	1800.42	1794.67
150,000	2802.13	2725.93	2700.62	2692.01

MONTHLY PAYMENTS
ANNUAL INTEREST RATE: 21.75 %

LOAN AMOUNT	LOAN MATURITY (YEARS)			
	15	20	25	30
50	0.95	0.92	0.92	0.91
100	1.89	1.84	1.83	1.82
200	3.78	3.68	3.65	3.64
300	5.67	5.52	5.47	5.45
400	7.55	7.35	7.29	7.27
500	9.44	9.19	9.11	9.08
600	11.33	11.03	10.93	10.90
700	13.21	12.87	12.75	12.71
800	15.10	14.70	14.57	14.53
900	16.99	16.54	16.39	16.34
1,000	18.87	18.38	18.21	18.16
2,000	37.74	36.75	36.42	36.31
3,000	56.61	55.12	54.63	54.46
4,000	75.48	73.49	72.84	72.62
5,000	94.35	91.86	91.05	90.77
6,000	113.22	110.23	109.25	108.92
7,000	132.09	128.61	127.46	127.08
8,000	150.96	146.98	145.67	145.23
9,000	169.83	165.35	163.88	163.38
10,000	188.69	183.72	182.09	181.54
20,000	377.38	367.44	364.17	363.07
30,000	566.07	551.15	546.25	544.60
40,000	754.76	734.87	728.33	726.13
50,000	943.45	918.58	910.41	907.67
60,000	1132.14	1102.30	1092.49	1089.20
70,000	1320.83	1286.01	1274.58	1270.73
80,000	1509.52	1469.73	1456.66	1452.26
90,000	1698.21	1653.44	1638.74	1633.79
100,000	1886.90	1837.16	1820.82	1815.33
150,000	2830.35	2755.73	2731.23	2722.99

LOAN PROGRESS TABLES
(Remaining Balance per $1,000 Original Loan)

Loan progress tables allow you to determine how much is still owed on a mortgage loan during the loan term. To use the tables you must know the following:

1. *The annual interest rate on the loan.* The rate is shown at the top of each table, and each table is for a different rate. Rates range from 7% to 21.75% by .25% intervals.

2. *The original amount borrowed.* The amounts in the table are per $1,000 of original loan. If the original principal was $30,000 then multiply the amount in the table by 30.

3. *The maturity of the loan.* The table shows amounts for 15, 20, 25 and 30 year maturities.

4. *The age of the loan.* This is the number of years since the loan was originated and is shown in the left-most column.

The amounts shown in the table are the remaining balance of the loan at the end of the period shown.

Example: Suppose you obtained a mortgage loan 3½ years ago for $48,500. The interest rate is 7% and the maturity is 20 years. How much do you still owe on the loan?

Find the 7% table. Look at the row for "3.5" age of loan. At the intersection of this row with the "20" column is the amount of 908.94. Multiply this amount by the number of thousands originally borrowed (48.5) to get $44,083.59, the existing balance of the loan.

Example: Suppose you want to know how much interest you paid last year on your mortgage loan so you can deduct the amount from your taxable income. The amount of interest is the difference between your total payments over the year and the amount the loan amortized principal. You can find this latter amount with aid of the table.

Suppose the loan had been originated 5 years ago for $50,000. The interest rate is 7% and maturity is 30 years. At the beginning of last year the loan was 4 years old. At that time the amount owed was $954.75 ("4.0" row, "30" column) per thousand, or $47,737.50 total (50 times 954.75). At the end of the year, the 5-year old loan had a balance of $941.32 per thousand, or $47,066.00. The balance amortized by $47,737.50 minus $47,066.00, or $671.50, during the year. The total monthly payments were $332.66 times 12, or $3,991.92. Total interest paid was $3,991.92 minus $671.50, or $3,320.42.

Example: Suppose you take out a loan today at 7% for 25 years. How long will it take to pay off half of the principal?

Look down the column for 25 year loans. At the 17 year row the amount is 518.41. This is slightly more than half the original $1,000 of principal. The 18 year row shows 468.29, which is less than half. Therefore, you will pay off half the principal some time during the 17th year of the loan.

REMAINING BALANCE PER $1000 OF ORIGINAL LOAN

ANNUAL INTEREST RATE: 7 %

AGE OF LOAN	LOAN MATURITY (YEARS)			
	15	20	25	30
0.5	980.79	988.31	992.48	995.01
1.0	960.90	976.21	984.70	989.84
1.5	940.31	963.68	976.64	984.49
2.0	918.98	950.70	968.30	978.95
2.5	896.89	937.26	959.66	973.21
3.0	874.02	923.35	950.71	967.27
3.5	850.34	908.94	941.44	961.12
4.0	825.82	894.02	931.85	954.75
4.5	800.42	878.57	921.91	948.15
5.0	774.13	862.57	911.62	941.32
6.0	718.70	828.84	889.93	926.92
7.0	659.27	792.68	866.68	911.47
8.0	595.54	753.90	841.74	894.92
9.0	527.20	712.32	815.01	877.16
10.0	453.93	667.74	786.33	858.12
11.0	375.35	619.93	755.59	837.71
12.0	291.10	568.66	722.62	815.82
13.0	200.75	513.69	687.27	792.35
14.0	103.88	454.75	649.37	767.18
15.0	0.00	391.54	608.72	740.19
16.0		323.77	565.14	711.25
17.0		251.09	518.41	680.22
18.0		173.16	468.29	646.94
19.0		89.60	414.56	611.26
20.0		0.00	356.94	573.00
21.0			295.15	531.98
22.0			228.90	487.98
23.0			157.86	440.81
24.0			81.68	390.23
25.0			0.00	335.99
26.0				277.83
27.0				215.47
28.0				148.60
29.0				76.89
30.0				0.00

REMAINING BALANCE PER $1000 OF ORIGINAL LOAN

ANNUAL INTEREST RATE: 7.25 %

AGE OF LOAN	LOAN MATURITY (YEARS)			
	15	20	25	30
0.5	981.20	988.66	992.77	995.25
1.0	961.70	976.90	985.28	990.32
1.5	941.49	964.70	977.51	985.21
2.0	920.53	952.06	969.46	979.92
2.5	898.80	938.96	961.11	974.43
3.0	876.27	925.37	952.45	968.73
3.5	852.92	911.28	943.47	962.83
4.0	828.70	896.67	934.16	956.71
4.5	803.59	881.52	924.51	950.37
5.0	777.56	865.82	914.51	943.79
6.0	722.59	832.66	893.38	929.90
7.0	663.49	797.01	870.67	914.96
8.0	599.97	758.70	846.26	898.91
9.0	531.68	717.50	820.01	881.65
10.0	458.28	673.23	791.80	863.10
11.0	379.37	625.63	761.48	843.16
12.0	294.55	574.46	728.88	821.73
13.0	203.37	519.46	693.83	798.69
14.0	105.36	460.34	656.16	773.92
15.0	0.00	396.79	615.67	747.29
16.0		328.47	572.14	718.67
17.0		255.03	525.35	687.90
18.0		176.08	475.06	654.83
19.0		91.22	420.99	619.28
20.0		0.00	362.87	581.06
21.0			300.39	539.98
22.0			233.23	495.82
23.0			161.03	448.35
24.0			83.42	397.32
25.0			0.00	342.47
26.0				283.50
27.0				220.12
28.0				151.98
29.0				78.73
30.0				0.00

REMAINING BALANCE PER $1000 OF ORIGINAL LOAN

ANNUAL INTEREST RATE: 7.5 %

AGE OF LOAN	LOAN MATURITY (YEARS)			
	15	20	25	30
0.5	981.59	988.99	993.05	995.48
1.0	962.49	977.57	985.84	990.78
1.5	942.65	965.71	978.35	985.91
2.0	922.06	953.40	970.58	980.85
2.5	900.69	940.61	962.52	975.60
3.0	878.50	927.35	954.14	970.14
3.5	855.46	913.57	945.45	964.48
4.0	831.55	899.27	936.42	958.61
4.5	806.73	884.43	927.05	952.51
5.0	780.96	869.02	917.33	946.17
6.0	726.44	836.42	896.75	932.78
7.0	667.69	801.29	874.57	918.34
8.0	604.38	763.43	850.68	902.78
9.0	536.15	722.64	824.93	886.02
10.0	462.63	678.67	797.18	867.95
11.0	383.40	631.29	767.27	848.48
12.0	298.02	580.24	735.04	827.50
13.0	206.01	525.22	700.32	804.89
14.0	106.85	465.93	662.89	780.52
15.0	0.00	402.03	622.56	754.27
16.0		333.18	579.10	725.97
17.0		258.98	532.27	695.48
18.0		179.02	481.80	662.62
19.0		92.86	427.41	627.21
20.0		0.00	368.80	589.05
21.0			305.64	547.93
22.0			237.57	503.62
23.0			164.22	455.86
24.0			85.18	404.40
25.0			0.00	348.95
26.0				289.18
27.0				224.78
28.0				155.38
29.0				80.59
30.0				0.00

REMAINING BALANCE PER $1000 OF ORIGINAL LOAN

ANNUAL INTEREST RATE: 7.75 %

AGE OF LOAN	LOAN MATURITY (YEARS)			
	15	20	25	30
0.5	981.98	989.32	993.32	995.70
1.0	963.26	978.22	986.38	991.22
1.5	943.80	966.69	979.17	986.57
2.0	923.57	954.70	971.67	981.74
2.5	902.54	942.24	963.88	976.72
3.0	880.69	929.28	955.78	971.50
3.5	857.98	915.82	947.36	966.07
4.0	834.37	901.83	938.61	960.43
4.5	809.83	887.28	929.52	954.57
5.0	784.33	872.17	920.07	948.48
6.0	730.26	840.12	900.03	935.56
7.0	671.86	805.50	878.39	921.61
8.0	608.77	768.11	855.00	906.54
9.0	540.61	727.71	829.74	890.25
10.0	466.97	684.06	802.45	872.66
11.0	387.42	636.91	772.97	853.66
12.0	301.49	585.97	741.12	833.13
13.0	208.65	530.95	706.71	810.95
14.0	108.35	471.50	669.54	786.99
15.0	0.00	407.28	629.38	761.11
16.0		337.90	586.00	733.14
17.0		262.95	539.14	702.93
18.0		181.97	488.51	670.30
19.0		94.50	433.81	635.04
20.0		0.00	374.72	596.96
21.0			310.89	555.81
22.0			241.93	511.36
23.0			167.43	463.34
24.0			86.95	411.46
25.0			0.00	355.42
26.0				294.87
27.0				229.46
28.0				158.80
29.0				82.47
30.0				0.00

REMAINING BALANCE PER $1000 OF ORIGINAL LOAN

ANNUAL INTEREST RATE: 8 %

AGE OF LOAN	LOAN MATURITY (YEARS)			
	15	20	25	30
0.5	982.37	989.64	993.58	995.91
1.0	964.02	978.86	986.91	991.65
1.5	944.93	967.65	979.96	987.21
2.0	925.06	955.97	972.73	982.60
2.5	904.38	943.82	965.21	977.80
3.0	882.86	931.18	957.38	972.80
3.5	860.46	918.02	949.23	967.60
4.0	837.16	904.33	940.75	962.19
4.5	812.90	890.08	931.92	956.56
5.0	787.66	875.26	922.74	950.70
6.0	734.06	843.77	903.24	938.25
7.0	676.01	809.66	882.11	924.77
8.0	613.14	772.73	859.24	910.18
9.0	545.05	732.73	834.46	894.37
10.0	471.31	689.41	807.63	877.25
11.0	391.45	642.49	778.58	858.71
12.0	304.97	591.68	747.11	838.62
13.0	211.30	536.65	713.03	816.88
14.0	109.86	477.06	676.12	793.32
15.0	0.00	412.52	636.14	767.82
16.0		342.62	592.85	740.19
17.0		266.92	545.97	710.27
18.0		184.94	495.19	677.87
19.0		96.16	440.20	642.78
20.0		0.00	380.65	604.78
21.0			316.15	563.62
22.0			246.30	519.05
23.0			170.65	470.78
24.0			88.73	418.50
25.0			0.00	361.88
26.0				300.56
27.0				234.16
28.0				162.24
29.0				84.35
30.0				0.00

REMAINING BALANCE PER $1000 OF ORIGINAL LOAN

ANNUAL INTEREST RATE: 8.25 %

AGE OF LOAN	LOAN MATURITY (YEARS)			
	15	20	25	30
0.5	982.75	989.95	993.84	996.11
1.0	964.77	979.49	987.42	992.05
1.5	946.04	968.58	980.73	987.83
2.0	926.52	957.22	973.76	983.42
2.5	906.19	945.38	966.49	978.83
3.0	885.00	933.04	958.92	974.05
3.5	862.92	920.19	951.04	969.07
4.0	839.91	906.79	942.82	963.88
4.5	815.94	892.83	934.26	958.47
5.0	790.97	878.29	925.34	952.84
6.0	737.82	847.35	906.36	940.85
7.0	680.13	813.76	885.75	927.83
8.0	617.49	777.29	863.38	913.70
9.0	549.48	737.69	839.09	898.36
10.0	475.65	694.70	812.72	881.70
11.0	395.48	648.02	784.09	863.62
12.0	308.45	597.35	753.00	843.98
13.0	213.96	542.34	719.25	822.66
14.0	111.38	482.60	682.61	799.52
15.0	0.00	417.76	642.83	774.39
16.0		347.35	599.64	747.11
17.0		270.91	552.75	717.49
18.0		187.92	501.84	685.33
19.0		97.82	446.57	650.42
20.0		0.00	386.57	612.52
21.0			321.42	571.36
22.0			250.69	526.68
23.0			173.89	478.18
24.0			90.52	425.51
25.0			0.00	368.34
26.0				306.26
27.0				238.86
28.0				165.69
29.0				86.25
30.0				0.00

REMAINING BALANCE PER $1000 OF ORIGINAL LOAN

ANNUAL INTEREST RATE: 8.5 %

AGE OF LOAN	LOAN MATURITY (YEARS)			
	15	20	25	30
0.5	983.12	990.26	994.08	996.30
1.0	965.51	980.10	987.91	992.44
1.5	947.13	969.50	981.47	988.41
2.0	927.97	958.44	974.75	984.21
2.5	907.97	946.90	967.74	979.83
3.0	887.11	934.86	960.43	975.26
3.5	865.34	922.30	952.80	970.49
4.0	842.64	909.20	944.84	965.51
4.5	818.95	895.53	936.53	960.32
5.0	794.24	881.27	927.87	954.90
6.0	741.56	850.87	909.40	943.36
7.0	684.22	817.79	889.30	930.79
8.0	621.82	781.78	867.43	917.11
9.0	553.90	742.59	843.62	902.23
10.0	479.97	699.94	817.70	886.02
11.0	399.52	653.51	789.50	868.39
12.0	311.95	602.98	758.80	849.20
13.0	216.64	547.99	725.39	828.31
14.0	112.90	488.13	689.03	805.57
15.0	0.00	422.99	649.45	780.83
16.0		352.08	606.37	753.90
17.0		274.91	559.49	724.58
18.0		190.92	508.46	692.68
19.0		99.50	452.92	657.95
20.0		0.00	392.48	620.16
21.0			326.69	579.03
22.0			255.08	534.26
23.0			177.14	485.53
24.0			92.32	432.50
25.0			0.00	374.78
26.0				311.95
27.0				243.58
28.0				169.16
29.0				88.16
30.0				0.00

REMAINING BALANCE PER $1000 OF ORIGINAL LOAN

ANNUAL INTEREST RATE: 8.75 %

AGE OF LOAN	LOAN MATURITY (YEARS)			
	15	20	25	30
0.5	983.48	990.56	994.32	996.48
1.0	966.23	980.69	988.38	992.81
1.5	948.21	970.39	982.19	988.98
2.0	929.39	959.63	975.71	984.97
2.5	909.73	948.38	968.95	980.78
3.0	889.19	936.64	961.88	976.41
3.5	867.74	924.37	954.50	971.85
4.0	845.33	911.56	946.79	967.08
4.5	821.92	898.18	938.74	962.09
5.0	797.47	884.20	930.33	956.89
6.0	745.26	854.34	912.37	945.77
7.0	688.29	821.77	892.77	933.65
8.0	626.12	786.22	871.39	920.41
9.0	558.30	747.44	848.05	905.98
10.0	484.29	705.13	822.60	890.22
11.0	403.55	658.96	794.82	873.04
12.0	315.45	608.58	764.51	854.28
13.0	219.32	553.62	731.45	833.82
14.0	114.44	493.65	695.37	811.49
15.0	0.00	428.21	656.00	787.13
16.0		356.82	613.05	760.56
17.0		278.92	566.18	731.56
18.0		193.92	515.05	699.91
19.0		101.19	459.25	665.39
20.0		0.00	398.38	627.72
21.0			331.96	586.62
22.0			259.49	541.77
23.0			180.41	492.84
24.0			94.14	439.46
25.0			0.00	381.20
26.0				317.65
27.0				248.30
28.0				172.64
29.0				90.08
30.0				0.00

REMAINING BALANCE PER $1000 OF ORIGINAL LOAN

ANNUAL INTEREST RATE: 9 %

AGE OF LOAN	LOAN MATURITY (YEARS)			
	15	20	25	30
0.5	983.84	990.85	994.55	996.66
1.0	966.95	981.27	988.84	993.17
1.5	949.28	971.26	982.88	989.52
2.0	930.79	960.79	976.64	985.70
2.5	911.46	949.84	970.12	981.70
3.0	891.25	938.38	963.29	977.52
3.5	870.11	926.41	956.16	973.15
4.0	847.99	913.88	948.69	968.58
4.5	824.87	900.77	940.89	963.80
5.0	800.68	887.07	932.73	958.80
6.0	748.93	857.75	915.26	948.11
7.0	692.32	825.68	896.15	936.41
8.0	630.41	790.60	875.25	923.61
9.0	562.68	752.23	852.40	909.61
10.0	488.61	710.26	827.39	894.30
11.0	407.58	664.35	800.05	877.55
12.0	318.96	614.14	770.13	859.23
13.0	222.02	559.22	737.41	839.20
14.0	115.98	499.14	701.62	817.28
15.0	0.00	433.43	662.48	793.31
16.0		361.55	619.66	767.09
17.0		282.94	572.82	738.40
18.0		196.94	521.60	707.03
19.0		102.88	465.56	672.72
20.0		0.00	404.27	635.19
21.0			337.23	594.13
22.0			263.90	549.23
23.0			183.69	500.11
24.0			95.96	446.38
25.0			0.00	387.62
26.0				323.34
27.0				253.03
28.0				176.13
29.0				92.01
30.0				0.00

REMAINING BALANCE PER $1000 OF ORIGINAL LOAN

ANNUAL INTEREST RATE: 9.25 %

AGE OF LOAN	LOAN MATURITY (YEARS)			
	15	20	25	30
0.5	984.20	991.13	994.77	996.83
1.0	967.65	981.84	989.29	993.51
1.5	950.32	972.11	983.55	990.03
2.0	932.17	961.92	977.54	986.39
2.5	913.17	951.26	971.25	982.58
3.0	893.27	940.09	964.66	978.58
3.5	872.44	928.39	957.76	974.40
4.0	850.62	916.14	950.54	970.03
4.5	827.77	903.32	942.97	965.44
5.0	803.85	889.89	935.05	960.64
6.0	752.57	861.10	918.07	950.35
7.0	696.33	829.53	899.45	939.07
8.0	634.67	794.91	879.03	926.69
9.0	567.05	756.96	856.64	913.12
10.0	492.91	715.34	832.09	898.25
11.0	411.61	669.70	805.17	881.93
12.0	322.47	619.66	775.65	864.05
13.0	224.72	564.78	743.28	844.43
14.0	117.53	504.61	707.79	822.92
15.0	0.00	438.63	668.88	799.34
16.0		366.29	626.20	773.48
17.0		286.96	579.41	745.12
18.0		199.97	528.10	714.03
19.0		104.59	471.84	679.93
20.0		0.00	410.15	642.55
21.0			342.50	601.55
22.0			268.32	556.60
23.0			186.98	507.31
24.0			97.80	453.27
25.0			0.00	394.00
26.0				329.02
27.0				257.76
28.0				179.62
29.0				93.95
30.0				0.00

REMAINING BALANCE PER $1000 OF ORIGINAL LOAN

ANNUAL INTEREST RATE: 9.5 %

AGE OF LOAN	LOAN MATURITY (YEARS)			
	15	20	25	30
0.5	984.54	991.40	994.98	996.99
1.0	968.34	982.39	989.72	993.83
1.5	951.35	972.94	984.20	990.52
2.0	933.53	963.03	978.41	987.06
2.5	914.86	952.65	972.35	983.42
3.0	895.28	941.76	965.99	979.60
3.5	874.74	930.34	959.32	975.61
4.0	853.22	918.37	952.33	971.41
4.5	830.65	905.81	945.00	967.02
5.0	806.99	892.65	937.31	962.41
6.0	756.17	864.39	920.81	952.51
7.0	700.31	833.32	902.66	941.63
8.0	638.91	799.17	882.72	929.67
9.0	571.41	761.63	860.79	916.53
10.0	497.21	720.36	836.70	902.08
11.0	415.64	675.00	810.20	886.19
12.0	325.99	625.14	781.08	868.73
13.0	227.43	570.32	749.07	849.54
14.0	119.09	510.07	713.88	828.44
15.0	0.00	443.83	675.20	805.24
16.0		371.03	632.69	779.75
17.0		290.99	585.95	751.72
18.0		203.02	534.57	720.92
19.0		106.31	478.09	687.05
20.0		0.00	416.01	649.82
21.0			347.77	608.90
22.0			272.75	563.92
23.0			190.29	514.47
24.0			99.64	460.12
25.0			0.00	400.37
26.0				334.69
27.0				262.50
28.0				183.14
29.0				95.90
30.0				0.00

REMAINING BALANCE PER $1000 OF ORIGINAL LOAN

ANNUAL INTEREST RATE: 9.75 %

AGE OF LOAN	LOAN MATURITY (YEARS)			
	15	20	25	30
0.5	984.88	991.67	995.18	997.14
1.0	969.02	982.93	990.13	994.14
1.5	952.36	973.75	984.82	991.00
2.0	934.87	964.12	979.25	987.69
2.5	916.52	954.00	973.41	984.22
3.0	897.25	943.38	967.27	980.58
3.5	877.02	932.24	960.82	976.76
4.0	855.78	920.54	954.06	972.74
4.5	833.49	908.26	946.96	968.53
5.0	810.09	895.37	939.51	964.11
6.0	759.74	867.62	923.47	954.59
7.0	704.26	837.05	905.79	944.11
8.0	643.12	803.36	886.32	932.55
9.0	575.74	766.24	864.85	919.82
10.0	501.49	725.33	841.20	905.79
11.0	419.67	680.25	815.14	890.32
12.0	329.51	630.57	786.42	873.28
13.0	230.15	575.82	754.76	854.51
14.0	120.66	515.50	719.89	833.81
15.0	0.00	449.02	681.45	811.01
16.0		375.76	639.10	785.88
17.0		295.03	592.42	758.19
18.0		206.07	540.99	727.68
19.0		108.03	484.31	694.05
20.0		0.00	421.85	656.99
21.0			353.03	616.16
22.0			277.18	571.16
23.0			193.60	521.57
24.0			101.50	466.93
25.0			0.00	406.71
26.0				340.36
27.0				267.23
28.0				186.65
29.0				97.85
30.0				0.00

REMAINING BALANCE PER $1000 OF ORIGINAL LOAN

ANNUAL INTEREST RATE: 10 %

AGE OF LOAN	LOAN MATURITY (YEARS)			
	15	20	25	30
0.5	985.22	991.93	995.38	997.29
1.0	969.68	983.45	990.53	994.44
1.5	953.35	974.54	985.43	991.45
2.0	936.19	965.17	980.07	988.30
2.5	918.15	955.33	974.43	984.99
3.0	899.19	944.98	968.51	981.52
3.5	879.26	934.10	962.29	977.86
4.0	858.32	922.67	955.74	974.02
4.5	836.30	910.65	948.87	969.99
5.0	813.17	898.02	941.64	965.74
6.0	763.28	870.80	926.06	956.60
7.0	708.18	840.72	908.84	946.49
8.0	647.31	807.50	889.83	935.33
9.0	580.06	770.79	868.82	923.00
10.0	505.77	730.24	845.61	909.38
11.0	423.70	685.45	819.98	894.33
12.0	333.03	635.96	791.66	877.71
13.0	232.88	581.30	760.37	859.34
14.0	122.23	520.90	725.81	839.06
15.0	0.00	454.19	687.62	816.64
16.0		380.49	645.44	791.89
17.0		299.07	598.85	764.54
18.0		209.13	547.37	734.32
19.0		109.77	490.50	700.94
20.0		0.00	427.68	664.07
21.0			358.28	623.33
22.0			281.62	578.33
23.0			196.92	528.62
24.0			103.36	473.70
25.0			0.00	413.03
26.0				346.01
27.0				271.97
28.0				190.18
29.0				99.82
30.0				0.00

REMAINING BALANCE PER $1000 OF ORIGINAL LOAN

ANNUAL INTEREST RATE: 10.25 %

AGE OF LOAN	LOAN MATURITY (YEARS)			
	15	20	25	30
0.5	985.55	992.19	995.57	997.43
1.0	970.34	983.96	990.92	994.72
1.5	954.33	975.31	986.01	991.88
2.0	937.49	966.20	980.85	988.88
2.5	919.76	956.62	975.42	985.73
3.0	901.11	946.54	969.71	982.41
3.5	881.48	935.92	963.70	978.92
4.0	860.82	924.75	957.37	975.25
4.5	839.08	913.00	950.71	971.38
5.0	816.20	900.63	943.71	967.31
6.0	766.79	873.92	928.57	958.52
7.0	712.07	844.33	911.81	948.79
8.0	651.47	811.57	893.25	938.01
9.0	584.36	775.28	872.70	926.08
10.0	510.03	735.10	849.93	912.86
11.0	427.72	690.60	824.72	898.22
12.0	336.56	641.31	796.80	882.01
13.0	235.61	586.73	765.88	864.05
14.0	123.81	526.29	731.64	844.17
15.0	0.00	459.35	693.72	822.15
16.0		385.22	651.72	797.76
17.0		303.12	605.21	770.76
18.0		212.20	553.71	740.85
19.0		111.51	496.66	707.72
20.0		0.00	433.49	671.04
21.0			363.53	630.42
22.0			286.06	585.43
23.0			200.25	535.61
24.0			105.23	480.43
25.0			0.00	419.32
26.0				351.65
27.0				276.71
28.0				193.71
29.0				101.79
30.0				0.00

REMAINING BALANCE PER $1000 OF ORIGINAL LOAN

ANNUAL INTEREST RATE: 10.5 %

AGE OF LOAN	LOAN MATURITY (YEARS)			
	15	20	25	30
0.5	985.87	992.43	995.76	997.56
1.0	970.98	984.46	991.29	994.99
1.5	955.29	976.06	986.58	992.29
2.0	938.77	967.21	981.61	989.44
2.5	921.35	957.88	976.38	986.43
3.0	903.00	948.06	970.87	983.27
3.5	883.66	937.70	965.07	979.93
4.0	863.29	926.79	958.95	976.42
4.5	841.83	915.30	952.50	972.72
5.0	819.21	903.18	945.71	968.82
6.0	770.27	876.98	931.02	960.38
7.0	715.93	847.88	914.70	951.00
8.0	655.61	815.58	896.59	940.60
9.0	588.64	779.71	876.48	929.05
10.0	514.28	739.90	854.15	916.22
11.0	431.74	695.69	829.37	901.99
12.0	340.10	646.62	801.85	886.18
13.0	238.36	592.13	771.30	868.63
14.0	125.40	531.65	737.38	849.15
15.0	0.00	464.49	699.73	827.52
16.0		389.94	657.93	803.51
17.0		307.17	611.51	776.85
18.0		215.28	559.99	747.25
19.0		113.26	502.79	714.39
20.0		0.00	439.28	677.91
21.0			368.77	637.41
22.0			290.49	592.45
23.0			203.59	542.53
24.0			107.11	487.11
25.0			0.00	425.58
26.0				357.27
27.0				281.44
28.0				197.24
29.0				103.77
30.0				0.00

REMAINING BALANCE PER $1000 OF ORIGINAL LOAN

ANNUAL INTEREST RATE: 10.75 %

AGE OF LOAN	LOAN MATURITY (YEARS)			
	15	20	25	30
0.5	986.19	992.67	995.93	997.69
1.0	971.61	984.95	991.65	995.25
1.5	956.24	976.79	987.12	992.68
2.0	940.02	968.19	982.35	989.97
2.5	922.91	959.11	977.31	987.11
3.0	904.86	949.54	972.00	984.09
3.5	885.82	939.44	966.39	980.90
4.0	865.73	928.79	960.48	977.54
4.5	844.54	917.55	954.24	974.00
5.0	822.18	905.69	947.66	970.26
6.0	773.71	879.98	933.39	962.15
7.0	719.76	851.37	917.52	953.13
8.0	659.72	819.52	899.84	943.09
9.0	592.90	784.08	880.17	931.92
10.0	518.53	744.64	858.28	919.48
11.0	435.75	700.74	833.92	905.64
12.0	343.63	651.88	806.81	890.23
13.0	241.11	597.50	776.63	873.08
14.0	127.00	536.98	743.04	854.00
15.0	0.00	469.62	705.66	832.76
16.0		394.66	664.06	809.12
17.0		311.22	617.76	782.81
18.0		218.37	566.23	753.53
19.0		115.02	508.87	720.95
20.0		0.00	445.04	684.68
21.0			374.00	644.31
22.0			294.94	599.39
23.0			206.94	549.39
24.0			109.00	493.74
25.0			0.00	431.81
26.0				362.88
27.0				286.16
28.0				200.78
29.0				105.76
30.0				0.00

REMAINING BALANCE PER $1000 OF ORIGINAL LOAN

ANNUAL INTEREST RATE: 11 %

AGE OF LOAN	LOAN MATURITY (YEARS)			
	15	20	25	30
0.5	986.50	992.91	996.10	997.81
1.0	972.24	985.42	991.99	995.50
1.5	957.17	977.50	987.64	993.06
2.0	941.26	969.15	983.05	990.48
2.5	924.45	960.32	978.21	987.75
3.0	906.70	950.99	973.08	984.87
3.5	887.95	941.14	967.67	981.83
4.0	868.14	930.74	961.96	978.62
4.5	847.22	919.75	955.92	975.23
5.0	825.12	908.14	949.55	971.65
6.0	777.12	882.93	935.70	963.86
7.0	723.56	854.80	920.25	955.18
8.0	663.81	823.41	903.01	945.49
9.0	597.14	788.39	883.78	934.69
10.0	522.76	749.32	862.32	922.63
11.0	439.77	705.73	838.38	909.17
12.0	347.17	657.09	811.67	894.16
13.0	243.86	602.83	781.87	877.41
14.0	128.60	542.29	748.62	858.72
15.0	0.00	474.74	711.52	837.87
16.0		399.37	670.12	814.61
17.0		315.28	623.94	788.66
18.0		221.46	572.42	759.70
19.0		116.79	514.93	727.39
20.0		0.00	450.78	691.34
21.0			379.22	651.12
22.0			299.38	606.25
23.0			210.29	556.19
24.0			110.90	500.33
25.0			0.00	438.00
26.0				368.47
27.0				290.89
28.0				204.33
29.0				107.75
30.0				0.00

REMAINING BALANCE PER $1000 OF ORIGINAL LOAN

ANNUAL INTEREST RATE: 11.25 %

AGE OF LOAN	LOAN MATURITY (YEARS)			
	15	20	25	30
0.5	986.80	993.14	996.27	997.93
1.0	972.85	985.88	992.32	995.73
1.5	958.09	978.20	988.15	993.41
2.0	942.48	970.08	983.74	990.96
2.5	925.97	961.49	979.07	988.37
3.0	908.51	952.41	974.13	985.62
3.5	890.04	942.80	968.91	982.72
4.0	870.51	932.64	963.39	979.65
4.5	849.86	921.90	957.55	976.41
5.0	828.02	910.54	951.38	972.97
6.0	780.49	885.82	937.94	965.50
7.0	727.32	858.16	922.91	957.15
8.0	667.86	827.23	906.10	947.81
9.0	601.36	792.64	887.30	937.36
10.0	526.97	753.94	866.27	925.67
11.0	443.77	710.66	842.75	912.59
12.0	350.71	662.26	816.44	897.97
13.0	246.63	608.12	787.01	881.61
14.0	130.21	547.56	754.10	863.32
15.0	0.00	479.83	717.29	842.86
16.0		404.07	676.11	819.97
17.0		319.34	630.06	794.37
18.0		224.56	578.55	765.74
19.0		118.56	520.94	733.72
20.0		0.00	456.50	697.90
21.0			384.42	657.84
22.0			303.81	613.03
23.0			213.65	562.91
24.0			112.80	506.86
25.0			0.00	444.16
26.0				374.03
27.0				295.60
28.0				207.87
29.0				109.75
30.0				0.00

REMAINING BALANCE PER $1000 OF ORIGINAL LOAN

ANNUAL INTEREST RATE: 11.5 %

| AGE OF LOAN | LOAN MATURITY (YEARS) | | | |
	15	20	25	30
0.5	987.10	993.36	996.43	998.04
1.0	973.45	986.32	992.64	995.96
1.5	958.99	978.87	988.64	993.75
2.0	943.67	970.99	984.40	991.42
2.5	927.46	962.63	979.90	988.95
3.0	910.29	953.79	975.15	986.34
3.5	892.11	944.43	970.11	983.57
4.0	872.86	934.51	964.78	980.64
4.5	852.47	924.01	959.13	977.53
5.0	830.89	912.89	953.15	974.25
6.0	783.83	888.65	940.11	967.08
7.0	731.06	861.47	925.50	959.04
8.0	671.90	830.99	909.11	950.03
9.0	605.56	796.82	890.73	939.93
10.0	531.17	758.51	870.12	928.60
11.0	447.77	715.55	847.02	915.90
12.0	354.25	667.38	821.11	901.66
13.0	249.40	613.37	792.06	885.69
14.0	131.83	552.81	759.49	867.79
15.0	0.00	484.90	722.97	847.71
16.0		408.77	682.03	825.20
17.0		323.40	636.11	799.97
18.0		227.67	584.63	771.67
19.0		120.34	526.91	739.93
20.0		0.00	462.19	704.36
21.0			389.62	664.46
22.0			308.24	619.73
23.0			217.01	569.58
24.0			114.71	513.34
25.0			0.00	450.28
26.0				379.58
27.0				300.31
28.0				211.42
29.0				111.75
30.0				0.00

REMAINING BALANCE PER $1000 OF ORIGINAL LOAN

ANNUAL INTEREST RATE: 11.75 %

AGE OF LOAN	LOAN MATURITY (YEARS)			
	15	20	25	30
0.5	987.40	993.57	996.58	998.14
1.0	974.04	986.76	992.95	996.17
1.5	959.87	979.53	989.11	994.08
2.0	944.85	971.87	985.03	991.86
2.5	928.93	963.75	980.71	989.51
3.0	912.04	955.14	976.13	987.02
3.5	894.15	946.01	971.27	984.38
4.0	875.17	936.33	966.12	981.58
4.5	855.05	926.07	960.66	978.61
5.0	833.72	915.19	954.87	975.46
6.0	787.13	891.43	942.22	968.59
7.0	734.76	864.72	928.01	960.86
8.0	675.90	834.69	912.03	952.18
9.0	609.73	800.95	894.07	942.41
10.0	535.36	763.01	873.89	931.44
11.0	451.76	720.38	851.20	919.11
12.0	357.80	672.45	825.69	905.24
13.0	252.17	618.58	797.02	889.65
14.0	133.45	558.02	764.80	872.14
15.0	0.00	489.96	728.58	852.45
16.0		413.45	687.86	830.31
17.0		327.45	642.10	805.43
18.0		230.79	590.66	777.47
19.0		122.13	532.84	746.03
20.0		0.00	467.84	710.70
21.0			394.79	670.99
22.0			312.67	626.35
23.0			220.37	576.17
24.0			116.62	519.76
25.0			0.00	456.37
26.0				385.10
27.0				305.00
28.0				214.96
29.0				113.76
30.0				0.00

REMAINING BALANCE PER $1000 OF ORIGINAL LOAN

ANNUAL INTEREST RATE: 12 %

AGE OF LOAN	LOAN MATURITY (YEARS)			
	15	20	25	30
0.5	987.69	993.78	996.73	998.24
1.0	974.61	987.18	993.25	996.37
1.5	960.74	980.17	989.56	994.39
2.0	946.01	972.73	985.64	992.28
2.5	930.37	964.84	981.49	990.05
3.0	913.77	956.46	977.07	987.67
3.5	896.15	947.56	972.39	985.16
4.0	877.45	938.11	967.41	982.48
4.5	857.60	928.09	962.14	979.64
5.0	836.52	917.44	956.53	976.63
6.0	790.40	894.15	944.27	970.04
7.0	738.44	867.91	930.45	962.61
8.0	679.88	838.34	914.88	954.24
9.0	613.89	805.01	897.33	944.81
10.0	539.54	767.46	877.56	934.18
11.0	455.75	725.15	855.29	922.20
12.0	361.34	677.47	830.18	908.71
13.0	254.96	623.75	801.89	893.50
14.0	135.08	563.21	770.02	876.37
15.0	0.00	494.99	734.10	857.06
16.0		418.13	693.63	835.30
17.0		331.51	648.02	810.78
18.0		233.91	596.64	783.16
19.0		123.93	538.73	752.03
20.0		0.00	473.48	716.95
21.0			399.95	677.42
22.0			317.10	632.88
23.0			223.74	582.69
24.0			118.54	526.14
25.0			0.00	462.41
26.0				390.60
27.0				309.69
28.0				218.51
29.0				115.77
30.0				0.00

REMAINING BALANCE PER $1000 OF ORIGINAL LOAN

ANNUAL INTEREST RATE: 12.25 %

AGE OF LOAN	LOAN MATURITY (YEARS)			
	15	20	25	30
0.5	987.97	993.98	996.87	998.33
1.0	975.18	987.59	993.54	996.56
1.5	961.59	980.80	990.00	994.68
2.0	947.15	973.57	986.23	992.68
2.5	931.79	965.90	982.24	990.56
3.0	915.48	957.74	977.99	988.30
3.5	898.13	949.07	973.47	985.90
4.0	879.70	939.85	968.67	983.34
4.5	860.11	930.06	963.57	980.63
5.0	839.29	919.65	958.14	977.75
6.0	793.64	896.82	946.25	971.43
7.0	742.07	871.04	932.82	964.29
8.0	683.82	841.91	917.65	956.22
9.0	618.02	809.01	900.51	947.11
10.0	543.69	771.85	881.15	936.82
11.0	459.73	729.87	859.28	925.20
12.0	364.88	682.45	834.58	912.07
13.0	257.74	628.88	806.67	897.23
14.0	136.72	568.36	775.15	880.47
15.0	0.00	500.01	739.54	861.55
16.0		422.79	699.32	840.16
17.0		335.56	653.88	816.01
18.0		237.03	602.55	788.72
19.0		125.73	544.57	757.90
20.0		0.00	479.08	723.09
21.0			405.09	683.76
22.0			321.52	639.33
23.0			227.11	589.15
24.0			120.47	532.46
25.0			0.00	468.42
26.0				396.08
27.0				314.36
28.0				222.06
29.0				117.79
30.0				0.00

REMAINING BALANCE PER $1000 OF ORIGINAL LOAN

ANNUAL INTEREST RATE: 12.5 %

AGE OF LOAN	LOAN MATURITY (YEARS)			
	15	20	25	30
0.5	988.25	994.18	997.00	998.42
1.0	975.74	987.99	993.81	996.75
1.5	962.43	981.40	990.42	994.96
2.0	948.26	974.39	986.80	993.06
2.5	933.19	966.93	982.96	991.04
3.0	917.15	958.99	978.87	988.89
3.5	900.08	950.54	974.51	986.60
4.0	881.92	941.55	969.88	984.17
4.5	862.59	931.98	964.95	981.58
5.0	842.02	921.80	959.70	978.82
6.0	796.84	899.44	948.17	972.76
7.0	745.68	874.11	935.12	965.90
8.0	687.74	845.43	920.34	958.13
9.0	622.13	812.95	903.61	949.33
10.0	547.84	776.18	884.65	939.37
11.0	463.70	734.53	863.19	928.09
12.0	368.43	687.37	838.88	915.31
13.0	260.53	633.96	811.36	900.85
14.0	138.36	573.48	780.19	884.46
15.0	0.00	505.00	744.90	865.91
16.0		427.44	704.93	844.90
17.0		339.62	659.67	821.11
18.0		240.16	608.41	794.17
19.0		127.54	550.37	763.67
20.0		0.00	484.64	729.12
21.0			410.21	690.00
22.0			325.93	645.69
23.0			230.48	595.53
24.0			122.40	538.71
25.0			0.00	474.38
26.0				401.53
27.0				319.02
28.0				225.60
29.0				119.80
30.0				0.00

REMAINING BALANCE PER $1000 OF ORIGINAL LOAN

ANNUAL INTEREST RATE: 12.75 %

AGE OF LOAN	LOAN MATURITY (YEARS)			
	15	20	25	30
0.5	988.52	994.37	997.13	998.51
1.0	976.29	988.38	994.08	996.92
1.5	963.25	981.99	990.82	995.23
2.0	949.36	975.19	987.35	993.43
2.5	934.57	967.94	983.65	991.50
3.0	918.80	960.21	979.71	989.46
3.5	902.01	951.98	975.52	987.28
4.0	884.11	943.21	971.05	984.95
4.5	865.04	933.86	966.28	982.48
5.0	844.72	923.91	961.21	979.84
6.0	800.01	902.00	950.04	974.03
7.0	749.25	877.13	937.36	967.44
8.0	691.63	848.89	922.96	959.96
9.0	626.22	816.84	906.62	951.47
10.0	551.96	780.45	888.07	941.83
11.0	467.67	739.14	867.01	930.88
12.0	371.97	692.24	843.10	918.46
13.0	263.33	639.01	815.96	904.35
14.0	140.00	578.57	785.15	888.34
15.0	0.00	509.97	750.17	870.16
16.0		432.08	710.46	849.53
17.0		343.67	665.39	826.10
18.0		243.29	614.22	799.51
19.0		129.35	556.13	769.32
20.0		0.00	490.18	735.05
21.0			415.32	696.14
22.0			330.33	651.97
23.0			233.86	601.84
24.0			124.33	544.92
25.0			0.00	480.30
26.0				406.95
27.0				323.67
28.0				229.14
29.0				121.83
30.0				0.00

REMAINING BALANCE PER $1000 OF ORIGINAL LOAN

ANNUAL INTEREST RATE: 13 %

AGE OF LOAN	LOAN MATURITY (YEARS)			
	15	20	25	30
0.5	988.79	994.56	997.26	998.59
1.0	976.82	988.76	994.33	997.09
1.5	964.06	982.57	991.21	995.48
2.0	950.45	975.96	987.88	993.77
2.5	935.92	968.92	984.32	991.95
3.0	920.43	961.40	980.53	990.00
3.5	903.90	953.38	976.49	987.92
4.0	886.27	944.83	972.18	985.70
4.5	867.46	935.70	967.57	983.34
5.0	847.39	925.97	962.67	980.82
6.0	803.15	904.51	951.84	975.26
7.0	752.80	880.08	939.52	968.93
8.0	695.50	852.29	925.51	961.72
9.0	630.29	820.66	909.55	953.53
10.0	556.08	784.66	891.40	944.20
11.0	471.62	743.69	870.74	933.58
12.0	375.51	697.07	847.23	921.50
13.0	266.13	644.01	820.47	907.75
14.0	141.66	583.63	790.02	892.11
15.0	0.00	514.91	755.36	874.30
16.0		436.71	715.92	854.03
17.0		347.71	671.04	830.97
18.0		246.43	619.96	804.73
19.0		131.17	561.84	774.86
20.0		0.00	495.69	740.87
21.0			420.40	702.19
22.0			334.73	658.17
23.0			237.23	608.07
24.0			126.27	551.06
25.0			0.00	486.18
26.0				412.34
27.0				328.31
28.0				232.68
29.0				123.85
30.0				0.00

REMAINING BALANCE PER $1000 OF ORIGINAL LOAN

ANNUAL INTEREST RATE: 13.25 %

AGE OF LOAN	LOAN MATURITY (YEARS) 15	20	25	30
0.5	989.05	994.74	997.38	998.67
1.0	977.35	989.12	994.57	997.24
1.5	964.85	983.12	991.58	995.72
2.0	951.51	976.72	988.38	994.10
2.5	937.25	969.87	984.97	992.36
3.0	922.03	962.56	981.32	990.51
3.5	905.76	954.75	977.43	988.53
4.0	888.39	946.41	973.27	986.42
4.5	869.84	937.50	968.82	984.16
5.0	850.02	927.98	964.07	981.75
6.0	806.24	906.96	953.59	976.42
7.0	756.30	882.98	941.63	970.35
8.0	699.33	855.62	927.98	963.41
9.0	634.33	824.41	912.41	955.50
10.0	560.17	788.80	894.65	946.48
11.0	475.57	748.18	874.38	936.19
12.0	379.05	701.84	851.26	924.44
13.0	268.94	648.96	824.89	911.04
14.0	143.32	588.64	794.80	895.76
15.0	0.00	519.83	760.47	878.32
16.0		441.32	721.30	858.42
17.0		351.75	676.62	835.73
18.0		249.57	625.65	809.83
19.0		132.99	567.50	780.29
20.0		0.00	501.15	746.59
21.0			425.46	708.14
22.0			339.11	664.27
23.0			240.60	614.23
24.0			128.22	557.14
25.0			0.00	492.01
26.0				417.70
27.0				332.93
28.0				236.21
29.0				125.88
30.0				0.00

REMAINING BALANCE PER $1000 OF ORIGINAL LOAN

ANNUAL INTEREST RATE: 13.5 %

AGE OF LOAN	LOAN MATURITY (YEARS)			
	15	20	25	30
0.5	989.30	994.92	997.49	998.74
1.0	977.87	989.48	994.81	997.39
1.5	965.63	983.67	991.94	995.95
2.0	952.55	977.45	988.87	994.41
2.5	938.56	970.80	985.59	992.76
3.0	923.60	963.69	982.08	991.00
3.5	907.60	956.08	978.33	989.12
4.0	890.49	947.95	974.32	987.10
4.5	872.19	939.25	970.03	984.95
5.0	852.62	929.95	965.44	982.64
6.0	809.31	909.37	955.28	977.54
7.0	759.78	885.83	943.67	971.71
8.0	703.13	858.90	930.38	965.04
9.0	638.34	828.11	915.19	957.41
10.0	564.25	792.90	897.81	948.68
11.0	479.50	752.62	877.94	938.70
12.0	382.59	706.56	855.21	927.29
13.0	271.75	653.88	829.22	914.23
14.0	144.98	593.63	799.49	899.30
15.0	0.00	524.72	765.49	882.23
16.0		445.92	726.61	862.70
17.0		355.79	682.14	840.37
18.0		252.71	631.28	814.83
19.0		134.82	573.11	785.61
20.0		0.00	506.59	752.20
21.0			430.50	714.00
22.0			343.49	670.30
23.0			243.98	620.32
24.0			130.16	563.16
25.0			0.00	497.79
26.0				423.03
27.0				337.53
28.0				239.74
29.0				127.91
30.0				0.00

REMAINING BALANCE PER $1000 OF ORIGINAL LOAN

ANNUAL INTEREST RATE: 13.75 %

AGE OF LOAN	LOAN MATURITY (YEARS)			
	15	20	25	30
0.5	989.56	995.09	997.60	998.81
1.0	978.37	989.83	995.03	997.53
1.5	966.40	984.19	992.29	996.17
2.0	953.58	978.16	989.34	994.71
2.5	939.85	971.70	986.19	993.14
3.0	925.15	964.79	982.82	991.47
3.5	909.41	957.38	979.20	989.67
4.0	892.55	949.45	975.33	987.75
4.5	874.51	940.97	971.19	985.70
5.0	855.18	931.88	966.75	983.49
6.0	812.34	911.72	956.92	978.61
7.0	763.22	888.61	945.64	973.01
8.0	706.90	862.12	932.71	966.59
9.0	642.33	831.75	917.89	959.23
10.0	568.30	796.92	900.89	950.80
11.0	483.43	757.00	881.41	941.12
12.0	386.12	711.22	859.07	930.03
13.0	274.56	658.74	833.46	917.32
14.0	146.65	598.57	804.09	902.74
15.0	0.00	529.59	770.43	886.02
16.0		450.49	731.83	866.86
17.0		359.82	687.58	844.89
18.0		255.85	636.84	819.70
19.0		136.66	578.67	790.82
20.0		0.00	511.98	757.71
21.0			435.52	719.75
22.0			347.85	676.23
23.0			247.35	626.33
24.0			132.11	569.12
25.0			0.00	503.53
26.0				428.33
27.0				342.11
28.0				243.26
29.0				129.93
30.0				0.00

REMAINING BALANCE PER $1000 OF ORIGINAL LOAN

ANNUAL INTEREST RATE: 14 %

AGE OF LOAN	LOAN MATURITY (YEARS)			
	15	20	25	30
0.5	989.80	995.25	997.71	998.88
1.0	978.87	990.16	995.25	997.67
1.5	967.15	984.71	992.62	996.38
2.0	954.58	978.85	989.79	994.99
2.5	941.11	972.58	986.77	993.51
3.0	926.67	965.86	983.52	991.91
3.5	911.19	958.65	980.04	990.21
4.0	894.59	950.92	976.31	988.37
4.5	876.79	942.64	972.31	986.41
5.0	857.71	933.76	968.03	984.31
6.0	815.33	914.02	958.50	979.63
7.0	766.62	891.35	947.56	974.26
8.0	710.64	865.28	934.98	968.09
9.0	646.30	835.33	920.52	960.99
10.0	572.34	800.89	903.90	952.84
11.0	487.34	761.32	884.80	943.46
12.0	389.65	715.84	862.85	932.69
13.0	277.37	663.56	837.62	920.31
14.0	148.32	603.48	808.62	906.07
15.0	0.00	534.43	775.29	889.72
16.0		455.06	736.98	870.92
17.0		363.84	692.95	849.31
18.0		259.00	642.35	824.47
19.0		138.50	584.19	795.93
20.0		0.00	517.34	763.12
21.0			440.51	725.41
22.0			352.21	682.08
23.0			250.72	632.27
24.0			134.07	575.02
25.0			0.00	509.22
26.0				433.60
27.0				346.68
28.0				246.78
29.0				131.96
30.0				0.00

REMAINING BALANCE PER $1000 OF ORIGINAL LOAN

ANNUAL INTEREST RATE: 14.25 %

AGE OF LOAN	LOAN MATURITY (YEARS)			
	15	20	25	30
0.5	990.04	995.41	997.81	998.94
1.0	979.36	990.49	995.46	997.80
1.5	967.89	985.20	992.94	996.57
2.0	955.57	979.53	990.23	995.26
2.5	942.35	973.44	987.32	993.85
3.0	928.17	966.90	984.20	992.34
3.5	912.94	959.89	980.85	990.71
4.0	896.59	952.35	977.26	988.97
4.5	879.05	944.27	973.40	987.09
5.0	860.21	935.59	969.26	985.08
6.0	818.29	916.28	960.04	980.61
7.0	770.00	894.02	949.41	975.46
8.0	714.35	868.39	937.18	969.52
9.0	650.24	838.84	923.07	962.68
10.0	576.36	804.81	906.83	954.80
11.0	491.25	765.59	888.11	945.72
12.0	393.18	720.40	866.54	935.25
13.0	280.19	668.34	841.69	923.20
14.0	150.00	608.36	813.05	909.31
15.0	0.00	539.24	780.06	893.30
16.0		459.61	742.05	874.86
17.0		367.86	698.26	853.61
18.0		262.14	647.79	829.13
19.0		140.34	589.65	800.93
20.0		0.00	522.66	768.43
21.0			445.48	730.98
22.0			356.55	687.84
23.0			254.08	638.13
24.0			136.03	580.86
25.0			0.00	514.87
26.0				438.83
27.0				351.23
28.0				250.29
29.0				134.00
30.0				0.00

REMAINING BALANCE PER $1000 OF ORIGINAL LOAN

ANNUAL INTEREST RATE: 14.5 %

AGE OF LOAN	LOAN MATURITY (YEARS)			
	15	20	25	30
0.5	990.28	995.57	997.91	999.00
1.0	979.83	990.81	995.66	997.92
1.5	968.61	985.69	993.24	996.76
2.0	956.54	980.18	990.65	995.51
2.5	943.58	974.27	987.85	994.18
3.0	929.64	967.92	984.86	992.74
3.5	914.66	961.09	981.63	991.19
4.0	898.57	953.75	978.17	989.53
4.5	881.27	945.86	974.44	987.74
5.0	862.67	937.38	970.44	985.83
6.0	821.22	918.48	961.52	981.55
7.0	773.34	896.65	951.21	976.60
8.0	718.03	871.43	939.31	970.90
9.0	654.15	842.30	925.56	964.30
10.0	580.36	808.66	909.67	956.69
11.0	495.14	769.80	891.33	947.89
12.0	396.71	724.91	870.14	937.73
13.0	283.01	673.07	845.67	925.99
14.0	151.68	613.19	817.40	912.44
15.0	0.00	544.02	784.75	896.78
16.0		464.14	747.04	878.70
17.0		371.86	703.48	857.81
18.0		265.29	653.17	833.68
19.0		142.19	595.06	805.82
20.0		0.00	527.94	773.63
21.0			450.42	736.45
22.0			360.87	693.51
23.0			257.45	643.92
24.0			137.98	586.63
25.0			0.00	520.46
26.0				444.03
27.0				355.76
28.0				253.80
29.0				136.03
30.0				0.00

REMAINING BALANCE PER $1000 OF ORIGINAL LOAN

ANNUAL INTEREST RATE: 14.75 %

AGE OF LOAN	LOAN MATURITY (YEARS)			
	15	20	25	30
0.5	990.51	995.72	998.00	999.05
1.0	980.30	991.11	995.85	998.03
1.5	969.32	986.16	993.54	996.94
2.0	957.50	980.82	991.05	995.76
2.5	944.78	975.08	988.37	994.49
3.0	931.09	968.91	985.48	993.12
3.5	916.36	962.26	982.38	991.65
4.0	900.51	955.11	979.04	990.07
4.5	883.46	947.41	975.45	988.36
5.0	865.11	939.13	971.59	986.53
6.0	824.11	920.64	962.95	982.44
7.0	776.64	899.22	952.95	977.70
8.0	721.68	874.42	941.38	972.21
9.0	658.04	845.70	927.97	965.86
10.0	584.35	812.45	912.45	958.50
11.0	499.02	773.95	894.48	949.98
12.0	400.23	729.37	873.67	940.12
13.0	285.83	677.75	849.57	928.70
14.0	153.37	617.98	821.67	915.47
15.0	0.00	548.78	789.37	900.16
16.0		468.65	751.96	882.43
17.0		375.87	708.65	861.90
18.0		268.43	658.50	838.13
19.0		144.04	600.43	810.60
20.0		0.00	533.19	778.73
21.0			455.33	741.83
22.0			365.19	699.10
23.0			260.81	649.63
24.0			139.94	592.34
25.0			0.00	526.01
26.0				449.20
27.0				360.27
28.0				257.29
29.0				138.06
30.0				0.00

REMAINING BALANCE PER $1000 OF ORIGINAL LOAN

ANNUAL INTEREST RATE: 15 %

AGE OF LOAN	LOAN MATURITY (YEARS)			
	15	20	25	30
0.5	990.74	995.87	998.09	999.11
1.0	980.76	991.41	996.04	998.14
1.5	970.01	986.61	993.82	997.10
2.0	958.43	981.44	991.43	995.99
2.5	945.96	975.87	988.86	994.78
3.0	932.51	969.87	986.09	993.48
3.5	918.03	963.40	983.11	992.09
4.0	902.43	956.43	979.89	990.58
4.5	885.62	948.93	976.43	988.96
5.0	867.50	940.84	972.69	987.21
6.0	826.97	922.74	964.34	983.29
7.0	779.91	901.73	954.64	978.75
8.0	725.30	877.35	943.38	973.48
9.0	661.90	849.04	930.32	967.35
10.0	588.31	816.18	915.15	960.25
11.0	502.89	778.05	897.54	952.00
12.0	403.74	733.78	877.11	942.43
13.0	288.66	682.39	853.39	931.31
14.0	155.07	622.74	825.86	918.41
15.0	0.00	553.51	793.90	903.44
16.0		473.14	756.80	886.06
17.0		379.86	713.74	865.89
18.0		271.58	663.76	842.47
19.0		145.89	605.74	815.29
20.0		0.00	538.39	783.74
21.0			460.22	747.12
22.0			369.49	704.61
23.0			264.16	655.26
24.0			141.91	597.99
25.0			0.00	531.51
26.0				454.34
27.0				364.76
28.0				260.78
29.0				140.09
30.0				0.00

REMAINING BALANCE PER $1000 OF ORIGINAL LOAN

ANNUAL INTEREST RATE: 15.25 %

AGE OF LOAN	LOAN MATURITY (YEARS)			
	15	20	25	30
0.5	990.96	996.01	998.18	999.16
1.0	981.21	991.70	996.21	998.25
1.5	970.70	987.05	994.09	997.26
2.0	959.35	982.04	991.80	996.20
2.5	947.11	976.64	989.34	995.06
3.0	933.91	970.80	986.67	993.83
3.5	919.67	964.51	983.80	992.50
4.0	904.31	957.73	980.70	991.06
4.5	887.74	950.41	977.36	989.52
5.0	869.87	942.51	973.76	987.85
6.0	829.79	924.80	965.68	984.11
7.0	783.15	904.20	956.27	979.75
8.0	728.88	880.22	945.33	974.68
9.0	665.73	852.32	932.59	968.79
10.0	592.25	819.86	917.78	961.93
11.0	506.75	782.08	900.53	953.94
12.0	407.25	738.13	880.47	944.65
13.0	291.48	686.98	857.12	933.84
14.0	156.76	627.46	829.96	921.26
15.0	0.00	558.20	798.34	906.62
16.0		477.61	761.56	889.59
17.0		383.84	718.76	869.77
18.0		274.72	668.95	846.71
19.0		147.75	610.99	819.87
20.0		0.00	543.55	788.64
21.0			465.08	752.31
22.0			373.77	710.02
23.0			267.51	660.82
24.0			143.87	603.57
25.0			0.00	536.95
26.0				459.43
27.0				369.23
28.0				264.26
29.0				142.12
30.0				0.00

REMAINING BALANCE PER $1000 OF ORIGINAL LOAN

ANNUAL INTEREST RATE: 15.5 %

AGE OF LOAN	LOAN MATURITY (YEARS)			
	15	20	25	30
0.5	991.18	996.14	998.26	999.20
1.0	981.65	991.98	996.38	998.34
1.5	971.37	987.48	994.35	997.41
2.0	960.25	982.63	992.16	996.41
2.5	948.25	977.38	989.79	995.33
3.0	935.29	971.71	987.23	994.16
3.5	921.29	965.59	984.47	992.89
4.0	906.17	958.98	981.49	991.53
4.5	889.84	951.85	978.27	990.05
5.0	872.20	944.14	974.79	988.46
6.0	832.58	926.81	966.97	984.88
7.0	786.36	906.61	957.85	980.71
8.0	732.44	883.04	947.21	975.84
9.0	669.54	855.55	934.81	970.16
10.0	596.18	823.48	920.33	963.54
11.0	510.59	786.07	903.45	955.81
12.0	410.76	742.43	883.75	946.80
13.0	294.31	691.52	860.78	936.28
14.0	158.46	632.14	833.98	924.02
15.0	0.00	562.87	802.71	909.71
16.0		482.07	766.25	893.02
17.0		387.81	723.71	873.55
18.0		277.87	674.09	850.84
19.0		149.61	616.20	824.35
20.0		0.00	548.68	793.45
21.0			469.91	757.41
22.0			378.04	715.36
23.0			270.86	666.31
24.0			145.84	609.09
25.0			0.00	542.35
26.0				464.49
27.0				373.67
28.0				267.73
29.0				144.15
30.0				0.00

REMAINING BALANCE PER $1000 OF ORIGINAL LOAN

ANNUAL INTEREST RATE: 15.75 %

AGE OF LOAN	LOAN MATURITY (YEARS)			
	15	20	25	30
0.5	991.39	996.28	998.34	999.25
1.0	982.09	992.25	996.54	998.44
1.5	972.02	987.90	994.60	997.56
2.0	961.14	983.19	992.50	996.61
2.5	949.37	978.10	990.23	995.58
3.0	936.64	972.60	987.77	994.47
3.5	922.88	966.65	985.12	993.27
4.0	908.00	960.21	982.24	991.97
4.5	891.90	953.25	979.14	990.56
5.0	874.50	945.72	975.78	989.04
6.0	835.33	928.78	968.22	985.63
7.0	789.52	908.97	959.38	981.63
8.0	735.96	885.80	949.04	976.95
9.0	673.32	858.71	936.95	971.48
10.0	600.07	827.03	922.81	965.09
11.0	514.42	789.99	906.28	957.61
12.0	414.26	746.67	886.95	948.87
13.0	297.13	696.01	864.35	938.64
14.0	160.17	636.77	837.91	926.69
15.0	0.00	567.50	807.00	912.70
16.0		486.50	770.85	896.36
17.0		391.77	728.58	877.24
18.0		281.00	679.15	854.88
19.0		151.47	621.35	828.73
20.0		0.00	553.76	798.16
21.0			474.71	762.41
22.0			382.28	720.60
23.0			274.20	671.71
24.0			147.80	614.54
25.0			0.00	547.69
26.0				469.51
27.0				378.10
28.0				271.19
29.0				146.18
30.0				0.00

REMAINING BALANCE PER $1000 OF ORIGINAL LOAN

ANNUAL INTEREST RATE: 16 %

AGE OF LOAN	\multicolumn{4}{c}{LOAN MATURITY (YEARS)}			
	15	20	25	30
0.5	991.60	996.41	998.41	999.29
1.0	982.51	992.52	996.70	998.52
1.5	972.67	988.30	994.84	997.69
2.0	962.01	983.74	992.83	996.79
2.5	950.47	978.81	990.65	995.82
3.0	937.97	973.46	988.29	994.77
3.5	924.44	967.67	985.74	993.62
4.0	909.80	961.40	982.97	992.39
4.5	893.94	954.62	979.98	991.05
5.0	876.77	947.27	976.74	989.60
6.0	838.05	930.70	969.43	986.33
7.0	792.66	911.28	960.86	982.50
8.0	739.45	888.51	950.81	978.01
9.0	677.07	861.82	939.04	972.75
10.0	603.95	830.54	925.23	966.58
11.0	518.24	793.86	909.05	959.34
12.0	417.75	750.86	890.08	950.86
13.0	299.96	700.46	867.84	940.92
14.0	161.87	641.37	841.77	929.27
15.0	0.00	572.11	811.21	915.61
16.0		490.91	775.39	899.60
17.0		395.73	733.39	880.82
18.0		284.14	684.16	858.82
19.0		153.34	626.45	833.02
20.0		0.00	558.80	802.78
21.0			479.49	767.32
22.0			386.52	725.77
23.0			277.53	677.05
24.0			149.77	619.94
25.0			0.00	552.99
26.0				474.50
27.0				382.50
28.0				274.65
29.0				148.21
30.0				0.00

REMAINING BALANCE PER $1000 OF ORIGINAL LOAN

ANNUAL INTEREST RATE: 16.25 %

AGE OF LOAN	LOAN MATURITY (YEARS)			
	15	20	25	30
0.5	991.81	996.53	998.49	999.33
1.0	982.93	992.77	996.85	998.61
1.5	973.30	988.70	995.07	997.82
2.0	962.86	984.28	993.14	996.97
2.5	951.54	979.49	991.05	996.05
3.0	939.28	974.30	988.79	995.05
3.5	925.98	968.67	986.33	993.96
4.0	911.57	962.56	983.67	992.79
4.5	895.94	955.95	980.79	991.51
5.0	879.00	948.78	977.66	990.13
6.0	840.73	932.58	970.59	987.01
7.0	795.76	913.54	962.29	983.34
8.0	742.91	891.17	952.53	979.03
9.0	680.80	864.88	941.06	973.96
10.0	607.81	833.98	927.58	968.01
11.0	522.04	797.67	911.74	961.01
12.0	421.24	755.00	893.13	952.79
13.0	302.79	704.86	871.26	943.13
14.0	163.59	645.93	845.55	931.77
15.0	0.00	576.68	815.35	918.43
16.0		495.30	779.85	902.74
17.0		399.67	738.13	884.31
18.0		287.28	689.11	862.66
19.0		155.21	631.50	837.21
20.0		0.00	563.80	807.30
21.0			484.23	772.15
22.0			390.74	730.85
23.0			280.86	682.31
24.0			151.74	625.27
25.0			0.00	558.23
26.0				479.46
27.0				386.88
28.0				278.09
29.0				150.24
30.0				0.00

REMAINING BALANCE PER $1000 OF ORIGINAL LOAN

ANNUAL INTEREST RATE: 16.5 %

AGE OF LOAN	LOAN MATURITY (YEARS)			
	15	20	25	30
0.5	992.01	996.65	998.56	999.37
1.0	983.33	993.02	996.99	998.69
1.5	973.92	989.08	995.29	997.94
2.0	963.70	984.80	993.44	997.14
2.5	952.60	980.15	991.44	996.26
3.0	940.56	975.11	989.27	995.31
3.5	927.49	969.64	986.91	994.28
4.0	913.31	963.70	984.34	993.16
4.5	897.91	957.25	981.56	991.95
5.0	881.20	950.25	978.55	990.63
6.0	843.38	934.41	971.71	987.65
7.0	798.83	915.75	963.67	984.14
8.0	746.33	893.77	954.19	980.00
9.0	684.50	867.87	943.02	975.12
10.0	611.65	837.37	929.86	969.38
11.0	525.83	801.43	914.36	962.61
12.0	424.72	759.08	896.11	954.64
13.0	305.62	709.21	874.59	945.25
14.0	165.30	650.44	849.25	934.19
15.0	0.00	581.22	819.40	921.15
16.0		499.67	784.23	905.80
17.0		403.59	742.80	887.71
18.0		290.41	693.99	866.40
19.0		157.08	636.49	841.30
20.0		0.00	568.75	811.73
21.0			488.95	776.89
22.0			394.93	735.84
23.0			284.18	687.49
24.0			153.71	630.53
25.0			0.00	563.42
26.0				484.37
27.0				391.24
28.0				281.52
29.0				152.27
30.0				0.00

REMAINING BALANCE PER $1000 OF ORIGINAL LOAN

ANNUAL INTEREST RATE: 16.75 %

AGE OF LOAN	LOAN MATURITY (YEARS)			
	15	20	25	30
0.5	992.20	996.77	998.62	999.41
1.0	983.73	993.26	997.13	998.76
1.5	974.52	989.45	995.50	998.06
2.0	964.52	985.30	993.73	997.30
2.5	953.64	980.79	991.81	996.47
3.0	941.82	975.90	989.72	995.57
3.5	928.98	970.58	987.46	994.59
4.0	915.02	964.80	984.99	993.52
4.5	899.86	958.51	982.31	992.37
5.0	883.38	951.69	979.40	991.11
6.0	846.00	936.20	972.80	988.26
7.0	801.86	917.92	965.00	984.90
8.0	749.73	896.32	955.80	980.93
9.0	688.17	870.82	944.92	976.24
10.0	615.46	840.70	932.08	970.70
11.0	529.60	805.13	916.92	964.16
12.0	428.20	763.12	899.01	956.43
13.0	308.45	713.51	877.86	947.30
14.0	167.02	654.92	852.88	936.53
15.0	0.00	585.73	823.38	923.80
16.0		504.01	788.54	908.77
17.0		407.51	747.40	891.02
18.0		293.54	698.81	870.06
19.0		158.95	641.43	845.30
20.0		0.00	573.66	816.06
21.0			493.63	781.53
22.0			399.12	740.76
23.0			287.50	692.60
24.0			155.68	635.73
25.0			0.00	568.56
26.0				489.24
27.0				395.57
28.0				284.94
29.0				154.29
30.0				0.00

REMAINING BALANCE PER $1000 OF ORIGINAL LOAN

ANNUAL INTEREST RATE: 17 %

AGE OF LOAN	LOAN MATURITY (YEARS)			
	15	20	25	30
0.5	992.39	996.88	998.69	999.44
1.0	984.12	993.49	997.26	998.83
1.5	975.12	989.80	995.70	998.17
2.0	965.32	985.79	994.01	997.45
2.5	954.66	981.42	992.17	996.66
3.0	943.06	976.67	990.17	995.81
3.5	930.44	971.50	987.99	994.88
4.0	916.71	965.87	985.61	993.87
4.5	901.77	959.75	983.03	992.77
5.0	885.52	953.08	980.23	991.57
6.0	848.58	937.95	973.85	988.85
7.0	804.86	920.03	966.30	985.63
8.0	753.09	898.82	957.36	981.82
9.0	691.81	873.70	946.77	977.31
10.0	619.25	843.97	934.24	971.96
11.0	533.36	808.77	919.40	965.64
12.0	431.67	767.10	901.84	958.15
13.0	311.27	717.76	881.05	949.28
14.0	168.74	659.35	856.43	938.79
15.0	0.00	590.20	827.28	926.36
16.0		508.34	792.78	911.65
17.0		411.41	751.93	894.24
18.0		296.67	703.57	873.62
19.0		160.83	646.31	849.21
20.0		0.00	578.53	820.31
21.0			498.28	786.10
22.0			403.28	745.59
23.0			290.80	697.64
24.0			157.65	640.87
25.0			0.00	573.65
26.0				494.08
27.0				399.88
28.0				288.35
29.0				156.32
30.0				0.00

REMAINING BALANCE PER $1000 OF ORIGINAL LOAN

ANNUAL INTEREST RATE: 17.25 %

AGE OF LOAN	LOAN MATURITY (YEARS)			
	15	20	25	30
0.5	992.58	996.99	998.75	999.47
1.0	984.50	993.72	997.38	998.90
1.5	975.70	990.15	995.90	998.27
2.0	966.11	986.26	994.28	997.59
2.5	955.66	982.03	992.51	996.84
3.0	944.28	977.41	990.59	996.04
3.5	931.88	972.39	988.49	995.15
4.0	918.37	966.91	986.21	994.19
4.5	903.65	960.95	983.73	993.14
5.0	887.62	954.45	981.02	992.00
6.0	851.13	939.65	974.86	989.41
7.0	807.82	922.10	967.54	986.33
8.0	756.42	901.26	958.86	982.67
9.0	695.42	876.54	948.56	978.33
10.0	623.02	847.19	936.33	973.18
11.0	537.10	812.36	921.82	967.06
12.0	435.12	771.02	904.60	959.81
13.0	314.10	721.96	884.16	951.19
14.0	170.47	663.74	859.90	940.97
15.0	0.00	594.64	831.11	928.84
16.0		512.63	796.94	914.45
17.0		415.30	756.39	897.36
18.0		299.79	708.26	877.09
19.0		162.70	651.14	853.02
20.0		0.00	583.35	824.46
21.0			502.90	790.57
22.0			407.42	750.34
23.0			294.10	702.60
24.0			159.61	645.94
25.0			0.00	578.69
26.0				498.88
27.0				404.16
28.0				291.75
29.0				158.34
30.0				0.00

REMAINING BALANCE PER $1000 OF ORIGINAL LOAN

ANNUAL INTEREST RATE: 17.5 %

AGE OF LOAN	LOAN MATURITY (YEARS)			
	15	20	25	30
0.5	992.77	997.10	998.81	999.50
1.0	984.88	993.94	997.50	998.96
1.5	976.27	990.48	996.08	998.37
2.0	966.88	986.72	994.53	997.72
2.5	956.64	982.62	992.84	997.02
3.0	945.47	978.14	991.00	996.25
3.5	933.29	973.25	988.98	995.41
4.0	920.00	967.92	986.79	994.50
4.5	905.51	962.11	984.40	993.50
5.0	889.70	955.77	981.79	992.42
6.0	853.65	941.32	975.83	989.94
7.0	810.75	924.12	968.75	986.99
8.0	759.72	903.66	960.32	983.48
9.0	699.00	879.31	950.29	979.31
10.0	626.77	850.35	938.37	974.34
11.0	540.82	815.89	924.17	968.43
12.0	438.58	774.90	907.29	961.40
13.0	316.93	726.12	887.20	953.04
14.0	172.19	668.09	863.30	943.09
15.0	0.00	599.05	834.86	931.25
16.0		516.91	801.03	917.16
17.0		419.18	760.78	900.41
18.0		302.91	712.89	880.47
19.0		164.58	655.92	856.75
20.0		0.00	588.14	828.53
21.0			507.49	794.96
22.0			411.54	755.01
23.0			297.39	707.49
24.0			161.58	650.95
25.0			0.00	583.68
26.0				503.64
27.0				408.42
28.0				295.14
29.0				160.36
30.0				0.00

REMAINING BALANCE PER $1000 OF ORIGINAL LOAN

ANNUAL INTEREST RATE: 17.75 %

AGE OF LOAN	LOAN MATURITY (YEARS)			
	15	20	25	30
0.5	992.95	997.20	998.86	999.53
1.0	985.24	994.15	997.62	999.02
1.5	976.83	990.81	996.26	998.46
2.0	967.64	987.17	994.78	997.85
2.5	957.60	983.19	993.15	997.18
3.0	946.65	978.84	991.39	996.46
3.5	934.68	974.09	989.45	995.66
4.0	921.61	968.91	987.34	994.79
4.5	907.33	963.25	985.04	993.84
5.0	891.74	957.07	982.52	992.81
6.0	856.13	942.94	976.77	990.44
7.0	813.65	926.10	969.91	987.62
8.0	762.98	906.00	961.73	984.26
9.0	702.56	882.04	951.98	980.24
10.0	630.49	853.46	940.34	975.46
11.0	544.53	819.37	926.46	969.75
12.0	442.02	778.71	909.91	962.94
13.0	319.75	730.23	890.17	954.82
14.0	173.92	672.39	866.62	945.13
15.0	0.00	603.42	838.54	933.58
16.0		521.16	805.05	919.80
17.0		423.04	765.10	903.37
18.0		306.02	717.46	883.77
19.0		166.46	660.64	860.39
20.0		0.00	592.87	832.51
21.0			512.05	799.26
22.0			415.65	759.60
23.0			300.67	712.30
24.0			163.55	655.89
25.0			0.00	588.61
26.0				508.36
27.0				412.66
28.0				298.51
29.0				162.37
30.0				0.00

REMAINING BALANCE PER $1000 OF ORIGINAL LOAN

ANNUAL INTEREST RATE: 18 %

AGE OF LOAN	LOAN MATURITY (YEARS)			
	15	20	25	30
0.5	993.12	997.30	998.91	999.56
1.0	985.60	994.35	997.73	999.08
1.5	977.38	991.13	996.43	998.55
2.0	968.38	987.60	995.01	997.97
2.5	958.55	983.74	993.46	997.34
3.0	947.80	979.52	991.76	996.65
3.5	936.04	974.91	989.90	995.90
4.0	923.19	969.87	987.87	995.07
4.5	909.13	964.36	985.66	994.17
5.0	893.76	958.33	983.23	993.18
6.0	858.58	944.53	977.68	990.93
7.0	816.51	928.03	971.04	988.23
8.0	766.22	908.30	963.10	985.00
9.0	706.08	884.71	953.61	981.14
10.0	634.19	856.51	942.26	976.53
11.0	548.23	822.80	928.69	971.01
12.0	445.45	782.48	912.46	964.42
13.0	322.57	734.29	893.07	956.53
14.0	175.66	676.66	869.88	947.10
15.0	0.00	607.76	842.15	935.83
16.0		525.38	809.00	922.36
17.0		426.89	769.36	906.24
18.0		309.13	721.97	886.98
19.0		168.34	665.31	863.95
20.0		0.00	597.57	836.41
21.0			516.57	803.48
22.0			419.73	764.12
23.0			303.95	717.05
24.0			165.51	660.78
25.0			0.00	593.49
26.0				513.05
27.0				416.87
28.0				301.87
29.0				164.38
30.0				0.00

REMAINING BALANCE PER $1000 OF ORIGINAL LOAN

ANNUAL INTEREST RATE: 18.25 %

AGE OF LOAN	LOAN MATURITY (YEARS)			
	15	20	25	30
0.5	993.29	997.40	998.97	999.58
1.0	985.95	994.55	997.83	999.13
1.5	977.91	991.43	996.59	998.63
2.0	969.11	988.02	995.23	998.09
2.5	959.48	984.28	993.75	997.49
3.0	948.93	980.19	992.12	996.83
3.5	937.38	975.71	990.34	996.12
4.0	924.74	970.80	988.39	995.33
4.5	910.90	965.43	986.25	994.48
5.0	895.74	959.55	983.91	993.54
6.0	860.99	946.07	978.55	991.38
7.0	819.34	929.92	972.12	988.80
8.0	769.42	910.55	964.42	985.71
9.0	709.58	887.34	955.18	982.00
10.0	637.86	859.51	944.12	977.55
11.0	551.91	826.17	930.85	972.23
12.0	448.88	786.20	914.95	965.84
13.0	325.40	738.30	895.90	958.19
14.0	177.39	680.88	873.06	949.01
15.0	0.00	612.06	845.69	938.02
16.0		529.58	812.88	924.84
17.0		430.72	773.55	909.04
18.0		312.23	726.42	890.11
19.0		170.22	669.93	867.42
20.0		0.00	602.22	840.22
21.0			521.06	807.62
22.0			423.79	768.55
23.0			307.21	721.72
24.0			167.48	665.60
25.0			0.00	598.33
26.0				517.70
27.0				421.06
28.0				305.23
29.0				166.40
30.0				0.00

REMAINING BALANCE PER $1000 OF ORIGINAL LOAN

ANNUAL INTEREST RATE: 18.5 %

AGE OF LOAN	LOAN MATURITY (YEARS) 15	20	25	30
0.5	993.46	997.49	999.01	999.61
1.0	986.29	994.74	997.93	999.18
1.5	978.44	991.73	996.75	998.71
2.0	969.82	988.42	995.45	998.19
2.5	960.38	984.80	994.02	997.63
3.0	950.04	980.83	992.46	997.01
3.5	938.69	976.48	990.75	996.33
4.0	926.26	971.71	988.88	995.59
4.5	912.63	966.48	986.82	994.77
5.0	897.70	960.75	984.57	993.87
6.0	863.37	947.58	979.39	991.82
7.0	822.13	931.76	973.17	989.35
8.0	772.58	912.75	965.69	986.38
9.0	713.05	889.91	956.71	982.82
10.0	641.51	862.46	945.92	978.54
11.0	555.56	829.48	932.96	973.39
12.0	452.29	789.86	917.38	967.21
13.0	328.21	742.26	898.66	959.78
14.0	179.13	685.06	876.17	950.85
15.0	0.00	616.33	849.15	940.13
16.0		533.76	816.68	927.24
17.0		434.54	777.67	911.76
18.0		315.33	730.80	893.16
19.0		172.10	674.49	870.81
20.0		0.00	606.82	843.95
21.0			525.52	811.68
22.0			427.84	772.91
23.0			310.47	726.33
24.0			169.44	670.36
25.0			0.00	603.11
26.0				522.30
27.0				425.22
28.0				308.56
29.0				168.40
30.0				0.00

REMAINING BALANCE PER $1000 OF ORIGINAL LOAN

ANNUAL INTEREST RATE: 18.75 %

AGE OF LOAN	LOAN MATURITY (YEARS)			
	15	20	25	30
0.5	993.63	997.58	999.06	999.63
1.0	986.63	994.93	998.03	999.23
1.5	978.95	992.01	996.90	998.78
2.0	970.52	988.82	995.65	998.30
2.5	961.28	985.31	994.29	997.76
3.0	951.13	981.46	992.79	997.17
3.5	939.99	977.23	991.15	996.53
4.0	927.76	972.59	989.35	995.82
4.5	914.34	967.50	987.37	995.05
5.0	899.62	961.91	985.20	994.20
6.0	865.72	949.05	980.20	992.24
7.0	824.89	933.56	974.18	989.87
8.0	775.72	914.90	966.93	987.03
9.0	716.49	892.43	958.19	983.61
10.0	645.14	865.36	947.67	979.48
11.0	559.21	832.75	935.00	974.51
12.0	455.70	793.48	919.74	968.53
13.0	331.03	746.17	901.36	961.32
14.0	180.87	689.20	879.22	952.63
15.0	0.00	620.57	852.55	942.17
16.0		537.91	820.42	929.58
17.0		438.35	781.73	914.40
18.0		318.42	735.13	896.13
19.0		173.98	678.99	874.11
20.0		0.00	611.38	847.60
21.0			529.95	815.66
22.0			431.86	777.19
23.0			313.71	730.86
24.0			171.40	675.05
25.0			0.00	607.83
26.0				526.87
27.0				429.35
28.0				311.89
29.0				170.41
30.0				0.00

REMAINING BALANCE PER $1000 OF ORIGINAL LOAN

ANNUAL INTEREST RATE: 19 %

AGE OF LOAN	LOAN MATURITY (YEARS)			
	15	20	25	30
0.5	993.79	997.67	999.10	999.65
1.0	986.96	995.11	998.12	999.27
1.5	979.45	992.29	997.04	998.85
2.0	971.21	989.20	995.85	998.39
2.5	962.15	985.80	994.54	997.89
3.0	952.20	982.06	993.11	997.33
3.5	941.26	977.96	991.53	996.72
4.0	929.24	973.45	989.80	996.05
4.5	916.03	968.49	987.90	995.31
5.0	901.51	963.05	985.81	994.50
6.0	868.04	950.48	980.98	992.63
7.0	827.62	935.32	975.16	990.37
8.0	778.82	917.01	968.12	987.65
9.0	719.89	894.90	959.63	984.36
10.0	648.74	868.20	949.38	980.38
11.0	562.83	835.96	936.99	975.59
12.0	459.10	797.04	922.04	969.79
13.0	333.85	750.04	903.99	962.80
14.0	182.61	693.29	882.19	954.35
15.0	0.00	624.77	855.87	944.15
16.0		542.03	824.10	931.84
17.0		442.13	785.72	916.97
18.0		321.51	739.39	899.02
19.0		175.86	683.45	877.34
20.0		0.00	615.90	851.17
21.0			534.34	819.56
22.0			435.86	781.40
23.0			316.95	735.33
24.0			173.37	679.69
25.0			0.00	612.51
26.0				531.40
27.0				433.46
28.0				315.20
29.0				172.41
30.0				0.00

REMAINING BALANCE PER $1000 OF ORIGINAL LOAN

ANNUAL INTEREST RATE: 19.25 %

AGE OF LOAN	LOAN MATURITY (YEARS) 15	20	25	30
0.5	993.94	997.75	999.15	999.67
1.0	987.28	995.28	998.21	999.31
1.5	979.95	992.56	997.18	998.92
2.0	971.88	989.57	996.04	998.48
2.5	963.01	986.27	994.79	998.00
3.0	953.24	982.65	993.41	997.48
3.5	942.50	978.66	991.90	996.90
4.0	930.68	974.28	990.24	996.26
4.5	917.68	969.45	988.40	995.56
5.0	903.38	964.15	986.39	994.79
6.0	870.32	951.88	981.73	993.01
7.0	830.32	937.04	976.10	990.85
8.0	781.89	919.07	969.28	988.24
9.0	723.27	897.32	961.02	985.08
10.0	652.32	870.99	951.02	981.25
11.0	566.44	839.12	938.93	976.62
12.0	462.49	800.55	924.28	971.01
13.0	336.66	753.86	906.56	964.22
14.0	184.35	697.34	885.10	956.01
15.0	0.00	628.93	859.13	946.07
16.0		546.13	827.70	934.03
17.0		445.90	789.65	919.47
18.0		324.59	743.60	901.83
19.0		177.74	687.85	880.49
20.0		0.00	620.37	854.66
21.0			538.70	823.39
22.0			439.84	785.54
23.0			320.17	739.72
24.0			175.32	684.26
25.0			0.00	617.14
26.0				535.89
27.0				437.54
28.0				318.50
29.0				174.41
30.0				0.00

REMAINING BALANCE PER $1000 OF ORIGINAL LOAN

ANNUAL INTEREST RATE: 19.5 %

AGE OF LOAN	LOAN MATURITY (YEARS)			
	15	20	25	30
0.5	994.10	997.83	999.19	999.69
1.0	987.59	995.45	998.29	999.35
1.5	980.43	992.82	997.31	998.98
2.0	972.54	989.92	996.22	998.57
2.5	963.85	986.73	995.02	998.12
3.0	954.27	983.22	993.70	997.62
3.5	943.73	979.35	992.25	997.07
4.0	932.11	975.09	990.65	996.46
4.5	919.31	970.39	988.89	995.80
5.0	905.21	965.22	986.95	995.06
6.0	872.58	953.24	982.46	993.36
7.0	832.98	938.71	977.01	991.30
8.0	784.93	921.08	970.39	988.80
9.0	726.62	899.69	962.36	985.76
10.0	655.87	873.73	952.62	982.08
11.0	570.03	842.23	940.80	977.61
12.0	465.86	804.01	926.46	972.18
13.0	339.47	757.63	909.06	965.60
14.0	186.10	701.35	887.95	957.61
15.0	0.00	633.06	862.33	947.92
16.0		550.20	831.24	936.16
17.0		449.66	793.51	921.89
18.0		327.66	747.74	904.57
19.0		179.63	692.20	883.56
20.0		0.00	624.80	858.07
21.0			543.02	827.13
22.0			443.79	789.60
23.0			323.39	744.05
24.0			177.28	688.78
25.0			0.00	621.72
26.0				540.34
27.0				441.60
28.0				321.79
29.0				176.41
30.0				0.00

REMAINING BALANCE PER $1000 OF ORIGINAL LOAN

ANNUAL INTEREST RATE: 19.75 %

AGE OF	LOAN MATURITY (YEARS)			
LOAN	15	20	25	30
0.5	994.25	997.91	999.23	999.71
1.0	987.90	995.61	998.37	999.39
1.5	980.90	993.07	997.43	999.04
2.0	973.18	990.27	996.39	998.65
2.5	964.67	987.18	995.25	998.22
3.0	955.28	983.77	993.98	997.75
3.5	944.93	980.02	992.59	997.23
4.0	933.51	975.87	991.05	996.66
4.5	920.91	971.30	989.36	996.02
5.0	907.02	966.26	987.49	995.32
6.0	874.80	954.57	983.15	993.70
7.0	835.60	940.35	977.88	991.73
8.0	787.93	923.05	971.47	989.34
9.0	729.94	902.01	963.66	986.42
10.0	659.40	876.42	954.17	982.87
11.0	573.60	845.28	942.63	978.56
12.0	469.23	807.41	928.59	973.31
13.0	342.27	761.35	911.50	966.92
14.0	187.85	705.31	890.73	959.16
15.0	0.00	637.15	865.45	949.71
16.0		554.25	834.71	938.22
17.0		453.40	797.31	924.24
18.0		330.73	751.82	907.24
19.0		181.51	696.49	886.56
20.0		0.00	629.18	861.40
21.0			547.31	830.80
22.0			447.73	793.58
23.0			326.59	748.31
24.0			179.24	693.23
25.0			0.00	626.24
26.0				544.75
27.0				445.63
28.0				325.06
29.0				178.40
30.0				0.00

REMAINING BALANCE PER $1000 OF ORIGINAL LOAN

ANNUAL INTEREST RATE: 20 %

AGE OF LOAN	LOAN MATURITY (YEARS)			
	15	20	25	30
0.5	994.39	997.99	999.26	999.73
1.0	988.20	995.77	998.45	999.43
1.5	981.36	993.31	997.55	999.10
2.0	973.81	990.61	996.56	998.73
2.5	965.48	987.61	995.46	998.32
3.0	956.27	984.31	994.25	997.88
3.5	946.11	980.66	992.91	997.38
4.0	934.88	976.64	991.44	996.84
4.5	922.48	972.19	989.81	996.24
5.0	908.79	967.28	988.01	995.57
6.0	876.99	955.86	983.83	994.03
7.0	838.20	941.95	978.73	992.14
8.0	790.90	924.98	972.51	989.85
9.0	733.23	904.29	964.92	987.05
10.0	662.91	879.06	955.68	983.63
11.0	577.15	848.29	944.40	979.47
12.0	472.59	810.77	930.65	974.39
13.0	345.08	765.02	913.89	968.20
14.0	189.59	709.24	893.44	960.65
15.0	0.00	641.21	868.51	951.44
16.0		558.27	838.12	940.22
17.0		457.12	801.05	926.53
18.0		333.78	755.85	909.84
19.0		183.39	700.73	889.49
20.0		0.00	633.52	864.67
21.0			551.57	834.40
22.0			451.64	797.50
23.0			329.78	752.50
24.0			181.19	697.63
25.0			0.00	630.72
26.0				549.13
27.0				449.64
28.0				328.32
29.0				180.39
30.0				0.00

REMAINING BALANCE PER $1000 OF ORIGINAL LOAN

ANNUAL INTEREST RATE: 20.25 %

AGE OF LOAN	LOAN MATURITY (YEARS)			
	15	20	25	30
0.5	994.54	998.06	999.30	999.74
1.0	988.50	995.92	998.52	999.46
1.5	981.82	993.55	997.66	999.15
2.0	974.43	990.93	996.71	998.80
2.5	966.27	988.03	995.67	998.42
3.0	957.24	984.83	994.51	998.00
3.5	947.26	981.29	993.22	997.53
4.0	936.23	977.38	991.81	997.01
4.5	924.03	973.05	990.24	996.44
5.0	910.54	968.26	988.51	995.81
6.0	879.14	957.12	984.47	994.33
7.0	840.76	943.51	979.54	992.54
8.0	793.84	926.86	973.51	990.34
9.0	736.49	906.52	966.14	987.65
10.0	666.38	881.65	957.13	984.36
11.0	580.69	851.24	946.12	980.34
12.0	475.93	814.08	932.66	975.43
13.0	347.88	768.65	916.21	969.43
14.0	191.34	713.12	896.10	962.09
15.0	0.00	645.24	871.51	953.12
16.0		562.26	841.46	942.16
17.0		460.83	804.72	928.75
18.0		336.84	759.82	912.37
19.0		185.27	704.92	892.34
20.0		0.00	637.82	867.86
21.0			555.80	837.93
22.0			455.53	801.35
23.0			332.96	756.63
24.0			183.14	701.97
25.0			0.00	635.15
26.0				553.46
27.0				453.62
28.0				331.57
29.0				182.37
30.0				0.00

REMAINING BALANCE PER $1000 OF ORIGINAL LOAN

ANNUAL INTEREST RATE: 20.5 %

AGE OF LOAN	LOAN MATURITY (YEARS)			
	15	20	25	30
0.5	994.68	998.13	999.33	999.76
1.0	988.78	996.07	998.59	999.49
1.5	982.26	993.78	997.77	999.20
2.0	975.04	991.24	996.87	998.87
2.5	967.04	988.44	995.86	998.51
3.0	958.19	985.34	994.75	998.11
3.5	948.40	981.90	993.52	997.66
4.0	937.55	978.10	992.16	997.17
4.5	925.55	973.88	990.65	996.63
5.0	912.26	969.22	988.98	996.03
6.0	881.27	958.35	985.09	994.63
7.0	843.29	945.03	980.32	992.91
8.0	796.75	928.70	974.48	990.80
9.0	739.72	908.70	967.32	988.22
10.0	669.84	884.19	958.55	985.06
11.0	584.20	854.15	947.79	981.18
12.0	479.26	817.34	934.62	976.43
13.0	350.67	772.23	918.47	970.61
14.0	193.09	716.95	898.69	963.48
15.0	0.00	649.22	874.45	954.74
16.0		566.22	844.74	944.03
17.0		464.51	808.33	930.91
18.0		339.88	763.72	914.83
19.0		187.15	709.06	895.12
20.0		0.00	642.07	870.97
21.0			559.98	841.38
22.0			459.39	805.12
23.0			336.13	760.69
24.0			185.09	706.24
25.0			0.00	639.52
26.0				557.76
27.0				457.57
28.0				334.80
29.0				184.35
30.0				0.00

REMAINING BALANCE PER $1000 OF ORIGINAL LOAN

ANNUAL INTEREST RATE: 20.75 %

AGE OF LOAN	LOAN MATURITY (YEARS)			
	15	20	25	30
0.5	994.81	998.20	999.36	999.77
1.0	989.06	996.21	998.66	999.52
1.5	982.69	994.00	997.88	999.24
2.0	975.63	991.55	997.01	998.94
2.5	967.80	988.83	996.05	998.59
3.0	959.13	985.82	994.99	998.21
3.5	949.51	982.49	993.81	997.79
4.0	938.86	978.79	992.50	997.33
4.5	927.05	974.70	991.05	996.81
5.0	913.95	970.16	989.44	996.24
6.0	883.36	959.55	985.69	994.90
7.0	845.79	946.51	981.08	993.26
8.0	799.63	930.50	975.42	991.25
9.0	742.92	910.84	968.46	988.77
10.0	673.26	886.68	959.92	985.72
11.0	587.70	857.00	949.42	981.99
12.0	482.58	820.55	936.52	977.39
13.0	353.46	775.76	920.68	971.75
14.0	194.85	720.75	901.22	964.82
15.0	0.00	653.17	877.32	956.31
16.0		570.16	847.96	945.85
17.0		468.18	811.88	933.00
18.0		342.91	767.57	917.22
19.0		189.03	713.14	897.84
20.0		0.00	646.28	874.02
21.0			564.14	844.77
22.0			463.24	808.83
23.0			339.29	764.69
24.0			187.04	710.46
25.0			0.00	643.85
26.0				562.02
27.0				461.50
28.0				338.02
29.0				186.33
30.0				0.00

REMAINING BALANCE PER $1000 OF ORIGINAL LOAN

ANNUAL INTEREST RATE: 21 %

AGE OF LOAN	LOAN MATURITY (YEARS)			
	15	20	25	30
0.5	994.95	998.27	999.39	999.79
1.0	989.34	996.34	998.72	999.55
1.5	983.12	994.21	997.98	999.29
2.0	976.21	991.84	997.15	999.00
2.5	968.55	989.21	996.23	998.67
3.0	960.04	986.30	995.21	998.31
3.5	950.61	983.06	994.08	997.92
4.0	940.14	979.47	992.82	997.48
4.5	928.51	975.49	991.43	996.98
5.0	915.62	971.06	989.89	996.44
6.0	885.43	960.71	986.27	995.17
7.0	848.25	947.96	981.81	993.60
8.0	802.47	932.26	976.32	991.67
9.0	746.09	912.93	969.57	989.29
10.0	676.67	889.13	961.24	986.36
11.0	591.18	859.81	951.00	982.76
12.0	485.90	823.71	938.38	978.32
13.0	356.25	779.25	922.84	972.85
14.0	196.60	724.51	903.70	966.11
15.0	0.00	657.09	880.13	957.82
16.0		574.07	851.11	947.61
17.0		471.84	815.38	935.04
18.0		345.94	771.37	919.55
19.0		190.91	717.18	900.48
20.0		0.00	650.44	877.00
21.0			568.26	848.08
22.0			467.06	812.47
23.0			342.44	768.62
24.0			188.98	714.62
25.0			0.00	648.13
26.0				566.24
27.0				465.40
28.0				341.22
29.0				188.31
30.0				0.00

REMAINING BALANCE PER $1000 OF ORIGINAL LOAN

ANNUAL INTEREST RATE: 21.25 %

AGE OF LOAN	LOAN MATURITY (YEARS)			
	15	20	25	30
0.5	995.08	998.33	999.42	999.80
1.0	989.61	996.48	998.78	999.58
1.5	983.53	994.42	998.07	999.33
2.0	976.78	992.13	997.28	999.05
2.5	969.28	989.58	996.40	998.75
3.0	960.94	986.76	995.43	998.41
3.5	951.68	983.62	994.34	998.03
4.0	941.39	980.13	993.14	997.61
4.5	929.96	976.25	991.80	997.15
5.0	917.26	971.95	990.31	996.63
6.0	887.46	961.85	986.82	995.42
7.0	850.68	949.38	982.51	993.92
8.0	805.28	933.98	977.20	992.07
9.0	749.23	914.98	970.63	989.79
10.0	680.04	891.52	962.53	986.97
11.0	594.63	862.57	952.52	983.50
12.0	489.19	826.82	940.18	979.20
13.0	359.03	782.69	924.93	973.90
14.0	198.35	728.21	906.11	967.36
15.0	0.00	660.96	882.88	959.28
16.0		577.95	854.21	949.32
17.0		475.47	818.81	937.01
18.0		348.96	775.10	921.82
19.0		192.79	721.16	903.06
20.0		0.00	654.56	879.91
21.0			572.35	851.33
22.0			470.86	816.05
23.0			345.58	772.49
24.0			190.92	718.73
25.0			0.00	652.35
26.0				570.42
27.0				469.27
28.0				344.41
29.0				190.28
30.0				0.00

REMAINING BALANCE PER $1000 OF ORIGINAL LOAN

ANNUAL INTEREST RATE: 21.5 %

AGE OF LOAN	LOAN MATURITY (YEARS)			
	15	20	25	30
0.5	995.20	998.39	999.45	999.81
1.0	989.87	996.60	998.84	999.60
1.5	983.94	994.62	998.16	999.37
2.0	977.33	992.40	997.41	999.11
2.5	969.99	989.94	996.57	998.82
3.0	961.82	987.20	995.63	998.50
3.5	952.73	984.16	994.59	998.14
4.0	942.62	980.77	993.43	997.75
4.5	931.38	977.00	992.15	997.30
5.0	918.87	972.80	990.72	996.81
6.0	889.47	962.95	987.35	995.66
7.0	853.08	950.76	983.19	994.23
8.0	808.06	935.66	978.04	992.46
9.0	752.34	916.99	971.66	990.27
10.0	683.39	893.88	963.77	987.56
11.0	598.07	865.28	954.01	984.20
12.0	492.48	829.88	941.93	980.05
13.0	361.81	786.09	926.98	974.92
14.0	200.11	731.88	908.48	968.56
15.0	0.00	664.81	885.58	960.70
16.0		581.80	857.24	950.97
17.0		479.09	822.18	938.93
18.0		351.97	778.79	924.02
19.0		194.67	725.09	905.58
20.0		0.00	658.64	882.75
21.0			576.40	854.51
22.0			474.64	819.56
23.0			348.70	776.30
24.0			192.86	722.78
25.0			0.00	656.54
26.0				574.57
27.0				473.13
28.0				347.59
29.0				192.24
30.0				0.00

REMAINING BALANCE PER $1000 OF ORIGINAL LOAN

ANNUAL INTEREST RATE: 21.75 %

AGE OF LOAN	LOAN MATURITY (YEARS)			
	15	20	25	30
0.5	995.33	998.45	999.48	999.82
1.0	990.13	996.73	998.90	999.63
1.5	984.33	994.81	998.25	999.41
2.0	977.88	992.67	997.53	999.16
2.5	970.69	990.29	996.72	998.89
3.0	962.68	987.63	995.83	998.58
3.5	953.77	984.68	994.83	998.25
4.0	943.83	981.39	993.72	997.87
4.5	932.77	977.72	992.48	997.45
5.0	920.45	973.64	991.11	996.98
6.0	891.44	964.03	987.86	995.88
7.0	855.45	952.10	983.84	994.52
8.0	810.81	937.31	978.85	992.82
9.0	755.43	918.95	972.66	990.72
10.0	686.72	896.18	964.98	988.12
11.0	601.49	867.94	955.45	984.88
12.0	495.75	832.90	943.63	980.87
13.0	364.58	789.43	928.97	975.90
14.0	201.86	735.51	910.78	969.73
15.0	0.00	668.62	888.22	962.07
16.0		585.63	860.22	952.57
17.0		482.68	825.49	940.79
18.0		354.97	782.41	926.17
19.0		196.54	728.97	908.03
20.0		0.00	662.67	885.54
21.0			580.42	857.63
22.0			478.39	823.00
23.0			351.82	780.05
24.0			194.79	726.77
25.0			0.00	660.67
26.0				578.67
27.0				476.95
28.0				350.76
29.0				194.21
30.0				0.00

MORTGAGE VALUE TABLES
(Value of Amortizing Mortgage Loans as Percentage of Face Value)

Mortgage loans can be an investment medium as well as a method for financing a home purchase. When viewed as an investment, a loan has a market value just as a share of stock or a bond. The value of the loan depends in part on the face interest rate of the loan compared with current interest rates. The following tables provide the relative value of mortgage loans for various combinations of face rates and market rates.

Some home sellers provide financing to the buyer to make their home more attractive on the market. The seller may hold the loan or sell it to investors in what is called the secondary market. These tables can be used to estimate how much the loan is worth to secondary market investors.

To use the tables, you need the following information:

1. *The interest rate on the loan* (face interest rate). Each page covers a different rate ranging from 6% to 17.75% in intervals of .25%.

2. *The yield demanded by secondary investors* (yield to maturity). Even though the loan is contracted at a certain interest rate, the yield may be raised or lowered by adjusting the price paid for the loan. The yield to maturity is the rate desired by the investor. Each page covers yields from 10 to 24.5% in .5% intervals.

3. *The remaining term of the loan.* How many years will the loan run after being purchased by the investor? The tables cover terms of 15, 20, 25, and 30 years. Use the column which is closest to the actual remaining term.

4. *The remaining balance of the loan* (face value). What is the balance of the loan when the investor makes the purchase? If some payments have already been made on the loan, the principal balance will be lower than the amount originally lent.

Example. A home seller provides a loan as part of the sales arrangement. After holding the loan for two years, the seller decides to sell the loan to secondary investors. The loan still has 23 years until maturity and a remaining principal balance of $45,000. The interest rate on the loan is 6%. If investors require a yield to maturity of 15% on 25-year amortizing home mortgage loans, what is the loan worth in the market?

Look at the first table. At the top is listed the "FACE INTEREST RATE" of 6%. Under the column for "YIELD TO MATURITY" find the yield of 15.0%. Follow this row over to the column under "TERM OF LOAN 25" (this is the closest to the actual term of 23 years). The value factor is 50.303. That is, the loan is worth 50.303 cents per dollar of face value. Multiply this percentage by the balance of the loan, or $45,000. The result is $22,636, which is the market value of the loan.

Example. A home seller is willing to provide financing to assist in making a sale. The seller makes an offer to provide a loan at 6% interest over a term of 20 years. The seller intends to sell the loan to investors who desire a yield to maturity of 12%. What should be the amount of the loan if the seller wants to get $50,000 cash from its sale?

Look at the table for "FACE INTEREST RATE" of 6%. Under the column "YIELD TO MATURITY" find the rate 12.0%. Follow the row to the column under "TERM OF LOAN 20." The value factor is 65.066. Divide the value desired, $50,000, by the percentage value factor, .65066, to obtain the result of $76,845. This is the face value of the loan which serves the seller's purpose.

VALUE OF AMORTIZING MORTGAGE LOANS
AS PERCENTAGE OF FACE VALUE

FACE INTEREST RATE: 6 %

YIELD TO MATURITY	TERM OF LOAN (YEARS)			
	15	20	25	30
10.0	78.527	74.240	70.903	68.319
10.5	76.339	71.759	68.239	65.543
11.0	74.244	69.409	65.737	62.957
11.5	72.236	67.180	63.386	60.543
12.0	70.312	65.066	61.174	58.287
12.5	68.466	63.058	59.091	56.177
13.0	66.695	61.151	57.127	54.199
13.5	64.996	59.338	55.274	52.344
14.0	63.365	57.613	53.524	50.600
14.5	61.798	55.971	51.869	48.961
15.0	60.293	54.407	50.303	47.416
15.5	58.847	52.917	48.820	45.960
16.0	57.456	51.495	47.414	44.584
16.5	56.118	50.139	46.079	43.284
17.0	54.831	48.843	44.812	42.054
17.5	53.593	47.605	43.607	40.888
18.0	52.400	46.422	42.460	39.782
18.5	51.251	45.289	41.368	38.732
19.0	50.144	44.205	40.327	37.734
19.5	49.077	43.167	39.334	36.784
20.0	48.047	42.172	38.387	35.879
20.5	47.055	41.218	37.481	35.017
21.0	46.097	40.302	36.615	34.194
21.5	45.172	39.423	35.786	33.407
22.0	44.279	38.579	34.993	32.656
22.5	43.417	37.767	34.232	31.936
23.0	42.583	36.987	33.503	31.247
23.5	41.777	36.235	32.803	30.587
24.0	40.998	35.512	32.130	29.953
24.5	40.245	34.816	31.484	29.345

VALUE OF AMORTIZING MORTGAGE LOANS
AS PERCENTAGE OF FACE VALUE

FACE INTEREST RATE: 6.25 %

YIELD TO MATURITY	TERM OF LOAN (YEARS)			
	15	20	25	30
10.0	79.789	75.742	72.594	70.161
10.5	77.566	73.211	69.866	67.310
11.0	75.437	70.813	67.305	64.654
11.5	73.397	68.539	64.898	62.175
12.0	71.441	66.382	62.633	59.859
12.5	69.566	64.334	60.500	57.691
13.0	67.767	62.388	58.490	55.660
13.5	66.041	60.538	56.592	53.755
14.0	64.383	58.779	54.800	51.965
14.5	62.791	57.104	53.106	50.281
15.0	61.262	55.508	51.503	48.695
15.5	59.792	53.987	49.984	47.199
16.0	58.379	52.537	48.545	45.786
16.5	57.020	51.153	47.178	44.451
17.0	55.713	49.831	45.880	43.188
17.5	54.454	48.568	44.647	41.990
18.0	53.242	47.361	43.473	40.855
18.5	52.074	46.206	42.355	39.776
19.0	50.950	45.100	41.289	38.751
19.5	49.865	44.040	40.273	37.776
20.0	48.820	43.025	39.302	36.847
20.5	47.811	42.052	38.375	35.961
21.0	46.838	41.118	37.488	35.115
21.5	45.898	40.221	36.640	34.308
22.0	44.991	39.359	35.827	33.536
22.5	44.114	38.531	35.049	32.797
23.0	43.268	37.735	34.302	32.090
23.5	42.449	36.969	33.585	31.412
24.0	41.657	36.231	32.897	30.761
24.5	40.891	35.520	32.235	30.137

VALUE OF AMORTIZING MORTGAGE LOANS
AS PERCENTAGE OF FACE VALUE

FACE INTEREST RATE: 6.5 %

| YIELD TO MATURITY | TERM OF LOAN (YEARS) | | | |
	15	20	25	30
10.0	81.063	77.260	74.305	72.025
10.5	78.805	74.679	71.513	69.098
11.0	76.642	72.233	68.891	66.371
11.5	74.569	69.913	66.427	63.827
12.0	72.582	67.713	64.109	61.449
12.5	70.677	65.624	61.926	59.224
13.0	68.849	63.639	59.868	57.139
13.5	67.095	61.752	57.926	55.183
14.0	65.411	59.957	56.092	53.345
14.5	63.794	58.248	54.358	51.616
15.0	62.241	56.621	52.717	49.988
15.5	60.747	55.070	51.162	48.452
16.0	59.312	53.590	49.688	47.003
16.5	57.931	52.178	48.290	45.632
17.0	56.602	50.830	46.961	44.335
17.5	55.323	49.542	45.699	43.106
18.0	54.092	48.310	44.497	41.940
18.5	52.906	47.132	43.353	40.833
19.0	51.763	46.004	42.262	39.781
19.5	50.662	44.923	41.221	38.779
20.0	49.599	43.888	40.228	37.825
20.5	48.575	42.895	39.279	36.916
21.0	47.586	41.942	38.372	36.048
21.5	46.631	41.027	37.503	35.219
22.0	45.709	40.148	36.671	34.427
22.5	44.819	39.304	35.874	33.668
23.0	43.959	38.491	35.110	32.942
23.5	43.127	37.710	34.376	32.246
24.0	42.322	36.957	33.672	31.578
24.5	41.544	36.232	32.995	30.937

VALUE OF AMORTIZING MORTGAGE LOANS
AS PERCENTAGE OF FACE VALUE

FACE INTEREST RATE: 6.75 %

YIELD TO MATURITY	TERM OF LOAN (YEARS)			
	15	20	25	30
10.0	82.347	78.792	76.033	73.908
10.5	80.053	76.160	73.176	70.905
11.0	77.856	73.665	70.493	68.107
11.5	75.751	71.300	67.972	65.496
12.0	73.732	69.056	65.600	63.056
12.5	71.797	66.925	63.366	60.772
13.0	69.940	64.901	61.260	58.633
13.5	68.158	62.977	59.273	56.626
14.0	66.448	61.146	57.396	54.740
14.5	64.805	59.404	55.622	52.966
15.0	63.227	57.744	53.943	51.295
15.5	61.710	56.162	52.352	49.719
16.0	60.251	54.653	50.844	48.232
16.5	58.848	53.213	49.413	46.825
17.0	57.499	51.838	48.054	45.494
17.5	56.200	50.525	46.761	44.233
18.0	54.949	49.268	45.532	43.037
18.5	53.744	48.067	44.361	41.901
19.0	52.583	46.916	43.245	40.821
19.5	51.464	45.814	42.180	39.793
20.0	50.385	44.758	41.164	38.815
20.5	49.344	43.745	40.192	37.881
21.0	48.340	42.774	39.264	36.991
21.5	47.370	41.841	38.375	36.140
22.0	46.434	40.945	37.524	35.327
22.5	45.529	40.083	36.709	34.549
23.0	44.655	39.255	35.926	33.804
23.5	43.810	38.458	35.176	33.089
24.0	42.993	37.690	34.455	32.404
24.5	42.202	36.951	33.762	31.746

VALUE OF AMORTIZING MORTGAGE LOANS
AS PERCENTAGE OF FACE VALUE

FACE INTEREST RATE: 7 %

YIELD TO MATURITY	TERM OF LOAN (YEARS)			
	15	20	25	30
10.0	83.642	80.340	77.779	75.812
10.5	81.312	77.656	74.856	72.731
11.0	79.081	75.112	72.112	69.861
11.5	76.942	72.700	69.533	67.182
12.0	74.892	70.412	67.106	64.680
12.5	72.926	68.240	64.821	62.337
13.0	71.040	66.176	62.667	60.143
13.5	69.230	64.214	60.634	58.084
14.0	67.493	62.347	58.714	56.150
14.5	65.824	60.570	56.899	54.330
15.0	64.221	58.878	55.181	52.616
15.5	62.680	57.265	53.554	51.000
16.0	61.199	55.726	52.011	49.474
16.5	59.774	54.258	50.548	48.031
17.0	58.403	52.856	49.157	46.666
17.5	57.084	51.517	47.835	45.372
18.0	55.813	50.236	46.577	44.145
18.5	54.589	49.011	45.379	42.980
19.0	53.410	47.838	44.238	41.872
19.5	52.273	46.714	43.149	40.818
20.0	51.177	45.637	42.109	39.814
20.5	50.120	44.605	41.115	38.857
21.0	49.100	43.614	40.166	37.944
21.5	48.115	42.663	39.257	37.071
22.0	47.164	41.749	38.386	36.237
22.5	46.245	40.870	37.552	35.439
23.0	45.357	40.026	36.751	34.674
23.5	44.499	39.213	35.984	33.941
24.0	43.669	38.430	35.246	33.238
24.5	42.866	37.677	34.537	32.564

VALUE OF AMORTIZING MORTGAGE LOANS
AS PERCENTAGE OF FACE VALUE

FACE INTEREST RATE: 7.25 %

YIELD TO MATURITY	TERM OF LOAN (YEARS)			
	15	20	25	30
10.0	84.949	81.903	79.543	77.735
10.5	82.582	79.166	76.554	74.576
11.0	80.316	76.573	73.748	71.633
11.5	78.144	74.114	71.110	68.887
12.0	76.062	71.782	68.628	66.320
12.5	74.065	69.567	66.291	63.919
13.0	72.150	67.463	64.088	61.669
13.5	70.312	65.463	62.009	59.557
14.0	68.547	63.560	60.046	57.574
14.5	66.852	61.748	58.189	55.708
15.0	65.224	60.023	56.433	53.951
15.5	63.659	58.379	54.769	52.294
16.0	62.155	56.810	53.191	50.729
16.5	60.708	55.314	51.694	49.249
17.0	59.315	53.885	50.272	47.849
17.5	57.975	52.519	48.920	46.523
18.0	56.685	51.213	47.634	45.265
18.5	55.442	49.964	46.409	44.070
19.0	54.244	48.768	45.241	42.934
19.5	53.090	47.623	44.127	41.853
20.0	51.977	46.525	43.064	40.824
20.5	50.903	45.472	42.048	39.843
21.0	49.867	44.462	41.077	38.906
21.5	48.866	43.492	40.147	38.011
22.0	47.900	42.561	39.257	37.156
22.5	46.967	41.665	38.403	36.337
23.0	46.066	40.804	37.585	35.554
23.5	45.194	39.976	36.800	34.802
24.0	44.351	39.178	36.045	34.082
24.5	43.536	38.410	35.320	33.390

VALUE OF AMORTIZING MORTGAGE LOANS
AS PERCENTAGE OF FACE VALUE

FACE INTEREST RATE: 7.5 %

YIELD TO MATURITY	TERM OF LOAN (YEARS) 15	20	25	30
10.0	86.265	83.479	81.324	79.676
10.5	83.862	80.690	78.268	76.438
11.0	81.560	78.047	75.398	73.422
11.5	79.354	75.541	72.702	70.607
12.0	77.240	73.163	70.165	67.976
12.5	75.212	70.906	67.775	65.515
13.0	73.267	68.761	65.523	63.209
13.5	71.401	66.723	63.398	61.045
14.0	69.609	64.783	61.390	59.012
14.5	67.888	62.937	59.492	57.099
15.0	66.235	61.178	57.696	55.298
15.5	64.645	59.502	55.995	53.599
16.0	63.118	57.904	54.382	51.996
16.5	61.648	56.378	52.851	50.479
17.0	60.234	54.922	51.397	49.044
17.5	58.873	53.530	50.015	47.685
18.0	57.563	52.199	48.700	46.395
18.5	56.301	50.926	47.448	45.170
19.0	55.085	49.707	46.254	44.006
19.5	53.912	48.539	45.115	42.899
20.0	52.782	47.420	44.028	41.844
20.5	51.692	46.347	42.989	40.838
21.0	50.639	45.318	41.996	39.878
21.5	49.624	44.329	41.046	38.961
22.0	48.643	43.380	40.135	38.084
22.5	47.695	42.467	39.263	37.245
23.0	46.779	41.590	38.426	36.441
23.5	45.894	40.745	37.623	35.671
24.0	45.038	39.932	36.852	34.933
24.5	44.210	39.149	36.111	34.223

VALUE OF AMORTIZING MORTGAGE LOANS
AS PERCENTAGE OF FACE VALUE

FACE INTEREST RATE: 7.75 %

YIELD TO MATURITY	TERM OF LOAN (YEARS)			
	15	20	25	30
10.0	87.593	85.071	83.122	81.636
10.5	85.153	82.228	79.998	78.319
11.0	82.816	79.535	77.066	75.228
11.5	80.576	76.981	74.309	72.344
12.0	78.429	74.558	71.716	69.649
12.5	76.370	72.258	69.274	67.127
13.0	74.395	70.072	66.972	64.764
13.5	72.500	67.995	64.799	62.546
14.0	70.680	66.018	62.748	60.463
14.5	68.933	64.137	60.808	58.504
15.0	67.254	62.345	58.972	56.658
15.5	65.641	60.637	57.233	54.918
16.0	64.089	59.008	55.584	53.275
16.5	62.597	57.453	54.020	51.721
17.0	61.162	55.969	52.534	50.251
17.5	59.780	54.550	51.121	48.858
18.0	58.449	53.194	49.777	47.536
18.5	57.168	51.897	48.497	46.282
19.0	55.933	50.655	47.277	45.089
19.5	54.742	49.465	46.113	43.954
20.0	53.595	48.325	45.002	42.873
20.5	52.487	47.231	43.940	41.842
21.0	51.419	46.182	42.925	40.859
21.5	50.387	45.175	41.953	39.919
22.0	49.391	44.207	41.023	39.021
22.5	48.429	43.277	40.131	38.161
23.0	47.499	42.383	39.276	37.338
23.5	46.601	41.522	38.455	36.549
24.0	45.732	40.693	37.667	35.792
24.5	44.891	39.895	36.910	35.065

VALUE OF AMORTIZING MORTGAGE LOANS
AS PERCENTAGE OF FACE VALUE

FACE INTEREST RATE: 8 %

YIELD TO MATURITY	TERM OF LOAN (YEARS)			
	15	20	25	30
10.0	88.930	86.676	84.936	83.613
10.5	86.453	83.780	81.744	80.216
11.0	84.080	81.036	78.748	77.050
11.5	81.806	78.434	75.931	74.096
12.0	79.626	75.965	73.281	71.335
12.5	77.536	73.621	70.786	68.752
13.0	75.531	71.394	68.433	66.332
13.5	73.607	69.278	66.214	64.061
14.0	71.760	67.264	64.117	61.928
14.5	69.985	65.347	62.135	59.921
15.0	68.281	63.521	60.259	58.031
15.5	66.643	61.781	58.482	56.248
16.0	65.068	60.121	56.798	54.565
16.5	63.553	58.537	55.199	52.974
17.0	62.096	57.025	53.680	51.468
17.5	60.693	55.580	52.237	50.041
18.0	59.342	54.198	50.863	48.688
18.5	58.041	52.876	49.555	47.403
19.0	56.787	51.610	48.309	46.181
19.5	55.578	50.398	47.119	45.018
20.0	54.413	49.236	45.984	43.911
20.5	53.289	48.122	44.899	42.856
21.0	52.204	47.053	43.862	41.848
21.5	51.157	46.027	42.869	40.886
22.0	50.146	45.041	41.918	39.966
22.5	49.169	44.093	41.007	39.085
23.0	48.225	43.182	40.133	38.242
23.5	47.312	42.305	39.295	37.434
24.0	46.430	41.461	38.489	36.659
24.5	45.576	40.648	37.715	35.915

VALUE OF AMORTIZING MORTGAGE LOANS
AS PERCENTAGE OF FACE VALUE

FACE INTEREST RATE: 8.25 %

YIELD TO MATURITY	TERM OF LOAN (YEARS)			
	15	20	25	30
10.0	90.279	88.295	86.767	85.607
10.5	87.764	85.345	83.506	82.129
11.0	85.355	82.549	80.445	78.888
11.5	83.046	79.899	77.568	75.863
12.0	80.834	77.384	74.861	73.037
12.5	78.712	74.996	72.311	70.392
13.0	76.676	72.728	69.908	67.914
13.5	74.723	70.572	67.641	65.589
14.0	72.847	68.520	65.499	63.405
14.5	71.046	66.568	63.474	61.350
15.0	69.316	64.708	61.558	59.415
15.5	67.653	62.935	59.743	57.590
16.0	66.054	61.244	58.022	55.866
16.5	64.516	59.631	56.389	54.237
17.0	63.037	58.090	54.837	52.695
17.5	61.613	56.618	53.363	51.235
18.0	60.241	55.210	51.960	49.849
18.5	58.920	53.864	50.623	48.533
19.0	57.648	52.574	49.350	47.282
19.5	56.421	51.340	48.135	46.092
20.0	55.238	50.156	46.975	44.959
20.5	54.097	49.021	45.867	43.878
21.0	52.995	47.932	44.807	42.846
21.5	51.932	46.887	43.793	41.861
22.0	50.906	45.882	42.822	40.919
22.5	49.914	44.917	41.891	40.018
23.0	48.956	43.989	40.998	39.154
23.5	48.029	43.096	40.142	38.327
24.0	47.134	42.236	39.319	37.533
24.5	46.267	41.407	38.528	36.771

VALUE OF AMORTIZING MORTGAGE LOANS
AS PERCENTAGE OF FACE VALUE

FACE INTEREST RATE: 8.5 %

YIELD TO MATURITY	TERM OF LOAN (YEARS)			
	15	20	25	30
10.0	91.637	89.928	88.613	87.618
10.5	89.085	86.923	85.283	84.058
11.0	86.640	84.076	82.157	80.741
11.5	84.296	81.377	79.218	77.645
12.0	82.050	78.815	76.454	74.753
12.5	79.896	76.384	73.850	72.046
13.0	77.830	74.073	71.396	69.510
13.5	75.848	71.877	69.080	67.130
14.0	73.944	69.788	66.893	64.894
14.5	72.116	67.799	64.825	62.791
15.0	70.360	65.905	62.868	60.810
15.5	68.672	64.099	61.014	58.942
16.0	67.048	62.377	59.256	57.179
16.5	65.488	60.734	57.589	55.511
17.0	63.986	59.165	56.004	53.933
17.5	62.540	57.665	54.498	52.438
18.0	61.148	56.231	53.065	51.020
18.5	59.807	54.860	51.701	49.673
19.0	58.515	53.547	50.400	48.393
19.5	57.270	52.289	49.159	47.175
20.0	56.069	51.084	47.974	46.015
20.5	54.911	49.928	46.843	44.908
21.0	53.793	48.819	45.760	43.853
21.5	52.714	47.754	44.725	42.844
22.0	51.672	46.731	43.733	41.880
22.5	50.665	45.748	42.782	40.958
23.0	49.693	44.802	41.871	40.074
23.5	48.752	43.893	40.996	39.227
24.0	47.843	43.017	40.156	38.415
24.5	46.964	42.173	39.348	37.635

VALUE OF AMORTIZING MORTGAGE LOANS
AS PERCENTAGE OF FACE VALUE

FACE INTEREST RATE: 8.75 %

YIELD TO MATURITY	TERM OF LOAN (YEARS)			
	15	20	25	30
10.0	93.006	91.574	90.475	89.645
10.5	90.415	88.514	87.075	86.003
11.0	87.934	85.615	83.883	82.609
11.5	85.555	82.866	80.882	79.441
12.0	83.276	80.258	78.060	76.482
12.5	81.090	77.782	75.401	73.712
13.0	78.993	75.429	72.896	71.117
13.5	76.980	73.193	70.531	68.683
14.0	75.048	71.065	68.298	66.395
14.5	73.193	69.040	66.186	64.244
15.0	71.410	67.111	64.188	62.217
15.5	69.697	65.272	62.296	60.306
16.0	68.050	63.519	60.501	58.501
16.5	66.466	61.845	58.798	56.795
17.0	64.941	60.248	57.181	55.181
17.5	63.474	58.721	55.643	53.651
18.0	62.061	57.261	54.180	52.200
18.5	60.700	55.864	52.787	50.822
19.0	59.389	54.527	51.459	49.512
19.5	58.125	53.246	50.192	48.266
20.0	56.907	52.019	48.982	47.079
20.5	55.731	50.842	47.827	45.947
21.0	54.596	49.712	46.722	44.867
21.5	53.501	48.628	45.664	43.835
22.0	52.444	47.587	44.652	42.849
22.5	51.422	46.585	43.681	41.905
23.0	50.435	45.623	42.750	41.001
23.5	49.480	44.696	41.857	40.135
24.0	48.558	43.804	40.999	39.303
24.5	47.665	42.945	40.175	38.506

VALUE OF AMORTIZING MORTGAGE LOANS
AS PERCENTAGE OF FACE VALUE

FACE INTEREST RATE: 9 %

YIELD TO MATURITY	TERM OF LOAN (YEARS)			
	15	20	25	30
10.0	94.384	93.233	92.351	91.687
10.5	91.755	90.118	88.881	87.962
11.0	89.237	87.167	85.622	84.490
11.5	86.823	84.368	82.560	81.251
12.0	84.510	81.712	79.679	78.224
12.5	82.291	79.191	76.965	75.391
13.0	80.164	76.796	74.408	72.737
13.5	78.121	74.519	71.994	70.247
14.0	76.161	72.353	69.714	67.908
14.5	74.278	70.291	67.559	65.707
15.0	72.469	68.327	65.520	63.634
15.5	70.730	66.455	63.588	61.680
16.0	69.058	64.670	61.756	59.834
16.5	67.451	62.966	60.018	58.089
17.0	65.904	61.339	58.367	56.438
17.5	64.415	59.785	56.797	54.873
18.0	62.981	58.298	55.304	53.389
18.5	61.600	56.876	53.881	51.980
19.0	60.270	55.515	52.526	50.640
19.5	58.987	54.211	51.233	49.366
20.0	57.750	52.961	49.998	48.152
20.5	56.557	51.763	48.819	46.994
21.0	55.406	50.613	47.691	45.889
21.5	54.294	49.509	46.611	44.834
22.0	53.221	48.449	45.578	43.825
22.5	52.184	47.429	44.587	42.860
23.0	51.182	46.449	43.637	41.935
23.5	50.214	45.506	42.725	41.049
24.0	49.277	44.598	41.849	40.199
24.5	48.371	43.723	41.008	39.383

VALUE OF AMORTIZING MORTGAGE LOANS
AS PERCENTAGE OF FACE VALUE

FACE INTEREST RATE: 9.25 %

YIELD TO MATURITY	TERM OF LOAN (YEARS)			
	15	20	25	30
10.0	95.774	94.906	94.243	93.745
10.5	93.106	91.735	90.701	89.936
11.0	90.551	88.731	87.376	86.386
11.5	88.102	85.882	84.251	83.074
12.0	85.754	83.179	81.311	79.979
12.5	83.503	80.612	78.542	77.083
13.0	81.344	78.174	75.932	74.370
13.5	79.272	75.856	73.469	71.824
14.0	77.282	73.651	71.142	69.432
14.5	75.371	71.552	68.943	67.182
15.0	73.536	69.553	66.862	65.062
15.5	71.772	67.648	64.890	63.064
16.0	70.075	65.830	63.021	61.177
16.5	68.444	64.096	61.247	59.393
17.0	66.874	62.440	59.562	57.704
17.5	65.363	60.857	57.960	56.105
18.0	63.908	59.344	56.436	54.587
18.5	62.507	57.897	54.985	53.146
19.0	61.157	56.511	53.602	51.777
19.5	59.855	55.184	52.282	50.473
20.0	58.600	53.912	51.022	49.232
20.5	57.390	52.692	49.818	48.048
21.0	56.221	51.522	48.667	46.919
21.5	55.094	50.398	47.566	45.840
22.0	54.005	49.318	46.511	44.808
22.5	52.953	48.281	45.500	43.821
23.0	51.936	47.283	44.531	42.876
23.5	50.953	46.323	43.600	41.970
24.0	50.003	45.398	42.707	41.101
24.5	49.084	44.508	41.848	40.266

VALUE OF AMORTIZING MORTGAGE LOANS
AS PERCENTAGE OF FACE VALUE

FACE INTEREST RATE: 9.5 %

YIELD TO MATURITY	TERM OF LOAN (YEARS)			
	15	20	25	30
10.0	97.172	96.591	96.148	95.816
10.5	94.465	93.364	92.535	91.923
11.0	91.873	90.306	89.142	88.295
11.5	89.388	87.407	85.954	84.910
12.0	87.006	84.655	82.954	81.746
12.5	84.722	82.043	80.129	78.786
13.0	82.531	79.562	77.467	76.013
13.5	80.429	77.203	74.954	73.411
14.0	78.410	74.959	72.580	70.966
14.5	76.472	72.823	70.337	68.666
15.0	74.609	70.788	68.213	66.500
15.5	72.819	68.849	66.202	64.457
16.0	71.098	66.999	64.295	62.528
16.5	69.443	65.234	62.485	60.705
17.0	67.851	63.549	60.766	58.979
17.5	66.318	61.938	59.132	57.344
18.0	64.842	60.398	57.577	55.793
18.5	63.420	58.925	56.097	54.321
19.0	62.050	57.515	54.685	52.921
19.5	60.729	56.164	53.339	51.589
20.0	59.456	54.869	52.054	50.320
20.5	58.228	53.628	50.826	49.110
21.0	57.042	52.436	49.651	47.956
21.5	55.898	51.293	48.528	46.853
22.0	54.793	50.194	47.451	45.798
22.5	53.726	49.138	46.420	44.790
23.0	52.694	48.122	45.431	43.823
23.5	51.697	47.145	44.482	42.897
24.0	50.733	46.204	43.570	42.009
24.5	49.800	45.298	42.694	41.156

VALUE OF AMORTIZING MORTGAGE LOANS
AS PERCENTAGE OF FACE VALUE

FACE INTEREST RATE: 9.75 %

YIELD TO MATURITY	TERM OF LOAN (YEARS)			
	15	20	25	30
10.0	98.582	98.290	98.067	97.901
10.5	95.835	95.006	94.382	93.923
11.0	93.205	91.894	90.922	90.217
11.5	90.684	88.943	87.670	86.758
12.0	88.268	86.144	84.611	83.526
12.5	85.951	83.486	81.729	80.501
13.0	83.728	80.961	79.013	77.667
13.5	81.595	78.560	76.450	75.008
14.0	79.547	76.277	74.029	72.510
14.5	77.581	74.103	71.741	70.161
15.0	75.691	72.033	69.575	67.947
15.5	73.875	70.059	67.524	65.860
16.0	72.129	68.177	65.578	63.889
16.5	70.450	66.381	63.733	62.026
17.0	68.835	64.666	61.979	60.263
17.5	67.279	63.027	60.313	58.592
18.0	65.782	61.460	58.727	57.008
18.5	64.339	59.961	57.217	55.503
19.0	62.950	58.526	55.777	54.073
19.5	61.610	57.151	54.404	52.711
20.0	60.318	55.834	53.093	51.415
20.5	59.072	54.570	51.840	50.179
21.0	57.869	53.358	50.643	48.999
21.5	56.709	52.194	49.496	47.873
22.0	55.588	51.076	48.399	46.795
22.5	54.505	50.002	47.347	45.764
23.0	53.458	48.968	46.338	44.777
23.5	52.447	47.974	45.370	43.831
24.0	51.469	47.017	44.440	42.923
24.5	50.522	46.095	43.546	42.052

VALUE OF AMORTIZING MORTGAGE LOANS
AS PERCENTAGE OF FACE VALUE

FACE INTEREST RATE: 10 %

YIELD TO MATURITY	TERM OF LOAN (YEARS) 15	20	25	30
10.0	100.000	100.000	100.000	100.000
10.5	97.214	96.659	96.242	95.937
11.0	94.546	93.493	92.714	92.151
11.5	91.989	90.491	89.398	88.618
12.0	89.538	87.643	86.278	85.316
12.5	87.188	84.939	83.340	82.227
13.0	84.933	82.370	80.570	79.332
13.5	82.769	79.927	77.957	76.616
14.0	80.692	77.604	75.489	74.065
14.5	78.697	75.393	73.155	71.665
15.0	76.780	73.286	70.946	69.404
15.5	74.938	71.278	68.854	67.272
16.0	73.167	69.363	66.871	65.259
16.5	71.464	67.536	64.989	63.356
17.0	69.825	65.791	63.201	61.555
17.5	68.247	64.124	61.501	59.848
18.0	66.728	62.529	59.884	58.230
18.5	65.265	61.004	58.344	56.693
19.0	63.855	59.544	56.876	55.232
19.5	62.496	58.146	55.476	53.841
20.0	61.186	56.805	54.139	52.517
20.5	59.922	55.520	52.862	51.255
21.0	58.702	54.287	51.641	50.050
21.5	57.525	53.103	50.472	48.899
22.0	56.387	51.965	49.353	47.798
22.5	55.289	50.872	48.280	46.746
23.0	54.228	49.820	47.251	45.737
23.5	53.201	48.809	46.264	44.771
24.0	52.209	47.835	45.316	43.843
24.5	51.249	46.897	44.404	42.953

VALUE OF AMORTIZING MORTGAGE LOANS
AS PERCENTAGE OF FACE VALUE

FACE INTEREST RATE: 10.25 %

YIELD TO MATURITY	TERM OF LOAN (YEARS)			
	15	20	25	30
10.0	101.428	101.722	101.946	102.111
10.5	98.602	98.323	98.115	97.962
11.0	95.896	95.103	94.518	94.096
11.5	93.302	92.049	91.137	90.489
12.0	90.816	89.152	87.957	87.117
12.5	88.432	86.401	84.962	83.963
13.0	86.146	83.788	82.138	81.007
13.5	83.951	81.304	79.474	78.234
14.0	81.844	78.941	76.957	75.629
14.5	79.820	76.691	74.578	73.178
15.0	77.877	74.548	72.327	70.869
15.5	76.008	72.506	70.194	68.692
16.0	74.212	70.558	68.172	66.637
16.5	72.484	68.699	66.253	64.694
17.0	70.822	66.924	64.431	62.854
17.5	69.222	65.228	62.698	61.112
18.0	67.681	63.606	61.049	59.459
18.5	66.197	62.055	59.479	57.890
19.0	64.767	60.570	57.983	56.398
19.5	63.389	59.147	56.556	54.978
20.0	62.060	57.784	55.193	53.626
20.5	60.777	56.476	53.891	52.337
21.0	59.540	55.222	52.645	51.106
21.5	58.346	54.017	51.454	49.931
22.0	57.192	52.860	50.313	48.808
22.5	56.078	51.748	49.219	47.732
23.0	55.002	50.678	48.171	46.703
23.5	53.961	49.649	47.164	45.716
24.0	52.955	48.659	46.197	44.769
24.5	51.981	47.704	45.268	43.860

VALUE OF AMORTIZING MORTGAGE LOANS
AS PERCENTAGE OF FACE VALUE

FACE INTEREST RATE: 10.5 %

YIELD TO MATURITY	TERM OF LOAN (YEARS) 15	20	25	30
10.0	102.866	103.457	103.905	104.235
10.5	100.000	100.000	100.000	100.000
11.0	97.255	96.725	96.334	96.054
11.5	94.625	93.619	92.888	92.371
12.0	92.104	90.672	89.647	88.929
12.5	89.686	87.875	86.594	85.709
13.0	87.367	85.217	83.716	82.692
13.5	85.141	82.690	81.001	79.861
14.0	83.004	80.287	78.436	77.202
14.5	80.952	77.999	76.011	74.700
15.0	78.981	75.819	73.716	72.343
15.5	77.086	73.742	71.543	70.121
16.0	75.264	71.761	69.482	68.023
16.5	73.512	69.871	67.526	66.039
17.0	71.826	68.065	65.669	64.162
17.5	70.203	66.340	63.903	62.383
18.0	68.640	64.691	62.222	60.696
18.5	67.135	63.113	60.622	59.094
19.0	65.685	61.602	59.097	57.571
19.5	64.287	60.156	57.642	56.122
20.0	62.939	58.769	56.253	54.741
20.5	61.639	57.439	54.926	53.425
21.0	60.384	56.163	53.657	52.169
21.5	59.173	54.938	52.443	50.970
22.0	58.003	53.761	51.280	49.823
22.5	56.873	52.630	50.165	48.725
23.0	55.781	51.543	49.096	47.674
23.5	54.726	50.496	48.070	46.667
24.0	53.705	49.488	47.085	45.700
24.5	52.718	48.518	46.138	44.773

VALUE OF AMORTIZING MORTGAGE LOANS
AS PERCENTAGE OF FACE VALUE

FACE INTEREST RATE: 10.75 %

YIELD TO MATURITY	TERM OF LOAN (YEARS)			
	15	20	25	30
10.0	104.312	105.203	105.876	106.371
10.5	101.407	101.688	101.897	102.049
11.0	98.623	98.357	98.162	98.022
11.5	95.956	95.199	94.650	94.263
12.0	93.399	92.203	91.347	90.752
12.5	90.947	89.358	88.237	87.465
13.0	88.596	86.655	85.304	84.386
13.5	86.339	84.086	82.537	81.497
14.0	84.172	81.641	79.924	78.783
14.5	82.091	79.315	77.453	76.230
15.0	80.091	77.099	75.115	73.825
15.5	78.170	74.987	72.900	71.558
16.0	76.322	72.972	70.800	69.416
16.5	74.546	71.050	68.807	67.392
17.0	72.836	69.214	66.914	65.476
17.5	71.190	67.460	65.115	63.661
18.0	69.606	65.783	63.403	61.940
18.5	68.080	64.178	61.772	60.305
19.0	66.609	62.642	60.218	58.750
19.5	65.192	61.171	58.736	57.272
20.0	63.825	59.761	57.320	55.863
20.5	62.506	58.408	55.968	54.520
21.0	61.234	57.111	54.675	53.238
21.5	60.005	55.865	53.437	52.014
22.0	58.819	54.669	52.252	50.844
22.5	57.673	53.518	51.117	49.724
23.0	56.566	52.412	50.027	48.651
23.5	55.496	51.348	48.982	47.623
24.0	54.461	50.323	47.978	46.637
24.5	53.459	49.337	47.013	45.690

VALUE OF AMORTIZING MORTGAGE LOANS
AS PERCENTAGE OF FACE VALUE

FACE INTEREST RATE: 11 %

YIELD TO MATURITY	TERM OF LOAN (YEARS)			
	15	20	25	30
10.0	105.768	106.960	107.859	108.518
10.5	102.822	103.386	103.805	104.109
11.0	100.000	100.000	100.000	100.000
11.5	97.295	96.789	96.423	96.166
12.0	94.703	93.743	93.058	92.583
12.5	92.217	90.850	89.889	89.231
13.0	89.832	88.103	86.902	86.090
13.5	87.544	85.490	84.083	83.142
14.0	85.346	83.005	81.421	80.373
14.5	83.236	80.640	78.904	77.769
15.0	81.209	78.387	76.522	75.316
15.5	79.261	76.239	74.265	73.002
16.0	77.388	74.191	72.126	70.817
16.5	75.586	72.236	70.096	68.752
17.0	73.853	70.370	68.168	66.798
17.5	72.184	68.587	66.335	64.946
18.0	70.577	66.881	64.590	63.190
18.5	69.030	65.250	62.929	61.522
19.0	67.539	63.688	61.346	59.936
19.5	66.101	62.193	59.836	58.428
20.0	64.715	60.759	58.394	56.991
20.5	63.378	59.384	57.016	55.620
21.0	62.088	58.065	55.699	54.313
21.5	60.843	56.798	54.438	53.064
22.0	59.640	55.582	53.231	51.870
22.5	58.478	54.412	52.074	50.727
23.0	57.356	53.288	50.964	49.633
23.5	56.270	52.206	49.900	48.584
24.0	55.221	51.164	48.877	47.578
24.5	54.206	50.161	47.894	46.612

VALUE OF AMORTIZING MORTGAGE LOANS
AS PERCENTAGE OF FACE VALUE

FACE INTEREST RATE: 11.25 %

YIELD TO MATURITY	TERM OF LOAN (YEARS) 15	20	25	30
10.0	107.234	108.729	109.853	110.676
10.5	104.247	105.096	105.725	106.179
11.0	101.386	101.654	101.850	101.989
11.5	98.644	98.390	98.207	98.078
12.0	96.015	95.293	94.779	94.424
12.5	93.495	92.353	91.552	91.005
13.0	91.077	89.560	88.509	87.802
13.5	88.757	86.904	85.639	84.796
14.0	86.529	84.378	82.927	81.972
14.5	84.390	81.973	80.363	79.315
15.0	82.335	79.683	77.937	76.813
15.5	80.360	77.500	75.639	74.454
16.0	78.460	75.418	73.460	72.226
16.5	76.634	73.431	71.392	70.120
17.0	74.876	71.534	69.429	68.126
17.5	73.184	69.721	67.561	66.238
18.0	71.556	67.987	65.785	64.446
18.5	69.987	66.329	64.093	62.745
19.0	68.475	64.742	62.481	61.128
19.5	67.018	63.221	60.942	59.590
20.0	65.612	61.764	59.474	58.124
20.5	64.257	60.366	58.071	56.727
21.0	62.949	59.025	56.729	55.393
21.5	61.686	57.738	55.445	54.119
22.0	60.467	56.501	54.216	52.901
22.5	59.289	55.312	53.037	51.736
23.0	58.150	54.169	51.907	50.620
23.5	57.050	53.069	50.822	49.550
24.0	55.986	52.010	49.781	48.524
24.5	54.957	50.990	48.780	47.539

VALUE OF AMORTIZING MORTGAGE LOANS
AS PERCENTAGE OF FACE VALUE

FACE INTEREST RATE: 11.5 %

YIELD TO MATURITY	TERM OF LOAN (YEARS)			
	15	20	25	30
10.0	108.709	110.508	111.859	112.844
10.5	105.680	106.816	107.656	108.259
11.0	102.780	103.317	103.709	103.987
11.5	100.000	100.000	100.000	100.000
12.0	97.336	96.853	96.510	96.275
12.5	94.780	93.864	93.224	92.788
13.0	92.329	91.025	90.126	89.522
13.5	89.977	88.326	87.202	86.457
14.0	87.719	85.759	84.441	83.578
14.5	85.550	83.315	81.831	80.869
15.0	83.467	80.987	79.360	78.318
15.5	81.464	78.768	77.020	75.913
16.0	79.539	76.652	74.801	73.641
16.5	77.687	74.633	72.696	71.494
17.0	75.906	72.705	70.696	69.461
17.5	74.191	70.862	68.795	67.536
18.0	72.539	69.100	66.986	65.709
18.5	70.949	67.415	65.264	63.975
19.0	69.416	65.801	63.622	62.326
19.5	67.939	64.256	62.055	60.757
20.0	66.514	62.775	60.560	59.263
20.5	65.140	61.354	59.131	57.838
21.0	63.814	59.991	57.765	56.478
21.5	62.534	58.683	56.458	55.180
22.0	61.298	57.426	55.206	53.938
22.5	60.104	56.218	54.006	52.750
23.0	58.950	55.056	52.855	51.612
23.5	57.835	53.938	51.751	50.521
24.0	56.756	52.861	50.690	49.475
24.5	55.712	51.825	49.670	48.471

VALUE OF AMORTIZING MORTGAGE LOANS
AS PERCENTAGE OF FACE VALUE

FACE INTEREST RATE: 11.75 %

YIELD TO MATURITY	TERM OF LOAN (YEARS)			
	15	20	25	30
10.0	110.192	112.299	113.877	115.023
10.5	107.123	108.547	109.597	110.350
11.0	104.183	104.992	105.580	105.995
11.5	101.365	101.620	101.803	101.931
12.0	98.664	98.422	98.251	98.133
12.5	96.074	95.385	94.905	94.580
13.0	93.590	92.500	91.751	91.250
13.5	91.205	89.758	88.775	88.126
14.0	88.916	87.148	85.964	85.192
14.5	86.718	84.665	83.306	82.431
15.0	84.606	82.299	80.791	79.830
15.5	82.576	80.045	78.409	77.378
16.0	80.625	77.894	76.150	75.063
16.5	78.748	75.842	74.007	72.874
17.0	76.942	73.883	71.971	70.802
17.5	75.203	72.010	70.036	68.839
18.0	73.530	70.220	68.194	66.978
18.5	71.917	68.507	66.440	65.210
19.0	70.364	66.867	64.769	63.529
19.5	68.866	65.297	63.174	61.930
20.0	67.422	63.792	61.652	60.407
20.5	66.029	62.348	60.198	58.955
21.0	64.685	60.963	58.807	57.569
21.5	63.388	59.634	57.476	56.245
22.0	62.135	58.356	56.201	54.979
22.5	60.924	57.128	54.980	53.768
23.0	59.755	55.948	53.808	52.608
23.5	58.624	54.812	52.684	51.497
24.0	57.531	53.718	51.604	50.430
24.5	56.473	52.664	50.566	49.406

VALUE OF AMORTIZING MORTGAGE LOANS
AS PERCENTAGE OF FACE VALUE

FACE INTEREST RATE: 12 %

YIELD TO MATURITY	TERM OF LOAN (YEARS)			
	15	20	25	30
10.0	111.684	114.099	115.904	117.211
10.5	108.573	110.287	111.549	112.449
11.0	105.593	106.675	107.460	108.011
11.5	102.737	103.250	103.616	103.870
12.0	100.000	100.000	100.000	100.000
12.5	97.375	96.915	96.595	96.379
13.0	94.857	93.983	93.385	92.986
13.5	92.440	91.197	90.356	89.803
14.0	90.120	88.546	87.494	86.812
14.5	87.892	86.022	84.790	83.999
15.0	85.752	83.619	82.230	81.349
15.5	83.694	81.328	79.805	78.850
16.0	81.716	79.143	77.506	76.491
16.5	79.814	77.058	75.325	74.260
17.0	77.984	75.067	73.253	72.149
17.5	76.222	73.165	71.283	70.149
18.0	74.525	71.346	69.408	68.252
18.5	72.891	69.605	67.623	66.450
19.0	71.317	67.940	65.922	64.738
19.5	69.799	66.344	64.299	63.108
20.0	68.335	64.815	62.750	61.556
20.5	66.923	63.348	61.269	60.076
21.0	65.561	61.941	59.854	58.664
21.5	64.246	60.590	58.499	57.315
22.0	62.976	59.292	57.202	56.025
22.5	61.749	58.044	55.959	54.791
23.0	60.564	56.845	54.766	53.609
23.5	59.418	55.691	53.622	52.476
24.0	58.309	54.579	52.523	51.389
24.5	57.237	53.509	51.466	50.346

VALUE OF AMORTIZING MORTGAGE LOANS
AS PERCENTAGE OF FACE VALUE

FACE INTEREST RATE: 12.25 %

YIELD TO MATURITY	TERM OF LOAN (YEARS) 15	20	25	30
10.0	113.185	115.911	117.942	119.409
10.5	110.032	112.038	113.510	114.557
11.0	107.012	108.368	109.349	110.036
11.5	104.118	104.889	105.438	105.817
12.0	101.344	101.587	101.758	101.875
12.5	98.684	98.453	98.293	98.186
13.0	96.132	95.475	95.027	94.729
13.5	93.683	92.644	91.944	91.486
14.0	91.331	89.951	89.033	88.440
14.5	89.073	87.388	86.280	85.574
15.0	86.904	84.946	83.676	82.874
15.5	84.819	82.619	81.208	80.328
16.0	82.815	80.400	78.869	77.925
16.5	80.887	78.281	76.649	75.652
17.0	79.032	76.259	74.541	73.502
17.5	77.246	74.326	72.536	71.464
18.0	75.527	72.478	70.629	69.531
18.5	73.871	70.710	68.812	67.696
19.0	72.275	69.018	67.081	65.951
19.5	70.737	67.397	65.430	64.291
20.0	69.254	65.843	63.853	62.710
20.5	67.823	64.354	62.347	61.202
21.0	66.442	62.924	60.906	59.764
21.5	65.109	61.552	59.528	58.389
22.0	63.822	60.233	58.208	57.075
22.5	62.579	58.966	56.942	55.818
23.0	61.378	57.747	55.729	54.614
23.5	60.216	56.575	54.565	53.460
24.0	59.093	55.446	53.446	52.353
24.5	58.007	54.358	52.371	51.290

VALUE OF AMORTIZING MORTGAGE LOANS
AS PERCENTAGE OF FACE VALUE

FACE INTEREST RATE: 12.5 %

YIELD TO MATURITY	TERM OF LOAN (YEARS)			
	15	20	25	30
10.0	114.695	117.732	119.990	121.615
10.5	111.500	113.798	115.481	116.673
11.0	108.440	110.071	111.248	112.069
11.5	105.507	106.537	107.269	107.772
12.0	102.696	103.184	103.525	103.757
12.5	100.000	100.000	100.000	100.000
13.0	97.414	96.976	96.677	96.480
13.5	94.932	94.100	93.541	93.177
14.0	92.550	91.365	90.579	90.074
14.5	90.262	88.761	87.779	87.155
15.0	88.064	86.281	85.129	84.405
15.5	85.951	83.917	82.619	81.813
16.0	83.919	81.663	80.239	79.364
16.5	81.966	79.512	77.980	77.050
17.0	80.086	77.457	75.835	74.860
17.5	78.276	75.494	73.796	72.785
18.0	76.534	73.617	71.855	70.816
18.5	74.856	71.821	70.007	68.947
19.0	73.239	70.103	68.246	67.170
19.5	71.680	68.456	66.566	65.479
20.0	70.177	66.878	64.962	63.869
20.5	68.728	65.365	63.429	62.333
21.0	67.329	63.913	61.964	60.868
21.5	65.978	62.519	60.561	59.468
22.0	64.674	61.180	59.218	58.130
22.5	63.414	59.892	57.931	56.849
23.0	62.196	58.655	56.697	55.623
23.5	61.020	57.464	55.512	54.448
24.0	59.881	56.317	54.374	53.320
24.5	58.781	55.212	53.281	52.238

VALUE OF AMORTIZING MORTGAGE LOANS
AS PERCENTAGE OF FACE VALUE

FACE INTEREST RATE: 12.75 %

YIELD TO MATURITY	TERM OF LOAN (YEARS)			
	15	20	25	30
10.0	116.213	119.563	122.048	123.830
10.5	112.976	115.568	117.462	118.798
11.0	109.875	111.783	113.156	114.110
11.5	106.904	108.194	109.108	109.735
12.0	104.055	104.789	105.301	105.647
12.5	101.324	101.555	101.715	101.821
13.0	98.704	98.484	98.335	98.237
13.5	96.189	95.564	95.145	94.874
14.0	93.775	92.786	92.132	91.714
14.5	91.456	90.142	89.284	88.742
15.0	89.229	87.623	86.589	85.942
15.5	87.088	85.223	84.035	83.302
16.0	85.030	82.933	81.615	80.810
16.5	83.050	80.748	79.317	78.453
17.0	81.146	78.662	77.136	76.223
17.5	79.312	76.668	75.061	74.110
18.0	77.547	74.762	73.088	72.106
18.5	75.847	72.938	71.208	70.202
19.0	74.209	71.193	69.416	68.393
19.5	72.629	69.521	67.707	66.672
20.0	71.106	67.918	66.076	65.032
20.5	69.637	66.381	64.517	63.468
21.0	68.220	64.907	63.026	61.976
21.5	66.851	63.491	61.600	60.551
22.0	65.530	62.131	60.234	59.189
22.5	64.253	60.824	58.925	57.885
23.0	63.020	59.567	57.669	56.636
23.5	61.827	58.357	56.464	55.439
24.0	60.674	57.193	55.307	54.291
24.5	59.559	56.071	54.195	53.189

VALUE OF AMORTIZING MORTGAGE LOANS
AS PERCENTAGE OF FACE VALUE

FACE INTEREST RATE: 13 %

YIELD TO MATURITY	TERM OF LOAN (YEARS)			
	15	20	25	30
10.0	117.740	121.404	124.115	126.052
10.5	114.460	117.347	119.451	120.930
11.0	111.319	113.504	115.072	116.158
11.5	108.308	109.860	110.956	111.704
12.0	105.422	106.402	107.084	107.543
12.5	102.654	103.119	103.437	103.649
13.0	100.000	100.000	100.000	100.000
13.5	97.452	97.035	96.756	96.577
14.0	95.006	94.214	93.693	93.360
14.5	92.658	91.529	90.796	90.335
15.0	90.401	88.972	88.055	87.485
15.5	88.232	86.535	85.459	84.798
16.0	86.147	84.210	82.997	82.260
16.5	84.141	81.991	80.661	79.861
17.0	82.212	79.873	78.442	77.591
17.5	80.354	77.849	76.332	75.440
18.0	78.566	75.913	74.325	73.400
18.5	76.843	74.061	72.414	71.462
19.0	75.183	72.289	70.592	69.621
19.5	73.583	70.591	68.854	67.868
20.0	72.040	68.964	67.195	66.199
20.5	70.552	67.403	65.610	64.608
21.0	69.116	65.906	64.094	63.089
21.5	67.729	64.469	62.643	61.638
22.0	66.390	63.088	61.254	60.251
22.5	65.097	61.760	59.923	58.924
23.0	63.847	60.484	58.646	57.653
23.5	62.639	59.256	57.420	56.434
24.0	61.471	58.073	56.243	55.266
24.5	60.341	56.934	55.112	54.144

VALUE OF AMORTIZING MORTGAGE LOANS
AS PERCENTAGE OF FACE VALUE

FACE INTEREST RATE: 13.25 %

YIELD TO MATURITY	TERM OF LOAN (YEARS)			
	15	20	25	30
10.0	119.275	123.254	126.191	128.283
10.5	115.952	119.136	121.449	123.070
11.0	112.770	115.234	116.997	118.213
11.5	109.720	111.534	112.812	113.681
12.0	106.796	108.023	108.875	109.446
12.5	103.993	104.690	105.168	105.483
13.0	101.304	101.524	101.673	101.770
13.5	98.723	98.514	98.375	98.285
14.0	96.245	95.650	95.260	95.012
14.5	93.866	92.924	92.315	91.933
15.0	91.580	90.328	89.528	89.033
15.5	89.383	87.854	86.888	86.298
16.0	87.270	85.493	84.385	83.716
16.5	85.238	83.241	82.010	81.275
17.0	83.284	81.090	79.754	78.964
17.5	81.402	79.035	77.609	76.775
18.0	79.590	77.070	75.569	74.699
18.5	77.845	75.190	73.625	72.727
19.0	76.164	73.391	71.773	70.853
19.5	74.543	71.667	70.006	69.069
20.0	72.980	70.015	68.319	67.370
20.5	71.472	68.431	66.707	65.751
21.0	70.017	66.911	65.166	64.205
21.5	68.612	65.451	63.691	62.729
22.0	67.256	64.049	62.279	61.317
22.5	65.946	62.702	60.925	59.966
23.0	64.680	61.406	59.627	58.673
23.5	63.456	60.159	58.381	57.433
24.0	62.272	58.958	57.184	56.244
24.5	61.128	57.802	56.034	55.102

VALUE OF AMORTIZING MORTGAGE LOANS
AS PERCENTAGE OF FACE VALUE

FACE INTEREST RATE: 13.5 %

YIELD TO MATURITY	TERM OF LOAN (YEARS)			
	15	20	25	30
10.0	120.818	125.113	128.276	130.521
10.5	117.452	120.933	123.455	125.217
11.0	114.229	116.972	118.930	120.276
11.5	111.139	113.216	114.676	115.664
12.0	108.178	109.653	110.674	111.355
12.5	105.338	106.270	106.905	107.323
13.0	102.614	103.056	103.352	103.545
13.5	100.000	100.000	100.000	100.000
14.0	97.490	97.093	96.833	96.670
14.5	95.080	94.326	93.840	93.537
15.0	92.764	91.691	91.007	90.586
15.5	90.539	89.179	88.323	87.804
16.0	88.399	86.783	85.779	85.176
16.5	86.341	84.497	83.365	82.692
17.0	84.361	82.313	81.072	80.342
17.5	82.455	80.227	78.891	78.114
18.0	80.620	78.233	76.817	76.002
18.5	78.852	76.324	74.841	73.996
19.0	77.149	74.498	72.959	72.089
19.5	75.507	72.748	71.162	70.274
20.0	73.924	71.071	69.448	68.546
20.5	72.396	69.463	67.809	66.898
21.0	70.923	67.920	66.242	65.325
21.5	69.500	66.438	64.743	63.823
22.0	68.126	65.015	63.307	62.387
22.5	66.799	63.647	61.931	61.012
23.0	65.517	62.332	60.612	59.696
23.5	64.277	61.066	59.345	58.435
24.0	63.078	59.848	58.129	57.225
24.5	61.918	58.674	56.960	56.063

VALUE OF AMORTIZING MORTGAGE LOANS
AS PERCENTAGE OF FACE VALUE

FACE INTEREST RATE: 13.75 %

YIELD TO	TERM OF LOAN (YEARS)			
MATURITY	15	20	25	30
10.0	122.369	126.982	130.369	132.766
10.5	118.960	122.739	125.470	127.371
11.0	115.696	118.719	120.871	122.344
11.5	112.566	114.907	116.547	117.654
12.0	109.567	111.291	112.480	113.270
12.5	106.691	107.857	108.650	109.169
13.0	103.932	104.595	105.039	105.326
13.5	101.284	101.494	101.632	101.720
14.0	98.742	98.543	98.414	98.332
14.5	96.301	95.735	95.371	95.146
15.0	93.956	93.060	92.492	92.144
15.5	91.702	90.511	89.765	89.314
16.0	89.534	88.079	87.179	86.641
16.5	87.450	85.759	84.725	84.115
17.0	85.444	83.543	82.395	81.724
17.5	83.514	81.426	80.179	79.458
18.0	81.655	79.401	78.071	77.309
18.5	79.865	77.464	76.063	75.268
19.0	78.139	75.610	74.149	73.329
19.5	76.476	73.835	72.324	71.483
20.0	74.873	72.133	70.581	69.725
20.5	73.326	70.500	68.916	68.048
21.0	71.833	68.934	67.324	66.449
21.5	70.392	67.431	65.800	64.921
22.0	69.001	65.986	64.341	63.460
22.5	67.657	64.598	62.942	62.062
23.0	66.358	63.263	61.601	60.723
23.5	65.102	61.978	60.314	59.440
24.0	63.888	60.742	59.078	58.209
24.5	62.713	59.550	57.890	57.027

VALUE OF AMORTIZING MORTGAGE LOANS
AS PERCENTAGE OF FACE VALUE

FACE INTEREST RATE: 14 %

YIELD TO MATURITY	TERM OF LOAN (YEARS)			
	15	20	25	30
10.0	123.928	128.859	132.470	135.017
10.5	120.476	124.554	127.492	129.531
11.0	117.169	120.474	122.819	124.419
11.5	114.000	116.606	118.426	119.649
12.0	110.963	112.936	114.293	115.191
12.5	108.050	109.451	110.401	111.020
13.0	105.256	106.141	106.732	107.112
13.5	102.575	102.994	103.270	103.445
14.0	100.000	100.000	100.000	100.000
14.5	97.528	97.150	96.908	96.759
15.0	95.153	94.436	93.983	93.707
15.5	92.870	91.849	91.212	90.828
16.0	90.675	89.381	88.584	88.110
16.5	88.564	87.026	86.091	85.541
17.0	86.533	84.778	83.723	83.110
17.5	84.578	82.629	81.471	80.806
18.0	82.695	80.575	79.329	78.620
18.5	80.882	78.610	77.289	76.545
19.0	79.135	76.728	75.344	74.572
19.5	77.451	74.926	73.489	72.695
20.0	75.827	73.199	71.719	70.907
20.5	74.260	71.543	70.027	69.202
21.0	72.748	69.953	68.409	67.576
21.5	71.289	68.428	66.860	66.022
22.0	69.880	66.962	65.378	64.536
22.5	68.519	65.553	63.957	63.114
23.0	67.203	64.198	62.594	61.753
23.5	65.932	62.895	61.286	60.448
24.0	64.702	61.640	60.030	59.196
24.5	63.512	60.431	58.823	57.994

VALUE OF AMORTIZING MORTGAGE LOANS
AS PERCENTAGE OF FACE VALUE

FACE INTEREST RATE: 14.25 %

YIELD TO	TERM OF LOAN (YEARS)			
MATURITY	15	20	25	30
10.0	125.495	130.745	134.580	137.275
10.5	121.999	126.376	129.522	131.697
11.0	118.651	122.237	124.774	126.500
11.5	115.442	118.312	120.311	121.650
12.0	112.366	114.589	116.113	117.118
12.5	109.416	111.053	112.159	112.877
13.0	106.587	107.694	108.431	108.903
13.5	103.871	104.501	104.914	105.175
14.0	101.264	101.463	101.592	101.672
14.5	98.761	98.572	98.451	98.377
15.0	96.356	95.818	95.479	95.274
15.5	94.044	93.193	92.664	92.347
16.0	91.821	90.689	89.995	89.584
16.5	89.683	88.300	87.462	86.972
17.0	87.627	86.018	85.056	84.499
17.5	85.647	83.838	82.768	82.157
18.0	83.741	81.754	80.592	79.935
18.5	81.905	79.760	78.519	77.825
19.0	80.135	77.851	76.544	75.819
19.5	78.430	76.022	74.660	73.911
20.0	76.785	74.270	72.860	72.093
20.5	75.199	72.590	71.141	70.360
21.0	73.668	70.977	69.498	68.706
21.5	72.190	69.429	67.925	67.126
22.0	70.763	67.942	66.419	65.615
22.5	69.385	66.512	64.975	64.170
23.0	68.053	65.138	63.590	62.786
23.5	66.765	63.815	62.262	61.459
24.0	65.520	62.542	60.986	60.186
24.5	64.315	61.315	59.759	58.964

VALUE OF AMORTIZING MORTGAGE LOANS
AS PERCENTAGE OF FACE VALUE

FACE INTEREST RATE: 14.5 %

YIELD TO MATURITY	TERM OF LOAN (YEARS)			
	15	20	25	30
10.0	127.070	132.639	136.696	139.539
10.5	123.530	128.207	131.560	133.869
11.0	120.140	124.008	126.737	128.586
11.5	116.890	120.027	122.204	123.656
12.0	113.776	116.249	117.939	119.049
12.5	110.789	112.662	113.923	114.739
13.0	107.924	109.255	110.137	110.699
13.5	105.175	106.015	106.565	106.910
14.0	102.535	102.933	103.190	103.349
14.5	100.000	100.000	100.000	100.000
15.0	97.565	97.206	96.981	96.845
15.5	95.224	94.543	94.121	93.870
16.0	92.973	92.003	91.410	91.062
16.5	90.809	89.579	88.837	88.406
17.0	88.726	87.265	86.394	85.893
17.5	86.722	85.053	84.070	83.512
18.0	84.792	82.938	81.860	81.253
18.5	82.932	80.915	79.754	79.109
19.0	81.141	78.979	77.748	77.070
19.5	79.414	77.124	75.834	75.130
20.0	77.749	75.346	74.006	73.282
20.5	76.143	73.641	72.261	71.520
21.0	74.593	72.005	70.591	69.839
21.5	73.096	70.435	68.993	68.233
22.0	71.651	68.926	67.463	66.698
22.5	70.256	67.476	65.997	65.228
23.0	68.907	66.081	64.591	63.821
23.5	67.603	64.740	63.241	62.472
24.0	66.342	63.448	61.945	61.179
24.5	65.122	62.203	60.699	59.937

VALUE OF AMORTIZING MORTGAGE LOANS
AS PERCENTAGE OF FACE VALUE

FACE INTEREST RATE: 14.75 %

YIELD TO MATURITY	TERM OF LOAN (YEARS)			
	15	20	25	30
10.0	128.652	134.541	138.821	141.809
10.5	125.068	130.046	133.604	136.047
11.0	121.636	125.787	128.706	130.678
11.5	118.346	121.748	124.103	125.668
12.0	115.193	117.916	119.772	120.986
12.5	112.169	114.278	115.693	116.605
13.0	109.268	110.821	111.848	112.500
13.5	106.484	107.536	108.220	108.649
14.0	103.812	104.410	104.794	105.030
14.5	101.245	101.434	101.554	101.627
15.0	98.780	98.600	98.488	98.421
15.5	96.410	95.899	95.584	95.397
16.0	94.131	93.323	92.831	92.543
16.5	91.940	90.864	90.218	89.844
17.0	89.831	88.516	87.736	87.290
17.5	87.802	86.273	85.377	84.870
18.0	85.847	84.128	83.132	82.575
18.5	83.965	82.076	80.994	80.395
19.0	82.151	80.112	78.956	78.323
19.5	80.403	78.230	77.012	76.352
20.0	78.717	76.427	75.156	74.474
20.5	77.091	74.697	73.383	72.684
21.0	75.521	73.038	71.688	70.975
21.5	74.007	71.445	70.065	69.343
22.0	72.544	69.915	68.512	67.782
22.5	71.130	68.444	67.023	66.289
23.0	69.765	67.029	65.594	64.859
23.5	68.445	65.668	64.224	63.489
24.0	67.168	64.358	62.907	62.174
24.5	65.933	63.095	61.642	60.912

VALUE OF AMORTIZING MORTGAGE LOANS
AS PERCENTAGE OF FACE VALUE

FACE INTEREST RATE: 15 %

YIELD TO MATURITY	TERM OF LOAN (YEARS)			
	15	20	25	30
10.0	130.242	136.452	140.952	144.084
10.5	126.613	131.892	135.655	138.230
11.0	123.138	127.573	130.682	132.775
11.5	119.808	123.476	126.008	127.684
12.0	116.616	119.590	121.610	122.927
12.5	113.554	115.900	117.469	118.476
13.0	110.618	112.395	113.565	114.305
13.5	107.800	109.062	109.882	110.392
14.0	105.094	105.892	106.402	106.716
14.5	102.496	102.874	103.113	103.257
15.0	100.000	100.000	100.000	100.000
15.5	97.601	97.260	97.051	96.928
16.0	95.294	94.647	94.256	94.028
16.5	93.075	92.154	91.603	91.286
17.0	90.941	89.773	89.083	88.691
17.5	88.886	87.498	86.687	86.232
18.0	86.908	85.322	84.408	83.900
18.5	85.002	83.241	82.237	81.685
19.0	83.166	81.249	80.168	79.580
19.5	81.396	79.341	78.194	77.577
20.0	79.690	77.512	76.310	75.669
20.5	78.043	75.758	74.510	73.850
21.0	76.455	74.075	72.788	72.114
21.5	74.921	72.459	71.141	70.456
22.0	73.440	70.907	69.563	68.870
22.5	72.009	69.415	68.051	67.353
23.0	70.627	67.981	66.601	65.900
23.5	69.290	66.600	65.210	64.507
24.0	67.998	65.271	63.873	63.172
24.5	66.748	63.991	62.589	61.889

VALUE OF AMORTIZING MORTGAGE LOANS
AS PERCENTAGE OF FACE VALUE

FACE INTEREST RATE: 15.25 %

YIELD TO MATURITY	TERM OF LOAN (YEARS) 15	20	25	30
10.0	131.839	138.370	143.090	146.365
10.5	128.166	133.746	137.713	140.418
11.0	124.649	129.366	132.664	134.876
11.5	121.277	125.212	127.919	129.705
12.0	118.046	121.271	123.455	124.873
12.5	114.947	117.529	119.251	120.351
13.0	111.975	113.975	115.288	116.115
13.5	109.122	110.595	111.548	112.139
14.0	106.383	107.380	108.016	108.405
14.5	103.753	104.320	104.677	104.892
15.0	101.226	101.406	101.517	101.583
15.5	98.798	98.628	98.523	98.462
16.0	96.463	95.978	95.685	95.516
16.5	94.217	93.449	92.992	92.731
17.0	92.056	91.035	90.434	90.095
17.5	89.976	88.728	88.002	87.597
18.0	87.974	86.522	85.688	85.228
18.5	86.045	84.411	83.485	82.978
19.0	84.186	82.391	81.384	80.840
19.5	82.395	80.456	79.381	78.805
20.0	80.667	78.601	77.468	76.867
20.5	79.000	76.823	75.640	75.019
21.0	77.392	75.116	73.892	73.255
21.5	75.840	73.478	72.220	71.571
22.0	74.341	71.904	70.619	69.960
22.5	72.892	70.391	69.084	68.419
23.0	71.493	68.936	67.612	66.943
23.5	70.140	67.536	66.199	65.528
24.0	68.832	66.189	64.842	64.171
24.5	67.566	64.891	63.538	62.869

VALUE OF AMORTIZING MORTGAGE LOANS
AS PERCENTAGE OF FACE VALUE

FACE INTEREST RATE: 15.5 %

YIELD TO MATURITY	TERM OF LOAN (YEARS) 15	20	25	30
10.0	133.443	140.295	145.234	148.651
10.5	129.726	135.608	139.776	142.611
11.0	126.165	131.166	134.652	136.983
11.5	122.753	126.954	129.836	131.731
12.0	119.482	122.959	125.305	126.823
12.5	116.346	119.165	121.038	122.231
13.0	113.337	115.561	117.016	117.928
13.5	110.450	112.134	113.220	113.891
14.0	107.678	108.875	109.635	110.098
14.5	105.015	105.772	106.246	106.530
15.0	102.458	102.817	103.038	103.169
15.5	100.000	100.000	100.000	100.000
16.0	97.636	97.313	97.119	97.008
16.5	95.363	94.750	94.386	94.179
17.0	93.177	92.302	91.789	91.502
17.5	91.071	89.962	89.321	88.965
18.0	89.044	87.726	86.972	86.559
18.5	87.092	85.586	84.736	84.274
19.0	85.211	83.538	82.604	82.102
19.5	83.397	81.576	80.570	80.036
20.0	81.648	79.695	78.629	78.067
20.5	79.962	77.892	76.774	76.190
21.0	78.334	76.162	75.000	74.399
21.5	76.763	74.500	73.302	72.688
22.0	75.245	72.904	71.677	71.053
22.5	73.779	71.371	70.119	69.487
23.0	72.363	69.896	68.625	67.989
23.5	70.994	68.476	67.191	66.552
24.0	69.669	67.110	65.814	65.174
24.5	68.389	65.794	64.490	63.850

VALUE OF AMORTIZING MORTGAGE LOANS
AS PERCENTAGE OF FACE VALUE

FACE INTEREST RATE: 15.75 %

YIELD TO MATURITY	TERM OF LOAN (YEARS)			
	15	20	25	30
10.0	135.055	142.228	147.385	150.941
10.5	131.293	137.476	141.847	144.808
11.0	127.689	132.973	136.647	139.093
11.5	124.236	128.704	131.759	133.760
12.0	120.926	124.653	127.161	128.777
12.5	117.751	120.807	122.831	124.114
13.0	114.706	117.153	118.749	119.745
13.5	111.784	113.679	114.897	115.646
14.0	108.978	110.375	111.259	111.794
14.5	106.284	107.229	107.819	108.171
15.0	103.696	104.234	104.564	104.759
15.5	101.208	101.378	101.481	101.541
16.0	98.816	98.654	98.558	98.502
16.5	96.515	96.055	95.784	95.630
17.0	94.302	93.573	93.149	92.912
17.5	92.171	91.202	90.644	90.336
18.0	90.120	88.934	88.260	87.893
18.5	88.144	86.765	85.991	85.573
19.0	86.240	84.689	83.827	83.367
19.5	84.404	82.700	81.763	81.269
20.0	82.635	80.793	79.793	79.270
20.5	80.927	78.965	77.911	77.364
21.0	79.280	77.211	76.111	75.546
21.5	77.690	75.527	74.388	73.808
22.0	76.154	73.909	72.738	72.148
22.5	74.670	72.354	71.157	70.558
23.0	73.237	70.859	69.641	69.036
23.5	71.851	69.420	68.186	67.577
24.0	70.511	68.035	66.788	66.178
24.5	69.215	66.700	65.445	64.834

VALUE OF AMORTIZING MORTGAGE LOANS
AS PERCENTAGE OF FACE VALUE

FACE INTEREST RATE: 16 %

YIELD TO MATURITY	TERM OF LOAN (YEARS) 15	20	25	30
10.0	136.673	144.168	149.542	153.236
10.5	132.866	139.351	143.922	147.010
11.0	129.219	134.787	138.646	141.208
11.5	125.725	130.459	133.687	135.794
12.0	122.375	126.353	129.022	130.735
12.5	119.162	122.454	124.628	126.001
13.0	116.081	118.751	120.487	121.566
13.5	113.124	115.230	116.578	117.404
14.0	110.284	111.880	112.887	113.494
14.5	107.558	108.692	109.397	109.816
15.0	104.938	105.655	106.094	106.352
15.5	102.421	102.761	102.966	103.085
16.0	100.000	100.000	100.000	100.000
16.5	97.672	97.365	97.185	97.084
17.0	95.432	94.850	94.512	94.324
17.5	93.276	92.446	91.970	91.709
18.0	91.200	90.147	89.552	89.229
18.5	89.200	87.949	87.249	86.874
19.0	87.273	85.844	85.054	84.635
19.5	85.416	83.828	82.960	82.504
20.0	83.625	81.895	80.961	80.475
20.5	81.897	80.042	79.051	78.541
21.0	80.230	78.264	77.224	76.694
21.5	78.621	76.557	75.477	74.931
22.0	77.067	74.917	73.803	73.244
22.5	75.565	73.341	72.199	71.631
23.0	74.115	71.825	70.660	70.086
23.5	72.712	70.367	69.184	68.605
24.0	71.356	68.963	67.766	67.184
24.5	70.044	67.610	66.403	65.820

VALUE OF AMORTIZING MORTGAGE LOANS
AS PERCENTAGE OF FACE VALUE

FACE INTEREST RATE: 16.25 %

YIELD TO MATURITY	TERM OF LOAN (YEARS)			
	15	20	25	30
10.0	138.299	146.115	151.704	155.535
10.5	134.446	141.233	146.004	149.216
11.0	130.756	136.608	140.651	143.327
11.5	127.220	132.221	135.621	137.832
12.0	123.830	128.059	130.888	132.697
12.5	120.579	124.108	126.430	127.892
13.0	117.461	120.355	122.229	123.390
13.5	114.469	116.786	118.264	119.165
14.0	111.596	113.391	114.519	115.197
14.5	108.837	110.160	110.979	111.464
15.0	106.186	107.082	107.629	107.947
15.5	103.639	104.148	104.455	104.631
16.0	101.189	101.350	101.446	101.500
16.5	98.833	98.680	98.591	98.541
17.0	96.567	96.131	95.879	95.740
17.5	94.385	93.694	93.300	93.085
18.0	92.284	91.365	90.847	90.568
18.5	90.261	89.136	88.511	88.177
19.0	88.311	87.003	86.284	85.905
19.5	86.432	84.960	84.160	83.742
20.0	84.619	83.001	82.132	81.683
20.5	82.871	81.123	80.194	79.719
21.0	81.184	79.321	78.341	77.845
21.5	79.556	77.591	76.568	76.055
22.0	77.983	75.929	74.870	74.343
22.5	76.464	74.331	73.243	72.706
23.0	74.996	72.795	71.682	71.137
23.5	73.577	71.317	70.184	69.634
24.0	72.205	69.894	68.746	68.192
24.5	70.877	68.523	67.363	66.808

VALUE OF AMORTIZING MORTGAGE LOANS
AS PERCENTAGE OF FACE VALUE

FACE INTEREST RATE: 16.5 %

YIELD TO MATURITY	TERM OF LOAN (YEARS)			
	15	20	25	30
10.0	139.931	148.069	153.873	157.839
10.5	136.033	143.122	148.091	151.425
11.0	132.300	138.434	142.662	145.449
11.5	128.721	133.989	137.559	139.873
12.0	125.292	129.772	132.759	134.662
12.5	122.002	125.768	128.238	129.786
13.0	118.848	121.964	123.976	125.217
13.5	115.820	118.348	119.955	120.930
14.0	112.913	114.908	116.156	116.903
14.5	110.121	111.633	112.565	113.114
15.0	107.440	108.514	109.167	109.546
15.5	104.862	105.541	105.948	106.181
16.0	102.384	102.706	102.896	103.004
16.5	100.000	100.000	100.000	100.000
17.0	97.707	97.416	97.249	97.157
17.5	95.499	94.947	94.634	94.464
18.0	93.374	92.587	92.146	91.909
18.5	91.326	90.328	89.776	89.483
19.0	89.354	88.167	87.517	87.177
19.5	87.452	86.096	85.363	84.983
20.0	85.618	84.111	83.306	82.892
20.5	83.849	82.208	81.340	80.900
21.0	82.142	80.382	79.461	78.998
21.5	80.495	78.629	77.663	77.181
22.0	78.904	76.944	75.940	75.444
22.5	77.366	75.325	74.290	73.782
23.0	75.881	73.769	72.707	72.191
23.5	74.445	72.271	71.187	70.665
24.0	73.057	70.829	69.728	69.202
24.5	71.714	69.439	68.326	67.797

VALUE OF AMORTIZING MORTGAGE LOANS
AS PERCENTAGE OF FACE VALUE

FACE INTEREST RATE: 16.75 %

YIELD TO MATURITY	TERM OF LOAN (YEARS)			
	15	20	25	30
10.0	141.570	150.030	156.046	160.146
10.5	137.626	145.017	150.183	153.639
11.0	133.849	140.267	144.677	147.576
11.5	130.229	135.763	139.502	141.917
12.0	126.759	131.490	134.634	136.630
12.5	123.431	127.433	130.049	131.683
13.0	120.240	123.579	125.727	127.047
13.5	117.176	119.915	121.649	122.698
14.0	114.235	116.429	117.797	118.612
14.5	111.411	113.111	114.155	114.768
15.0	108.698	109.951	110.709	111.147
15.5	106.090	106.939	107.445	107.733
16.0	103.583	104.066	104.350	104.509
16.5	101.171	101.324	101.413	101.462
17.0	98.851	98.706	98.623	98.578
17.5	96.618	96.204	95.971	95.845
18.0	94.467	93.813	93.447	93.253
18.5	92.396	91.524	91.044	90.791
19.0	90.400	89.334	88.754	88.451
19.5	88.476	87.236	86.568	86.225
20.0	86.621	85.225	84.482	84.104
20.5	84.831	83.296	82.489	82.082
21.0	83.105	81.446	80.583	80.153
21.5	81.438	79.670	78.760	78.309
22.0	79.828	77.963	77.013	76.547
22.5	78.273	76.323	75.339	74.861
23.0	76.770	74.745	73.734	73.246
23.5	75.317	73.228	72.193	71.698
24.0	73.912	71.766	70.713	70.213
24.5	72.554	70.359	69.291	68.788

VALUE OF AMORTIZING MORTGAGE LOANS
AS PERCENTAGE OF FACE VALUE

FACE INTEREST RATE: 17 %

| YIELD TO MATURITY | TERM OF LOAN (YEARS) | | | |
	15	20	25	30
10.0	143.215	151.996	158.225	162.457
10.5	139.226	146.918	152.279	155.856
11.0	135.405	142.106	146.697	149.705
11.5	131.742	137.543	141.450	143.965
12.0	128.232	133.214	136.514	138.602
12.5	124.866	129.104	131.865	133.583
13.0	121.637	125.199	127.483	128.881
13.5	118.538	121.487	123.348	124.468
14.0	115.563	117.955	119.442	120.323
14.5	112.706	114.594	115.749	116.424
15.0	109.961	111.392	112.255	112.751
15.5	107.323	108.340	108.945	109.288
16.0	104.787	105.430	105.807	106.017
16.5	102.347	102.652	102.829	102.926
17.0	100.000	100.000	100.000	100.000
17.5	97.741	97.466	97.311	97.228
18.0	95.565	95.042	94.752	94.598
18.5	93.470	92.724	92.315	92.101
19.0	91.451	90.505	89.993	89.728
19.5	89.504	88.379	87.777	87.469
20.0	87.628	86.342	85.662	85.318
20.5	85.817	84.388	83.641	83.267
21.0	84.070	82.514	81.709	81.309
21.5	82.384	80.714	79.859	79.439
22.0	80.755	78.985	78.088	77.652
22.5	79.182	77.323	76.391	75.941
23.0	77.662	75.725	74.763	74.303
23.5	76.193	74.188	73.201	72.733
24.0	74.772	72.707	71.701	71.227
24.5	73.397	71.281	70.259	69.781

VALUE OF AMORTIZING MORTGAGE LOANS
AS PERCENTAGE OF FACE VALUE

FACE INTEREST RATE: 17.25 %

YIELD TO MATURITY	TERM OF LOAN (YEARS)			
	15	20	25	30
10.0	144.868	153.970	160.409	164.771
10.5	140.832	148.825	154.381	158.076
11.0	136.967	143.951	148.722	151.838
11.5	133.262	139.329	143.402	146.016
12.0	129.712	134.943	138.398	140.576
12.5	126.307	130.780	133.685	135.486
13.0	123.040	126.824	129.242	130.717
13.5	119.906	123.064	125.050	126.242
14.0	116.896	119.487	121.091	122.037
14.5	114.006	116.082	117.347	118.082
15.0	111.230	112.838	113.804	114.357
15.5	108.561	109.747	110.449	110.845
16.0	105.996	106.799	107.267	107.528
16.5	103.528	103.985	104.248	104.392
17.0	101.154	101.298	101.380	101.425
17.5	98.868	98.731	98.654	98.613
18.0	96.668	96.276	96.060	95.946
18.5	94.548	93.928	93.589	93.413
19.0	92.506	91.680	91.235	91.006
19.5	90.537	89.527	88.989	88.715
20.0	88.639	87.463	86.844	86.533
20.5	86.807	85.484	84.796	84.453
21.0	85.040	83.585	82.836	82.468
21.5	83.334	81.762	80.962	80.571
22.0	81.687	80.010	79.166	78.758
22.5	80.096	78.327	77.446	77.023
23.0	78.558	76.708	75.795	75.362
23.5	77.072	75.151	74.211	73.769
24.0	75.634	73.651	72.690	72.241
24.5	74.244	72.207	71.229	70.775

VALUE OF AMORTIZING MORTGAGE LOANS
AS PERCENTAGE OF FACE VALUE

FACE INTEREST RATE: 17.5 %

YIELD TO MATURITY	TERM OF LOAN (YEARS) 15	20	25	30
10.0	146.526	155.949	162.598	167.089
10.5	142.444	150.738	156.488	160.300
11.0	138.535	145.801	150.751	153.974
11.5	134.788	141.120	145.359	148.070
12.0	131.197	136.678	140.286	142.554
12.5	127.752	132.461	135.509	137.392
13.0	124.449	128.455	131.006	132.555
13.5	121.278	124.646	126.757	128.017
14.0	118.234	121.023	122.743	123.754
14.5	115.311	117.574	118.948	119.743
15.0	112.503	114.289	115.357	115.966
15.5	109.804	111.158	111.956	112.404
16.0	107.209	108.171	108.731	109.040
16.5	104.713	105.322	105.670	105.861
17.0	102.312	102.600	102.764	102.851
17.5	100.000	100.000	100.000	100.000
18.0	97.774	97.514	97.371	97.295
18.5	95.630	95.135	94.866	94.727
19.0	93.565	92.858	92.480	92.286
19.5	91.574	90.677	90.203	89.963
20.0	89.653	88.587	88.029	87.750
20.5	87.801	86.583	85.953	85.641
21.0	86.014	84.659	83.967	83.628
21.5	84.288	82.813	82.066	81.704
22.0	82.622	81.039	80.246	79.866
22.5	81.013	79.334	78.502	78.107
23.0	79.457	77.694	76.829	76.422
23.5	77.954	76.117	75.224	74.807
24.0	76.500	74.598	73.682	73.257
24.5	75.093	73.135	72.200	71.770

VALUE OF AMORTIZING MORTGAGE LOANS
AS PERCENTAGE OF FACE VALUE

FACE INTEREST RATE: 17.75 %

YIELD TO MATURITY	TERM OF LOAN (YEARS)			
	15	20	25	30
10.0	148.191	157.934	164.791	169.410
10.5	144.063	152.657	158.599	162.526
11.0	140.109	147.657	152.785	156.112
11.5	136.319	142.916	147.320	150.127
12.0	132.687	138.418	142.179	144.534
12.5	129.204	134.147	137.337	139.300
13.0	125.863	130.090	132.773	134.396
13.5	122.656	126.233	128.466	129.795
14.0	119.578	122.563	124.398	125.473
14.5	116.621	119.070	120.553	121.407
15.0	113.781	115.744	116.913	117.577
15.5	111.052	112.573	113.466	113.965
16.0	108.427	109.548	110.197	110.555
16.5	105.903	106.662	107.096	107.331
17.0	103.474	103.906	104.150	104.280
17.5	101.136	101.273	101.349	101.389
18.0	98.885	98.755	98.684	98.647
18.5	96.717	96.346	96.146	96.043
19.0	94.628	94.041	93.727	93.568
19.5	92.614	91.832	91.420	91.213
20.0	90.672	89.715	89.217	88.969
20.5	88.799	87.685	87.112	86.830
21.0	86.991	85.737	85.099	84.789
21.5	85.246	83.867	83.173	82.839
22.0	83.561	82.071	81.329	80.975
22.5	81.933	80.344	79.561	79.191
23.0	80.360	78.683	77.866	77.483
23.5	78.840	77.086	76.239	75.846
24.0	77.369	75.547	74.676	74.275
24.5	75.947	74.066	73.174	72.767

481

PREMIUMS FOR ASSUMABLE LOANS
(Maximum Premiums for Assumable Loans as Percentage of Loan Balance)

Homes are often sold with a provision for the buyer to assume the existing mortgage, rather than arrange new financing. Some older loans carry interest rates below the rates charged on new loans. When the buyer assumes such a loan (and the lender does not have the authority to escalate the rate), monthly loan payments will be lower than for a comparable loan at the higher market rate of interest. Consequently, buyers are often willing to pay a higher price for the home because of the assumable mortgage.

The tables which follow provide indications of the highest additional price sellers should expect to receive for specific assumable loans. At the premium shown in the table, a buyer would be indifferent between assuming the loan and arranging new financing, assuming the buyer has enough additional cash to pay the premium. In the actual market, the price will be set through negotiation between buyer and seller, so the actual premium paid for the favorable assumption tends to be lower than the maximum indicated in the table.

To use the tables, you need the following information:

1. *The market value of the home with new financing.* How much would the home be worth if the assumable loan did not exist? A knowledgeable real estate appraiser should be able to provide an indication.

2. *The interest rate on new financing* (current rate). What is the current interest rate on new mortgage loans with a maturity similar to the remaining term on the assumable loan? The tables cover current rates ranging from 7% to 21.5% in .5% intervals.

3. *The interest rate on the assumable loan* (face interest rate). This is the rate you are paying on the existing loan and that the buyer will be paying on the assumed loan. In some cases, lenders may raise the rate above what the seller has paid but keep it below that of new financing. The rate charged to the buyer is the rate to use. The tables cover face rates from 6% to 17.75% in intervals of .25%.

4. *The remaining term of the existing loan.* How many more years are left on the loan that will be assumed? The tables cover terms of 15, 20, 25, and 30 years. Select the term which is closest to the actual remaining term on the loan.

5. *The remaining balance of the assumable loan.* How much is still owed on the existing loan? This represents the amount of the purchase price that will be covered by the assumed loan.

Example. A home is valued at $60,000. The owner has an assumable loan with a remaining principal balance of $30,000 and a 21-year remaining term. The loan may be assumed at the existing interest rate of 6%. What is the maximum price the seller can expect to receive if the current market interest rate for 20-year loans is 14%?

Look at the first table covering face interest rates of 6%. Look down the "CURRENT RATE" column to find 14.00%. Follow this row over to the column under 20-year remaining term. (The table has no 21-year remaining term column, so use the column which most closely matches the actual remaining term in the problem.) The premium listed in the table is 42.387%. Multiply this percentage by the remaining balance of the assumed loan, or $30,000. The result is $12,716 which is added to the home's market value of $60,000. The home could sell for as much as $72,716 owing to the assumable loan.

Example. A home is for sale. The seller wants $70,000 cash which is in line with prices of similar homes on the market. Alternatively, the seller is willing to provide financing for $50,000 of the price with an amortizing loan at 10% interest over 25 years. If the financing is included, the seller will demand a higher price. If current mortgage interest rates for 25-year loans is 15%, what is the highest price a buyer should pay under the favorable financing arrangement?

Look for the table with a "FACE INTEREST RATE" of 10%. Follow down the "CURRENT RATE" column to find 15.00%. Follow this row to the "25" column and read the premium of 29.054%. Multiply this percentage by the balance of $50,000 to obtain the amount of $14,527. The buyer could pay up to $70,000 plus $14,527, or $84,527, for the home with the seller financing.

MAXIMUM PREMIUM FOR ASSUMABLE LOANS
AS PERCENTAGE OF LOAN BALANCE

FACE INTEREST RATE: 6 %

CURRENT RATE	REMAINING TERM OF LOAN (YEARS)			
	15	20	25	30
7.0	6.116	7.593	8.840	9.883
7.5	8.970	11.068	12.813	14.254
8.0	11.698	14.348	16.521	18.291
8.5	14.307	17.445	19.985	22.026
9.0	16.801	20.372	23.224	25.487
9.5	19.188	23.140	26.256	28.697
10.0	21.473	25.760	29.097	31.681
10.5	23.661	28.241	31.761	34.457
11.0	25.756	30.591	34.263	37.043
11.5	27.764	32.820	36.614	39.457
12.0	29.688	34.934	38.826	41.713
12.5	31.534	36.942	40.909	43.823
13.0	33.305	38.849	42.873	45.801
13.5	35.004	40.662	44.726	47.656
14.0	36.635	42.387	46.476	49.400
14.5	38.202	44.029	48.131	51.039
15.0	39.707	45.593	49.697	52.584
15.5	41.153	47.083	51.180	54.040
16.0	42.544	48.505	52.586	55.416
16.5	43.882	49.861	53.921	56.716
17.0	45.169	51.157	55.188	57.946
17.5	46.407	52.395	56.393	59.112
18.0	47.600	53.578	57.540	60.218
18.5	48.749	54.711	58.632	61.268
19.0	49.856	55.795	59.673	62.266
19.5	50.923	56.833	60.666	63.216
20.0	51.953	57.828	61.613	64.121
20.5	52.945	58.782	62.519	64.983
21.0	53.903	59.698	63.385	65.806
21.5	54.828	60.577	64.214	66.593

MAXIMUM PREMIUM FOR ASSUMABLE LOANS
AS PERCENTAGE OF LOAN BALANCE

FACE INTEREST RATE: 6.25 %

CURRENT RATE	REMAINING TERM OF LOAN (YEARS)			
	15	20	25	30
7.0	4.607	5.723	6.666	7.453
7.5	7.507	9.269	10.734	11.942
8.0	10.279	12.615	14.531	16.088
8.5	12.930	15.775	18.077	19.924
9.0	15.464	18.761	21.393	23.478
9.5	17.889	21.586	24.497	26.775
10.0	20.211	24.258	27.406	29.839
10.5	22.434	26.789	30.134	32.690
11.0	24.563	29.187	32.695	35.346
11.5	26.603	31.461	35.102	37.825
12.0	28.559	33.618	37.367	40.141
12.5	30.434	35.666	39.500	42.309
13.0	32.233	37.612	41.510	44.340
13.5	33.959	39.462	43.408	46.245
14.0	35.617	41.221	45.200	48.035
14.5	37.209	42.897	46.894	49.719
15.0	38.738	44.492	48.497	51.305
15.5	40.208	46.013	50.016	52.801
16.0	41.621	47.463	51.455	54.214
16.5	42.980	48.847	52.822	55.549
17.0	44.287	50.169	54.120	56.812
17.5	45.546	51.432	55.353	58.010
18.0	46.758	52.639	56.527	59.145
18.5	47.926	53.794	57.645	60.224
19.0	49.050	54.900	58.711	61.249
19.5	50.135	55.960	59.727	62.224
20.0	51.180	56.975	60.698	63.153
20.5	52.189	57.948	61.625	64.039
21.0	53.162	58.882	62.512	64.885
21.5	54.102	59.779	63.360	65.692

MAXIMUM PREMIUM FOR ASSUMABLE LOANS
AS PERCENTAGE OF LOAN BALANCE

FACE INTEREST RATE: 6.5 %

CURRENT RATE	REMAINING TERM OF LOAN (YEARS)			
	15	20	25	30
7.0	3.083	3.834	4.467	4.995
7.5	6.030	7.450	8.631	9.603
8.0	8.846	10.863	12.517	13.859
8.5	11.539	14.087	16.147	17.797
9.0	14.114	17.133	19.541	21.445
9.5	16.578	20.014	22.718	24.830
10.0	18.937	22.740	25.695	27.975
10.5	21.195	25.321	28.487	30.902
11.0	23.358	27.767	31.109	33.629
11.5	25.431	30.087	33.573	36.173
12.0	27.418	32.287	35.891	38.551
12.5	29.323	34.376	38.074	40.776
13.0	31.151	36.361	40.132	42.861
13.5	32.905	38.248	42.074	44.817
14.0	34.589	40.043	43.908	46.655
14.5	36.206	41.752	45.642	48.384
15.0	37.759	43.379	47.283	50.012
15.5	39.253	44.930	48.838	51.548
16.0	40.688	46.410	50.312	52.997
16.5	42.069	47.822	51.710	54.368
17.0	43.398	49.170	53.039	55.665
17.5	44.677	50.458	54.301	56.894
18.0	45.908	51.690	55.503	58.060
18.5	47.094	52.868	56.647	59.167
19.0	48.237	53.996	57.738	60.219
19.5	49.338	55.077	58.779	61.221
20.0	50.401	56.112	59.772	62.175
20.5	51.425	57.105	60.721	63.084
21.0	52.414	58.058	61.628	63.952
21.5	53.369	58.973	62.497	64.781

MAXIMUM PREMIUM FOR ASSUMABLE LOANS
AS PERCENTAGE OF LOAN BALANCE

FACE INTEREST RATE: 6.75 %

CURRENT RATE	REMAINING TERM OF LOAN (YEARS)			
	15	20	25	30
7.0	1.548	1.926	2.245	2.511
7.5	4.541	5.614	6.506	7.239
8.0	7.402	9.095	10.482	11.607
8.5	10.138	12.383	14.197	15.648
9.0	12.753	15.489	17.670	19.391
9.5	15.257	18.427	20.921	22.864
10.0	17.653	21.208	23.967	26.092
10.5	19.947	23.840	26.824	29.095
11.0	22.144	26.335	29.507	31.893
11.5	24.249	28.700	32.028	34.504
12.0	26.268	30.944	34.400	36.944
12.5	28.203	33.075	36.634	39.228
13.0	30.060	35.099	38.740	41.367
13.5	31.842	37.023	40.727	43.374
14.0	33.552	38.854	42.604	45.260
14.5	35.195	40.596	44.378	47.034
15.0	36.773	42.256	46.057	48.705
15.5	38.290	43.838	47.648	50.281
16.0	39.749	45.347	49.156	51.768
16.5	41.152	46.787	50.587	53.175
17.0	42.501	48.162	51.946	54.506
17.5	43.800	49.476	53.239	55.767
18.0	45.051	50.732	54.468	56.963
18.5	46.256	51.933	55.639	58.099
19.0	47.417	53.084	56.755	59.179
19.5	48.536	54.186	57.820	60.207
20.0	49.615	55.242	58.836	61.185
20.5	50.656	56.255	59.808	62.119
21.0	51.660	57.226	60.736	63.009
21.5	52.630	58.159	61.625	63.860

MAXIMUM PREMIUM FOR ASSUMABLE LOANS
AS PERCENTAGE OF LOAN BALANCE

FACE INTEREST RATE: 7 %

CURRENT RATE	REMAINING TERM OF LOAN (YEARS)			
	15	20	25	30
7.0	0.000	0.000	0.000	0.000
7.5	3.040	3.760	4.359	4.850
8.0	5.946	7.310	8.427	9.330
8.5	8.725	10.662	12.226	13.475
9.0	11.381	13.829	15.779	17.315
9.5	13.924	16.825	19.105	20.878
10.0	16.358	19.660	22.221	24.188
10.5	18.688	22.344	25.144	27.269
11.0	20.919	24.888	27.888	30.139
11.5	23.058	27.300	30.467	32.818
12.0	25.108	29.588	32.894	35.320
12.5	27.074	31.760	35.179	37.663
13.0	28.960	33.824	37.333	39.857
13.5	30.770	35.786	39.366	41.916
14.0	32.507	37.653	41.286	43.850
14.5	34.176	39.430	43.101	45.670
15.0	35.779	41.122	44.819	47.384
15.5	37.320	42.735	46.446	49.000
16.0	38.801	44.274	47.989	50.526
16.5	40.226	45.742	49.452	51.969
17.0	41.597	47.144	50.843	53.334
17.5	42.916	48.483	52.165	54.628
18.0	44.187	49.764	53.423	55.855
18.5	45.411	50.989	54.621	57.020
19.0	46.590	52.162	55.762	58.128
19.5	47.727	53.286	56.851	59.182
20.0	48.823	54.363	57.891	60.186
20.5	49.880	55.395	58.885	61.143
21.0	50.900	56.386	59.834	62.056
21.5	51.885	57.337	60.743	62.929

MAXIMUM PREMIUM FOR ASSUMABLE LOANS
AS PERCENTAGE OF LOAN BALANCE

FACE INTEREST RATE: 7.25 %

CURRENT RATE	REMAINING TERM OF LOAN (YEARS)			
	15	20	25	30
7.0	-1.562	-1.945	-2.268	-2.537
7.5	1.526	1.888	2.190	2.436
8.0	4.477	5.507	6.350	7.030
8.5	7.299	8.924	10.236	11.280
9.0	9.997	12.153	13.869	15.218
9.5	12.579	15.207	17.270	18.871
10.0	15.051	18.097	20.457	22.265
10.5	17.418	20.834	23.446	25.424
11.0	19.684	23.427	26.252	28.367
11.5	21.856	25.886	28.890	31.113
12.0	23.939	28.218	31.372	33.680
12.5	25.935	30.433	33.709	36.081
13.0	27.850	32.537	35.912	38.331
13.5	29.688	34.537	37.991	40.443
14.0	31.453	36.440	39.954	42.426
14.5	33.148	38.252	41.811	44.292
15.0	34.776	39.977	43.567	46.049
15.5	36.341	41.621	45.231	47.706
16.0	37.845	43.190	46.809	49.271
16.5	39.292	44.686	48.306	50.751
17.0	40.685	46.115	49.728	52.151
17.5	42.025	47.481	51.080	53.477
18.0	43.315	48.787	52.366	54.735
18.5	44.558	50.036	53.591	55.930
19.0	45.756	51.232	54.759	57.066
19.5	46.910	52.377	55.873	58.147
20.0	48.023	53.475	56.936	59.176
20.5	49.097	54.528	57.952	60.157
21.0	50.133	55.538	58.923	61.094
21.5	51.134	56.508	59.853	61.989

MAXIMUM PREMIUM FOR ASSUMABLE LOANS
AS PERCENTAGE OF LOAN BALANCE

FACE INTEREST RATE: 7.5 %

CURRENT RATE	REMAINING TERM OF LOAN (YEARS)			
	15	20	25	30
7.0	-3.135	-3.907	-4.557	-5.097
7.5	0.000	0.000	0.000	0.000
8.0	2.997	3.688	4.253	4.709
8.5	5.863	7.171	8.226	9.065
9.0	8.603	10.462	11.941	13.100
9.5	11.225	13.575	15.418	16.845
10.0	13.735	16.521	18.676	20.324
10.5	16.138	19.310	21.732	23.562
11.0	18.440	21.953	24.602	26.578
11.5	20.646	24.459	27.298	29.393
12.0	22.760	26.837	29.835	32.024
12.5	24.788	29.094	32.225	34.485
13.0	26.733	31.239	34.477	36.791
13.5	28.599	33.277	36.602	38.955
14.0	30.391	35.217	38.610	40.988
14.5	32.112	37.063	40.508	42.901
15.0	33.765	38.822	42.304	44.702
15.5	35.355	40.498	44.005	46.401
16.0	36.882	42.096	45.618	48.005
16.5	38.352	43.622	47.149	49.521
17.0	39.766	45.078	48.603	50.956
17.5	41.127	46.470	49.985	52.315
18.0	42.437	47.801	51.300	53.605
18.5	43.699	49.074	52.552	54.830
19.0	44.915	50.293	53.746	55.994
19.5	46.088	51.461	54.885	57.101
20.0	47.218	52.580	55.972	58.156
20.5	48.308	53.653	57.011	59.162
21.0	49.361	54.682	58.004	60.122
21.5	50.376	55.671	58.954	61.039

MAXIMUM PREMIUM FOR ASSUMABLE LOANS
AS PERCENTAGE OF LOAN BALANCE

FACE INTEREST RATE: 7.75 %

CURRENT RATE	REMAINING TERM OF LOAN (YEARS)			
	15	20	25	30
7.0	-4.723	-5.888	-6.870	-7.682
7.5	-1.539	-1.907	-2.211	-2.460
8.0	1.504	1.852	2.136	2.365
8.5	4.414	5.401	6.197	6.828
9.0	7.196	8.755	9.993	10.963
9.5	9.858	11.927	13.548	14.799
10.0	12.407	14.929	16.878	18.364
10.5	14.847	17.772	20.002	21.681
11.0	17.184	20.465	22.934	24.772
11.5	19.424	23.019	25.691	27.656
12.0	21.571	25.442	28.284	30.351
12.5	23.630	27.742	30.726	32.873
13.0	25.605	29.928	33.028	35.236
13.5	27.500	32.005	35.201	37.454
14.0	29.320	33.982	37.252	39.537
14.5	31.067	35.863	39.192	41.496
15.0	32.746	37.655	41.028	43.342
15.5	34.359	39.363	42.767	45.082
16.0	35.911	40.992	44.416	46.725
16.5	37.403	42.547	45.980	48.279
17.0	38.838	44.031	47.466	49.749
17.5	40.220	45.450	48.879	51.142
18.0	41.551	46.806	50.223	52.464
18.5	42.832	48.103	51.503	53.718
19.0	44.067	49.345	52.723	54.911
19.5	45.258	50.535	53.887	56.046
20.0	46.405	51.675	54.998	57.127
20.5	47.513	52.769	56.060	58.158
21.0	48.581	53.818	57.075	59.141
21.5	49.613	54.825	58.047	60.081

MAXIMUM PREMIUM FOR ASSUMABLE LOANS
AS PERCENTAGE OF LOAN BALANCE

FACE INTEREST RATE: 8 %

CURRENT RATE	REMAINING TERM OF LOAN (YEARS)			
	15	20	25	30
7.0	-6.322	-7.886	-9.202	-10.290
7.5	-3.090	-3.829	-4.442	-4.941
8.0	0.000	0.000	0.000	0.000
8.5	2.954	3.617	4.149	4.571
9.0	5.779	7.034	8.029	8.806
9.5	8.482	10.266	11.661	12.736
10.0	11.070	13.324	15.064	16.387
10.5	13.547	16.220	18.256	19.784
11.0	15.920	18.964	21.252	22.950
11.5	18.194	21.566	24.069	25.904
12.0	20.374	24.035	26.719	28.665
12.5	22.464	26.379	29.214	31.248
13.0	24.469	28.606	31.567	33.668
13.5	26.393	30.722	33.786	35.939
14.0	28.240	32.736	35.883	38.072
14.5	30.015	34.653	37.865	40.079
15.0	31.719	36.479	39.741	41.969
15.5	33.357	38.219	41.518	43.752
16.0	34.932	39.879	43.202	45.435
16.5	36.447	41.463	44.801	47.026
17.0	37.904	42.975	46.320	48.532
17.5	39.307	44.420	47.763	49.959
18.0	40.658	45.802	49.137	51.312
18.5	41.959	47.124	50.445	52.597
19.0	43.213	48.390	51.691	53.819
19.5	44.422	49.602	52.881	54.982
20.0	45.587	50.764	54.016	56.089
20.5	46.711	51.878	55.101	57.144
21.0	47.796	52.947	56.138	58.152
21.5	48.843	53.973	57.131	59.114

MAXIMUM PREMIUM FOR ASSUMABLE LOANS
AS PERCENTAGE OF LOAN BALANCE

FACE INTEREST RATE: 8.25 %

CURRENT RATE	REMAINING TERM OF LOAN (YEARS)			
	15	20	25	30
7.0	-7.934	-9.902	-11.555	-12.921
7.5	-4.653	-5.769	-6.693	-7.445
8.0	-1.516	-1.868	-2.155	-2.385
8.5	1.483	1.816	2.084	2.295
9.0	4.350	5.297	6.047	6.631
9.5	7.095	8.589	9.757	10.654
10.0	9.721	11.705	13.233	14.393
10.5	12.236	14.655	16.494	17.871
11.0	14.645	17.451	19.555	21.112
11.5	16.954	20.101	22.433	24.137
12.0	19.166	22.616	25.139	26.963
12.5	21.288	25.004	27.689	29.608
13.0	23.324	27.272	30.092	32.086
13.5	25.277	29.428	32.359	34.411
14.0	27.153	31.480	34.501	36.595
14.5	28.954	33.432	36.526	38.650
15.0	30.684	35.292	38.442	40.585
15.5	32.347	37.065	40.257	42.410
16.0	33.946	38.756	41.978	44.134
16.5	35.484	40.369	43.611	45.763
17.0	36.963	41.910	45.163	47.305
17.5	38.387	43.382	46.637	48.765
18.0	39.759	44.790	48.040	50.151
18.5	41.080	46.136	49.377	51.467
19.0	42.352	47.426	50.650	52.718
19.5	43.579	48.660	51.865	53.908
20.0	44.762	49.844	53.025	55.041
20.5	45.903	50.979	54.133	56.122
21.0	47.005	52.068	55.193	57.154
21.5	48.068	53.113	56.207	58.139

MAXIMUM PREMIUM FOR ASSUMABLE LOANS
AS PERCENTAGE OF LOAN BALANCE

FACE INTEREST RATE: 8.5 %

CURRENT RATE	REMAINING TERM OF LOAN (YEARS)			
	15	20	25	30
7.0	-9.559	-11.934	-13.929	-15.574
7.5	-6.228	-7.725	-8.963	-9.969
8.0	-3.044	-3.752	-4.329	-4.790
8.5	0.000	0.000	0.000	0.000
9.0	2.910	3.545	4.047	4.438
9.5	5.696	6.899	7.836	8.555
10.0	8.363	10.072	11.387	12.382
10.5	10.915	13.077	14.717	15.942
11.0	13.360	15.924	17.843	19.259
11.5	15.704	18.623	20.782	22.355
12.0	17.950	21.185	23.546	25.247
12.5	20.104	23.616	26.150	27.954
13.0	22.170	25.927	28.604	30.490
13.5	24.152	28.123	30.920	32.870
14.0	26.056	30.212	33.107	35.106
14.5	27.884	32.201	35.175	37.209
15.0	29.640	34.095	37.132	39.190
15.5	31.328	35.901	38.986	41.058
16.0	32.952	37.623	40.744	42.821
16.5	34.512	39.266	42.411	44.489
17.0	36.014	40.835	43.996	46.067
17.5	37.460	42.335	45.502	47.562
18.0	38.852	43.769	46.935	48.980
18.5	40.193	45.140	48.299	50.327
19.0	41.485	46.453	49.600	51.607
19.5	42.730	47.711	50.841	52.825
20.0	43.931	48.916	52.026	53.985
20.5	45.089	50.072	53.157	55.092
21.0	46.207	51.181	54.240	56.147
21.5	47.286	52.246	55.275	57.156

MAXIMUM PREMIUM FOR ASSUMABLE LOANS
AS PERCENTAGE OF LOAN BALANCE

FACE INTEREST RATE: 8.75 %

CURRENT RATE	REMAINING TERM OF LOAN (YEARS) 15	20	25	30
7.0	-11.195	-13.983	-16.323	-18.247
7.5	-7.814	-9.697	-11.252	-12.512
8.0	-4.583	-5.651	-6.521	-7.214
8.5	-1.493	-1.830	-2.101	-2.313
9.0	1.461	1.780	2.032	2.227
9.5	4.288	5.194	5.900	6.440
10.0	6.994	8.426	9.525	10.355
10.5	9.585	11.486	12.925	13.997
11.0	12.066	14.385	16.117	17.391
11.5	14.445	17.134	19.118	20.559
12.0	16.724	19.742	21.940	23.518
12.5	18.910	22.218	24.599	26.288
13.0	21.007	24.571	27.104	28.883
13.5	23.020	26.807	29.469	31.317
14.0	24.952	28.935	31.702	33.605
14.5	26.807	30.960	33.814	35.756
15.0	28.590	32.889	35.812	37.783
15.5	30.303	34.728	37.704	39.694
16.0	31.950	36.481	39.499	41.499
16.5	33.534	38.155	41.202	43.205
17.0	35.059	39.752	42.819	44.819
17.5	36.526	41.279	44.357	46.349
18.0	37.939	42.739	45.820	47.800
18.5	39.300	44.136	47.213	49.178
19.0	40.611	45.473	48.541	50.488
19.5	41.875	46.754	49.808	51.734
20.0	43.093	47.981	51.018	52.921
20.5	44.269	49.158	52.173	54.053
21.0	45.404	50.288	53.278	55.133
21.5	46.499	51.372	54.336	56.165

MAXIMUM PREMIUM FOR ASSUMABLE LOANS
AS PERCENTAGE OF LOAN BALANCE

FACE INTEREST RATE: 9 %

CURRENT RATE	REMAINING TERM OF LOAN (YEARS)			
	15	20	25	30
7.0	-12.843	-16.049	-18.735	-20.941
7.5	-9.412	-11.685	-13.560	-15.075
8.0	-6.133	-7.566	-8.730	-9.657
8.5	-2.998	-3.676	-4.218	-4.644
9.0	0.000	0.000	0.000	0.000
9.5	2.869	3.477	3.949	4.309
10.0	5.616	6.767	7.649	8.313
10.5	8.245	9.882	11.120	12.038
11.0	10.763	12.833	14.378	15.510
11.5	13.177	15.632	17.440	18.749
12.0	15.490	18.288	20.321	21.776
12.5	17.709	20.809	23.035	24.609
13.0	19.836	23.204	25.592	27.263
13.5	21.879	25.481	28.006	29.753
14.0	23.839	27.647	30.286	32.092
14.5	25.722	29.709	32.441	34.293
15.0	27.531	31.673	34.480	36.366
15.5	29.270	33.545	36.412	38.320
16.0	30.942	35.330	38.244	40.166
16.5	32.549	37.034	39.982	41.911
17.0	34.096	38.661	41.633	43.562
17.5	35.585	40.215	43.203	45.127
18.0	37.019	41.702	44.696	46.611
18.5	38.400	43.124	46.119	48.020
19.0	39.730	44.485	47.474	49.360
19.5	41.013	45.789	48.767	50.634
20.0	42.250	47.039	50.002	51.848
20.5	43.443	48.237	51.181	53.006
21.0	44.594	49.387	52.309	54.111
21.5	45.706	50.491	53.389	55.166

MAXIMUM PREMIUM FOR ASSUMABLE LOANS
AS PERCENTAGE OF LOAN BALANCE

FACE INTEREST RATE: 9.25 %

CURRENT RATE	REMAINING TERM OF LOAN (YEARS)			
	15	20	25	30
7.0	-14.504	-18.131	-21.167	-23.655
7.5	-11.023	-13.689	-15.886	-17.657
8.0	-7.696	-9.496	-10.957	-12.117
8.5	-4.514	-5.536	-6.353	-6.992
9.0	-1.472	-1.795	-2.048	-2.244
9.5	1.439	1.744	1.981	2.162
10.0	4.226	5.094	5.757	6.255
10.5	6.894	8.265	9.299	10.064
11.0	9.449	11.269	12.624	13.614
11.5	11.898	14.118	15.749	16.926
12.0	14.246	16.821	18.689	20.021
12.5	16.497	19.388	21.458	22.917
13.0	18.656	21.826	24.068	25.630
13.5	20.728	24.144	26.531	28.176
14.0	22.718	26.349	28.858	30.568
14.5	24.629	28.448	31.057	32.818
15.0	26.464	30.447	33.138	34.938
15.5	28.228	32.352	35.110	36.936
16.0	29.925	34.170	36.979	38.823
16.5	31.556	35.904	38.753	40.607
17.0	33.126	37.560	40.438	42.296
17.5	34.637	39.143	42.040	43.895
18.0	36.092	40.656	43.564	45.413
18.5	37.493	42.103	45.015	46.854
19.0	38.843	43.489	46.398	48.223
19.5	40.145	44.816	47.718	49.527
20.0	41.400	46.088	48.978	50.768
20.5	42.610	47.308	50.182	51.952
21.0	43.779	48.478	51.333	53.081
21.5	44.906	49.602	52.434	54.160

MAXIMUM PREMIUM FOR ASSUMABLE LOANS
AS PERCENTAGE OF LOAN BALANCE

FACE INTEREST RATE: 9.5 %

CURRENT RATE	REMAINING TERM OF LOAN (YEARS)			
	15	20	25	30
7.0	-16.176	-20.229	-23.617	-26.387
7.5	-12.644	-15.708	-18.228	-20.257
8.0	-9.268	-11.440	-13.200	-14.594
8.5	-6.040	-7.410	-8.503	-9.356
9.0	-2.954	-3.602	-4.111	-4.503
9.5	0.000	0.000	0.000	0.000
10.0	2.828	3.409	3.852	4.184
10.5	5.535	6.636	7.465	8.077
11.0	8.127	9.694	10.858	11.705
11.5	10.612	12.593	14.046	15.090
12.0	12.994	15.345	17.046	18.254
12.5	15.278	17.957	19.871	21.214
13.0	17.469	20.438	22.533	23.987
13.5	19.571	22.797	25.046	26.589
14.0	21.590	25.041	27.420	29.034
14.5	23.528	27.177	29.663	31.334
15.0	25.391	29.212	31.787	33.500
15.5	27.181	31.151	33.798	35.543
16.0	28.902	33.001	35.705	37.472
16.5	30.557	34.766	37.515	39.295
17.0	32.149	36.451	39.234	41.021
17.5	33.682	38.062	40.868	42.656
18.0	35.158	39.602	42.423	44.207
18.5	36.580	41.075	43.903	45.679
19.0	37.950	42.485	45.315	47.079
19.5	39.271	43.836	46.661	48.411
20.0	40.544	45.131	47.946	49.680
20.5	41.772	46.372	49.174	50.890
21.0	42.958	47.564	50.349	52.044
21.5	44.102	48.707	51.472	53.147

MAXIMUM PREMIUM FOR ASSUMABLE LOANS
AS PERCENTAGE OF LOAN BALANCE

FACE INTEREST RATE: 9.75 %

CURRENT RATE	REMAINING TERM OF LOAN (YEARS)			
	15	20	25	30
7.0	-17.861	-22.342	-26.085	-29.138
7.5	-14.278	-17.742	-20.589	-22.875
8.0	-10.853	-13.399	-15.460	-17.089
8.5	-7.578	-9.298	-10.669	-11.736
9.0	-4.447	-5.423	-6.190	-6.778
9.5	-1.450	-1.758	-1.996	-2.177
10.0	1.418	1.710	1.933	2.099
10.5	4.165	4.994	5.618	6.077
11.0	6.795	8.106	9.078	9.783
11.5	9.316	11.057	12.330	13.242
12.0	11.732	13.856	15.389	16.474
12.5	14.049	16.514	18.271	19.499
13.0	16.272	19.039	20.987	22.333
13.5	18.405	21.440	23.550	24.992
14.0	20.453	23.723	25.971	27.490
14.5	22.419	25.897	28.259	29.839
15.0	24.309	27.967	30.425	32.053
15.5	26.125	29.941	32.476	34.140
16.0	27.871	31.823	34.422	36.111
16.5	29.550	33.619	36.267	37.974
17.0	31.165	35.334	38.021	39.737
17.5	32.721	36.973	39.687	41.408
18.0	34.218	38.540	41.273	42.992
18.5	35.661	40.039	42.783	44.497
19.0	37.050	41.474	44.223	45.927
19.5	38.390	42.849	45.596	47.289
20.0	39.682	44.166	46.907	48.585
20.5	40.928	45.430	48.160	49.821
21.0	42.131	46.642	49.357	51.001
21.5	43.291	47.806	50.504	52.127

MAXIMUM PREMIUM FOR ASSUMABLE LOANS
AS PERCENTAGE OF LOAN BALANCE

FACE INTEREST RATE: 10 %

CURRENT RATE	REMAINING TERM OF LOAN (YEARS)			
	15	20	25	30
7.0	-19.557	-24.471	-28.570	-31.906
7.5	-15.922	-19.791	-22.965	-25.509
8.0	-12.448	-15.373	-17.736	-19.599
8.5	-9.126	-11.200	-12.850	-14.131
9.0	-5.950	-7.258	-8.283	-9.067
9.5	-2.910	-3.529	-4.007	-4.367
10.0	0.000	0.000	0.000	0.000
10.5	2.786	3.341	3.758	4.063
11.0	5.454	6.507	7.286	7.849
11.5	8.011	9.509	10.602	11.382
12.0	10.462	12.357	13.722	14.684
12.5	12.812	15.061	16.660	17.773
13.0	15.067	17.630	19.430	20.668
13.5	17.231	20.073	22.043	23.384
14.0	19.308	22.396	24.511	25.935
14.5	21.303	24.607	26.845	28.335
15.0	23.220	26.714	29.054	30.596
15.5	25.062	28.722	31.146	32.728
16.0	26.833	30.637	33.129	34.741
16.5	28.536	32.464	35.011	36.644
17.0	30.175	34.209	36.799	38.445
17.5	31.753	35.876	38.499	40.152
18.0	33.272	37.471	40.116	41.770
18.5	34.735	38.996	41.656	43.307
19.0	36.145	40.456	43.124	44.768
19.5	37.504	41.854	44.524	46.159
20.0	38.814	43.195	45.861	47.483
20.5	40.078	44.480	47.138	48.745
21.0	41.298	45.713	48.359	49.950
21.5	42.475	46.897	49.528	51.101

MAXIMUM PREMIUM FOR ASSUMABLE LOANS
AS PERCENTAGE OF LOAN BALANCE

FACE INTEREST RATE: 10.25 %

CURRENT RATE	REMAINING TERM OF LOAN (YEARS)			
	15	20	25	30
7.0	-21.264	-26.615	-31.071	-34.691
7.5	-17.577	-21.854	-25.358	-28.158
8.0	-14.053	-17.360	-20.026	-22.124
8.5	-10.684	-13.115	-15.046	-16.541
9.0	-7.462	-9.105	-10.390	-11.369
9.5	-4.379	-5.312	-6.030	-6.570
10.0	-1.428	-1.722	-1.946	-2.111
10.5	1.398	1.677	1.885	2.038
11.0	4.104	4.897	5.482	5.904
11.5	6.698	7.951	8.863	9.511
12.0	9.184	10.848	12.043	12.883
12.5	11.568	13.599	15.038	16.037
13.0	13.854	16.212	17.862	18.993
13.5	16.049	18.696	20.526	21.766
14.0	18.156	21.059	23.043	24.371
14.5	20.180	23.309	25.422	26.822
15.0	22.123	25.452	27.673	29.131
15.5	23.992	27.494	29.806	31.308
16.0	25.788	29.442	31.828	33.363
16.5	27.516	31.301	33.747	35.306
17.0	29.178	33.076	35.569	37.146
17.5	30.778	34.772	37.302	38.888
18.0	32.319	36.394	38.951	40.541
18.5	33.803	37.945	40.521	42.110
19.0	35.233	39.430	42.017	43.602
19.5	36.611	40.853	43.444	45.022
20.0	37.940	42.216	44.807	46.374
20.5	39.223	43.524	46.109	47.663
21.0	40.460	44.778	47.355	48.894
21.5	41.654	45.983	48.546	50.069

MAXIMUM PREMIUM FOR ASSUMABLE LOANS
AS PERCENTAGE OF LOAN BALANCE

FACE INTEREST RATE: 10.5 %

CURRENT RATE	REMAINING TERM OF LOAN (YEARS)			
	15	20	25	30
7.0	-22.983	-28.774	-33.590	-37.492
7.5	-19.244	-23.932	-27.767	-30.824
8.0	-15.670	-19.361	-22.333	-24.664
8.5	-12.253	-15.044	-17.256	-18.965
9.0	-8.986	-10.965	-12.511	-13.686
9.5	-5.859	-7.108	-8.068	-8.787
10.0	-2.866	-3.457	-3.905	-4.235
10.5	0.000	0.000	0.000	0.000
11.0	2.745	3.275	3.666	3.946
11.5	5.375	6.381	7.112	7.629
12.0	7.896	9.328	10.353	11.071
12.5	10.314	12.125	13.406	14.291
13.0	12.633	14.783	16.284	17.308
13.5	14.859	17.310	18.999	20.139
14.0	16.996	19.713	21.564	22.798
14.5	19.048	22.001	23.989	25.300
15.0	21.019	24.181	26.284	27.657
15.5	22.914	26.258	28.457	29.879
16.0	24.736	28.239	30.518	31.977
16.5	26.488	30.129	32.474	33.961
17.0	28.174	31.935	34.331	35.838
17.5	29.797	33.660	36.097	37.617
18.0	31.360	35.309	37.778	39.304
18.5	32.865	36.887	39.378	40.906
19.0	34.315	38.398	40.903	42.429
19.5	35.713	39.844	42.358	43.878
20.0	37.061	41.231	43.747	45.259
20.5	38.361	42.561	45.074	46.575
21.0	39.616	43.837	46.343	47.831
21.5	40.827	45.062	47.557	49.030

MAXIMUM PREMIUM FOR ASSUMABLE LOANS
AS PERCENTAGE OF LOAN BALANCE

FACE INTEREST RATE: 10.75 %

CURRENT RATE	REMAINING TERM OF LOAN (YEARS)			
	15	20	25	30
7.0	-24.712	-30.947	-36.124	-40.309
7.5	-20.921	-26.023	-30.190	-33.505
8.0	-17.297	-21.375	-24.653	-27.218
8.5	-13.832	-16.985	-19.481	-21.403
9.0	-10.519	-12.838	-14.645	-16.015
9.5	-7.348	-8.915	-10.118	-11.016
10.0	-4.312	-5.203	-5.876	-6.371
10.5	-1.407	-1.688	-1.897	-2.049
11.0	1.377	1.643	1.838	1.978
11.5	4.044	4.801	5.350	5.737
12.0	6.601	7.797	8.653	9.248
12.5	9.053	10.642	11.763	12.535
13.0	11.404	13.345	14.696	15.614
13.5	13.661	15.914	17.463	18.503
14.0	15.828	18.359	20.076	21.217
14.5	17.909	20.685	22.547	23.770
15.0	19.909	22.901	24.885	26.175
15.5	21.830	25.013	27.100	28.442
16.0	23.678	27.028	29.200	30.584
16.5	25.454	28.950	31.193	32.608
17.0	27.164	30.786	33.086	34.524
17.5	28.810	32.540	34.885	36.339
18.0	30.394	34.218	36.597	38.060
18.5	31.920	35.822	38.228	39.695
19.0	33.391	37.358	39.782	41.250
19.5	34.808	38.829	41.264	42.728
20.0	36.175	40.239	42.680	44.137
20.5	37.494	41.592	44.032	45.480
21.0	38.766	42.889	45.325	46.762
21.5	39.995	44.135	46.563	47.986

MAXIMUM PREMIUM FOR ASSUMABLE LOANS
AS PERCENTAGE OF LOAN BALANCE

FACE INTEREST RATE: 11 %

CURRENT RATE	REMAINING TERM OF LOAN (YEARS)			
	15	20	25	30
7.0	-26.453	-33.134	-38.673	-43.141
7.5	-22.609	-28.128	-32.629	-36.199
8.0	-18.934	-23.402	-26.988	-29.786
8.5	-15.421	-18.940	-21.719	-23.853
9.0	-12.061	-14.723	-16.792	-18.357
9.5	-8.846	-10.734	-12.180	-13.257
10.0	-5.768	-6.960	-7.859	-8.518
10.5	-2.822	-3.386	-3.805	-4.109
11.0	0.000	0.000	0.000	0.000
11.5	2.705	3.211	3.577	3.834
12.0	5.297	6.257	6.942	7.417
12.5	7.783	9.150	10.111	10.769
13.0	10.168	11.897	13.098	13.910
13.5	12.456	14.510	15.917	16.858
14.0	14.654	16.995	18.579	19.627
14.5	16.764	19.360	21.096	22.231
15.0	18.791	21.613	23.478	24.684
15.5	20.739	23.761	25.735	26.998
16.0	22.612	25.809	27.874	29.183
16.5	24.414	27.764	29.904	31.248
17.0	26.147	29.630	31.832	33.202
17.5	27.816	31.413	33.665	35.054
18.0	29.423	33.119	35.410	36.810
18.5	30.970	34.750	37.071	38.478
19.0	32.461	36.312	38.654	40.064
19.5	33.899	37.807	40.164	41.572
20.0	35.285	39.241	41.606	43.009
20.5	36.622	40.616	42.984	44.380
21.0	37.912	41.935	44.301	45.687
21.5	39.157	43.202	45.562	46.936

MAXIMUM PREMIUM FOR ASSUMABLE LOANS
AS PERCENTAGE OF LOAN BALANCE

FACE INTEREST RATE: 11.25 %

CURRENT RATE	REMAINING TERM OF LOAN (YEARS)			
	15	20	25	30
7.0	-28.206	-35.336	-41.238	-45.988
7.5	-24.308	-30.247	-35.082	-38.908
8.0	-20.582	-25.443	-29.337	-32.367
8.5	-17.020	-20.907	-23.970	-26.316
9.0	-13.614	-16.620	-18.952	-20.710
9.5	-10.355	-12.566	-14.255	-15.509
10.0	-7.234	-8.729	-9.853	-10.676
10.5	-4.247	-5.096	-5.725	-6.179
11.0	-1.386	-1.654	-1.850	-1.989
11.5	1.356	1.610	1.793	1.922
12.0	3.985	4.707	5.221	5.576
12.5	6.505	7.647	8.448	8.995
13.0	8.923	10.440	11.491	12.198
13.5	11.243	13.096	14.361	15.204
14.0	13.471	15.622	17.073	18.028
14.5	15.610	18.027	19.637	20.685
15.0	17.665	20.317	22.063	23.187
15.5	19.640	22.500	24.361	25.546
16.0	21.540	24.582	26.540	27.774
16.5	23.366	26.569	28.608	29.880
17.0	25.124	28.466	30.571	31.874
17.5	26.816	30.279	32.439	33.762
18.0	28.444	32.013	34.215	35.554
18.5	30.013	33.671	35.907	37.255
19.0	31.525	35.258	37.519	38.872
19.5	32.982	36.779	39.058	40.410
20.0	34.388	38.236	40.526	41.876
20.5	35.743	39.634	41.929	43.273
21.0	37.051	40.975	43.271	44.607
21.5	38.314	42.262	44.555	45.881

MAXIMUM PREMIUM FOR ASSUMABLE LOANS
AS PERCENTAGE OF LOAN BALANCE

FACE INTEREST RATE: 11.5 %

CURRENT RATE	REMAINING TERM OF LOAN (YEARS)			
	15	20	25	30
7.0	-29.968	-37.551	-43.817	-48.848
7.5	-26.017	-32.379	-37.549	-41.629
8.0	-22.240	-27.496	-31.698	-34.960
8.5	-18.629	-22.885	-26.234	-28.791
9.0	-15.176	-18.529	-21.124	-23.076
9.5	-11.872	-14.408	-16.341	-17.772
10.0	-8.709	-10.508	-11.859	-12.844
10.5	-5.680	-6.816	-7.656	-8.259
11.0	-2.780	-3.317	-3.709	-3.987
11.5	0.000	0.000	0.000	0.000
12.0	2.664	3.147	3.490	3.726
12.5	5.220	6.136	6.776	7.212
13.0	7.671	8.975	9.874	10.478
13.5	10.023	11.674	12.798	13.543
14.0	12.281	14.241	15.559	16.422
14.5	14.450	16.685	18.169	19.131
15.0	16.533	19.013	20.640	21.682
15.5	18.536	21.232	22.980	24.087
16.0	20.461	23.348	25.199	26.359
16.5	22.313	25.367	27.304	28.506
17.0	24.094	27.295	29.304	30.539
17.5	25.809	29.138	31.205	32.464
18.0	27.461	30.900	33.014	34.291
18.5	29.051	32.585	34.736	36.025
19.0	30.584	34.199	36.378	37.674
19.5	32.061	35.744	37.945	39.243
20.0	33.486	37.225	39.440	40.737
20.5	34.860	38.646	40.869	42.162
21.0	36.186	40.009	42.235	43.522
21.5	37.466	41.317	43.542	44.820

MAXIMUM PREMIUM FOR ASSUMABLE LOANS
AS PERCENTAGE OF LOAN BALANCE

FACE INTEREST RATE: 11.75 %

CURRENT RATE	REMAINING TERM OF LOAN (YEARS)			
	15	20	25	30
7.0	-31.742	-39.780	-46.411	-51.722
7.5	-27.737	-34.524	-40.029	-44.364
8.0	-23.909	-29.562	-34.073	-37.566
8.5	-20.248	-24.877	-28.510	-31.277
9.0	-16.749	-20.449	-23.309	-25.452
9.5	-13.399	-16.262	-18.439	-20.046
10.0	-10.192	-12.299	-13.877	-15.023
10.5	-7.123	-8.547	-9.597	-10.349
11.0	-4.183	-4.992	-5.580	-5.995
11.5	-1.365	-1.620	-1.803	-1.931
12.0	1.336	1.578	1.749	1.867
12.5	3.926	4.615	5.095	5.420
13.0	6.410	7.500	8.249	8.750
13.5	8.795	10.242	11.225	11.874
14.0	11.084	12.852	14.036	14.808
14.5	13.282	15.335	16.694	17.569
15.0	15.394	17.701	19.209	20.170
15.5	17.424	19.955	21.591	22.622
16.0	19.375	22.106	23.850	24.937
16.5	21.252	24.158	25.993	27.126
17.0	23.058	26.117	28.029	29.198
17.5	24.797	27.990	29.964	31.161
18.0	26.470	29.780	31.806	33.022
18.5	28.083	31.493	33.560	34.790
19.0	29.636	33.133	35.231	36.471
19.5	31.134	34.703	36.826	38.070
20.0	32.578	36.208	38.348	39.593
20.5	33.971	37.652	39.802	41.045
21.0	35.315	39.037	41.193	42.431
21.5	36.612	40.366	42.524	43.755

MAXIMUM PREMIUM FOR ASSUMABLE LOANS
AS PERCENTAGE OF LOAN BALANCE

FACE INTEREST RATE: 12 %

CURRENT RATE	REMAINING TERM OF LOAN (YEARS)			
	15	20	25	30
7.0	-33.526	-42.021	-49.018	-54.608
7.5	-29.467	-36.681	-42.522	-47.110
8.0	-25.586	-31.640	-36.461	-40.183
8.5	-21.876	-26.879	-30.798	-33.775
9.0	-18.329	-22.381	-25.504	-27.838
9.5	-14.934	-18.126	-20.548	-22.330
10.0	-11.684	-14.099	-15.904	-17.211
10.5	-8.573	-10.287	-11.549	-12.449
11.0	-5.593	-6.675	-7.460	-8.011
11.5	-2.737	-3.250	-3.616	-3.870
12.0	0.000	0.000	0.000	0.000
12.5	2.625	3.085	3.405	3.621
13.0	5.143	6.017	6.615	7.014
13.5	7.560	8.803	9.644	10.197
14.0	9.880	11.454	12.506	13.188
14.5	12.108	13.978	15.210	16.001
15.0	14.248	16.381	17.770	18.651
15.5	16.306	18.672	20.195	21.150
16.0	18.284	20.857	22.494	23.509
16.5	20.186	22.942	24.675	25.740
17.0	22.016	24.933	26.747	27.851
17.5	23.778	26.835	28.717	29.851
18.0	25.475	28.654	30.592	31.748
18.5	27.109	30.395	32.377	33.550
19.0	28.683	32.060	34.078	35.262
19.5	30.201	33.656	35.701	36.892
20.0	31.665	35.185	37.250	38.444
20.5	33.077	36.652	38.731	39.924
21.0	34.439	38.059	40.146	41.336
21.5	35.754	39.410	41.501	42.685

MAXIMUM PREMIUM FOR ASSUMABLE LOANS
AS PERCENTAGE OF LOAN BALANCE

FACE INTEREST RATE: 12.25 %

CURRENT RATE	REMAINING TERM OF LOAN (YEARS)			
	15	20	25	30
7.0	-35.321	-44.275	-51.638	-57.507
7.5	-31.207	-38.850	-45.028	-49.868
8.0	-27.274	-33.729	-38.860	-42.811
8.5	-23.514	-28.893	-33.098	-36.283
9.0	-19.920	-24.323	-27.711	-30.235
9.5	-16.479	-20.001	-22.668	-24.623
10.0	-13.185	-15.911	-17.942	-19.409
10.5	-10.032	-12.038	-13.510	-14.557
11.0	-7.012	-8.368	-9.349	-10.036
11.5	-4.118	-4.889	-5.438	-5.817
12.0	-1.344	-1.587	-1.758	-1.875
12.5	1.316	1.547	1.707	1.814
13.0	3.868	4.525	4.973	5.271
13.5	6.317	7.356	8.056	8.514
14.0	8.669	10.049	10.967	11.560
14.5	10.927	12.612	13.720	14.426
15.0	13.096	15.054	16.324	17.126
15.5	15.181	17.381	18.792	19.672
16.0	17.185	19.600	21.131	22.075
16.5	19.113	21.719	23.351	24.348
17.0	20.968	23.741	25.459	26.498
17.5	22.754	25.674	27.464	28.536
18.0	24.473	27.522	29.371	30.469
18.5	26.129	29.290	31.188	32.304
19.0	27.725	30.982	32.919	34.049
19.5	29.263	32.603	34.570	35.709
20.0	30.746	34.157	36.147	37.290
20.5	32.177	35.646	37.653	38.798
21.0	33.558	37.076	39.094	40.236
21.5	34.891	38.448	40.472	41.611

MAXIMUM PREMIUM FOR ASSUMABLE LOANS
AS PERCENTAGE OF LOAN BALANCE

FACE INTEREST RATE: 12.5 %

CURRENT RATE	REMAINING TERM OF LOAN (YEARS)			
	15	20	25	30
7.0	-37.126	-46.543	-54.271	-60.417
7.5	-32.957	-41.032	-47.547	-52.637
8.0	-28.972	-35.831	-41.271	-45.450
8.5	-25.162	-30.918	-35.409	-38.801
9.0	-21.519	-26.277	-29.929	-32.641
9.5	-18.033	-21.887	-24.798	-26.926
10.0	-14.695	-17.732	-19.990	-21.615
10.5	-11.500	-13.798	-15.481	-16.673
11.0	-8.440	-10.071	-11.248	-12.069
11.5	-5.507	-6.537	-7.269	-7.772
12.0	-2.696	-3.184	-3.525	-3.757
12.5	0.000	0.000	0.000	0.000
13.0	2.586	3.024	3.323	3.520
13.5	5.068	5.900	6.459	6.823
14.0	7.450	8.635	9.421	9.926
14.5	9.738	11.239	12.221	12.845
15.0	11.936	13.719	14.871	15.595
15.5	14.049	16.083	17.381	18.187
16.0	16.081	18.337	19.761	20.636
16.5	18.034	20.488	22.020	22.950
17.0	19.914	22.543	24.165	25.140
17.5	21.724	24.506	26.204	27.215
18.0	23.466	26.383	28.145	29.184
18.5	25.144	28.179	29.993	31.053
19.0	26.761	29.897	31.754	32.830
19.5	28.320	31.544	33.434	34.521
20.0	29.823	33.122	35.038	36.131
20.5	31.272	34.635	36.571	37.667
21.0	32.671	36.087	38.036	39.132
21.5	34.022	37.481	39.439	40.532

MAXIMUM PREMIUM FOR ASSUMABLE LOANS
AS PERCENTAGE OF LOAN BALANCE

FACE INTEREST RATE: 12.75 %

CURRENT RATE	REMAINING TERM OF LOAN (YEARS)			
	15	20	25	30
7.0	-38.941	-48.822	-56.917	-63.338
7.5	-34.717	-43.226	-50.077	-55.417
8.0	-30.679	-37.943	-43.694	-48.098
8.5	-26.819	-32.954	-37.731	-41.328
9.0	-23.128	-28.241	-32.157	-35.057
9.5	-19.595	-23.782	-26.938	-29.237
10.0	-16.213	-19.563	-22.048	-23.829
10.5	-12.976	-15.568	-17.462	-18.798
11.0	-9.875	-11.783	-13.156	-14.110
11.5	-6.904	-8.194	-9.108	-9.735
12.0	-4.055	-4.788	-5.301	-5.647
12.5	-1.324	-1.555	-1.715	-1.821
13.0	1.296	1.516	1.665	1.763
13.5	3.811	4.436	4.855	5.126
14.0	6.225	7.214	7.868	8.286
14.5	8.544	9.858	10.716	11.258
15.0	10.771	12.377	13.411	14.058
15.5	12.912	14.777	15.965	16.698
16.0	14.970	17.067	18.385	19.190
16.5	16.950	19.252	20.683	21.547
17.0	18.854	21.338	22.864	23.777
17.5	20.688	23.332	24.939	25.890
18.0	22.453	25.238	26.912	27.894
18.5	24.153	27.062	28.792	29.798
19.0	25.791	28.807	30.584	31.607
19.5	27.371	30.479	32.293	33.328
20.0	28.894	32.082	33.924	34.968
20.5	30.363	33.619	35.483	36.532
21.0	31.780	35.093	36.974	38.024
21.5	33.149	36.509	38.400	39.449

MAXIMUM PREMIUM FOR ASSUMABLE LOANS
AS PERCENTAGE OF LOAN BALANCE

FACE INTEREST RATE: 13 %

CURRENT RATE	REMAINING TERM OF LOAN (YEARS)			
	15	20	25	30
7.0	-40.766	-51.113	-59.574	-66.270
7.5	-36.486	-45.431	-52.619	-58.206
8.0	-32.396	-40.067	-46.127	-50.757
8.5	-28.484	-35.001	-40.064	-43.865
9.0	-24.745	-30.215	-34.395	-37.481
9.5	-21.166	-25.688	-29.088	-31.557
10.0	-17.740	-21.404	-24.115	-26.052
10.5	-14.460	-17.347	-19.451	-20.930
11.0	-11.319	-13.504	-15.072	-16.158
11.5	-8.308	-9.860	-10.956	-11.704
12.0	-5.422	-6.402	-7.084	-7.543
12.5	-2.654	-3.119	-3.437	-3.649
13.0	0.000	0.000	0.000	0.000
13.5	2.548	2.965	3.244	3.423
14.0	4.994	5.786	6.307	6.640
14.5	7.342	8.471	9.204	9.665
15.0	9.599	11.028	11.945	12.515
15.5	11.768	13.465	14.541	15.202
16.0	13.853	15.790	17.003	17.740
16.5	15.859	18.009	19.339	20.139
17.0	17.788	20.127	21.558	22.409
17.5	19.646	22.151	23.668	24.560
18.0	21.434	24.087	25.675	26.600
18.5	23.157	25.939	27.586	28.538
19.0	24.817	27.711	29.408	30.379
19.5	26.417	29.409	31.146	32.132
20.0	27.960	31.036	32.805	33.801
20.5	29.448	32.597	34.390	35.392
21.0	30.884	34.094	35.906	36.911
21.5	32.271	35.531	37.357	38.362

MAXIMUM PREMIUM FOR ASSUMABLE LOANS
AS PERCENTAGE OF LOAN BALANCE

FACE INTEREST RATE: 13.25 %

CURRENT RATE	REMAINING TERM OF LOAN (YEARS)			
	15	20	25	30
7.0	-42.601	-53.416	-62.243	-69.212
7.5	-38.266	-47.647	-55.171	-61.006
8.0	-34.122	-42.202	-48.572	-53.424
8.5	-30.160	-37.059	-42.407	-46.411
9.0	-26.371	-32.200	-36.643	-39.914
9.5	-22.746	-27.604	-31.247	-33.885
10.0	-19.275	-23.254	-26.191	-28.283
10.5	-15.952	-19.136	-21.449	-23.070
11.0	-12.770	-15.234	-16.997	-18.213
11.5	-9.720	-11.534	-12.812	-13.681
12.0	-6.796	-8.023	-8.875	-9.446
12.5	-3.993	-4.690	-5.168	-5.483
13.0	-1.304	-1.524	-1.673	-1.770
13.5	1.277	1.486	1.625	1.715
14.0	3.755	4.350	4.740	4.988
14.5	6.134	7.076	7.685	8.067
15.0	8.420	9.672	10.472	10.967
15.5	10.617	12.146	13.112	13.702
16.0	12.730	14.507	15.615	16.284
16.5	14.762	16.759	17.990	18.725
17.0	16.716	18.910	20.246	21.036
17.5	18.598	20.965	22.391	23.225
18.0	20.410	22.930	24.431	25.301
18.5	22.155	24.810	26.375	27.273
19.0	23.836	26.609	28.227	29.147
19.5	25.457	28.333	29.994	30.931
20.0	27.020	29.985	31.681	32.630
20.5	28.528	31.569	33.293	34.249
21.0	29.983	33.089	34.834	35.795
21.5	31.388	34.549	36.309	37.271

MAXIMUM PREMIUM FOR ASSUMABLE LOANS
AS PERCENTAGE OF LOAN BALANCE

FACE INTEREST RATE: 13.5 %

CURRENT RATE	REMAINING TERM OF LOAN (YEARS)			
	15	20	25	30
7.0	-44.446	-55.730	-64.924	-72.164
7.5	-40.054	-49.874	-57.735	-63.814
8.0	-35.857	-44.347	-51.026	-56.101
8.5	-31.843	-39.126	-44.759	-48.965
9.0	-28.006	-34.194	-38.900	-42.354
9.5	-24.333	-29.529	-33.415	-36.220
10.0	-20.818	-25.113	-28.276	-30.521
10.5	-17.452	-20.933	-23.455	-25.217
11.0	-14.229	-16.972	-18.930	-20.276
11.5	-11.139	-13.216	-14.676	-15.664
12.0	-8.178	-9.653	-10.674	-11.355
12.5	-5.338	-6.270	-6.905	-7.323
13.0	-2.614	-3.056	-3.352	-3.545
13.5	0.000	0.000	0.000	0.000
14.0	2.510	2.907	3.167	3.330
14.5	4.920	5.674	6.160	6.463
15.0	7.236	8.309	8.993	9.414
15.5	9.461	10.821	11.677	12.196
16.0	11.601	13.217	14.221	14.824
16.5	13.659	15.503	16.635	17.308
17.0	15.639	17.687	18.928	19.658
17.5	17.545	19.773	21.109	21.886
18.0	19.380	21.767	23.183	23.998
18.5	21.148	23.676	25.159	26.004
19.0	22.851	25.502	27.041	27.911
19.5	24.493	27.252	28.838	29.726
20.0	26.076	28.929	30.552	31.454
20.5	27.604	30.537	32.191	33.102
21.0	29.077	32.080	33.758	34.675
21.5	30.500	33.562	35.257	36.177

MAXIMUM PREMIUM FOR ASSUMABLE LOANS
AS PERCENTAGE OF LOAN BALANCE

FACE INTEREST RATE: 13.75 %

CURRENT RATE	REMAINING TERM OF LOAN (YEARS)			
	15	20	25	30
7.0	-46.301	-58.056	-67.615	-75.125
7.5	-41.853	-52.113	-60.309	-66.632
8.0	-37.601	-46.503	-53.491	-58.786
8.5	-33.536	-41.204	-47.122	-51.527
9.0	-29.650	-36.198	-41.167	-44.803
9.5	-25.930	-31.463	-35.593	-38.563
10.0	-22.369	-26.982	-30.369	-32.765
10.5	-18.960	-22.739	-25.470	-27.371
11.0	-15.696	-18.719	-20.871	-22.344
11.5	-12.566	-14.907	-16.547	-17.654
12.0	-9.567	-11.291	-12.480	-13.270
12.5	-6.691	-7.857	-8.650	-9.169
13.0	-3.932	-4.595	-5.039	-5.326
13.5	-1.284	-1.494	-1.632	-1.720
14.0	1.258	1.457	1.586	1.668
14.5	3.699	4.265	4.629	4.854
15.0	6.044	6.940	7.508	7.856
15.5	8.298	9.489	10.235	10.686
16.0	10.466	11.921	12.821	13.359
16.5	12.550	14.241	15.275	15.885
17.0	14.556	16.457	17.605	18.276
17.5	16.486	18.574	19.821	20.542
18.0	18.345	20.599	21.929	22.691
18.5	20.135	22.536	23.937	24.732
19.0	21.860	24.390	25.851	26.671
19.5	23.524	26.165	27.676	28.517
20.0	25.127	27.867	29.419	30.275
20.5	26.674	29.500	31.084	31.952
21.0	28.167	31.066	32.676	33.551
21.5	29.608	32.569	34.200	35.079

MAXIMUM PREMIUM FOR ASSUMABLE LOANS
AS PERCENTAGE OF LOAN BALANCE

FACE INTEREST RATE: 14 %

CURRENT RATE	REMAINING TERM OF LOAN (YEARS)			
	15	20	25	30
7.0	-48.165	-60.393	-70.317	-78.095
7.5	-43.660	-54.361	-62.893	-69.458
8.0	-39.354	-48.668	-55.965	-61.479
8.5	-35.238	-43.292	-49.493	-54.097
9.0	-31.302	-38.212	-43.443	-47.258
9.5	-27.534	-33.407	-37.778	-40.913
10.0	-23.928	-28.859	-32.470	-35.017
10.5	-20.476	-24.554	-27.492	-29.531
11.0	-17.169	-20.474	-22.819	-24.419
11.5	-14.000	-16.606	-18.426	-19.649
12.0	-10.963	-12.936	-14.293	-15.191
12.5	-8.050	-9.451	-10.401	-11.020
13.0	-5.256	-6.141	-6.732	-7.112
13.5	-2.575	-2.994	-3.270	-3.445
14.0	0.000	0.000	0.000	0.000
14.5	2.472	2.850	3.092	3.241
15.0	4.847	5.564	6.017	6.293
15.5	7.130	8.151	8.788	9.172
16.0	9.325	10.619	11.416	11.890
16.5	11.436	12.974	13.909	14.459
17.0	13.467	15.222	16.277	16.890
17.5	15.422	17.371	18.529	19.194
18.0	17.305	19.425	20.671	21.380
18.5	19.118	21.390	22.711	23.455
19.0	20.865	23.272	24.656	25.428
19.5	22.549	25.074	26.511	27.305
20.0	24.173	26.801	28.281	29.093
20.5	25.740	28.457	29.973	30.798
21.0	27.252	30.047	31.591	32.424
21.5	28.711	31.572	33.140	33.978

MAXIMUM PREMIUM FOR ASSUMABLE LOANS
AS PERCENTAGE OF LOAN BALANCE

FACE INTEREST RATE: 14.25 %

CURRENT RATE	REMAINING TERM OF LOAN (YEARS)			
	15	20	25	30
7.0	-50.038	-62.740	-73.028	-81.074
7.5	-45.476	-56.620	-65.486	-72.292
8.0	-41.116	-50.844	-58.448	-64.179
8.5	-36.947	-45.389	-51.873	-56.674
9.0	-32.962	-40.234	-45.726	-49.721
9.5	-29.147	-35.359	-39.972	-43.270
10.0	-25.495	-30.745	-34.580	-37.275
10.5	-21.999	-26.376	-29.522	-31.697
11.0	-18.651	-22.237	-24.774	-26.500
11.5	-15.442	-18.312	-20.311	-21.650
12.0	-12.366	-14.588	-16.113	-17.118
12.5	-9.416	-11.053	-12.159	-12.877
13.0	-6.587	-7.694	-8.431	-8.903
13.5	-3.871	-4.501	-4.914	-5.175
14.0	-1.264	-1.463	-1.592	-1.672
14.5	1.239	1.428	1.549	1.623
15.0	3.644	4.182	4.521	4.726
15.5	5.956	6.807	7.336	7.653
16.0	8.179	9.311	10.005	10.416
16.5	10.317	11.700	12.538	13.028
17.0	12.373	13.982	14.944	15.501
17.5	14.353	16.162	17.232	17.843
18.0	16.259	18.246	19.408	20.065
18.5	18.095	20.240	21.481	22.175
19.0	19.865	22.149	23.456	24.181
19.5	21.570	23.978	25.341	26.089
20.0	23.215	25.730	27.140	27.907
20.5	24.801	27.410	28.859	29.640
21.0	26.332	29.023	30.502	31.294
21.5	27.810	30.571	32.075	32.874

MAXIMUM PREMIUM FOR ASSUMABLE LOANS
AS PERCENTAGE OF LOAN BALANCE

FACE INTEREST RATE: 14.5 %

CURRENT RATE	REMAINING TERM OF LOAN (YEARS)			
	15	20	25	30
7.0	-51.921	-65.098	-75.750	-84.060
7.5	-47.302	-58.889	-68.089	-75.133
8.0	-42.887	-53.029	-60.940	-66.887
8.5	-38.666	-47.495	-54.262	-59.258
9.0	-34.630	-42.266	-48.019	-52.190
9.5	-30.767	-37.320	-42.173	-45.633
10.0	-27.070	-32.639	-36.696	-39.539
10.5	-23.530	-28.207	-31.560	-33.869
11.0	-20.140	-24.008	-26.737	-28.586
11.5	-16.890	-20.027	-22.204	-23.656
12.0	-13.776	-16.249	-17.939	-19.049
12.5	-10.789	-12.662	-13.923	-14.739
13.0	-7.924	-9.255	-10.137	-10.699
13.5	-5.175	-6.015	-6.565	-6.910
14.0	-2.535	-2.933	-3.190	-3.349
14.5	0.000	0.000	0.000	0.000
15.0	2.435	2.794	3.019	3.155
15.5	4.776	5.457	5.879	6.130
16.0	7.027	7.997	8.590	8.938
16.5	9.191	10.421	11.163	11.594
17.0	11.274	12.735	13.606	14.107
17.5	13.278	14.947	15.930	16.488
18.0	15.208	17.062	18.140	18.747
18.5	17.068	19.085	20.246	20.891
19.0	18.859	21.021	22.252	22.930
19.5	20.586	22.876	24.166	24.870
20.0	22.251	24.654	25.994	26.718
20.5	23.857	26.359	27.739	28.480
21.0	25.407	27.995	29.409	30.161
21.5	26.904	29.565	31.007	31.767

MAXIMUM PREMIUM FOR ASSUMABLE LOANS
AS PERCENTAGE OF LOAN BALANCE

FACE INTEREST RATE: 14.75 %

CURRENT RATE	REMAINING TERM OF LOAN (YEARS)			
	15	20	25	30
7.0	-53.812	-67.465	-78.481	-87.054
7.5	-49.136	-61.168	-70.701	-77.982
8.0	-44.666	-55.224	-63.441	-69.602
8.5	-40.393	-49.610	-56.659	-61.848
9.0	-36.306	-44.306	-50.319	-54.666
9.5	-32.396	-39.289	-44.383	-48.002
10.0	-28.652	-34.541	-38.821	-41.809
10.5	-25.068	-30.046	-33.604	-36.047
11.0	-21.636	-25.787	-28.706	-30.678
11.5	-18.346	-21.748	-24.103	-25.668
12.0	-15.193	-17.916	-19.772	-20.986
12.5	-12.169	-14.278	-15.693	-16.605
13.0	-9.268	-10.821	-11.848	-12.500
13.5	-6.484	-7.536	-8.220	-8.649
14.0	-3.812	-4.410	-4.794	-5.030
14.5	-1.245	-1.434	-1.554	-1.627
15.0	1.220	1.400	1.512	1.579
15.5	3.590	4.101	4.416	4.603
16.0	5.869	6.677	7.169	7.457
16.5	8.060	9.136	9.782	10.156
17.0	10.169	11.484	12.264	12.710
17.5	12.198	13.727	14.623	15.130
18.0	14.153	15.872	16.868	17.425
18.5	16.035	17.924	19.006	19.605
19.0	17.849	19.888	21.044	21.677
19.5	19.597	21.770	22.988	23.648
20.0	21.283	23.573	24.844	25.526
20.5	22.909	25.303	26.617	27.316
21.0	24.479	26.962	28.312	29.025
21.5	25.993	28.555	29.935	30.657

MAXIMUM PREMIUM FOR ASSUMABLE LOANS
AS PERCENTAGE OF LOAN BALANCE

FACE INTEREST RATE: 15 %

CURRENT RATE	REMAINING TERM OF LOAN (YEARS)			
	15	20	25	30
7.0	-55.712	-69.843	-81.221	-90.056
7.5	-50.979	-63.456	-73.322	-80.838
8.0	-46.453	-57.428	-65.950	-72.323
8.5	-42.127	-51.734	-59.064	-64.445
9.0	-37.990	-46.355	-52.626	-57.148
9.5	-34.031	-41.267	-46.599	-50.376
10.0	-30.242	-36.452	-40.952	-44.084
10.5	-26.613	-31.892	-35.655	-38.230
11.0	-23.138	-27.573	-30.682	-32.775
11.5	-19.808	-23.476	-26.008	-27.684
12.0	-16.616	-19.590	-21.610	-22.927
12.5	-13.554	-15.900	-17.469	-18.476
13.0	-10.618	-12.395	-13.565	-14.305
13.5	-7.800	-9.062	-9.882	-10.392
14.0	-5.094	-5.892	-6.402	-6.716
14.5	-2.496	-2.874	-3.113	-3.257
15.0	0.000	0.000	0.000	0.000
15.5	2.399	2.740	2.949	3.072
16.0	4.706	5.353	5.744	5.972
16.5	6.925	7.846	8.397	8.714
17.0	9.059	10.227	10.917	11.309
17.5	11.114	12.502	13.313	13.768
18.0	13.092	14.678	15.592	16.100
18.5	14.998	16.759	17.763	18.315
19.0	16.834	18.751	19.832	20.420
19.5	18.604	20.659	21.806	22.423
20.0	20.310	22.488	23.690	24.331
20.5	21.957	24.242	25.490	26.150
21.0	23.545	25.925	27.212	27.886
21.5	25.079	27.541	28.859	29.544

MAXIMUM PREMIUM FOR ASSUMABLE LOANS
AS PERCENTAGE OF LOAN BALANCE

FACE INTEREST RATE: 15.25 %

CURRENT RATE	REMAINING TERM OF LOAN (YEARS)			
	15	20	25	30
7.0	-57.622	-72.230	-83.970	-93.064
7.5	-52.830	-65.754	-75.951	-83.701
8.0	-48.250	-59.641	-68.467	-75.051
8.5	-43.870	-53.867	-61.477	-67.048
9.0	-39.683	-48.412	-54.941	-59.635
9.5	-35.675	-43.253	-48.823	-52.757
10.0	-31.839	-38.370	-43.090	-46.365
10.5	-28.166	-33.746	-37.713	-40.418
11.0	-24.649	-29.366	-32.664	-34.876
11.5	-21.277	-25.212	-27.919	-29.705
12.0	-18.046	-21.271	-23.455	-24.873
12.5	-14.947	-17.529	-19.251	-20.351
13.0	-11.975	-13.975	-15.288	-16.115
13.5	-9.122	-10.595	-11.548	-12.139
14.0	-6.383	-7.380	-8.016	-8.405
14.5	-3.753	-4.320	-4.677	-4.892
15.0	-1.226	-1.406	-1.517	-1.583
15.5	1.202	1.372	1.477	1.538
16.0	3.537	4.022	4.315	4.484
16.5	5.783	6.551	7.008	7.269
17.0	7.944	8.965	9.566	9.905
17.5	10.024	11.272	11.998	12.403
18.0	12.026	13.478	14.312	14.772
18.5	13.955	15.589	16.515	17.022
19.0	15.814	17.609	18.616	19.160
19.5	17.605	19.544	20.619	21.195
20.0	19.333	21.399	22.532	23.133
20.5	21.000	23.177	24.360	24.981
21.0	22.608	24.884	26.108	26.745
21.5	24.160	26.522	27.780	28.429

MAXIMUM PREMIUM FOR ASSUMABLE LOANS
AS PERCENTAGE OF LOAN BALANCE

FACE INTEREST RATE: 15.5 %

CURRENT RATE	REMAINING TERM OF LOAN (YEARS)			
	15	20	25	30
7.0	-59.540	-74.627	-86.727	-96.079
7.5	-54.690	-68.060	-78.588	-86.569
8.0	-50.053	-61.862	-70.992	-77.784
8.5	-45.621	-56.008	-63.897	-69.657
9.0	-41.383	-50.477	-57.263	-62.128
9.5	-37.326	-45.246	-51.053	-55.142
10.0	-33.443	-40.295	-45.234	-48.651
10.5	-29.726	-35.608	-39.776	-42.611
11.0	-26.165	-31.166	-34.652	-36.983
11.5	-22.753	-26.954	-29.836	-31.731
12.0	-19.482	-22.959	-25.305	-26.823
12.5	-16.346	-19.165	-21.038	-22.231
13.0	-13.337	-15.561	-17.016	-17.928
13.5	-10.450	-12.134	-13.220	-13.891
14.0	-7.678	-8.875	-9.635	-10.098
14.5	-5.015	-5.772	-6.246	-6.530
15.0	-2.458	-2.817	-3.038	-3.169
15.5	0.000	0.000	0.000	0.000
16.0	2.364	2.687	2.881	2.992
16.5	4.637	5.250	5.614	5.821
17.0	6.823	7.698	8.211	8.498
17.5	8.929	10.038	10.679	11.035
18.0	10.956	12.274	13.028	13.441
18.5	12.908	14.414	15.264	15.726
19.0	14.789	16.462	17.396	17.898
19.5	16.603	18.425	19.430	19.964
20.0	18.352	20.305	21.371	21.933
20.5	20.038	22.108	23.226	23.810
21.0	21.666	23.838	25.000	25.601
21.5	23.237	25.500	26.698	27.312

MAXIMUM PREMIUM FOR ASSUMABLE LOANS
AS PERCENTAGE OF LOAN BALANCE

FACE INTEREST RATE: 15.75 %

CURRENT RATE	REMAINING TERM OF LOAN (YEARS)			
	15	20	25	30
7.0	-61.467	-77.033	-89.492	-99.100
7.5	-56.558	-70.376	-81.233	-89.444
8.0	-51.866	-64.092	-73.525	-80.524
8.5	-47.380	-58.158	-66.324	-72.271
9.0	-43.090	-52.551	-59.592	-64.626
9.5	-38.985	-47.247	-53.290	-57.533
10.0	-35.055	-42.228	-47.385	-50.941
10.5	-31.293	-37.476	-41.847	-44.808
11.0	-27.689	-32.973	-36.647	-39.093
11.5	-24.236	-28.704	-31.759	-33.760
12.0	-20.926	-24.653	-27.161	-28.777
12.5	-17.751	-20.807	-22.831	-24.114
13.0	-14.706	-17.153	-18.749	-19.745
13.5	-11.784	-13.679	-14.897	-15.646
14.0	-8.978	-10.375	-11.259	-11.794
14.5	-6.284	-7.229	-7.819	-8.171
15.0	-3.696	-4.234	-4.564	-4.759
15.5	-1.208	-1.378	-1.481	-1.541
16.0	1.184	1.346	1.442	1.498
16.5	3.485	3.945	4.216	4.370
17.0	5.698	6.427	6.851	7.088
17.5	7.829	8.798	9.356	9.664
18.0	9.880	11.066	11.740	12.107
18.5	11.856	13.235	14.009	14.427
19.0	13.760	15.311	16.173	16.633
19.5	15.596	17.300	18.237	18.731
20.0	17.365	19.207	20.207	20.730
20.5	19.073	21.035	22.089	22.636
21.0	20.720	22.789	23.889	24.454
21.5	22.310	24.473	25.612	26.192

MAXIMUM PREMIUM FOR ASSUMABLE LOANS
AS PERCENTAGE OF LOAN BALANCE

FACE INTEREST RATE: 16 %

CURRENT RATE	REMAINING TERM OF LOAN (YEARS)			
	15	20	25	30
7.0	-63.402	-79.448	-92.265	-102.127
7.5	-58.434	-72.700	-83.885	-92.324
8.0	-53.686	-66.331	-76.064	-83.268
8.5	-49.146	-60.315	-68.758	-74.890
9.0	-44.805	-54.632	-61.928	-67.129
9.5	-40.650	-49.256	-55.534	-59.928
10.0	-36.673	-44.168	-49.542	-53.236
10.5	-32.866	-39.351	-43.922	-47.010
11.0	-29.219	-34.787	-38.646	-41.208
11.5	-25.725	-30.459	-33.687	-35.794
12.0	-22.375	-26.353	-29.022	-30.735
12.5	-19.162	-22.454	-24.628	-26.001
13.0	-16.081	-18.751	-20.487	-21.566
13.5	-13.124	-15.230	-16.578	-17.404
14.0	-10.284	-11.880	-12.887	-13.494
14.5	-7.558	-8.692	-9.397	-9.816
15.0	-4.938	-5.655	-6.094	-6.352
15.5	-2.421	-2.761	-2.966	-3.085
16.0	0.000	0.000	0.000	0.000
16.5	2.328	2.635	2.815	2.916
17.0	4.568	5.150	5.488	5.676
17.5	6.724	7.554	8.030	8.291
18.0	8.800	9.853	10.448	10.771
18.5	10.800	12.051	12.751	13.126
19.0	12.727	14.156	14.946	15.365
19.5	14.584	16.172	17.040	17.496
20.0	16.375	18.105	19.039	19.525
20.5	18.103	19.958	20.949	21.459
21.0	19.770	21.736	22.776	23.306
21.5	21.379	23.443	24.523	25.069

MAXIMUM PREMIUM FOR ASSUMABLE LOANS
AS PERCENTAGE OF LOAN BALANCE

FACE INTEREST RATE: 16.25 %

CURRENT RATE	REMAINING TERM OF LOAN (YEARS)			
	15	20	25	30
7.0	-65.345	-81.871	-95.046	-105.160
7.5	-60.319	-75.032	-86.544	-95.210
8.0	-55.513	-68.577	-78.610	-86.018
8.5	-50.919	-62.480	-71.199	-77.514
9.0	-46.527	-56.720	-64.270	-69.637
9.5	-42.323	-51.271	-57.783	-62.327
10.0	-38.299	-46.115	-51.704	-55.535
10.5	-34.446	-41.233	-46.004	-49.216
11.0	-30.756	-36.608	-40.651	-43.327
11.5	-27.220	-32.221	-35.621	-37.832
12.0	-23.830	-28.059	-30.888	-32.697
12.5	-20.579	-24.108	-26.431	-27.892
13.0	-17.461	-20.355	-22.229	-23.390
13.5	-14.469	-16.786	-18.264	-19.165
14.0	-11.596	-13.391	-14.519	-15.197
14.5	-8.837	-10.160	-10.979	-11.464
15.0	-6.186	-7.082	-7.629	-7.947
15.5	-3.639	-4.148	-4.455	-4.631
16.0	-1.189	-1.350	-1.446	-1.500
16.5	1.167	1.320	1.409	1.459
17.0	3.433	3.869	4.121	4.260
17.5	5.615	6.306	6.700	6.915
18.0	7.716	8.635	9.153	9.432
18.5	9.739	10.864	11.489	11.823
19.0	11.689	12.997	13.716	14.095
19.5	13.568	15.040	15.840	16.258
20.0	15.381	16.999	17.868	18.317
20.5	17.129	18.877	19.806	20.281
21.0	18.816	20.679	21.659	22.155
21.5	20.444	22.409	23.432	23.945

MAXIMUM PREMIUM FOR ASSUMABLE LOANS
AS PERCENTAGE OF LOAN BALANCE

FACE INTEREST RATE: 16.5 %

CURRENT RATE	REMAINING TERM OF LOAN (YEARS)			
	15	20	25	30
7.0	-67.297	-84.304	-97.834	-108.198
7.5	-62.211	-77.373	-89.210	-98.101
8.0	-57.349	-70.831	-81.163	-88.773
8.5	-52.701	-64.653	-73.646	-80.143
9.0	-48.257	-58.816	-66.618	-72.149
9.5	-44.003	-53.294	-60.038	-64.731
10.0	-39.931	-48.069	-53.873	-57.839
10.5	-36.033	-43.122	-48.091	-51.425
11.0	-32.300	-38.434	-42.662	-45.449
11.5	-28.721	-33.989	-37.559	-39.873
12.0	-25.292	-29.772	-32.759	-34.662
12.5	-22.002	-25.768	-28.238	-29.786
13.0	-18.848	-21.964	-23.976	-25.217
13.5	-15.820	-18.348	-19.955	-20.930
14.0	-12.913	-14.908	-16.156	-16.903
14.5	-10.121	-11.633	-12.565	-13.114
15.0	-7.440	-8.514	-9.167	-9.546
15.5	-4.862	-5.541	-5.948	-6.181
16.0	-2.384	-2.706	-2.896	-3.004
16.5	0.000	0.000	0.000	0.000
17.0	2.293	2.584	2.751	2.843
17.5	4.501	5.053	5.366	5.536
18.0	6.626	7.413	7.854	8.091
18.5	8.674	9.672	10.224	10.517
19.0	10.646	11.833	12.483	12.823
19.5	12.548	13.904	14.637	15.017
20.0	14.382	15.889	16.694	17.108
20.5	16.151	17.792	18.660	19.100
21.0	17.858	19.618	20.539	21.002
21.5	19.505	21.371	22.337	22.819

MAXIMUM PREMIUM FOR ASSUMABLE LOANS
AS PERCENTAGE OF LOAN BALANCE

FACE INTEREST RATE: 16.75 %

CURRENT RATE	REMAINING TERM OF LOAN (YEARS)			
	15	20	25	30
7.0	-69.256	-86.744	-100.628	-111.242
7.5	-64.111	-79.721	-91.883	-100.997
8.0	-59.192	-73.093	-83.722	-91.532
8.5	-54.489	-66.833	-76.099	-82.777
9.0	-49.993	-60.918	-68.971	-74.666
9.5	-45.689	-55.324	-62.299	-67.139
10.0	-41.570	-50.030	-56.046	-60.146
10.5	-37.626	-45.017	-50.183	-53.639
11.0	-33.849	-40.267	-44.677	-47.576
11.5	-30.229	-35.763	-39.502	-41.917
12.0	-26.759	-31.490	-34.634	-36.630
12.5	-23.431	-27.433	-30.049	-31.683
13.0	-20.240	-23.579	-25.727	-27.047
13.5	-17.176	-19.915	-21.649	-22.698
14.0	-14.235	-16.429	-17.797	-18.612
14.5	-11.411	-13.111	-14.155	-14.768
15.0	-8.698	-9.951	-10.709	-11.147
15.5	-6.090	-6.939	-7.445	-7.733
16.0	-3.583	-4.066	-4.350	-4.509
16.5	-1.171	-1.324	-1.413	-1.462
17.0	1.149	1.294	1.377	1.422
17.5	3.382	3.796	4.029	4.155
18.0	5.533	6.187	6.553	6.747
18.5	7.604	8.476	8.956	9.209
19.0	9.600	10.666	11.246	11.549
19.5	11.524	12.764	13.432	13.775
20.0	13.379	14.775	15.518	15.896
20.5	15.169	16.704	17.511	17.918
21.0	16.895	18.554	19.417	19.847
21.5	18.562	20.330	21.240	21.691

MAXIMUM PREMIUM FOR ASSUMABLE LOANS
AS PERCENTAGE OF LOAN BALANCE

FACE INTEREST RATE: 17 %

CURRENT RATE	REMAINING TERM OF LOAN (YEARS)			
	15	20	25	30
7.0	-71.223	-89.192	-103.430	-114.290
7.5	-66.018	-82.077	-94.562	-103.897
8.0	-61.042	-75.362	-86.287	-94.296
8.5	-56.285	-69.020	-78.558	-85.414
9.0	-51.736	-63.028	-71.331	-77.186
9.5	-47.383	-57.360	-64.565	-69.551
10.0	-43.215	-51.996	-58.225	-62.457
10.5	-39.226	-46.918	-52.279	-55.856
11.0	-35.405	-42.106	-46.697	-49.705
11.5	-31.742	-37.543	-41.450	-43.965
12.0	-28.232	-33.214	-36.514	-38.602
12.5	-24.866	-29.104	-31.865	-33.583
13.0	-21.637	-25.199	-27.483	-28.881
13.5	-18.538	-21.487	-23.348	-24.468
14.0	-15.563	-17.955	-19.442	-20.323
14.5	-12.706	-14.594	-15.749	-16.424
15.0	-9.961	-11.392	-12.255	-12.751
15.5	-7.323	-8.340	-8.945	-9.288
16.0	-4.787	-5.430	-5.807	-6.017
16.5	-2.347	-2.652	-2.829	-2.926
17.0	0.000	0.000	0.000	0.000
17.5	2.259	2.534	2.689	2.772
18.0	4.435	4.958	5.248	5.402
18.5	6.530	7.276	7.685	7.899
19.0	8.549	9.495	10.007	10.272
19.5	10.496	11.621	12.223	12.531
20.0	12.372	13.658	14.338	14.682
20.5	14.183	15.612	16.359	16.733
21.0	15.930	17.486	18.291	18.691
21.5	17.616	19.286	20.141	20.561

MAXIMUM PREMIUM FOR ASSUMABLE LOANS
AS PERCENTAGE OF LOAN BALANCE

FACE INTEREST RATE: 17.25 %

CURRENT RATE	REMAINING TERM OF LOAN (YEARS)			
	15	20	25	30
7.0	-73.199	-91.648	-106.237	-117.343
7.5	-67.933	-84.441	-97.248	-106.802
8.0	-62.900	-77.639	-88.859	-97.064
8.5	-58.088	-71.214	-81.022	-88.055
9.0	-53.487	-65.144	-73.695	-79.710
9.5	-49.083	-59.403	-66.836	-71.966
10.0	-44.868	-53.970	-60.409	-64.771
10.5	-40.832	-48.825	-54.381	-58.076
11.0	-36.967	-43.951	-48.722	-51.838
11.5	-33.262	-39.329	-43.402	-46.016
12.0	-29.712	-34.943	-38.398	-40.576
12.5	-26.307	-30.780	-33.685	-35.486
13.0	-23.040	-26.824	-29.242	-30.717
13.5	-19.906	-23.064	-25.050	-26.242
14.0	-16.896	-19.487	-21.091	-22.037
14.5	-14.006	-16.082	-17.347	-18.082
15.0	-11.230	-12.838	-13.804	-14.357
15.5	-8.561	-9.747	-10.449	-10.845
16.0	-5.996	-6.799	-7.267	-7.528
16.5	-3.528	-3.985	-4.248	-4.392
17.0	-1.154	-1.298	-1.380	-1.425
17.5	1.132	1.269	1.346	1.387
18.0	3.332	3.724	3.940	4.054
18.5	5.452	6.072	6.411	6.587
19.0	7.494	8.320	8.765	8.994
19.5	9.463	10.473	11.011	11.285
20.0	11.361	12.537	13.156	13.467
20.5	13.193	14.516	15.204	15.547
21.0	14.960	16.415	17.164	17.532
21.5	16.666	18.238	19.038	19.429

MAXIMUM PREMIUM FOR ASSUMABLE LOANS
AS PERCENTAGE OF LOAN BALANCE

FACE INTEREST RATE: 17.5 %

CURRENT	REMAINING TERM OF LOAN (YEARS)			
RATE	15	20	25	30
7.0	-75.182	-94.111	-109.051	-120.400
7.5	-69.856	-86.812	-99.939	-109.711
8.0	-64.765	-79.922	-91.435	-99.836
8.5	-59.898	-73.415	-83.492	-90.701
9.0	-55.244	-67.267	-76.065	-82.238
9.5	-50.790	-61.452	-69.113	-74.385
10.0	-46.526	-55.949	-62.598	-67.089
10.5	-42.444	-50.738	-56.488	-60.300
11.0	-38.535	-45.801	-50.751	-53.974
11.5	-34.788	-41.120	-45.359	-48.070
12.0	-31.196	-36.678	-40.286	-42.554
12.5	-27.752	-32.461	-35.509	-37.392
13.0	-24.449	-28.455	-31.006	-32.555
13.5	-21.278	-24.646	-26.756	-28.017
14.0	-18.234	-21.023	-22.743	-23.754
14.5	-15.311	-17.574	-18.948	-19.743
15.0	-12.503	-14.289	-15.357	-15.966
15.5	-9.804	-11.158	-11.956	-12.404
16.0	-7.209	-8.171	-8.731	-9.040
16.5	-4.713	-5.322	-5.670	-5.861
17.0	-2.312	-2.600	-2.764	-2.851
17.5	0.000	0.000	0.000	0.000
18.0	2.226	2.486	2.629	2.705
18.5	4.370	4.865	5.134	5.273
19.0	6.435	7.142	7.520	7.714
19.5	8.427	9.323	9.797	10.037
20.0	10.347	11.413	11.971	12.250
20.5	12.199	13.417	14.048	14.359
21.0	13.986	15.341	16.033	16.372
21.5	15.712	17.187	17.934	18.296

MAXIMUM PREMIUM FOR ASSUMABLE LOANS
AS PERCENTAGE OF LOAN BALANCE

FACE INTEREST RATE: 17.75 %

CURRENT RATE	REMAINING TERM OF LOAN (YEARS)			
	15	20	25	30
7.0	-77.172	-96.582	-111.871	-123.461
7.5	-71.786	-89.190	-102.636	-112.624
8.0	-66.637	-82.213	-94.018	-102.612
8.5	-61.714	-75.623	-85.967	-93.350
9.0	-57.008	-69.397	-78.440	-84.769
9.5	-52.503	-63.507	-71.394	-76.808
10.0	-48.191	-57.934	-64.791	-69.410
10.5	-44.063	-52.657	-58.599	-62.526
11.0	-40.109	-47.657	-52.785	-56.112
11.5	-36.319	-42.916	-47.320	-50.127
12.0	-32.687	-38.418	-42.179	-44.534
12.5	-29.204	-34.147	-37.337	-39.300
13.0	-25.863	-30.090	-32.773	-34.396
13.5	-22.656	-26.233	-28.466	-29.795
14.0	-19.578	-22.563	-24.398	-25.473
14.5	-16.621	-19.070	-20.553	-21.407
15.0	-13.781	-15.744	-16.913	-17.577
15.5	-11.052	-12.573	-13.466	-13.965
16.0	-8.427	-9.548	-10.197	-10.555
16.5	-5.903	-6.662	-7.096	-7.331
17.0	-3.474	-3.906	-4.150	-4.280
17.5	-1.136	-1.273	-1.349	-1.389
18.0	1.115	1.245	1.316	1.353
18.5	3.283	3.654	3.854	3.957
19.0	5.372	5.959	6.273	6.432
19.5	7.386	8.168	8.580	8.787
20.0	9.328	10.285	10.783	11.031
20.5	11.201	12.315	12.888	13.170
21.0	13.009	14.263	14.901	15.211
21.5	14.754	16.133	16.827	17.161

DISCOUNT POINT TABLE
(Effective Annual Interest Rates on Loan Held to Maturity)

The following tables indicate the effective interest rate paid over the term of a mortgage loan when discount points are charged at origination. Discount points are commonly charged to either or both the seller and buyer when a home mortgage loan is made. Each point is equal to 1% of the amount borrowed on the loan. Points are generally considered interest. Their effect is to raise the interest rate above the rate stated in the mortgage contract. The tables assume that loans run to their full amortization term. If the loan is paid off before maturity, the effective rate is higher than that shown in the table. The difference is not substantial, however, unless the loan is paid off in the early part of the term.

To use the table, you must know the following items:

1. *The loan maturity.* There are two tables each for loans with maturities of 15, 20, 25, and 30 years.

2. *The contract or face rate of interest.* This is the rate of interest stated in the mortgage contract. Contract rates are shown in the left-most column of each table. One table covers rates from 7% to 13.75% and the other from 14% to 20.75% in .25% increments.

3. *The number of discount points charged.* These are listed in the heading of each table and vary from 1 to 5 points.

Example: A loan with a maturity of 15 years is originated at a contract rate of 10%. If three points are charged and the loan is held to maturity, what is the effective annual rate of interest? ·

Look at the first table for 15-year loans. Find "10.00" in the column under "CONTRACT RATE." Follow this row across to the column under "3 DISCOUNT POINTS." This is the effective interest rate of 10.54%

Example. A loan is originated for 15 years at a contract interest rate of 14. 5%. If the lender wants to earn an effective rate of 15.5% on the loan, how many discount points should be charged?

Look at the second table for 15-year loans. Find the row under "CONTRACT RATE" for 14.50%. Follow this row across until a rate of at least 15.5% is found. The column under "5 DISCOUNT POINTS" shows an effective rate of 15.55%, so the lender should charge 5 points.

EFFECTIVE ANNUAL INTEREST RATE
ON LOAN HELD TO MATURITY
(ANNUAL PERCENTAGE RATE)

LOAN TERM: 15 YEARS

CONTRACT RATE	DISCOUNT POINTS				
	1	2	3	4	5
7.00	7.16	7.33	7.49	7.66	7.83
7.25	7.41	7.58	7.75	7.92	8.09
7.50	7.66	7.83	8.00	8.17	8.35
7.75	7.92	8.08	8.25	8.43	8.60
8.00	8.17	8.34	8.51	8.68	8.86
8.25	8.42	8.59	8.76	8.94	9.12
8.50	8.67	8.84	9.02	9.19	9.37
8.75	8.92	9.09	9.27	9.45	9.63
9.00	9.17	9.35	9.52	9.70	9.89
9.25	9.42	9.60	9.78	9.96	10.14
9.50	9.67	9.85	10.03	10.21	10.40
9.75	9.93	10.10	10.29	10.47	10.66
10.00	10.18	10.36	10.54	10.72	10.91
10.25	10.43	10.61	10.79	10.98	11.17
10.50	10.68	10.86	11.05	11.24	11.43
10.75	10.93	11.11	11.30	11.49	11.68
11.00	11.18	11.37	11.56	11.75	11.94
11.25	11.43	11.62	11.81	12.00	12.20
11.50	11.69	11.87	12.06	12.26	12.46
11.75	11.94	12.13	12.32	12.51	12.71
12.00	12.19	12.38	12.57	12.77	12.97
12.25	12.44	12.63	12.83	13.03	13.23
12.50	12.69	12.88	13.08	13.28	13.49
12.75	12.94	13.14	13.34	13.54	13.74
13.00	13.19	13.39	13.59	13.79	14.00
13.25	13.45	13.64	13.85	14.05	14.26
13.50	13.70	13.90	14.10	14.31	14.52
13.75	13.95	14.15	14.35	14.56	14.77

EFFECTIVE ANNUAL INTEREST RATE
ON LOAN HELD TO MATURITY
(ANNUAL PERCENTAGE RATE)

LOAN TERM: 15 YEARS

CONTRACT RATE	DISCOUNT POINTS				
	1	2	3	4	5
14.00	14.20	14.40	14.61	14.82	15.03
14.25	14.45	14.66	14.86	15.08	15.29
14.50	14.70	14.91	15.12	15.33	15.55
14.75	14.95	15.16	15.37	15.59	15.81
15.00	15.21	15.42	15.63	15.84	16.07
15.25	15.46	15.67	15.88	16.10	16.32
15.50	15.71	15.92	16.14	16.36	16.58
15.75	15.96	16.18	16.39	16.61	16.84
16.00	16.21	16.43	16.65	16.87	17.10
16.25	16.46	16.68	16.90	17.13	17.36
16.50	16.72	16.94	17.16	17.38	17.62
16.75	16.97	17.19	17.41	17.64	17.87
17.00	17.22	17.44	17.67	17.90	18.13
17.25	17.47	17.69	17.92	18.16	18.39
17.50	17.72	17.95	18.18	18.41	18.65
17.75	17.97	18.20	18.43	18.67	18.91
18.00	18.23	18.46	18.69	18.93	19.17
18.25	18.48	18.71	18.94	19.18	19.43
18.50	18.73	18.96	19.20	19.44	19.69
18.75	18.98	19.22	19.45	19.70	19.95
19.00	19.23	19.47	19.71	19.96	20.20
19.25	19.48	19.72	19.97	20.21	20.46
19.50	19.74	19.98	20.22	20.47	20.72
19.75	19.99	20.23	20.48	20.73	20.98
20.00	20.24	20.48	20.73	20.98	21.24
20.25	20.49	20.74	20.99	21.24	21.50
20.50	20.74	20.99	21.24	21.50	21.76
20.75	21.00	21.24	21.50	21.76	22.02

EFFECTIVE ANNUAL INTEREST RATE
ON LOAN HELD TO MATURITY
(ANNUAL PERCENTAGE RATE)

LOAN TERM: 20 YEARS

CONTRACT RATE	DISCOUNT POINTS				
	1	2	3	4	5
7.00	7.13	7.26	7.40	7.53	7.67
7.25	7.38	7.51	7.65	7.79	7.93
7.50	7.63	7.77	7.90	8.04	8.18
7.75	7.88	8.02	8.16	8.30	8.44
8.00	8.14	8.27	8.41	8.55	8.70
8.25	8.39	8.53	8.67	8.81	8.96
8.50	8.64	8.78	8.92	9.07	9.21
8.75	8.89	9.03	9.18	9.32	9.47
9.00	9.14	9.28	9.43	9.58	9.73
9.25	9.39	9.54	9.68	9.83	9.99
9.50	9.64	9.79	9.94	10.09	10.24
9.75	9.90	10.04	10.19	10.35	10.50
10.00	10.15	10.30	10.45	10.60	10.76
10.25	10.40	10.55	10.70	10.86	11.02
10.50	10.65	10.80	10.96	11.11	11.27
10.75	10.90	11.06	11.21	11.37	11.53
11.00	11.15	11.31	11.47	11.63	11.79
11.25	11.40	11.56	11.72	11.88	12.05
11.50	11.66	11.81	11.98	12.14	12.31
11.75	11.91	12.07	12.23	12.40	12.57
12.00	12.16	12.32	12.49	12.65	12.82
12.25	12.41	12.57	12.74	12.91	13.08
12.50	12.66	12.83	13.00	13.17	13.34
12.75	12.91	13.08	13.25	13.42	13.60
13.00	13.17	13.33	13.51	13.68	13.86
13.25	13.42	13.59	13.76	13.94	14.12
13.50	13.67	13.84	14.02	14.19	14.38
13.75	13.92	14.09	14.27	14.45	14.63

EFFECTIVE ANNUAL INTEREST RATE
ON LOAN HELD TO MATURITY
(ANNUAL PERCENTAGE RATE)

LOAN TERM: 20 YEARS

CONTRACT RATE	DISCOUNT POINTS				
	1	2	3	4	5
14.00	14.17	14.35	14.53	14.71	14.89
14.25	14.42	14.60	14.78	14.97	15.15
14.50	14.68	14.86	15.04	15.22	15.41
14.75	14.93	15.11	15.29	15.48	15.67
15.00	15.18	15.36	15.55	15.74	15.93
15.25	15.43	15.62	15.80	16.00	16.19
15.50	15.68	15.87	16.06	16.25	16.45
15.75	15.94	16.12	16.32	16.51	16.71
16.00	16.19	16.38	16.57	16.77	16.97
16.25	16.44	16.63	16.83	17.03	17.23
16.50	16.69	16.89	17.08	17.28	17.49
16.75	16.94	17.14	17.34	17.54	17.75
17.00	17.19	17.39	17.59	17.80	18.01
17.25	17.45	17.65	17.85	18.06	18.27
17.50	17.70	17.90	18.11	18.32	18.53
17.75	17.95	18.15	18.36	18.57	18.79
18.00	18.20	18.41	18.62	18.83	19.05
18.25	18.45	18.66	18.87	19.09	19.31
18.50	18.71	18.92	19.13	19.35	19.57
18.75	18.96	19.17	19.39	19.61	19.83
19.00	19.21	19.42	19.64	19.86	20.09
19.25	19.46	19.68	19.90	20.12	20.35
19.50	19.71	19.93	20.15	20.38	20.61
19.75	19.97	20.19	20.41	20.64	20.87
20.00	20.22	20.44	20.67	20.90	21.13
20.25	20.47	20.70	20.92	21.16	21.39
20.50	20.72	20.95	21.18	21.42	21.66
20.75	20.97	21.20	21.44	21.67	21.92

EFFECTIVE ANNUAL INTEREST RATE
ON LOAN HELD TO MATURITY
(ANNUAL PERCENTAGE RATE)

LOAN TERM: 25 YEARS

CONTRACT RATE	DISCOUNT POINTS				
	1	2	3	4	5
7.00	7.11	7.23	7.34	7.46	7.58
7.25	7.36	7.48	7.59	7.71	7.83
7.50	7.61	7.73	7.85	7.97	8.09
7.75	7.87	7.98	8.10	8.23	8.35
8.00	8.12	8.24	8.36	8.48	8.61
8.25	8.37	8.49	8.61	8.74	8.86
8.50	8.62	8.74	8.87	8.99	9.12
8.75	8.87	9.00	9.12	9.25	9.38
9.00	9.12	9.25	9.38	9.51	9.64
9.25	9.38	9.50	9.63	9.76	9.90
9.50	9.63	9.76	9.89	10.02	10.16
9.75	9.88	10.01	10.14	10.28	10.41
10.00	10.13	10.26	10.40	10.53	10.67
10.25	10.38	10.52	10.65	10.79	10.93
10.50	10.63	10.77	10.91	11.05	11.19
10.75	10.88	11.02	11.16	11.30	11.45
11.00	11.14	11.28	11.42	11.56	11.71
11.25	11.39	11.53	11.67	11.82	11.97
11.50	11.64	11.78	11.93	12.08	12.23
11.75	11.89	12.04	12.18	12.33	12.49
12.00	12.14	12.29	12.44	12.59	12.74
12.25	12.40	12.54	12.69	12.85	13.00
12.50	12.65	12.80	12.95	13.11	13.26
12.75	12.90	13.05	13.21	13.36	13.52
13.00	13.15	13.30	13.46	13.62	13.78
13.25	13.40	13.56	13.72	13.88	14.04
13.50	13.65	13.81	13.97	14.14	14.30
13.75	13.91	14.07	14.23	14.39	14.56

EFFECTIVE ANNUAL INTEREST RATE
ON LOAN HELD TO MATURITY
(ANNUAL PERCENTAGE RATE)

LOAN TERM: 25 YEARS

CONTRACT RATE	DISCOUNT POINTS				
	1	2	3	4	5
14.00	14.16	14.32	14.48	14.65	14.82
14.25	14.41	14.57	14.74	14.91	15.08
14.50	14.66	14.83	15.00	15.17	15.34
14.75	14.91	15.08	15.25	15.43	15.60
15.00	15.17	15.34	15.51	15.68	15.86
15.25	15.42	15.59	15.77	15.94	16.12
15.50	15.67	15.84	16.02	16.20	16.39
15.75	15.92	16.10	16.28	16.46	16.65
16.00	16.17	16.35	16.53	16.72	16.91
16.25	16.43	16.61	16.79	16.98	17.17
16.50	16.68	16.86	17.05	17.24	17.43
16.75	16.93	17.12	17.30	17.49	17.69
17.00	17.18	17.37	17.56	17.75	17.95
17.25	17.44	17.62	17.82	18.01	18.21
17.50	17.69	17.88	18.07	18.27	18.47
17.75	17.94	18.13	18.33	18.53	18.73
18.00	18.19	18.39	18.59	18.79	19.00
18.25	18.44	18.64	18.84	19.05	19.26
18.50	18.70	18.90	19.10	19.31	19.52
18.75	18.95	19.15	19.36	19.57	19.78
19.00	19.20	19.40	19.61	19.82	20.04
19.25	19.45	19.66	19.87	20.08	20.30
19.50	19.70	19.91	20.13	20.34	20.56
19.75	19.96	20.17	20.38	20.60	20.83
20.00	20.21	20.42	20.64	20.86	21.09
20.25	20.46	20.68	20.90	21.12	21.35
20.50	20.71	20.93	21.15	21.38	21.61
20.75	20.97	21.19	21.41	21.64	21.87

EFFECTIVE ANNUAL INTEREST RATE
ON LOAN HELD TO MATURITY
(ANNUAL PERCENTAGE RATE)

LOAN TERM: 30 YEARS

CONTRACT RATE	DISCOUNT POINTS				
	1	2	3	4	5
7.00	7.10	7.20	7.30	7.41	7.52
7.25	7.35	7.45	7.56	7.67	7.77
7.50	7.60	7.71	7.81	7.92	8.03
7.75	7.85	7.96	8.07	8.18	8.29
8.00	8.11	8.21	8.32	8.44	8.55
8.25	8.36	8.47	8.58	8.69	8.81
8.50	8.61	8.72	8.83	8.95	9.07
8.75	8.86	8.97	9.09	9.21	9.32
9.00	9.11	9.23	9.34	9.46	9.58
9.25	9.36	9.48	9.60	9.72	9.84
9.50	9.62	9.73	9.85	9.98	10.10
9.75	9.87	9.99	10.11	10.23	10.36
10.00	10.12	10.24	10.37	10.49	10.62
10.25	10.37	10.50	10.62	10.75	10.88
10.50	10.62	10.75	10.88	11.01	11.14
10.75	10.88	11.00	11.13	11.26	11.40
11.00	11.13	11.26	11.39	11.52	11.66
11.25	11.38	11.51	11.64	11.78	11.92
11.50	11.63	11.76	11.90	12.04	12.18
11.75	11.88	12.02	12.16	12.30	12.44
12.00	12.13	12.27	12.41	12.55	12.70
12.25	12.39	12.53	12.67	12.81	12.96
12.50	12.64	12.78	12.92	13.07	13.22
12.75	12.89	13.03	13.18	13.33	13.48
13.00	13.14	13.29	13.44	13.59	13.74
13.25	13.39	13.54	13.69	13.85	14.00
13.50	13.65	13.80	13.95	14.10	14.26
13.75	13.90	14.05	14.21	14.36	14.52

EFFECTIVE ANNUAL INTEREST RATE
ON LOAN HELD TO MATURITY
(ANNUAL PERCENTAGE RATE)

LOAN TERM: 30 YEARS

CONTRACT RATE	DISCOUNT POINTS				
	1	2	3	4	5
14.00	14.15	14.31	14.46	14.62	14.78
14.25	14.40	14.56	14.72	14.88	15.05
14.50	14.66	14.81	14.97	15.14	15.31
14.75	14.91	15.07	15.23	15.40	15.57
15.00	15.16	15.32	15.49	15.66	15.83
15.25	15.41	15.58	15.74	15.92	16.09
15.50	15.66	15.83	16.00	16.17	16.35
15.75	15.92	16.09	16.26	16.43	16.61
16.00	16.17	16.34	16.51	16.69	16.87
16.25	16.42	16.59	16.77	16.95	17.14
16.50	16.67	16.85	17.03	17.21	17.40
16.75	16.92	17.10	17.29	17.47	17.66
17.00	17.18	17.36	17.54	17.73	17.92
17.25	17.43	17.61	17.80	17.99	18.18
17.50	17.68	17.87	18.06	18.25	18.45
17.75	17.93	18.12	18.31	18.51	18.71
18.00	18.19	18.38	18.57	18.77	18.97
18.25	18.44	18.63	18.83	19.03	19.23
18.50	18.69	18.89	19.08	19.29	19.49
18.75	18.94	19.14	19.34	19.55	19.76
19.00	19.20	19.40	19.60	19.81	20.02
19.25	19.45	19.65	19.86	20.07	20.28
19.50	19.70	19.90	20.11	20.33	20.54
19.75	19.95	20.16	20.37	20.59	20.81
20.00	20.21	20.41	20.63	20.85	21.07
20.25	20.46	20.67	20.88	21.11	21.33
20.50	20.71	20.92	21.14	21.37	21.59
20.75	20.96	21.18	21.40	21.62	21.85

GRADUATED PAYMENT MORTGAGES
(Monthly Payment per $1,000 of Principal)

The following tables allow you to compute a payment schedule for a common form of graduated payment mortgage loan. This type of loan features a 5-year period in the beginning of the loan term in which monthly payments are lower than with a conventional fixed-payment loan. For each year of this period, monthly payments are increased by 7.5% compared with the previous year. The payment reaches its highest level in the sixth year and is constant over the remaining term of the loan.

The table allows you to calculate what the payments will be for each year of the initial term and the constant payment for the remaining term. You will need the following information:

1. *The interest rate on the loan.* Interest rates ranging from 8% to 21.75% in .25% intervals are listed in the left-most column of the tables.

2. *The amount of the loan.* The factors in the tables represent the monthly payment in dollars for each thousand dollars of original loan principal. To calculate the payments for your loan, you must multiply the factor by the number of thousands in the loan amount.

Example. A graduated payment mortgage, following the form of FHA 245 plan III, is originated at 12% interest. The amount of the loan is $55,500. What is the monthly payment in the first year? In the sixth year?

Find the column under "INTEREST RATE" and look for the rate of 12.00%. Follow this row to the column under "YEAR 1st." The factor is 7.91. Multiply this factor by 55.5 to obtain the first-year payment of $439.01.

Now follow the row for the 12% interest rate to the column under "YEAR 6-30." The factor shown is 11.36. Multiplying this factor by 55.5 gives $630.48, the payment in the sixth year and every year thereafter.

Example. You can afford to pay up to $400 in monthly payments in the first year. If the interest rate on graduated payment mortgages is 15%, how much can you afford to borrow?

Look under "INTEREST RATE" to find 15.00 (second page of tables). The factor under the 1st year is 9.90. Divide $400 by the factor to obtain 40.4. Multiply this figure by $1,000 to obtain the maximum loan you can afford, $40,400.

GRADUATED PAYMENT MORTGAGE

MONTHLY PAYMENT PER $1000 OF PRINCIPAL
FHA 245 PLAN III
LOAN TERM = 30 YEARS

INTEREST RATE	1st	2nd	3rd	4th	5th	6-30
8.00	5.51	5.92	6.37	6.85	7.36	7.91
8.25	5.65	6.07	6.53	7.02	7.55	8.11
8.50	5.79	6.23	6.69	7.19	7.73	8.31
8.75	5.93	6.38	6.86	7.37	7.93	8.52
9.00	6.08	6.53	7.02	7.55	8.12	8.73
9.25	6.22	6.69	7.19	7.73	8.31	8.94
9.50	6.37	6.85	7.36	7.92	8.51	9.15
9.75	6.52	7.01	7.54	8.10	8.71	9.36
10.00	6.67	7.17	7.71	8.29	8.91	9.58
10.25	6.82	7.33	7.88	8.47	9.11	9.79
10.50	6.97	7.50	8.06	8.66	9.31	10.01
10.75	7.13	7.66	8.24	8.85	9.52	10.23
11.00	7.28	7.83	8.42	9.05	9.73	10.46
11.25	7.44	8.00	8.60	9.24	9.93	10.68
11.50	7.60	8.17	8.78	9.44	10.14	10.90
11.75	7.75	8.34	8.96	9.63	10.36	11.13
12.00	7.91	8.51	9.15	9.83	10.57	11.36
12.25	8.07	8.68	9.33	10.03	10.78	11.59
12.50	8.24	8.85	9.52	10.23	11.00	11.82
12.75	8.40	9.03	9.71	10.43	11.22	12.06
13.00	8.56	9.20	9.89	10.64	11.43	12.29
13.25	8.73	9.38	10.08	10.84	11.65	12.53
13.50	8.89	9.56	10.28	11.05	11.87	12.77
13.75	9.06	9.74	10.47	11.25	12.10	13.00
14.00	9.23	9.92	10.66	11.46	12.32	13.24
14.25	9.39	10.10	10.86	11.67	12.54	13.49
14.50	9.56	10.28	11.05	11.88	12.77	13.73
14.75	9.73	10.46	11.25	12.09	13.00	13.97

GRADUATED PAYMENT MORTGAGE

MONTHLY PAYMENT PER $1000 OF PRINCIPAL
FHA 245 PLAN III
LOAN TERM = 30 YEARS

INTEREST RATE	1st	2nd	3rd	4th	5th	6-30
15.00	9.90	10.65	11.44	12.30	13.22	14.22
15.25	10.07	10.83	11.64	12.51	13.45	14.46
15.50	10.25	11.01	11.84	12.73	13.68	14.71
15.75	10.42	11.20	12.04	12.94	13.91	14.96
16.00	10.59	11.39	12.24	13.16	14.15	15.21
16.25	10.77	11.57	12.44	13.37	14.38	15.46
16.50	10.94	11.76	12.64	13.59	14.61	15.71
16.75	11.12	11.95	12.85	13.81	14.85	15.96
17.00	11.29	12.14	13.05	14.03	15.08	16.21
17.25	11.47	12.33	13.25	14.25	15.32	16.47
17.50	11.65	12.52	13.46	14.47	15.55	16.72
17.75	11.82	12.71	13.66	14.69	15.79	16.98
18.00	12.00	12.90	13.87	14.91	16.03	17.23
18.25	12.18	13.10	14.08	15.13	16.27	17.49
18.50	12.36	13.29	14.29	15.36	16.51	17.75
18.75	12.54	13.48	14.49	15.58	16.75	18.01
19.00	12.72	13.68	14.70	15.81	16.99	18.27
19.25	12.90	13.87	14.91	16.03	17.23	18.53
19.50	13.09	14.07	15.12	16.26	17.48	18.79
19.75	13.27	14.26	15.33	16.48	17.72	19.05
20.00	13.45	14.46	15.54	16.71	17.96	19.31
20.25	13.63	14.66	15.76	16.94	18.21	19.57
20.50	13.82	14.85	15.97	17.17	18.45	19.84
20.75	14.00	15.05	16.18	17.39	18.70	20.10
21.00	14.19	15.25	16.39	17.62	18.95	20.37
21.25	14.37	15.45	16.61	17.85	19.19	20.63
21.50	14.56	15.65	16.82	18.08	19.44	20.90
21.75	14.74	15.85	17.04	18.31	19.69	21.16

DEPRECIATION PERCENTAGES
Economic Recovery Tax Act of 1981 as modified
by The Tax Reform Act of 1984
and
Standard Accounting Depreciation

The body of these tables shows the percentage of depreciation that may be claimed in a year for assets eligible for depreciation. The tables shown here include those offered by the Tax Reform Act of 1984 and those used for standard accounting purposes.

Depreciation deductions may be claimed for tax purposes on most structural assets or equipment used in a trade or business. These deductions may be thought of as providing a tax incentive for the use of productive assets, allowing for the cost of assets to be recovered over time, or as an allowance for exhaustion, wear and tear and normal obsolescence.

To be eligible for depreciation deductions, an asset must be used in a trade or business or held for the production of income. This excludes personal cars or residences since they are not used in a trade or business. It also excludes land since land does not wear out. For example, a tractor that is used to farm land or clear land for sale as a subdivision is eligible for depreciation. The land itself is considered nonwasting and is not eligible for depreciation. A single family home that is rented to a tenant can be depreciated, but not the land under it.

Depreciation under the Tax Reform Act of 1984. The Tax Reform Act of 1984 (TRA) prescribed the percentage of asset cost that may be depreciated each year. This is based on the class of property. Classes include 3-, 5-, 10-, and 18-year life property. Most buildings fall in the 18-year category. The percentage of depreciation to be claimed is shown.

For personal property, such as refrigerators and furniture, the annual depreciation percentage under TRA will vary depending on the year it is placed in service. For real estate, the percentage will vary depending upon the month placed in service.

You may use either these tables or an alternative straight-line amount. To use the tables you need to know the year the property was placed in service (for buildings the month is needed), the recovery class, and asset cost. Select the appropriate table considering the year and class of property. For most personal property (short-lived) find the intersection of the class life (year) with the year of use. Apply the percentage in the table to the asset cost. For a building, find the column for the month it is placed in service. Multiply the percentage by the building cost to derive the annual depreciation allowance.

Standard accounting depreciation tables. Tables are also provided for standard accounting depreciation. They reflect the deduction percentages for straight-line, 125%, 150%, and 200% declining balance depreciation and sum-of-the-years' digits.

Example. A warehouse was acquired in July 1984 for $1,000,000, exclusive of land. How much depreciation may be deducted under TRA in

1984 and 1985? Turn to the page which offers recovery amounts for buildings other than low-income housing. The intersection of July with year 1 offers the number 4. Thus, 4% of the asset cost, or $40,000 for the warehouse, is deductible in 1984. The intersection of July with recovery year 2 offers 9. Therefore 9% of the asset cost, or $90,000, may be deducted in the second year (1985).

Example. What are the first and second year deductions for furniture that cost $500 and was placed in service in 1985? Most furniture is in the 5-year property class. Find the page that offers property placed in service in 1985. Then find the column for 5-year property. The appropriate first year percentage is 18. Then 18 percent of its cost may be deducted in 1985 regardless of the month of acquisition. This is a $90 deduction. The second year percentage is 33. The second year deduction is 33% of $500 or $165.

Example. What is the accounting deduction for depreciation on a $100,000 asset that has a 25-year depreciable life? Use the straight-line and double-declining methods for the first 2 years. Turn to the page that shows accounting methods with a 25-year life. Read the intersection of "YEAR" with the method. For straight-line, it is 4.00% per year, or $4,000 for a $100,000 asset. Using 200% declining balance it is 8.00% the first year ($8,000) and 7.36% ($7,360) the second.

DEPRECIATION PERCENTAGES
UNDER ACCELERATED COST RECOVERY SYSTEM

FOR PROPERTY PLACED IN SERVICE FROM 1981 to 1984

	Class of property			
Recovery year	3-year	5-year	10-year	15-year public utility
1	25	15	8	5
2	38	22	14	10
3	37	21	12	9
4	—	21	10	8
5	—	21	10	7
6	—	—	10	7
7	—	—	9	6
8	—	—	9	6
9	—	—	9	6
10	—	—	9	6
11	—	—	—	6
12	—	—	—	6
13	—	—	—	6
14	—	—	—	6
15	—	—	—	6

DEPRECIATION PERCENTAGES
UNDER ACCELERATED COST RECOVERY SYSTEM

FOR PROPERTY PLACED IN SERVICE IN 1985

		Class of property		
Recovery year	3-year	5-year	10-year	15-year public utility
1	29	18	9	6
2	47	33	19	12
3	24	25	16	12
4	—	16	14	11
5	—	8	12	10
6	—	—	10	9
7	—	—	8	8
8	—	—	6	7
9	—	—	4	6
10	—	—	2	5
11	—	—	—	4
12	—	—	—	4
13	—	—	—	3
14	—	—	—	2
15	—	—	—	1

FOR PROPERTY PLACED IN SERVICE AFTER 1985

1	33	20	10	7
2	45	32	18	12
3	22	24	16	12
4	—	16	14	11
5	—	8	12	10
6	—	—	10	9
7	—	—	8	8
8	—	—	6	7
9	—	—	4	6
10	—	—	2	5
11	—	—	—	4
12	—	—	—	3
13	—	—	—	3
14	—	—	—	2
15	—	—	—	1

DEPRECIATION PERCENTAGES FOR BUILDINGS UNDER THE ACCELERATED COST RECOVERY SYSTEM

RECOVERY PERCENTAGES FOR BUILDINGS PLACED IN SERVICE AFTER JUNE 22, 1984 (EXCEPT LOW-INCOME HOUSING)

Applicable percentage
(Use the column for the month in the first year the property is placed in service)

Recovery year	Jan	Feb	Mar	Apr	May	Jun	Jul	Aug	Sep	Oct	Nov	Dec
1	9	9	8	7	6	5	4	4	3	2	1	0.4
2	9	9	9	9	9	9	9	9	9	10	10	10.0
3	8	8	8	8	8	8	8	8	9	9	9	9.0
4	7	7	7	8	7	8	8	8	8	8	8	8.0
5	7	7	7	7	7	7	7	7	7	7	7	7.0
6	6	6	6	6	6	6	6	6	6	6	6	6.0
7	5	5	5	5	6	6	6	6	6	6	6	6.0
8	5	5	5	5	5	5	5	5	5	5	5	5.0
9	5	5	5	5	5	5	5	5	5	5	5	5.0
10	5	5	5	5	5	5	5	5	5	5	5	5.0
11	5	5	5	5	5	5	5	5	5	5	5	5.0
12	5	5	5	5	5	5	5	5	5	5	5	5.0
13	4	4	4	5	4	4	5	4	4	4	5	5.0
14	4	4	4	4	4	4	4	4	4	4	4	4.0
15	4	4	4	4	4	4	4	4	4	4	4	4.0
16	4	4	4	4	4	4	4	4	4	4	4	4.0
17	4	4	4	4	4	4	4	4	4	4	4	4.0
18	4	3	4	4	4	4	4	4	4	4	4	4.0
19	1	1	1	1	2	2	2	3	3	3	3	3.6

DEPRECIATION PERCENTAGES FOR BUILDINGS UNDER THE ACCELERATED COST RECOVERY SYSTEM

RECOVERY PERCENTAGES FOR LOW-INCOME HOUSING

Applicable percentage
(Use the column for the month in the first year the property is placed in service)

Recovery year	Jan	Feb	Mar	Apr	May	Jun	Jul	Aug	Sep	Oct	Nov	Dec
1	13	12	11	10	9	8	7	6	4	3	2	1
2	12	12	12	12	12	12	12	13	13	13	13	13
3	10	10	10	10	11	11	11	11	11	11	11	11
4	9	9	9	9	9	9	9	9	10	10	10	10
5	8	8	8	8	8	8	8	8	8	8	8	9
6	7	7	7	7	7	7	7	7	7	7	7	7
7	6	6	6	6	6	6	6	6	6	6	6	6
8	5	5	5	5	5	5	5	5	5	5	6	6
9	5	5	5	5	5	5	5	5	5	5	5	5
10	5	5	5	5	5	5	5	5	5	5	5	5
11	4	5	5	5	5	5	5	5	5	5	5	5
12	4	4	4	4	4	4	4	4	5	5	5	5
13	4	4	4	4	4	4	4	4	4	4	4	4
14	4	4	4	4	4	4	4	4	4	4	4	4
15	4	4	4	4	4	4	4	4	4	4	4	4
16	—	—	1	1	2	2	2	3	3	3	4	4

DEPRECIATION PERCENTAGES UNDER
ACCOUNTING METHODS

3-YEAR USEFUL LIFE

Year	Straight-Line Rate: 33.33%	125% Decl Bal Rate: 41.67	150% Decl Bal Rate: 50.00%	200% Decl Bal Rate: 66.67%	Sum-of-the-Years Digits
1	33.333	41.667	50.000	66.667	50.000
2	33.333	24.306	25.000	22.222	33.333
3	33.333	14.178	12.500	7.407	16.667

4-YEAR USEFUL LIFE

Year	Straight-Line Rate: 25.00%	125% Decl Bal Rate: 31.25	150% Decl Bal Rate: 37.50%	200% Decl Bal Rate: 50.00%	Sum-of-the-Years Digits
1	25.000	31.250	37.500	50.000	40.000
2	25.000	21.484	23.438	25.000	30.000
3	25.000	14.771	14.648	12.500	20.000
4	25.000	10.155	9.155	6.250	10.000

5-YEAR USEFUL LIFE

Year	Straight-Line Rate: 20.00%	125% Decl Bal Rate: 25.00	150% Decl Bal Rate: 30.00%	200% Decl Bal Rate: 40.00%	Sum-of-the-Years Digits
1	20.000	25.000	30.000	40.000	33.333
2	20.000	18.750	21.000	24.000	26.667
3	20.000	14.063	14.700	14.400	20.000
4	20.000	10.547	10.290	8.640	13.333
5	20.000	7.910	7.203	5.184	6.667

DEPRECIATION PERCENTAGES UNDER ACCOUNTING METHODS

10-YEAR USEFUL LIFE

Year	Straight-Line Rate: 10.00%	125% Decl Bal Rate: 12.50	150% Decl Bal Rate: 15.00%	200% Decl Bal Rate: 20.00%	Sum-of-the-Years Digits
1	10.000	12.500	15.000	20.000	18.182
2	10.000	10.937	12.750	16.000	16.364
3	10.000	9.570	10.837	12.800	14.545
4	10.000	8.374	9.212	10.240	12.727
5	10.000	7.327	7.830	8.192	10.909
6	10.000	6.411	6.656	6.554	9.091
7	10.000	5.610	5.657	5.243	7.273
8	10.000	4.909	4.809	4.194	5.455
9	10.000	4.295	4.087	3.355	3.636
10	10.000	3.758	3.474	2.684	1.818

12-YEAR USEFUL LIFE

Year	Straight-Line Rate: 8.33%	125% Decl Bal Rate: 10.42	150% Decl Bal Rate: 12.50%	200% Decl Bal Rate: 16.67%	Sum-of-the-Years Digits
1	8.333	10.417	12.500	16.667	15.385
2	8.333	9.332	10.937	13.889	14.103
3	8.333	8.360	9.570	11.574	12.821
4	8.333	7.489	8.374	9.645	11.538
5	8.333	6.709	7.327	8.038	10.256
6	8.333	6.010	6.411	6.698	8.974
7	8.333	5.384	5.610	5.582	7.692
8	8.333	4.823	4.909	4.651	6.410
9	8.333	4.321	4.295	3.876	5.128
10	8.333	3.871	3.758	3.230	3.846
11	8.333	3.467	3.288	2.692	2.564
12	8.333	3.106	2.877	2.243	1.282

DEPRECIATION PERCENTAGES UNDER
ACCOUNTING METHODS

15-YEAR USEFUL LIFE

Year	Straight-Line Rate: 6.67%	125% Decl Bal Rate: 8.33%	150% Decl Bal Rate: 10.00%	200% Decl Bal Rate: 13.33%	Sum-of-the-Years Digits
1	6.667	8.333	10.000	13.333	12.500
2	6.667	7.639	9.000	11.556	11.667
3	6.667	7.002	8.100	10.015	10.833
4	6.667	6.419	7.290	8.680	10.000
5	6.667	5.884	6.561	7.522	9.167
6	6.667	5.394	5.905	6.519	8.333
7	6.667	4.944	5.314	5.650	7.500
8	6.667	4.532	4.783	4.897	6.667
9	6.667	4.154	4.305	4.244	5.833
10	6.667	3.808	3.874	3.678	5.000
11	6.667	3.491	3.487	3.188	4.167
12	6.667	3.200	3.138	2.763	3.333
13	6.667	2.933	2.824	2.394	2.500
14	6.667	2.689	2.542	2.075	1.667
15	6.667	2.465	2.288	1.798	0.833

DEPRECIATION PERCENTAGES UNDER
ACCOUNTING METHODS

20-YEAR USEFUL LIFE

Year	Straight-Line Rate: 5.00%	125% Decl Bal Rate: 6.25%	150% Decl Bal Rate: 7.50%	200% Decl Bal Rate: 10.00%	Sum-of-the-Years Digits
1	5.000	6.250	7.500	10.000	9.524
2	5.000	5.859	6.937	9.000	9.048
3	5.000	5.493	6.417	8.100	8.571
4	5.000	5.150	5.936	7.290	8.095
5	5.000	4.828	5.491	6.561	7.619
6	5.000	4.526	5.079	5.905	7.143
7	5.000	4.243	4.698	5.314	6.667
8	5.000	3.978	4.346	4.783	6.190
9	5.000	3.729	4.020	4.305	5.714
10	5.000	3.496	3.718	3.874	5.238
11	5.000	3.278	3.439	3.487	4.762
12	5.000	3.073	3.181	3.138	4.286
13	5.000	2.881	2.943	2.824	3.810
14	5.000	2.701	2.722	2.542	3.333
15	5.000	2.532	2.518	2.288	2.857
16	5.000	2.374	2.329	2.059	2.381
17	5.000	2.225	2.154	1.853	1.905
18	5.000	2.086	1.993	1.668	1.429
19	5.000	1.956	1.843	1.501	0.952
20	5.000	1.834	1.705	1.351	0.476

DEPRECIATION PERCENTAGES UNDER ACCOUNTING METHODS

25-YEAR USEFUL LIFE

Year	Straight-Line Rate: 4.00%	125% Decl Bal Rate: 5.00%	150% Decl Bal Rate: 6.00%	200% Decl Bal Rate: 8.00%	Sum-of-the-Years Digits
1	4.00	5.000	6.000	8.000	7.692
2	4.00	4.750	5.640	7.360	7.385
3	4.00	4.512	5.302	6.771	7.077
4	4.00	4.287	4.984	6.230	6.769
5	4.00	4.073	4.684	5.731	6.462
6	4.00	3.869	4.403	5.273	6.154
7	4.00	3.675	4.139	4.851	5.846
8	4.00	3.492	3.891	4.463	5.538
9	4.00	3.317	3.657	4.106	5.231
10	4.00	3.151	3.438	3.777	4.923
11	4.00	2.994	3.232	3.475	4.615
12	4.00	2.844	3.038	3.197	4.308
13	4.00	2.702	2.856	2.941	4.000
14	4.00	2.567	2.684	2.706	3.692
15	4.00	2.438	2.523	2.490	3.385
16	4.00	2.316	2.372	2.290	3.077
17	4.00	2.201	2.229	2.107	2.769
18	4.00	2.091	2.096	1.939	2.462
19	4.00	1.986	1.970	1.783	2.154
20	4.00	1.887	1.852	1.641	1.846
21	4.00	1.792	1.741	1.510	1.538
22	4.00	1.703	1.636	1.389	1.231
23	4.00	1.618	1.538	1.278	0.923
24	4.00	1.537	1.446	1.175	0.615
25	4.00	1.460	1.359	1.081	0.308

DEPRECIATION PERCENTAGES UNDER
ACCOUNTING METHODS

30-YEAR USEFUL LIFE

Year	Straight-Line Rate: 3.33%	125% Decl Bal Rate: 4.17%	150% Decl Bal Rate: 5.00%	200% Decl Bal Rate: 6.67%	Sum-of-the-Years Digits
1	3.333	4.167	5.000	6.667	6.452
2	3.333	3.993	4.750	6.222	6.237
3	3.333	3.827	4.517	5.807	6.022
4	3.333	3.667	4.287	5.420	5.806
5	3.333	3.514	4.073	5.059	5.591
6	3.333	3.368	3.869	4.722	5.376
7	3.333	3.228	3.675	4.407	5.161
8	3.333	3.093	3.492	4.113	4.946
9	3.333	2.964	3.317	3.839	4.731
10	3.333	2.841	3.151	3.583	4.516
11	3.333	2.722	2.994	3.344	4.301
12	3.333	2.609	2.844	3.121	4.086
13	3.333	2.500	2.702	2.913	3.871
14	3.333	2.396	2.567	2.719	3.656
15	3.333	2.296	2.438	2.538	3.441
16	3.333	2.201	2.316	2.368	3.226
17	3.333	2.109	2.201	2.211	3.011
18	3.333	2.021	2.091	2.063	2.796
19	3.333	1.937	1.986	1.926	2.581
20	3.333	1.856	1.887	1.797	2.366
21	3.333	1.779	1.792	1.677	2.151
22	3.333	1.705	1.703	1.566	1.935
23	3.333	1.634	1.618	1.461	1.720
24	3.333	1.566	1.537	1.364	1.505
25	3.333	1.500	1.460	1.273	1.290
26	3.333	1.438	1.387	1.188	1.075
27	3.333	1.378	1.318	1.109	0.860
28	3.333	1.320	1.252	1.035	0.645
29	3.333	1.265	1.189	0.966	0.430
30	3.333	1.213	1.130	0.902	0.215

DEPRECIATION PERCENTAGES UNDER ACCOUNTING METHODS

33.3-YEAR USEFUL LIFE

Year	Straight-Line Rate: 3.00%	125% Decl Bal Rate: 3.75%	150% Decl Bal Rate: 4.50%	200% Decl Bal Rate: 6.00%	Sum-of-the-Years Digits
1	3.000	3.750	4.500	6.000	5.602
2	3.000	3.609	4.298	5.640	5.434
3	3.000	3.474	4.104	5.302	5.266
4	3.000	3.344	3.919	4.984	5.098
5	3.000	3.218	3.743	4.684	4.930
6	3.000	3.098	3.575	4.403	4.762
7	3.000	2.982	3.414	4.139	4.594
8	3.000	2.870	3.260	3.891	4.426
9	3.000	2.762	3.113	3.657	4.258
10	3.000	2.659	2.973	3.438	4.090
11	3.000	2.559	2.840	3.232	3.922
12	3.000	2.463	2.712	3.038	3.754
13	3.000	2.371	2.590	2.856	3.585
14	3.000	2.282	2.473	2.684	3.417
15	3.000	2.196	2.362	2.523	3.249
16	3.000	2.114	2.256	2.372	3.081
17	3.000	2.034	2.154	2.229	2.913
18	3.000	1.958	2.057	2.096	2.745
19	3.000	1.885	1.965	1.970	2.577
20	3.000	1.814	1.876	1.852	2.409
21	3.000	1.746	1.792	1.741	2.241
22	3.000	1.681	1.711	1.636	2.073
23	3.000	1.618	1.634	1.538	1.905
24	3.000	1.557	1.561	1.446	1.737
25	3.000	1.498	1.490	1.359	1.569
26	3.000	1.442	1.423	1.277	1.401
27	3.000	1.388	1.359	1.201	1.232
28	3.000	1.336	1.298	1.129	1.064
29	3.000	1.286	1.240	1.061	0.896
30	3.000	1.238	1.184	0.997	0.728
31	3.000	1.191	1.131	0.938	0.560
32	3.000	1.147	1.080	0.881	0.392
33	3.000	1.104	1.031	0.828	0.224
34	1.000	0.354	0.328	0.260	0.019

DEPRECIATION PERCENTAGES UNDER ACCOUNTING METHODS

40-YEAR USEFUL LIFE

Year	Straight-Line Rate: 2.50%	125% Decl Bal Rate: 3.12%	150% Decl Bal Rate: 3.75%	200% Decl Bal Rate: 5.00%	Sum-of-the-Years Digits
1	2.500	3.125	3.750	5.000	4.878
2	2.500	3.027	3.609	4.750	4.756
3	2.500	2.933	3.474	4.512	4.634
4	2.500	2.841	3.344	4.287	4.512
5	2.500	2.752	3.218	4.073	4.390
6	2.500	2.666	3.098	3.869	4.268
7	2.500	2.583	2.982	3.675	4.146
8	2.500	2.502	2.870	3.492	4.024
9	2.500	2.424	2.762	3.317	3.902
10	2.500	2.348	2.659	3.151	3.780
11	2.500	2.275	2.559	2.994	3.659
12	2.500	2.204	2.463	2.844	3.537
13	2.500	2.135	2.371	2.702	3.415
14	2.500	2.068	2.282	2.567	3.293
15	2.500	2.004	2.196	2.438	3.171
16	2.500	1.941	2.114	2.316	3.049
17	2.500	1.880	2.034	2.201	2.927
18	2.500	1.822	1.958	2.091	2.805
19	2.500	1.765	1.885	1.986	2.683
20	2.500	1.710	1.814	1.887	2.561
21	2.500	1.656	1.746	1.792	2.439
22	2.500	1.604	1.681	1.703	2.317
23	2.500	1.554	1.618	1.618	2.195
24	2.500	1.506	1.557	1.537	2.073
25	2.500	1.459	1.498	1.460	1.951
26	2.500	1.413	1.442	1.387	1.829
27	2.500	1.369	1.388	1.318	1.707
28	2.500	1.326	1.336	1.252	1.585
29	2.500	1.285	1.286	1.189	1.463
30	2.500	1.244	1.238	1.130	1.341

DEPRECIATION PERCENTAGES UNDER
ACCOUNTING METHODS

40-YEAR USEFUL LIFE

Year	Straight-Line Rate: 2.50%	125% Decl Bal Rate: 3.12%	150% Decl Bal Rate: 3.75%	200% Decl Bal Rate: 5.00%	Sum-of-the-Years Digits
31	2.500	1.206	1.191	1.073	1.220
32	2.500	1.168	1.147	1.020	1.098
33	2.500	1.131	1.104	0.969	0.976
34	2.500	1.096	1.062	0.920	0.854
35	2.500	1.062	1.022	0.874	0.732
36	2.500	1.029	0.984	0.830	0.610
37	2.500	0.996	0.947	0.789	0.488
38	2.500	0.965	0.912	0.749	0.366
39	2.500	0.935	0.878	0.712	0.244
40	2.500	0.906	0.845	0.676	0.122

PRORATION PERCENTAGES

The following tables allow you to prorate expenses for closing dates within the 365-day calendar year. Using the percentages in the tables, you may calculate how much of prepaid or postpaid property expenses should be allocated to the buying and selling party. To use the tables, you need the following information:

1. *The closing date.* The day of the month on which the property is to be closed. According to convention the day of closing is allocated to the seller. This is reflected in the tables.

2. *When the expense was paid or is due to be paid.* Has the seller paid the expense covering the entire year or will the bill fall due after the closing and be paid by the buyer?

3. *The amount of the expense.* The expense should cover the calendar year in which the closing takes place. If the expense covers multiple years, use only that portion which covers the year of closing.

Example. Brown sells a home to Jones. The closing is scheduled for May 22. In January, Brown paid an insurance premium covering the entire calendar year in the amount of $200. Property taxes for the year are due on November 1 and will be paid by the buyer. The tax bill is expect to be $500. How should these expenses be prorated at the closing?

The insurance premium was paid by Brown, the seller. Brown should get a credit for the premium less the proportion covering the time the home was owned by Brown. Look at the tables and find the column marked "MAY." Follow this column down to the 22 under the column "DAY OF MO." This is the percentage of the year from January 1 through May 22, the day of closing. The percentage is 38.90%. Brown has used 38.9% of the insurance, the premium for which is .389 times $200, or $77.80. Brown gets a credit for the remaining $122.20 of the prepaid premium.

The same percentage is used to prorate the tax expense. Brown is debited for 38.9% of the $500 bill which covers the time Brown owned the home. Accordingly, Brown's closing statement is reduced by .389 times $500, or $194.50.

PRORATION PERCENTAGES
DAYS FROM JANUARY 1

DAY OF MO.	JAN	FEB	MARCH	APRIL	MAY	JUNE
1	0.27	8.77	16.44	24.93	33.15	41.64
2	0.55	9.04	16.71	25.21	33.42	41.92
3	0.82	9.32	16.99	25.48	33.70	42.19
4	1.10	9.59	17.26	25.75	33.97	42.47
5	1.37	9.86	17.53	26.03	34.25	42.74
6	1.64	10.14	17.81	26.30	34.52	43.01
7	1.92	10.41	18.08	26.58	34.79	43.29
8	2.19	10.68	18.36	26.85	35.07	43.56
9	2.47	10.96	18.63	27.12	35.34	43.84
10	2.74	11.23	18.90	27.40	35.62	44.11
11	3.01	11.51	19.18	27.67	35.89	44.38
12	3.29	11.78	19.45	27.95	36.16	44.66
13	3.56	12.05	19.73	28.22	36.44	44.93
14	3.84	12.33	20.00	28.49	36.71	45.21
15	4.11	12.60	20.27	28.77	36.99	45.48
16	4.38	12.88	20.55	29.04	37.26	45.75
17	4.66	13.15	20.82	29.32	37.53	46.03
18	4.93	13.42	21.10	29.59	37.81	46.30
19	5.21	13.70	21.37	29.86	38.08	46.58
20	5.48	13.97	21.64	30.14	38.36	46.85
21	5.75	14.25	21.92	30.41	38.63	47.12
22	6.03	14.52	22.19	30.68	38.90	47.40
23	6.30	14.79	22.47	30.96	39.18	47.67
24	6.58	15.07	22.74	31.23	39.45	47.95
25	6.85	15.34	23.01	31.51	39.73	48.22
26	7.12	15.62	23.29	31.78	40.00	48.49
27	7.40	15.89	23.56	32.05	40.27	48.77
28	7.67	16.16	23.84	32.33	40.55	49.04
29	7.95		24.11	32.60	40.82	49.32
30	8.22		24.38	32.88	41.10	49.59
31	8.49		24.66		41.37	

PRORATION PERCENTAGES
DAYS FROM JANUARY 1

DAY OF MO.	JULY	AUG	SEPT	OCT	NOV	DEC
1	49.86	58.36	66.85	75.07	83.56	91.78
2	50.14	58.63	67.12	75.34	83.84	92.05
3	50.41	58.90	67.40	75.62	84.11	92.33
4	50.68	59.18	67.67	75.89	84.38	92.60
5	50.96	59.45	67.95	76.16	84.66	92.88
6	51.23	59.73	68.22	76.44	84.93	93.15
7	51.51	60.00	68.49	76.71	85.21	93.42
8	51.78	60.27	68.77	76.99	85.48	93.70
9	52.05	60.55	69.04	77.26	85.75	93.97
10	52.33	60.82	69.32	77.53	86.03	94.25
11	52.60	61.10	69.59	77.81	86.30	94.52
12	52.88	61.37	69.86	78.08	86.58	94.79
13	53.15	61.64	70.14	78.36	86.85	95.07
14	53.42	61.92	70.41	78.63	87.12	95.34
15	53.70	62.19	70.68	78.90	87.40	95.62
16	53.97	62.47	70.96	79.18	87.67	95.89
17	54.25	62.74	71.23	79.45	87.95	96.16
18	54.52	63.01	71.51	79.73	88.22	96.44
19	54.79	63.29	71.78	80.00	88.49	96.71
20	55.07	63.56	72.05	80.27	88.77	96.99
21	55.34	63.84	72.33	80.55	89.04	97.26
22	55.62	64.11	72.60	80.82	89.32	97.53
23	55.89	64.38	72.88	81.10	89.59	97.81
24	56.16	64.66	73.15	81.37	89.86	98.08
25	56.44	64.93	73.42	81.64	90.14	98.36
26	56.71	65.21	73.70	81.92	90.41	98.63
27	56.99	65.48	73.97	82.19	90.68	98.90
28	57.26	65.75	74.25	82.47	90.96	99.18
29	57.53	66.03	74.52	82.74	91.23	99.45
30	57.81	66.30	74.79	83.01	91.51	99.73
31	58.08	66.58		83.29		100.00

APPENDIX

House Cross Section

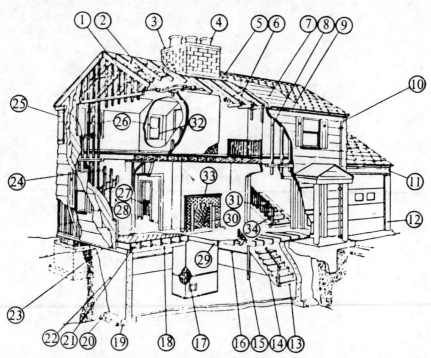

Description of Number Parts in House

1—Collar beam
2—Ceiling joist
3—Chimney cap
4—Chimney pots
5—Chimney flashing
6—Rafters
7—Roof boards
8—Stud
9—Eave trough or gutter
10—Downspout or leader gooseneck
11—Frieze
12—Door jamb
13—Basement stair riser
14—Stair stringer
15—Girder post
16—Chair rail
17—Furring strips
18—Girder
19—Footing for foundation wall
20—Foundation drain tile
21—Diagonal subflooring
22—Foundation wall
23—Termite shield
24—Wall studs
25—Pilaster
26—Window casing
27—Wainscoting
28—Baseboard
29—Floor joists
30—Fire brick
31—Newel cap
32—Mantel
33—Window sash
34—Newel

FIGURE 188

From Boyce's *Real Estate Appraisal Terminology,* Copyright 1975, The American Institute of Real Estate Appraisers and The Society of Real Estate Appraisers. Reprinted with permission from Ballinger Publishing Company.

ABBREVIATIONS

A/C   air conditioning

ACRS   accelerated cost recovery system

ADR   asset depreciation range

AIREA   American Institute of Real Estate Appraisers

ALTA   American Land Title Association

AMI   alternative mortgage instrument

AML   adjustable mortgage loan

APA   American Planning Association

app   appreciation (in appraisal terminology)

APR   annual percentage rate

AREUEA   American Real Estate and Urban Economics Association

ARM   adjustable rate mortgage

ASA   American Society of Appraisers

ASREC   American Society of Real Estate Counselors

BOMA   Building Owners and Managers Association

CAI   Community Associations Institute

CBD   central business district

CCIM   Certified Commercial-Investment Member (RNMI)

CD   certificate of deposit

CPI   consumer price index (see cost of living index)

CPM   Certified Property Manager (IREM)

CRB   Certified Real Estate Brokerage Manager (RNMI)

CRE   Counselor in Real Estate (ASREC)

CRS   Certified Residential Specialist (RNMI)

DCR   debt coverage ratio

dep   depreciation (in appraisal terminology)

EIS   environmental impact statement

EPA   Environmental Protection Agency

FAR   floor-area ratio

FDIC   Federal Deposit Insurance Corporation

FHA   Federal Housing Administration

FHLB   Federal Home Loan Bank

FHLMC   Federal Home Loan Mortgage Corporation (Freddie Mac)

FmHA   Farmers Home Administration

FMRR   financial management rate of return

FMV   fair market value

FNMA   Federal National Mortgage Association (Fannie Mae)

FPM   flexible payment mortgage

FSLIC   Federal Savings and Loan Insurance Corporation

FTC   Federal Trade Commission

FY   fiscal year

GEM   growing equity mortgage

GIM   gross income multiplier

GNMA   Government National Mortgage Association (Ginnie Mae)

GPM   graduated payment mortgage

GRI   Graduate, Realtors® Institute

GRM   gross rent multiplier

HOW   homeowners warranty

HUD   Department of Housing and Urban Development

HVAC   heating, ventilation, and air conditioning

IAAO   International Association of Assessing Officers

IRA   individual retirement account

IREM   Institute of Real Estate Management

IRR   internal rate of return

IRS   Internal Revenue Service

IRWA   International Right-of-Way Association

L/V   loan-to-value ratio

MAI   Member, Appraisal Institute (AIREA)

MBA   Mortgage Bankers Association of America

MGIC   Mortgage Guaranty Insurance Corporation

MLS   multiple listing service

MMC   money market certificate of deposit

NAA   National Apartment Association

NACORE   National Association of Corporate Real Estate Executives

NAHB   National Association of Home Builders

NAR   National Association of Realtors®

NAREB   National Association of Real Estate Brokers

NARELLO   National Association of Real Estate Licensing Law Officials

NOI   net operating income

NOW   negotiable order of withdrawal (account)

NPV   net present value

OAR   overall rate of capitalization

OILSR   Office of Interstate Land Sales Registration

PAM   pledged account mortgage

P & I   principal and interest (payment)

PITI   principal, interest, taxes and insurance (payment)

PMI   private mortgage insurance

PUD   planned unit development

RAM   reverse annuity mortgage

REIT   real estate investment trust

RESPA   Real Estate Settlement Procedures Act

RESSI   Real Estate Securities and Syndication Institute

RM   Residential Member (AIREA)

RNMI   Realtors® National Marketing Institute

RRM   renegotiated rate mortgage

R/W   right-of-way

SAM   shared appreciation mortgage

SBA   Small Business Administration

SEC   Securities and Exchange Commission

SIR   Society of Industrial Realtors®

S&L   savings and loan association

SMSA   standard metropolitan statistical area

SRA   Senior Residential Appraiser (SREA)

SREA   Senior Real Estate Analyst (SREA)

SREA   Society of Real Estate Appraisers

SRPA   Senior Real Property Appraiser (SREA)

SYD   sum-of-the-years-digits (method of depreciation)

TDR   transferable development rights

TIL   truth-in-lending law

UCC   Uniform Commercial Code

ULI   Urban Land Institute

VA   Veterans Administration

VRM   variable rate mortgage

WCR   Women's Council of Realtors

YTM   yield to maturity

MEASUREMENT TABLES

ENGLISH SYSTEM

Linear Measure

12 inches (in or ″)	= 1 foot (ft or ′)
3 feet	= 1 yard (yd)
5½ yards	= 1 rod (rd), pole, or perch (16½ feet)
40 rods	= 1 furlong (fur)
	= 220 yards
	= 660 feet
6076.11549 feet	= 1 international nautical mile

Gunter's or Surveyor's Chain Measure

7.92 inches (in)	= 1 link
100 links	= 1 chain (ch)
	= 4 rods
	= 66 feet
80 chains	= 1 statute mile (mi)
	= 320 rods
	= 5,280 feet

Area Measure

Squares and cubes of units are sometimes abbreviated by using "superior" figures. For example, ft^2 means square foot, and ft^3 means cubic foot.

144 square inches	= 1 square foot (ft^2)
9 square feet	= 1 square yard (yd^2)
	= 1,296 square inches
30¼ square yards	= 1 square rod (rd^2)
	= 272¼ square feet
160 square rods	= 1 acre
	= 4,840 square yards
	= 43,560 square feet
640 acres	= 1 square mile (mi^2)
1 mile square	= 1 section (of land)
6 miles square	= 1 township
	= 36 sections
	= 36 square miles

METRIC SYSTEM

Linear Measure

10 millimeters (mm)	= 1 centimeter (cm)
10 centimeters	= 1 decimeter (dm)
	= 100 millimeters
10 decimeters	= 1 meter (m)
	= 1,000 millimeters
10 meters	= 1 dekameter (dam)
10 dekameters	= 1 hectometer (hm)
	= 100 meters
10 hectometers	= 1 kilometer (km)
	= 1,000 meters

Area Measure

100 square millimeters (mm^2)	= 1 square centimeter (cm^2)
10,000 square centimeters	= 1 square meter (m^2)
	= 1,000,000 square millimeters
100 square meters	= 1 are (a)
100 ares	= 1 hectare (ha)
	= 10,000 square meters
100 hectares	= 1 square kilometer (km^2)
	= 1,000,000 square meters

EQUIVALENTS BETWEEN ENGLISH AND METRIC SYSTEMS

Lengths

angstrom	= 0.1 nanometer (exactly)
	= 0.000 1 micron (exactly)
	= 0.000 000 1 millimeter (exactly)
	= 0.000 000 004 inch
1 cable's length	= 120 fathoms
	= 720 feet
	= 219.456 meters (exactly)
1 centimeter (cm)	= 0.3937 inch
1 chain (ch), (Gunter's or surveyor's)	= 66 feet
	= 20.1168 meters (exactly)
1 chain (engineer's)	= 100 feet
	= 30.48 meters (exactly)
1 decimeter (dm)	= 3.937 inches
1 dekameter (dam)	= 32.808 feet
1 fathom	= 6 feet
	= 1.8288 meters (exactly)

EQUIVALENTS BETWEEN ENGLISH AND METRIC SYSTEMS

Lengths

1 foot (ft)	= 0.3048 meters (exactly)
1 inch (in)	= 2.54 centimeters (exactly)
1 kilometer (km)	= 0.621 mile
	= 3,280.8 feet
1 league (land)	= 3 statute miles
	= 4.828 kilometers
1 link (Gunter's or surveyor's)	= 7.92 inches
	= 0.201 meter
1 link (engineer's)	= 1 foot
	= 0.305 meter
1 meter (m)	= 39.37 inches
	= 1.094 yards
1 mile (mi) (statute or land)	= 5,280 feet
	= 1.609 kilometers
1 international nautical mile	= 1,852 kilometers (exactly)
(INM)	= 1.150779 statute miles
	= 6,076.11549 feet
1 rod (rd), pole, or perch	= 16½ feet
	= 5½ yards
	= 5.029 meters
1 yard (yd)	= 0.9144 meter (exactly)

Areas or Surfaces

1 acre	= 43,560 square feet
	= 4,840 square yards
	= 0.405 hectare
1 are (a) (100 square meters)	= 119.599 square yards
	= 0.025 acre
1 hectare (ha) (10,000 square meters)	= 2.471 acres
[1 square (building)]	= 100 square feet
1 square centimeter (cm^2)	= 0.155 square inch
1 square decimeter (dm^2)	= 15.500 square inches
1 square foot (ft^2)	= 929.030 square centimeters
1 square inch (in^2)	= 6.452 square centimeters
1 square kilometer (km^2)	= 247.105 acres
	= 0.386 square mile
	= 1,196 square yards
1 square meter (m^2)	= 10.764 square feet
1 square mile (mi^2)	= 640 acres 258.999 hectares
1 square millimeter (mm^2)	= 0.002 square inch
1 square rod (rd^2), sq. pole, or sq. perch	= 25.293 square meters
1 square yard (yd^2)	= 0.836 square meter

MATHEMATICAL FORMULAS

To find the **CIRCUMFERENCE** of a:

Circle—Multiply the diameter by 3.14159265 (usually 3.1416).

To find the **AREA** of a:

Circle—Multiply the square of the diameter by .785398 (usually .7854).

Rectangle—Multiply the length of the base by the height.

Sphere (surface)—Multiply the square of the radius by 3.1416 and multiply by 4.

Square—Square the length of one side.

Trapezoid—Add the length of the 2 parallel sides, multiply by the height and divide by 2.

Triangle—Multiply the length of the base by the height and divide by 2.